*"Value-packed, accurate, comprehensive..."*

—*Los Angeles Times*

*"Unbeatable..."*

—*The Washington Post*

# Let's Go
# PARIS

**is the best book for anyone traveling on a budget. Here's why:**

## ■ No other guidebook has as many budget listings.

For example: We list 50 hostels and hotels for under $30 a night. We tell you how to get there the cheapest way, whether by bus, plane, or bike, and where to get an inexpensive and satisfying meal once you've arrived. We give hundreds of money-saving tips that anyone can use, plus invaluable advice on discounts and deals for students, children, families, and senior travelers.

## ■ Let's Go researchers have to make it on their own.

Our Harvard-Radcliffe researcher-writers travel on budgets as tight as your own—no expense accounts, no free hotel rooms.

## ■ Let's Go is completely revised each year.

We don't just update the prices, we go back to the place. If a charming café has become an overpriced tourist trap, we'll replace the listing with a new and better one.

## ■ No other guidebook includes all this:

Honest, engaging coverage of the city and beyond; up-to-the-minute prices, directions, addresses, phone numbers, and opening hours; in-depth essays on local culture, history, and politics; comprehensive listings on transportation within and outside the city; straight advice on budget accommodations, sights, nightlife, food, and drink; detailed city and regional maps; and much more.

## ■ Let's Go is for anyone who wants to see Paris on a budget.

# Books by Let's Go, Inc.

## EUROPE

Let's Go: Europe

Let's Go: Austria

Let's Go: Britain & Ireland

Let's Go: France

Let's Go: Germany & Switzerland

Let's Go: Greece & Turkey

Let's Go: Ireland

Let's Go: Italy

Let's Go: London

Let's Go: Paris

Let's Go: Rome

Let's Go: Spain & Portugal

## NORTH & CENTRAL AMERICA

Let's Go: USA & Canada

Let's Go: Alaska & The Pacific Northwest

Let's Go: California & Hawaii

Let's Go: New York City

Let's Go: Washington, D.C.

Let's Go: Mexico

## MIDDLE EAST & ASIA

Let's Go: Israel & Egypt

Let's Go: Thailand

# Let's Go

The Budget Guide to

## PARIS

# 1994

**Natasha Hanna Leland**
Editor

**Verity Winship**
Assistant Editor

Written by
Let's Go, Inc.
A subsidiary of
Harvard Student Agencies, Inc.

## M
**Macmillan Reference**

## HELPING LET'S GO

If you have suggestions or corrections, or just want to share your discoveries, drop us a line. We read every piece of correspondence, whether a 10-page letter, a velveteen Elvis postcard, or, as in one case, a collage. All suggestions are passed along to our researcher-writers. Please note that mail received after May 5, 1994 will probably be too late for the 1995 book, but will be retained for the following edition. Address mail to:

> **Let's Go: Paris**
> **Let's Go, Inc.**
> **1 Story Street**
> **Cambridge, MA 02138**
> **USA**

In addition to the invaluable travel advice our readers share with us, many are kind enough to offer their services as researchers or editors. Unfortunately, the charter of Let's Go, Inc. and Harvard Student Agencies, Inc. enables us to employ only currently enrolled Harvard students.

Published in Great Britain 1994 by Pan Macmillan Ltd., Cavaye Place, London SW10 9PG.

10 9 8 7 6 5 4 3 2 1

Maps by David Lindroth, copyright © 1994, 1993 by St. Martin's Press, Inc.

Printed in the United States of America by St. Martin's Press, Inc.

ISBN: 0-333-61165-9

Let's Go: **Paris** is written by the Publishing Division of Let's Go, Inc., 1 Story Street, Cambridge, MA 02138.

Let's Go® is a registered trademark of Let's Go, Inc. Printed in the U.S.A. on recycled paper with biodegradable soy ink.

# ■ Acknowledgments

It almost was not. It certainly wouldn't have been, without the dedication, skill, and humor of the three Paris researchers. **Nancy Hopkins** rewrote entire introductions in her flowing and natural (and legible) prose as if she had spent hours on each one—we honestly don't know how she did it. Nancy's light-hearted attitude raised our spirits, and her reassuring advice is sure to brighten the days of many a tired tourist. **Brian Martin,** with the energy of a freight train gone berserk, wrote hilarious "fabulous" prose with a soft spot for the confused tourist. Brian at the Louvre, Brian at Versailles, Brian at Euro Disney®; we think he should write his own companion travel guide. **Miranda Spieler** had the dedication of a historian and a friend. She analyzed the nature of her *arrondissements* with the understanding of a Parisian, the insight of a foreigner, and a subtlety which is a sign of true brilliance. Fearless, she attacked each section with equal rigor, leaving bars and tidbits of urban legend in her wake.

Nina Nowak's kind words comforted researchers and editors alike. Her knowledge of life in the field was invaluable as was her concern for the reader. Always eager to help, Nina was a continual force in the office. As was **Ed Owen,** the man who made it all happen. Never ruffled, his patience and expertise overcame any technical glitches. **Sue Krause** and **Anne Chisholm,** both ever-organized, made our lives in the office so much easier. **Mark Templeton's** gentle diplomacy smoothed the relationship with the powers that be. To everyone else in the office, especially those who understand what it means to be a city guide, our utmost gratitude and apologies.

—NHL and VW

What to write? Verity, I have thought over and over about how to thank you. And I do thank you—for everything, but most especially for your companionship. You know even better than I do what my summer would have been like without you. You are funny, comforting, brilliant, perceptive, dedicated, understanding, generous, meticulous, serene, and yet you still put up with me. Paris, you bewilder me and force me to love you. *Je bois cet alcool brulant comme ma vie...* Mummy, I know now you are French—can you feel my heart too is in Paris? To all the members of what I consider my family (and most especially to Olivia) I really do love you and thank you for all you have taught me. To my friends—you know who you are— I have missed you.

—NHL

Many thanks to Natasha for her weightlifting, odd humor, and friendship—and, of course, her fine editing. To my parents who introduced me to Paris. And to Sergio who, even from a distance, kept me from becoming too irritable.

—VW

# About Let's Go

Back in 1960, a few students at Harvard got together to produce a 20-page pamphlet offering a collection of tips on budget travel in Europe. For three years, Harvard Student Agencies, a student-run nonprofit corporation, had been doing a brisk business booking charter flights to Europe; this modest, mimeographed packet was offered to passengers as an extra. The following year, students traveling to Europe researched the first full-fledged edition of *Let's Go: Europe*, a pocket-sized book featuring advice on shoestring travel, irreverent write-ups of sights, and a decidedly youthful slant.

Throughout the 60s, the guides reflected the times: one section of the 1968 *Let's Go: Europe* talked about "Street Singing in Europe on No Dollars a Day." During the 70s, *Let's Go* gradually became a large-scale operation, adding regional European guides and expanding coverage into North Africa and Asia. The 80s saw the arrival of *Let's Go: USA & Canada* and *Let's Go: Mexico*, as well as regional North American guides; in the 90s we introduced five in-depth city guides to Paris, London, Rome, New York, and Washington, DC.

This year we're proud to announce three new guides: *Let's Go: Austria* (including Prague and Budapest), *Let's Go: Ireland*, and *Let's Go: Thailand* (including Honolulu, Tokyo, and Singapore), bringing our total number of titles up to twenty.

We've seen a lot in thirty-four years. *Let's Go: Europe* is now the world's #1 best selling international guide, translated into seven languages. And our guides are still researched, written, and produced entirely by students who know first-hand how to see the world on the cheap.

Every spring, we recruit nearly 100 researchers and an editorial team of 50 to write our books anew. Come summertime, after several months of training, researchers hit the road for seven weeks of exploration, from Bangkok to Budapest, Anchorage to Ankara. With pen and notebook in hand, a few changes of underwear stuffed in our backpacks, and a budget as tight as yours, we visit every *pensione*, *palapa*, pizzeria, café, club, campground, or castle we can find to make sure you'll get the most out of *your* trip.

We've put the best of our discoveries into the book you're now holding. A brand-new edition of each guide hits the shelves every year, only months after it was researched, so you know you're getting the most reliable, up-to-date, and comprehensive information available. And even as you read this, work on next year's editions is well underway.

At *Let's Go*, we think of budget travel not only as a means of cutting down on costs, but as a way of breaking down a few walls as well. Living cheap and simple on the road brings you closer to the real people and places you've been saving up to visit. This book will ease your anxieties and answer your questions about the basics—to help *you* get off the beaten track and explore. We encourage you to put *Let's Go* away now and then and strike out on your own. As any seasoned traveler will tell you, the best discoveries are often those you make yourself. If you find something worth sharing, drop us a line and let us know. We're at Let's Go, Inc., 1 Story Street, Cambridge, MA, 02138, USA.

Happy travels!

# We can wire money to every major city in Europe almost as fast as you can say, "Zut alors! J'ai perdu mes valises".

How fast? We can send money in 10 minutes or less, to 13,500 locations in over 68 countries. That's faster than any other international money transfer service. And when you're *sans* luggage, every minute counts.

For more information contact our Customer Service Office in Paris at 33-1-47777000 or visit your nearest American Express® Travel Service Office. In the U.S. call 1-800-MONEYGRAM.

## AMERICAN EXPRESS *MoneyGram*™

### INTERNATIONAL MONEY TRANSFERS.

# Contents

# Maps

# How To Use This Book

Paris has been the subject of thousands of books about aspects of its varied life, from its Roman past, to the cafés of the 1880s, to today's bustling nightlife and art and architecture. We give you a sense of the city's history and where to find its traces, and we help you budget time and money. This book is designed to give both first-time visitors and long-time friends an introduction to Paris's (budget) riches.

**Paris: An Introduction** fills you in on Paris's history, politics, architecture, art, and literary life. **Essentials** offers practical advice for before you go and after you arrive. **Planning Your Trip,** with its helpful information on necessary documents, useful maps, and currency will help you think ahead. **Getting There** gives tips about budget travel to Paris. **Once There** provides information on useful organizations in Paris, emergency services, and the layout of the city. We cover *métro,* bus, and other services that will help you get around. We offer special tips and resources for students, seniors, families, women, and other travelers with specific needs.

In the **Accommodations** section, hotels, hostels, and *foyers* are listed in the order of value, based on price, location, safety, and comfort, as determined by our researcher-writers. **Food and Drink** includes restaurant reviews organized by *arrondissement* and accompanied by a full list cross-referenced by type of food, price, hours, and atmosphere. We also list cafés, wine bars, sweet shops, and groceries. Organized by *arrondissement,* the **Sights** section gives a sense of the hidden and not-so-hidden treasures in Paris's different neighborhoods. **Museums** get a section of their own, with detailed descriptions of the large museums—the Louvre, Musée d'Orsay, and more—and informative listings of smaller collections for every taste. **Entertainment** is chock full of film, theater, music, and dance. It includes listings of both participatory and spectator sports, and for the less *sportif,* a sampling of Paris's finest bars. **Shopping,** entertainment for some, includes the city's major department stores as well as harder to find specialty shops, book stores, and street markets. Our section on **Bisexual, Gay, and Lesbian Paris** offers information on social services and entertainment. For those who want to see another part of France, our many **Daytrips** include châteaux, cathedrals, and even theme park fun. Check out our **Appendices** for useful phrases and our extensive menu reader.

# Paris:
# An Introduction

*A Paris on peut s'amuser, s'ennuyer, rire, pleurer, faire tout ce qui vous plaît; nul ne vous jette un regard car il y a des milliers qui y font la même chose et chacun a sa manière.*
*(In Paris you can enjoy yourself, bore yourself, laugh, cry, do all that pleases you, and no one casts a glance at you because there are thousands who do the same thing and each one in her own way.)*
—Frédéric Chopin, 1831

In the midst of Paris's layers of activity, it is for the individual to create a distinctive niche in both the city's reality and in its mystique. Paris is a place that exists in most peoples' imaginations before they ever see the city—Paris as the City of Lights, the romantic Paris of the movies, the vibrant and mysterious city described in centuries of books and letters. The actual city, though different from the imaginary one, is not a disappointment. The city is constantly evolving. It is the center of the changing French political landscape, ground for artistic innovation as well as tradition, and home to a diverse population.

Today Parisians go about their daily lives, crowding into the same cafés where Picasso and Matisse met, erecting barricades on the same streets as they did during the French revolution. Baudelaire called Paris a "teeming city, city full of dreams, where the specter in full daylight, accosts the passerby." These phantoms are part of the city's mystery. And while Paris may not be the mythic city of dreams (it is quite possible to go to Paris and not fall in love; you may not even finish your novel), its complexities are part of its charm, and the web of myth is part of its everyday realities. It is, in Hemingway's words, "a moveable feast," a city with a flavor so irresistible that once you taste it, you will carry memories of the experience around with you forever after.

## ■ History

*To have been Lutèce and to have become Paris—what could be a more magnificent symbol! To have been mud and to have become spirit!*
—Victor Hugo

In the beginning, there was a crossroads and an island, the Ile de la Cité, home to a tribe called the Parisii. The Parisii's *Loutonheze*, "a dwelling in the midst of the waters," became the Roman *Lutetia* (Lutèce), and in the Middle Ages, the ruling Franks shortened *Lutetia Parisiorum* to a simple *Paris*. Its regional power dates to 987 when Hugh Capet, count of Paris, became King of France and brought prestige to the tiny medieval town by making it his capital. Over the years, prestige has had its price; as the capital of France, Paris has borne the brunt of fighting between monarchs, the citizens of Paris, and lords and, during the Hundred Years War (1337-1453), with England. During this war, the now mythic Jeanne d'Arc, who allied with the French King Charles VII against Henry V of England, was wounded on the streets of Paris.

Religion was at the center of daily life in the Middle Ages and the Renaissance. Nascent strands of Protestantism fomented strife across France in the late 16th century. During this period, Cathérine de Médicis, Henri II's wife then widow, ruled France through her sons. Concerned by a rising Huguenot (French Protestant) power, she married her daughter to the Protestant Henri of Navarre (later Henri IV).

# Paris: Map of Maps

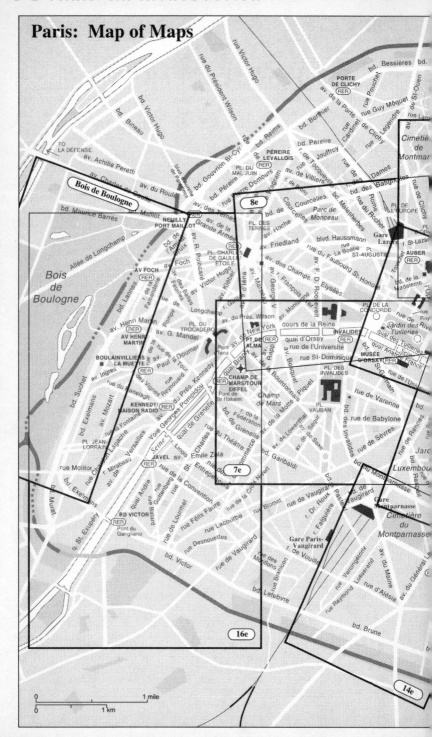

When all of the leading Protestants in France had assembled in Paris for the wedding, she signaled the start of the St-Bartholomew's Day Massacre. A wild Parisian mob slaughtered some 2000 Huguenots. When Henri IV acceded to the throne in 1589, he converted to Catholicism, waving off the magnitude of his decision with a nonchalant *"Paris vaut bien une Messe"* (Paris is well worth a mass).

The 17th century was a period of burgeoning absolutism. Cardinal Richelieu, first minister to Louis XIII, began to fashion the greatest absolutist state Europe has ever seen, a nation where sovereignty rested solely and entirely with the monarch. The power of the king reached its height during the reign of Louis XIV, the *Roi Soleil* (the Sun King), who rose to the throne as a five-year-old in 1642 and ruled for 72 years. In 1648, fines on Parisian homeowners drove the city to the barricades in a revolt known as the Fronde. In retreat from the rebellious city, Louis XIV moved his capital to Versailles. The palace became a showcase for regal opulence and noble privilege as the king surrounded himself with exquisite luxuries and submissive nobles. Marie-Antoinette, Louis XIV's equally extravagant queen, lives on in paintings and in popular legend—"let them eat cake" is her infamous line. The Sun King's great-grandson, Louis XV, continued the tradition of expensive wars and lavish consumption into the late 18th century. His mistresses, including Madame de Pompadour and Madame du Barry, were notorious for their "power behind the throne."

Discontent with the monarchy, its policies, and its excesses contributed to the French Revolution. The Revolution's declared goal was twofold, at once destructive and constructive: to tear down the vestiges of feudalism and to erect in its place a new society built on the tripartite ideal of *liberté, égalité,* and *fraternité.* On July 14, 1789, an impatient mob stormed the Bastille to seize its gunpowder. The French now celebrate July 14 (*le quatorze juillet*) as the *Fête Nationale,* Bastille Day. In September 1792, efforts at revolt were successful and the French republic was declared. Major reforms, such as the abolition of guilds and the dismantling of the Church, transformed the nation, but could not bring lasting peace to Paris. In 1793, the radical Jacobin faction, led by Maximilien Robespierre and his Committee of Public Safety, took over the Convention and began a period of suppression and mass execution known as the Terror. The Jacobins guillotined the king and queen, their enemies, and eventually each other. The place de la Concorde, now a glorified traffic circle, was once the site for more than 1300 beheadings. Thankfully, such a system did not last, and the leading Jacobins were arrested in the revolutionary month of Thermidor (August 1793).

An exhausted French people yearned for stability and welcomed the rise of a man they felt could achieve it: Napoleon Bonaparte. This famed military commander and megalomaniac took power in a coup in 1799 and by 1804 had declared himself emperor. Napoleon established a strong central bureaucracy and a system of law that still lies at the foundation of legal systems around the world. He was not satisfied with ruling France alone, and soon initiated a series of military campaigns that nearly yielded him hegemony over the entire European continent. Apart from a brief return to monarchy (Louis XVIII), Napoleon ruled until his ultimate defeat at Waterloo in 1815. Power then passed to Louis-Philippe, whose July Monarchy was seen as a compromise between the Bourbon kings' autocracy and the Republic's excess. Louis-Philippe was to be a "citizen-king," king not of France, but of the French; in a symbolic gesture, he kept the revolutionary tricolor as his flag.

Revolution hit again in 1848 when veterans of a 1830 revolt joined students in a march on the Chambre des Députés, demanding a republic. Louis-Philippe abdicated peacefully, and the Second Republic was declared. Even more than in 1792, the change in regime had been determined solely by events in the capital. Despite Paris's power, in 1851 an anti-Parisian, conservative peasantry elected to the presidency an ambitious man named Louis-Napoleon Bonaparte. Aided by his popular slogan *"l'Empire c'est la paix"* (the Empire means peace), he successfully proclaimed himself Emperor Napoleon III. His downfall came soon after he launched the Franco-Prussian War in July 1870; he was captured by the Prussians and deposed.

Paris's revolutionary tradition continued into the Third Republic with the establishment of the Paris Commune in 1871. For four months a committee of leftist politicians held power, temporarily replacing the extremely conservative regime led by Adolphe Thiers. The Commune threw up barricades to defend against the inroads of the expelled government, but the wide boulevards designed by Baron Haussmann enabled the regulars to outflank the defenders. The crushing of the Commune broke both the power of Paris over the provinces and of the Parisian proletariat over the city. Into the beginning of the next century France ambled along, through both conservative and liberal regimes, under the republican tricolor.

World War I touched Paris only indirectly. Fears that the German army deployed in northern France would attack the capital proved to be unfounded. By 1916, despite occasional air raids, the theaters, cinemas, and galleries of Paris were joyously humming again. In the immediate aftermath of the war, Paris basked in its role as a European political center. Delegates from around the world arrived to redraw the map of Europe at the Paris Peace Conference, eventually producing the flawed Treaty of Versailles.

After a brief period (1936-37) of rule by the Popular Front, a coalition of the political left formed in response to the rise of the Nazis in Germany, Paris entered the turmoil of World War II. On June 14, 1940, German armies swept into Paris and the French government fled into exile in the small town of Vichy. Because it lay at the heart of occupied France, Paris swarmed with officials, diplomats, and spies sent from Berlin, Vichy, and the rest of the world. Well-attended exhibits purported to show the evils of Freemasonry, Bolshevism, and international Jewry, and a detention center was set up just outside Paris in Compiègne. Meanwhile, the leader of the Résistance, Général Charles de Gaulle, having escaped to London, declared his Comité National Français to be the government-in-exile. Paris's destruction in World War II was narrowly avoided. Hitler ordered the destruction of the French capital in the summer of 1944, but his garrison commander evaded the order, and Paris was preserved. The horrors of the Nazi occupation made the liberation of Paris, in contrast, one of the most glorious moments in the city's history. Allied armies, sweeping east from the Normandy beachheads, marched through Paris in August 1944. This period left its mark on Paris and the Parisians: Vichy collaboration with the Nazis has left still tender scars. Today's government has attempted to bring to trial high-ranking officials of the Vichy government, including Vichy police chief Réné Bousquet, who was murdered in June 1993 before he could be tried.

Soon after the war, the Fourth Republic was declared, with de Gaulle as its president. Its 12-year reign (1946-58) saw the reconstruction of French transport and industry, the formation of the European Economic Community (EEC) in 1957, and the collapse of the French Empire in Indochina, Tunisia, and Morocco. Problems with the colonial empire plagued the regime, and a 1958 revolution in Algeria triggered its collapse. After a period of personal rule by de Gaulle, the constitution of the Fifth (and current) Republic was approved in 1958.

Paris was the center of student revolts in the 1960s. In May 1968, university students, frustrated by sexual segregation, an outdated curriculum, and the threat of a reduction in the number of students allowed to matriculate, seized the Sorbonne, launching a student revolt. Classic barricades were erected in the *quartier latin*. During the month of May, the situation escalated; police used tear gas and clubs to storm the barricades, while students fought back by throwing Molotov cocktails and lighting cars on fire. Though none were killed, hundreds of students and police officers were wounded in the fighting. Workers in state industries went on strike in support of the students, nearly paralyzing the whole country. Government officials, planning for the worst, arranged for tanks and commando units to be brought into the city in the event of a Communist insurrection. But a march of hundreds of thou-

POLITICS

sands of de Gaulle's supporters down the Champs-Elysées confirmed public support of the government, extinguishing the revolt.

## ■ Politics

The French political system blends the traditional European parliamentary system with the American system of an independent executive. Parliament—made up of the *sénat* and the Assemblée Nationale, both elected by universal suffrage—holds legislative power. The Assemblée is housed in the Palais Bourbon in the 7*ème arrondissement*; the *sénat* meets in the Palais du Luxembourg in the 6*ème*. The President, who is elected by popular vote for a seven-year term, holds executive power. The President appoints a Council of Ministers, headed by the Prime Minister, which manages the country and is responsible to Parliament. Depending on the composition of the Assemblée, the balance of power lies alternately with the President or the Prime Minister, a system designed to prevent legislative gridlock.

France's political parties include two center-right parties, the Union pour la Démocracie Française (UDF) and the Rassemblement pour la République (RPR). Jacques Chirac, prime minister between 1986 and 1988 and mayor since 1977, leads the RPR. The Socialists and the Communists are the major parties on the left. The Communist Party was a political force to be reckoned with until their decline in the polls in the early 80s; in the March 1992 elections, they got merely 9% of the vote. Many of the voters for the Communist Party inhabit the outlying districts including the 12*ème* and the 20*ème arrondissements*. The former faubourg St-Antoine, now the 12*ème arrondissement*, forms part of what is known at the "red belt" because of its voting habits and history of revolt. The ecologists are not particularly well-organized in France; the two Green parties are politically opposed.

The Socialist Party, with François Mitterrand at its helm, swept to power in 1981, capturing both the Assemblée Nationale and the presidency. Within weeks they had raised the minimum wage and added a fifth week to the French worker's annual vacation. Despite these successes, Socialists suffered serious setbacks in local and European parliamentary elections soon after Mitterrand enacted deflationary policies in response to a 1983 economic recession. A new racist, ultra-rightist, ultra-nationalist party called the Front National (National Front) emerged in the 1986 legislative elections, reflecting the social strife of the last decade. Its leader, Jean-Marie Le Pen, ran for office with the slogan "*La France pour les français*"—France for the French, with a very narrow interpretation of Frenchness. Despite his visibility, Le Pen only gained 10% of the vote that year. Two years later, Mitterrand won re-election to a second seven-year term and appointed France's first woman Prime Minister, Edith Cresson (she stepped down in March 1992).

Pierre Bérégovoy replaced Cresson, announcing his mission to "lance the abscess of corruption." This was easier said than done. The Socialist Party continued to be tainted by scandal to the point that Bérégovoy himself was accused of improper behavior—accepting a free loan from a friend who was later accused of insider trading. His constituency forgave him; they soon reelected him to Parliament. Bérégovoy committed suicide in May 1993 following the Socialist Party's greatest defeat in 25 years in the March elections.

The conservative former finance minister Edouard Balladur became Prime Minister after the Socialist defeat. This heralded a still continuing period of (often uneasy) *cohabitation* between the Socialist President and the conservative Prime Minister. France's troubled economy is one of Balladur's most daunting tasks; the unemployment level in May 1993 was 10.7%, and both it and the deficit continue to increase. Despite his initiation of programs to tax petrol and alcohol and to cut health care spending, Balladur's approval ratings have remained at 70% of the electorate.

Tough economic times have exacerbated problems of racism and nationalism. Workers from France's African and Asian colonies migrated to Paris after World War II. In the early 1970s, amid the oil shock, the government decided to halt the flow of immigrants, and since then very few have come, except for the families of male workers already in France. Today, almost half of the immigrants in France live in or around Paris—particularly in the 13ème, 19ème, and 20ème arrondissements, as well as in the suburbs—making up 13% of the city's population. The amount of immigration has not increased over time, but the composition has: race has become an issue as immigrants hail from Arab and African nations rather than from Europe. Neither the immigrants nor their French-born children are citizens, but members of the second generation born in France are. Recent laws limit the ability to gain citizenship. Even non-citizens, however, receive many benefits of the welfare state. In part because of this, immigrants have encountered a great deal of hostility, especially from the Front National, which has called for citizens to be given preference in housing, jobs, and schooling, and for immigrants to be denied welfare payments.

The French economy is in transition. One of the government's projects is the privatization of many public companies. A law has been drafted that would allow the government to sell 21 French state-owned firms including Renault, Air France, Crédit Lyonnais, and others. In a trial run the government sold off their holdings (little more than 25%) of Crédit Local de France. The program is scheduled to begin in full force in September, 1993.

Economic conditions and policies in France are tied to its relationship with other European countries. The French have been a major force in the development of the European Economic Community (EEC), first formed in 1957. In January of 1992, France, along with 12 other EEC member-nations, began a program of tariff reduction that will eventually allow goods and workers to pass freely from nation to nation. A recent agreement has also set Europe in motion towards monetary union, whereby all member countries would use a common currency, controlled by a single central bank. Some historians believe this "shared sovereignty" marks the first step towards an ultimate political union. Progress has been slowed by economic recession. The year 1993, the first year of the European Community's single market, saw the worst recession in 20 years; economic conditions have fueled national and international debate about the Maastricht treaty and the unity it could bring. France's position in the EEC has an impact on domestic politics: long-time enemies Jacques Chirac and former president Giscard d'Estaing both vie for a position on the European parliament, in part because the EEC representative will likely run against Socialist presidential candidate Michel Rocard in the next elections.

## ■ Architecture and Urban Design

New and old exist side by side in Paris. Roman ruins lie next to or underneath Art Nouveau, and single buildings have been made and remade over centuries. Different elements of the Palais du Louvre date from the 12th century, from the 1980s, and from almost every century in between. The cityscape has also evolved over time as tastes have changed and as Paris's growing population has pushed at the boundaries of the city, outgrowing a series of city walls.

The Romans transformed Paris from a collection of fishing huts into a place of civilization, a title the city has prided itself on ever since. They rebuilt the city in their own image, with vineyards, an arena, and a perpendicular street plan. Traces of the Romans' Greek-inspired pristine forms and simple geometry exist in such diverse buildings as the 17th-century Cour Carrée of the Louvre and Napoleon's triumphal arches. An early type of architecture modeled after Roman basilicas blossomed into the massive Romanesque cathedrals of the 11th century. The oldest parts of St-Germain-des-Prés show the immense walls and semicircular arches characteristic of this style. The prosperity of the 12th century allowed the invention of a new, far more ornate architectural style—the Gothic. From this period Paris boasts St-Denis, Europe's first Gothic cathedral, as well as the jewel-like Sainte-Chapelle.

The 12th century also saw the basic segregation of functions that still characterizes the city. King Philippe-Auguste established the political and ecclesiastical institutions on Ile de la Cité, academic on the Left Bank, and commercial on the Right Bank. By the 14th century, Paris's 80,000 inhabitants made it one of the great cities of Europe. To cope with this growth, Charles V replaced an earlier wall with a new, larger wall on the Right Bank. Though it was destroyed in the 17th century, its outline defines the northern and eastern borders of the third *arrondissement*. The color of present day Paris dates back to the 16th century when fire regulations decreed that wooden exteriors had to be plastered over, creating a gray city. The late 16th and early 17th century saw the construction of the Pont Neuf, the Palais du Luxembourg, and the Palais Royal, as well as the widening of Paris's streets. Meanwhile the city's population skyrocketed, reaching almost 400,000 by the mid-17th century.

The 17th century—reign of the Sun King, Versailles, and the Absolute Monarchy— ushered in the age of the Baroque. In place of the Gothic architecture banned by Louis XIV, Italianate domes popped up across the city. Le Nôtre, Le Brun, and Le Vau reigned as the triumvirate of French art, designing respectively the gardens, architecture, and all-important interior paintings of Versailles and château Vaux-le-Vicomte. Paris had become the largest city in Europe. Earlier walls became wide streets to accommodate the growing population. This process continued into the following centuries: a wall constructed in the late 18th century was replaced by the "exterior boulevards" in the 19th. The outer borders of the eighth, ninth, tenth, and eleventh *arrondissements* as well as the bd. St-Jacques, bd. de Grenelle, and other streets on the Left Bank have their origins in this replacement.

Not too surprisingly, destruction outweighed construction during the French Revolution. Most of its impressive architectural achievements were temporary: an artificial mountain on the Champ de Mars, a cardboard Neoclassical interior for Notre-Dame, and various plaster statues of Liberty. More lasting were the various defacements, especially of kings' statues and churches. At the same time, the Jacobins were not too busy beheading people to open up to development parts of the city center previously owned by the Church and nobility. Napoleon made further improvements in the early 19th century; he planned cemeteries, dug sewers, numbered houses, widened the streets, and brought back the plunder of a continent to the Louvre.

Despite two bloody revolutions, the early 19th century was a prosperous time for Paris. The government's decision that France's major railroads would all terminate in the capital guaranteed Paris's position at the center of the French economy in the new industrial age. Paris thrived as the center of manufacture, a magnet attracting thousands of migrants from the provinces. It continued to be innovative in architecture, adopting the (now ubiquitous) apartment building, a form which was imitated throughout the world. The products of industrialization made many living quarters more pleasant—glass became cheaper and windows proliferated. But unchecked growth continued to swamp improvements, and many of Paris's one million people lived in congested slums.

Though traces of the past abound, parts of pre-19th century Paris would be virtually unrecognizable to a modern visitor. Today's city is the Paris remade under the (somewhat dictatorial) direction of Baron Georges-Eugène Haussmann. From 1852 to 1870, Haussmann transformed Paris from an intimate medieval city to a bustling modern metropolis. Commissioned by the government to modernize the city, Haussmann tore long, straight boulevards through the tangled clutter and narrow alleys of old Paris, creating a unified network of *grands boulevards*. These avenues were designed not only to increase circulation of goods and people, but to make Paris a work of art, a splendid capital worthy of France. Not incidently, the wide avenues and oblique intersections also impeded insurrection, limiting once and for all the effectiveness of street barricades.

The changes during this period were momentous. The city doubled its area and Haussmann shifted the boundaries of the 20 existing *quartiers,* establishing Paris's present organization into 20 *arrondissements.* Five of Paris's seven hills were leveled; only Montmartre and the Montagne Ste-Geneviève remain. Twelve thousand structures were destroyed and 136km of straight avenues created. Wide sidewalks (demolished in the next century to make room for automobiles) encouraged strollers, sidewalk cafés, kiosks, and general crowds, giving birth to Paris's famed street culture. But the transformation was not without its costs. Intimate neighborhoods were destroyed by the lacerations of the avenue de l'Opéra and the boulevard St-Michel. Their homes demolished to make room for the boulevards and luxury apartments, the workers of Paris were forced eastward to Belleville and beyond.

The transformation of Paris continued along the same lines into the early 20th century. Traffic circles, varied façades, electrical lamps, and elevators became important elements in the development of the city's appearance. Paris continued to establish itself as an international center of innovation with the Exhibitions of 1889 and 1900. Both left several quintessentially Parisian landmarks in their wake: the *Métropolitain,* the Grand and Petit Palais, and of course, the Eiffel Tower, a celebration of steel construction.

Paris's cityscape and its architectural styles survived two world wars fundamentally unchanged. In the interwar period, a few radical architects began to focus on new building materials. Le Corbusier, a Swiss citizen who lived and built in Paris, was a pioneer in the new material of reinforced concrete. During the postwar years, architects began to make buildings that would stand out, rather than blend in. Most of the changes were made in the outer *arrondissements,* like the 13*ème* and the 17*ème,* leaving the historic core relatively intact. The old market place of Les Halles, now a subterranean shopping mall, was torn down, and the *quais* of the Left Bank, like those of the Right, were almost converted into expressways—acts that inspired calls for conservation.

Paris's growth was not restricted to its center. Its history of expansion into the surrounding territory dates back to the emergence of working-class districts (*faubourgs*) in the late 18th century. In the 19th century, technical innovations made the suburbs more inviting by enabling workers to commute from the outer districts and suburbs to jobs in the city. During the 50s and 60s, the government sponsored housing developments and a plan for a ring of "new towns" surrounding Paris. Five of these towns have been built, including Marne-la-Vallée, now the home of Euro Disneyland® Park. Parisian suburbs, often the only source of affordable housing, are home mainly to the working class and immigrants. As high rents have pushed the working class out to the suburbs, Paris's middle class has gentrified the old workers' quarters, making them tidy but, some would say, dull.

The last two decades may go down in history as one of the greatest periods of building in Paris. Presidents Giscard d'Estaing and Mitterrand have been enthusiasts of dramatic architectural endeavors. Mitterrand initiated the famous (some say infamous) 15 billion franc Grands Projets program to provide a series of modern monuments symbolic of France's role at the center of art, politics, and the world economy. From La Défense to La Villette, these government offices, museums, and public buildings constitute some of the boldest and most controversial additions to the city. I.M. Pei's 1989 modernist glass pyramid, part of the program, was planted smack in the middle of the courtyard of the Louvre. One of the most recent Mitterrand-sponsored projects is construction of the Bibliothèque Nationale, part of a massive urban renewal project called ZAC (zone d'aménagement concerte) Seine-Rive Gauche. The library's design by architect Dominique Perrault has prompted ongoing debate. Whether Paris should be preserved as a city of another era (or eras) or be host to sometimes jarringly innovative projects, and who should make these aesthetic and economic decisions remain the subjects of a lively public dialogue.

# ■ The Arts

Many of Paris's early examples of visual arts and elements of architecture are objects of ecclesiastical worship. They can be seen in today's Paris in the stunning stained glass which illustrates the stories of the Bible at Chartres, Sainte-Chapelle, and Notre-Dame, or in the intricately carved stone façades of these and other early churches. Medieval works exist side by side with the more secular work of the Renaissance. A new emphasis on Humanism, coupled with a nostalgia for the classical past, strongly colored the art of the Renaissance. Italy was its artistic center; even François I imported Italian artists to decorate his palace at Fontainebleau in the latest Mannerist (consciously "artificial") style.

Under Louis XIV, an indigenous French art flourished and eventually rose to European dominance. The center of Western art shifted decisively from Rome to Paris where, many would say, it has remained to this day. Nicolas Poussin elaborated the theory of the "grand manner," with its huge canvases and panoramic subjects taken from mythology and history. The French Académie Royale, founded in 1648, came to value this style above all others and all subsequent French painters had to contend with these weighty "academic" precepts. Claude Lorraine's idyllic landscapes defined the Académie's landscape tradition. In 1725, the Académie inaugurated annual Salons, held in the vacant halls of the Louvre.

A sober 18th-century bourgeoisie admired the scenes of everyday life by Chardin and Greuze before turning its attention to the moral history paintings of David. Meanwhile the French aristocracy, continuing on its course of extravagance and dissolution, employed Rococo artists like Boucher and Fragonard to decorate its gold-embossed salons and bedrooms with flying cherubs and mischievous escapades. Watteau painted the *fêtes* and secret *rendez-vous* of the aristocracy as a magnificently theatrical display. Elisabeth Vigée-Lebrun painted the French nobility with a charm that many years later earned her a great success with the court of Russia.

Art during the Revolution, with its emphasis on classical style and public display, was a far cry from the Rococo. Ceremonies, with elaborate Neoclassical props and costumes planned by David, fêted such important state occasions as the transfer of Voltaire's body to the Panthéon. David himself joined the Jacobin party, painting such striking works as *The Oath in the Tennis Court* and *The Dead Marat*. In 1793—the year of the Terror—the Louvre opened the Royal collection to the public, providing the beginnings of what would become the world's most famous art museum. After being imprisoned (and then released) by the Directory in 1794, David changed allegiance, moving to the camp of the Corsican Emperor-to-be and painting for him the monumental *Coronation of Napoleon*. Napoleon's regime sponsored a Neoclassicism in all realms of visual art, with Egyptian and Greek motifs (the Empire style) expressing his idea of himself as the spiritual son of the Roman emperors.

The period of the Restoration and July Monarchy marked the division that would define the rest of the century: the Classical school led by Jean-Auguste Dominique Ingres, a student of David, and the Romantic school led by Eugène Delacroix. Ingres's use of sinuous lines and sensual surfaces sharply contrasted with Delacroix's emphasis on brilliant colors, dramatic movement, and emotional excess. Chopin, a Polish-born composer, brought Romanticism to music with his sensitive, highly personal piano serenades. Meanwhile the invention of photography by Parisians Nièpce and Daguerre provided a new artistic medium, sparking an intense debate over the relative merits of painting and photography.

Napoleon III's declaration of the Second Empire spawned a generation of artists who were utterly disillusioned with a government that no longer represented their ideals. Like the itinerant gypsies after which they were named, the Bohemians proclaimed for themselves a life free from normal conventions. This "race of obstinate dreamers for whom art has remained a faith and not a career" gathered in the cafés of the *quartier latin* and starved proudly in the garrets of Paris. Charles Baudelaire, Champfleury, Nadar, and Rodolphe Bresdin were but a few of the famous characters whose way of life was made famous in Henry Murger's bestselling *Scènes de la Vie de Bohème* (later turned into Puccini's opera, *La Bohème*).

While urban Bohemians starved in the attics of Paris, artists like Millet and Rousseau followed the Romantics' urge to escape from nature, retreating to Barbizon to paint the forêt de Fontainebleau and the French peasantry. Influenced by the social-Utopian theories of Charles Fourier, Gustave Courbet rejected Academic historical painting in favor of a "living art" that would portray what he saw around him. As Europe spread its tentacles across the globe in the 19th century, the East became an inspiration for fashion, painting, and the decorative arts. Academic artists like Jean-Léon Gérôme created lush scenes of Turkish baths and snake-charmers. Japanese *ukiyoe* prints inundated the market from 1853 on, inspiring the nascent Impressionists.

Claude Monet, Pierre-Auguste Renoir, and Frédéric Bazille met during the 1860s in Paris and began to develop their now-famous technique. Used to the smooth surfaces and clear-cut lines of Academic painting, critics objected to the "mess"—the rough brushwork and the sketchy quality—the soon-to-be Impressionists produced. Edouard Manet's *Déjeuner sur l'Herbe* was refused by the Salon of 1863; in defiance he exhibited his painting just outside in a separate *"Salon des Refusés* (Salon of the Rejected), with a 50 centimes entrance fee.

The Third Republic (1870-1940) is seen by many as the age of Impressionism. Monet, increasingly the head of this group of young radicals, and Camille Pissaro established their own exhibition in 1874, sick of juries, official competition, and establishment taste. Housed in the former photographic studio of Nadar, the exhibit consisted of 165 canvases of which one was Monet's *Impression: Sunrise*. A snide critic made fun of this canvas, labeling its creator an "Impressionist." Monet and his colleagues gleefully adopted this name, and the show became an annual event. The newly dubbed Impressionists set about playing with light and color to capture perceived reality. For the first time, the crowd—already so aptly described by Hugo and in Baudelaire's *Les Fleurs du Mal*—became a subject worthy of painting. Impressionist paintings, like Manet's *A Bar at the Folies-Bergères* (1882) and Degas's *The Glass of Absinthe* (1876), focused on cafés, balls, cabarets, and ballets. At the same time, a new interest in the countryside created an ideal arena for the Impressionists' credo of *plein air* (open-air) painting.

The inheritors of Impressionism, a highly individualistic group of artists labeled the Post-Impressionists, explored more and more abstract issues of color, light, and planar geometry, anticipating the 20th century's movement to Cubism and abstract art. Both Paul Cézanne and Vincent Van Gogh went past Impressionism to explore their own unique visions—from Van Gogh's brilliant color and deeply spiritual views of nature to Cézanne's geometric reconstruction of landscape and form. Paul Gauguin, to whom Van Gogh mailed his severed ear, left a family and a highly successful career as a stockbroker to paint the peasants of Brittany and the "natives" of Tahiti. Meanwhile, Pointillists like Seurat explored a highly scientific type of painting, with works made up of tiny dots in primary colors. In sculpture, official commissions (exemplified by the extravagant, allegorical creations of Carpeaux) abounded, while Rodin, with the aid of Camille Claudel, focused on a highly energetic, muscular shaping of bronze and stone.

During the last decades of the 19th century, Bohemia had moved outside Haussmann's city to the cabarets and cafés of Montmartre—an oasis for artists and bourgeois alike from the sterility of the modern city below. Offenbach composed his celebrated cancan; Toulouse-Lautrec captured the spirit and flashy theatricality of the Belle Epoque in the vibrant silkscreen posters that covered Paris, as well as in his starkly linear paintings of brothels, circuses, and cabarets. "Impressionist" composers like Debussy and Ravel in turn evoked the sounds of the ocean, the winds, and the rising sun. At the same time, Nietzsche's philosophy, rooted in a belief in artifice, in surface, and in the rejection of decayed traditions, formed the basis of a new, decorative style—Art Nouveau. Art Nouveau quickly embraced architecture, furniture, lamps, jewelry, fashion, and book illustration in its search for an all-conclusive aesthetic in which style was more important than function.

The 20th century brought a deeply self-conscious, chaotic art world, following the generation just before in its search for a new and *modern* art. Erik Satie, a wandering Bohemian of Montmartre, composed his pensive, ponderous *Gymnopèdes*. A young group of artists led by Henri Matisse and inspired by Gauguin painted with increasingly brilliant colors and decorative surfaces. Critics labeled them the *fauves* (wild beasts), yet their "wildness" barely hinted at the extreme to which Pablo Picasso and George Braque would carry art with their Cubist experiments of 1907 to 1914. Together with Braque and a poet friend—Guillaume Apollinaire—Picasso formulated rigid precepts for the movement: Cubist painting sought to represent the idea of an object, rather than the object itself. In order to represent a three-dimensional "idea" on a flat canvas, Picasso presented his subjects from several angles at once. Marcel Duchamp added an element of dynamic movement to Cubism with paintings like *Nude Descending a Staircase*. Utrillo and Man Ray formed part of the same set, while Eugène Atget, a photographer who documented the streets and shop fronts of Paris, provided Picasso and his friends with photographic "sketches" to use as a basis for their art. Marc Chagall and Giorgio de Chirico immigrated to Paris from Russia and Italy and brought with them their own visions; Chagall created his Cubist fairy-tale pictures of Russian villages and Jewish legends, while de Chirico painted his strange, often haunting images that anticipated Surrealism.

On the eve of World War I, Paris argued over such *ballets russes* as Debussy's *L'Après-midi d'un faune* (1912), danced and choreographed by the famous Nijinsky. Debussy's symphonic setting of Mallarmé's poem, with the flute taking the role of Pan, provided perhaps the era's most perfect expression of the union between musical sound and words, while Nijinsky's highly erotic choreography caused a truly magnificent scandal. Yet no one was prepared for the 1913 opening of Stravinsky's *Rites of Spring,* which blew apart traditional precepts of music and ballet with its iconoclastic use of atonalities, a non-plot, and violently ungraceful choreography. The opening show on May 29, 1913 at the Théâtre des Champs-Elysées erupted almost immediately into an uproar; to Stravinsky's amazement, the conductor kept going and was able (amid catcalls, fights, whistles, and applause) to finish the show.

In 1917 came the *ballet russes*'s final great triumph—*Parade,* written by the poet Jean Cocteau, inspired by the audience "participation" at the opening of *Rites of Spring,* with music by Erik Satie, Cubist costumes and set by Picasso, and choreography by Nijinsky. As the war continued, however, the Cubists and their circle dispersed, and Apollinaire died at the front. Horrified by the slaughter of the war, Duchamp switched from painting his futurist machine-worshiping images to leading the Dadäists, a group of artists who focused on nonsense and non-art—drawing a mustache on a picture of the Mona Lisa and exhibiting a urinal titled *La Fontaine*.

In 1924, André Breton published his *Surrealist Manifesto* and launched the Surrealist movement among a group of former Dadäists. The Surrealists claimed to create an art of the subconscious, seeking out the dream world that was more real than the rational world around them. René Magritte, Salvador Dalí, Yves Tanguy, and Max Ernst painted and etched their playful images of top hats, castles, angels, misplaced nude bodies, and melting clocks. Many constructed Surrealist "objects"—modifications of ready-made things. Meret Oppenheim's *Furred Teacup* and Man Ray's nail-studded iron, *The Gift,* were both playful and somewhat menacing. Cocteau, now a full-fledged Surrealist, wrote *Les Enfants Terribles* and produced such dreamily evocative films as *La Belle et la Bête*.

During the 30s, photographers like Brassaï and Kertész, both emigrants from Hungary, recorded the streets and *quartiers* of Paris, especially Montmartre, in black and white. Jean Renoir (son of the painter) made his poetic, witty films which investigated the state of culture in the 20th century; *Boudu is Saved from Drowning* (the original version of *Down and Out in Beverly Hills)* tells the story of a beggar saved from the Seine and taken in by a book-seller. *La Grande Illusion,* on a more serious level, presents the interactions of three French prisoners of war, each from radically different social backgrounds, with the aristocratic German head of their World War I camp. In 1937, Picasso exhibited the huge and violent mural *Guernica* at the Paris International Exposition, in the pavilion of the Spanish Republic. Based on the bombing of a Basque town during the Spanish Civil War, *Guernica* provided the century's most conclusive condemnation of the horrors of the war—three years before the Germans invaded Paris, bringing on the brutality of World War II.

As the Germans advanced on Paris, the masterpieces of the Louvre, except for the *Nike,* which was too heavy, were evacuated to the provinces. Within days of the German entry into Paris, the invaders filled the Opéra and the theaters, which staged uncontroversial farces to avoid offense. Braque and Picasso kept painting, and musicians pulled out their Wagner and Beethoven scores. Jacques Prévert and Marcel Carné teamed up to create two films, *The Devil's Envoy* (1942) and the epic *Children of Paradise* (1945). Edith Piaf and Maurice Chevalier sang in the music halls. In May 27, 1943, hundreds of "degenerate" paintings by Miró, Picasso, Ernst, Klee, and Léger were destroyed in a bonfire in the garden of the Jeu de Paume. Tens of thousands more "respectable" masterpieces belonging to Jewish collectors were appropriated and shipped to Germany, but were returned after the war.

Post-war Paris was filled with the sounds of jazz, imported from America to Paris, where musicians like Louis Armstrong found a far more receptive audience than they could have hoped for in the States. New Wave movies, inspired by American gangster films and Alfred Hitchcock, burst into the cinematic scene in the 50s, using black and white to capture the fragmented, hurried quality of life on the edge. François Truffaut's *The 400 Blows,* Alain Resnais's *Hiroshima mon Amour,* and Jean-Luc Godard's *A bout de souffle,* all made in 1959 are examples of this style.

Look in the contemporary arts galleries all over Paris to get an idea of the eclecticism that has characterized the visual arts in the last decade, as artists search for a new medium to express the postmodern culture of the 1980s and 90s. Minimalist artist Christo, originally from Bulgaria, received permission to wrap the Pont Neuf in pink plastic. But even this is *passé.* The new-age synthesizer music of Jean-Michel Jarre is the equivalent of buildings like the Arche de la Défense in its expression of the sleek, commodities-oriented quality of modern French culture. The same idea was expressed in Jean-Jacques Beineix's film *Diva,* with its complex plot, black humor, refined symbolism, and thrilling scenes of Paris, above-ground and below.

## ■ Literary Paris

Paris has long been a center for literary life. During the Middle Ages, the Sorbonne (recognized by the pope in 1209) and other academies attracted such intellectual giants as Pierre Abélard (of the celebrated romance with Héloïse), St-Thomas d'Aquin, and Roger Bacon to a city that had become Europe's most prestigious center for theological study. The Humanism of 15th-century Renaissance, coupled with the invention of the printing press in about 1450, resulted in a widely circulated literature addressing the foundations of human nature. These concerns continued into the 16th century in Rabelais's social satire, Calvin's reformist works, and Montaigne's personal essays. The *Très Riches Heures du Duc de Berry,* an illuminated prayer book now in the collection of the Chantilly museum, ushered in the Northern Renaissance with its naturalistic portrayal of the labors of the months.

Within the walls of the aristocracy's elaborate palaces, a system of patronage tied the age's most respected literati to the whim of their ruler. The rigidly rhythmed tragedies of Corneille and Racine explored the issues of love, honor, and duty. Molière's brilliant satires were performed in the gardens of Vaux-le-Vicomte and Versailles and, sponsored by the king's cousin, at the prestigious Comédie Française. La Fontaine read his highly moralistic fables in the salons of the immoral aristocracy, who were in turn serenaded by the operas of Jean-Baptiste Lully. Pascal, in his pessimistic *Pensées,* anticipated Romanticism when he wrote "the heart has its reasons of which reason knows nothing," while his colleague Descartes ushered in the Enlightenment with a more intellectual "I think, therefore I am." Commentary on the leading intellectuals of the day is provided by *salon* hostess Mme. de Sévigné, who recorded her reflections in hundreds of letters to her daughter. All this was regulated by the newly formed Académie Française (1635), which gathered 40 men to regulate and codify French literature, grammar, spelling, and rhetoric. The rules and standards they set loosely at this time would soon solidify into rigid regulations, launching the "Classical" age of French literature. The *académie* has ever since righteously preserved the tradition of classical French letters, with Racine's *Phèdre* as its Bible and the crystal clear poetry of Malherbe as its *Book of Songs*.

In 1666, Colbert founded the Académie des Sciences to argue over such important issues as whether a dead fish weighs more than a live fish (actually weighing two such fish was *not* considered conclusive evidence). The publication of Newton's *Principia* in 1687 ushered in an era of faith in the power of reason known as the Enlightenment. Voltaire declared that "if God did not exist, we would have to invent Him." A generation later, Diderot gathered around him a group of young intellectuals, intent on creating the *Encyclopédie,* a multi-volume work that sought to catalogue, systematize, and rationalize the whole of human knowledge. Rousseau's *Social Contract* and autobiographical *Confessions* rejected this rationality entirely, claiming that a return to nature alone could save human nature, long corrupted by modern society.

Beaumarchais's *Marriage of Figaro,* produced in 1784, was hugely popular with nobility and working class alike, yet its sharp wit and eloquent dialogues held an open condemnation of the aristocracy. Louis XVI, when he first heard the play, exclaimed prophetically "the Bastille would have to be destroyed if the performance of the play is not to have dangerous consequences;" the playwright was imprisoned, not in the Bastille as protocol dictated, but in the St-Lazare prison for delinquent boys. Choderlos de Laclos illuminated the same world, part sparkling wit, part licentiousness, part emptiness, in his controversial *Dangerous Liaisons.*

Deeply influenced by a spirit of Romanticism creeping in from Germany, from England, and from Jean-Jacques Rousseau, the 19th century in France began with a new literary movement. The Romantic movement came to a focus in the essays of Mme. de Staël and the novels of Chateaubriand. Chateaubriand's description of an isolated, melancholy young hero in *René* provided perhaps the first example of the *mal du siècle*—a feeling of disillusionment and alienation among 19th-century literati, rooted in the conviction that their century was a dying age. The *petit cénacle,* a group of poets led by Victor Hugo and including Gérard de Nerval and Théophile Gautier, espoused an emotional, lyrical style. Alfred de Vigny's *Chatterton* blamed society for the tragic suicide of a young, idealistic poet. Alfred de Musset eloquently expressed the gloomy outlook of his contemporaries when he declared that "I came too late in a century that is too old."

The prolific Honoré de Balzac rejected the Romanticism of his peers, focusing on the harsh realities of bourgeois society under Louis-Philippe, the "citizen-king." His *Comédie Humaine*—a series of novels that attempted to describe all of Parisian society—covered everyone from the melancholy poet to the bejeweled courtesan and the *nouveau riche* noble. At the same time, George Sand, the preeminent female literary figure of the 19th century, was celebrated for her *romans champêtres* (pastoral novels) and for her scandalous habit of wearing trousers and smoking cigars. She kept equally well-known company, spending nine years as Chopin's on-again-off-again lover. A second affair, between Sand and de Musset, ended unhappily—in the best of romantic traditions, both used the failed romance as a subject for their next books.

The birth of the Second Republic in 1848 brought sudden hope to the melancholy circle of Romantics headed by Hugo. Alphonse de Lamartine, a poet known for his lyrical, soul-searching verses, turned to radical politics, becoming a member of the provisional government, and then the short-lived Legislature. Hugo himself served in the Assemblée Nationale, eloquently defending the cause of "*liberté*." Louis-Napoleon Bonaparte's coup d'état ended their short-lived political careers. Lamartine fled to the country; Hugo was exiled and spent the next 19 years on the isle of Guernsey, where he penned *Les Châtîments,* a book of vehemently anti-Bonaparte poems.

Hugo's exile became the clarion-call for a new generation of artists utterly disillusioned with a government that no longer represented their ideals. Their world, together with that of the bourgeois society they rejected, was described by Emile Zola in his *Rougon-Macquart* series. Inspired by Balzac's *Comédie Humaine,* Zola added a newly "scientific" element of detail and called his movement Naturalism. Flaubert's *Madame Bovary,* published in 1857 and charged with "offense to public and religious morality and to good morals," caused a sensational trial.

At the same time, Charles Baudelaire led the way to modernism with his perverse, disturbingly beautiful *Fleurs du Mal* (Flowers of Evil), a collection of poems that focused on the sordid world of modern Paris, seen through the eyes of the elderly, the poor, the prostitutes, and, amid all these, the poet. With this alternative guidebook to Paris, the *flâneur* (wanderer) came into being—the Bohemian ideal of someone who wanders endlessly without direction, roaming among the crowds, yet standing apart from them. In August 1857, half a year after the *Madame Bovary* trial, *Les Fleurs du Mal* was put on trial for the same charge; the same prosecutor this time succeeded. Baudelaire was fined and six poems were censored from his book, not to be reinstated until a second trial in 1949.

As the century closed, a circle of Symbolist poets—Verlaine, Rimbaud, and, later, Mallarmé—followed Baudelaire to create a "musical" poetry, founded in sounds and images *(vers libérés)* rather than in meaning, reaching its epitome in Mallarmé's *l'Après-midi d'un faune.* Rimbaud's career as a poet was precocious and short; he began writing at fifteen only to abandon it later for life as a gunrunner and explorer in the depths of Abysinnia. Rimbaud's involvement with the Parisian poetry scene included a stormy relationship with fellow poet Verlaine; the relationship ended violently when Verlaine wounded Rimbaud in a drunken quarrel. Rimbaud's work (and his life) had a strong and lasting influence on modern French poetry.

Politics and the artistic and literary worlds overlapped as Paris erupted into the controversy of the Dreyfus Affair in 1898. The affair set the Rightists and anti-Semites, who believed Jewish army captain Alfred Dreyfus a traitor, against Leftists of various types. Emile Zola published *J'accuse*—a letter that accused the government of a huge cover-up that had made Dreyfus into a national scapegoat. Artists and writers took sides in a public dialogue that swept Paris. Manet, Pissaro, Signac, and Mary Cassatt joined Zola in the *dreyfusard* camp; Cézanne, Renoir, Rodin, and the anti-Semitic Degas joined the *anti-dreyfusards.*

In 1909, André Gide, whose own novels and journals reflected a pure, classical detachment, founded the *Nouvelle Revue Française,* a journal which would become *the* grounding board for up-and-coming writers in the inter-war period. In the years between 1913 and 1927, Marcel Proust wrote his monumental *Remembrance of Things Past,* a semi-autobiographical summation of the Belle Epoque and its complex social undercurrents. Proust sent his first chapter to the *Nouvelle Revue;* in one of history's great miscalculations, Gide refused the piece without even unwrapping the package, claiming that the aristocratic Proust—"a snob, a dilettante, and a man-about-town"—was incapable of producing good literature. The journal's history was not always illustrious: under a collaborationist editor during World War II, the journal promoted fascism as an alternative to communism.

Colette's multi-layered descriptions of the sensual world of Paris in the 20s were unique in their focus on issues of love and sexuality, especially between women. Besides her, the 1920s and 30s were the decades of the expatriates. Even before the war, much of the cutting edge had belonged to foreigners, such as Stravinsky and Picasso. After the Armistice, a "lost generation" of literati streamed in from America and western Europe—James Joyce, Ernest Hemingway, Ford Madox Ford, Ezra Pound, Gertrude Stein, and F. Scott Fitzgerald among them. The Americans, above all, sought a freedom in Paris they could not find at home—and enjoyed the power of the American dollar against the highly devalued French franc. Gertrude Stein expressed the feelings of her fellow expatriates: "America is my country, but Paris is my home town." Soon they were joined by a different kind of migrant: refugees from the tyrannical states that were sprouting up around Europe. Walter Benjamin, for example, fled to Paris from Nazi Germany, only to flee again (unsuccessfully) after the fall of France. Robert Capa, a Hungarian Jew who grew up in Germany, escaped to Paris before beginning his twenty years as a war photographer.

The years before World War II were marked by the beginnings of Existentialism, led by Jean-Paul Sartre. Sartre's *Being and Nothingness,* written at Café de Flore in the midst of the Occupation, became the veritable encyclopedia of Existentialism. Albert Camus published *The Stranger* in 1942, telling the story of the young Meursault who is fundamentally incapable of relating to his fellow human beings. After the war Paris was still the city of the Existentialists, who met at the cafés of Montparnasse to discuss the absurdity and meaninglessness of the world around them. Sartre published *Huis Clos* in 1945, with its telling assertion that *"L'Enfer, c'est les autres"* (Hell is other people). Simone de Beauvoir, his lifetime companion, wrote the significant feminist work *The Second Sex,* as well as existentialist novels. Camus's *The Plague* (1947) provided the spiritual summation of the movement, with its description of a town quarantined by a renewed epidemic of the bubonic plague. Paris moved into the 1950s with the absurdist plays of Eugène Ionesco and expatriate Samuel Beckett. Ionesco's plays *The Bald Soprano* and *The Lesson* have been running for 34 years in the *quartier latin's* Théâtre de la Huchette.

Despite philosophies which deemphasized the meaning of political events, politics and the arts and letters mixed as the Fourth Republic (1947-58) witnessed the collapse of the French Empire in Indochina, Tunisia, and Morocco. By 1958, France, reluctant to give up control, was embroiled in a war in Algeria. Writers of the political left in Paris, such as Sartre, made an outcry, torn between loyalty to the French government and their desire to condemn imperialism.

While Sartre and Camus preserved somewhat traditional literary styles, experimental writing in the 50s and 60s produced the *nouveau roman* (the new novel), which abandoned conventional narrative techniques, embracing subject matter previously considered trivial and mundane. Among its best known exponents are Alain Robbe-Grillet, Nathalie Sarraute, and Marguerite Duras. Sarraute presents character dialogue with an emphasis on *sous conversation* (what people think as they converse) as opposed to spoken dialogue. Marguerite Duras's novels and her script for the haunting film *Hiroshima Mon Amour* claim to present the abstract painting of literature. In a less abstract vein, Georges Simenon has described the streets of Paris relentlessly perused by his detective hero, Inspector Maigret. France is also home to many of the great names in modern philosophy—Lacan, Foucault, Saussure, Barthes, Baudrillard, and Derrida have been at the center of such movements as Cultural Criticism, Semiology, Structuralism, and Deconstructionism. For more on the latest in French writing (in French), check the list of best sellers in the weekly magazine *Livre,* or look for reviews in the literary section of a French newspaper.

## ■ La Politesse and Other Necessities

### MANNERS

Many visitors from abroad or even from the French provinces have returned with stories of the Parisians' xenophobia and snobbery. These tall tales of Parisian discourtesy may come true if you address people in English without the prefatory *"Parlez-vous anglais, Madame/Monsieur?"* Although some Parisians have the somewhat annoying habit of answering all queries in English, even the simplest of efforts to speak French will be appreciated. Be lavish with your *Monsieurs, Madames,* and *Mademoiselles*—unlike English, French demands use of titles when addressing strangers—and greet everyone with a friendly *bonjour* or *bonsoir.* When you do encounter rude locals, consider their point of view. Every summer, tourists more than double the city's population. Many do not speak French and are unwilling to accept the challenge of dealing with people who do not understand them. Parisians have a soft spot for those who wish to share their love of French language and culture, but Paris is not about to pamper you.

## LANGUAGE

> *Il n'est bon bec que de Paris (There is no good speech except from Paris)*
> —François Villon, 1461

For centuries, France has been a country obsessed with language. Spelling changes proposed by the state in the 1980s brought die-hard purists to the brink of riot. All such changes occur under the watchful eye of the Académie Française, which compiles the French dictionary and oversees the language. In the summer of 1992, the Assemblée Nationale added a line to the constitution: French is now the undisputable official language of France. Parisian French, although full of anglicisms, remains the "official" dialect. Like the city itself, the language of Paris was instrumental in forging the political unity of the nation and in creating its national culture. The Jules Ferry laws of the Third Republic sent state-employed instructors to spread the Parisian lingo and culture through the provinces. While a regional twang still lingers in the southwest, the Parisian pronunciation, like the BBC accent among the British, endures as the standard of excellence.

While English-speaking visitors may find themselves occasional targets of ridicule, don't despair. Paris is also a city for tourists, highly adapted to the needs of the multilingual crowds it receives each year. You will find a wide variety of English-language signs, tours, and brochures, and should have no trouble finding your way around and making yourself understood. Most major sites offer guided tours in English, or at least printed English translations.

LA POLITESSE

# ■ Essentials

## ■■■ PLANNING YOUR TRIP

> Note: In Paris addresses "Mo." indicates the nearest *métro* stop. The postal code of Paris addresses is formed by affixing the two-digit *arrondissement* number to 750. Thus, the postal code of an address in the 8*ème* (eighth *arrondissement*) is 75008. An international telephone call to Paris requires dialing 33 (France code) plus 1 (Paris code) before the 8-digit number (see Essentials—Communications for more information).

### ■ Useful Addresses and Publications

Research your trip early. The government and private agencies listed below will provide useful information.

### FRENCH GOVERNMENT SERVICES

The French government is well aware of the benefits of tourism for the country's economy, and will gladly provide prospective visitors a panoply of pamphlets and an inundation of information.

**French Government Tourist Office:** Write for information on any region of France, festival dates, and tips for travelers with disabilities. **U.S.,** 610 Fifth Ave., New York, NY 10020 (tel. nationwide (900) 990-0040, 50¢/min.). **Canada,** 1981, av. McGill College, #490, Montréal, Qué. H3A 2W9 (tel. (514) 288-4264). **U.K.,** 178 Piccadilly, London W1V OAL (tel. (071) 629 1272). In **Ireland,** citizens should consult the Consular Section within the French Embassy at 36 Ailesbury Rd., Ballsbridge, Dublin 4 (tel. (353) 1 77 18 71). **Australia,** BNP Building, 12th Fl., 12 Castlereagh St., Sydney, NSW 2000 (tel. (02) 231 52 44). For information and visas **New Zealanders** should contact this branch or the Consular Section within the French Embassy at 1 Willeston St., Wellington (tel. (64) 4 4720 200).

**Cultural Services of the French Embassy: U.S.,** 972 Fifth Ave., New York, NY 10021 (tel. (212) 439-1400). **U.K.,** 23 Cromwell Rd., London SW7 2EL (tel. (071) 581 5292). General information about France including culture, student employment, and educational possibilities.

### FRENCH CONSULATES

While not laden with colorful brochures, the French consulate in your home country can supply you with important legal information concerning your trip, arrange for necessary visas, and direct you toward a wealth of other information about tourism, education, and employment in France. Write or call for more information.

**U.S., Consulate General:** 3 Commonwealth Ave., Boston, MA 02116 (tel. (617) 266-1680); Visa Section, 20 Park Plaza, Statler Bldg., 11th Fl., Boston, MA 02116 (tel. (617) 482-3650 for a recording of general information, (617) 482-2864 for specific inquiries; open 8am-noon). There are 12 branch offices across the U.S.; contact the Consulate General to locate the branch nearest you. **Canada,** 2, Elysée, Place Bonaventure, BP 202 Montréal, Qué. H5A 1B1 (tel. (514) 878-4381); other consulates in Moncton, Québec City, Toronto, Edmonton, and Vancouver; French Embassy in Ottawa. **U.K.,** 21 Cromwell Rd., London SW7 2DQ (tel. (071) 581 5292); Visa Section, 6A Cromwell Pl., London SW7 2EW (tel. (089) 820 0289). **Irish** residents in the U.K. should address inquiries to this consulate. In Ireland, citizens should consult the Consular Section within the French Embassy at 36 Ailesbury Rd., Ballsbridge, Dublin 4 (tel. (353) 1 77 18 71), or the antenna office at 35 Lower Abbey St., Dublin 1 (tel. (353) 1 77 18 71). **Australia,** 31 Market St., 26th Fl., Sydney, NSW 2000 (tel. (02) 261 5931 or (02) 261 5779). **New Zealand,** 1 Willeston St., Wellington (tel. (64) 4 4720 200).

## USEFUL TRAVEL ORGANIZATIONS

**Campus Travel.** A new travel service, it offers special student and youth fares on travel by plane, train, boat, and bus, as well as flexible airline tickets. Also provides discount and ID cards for youths, special travel insurance for students and those under 35, and maps and guides. Office at 52 Grosvenor Gardens, London SW1W 0AG (tel. (071) 730 8832; fax (071) 730 5739).

**Council on International Educational Exchange (CIEE/Council Travel).** Provides low-cost travel arrangements, books (including *Let's Go)*, and gear. Operates 43 offices throughout the U.S., including those listed below and branches in Chicago, IL; Dallas, TX; Portland, OR; Seattle, WA; Providence, RI; Cambridge, MA; San Diego, San Francisco, Berkeley, La Jolla, and Long Beach, CA. **Boston,** 729 Boylston St., #201, MA 02116 (tel. (617) 266-1926; fax (617) 266 7168); **Los Angeles,** 1093 Broxton Ave., #220, CA 90024 (tel. (310) 208-3551). **New York,** 205 E. 42nd St., NY 10017 (tel. (212) 661-1450).

**Council on International Educational Exchange (CIEE)** has **affiliates** abroad that charter airline tickets, arrange homestays, and sell international student ID cards, travel literature, insurance, and hostel cards. CIEE also helps students secure work visas and find employment through its work-exchange programs. In **Australia,** contact SSA Swap Program, P.O. Box 399 or 220 Faraday St. (1st Fl.), Carlton South, Melbourne, Victoria 3053 (tel. (03) 348 17 77). In the **U.K.,** contact London Student Travel, 52 Grosvenor Gardens, London WC1 (tel. (071) 730 34 02). In **Canada,** write to Travel CUTS (Canadian University Travel Services Ltd.), 187 College St., Toronto, Ont. M5T 1P7 (tel. (416) 979-2406). If you can't locate an affiliated office in your country, contact CIEE's main office: 205 E. 42nd St., New York, NY 10017 (tel. (212) 661-1450, (800) 223-7402 for charter flight tickets only), or the **International Student Travel Confederation,** listed below.

**Council Travel** and **Council Charter.** 2 budget subsidiaries of CIEE. Council Travel sells Eurail and BritRail passes, guidebooks, travel gear, discounted flights, ISIC, FIYTO, and ITIC cards, and HI memberships. Publishes *Council Travel's Budget Traveler* newsletter. Offices in the **U.S.** include ones in New York, Boston, Los Angeles, Chicago, San Francisco, and Austin. Also in **U.K.** at 28A Poland St., London W1V 3DB (tel. (071) 437 7767).

**Educational Travel Centre (ETC),** 438 North Frances St., Madison, WI 53703 (tel. (608) 256-5551). Flight information, HI/AYH cards, Eurail and regional rail passes.

**International Student Exchange Flights (ISE),** 5010 E. Shea Blvd., #A104, Scottsdale, AZ 85254 (tel. (602) 951-1177). Budget student flights, BritRail and Eurail passes, traveler's checks, and travel guides. Free catalogue.

**International Student Travel Confederation (ISTC),** Store Kongensgade 40H, 1264 Copenhagen K, Denmark (tel. 45 33 93 93 03). Applications have detailed specific requirements.US$14. Cards are valid Sept.-Dec. of the next year.

**Let's Go Travel,** Harvard Student Agencies, Inc., 53 Church St., Cambridge, MA 02138 (tel. (617) 495-9649 or (800) 553-8746). They sell plane tickets, railpasses, HI/AYH memberships, ISIC, ITIC, and IYC cards, traveling gear, and travel guides.

**London Student Travel,** 52 Grosvenor Gardens, London WC1 (tel. (071) 730 3402); in Ireland, **USIT Ltd.,** Aston Quay, O'Connell Bridge, Dublin 2 (tel. (01) 679 8833; fax (01) 677 8843).

**SSA Swap Program,** P.O. Box 399 or 220 Faraday St. (1 Fl.), Carlton South, Melbourne, Victoria, 3053 Australia (tel. (03) 348 17 77).

**STA Travel,** a worldwide youth travel organization. Offers bargain flights, railpasses, accommodations, tours, insurance, and ISICs. 10 offices in the **U.S.,** including 17 E. 45th St., New York, NY 10017 (tel. (212) 986-9643 or (800) 777-0112), and 7202 Melrose Ave., Los Angeles, CA 90046 (tel. (213) 934-8722). In the **U.K.,** STA's main office is at 86 Old Brompton Rd., London SW7 3LQ.

# LET'S USE CTS

**Travel CUTS** (Canadian University Travel Services Ltd.), 187 College St., Toronto, Ont. M5T 1P7 (tel. (416) 979-2406). In the **U.K.,** 295-A Regent St., London W1R 7YA (tel. (071) 637 3161). Does many wonderful things including offering discounted transatlantic flights with special student fares and discount rail passes. Sells ISIC, FIYTO, and HI hostel cards. Student Work Abroad Program (SWAP). *The Student Traveller* is available free at all 35 offices across Canada.

## Hostel Associations

**Hostelling International (HI)** is the new and universal trademark name adopted by the International Youth Hostel Federation (IYHF). The 6000 official youth hostels worldwide will normally display the new HI logo (a blue triangle) alongside the symbol of one of the 70 national hostel association.

A one-year Hostelling International (HI) membership permits you to stay at youth hostels in Paris at reasonable prices. Despite the name, you need not be a youth; travelers over 25 pay only a slight surcharge for a bed. You can save yourself potential trouble by procuring a membership card before you leave home; some hostels do not sell them on the spot. (For more details on youth hostels, see Accommodations.)

The guide *Budget Accommodation Vol. 1: Europe and the Mediterranean* (US$13.95, including postage and handling) lists up-to-date information on HI hostels.

One-year hostel membership cards are available from some travel agencies, including Council Travel, Let's Go Travel, and STA Travel, and from the following organizations:

**Hostelling International (HI),** headquarters, 9 Guessens Rd., Welwyn Garden City, Hertfordshire AL8 6QW, England (tel. (44) (0707) 33 24 87).

**American Youth Hostels (AYH),** 733 15th St. N.W., #840, Washington, DC 20005 (tel. (202) 783-6161; fax (202) 783-6171); also dozens of regional offices across the U.S. (call above number for information). AYH is the U.S. member of HI. Cards cost US$25 (renewals US$20, under 18 US$10, over 54 US$15, family cards US$35). 200 hostels in U.S. Contact AYH for ISICs, student and charter flights, travel equipment, and literature on budget travel.

**Hostelling International—Canada (HIC),** National Office, 1600 James Naismith Dr., #608, Gloucester, Ottawa, Ont. K1B 5N4 (tel. (613) 748 5638). 1-yr. membership fee CDN$26.75, under 18 CDN$12.84, 2-yr. CDN$37.45.

**Fédération Unie des Auberges de Jeunesse (FUAJ),** 27, rue Pajol, 75018 Paris (tel. 46 07 00 01; Mo. La Chapelle).

**Youth Hostels Association of England and Wales (YHA),** Trevelyan House, 8 St. Stephen's Hill, St. Albans, Herts AL1 2DY (tel. (0727) 855 215), or 14 Southampton St., Covent Garden, London WC2E 7HY (tel. (071) 836 1036). Fee £9, under 18 £3.

**Scottish Youth Hostel Association (SYHA),** 7 Glebe Crescent, Sterling FK8 2JA (tel. (0786) 511 81).

**An Oíge (Irish Youth Hostel Association),** 61 Mountjoy St., Dublin 7 (tel. (01) 304555; fax (01) 305808). Fee IR£9, under 18 IR£3.

**Youth Hostel Association of Northern Ireland (YHANI),** 56 Bradbury Pl., Belfast BT7 1RU (tel. (0232) 324 733).

**Australian Youth Hostels Association (AYHA),** Level 3, 10 Mallett St., Camperdown, NSW 2050 Australia (tel. (02) 565 1699; fax (02) 565 1325). Membership card AUS$40 for Australians for use overseas; AUS$24 for overseas visitors.

**Youth Hostels Association of New Zealand (YHANZ),** P.O. Box 436, 173 Gloucester St., Christchurch 1, New Zealand (tel. 64 3 379 99 70; fax 64 3 365 44 76).

## BOOKS, GUIDES, MAPS, ETC.

**Animal and Plant Health Inspection Service,** U.S. Dept. of Agriculture, 6505 Belcrest Road, Hyattsville, MD 20782-2058. Provides information about restrictions in the wildlife trade, as well as a pamphlet entitled *Travelers' Tips on Bringing Food, Plant, and Animal Products into the United States.*

**The European Association of Music Festivals,** 122, rue de Lausanne, 1202 Geneva, Switzerland (tel. (22) 732 28 03; fax (22) 738 40 12), publishes the booklet *Festivals,* which lists the dates and programs of major European music and theater festivals.

**Forsyth Travel Library,** P.O. Box 2975, Shawnee Mission, KS 66201 (tel. (800) 367-7984). Call or write for their catalogue of maps, railpasses, and timetables.

**Hippocrene Books, Inc.,** 171 Madison Ave., New York NY 10016 (tel. (212) 685-4371; orders (718) 454-2360; fax (718) 454-1391). Free catalogue. Publishes travel reference books, travel guides, maps, and foreign language dictionaries.

**Press and Information Division of the French Embassy,** 4101 Reservoir Rd. N.W., Washington, DC 20007 (tel. (202) 944-6048). Write for information about political, social, and economic aspects of France. Publishes a bi-weekly newsletter, *News from France,* as well as *France Magazine.*

**Superintendent of Documents,** U.S. Government Printing Office, Washington, DC 20402 (tel. (202) 783-3238), prints another helpful, regionally specific publication, *Tips for Travelers* (US$1).

**Travelling Books,** P.O. Box 77114, Seattle, WA 98177 (tel. (206) 367-5848), publishes a catalogue of guides which will make the traveler weep with wanderlust.

**Wide World Books and Maps,** 1911 N. 45th St., Seattle, WA 98103 (tel. (206) 634-3453). Write them for hard-to-find maps. Open Mon.-Fri. 10am-7pm, Sat. 10am-6pm, Sun. noon-5pm.

# ■ Documents and Formalities

Remember to file all applications several weeks or even months before your planned departure date. Most offices suggest that you apply in the winter off-season (Aug.-Dec.) for speedier service. When you travel, always carry on your person two or more forms of identification, including at least one photo ID. Many establishments, especially banks, require several IDs before cashing traveler's checks. It is useful to carry extra passport-size photos to affix to the various IDs you will eventually acquire.

## PASSPORTS

You need a valid passport to enter France and to re-enter your own country. Photocopy the page of your passport that contains your photograph and identifying information; your passport number is especially important. Consulates recommend that you carry an expired passport or an official copy of your birth certificate in your baggage separate from other documents. Losing your passport can be a nightmare. It may take weeks to process a replacement. Some consulates can issue new passports within two days if you give them proof of citizenship. In an emergency, immediate temporary traveling papers may permit you to return to your home country.

**Applying for a passport** is complicated, so make sure your questions are answered in advance. All the countries listed below require various forms of identification, two recent, identical passport-sized photographs, and a fee, along with the completed application form; be sure to contact your local passport office for more specific information.

**U.S. citizens** may apply for a passport at any one of several thousand federal or state **courthouses** or **post offices** authorized to accept passport applications or at a **U.S. Passport Agency.** Refer to the "U.S. Government, State Department" section of the telephone directory or call your local post office for addresses.

File your application as early as possible. Processing usually takes three to four weeks, perhaps fewer from a Passport Agency. Passports are processed according to the departure date indicated on the application form. During peak travel season (March-Aug.) processing may take even longer. Passport agencies also offer **rush service:** if you have proof (e.g. an airplane ticket) that you are departing within five working days, a Passport Agency will issue a passport while you wait.

U.S. embassies and consulates in Paris can usually issue new passports, given proof of citizenship. For more **information**, contact the U.S. Passport Information's helpful 24-hour recorded message (tel. (202) 647-0518) or call the recorded message of the passport agency nearest you.

**Canadian application** forms in English and French are available at all passport offices, post offices, and most travel agencies. Citizens may apply in person at any one of 29 regional passport offices across Canada. You can apply by mail to Passport Office, External Affairs, Ottawa, Ont. K1A OG3. The processing time is approximately five business days for in-person applications and three weeks for mailed ones. If a passport is lost abroad, Canadians must be able to prove citizenship with another document. For additional **information**, call the 24-hour number (tel. (800) 567-6868). Refer to the booklet *Bon Voyage, But...* for further help and a list of Canadian embassies and consulates abroad. It is available free of charge from any passport office or from: Info-Export (BPTE), External Affairs, Ottawa, Ont. K1A OG2.

**British citizens** can obtain either a full passport or a more restricted Visitor's Passport. For a **full passport** (fee £18), apply in person or by mail to the London Passport Office or by mail to a passport office located in Liverpool, Newport, Peterborough, Glasgow, or Belfast. Processing usually takes four to six weeks. The London office offers same-day walk-in rush service; arrive early. For a **Visitor's Passport** (around £9), valid for one year in Western Europe only, apply in person at major post offices.

**Irish citizens** can apply by mail to one of the following two passport offices: Dept. of Foreign Affairs, Passport Office, Setanta Centre, Molesworth St., Dublin 2 (tel. (01) 6711633), or Passport Office, 1A South Mall, Cork (tel. (021) 272 525). Obtain an application form at a local Garda station or request one from a passport office.

**Australian citizens** must apply for a passport in person at a local post office, a passport office, or an Australian diplomatic mission overseas. An appointment may be necessary at all three; call the toll-free information service for details (tel. 13 12 32).

Applicants for **New Zealand passports** must contact their local Link Centre, travel agent, or New Zealand Representative for an application form. Mail it to the New Zealand Passport Office, Documents of National Identity Division, Dept. of Internal Affairs, Box 10-526, Wellington (tel. (04) 474 81 00). The application fee is NZ$56.25 for an application lodged in New Zealand and NZ$110 for one lodged overseas.

**South African citizens** can apply for a passport (30R) at any Home Affairs Office.

## VISAS

A visa is an endorsement that a foreign government stamps into a passport; it allows the bearer to stay in that country for a specified purpose and period of time. Visas are currently required of all visitors to France, except those from EC member countries, as well as the U.S., Canada, New Zealand, Andorra, Austria, Czech Republic, the Greek half of Cyprus, Finland, Hungary, Iceland, Japan, Republic of Korea, Liechtenstein, Malta, Monaco, Norway, Poland, San Marino, Slovak Republic, Sweden, and Switzerland. Note that Australia is distinctly absent from this list. A visa is required of *anyone* planning to stay more than three months (see below). It must be obtained from the French consulate in your home country.

Requirements for a long-stay visa vary with the nature of the stay: work, study, or *au pair*. Apply to the nearest French consulate at least three months in advance. For a **student visa,** you must present a passport valid until at least 90 days after the date you plan to leave France, a letter of acceptance with the exact dates of study, a financial guarantee for US$600 per month above room and board (a notarized note from parents is adequate), proof of medical insurance covering the whole stay in France, an application available from the consulate, a passport photo, and a fee (currently US$60). For an *au pair* stay of more than three months, an **au pair's visa** is required. *Au pairs* must be students for the whole time they are *au pairs.* The visa requirements are the same as those for students, although an *au pair* contract can substitute for the financial guarantee. French employers must initiate the process of obtaining a **work visa.** Contact a French consulate for more details. Note that it is illegal for foreign students to work during the school year, although they can receive permission from their local *Direction départementale du travail et de la main-d'oeuvre étrangère* to work in summer (see below).

In addition to securing a visa, if you are staying longer than 90 days in France you must obtain a **carte de séjour** (residency permit) once in France. Report to the **Préfecture de Paris,** 17, bd. Morland, *4ème* (tel. 53 71 51 68; open 8:30am-6pm). Here you must present the same information required for a student visa as well as six (yes, six) application forms completed in French and six passport photos. Be prepared to stand in line, perhaps repeatedly. Bring your Proust.

For more information, send for the U.S. government pamphlet *Foreign Visa Requirements.* Mail a check for 50¢ to Consumer Information Center, Dept. 454V, Pueblo, CO 81009 (tel. (719) 948-3334). The company **Visa Center, Inc.,** 507 Fifth Ave., #904, New York, NY 10017 (tel. (212) 986-0924), secures visas for travel to and from all possible countries. Average cost for a U.S. citizen is US$15-20 per visa.

## YOUTH AND STUDENT IDENTIFICATION

In the world of budget travel, youth has its privileges. In many cases, establishments will honor a student ID from your college or university for student discounts. Two main forms of student and youth identification are accepted worldwide; they are extremely useful, especially for the insurance packages that accompany them.

The **International Student Identity Card (ISIC)** is the most widely accepted form of student identification. This card can garner you discounts for sights, theaters, museums, accommodations, train, ferry, and airplane travel, and other services in Paris. Present the card wherever you go, and always ask about discounts. The ISIC (US$15) also provides accident insurance of up to US$3000 and US$100 per day of in-hospital care for up to 60 days. In addition, cardholders have access to a toll-free Traveler's Assistance hotline whose multilingual staff can provide help in emergencies overseas.

The student travel offices which issue ISICs include Council Travel, Let's Go Travel, and Student Travel Network in the U.S.; Travel CUTS in Canada; and organizations under the auspices of the International Student Travel Confederation (ISTC) around the world (see Useful Addresses and Publications). The *International Student Identity Card Handbook* lists by country some of the available discounts.

Because of the proliferation of phony and improperly issued ISIC cards, many airlines and some other services now require double proof of student identity. It is wise to have a signed letter from the registrar and stamped with the school seal attesting to your student status, or to carry your school ID card. The new **International Teacher Identity Card (ITIC)** (US$16) offers identical discounts, in theory, but because of its recent introduction many establishments are reluctant to honor it.

**Federation of International Youth Travel Organizations (FIYTO)** issues its own discount card to travelers who are not students but are under 26. Also known as the **International Youth Discount Travel Card** or the **GO 25 Card,** this one-year card offers many of the same benefits as the ISIC. Most organizations that sell the ISIC also sell the Go 25 Card. A free brochure that lists discounts is also provided. The fee is US$10, CDN$12, or £4. For more information, contact FIYTO at Bredgage 25H, DK-1260, Copenhagen K, Denmark (tel. (45) 33 33 96 00; fax (45) 33 93 96 76).

## INTERNATIONAL DRIVER'S LICENSE

An International Driving Permit is not usually required to drive in France, but is recommended if you don't speak French. Most rental agencies will not ask to see the permit but will want to see a valid driver's license.

Your IDP must be issued in your own country before you depart. U.S. license holders can obtain an International Driving Permit (US$10), valid for one year, at

# Always travel with a friend.

Get the International
Student Identity Card,
recognized worldwide.

For information call toll-free **1-800-GET-AN-ID**.
or contact any Council Travel office. (See inside front cover.)

 **Council on International Educational Exchange**
205 East 42nd Street, New York, NY 10017

any **American Automobile Association (AAA)** office or by writing to its main office, AAA Florida, Travel Agency Services Department, 1000 AAA Drive, Heathrow, FL 32746-5080 (tel. (800) 222-4357 or (407) 444-7883; fax (407) 444-7380). For further information, contact a local AAA office. You may also procure an IDP from the **American Automobile Touring Alliance,** Bayside Plaza, 188 The Embarcadero, San Francisco, CA 94105. Canadians can obtain an IDP (CDN$10) through any **Canadian Automobile Association (CAA)** branch office in Canada, or by writing to CAA Toronto, 60 Commerce Valley Dr. E., Markham, Ont. L3T 7P9 (tel. (416) 771-3170).

Most credit cards cover standard insurance. If you drive your own car or rent or borrow one, you will need a **green card,** or **International Insurance Certificate,** to prove that you have liability insurance. The application forms are available at any AAA or CAA office or the car rental agency; most agencies include coverage in their prices. If you lease a car, you can obtain a green card from the dealer. Even if your auto insurance applies abroad, you will need a green card to certify this to foreign officials.

## CUSTOMS

Don't be alarmed by customs procedures. The many regulations of customs and duties hardly pose a threat to the budget traveler. Most countries prohibit or restrict the importation of firearms, explosives, ammunition, fireworks, controlled drugs, most plants and animals, lottery tickets, and obscene literature and films. To avoid problems when you transport prescription drugs, ensure that the bottles are clearly marked, and carry a copy of the prescription to show the customs officer.

Anything exceeding the allowance of what a visitor can bring into France is charged a duty. Among other things, if you are bringing in more than 200 cigarettes, 2L of wine, 1L of alcohol over 38.8 proof, or 50g of perfume, you must declare such items. Drug trafficking is illegal in France. Write the Bureau of Consular Affairs, Public Affairs #5807, Dept. of State, Washington, DC 20520, for more information and the pamphlet *Travel Warning on Drugs Abroad.*

Upon returning home, you must declare all articles you acquired abroad and must pay a duty on the value of those articles that exceeds the allowance established by your country's customs service. Holding onto receipts for purchases made abroad will help establish values when you return. Make a list of any valuables that you carry with you from home; if you register this list with customs before your departure, you will avoid import duty charges and ensure an easy passage upon your return.

Keep in mind that goods and gifts purchased at duty-free shops abroad are not exempt from duty or sales tax at your point of return; you must declare these items along with other purchases. For a complete and specific list of what can and cannot be brought back home, contact your local customs service.

**U.S. citizens** can mail unsolicited gifts duty-free if they are worth less than US$50, though you may not mail liquor, tobacco, or perfume. Officials occasionally spot-check parcels, so mark the price and nature of the gift and the words "Unsolicited Gift" on the package. If you send back a non-gift parcel or a gift worth more than US$50, the Postal Service will collect a duty for its value plus a handling charge to deliver it. If you mail home personal goods of U.S. origin, you can avoid duty charges by marking the package "American goods returned." For more information, consult the brochure *Know Before You Go,* available from R. Woods, Consumer Information Center, Pueblo, CO 81009 (item 477Y). You can direct other questions to the U.S. Customs Service, P.O. Box 7407, Washington, DC 20044 (tel. (202) 927-6724). Foreign nationals living in the U.S. are subject to different regulations; refer to the leaflet *Customs Hints for Visitors (Nonresidents).*

**Canadian citizens** who remain abroad for at least one week may bring back up to CDN$300 worth of goods duty-free once every calendar year. For more information, contact External Affairs, Communications Branch, Mackenzie Ave., Ottawa, Ont. K1A 0l5 (tel. (613) 957-0275).

**EC nationals** who travel between EC countries no longer need to declare the goods they purchase abroad. For information about **U.K. customs,** contact Her Majesty's Customs and Excise, Custom House, Heathrow Airport North, Hounslow, Middlesex, TW6 2LA (tel. (081) 750 1603; fax (081) 750 1549). *HM Customs & Excise Notice 1* explains the allowances for people travelling to the U.K. both from within and without the European Community. For more information about **Irish customs**, contact The Revenue Commissioners, Dublin Castle (tel. (01) 679 2777; fax (01) 671 2021).

**Australian citizens** may import AUS$400 of goods duty-free. For information, contact the nearest Australian consulate. Each **New Zealand citizen** may bring home up to NZ$700 worth of goods duty-free. For more information, consult the *New Zealand Customs Guide for Travelers* or contact New Zealand Customs, 50 Anzac Ave., Box 29, Auckland (tel. (09) 377 35 20; fax (09) 309 2978).

Each **South African citizen** may import up to a value of R500. For more information contact The Commissioner for Customs and Excise, Private Bag X47, Pretoria, 0001. Write for the pamphlet *South African Customs Information*. South Africans residing in the U.S. should contact the South African Mission, 3201 New Mexico Ave. N.W., #390, Washington, DC 20016 (tel. (202) 232-4400; fax (202) 364-6008).

# ■ Money

## CURRENCY AND EXCHANGE

| | |
|---|---|
| **US$1 = 6.06F** | **1F = US$0.16** |
| **CDN$1 = 4.61F** | **1F = CDN$0.22** |
| **UK£1 = 8.86F** | **1F = UK£0.11** |
| **IR£1 = 8.27F** | **1F = IR£.12** |
| **AUS$1 = 4.11F** | **1F = AUS$0.24** |
| **NZ$1 = 3.34F** | **1F = NZ$0.30** |
| **SAR1 = 1.80F** | **1F = SAR0.56** |

---

### A Note on Prices and Currency

The information in this book was researched in the summer of 1993. Since then, inflation will have raised most prices at least 10%. The exchange rates listed were compiled on August 17, 1993. Since rates fluctuate considerably, confirm them before you go by checking a national newspaper.

---

The basic unit of currency in France is the franc, divided into 100 centimes, and issued in both coins and paper notes. The smallest unit of French currency is the five-centime piece. The new franc, equal to 100 old francs, was issued in 1960.

Remember that it is usually more expensive to buy foreign currency than it is to buy domestic; therefore francs will be less costly in France than at home. Converting a small amount of money before you go, however, will allow you to breeze through the airport while others languish in exchange counter lines. This is also a good practice in case you find yourself stuck with no money after banking hours or on a holiday.

When looking to change money in Paris, try to approach the event with the spirit of competition. Not every *bureau de change* offers the same rates and most do not charge commission. Don't be fooled by what seem like fantastic rates. Make sure that no strings (like having to exchange at least 15,000F worth of currency) apply. The best rates in town are found around the Opéra on rue Scribe, rue Auber, and rue de la Paix. Many post offices will change cash and American Express Traveler's Cheques at competitive rates and without commission; bureaus at train stations and airports tend to offer less favorable rates. Most banks are open 9am-noon and 2-4:30pm, but not all exchange currency. Check before you get in line.

MONEY

**American Express:** 11, rue Scribe, 9ème (tel. 47 77 77 07). Mo. Opéra or Auber. Across from the back of the Opéra. No commission on AmEx Traveler's Cheques, 5F20 commission on all other transactions. Mediocre exchange rates. Cardholders can cash a personal check from a U.S. bank account every 21 days; bring your passport. Mobbed during the summer, especially Mon. and Fri.-Sat. They will hold mail for you without charge if you have their card or Traveler's Cheques; otherwise 5F per inquiry. Upstairs open for currency exchange daily 7:30am-7pm. Downstairs serves cardholders, receives money grams, and distributes *poste restante* daily 9am-5:30pm.

**Change Automatique,** 66, av. des Champs-Elysées, 8ème. Mo. George V. An automatic machine that accepts 5, 10, or 20 dollar bills and 50 or 100 German mark, 50 or 100 Swiss franc, and 50,000 or 100,000 Italian lire notes. Rates and commission posted above "insert bill" slot. Not the best rates in town. Open 24 hrs.

**At Train Stations:** Remember these offices offer less-than-attractive rates intended for impatient travelers. **Gare d'Austerlitz,** 13ème (tel. 45 84 91 40). Open daily 7am-9pm. **Gare de Lyon,** 12ème (tel. 43 41 52 70). Open daily 7am-11pm. **Gare de l'Est,** 10ème (tel. 46 07 66 84). Open Mon.-Fri. 9am-6:30pm, Sat. 9:30am-5:30pm. **Gare du Nord,** 10ème (tel. 42 80 11 50). Open daily 6:15am-11:30pm. **Gare St-Lazare,** 8ème (tel. 43 87 72 51). Open daily 7am-9pm.

**At Airports:** Also not the best place to change your currency. Exchange just enough to get to Paris and change the rest within the city. **Orly-Sud:** open daily 6am-11:30pm. **Roissy-Charles de Gaulle:** open daily 6am-11:30pm.

## TRAVELER'S CHECKS

Traveler's checks are the safest way to carry large sums of money. They are refundable if lost or stolen, and many issuing agencies offer additional services such as refund hotlines, message relaying, travel insurance, and emergency assistance. Most tourist establishments will accept traveler's checks and almost any bank will cash them. Usually banks sell traveler's checks for a 1-2% commission, although your own bank may waive the surcharge. Buying checks in small denominations (US$20 checks rather than US$50 ones or higher) is safer and more convenient—otherwise, after a small purchase, you'll still be carrying around a large amount of cash. Be prepared to convert at least US$100 into traveler's checks; most places will not exchange less than that.

Refunds on lost or stolen checks can be time-consuming. To accelerate the process and avoid red tape, keep check receipts and a record of which checks you've cashed. When you buy your checks, ask for a list of refund centers. Leave a photocopy of check serial numbers with someone at home as back-up in case you lose your copy. Never countersign checks until you're prepared to cash them.

Finally, consider purchasing traveler's checks in francs. Most companies offer their checks in several currencies. While U.S. citizens can easily exchange dollars for francs in France, South Africans, New Zealanders, and Australians may have difficulty exchanging their currencies. Dealing with double exchange rates can be expensive. In smaller French cities and towns, as in stores and restaurants, it is often easier to exchange checks in francs. In addition, you avoid the hassle of worrying about exchange rates. Most banks will cash French franc traveler's checks commission-free (be sure to ask, however, *before* you give them your money).

**American Express:** AmEx Traveler's Cheques are the most widely recognized worldwide and easiest to replace if lost or stolen—just call the information number or the AmEx Travel office nearest you. AmEx offices cash their own Cheques commission-free and sell Cheques which can be signed by either of two people traveling together. Cheques available in 7 currencies. American Automobile Association members can obtain AmEx Traveler's Cheques commission-free at AAA offices. Call and ask for AmEx's booklet *Traveler's Companion* which gives travel office addresses and stolen Cheque hotlines for each European country. Call (800) 221-7282 in the U.S. and Canada; (0800) 52 13 13 in the U.K.; (02) 886 0689

# Don't forget to write.

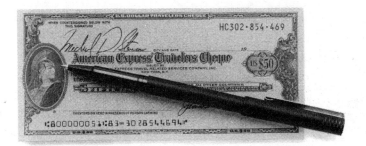

Now that you've said, "Let's go," it's time to say
"Let's get American Express® Travelers Cheques." If they are lost or
stolen, you can get a fast and full refund virtually anywhere you
travel. So before you leave be sure and write.

MONEY

in Australia, New Zealand, and the South Pacific with questions or to report lost or stolen Cheques. Elsewhere, call U.S. collect (801) 964-6665.

**Barclays Bank:** sells Visa traveler's checks. For lost or stolen checks, call Visa (tel. (800) 645-6556); for Barclays information specifically, call (800) 221-2426 in the U.S. and Canada call (202) 67 12 12 in the U.K.; from elsewhere call New York collect at (212) 858-8500. Branches throughout Britain. Commission on purchase of checks varies (usually 1-3%). Barclays branches cash Barclays-Visa and any other Visa brand traveler's checks for free. Checks in 4 currencies.

**Citicorp:** sells Visa traveler's checks. Call (800) 645-6556 in the U.S. and Canada, (071) 982 4040 in London, from abroad call collect (813) 623-1709. Commission is 1-2% on check purchases. Check holders are automatically enrolled in **Travel Assist Hotline** (800) 523-1199 for 45 days after checks are purchased. This service provides travelers with English-speaking doctor, lawyer, and interpreter referrals as well as traveler's check refund assistance. Citicorp also has a World Courier Service which guarantees hand delivery of traveler's checks anywhere in the world.

**Mastercard International:** tel. (800) 223-9920 in the U.S. and Canada, from abroad call collect (609) 987-7300. Commission varies from 1-2% for purchases depending on the bank. Issued in U.S. dollars only.

**Thomas Cook:** Thomas Cook and Mastercard International have formed a "global alliance"—Thomas Cook distributes traveler's checks with both the Mastercard and Thomas Cook names printed on them. Thomas Cook handles the distribution of checks in U.S. dollars as well as checks in 10 other currencies. Call (800) 223-7373 for refunds in U.S., (800) 223-4030 for orders. From elsewhere call collect (212) 974-5696. Some Thomas Cook Currency Services offices do not charge any fee for purchase of checks, while some charge a 1-2% commission. You can buy Mastercard traveler's checks from Thomas Cook at any bank displaying a Mastercard sign.

**Visa:** Visa and Barclay's Bank have formed a team, similar to the Thomas Cook/Mastercard alliance, by which Visa checks can be cashed for free at any Barclay's bank. Call (800) 227-6811 in the U.S. and Canada; from abroad, call New York collect (212) 858-8500 or London (071) 937 8091.

## CREDIT CARDS

Credit cards in Europe do everything they do in America. **Mastercard** and **Visa** are the most welcomed in shops and hotels; heavy surcharges keep small businesses out of the American Express loop. Yet all three major credit cards offer instant cash advances from banks and teller machines throughout Western Europe, in local currency. Nearly 800 banks in France, indicated by the sticker *CB/VISA ou EC,* will allow you to withdraw money at a teller with a Visa or AmEx card. Keep in mind that Mastercard and Visa have aliases here, Eurocard and Carte Bleue, respectively; some cashiers may not know this until they check their manual.

Credit cards are also invaluable in an emergency—an unexpected hospital bill or the more prosaic loss of traveler's checks—which may leave you temporarily without other resources. Try to pay for large purchases abroad by credit card; the credit card company gets a better exchange rate than you would have. In the Paris office, **American Express** cardholders can cash up to US$1000 in personal checks (US$5000 for gold card holders) every three weeks. With someone feeding money into your account back home, this can be one of the easiest and cheapest ways to send money overseas. Global Assist, a 24-hour hotline offering information and legal assistance in emergencies, is also available to cardholders (tel. (800) 333-2639 in U.S. and Canada; from abroad call collect (202) 554-2639). Call **American Express Travel Service** (tel. (800) 221-7282) for more information on services, or consult their *Traveler's Companion* booklet which lists full-service offices worldwide. If you lose your American Express Card, call 47 77 72 00. For lost Visa Cards call 42 77 11 90.

M O N E Y

## CASH CARDS

**Automatic Teller Machines**—popularly called ATMs—are widespread within Paris, and in the last years huge advances have been made in the extension of the **Cirrus** network (tel. (800) 4-CIRRUS (424-7787)) to European countries. Depending on the system that your bank at home uses, you will probably be able to access your own personal bank account whenever you're in need of funds. Keep in mind that the ATM machines get the wholesale exchange rate which is generally 5% better than the retail rate most banks use (which is better than the rate most *bureaux de change* use). **American Express** card holders can sign up for AmEx's Express Cash service through which you can access cash from your account at any ATM with the AmEx trademark. American Express cards work in ATMs at **Credit Lyonnais** banks, as well as at AmEx offices and major airports. Each transaction costs a minimum US$2.50 (max. US$10.00) plus conversion fees and interest. For a list of ATMs where you can use your card, call AmEx at (800) CASH-NOW (227-4669) and they'll send you a list of participating machines. Make sure to set up your Express Cash account a few weeks before you plan to travel. **Visa** cards can access ATM networks in 40 countries around the world (usually Cirrus, but it varies according to the issuing bank). **Mastercard** functions in essentially the same way as Visa. Be sure to contact your issuer before you travel in order to get the **Personal Identification Number (PIN)** essential for ATM use. There are no letters on European bank machines, so persons with words for passwords should figure out the corresponding numbers before leaving home. Don't rely too heavily on automation. There is often a limit on the amount of money you can withdraw per day, and computer network failures are not uncommon.

In Paris, **Crédit Mutuel's Minibanque/24** and **Crédit Agricole** teller machines are on the CIRRUS network. Consult Crédit Agricole's brochure *Rencontrez un specialiste* for the location of its ATM machines.

## SENDING MONEY ABROAD

Sending money overseas is a complicated, expensive, and often extremely frustrating adventure. Do your best to avoid it; carry a credit card or a separate stash of emergency traveler's checks. The easiest way to obtain money from home is to bring an **American Express Card.** AmEx allows green-card holders to draw cash from their checking accounts at any of its major offices (up to US$1000 every seven days; no service charge, no interest). Otherwise, money can be wired abroad through international money transfer services operated by American Express or Western Union.

**American Express** offers a MoneyGram service by which US$100-7450 may be sent abroad. MoneyGrams sent from the U.S. to France arrive in 10 minutes at the designated AmEx office. It costs US$40 to send US$500 and US$70 to send US$1000. The money is disbursed in traveler's checks. For more information, call the American Express MoneyGram Customer Service toll-free number: (800) 543-4080; in Canada (800) 933-3278. This service operates only between American Express offices proper, not their representatives, and is available for non-card holders. Not every office in France can receive MoneyGrams; check carefully.

**Western Union** (tel. (800) 225-5227) offers a similar service for cabling money abroad to any of 15 cities in France. In the U.S., call Western Union any time at (800) 325-6000 to cable money with your **Visa** or **Mastercard.** For payment with credit card it costs US$50 to send US$500 and US$60 for US$1000. The cabled money can be retrieved with proper identification from any of four locations at Banque Rivaud in Paris. It should arrive, in francs, within minutes.

If you're staying in France long enough to have a personal bank account, a cheaper alternative may be to **cable money**. Tell your home bank the amount you need and the name and address of the receiving bank (a bank with an international department), together with the destination account number. Give the same information to whoever is sending you money from their own account. Transfer can take up to a few days; the fee is usually a flat US$20-30. Outside an American Express office, don't try to cash checks in foreign currencies; they often take weeks and a US$30 fee to clear.

Finally, if you find yourself in a life-or-death situation, you can usually have money sent through your government's diplomatic mission in Paris. Citizens of the United States who are desperate should turn to a U.S. Consular section of the U.S. Embassy or Consulate, which will assist by contacting friends or family in the U.S. and arranging for them to send money. In emergencies, U.S. citizens can have money sent via the State Department's **Citizens Emergency Center,** Dept. of State, 2201 C St. N.W., Washington, DC 20520 (tel. (202) 647-5225, after-hours and holiday emergencies tel. (202) 647-4000). This service provides, among other things, repatriation loans to pay for destitute Americans' direct return to the U.S. More information can be found in the pamphlet *The Citizens Emergency Center.* Order it from the Bureau of Consular Affairs, Public Affairs Staff, U.S. Dept. of State, Washington, DC 20570-4818.

## OPENING A BANK ACCOUNT

If you are planning a long-term stay in Paris and have fairly liquid assets, consider opening a bank account. Foreigners can open non-resident bank accounts, but banks expect that these will be long-term (a few years) and often require a hefty opening deposit, and the maintenance of a high minimum balance (30,000F). Go to main bank offices near the Opéra to inquire about such accounts—neighborhood branches without a foreign affairs department are not equipped to provide such services.

## VALUE-ADDED TAX

Value-Added Tax (called TVA in France) is a varying sales tax levied especially in the EEC. The French rate is 18.6% on all goods except books, food, and medicine. There is a 33% luxury tax on such items as videocassettes, watches, jewelry, and cameras.

If you spend more than 2000F (4200F for EC members) in a particular store, you can participate in a complex over-the-counter export program for foreign shoppers that exempts you from paying TVA. Ask the store for an official *formulaire de détaxe pour l'exportation* (detax invoice) and a stamped envelope. At the border, show the invoices and your purchases to the French customs officials, who will stamp the invoices. (Make sure you leave all the articles you have purchased near the top of your suitcase.) If you're at an airport, look for the window labeled *douane de détaxe,* and be sure to budget at least an hour for the intricacies of the French bureaucracy. On a train, find an official (they won't find you) or get off at a station close to the border. Then send a copy back to the vendor. With this official TVA-exempt proof, they will refund the agreed amount. The refunds are sent to your bank account and not to your address, a process which may take as much as six months. Upon returning to your country, you may have to pay customs charges if your purchases amount to more than the allotted amount (US$400), but this often falls short of the VAT refund.

# ■ Health and Insurance

Common sense is the simplest prescription for good health while you travel: eat well, drink enough, get enough sleep, and don't overexert yourself. All food, including seafood, dairy products, and fresh produce, is normally safe in Paris. The water is chlorinated and also quite safe; to avoid the infamous traveler's diarrhea, you may want to drink mineral water for the first day or two while your body adjusts to new bacteria.

Although no special immunizations are necessary for travel to France, be sure that your **inoculations** are up-to-date. Typhoid shots remain good for three years, tetanus for 10.

Always go prepared with any **medication** you may need while away. Carry up-to-date prescriptions and/or a statement (with a translated version) from your doctor, especially if you use insulin, syringes, or any narcotic drug. Keep all medicines in your carry-on luggage. Matching prescriptions with foreign equivalents may be difficult.

If you wear **glasses** or **contact lenses,** take an extra prescription with you. Bring along adequate supplies of your cleaning solutions. For heat disinfection you'll need outlet and low-watt voltage adapters. In general, use chemicals if you can while you're traveling; even with a converter, heat-disinfecting units don't always work the same way in Europe. Many, for example, will not shut off automatically.

Any traveler with a medical condition that cannot be easily recognized (i.e. diabetes, epilepsy, heart conditions, allergies to antibiotics) may want to obtain a **Medic Alert Identification Tag.** In an emergency, their internationally recognized tag indicates the nature of the bearer's problem and provides the number of Medic Alert's 24-hour hotline. Lifetime membership (tag, annually-updated wallet card, and hotline access) begins at US$35. Contact Medic Alert Foundation, P.O. Box 1009, Turlock, CA 95381-1009 (tel. (800) 432-5378). The **American Diabetes Association,** 1660 Duke St., Alexandria, VA 22314 (tel. (800) 232-3472), provides copies of an article "Travel and Diabetes" and diabetic ID cards.

All travelers should be concerned about **Acquired Immune Deficiency Syndrome (AIDS),** called *le SIDA* in French. The Center for Disease Control's **AIDS Hotline** provides information on AIDS in the U.S. and can refer you to other organizations with information on France (tel. (800) 342-2437; TTD (800) 243-7889). Call the **U.S. State Department** for country-specific restrictions for HIV-positive travelers (tel. (202) 647-1488; fax (202) 647-3000 or write Bureau of Consular Affairs, #5807, Dept. of State, Washington, DC 20520). The **World Health Organization** provides written material on AIDS internationally (tel. (202) 861-3200).

**Contraception** is readily available in most pharmacies. Condoms, called *préservatifs* (pray-zehr-vah-TEEF) can be bought at most pharmacies, but you have to ask at the counter. The French branch of the International Planned Parenthood Federation, the **Mouvement Français pour le Planning Familiale (MFPF)** (tel. 48 07 29 10; fax 47 00 79 77), can provide more information.

**Abortion** is legal in France, and is performed on request. The controversial abortion pill RU486 is both legal and practiced. The **National Abortion Federation's hotline** (tel. (800) 772-9100, Mon.-Fri. 9:30am-5:30pm) can direct you to organizations which provide information on abortion in France.

For additional information before you go, you may wish to contact the **International Association for Medical Assistance to Travelers (IAMAT).** IAMAT provides brochures on health for travelers, an ID card, a chart detailing advisable immunizations for 200 countries, and a directory of English-speaking physicians who have had medical training in Europe or North America. Membership to the organization is free (although donations are welcome) and doctors are on call 24 hours. Contact chapters in the **U.S.,** 417 Center St., Lewiston, NY, 14092, (tel. (716) 754-4883); in **Canada,** 40 Regal Rd. Guelph, Ont. N1K 1B5, (tel. (519) 836-0102), and 1287 St. Clair Ave. West, Toronto, M6E 1B8 (tel. (416) 652-0137); in **New Zealand,** P.O. Box 5049, 438 Pananui Rd., Christchurch 5 (tel. (03) 352 9053; fax (03) 352 4630).

For more information, write the **Superintendent of Documents.** Their publication *Health Information for International Travel* (US$5) details immunization requirements and other health precautions for travelers.

Beware of unnecessary insurance coverage—your current policies might well extend to many travel-related accidents. **Medical insurance** often covers costs incurred abroad. **Medicare** does not cover travel to Paris. Canadians are protected by their home province's health insurance plan: check with the provincial Ministry of Health or Health Plan Headquarters. Your **homeowners' insurance** may cover theft during travel. Homeowners are generally covered against loss of travel documents up to about US$500. ISIC, CIEE, STA and AmEx provide varying levels of insurance (see Useful Travel Organizations above).

Remember that insurance companies usually require a copy of the police report for thefts, or evidence of having paid medical expenses before they will honor a claim, and may have time limits on filing for reimbursement. Have all documents written in English to avoid possible translating fees. Always carry policy numbers and proof of insurance. Note that some of the plans listed below offer cash advances or guaranteed bills; check with each insurance carrier for specific restrictions.

## SAFETY AND SECURITY

Paris has much less violent crime than its American big-city equivalents, but crime on the whole is disturbingly on the rise. A few precautions will see you safely through your travels more effectively than constant paranoia. Take as few valuables as possible; flashy jewelry and big cameras will draw unwanted attention. Keep all valuables with you whenever you leave your room, even if it has a lock, as others may have a pass-key. At night, sleep with valuables on your person. Carry all your valuables (including your passport, railpass, traveler's checks, and airline ticket) either in a **money belt** or **neckpouch** stashed securely inside your clothing. These will protect you from thieves who use razors to slash open backpacks and fanny packs.

Like so much else, **pickpocketing** has been brought to a fine art in Paris. Parisian pickpockets are fast, practiced, and professional. Pros can unzip a bag in just a few seconds, so wear yours with the opening against your body. Threading a safety pin or keyring through both zippers on a pack makes it difficult to open quickly. Thieves often work in pairs, one providing a distraction and the other grabbing your wallet or purse. Some street children will do anything to distract you. In busy areas, walk quickly and purposefully. Thieves in *métro* stations may try to grab your bag as you walk through the turnstile or as you board the subway, just before the doors close.

Photocopy all important documents such as your passport, identification, credit cards, and traveler's checks' serial numbers. If you are robbed, check your surroundings carefully. Thieves may throw away your wallet after taking the cash, and you might be able to retrieve non-cash items such as credit cards. Report the theft to the police station in the area where it occurred. Be insistent; a police report may be necessary to claim stolen traveler's checks.

Especially if you are traveling alone, be sure that someone knows your itinerary. Never say that you're traveling alone. Steer clear of empty train compartments, and avoid large *métro* stations after dark. Ask the managers of your hotel, hostel, or *foyer* for advice on specific areas, and consider staying in places with a curfew or night attendant. Some cheap accommodations may entail more risks than savings; when traveling alone, you may want to forego dives and city outskirts.

There is no sure-fire set of precautions that will protect you from all situations you might encounter when you travel. A good self-defense course will give you more concrete ways to react to different types of aggression, but it might cost you more money than your trip. **Model Mugging** (East Coast tel. (617) 232-2900; Midwest tel. (312) 338-4545; West Coast tel. (415) 592-7300), a U.S. organization with offices in several major cities, teaches a comprehensive course on self-defense (course prices US$400-500). Women's and men's courses offered. Community colleges frequently offer self-defense courses at more affordable prices. **U.S. Department of State's** (tel. (202) 783-3238) pamphlet *A Safe Trip Abroad* (US$1) summarizes safety information for travelers. It is available by calling the above number or by writing the Superintendent of Documents, U.S. Government Printing Office, Washington, DC 20402. For an official Department of State travel advisory on France call their 24-hour hotline at (202) 647-5225. Pamphlets on traveling to specific areas are also available. More complete information may be found in *Travel Safety: Security and Safeguards at Home and Abroad*, published by **Hippocrene Books, Inc.,** 171 Madison Ave., New York, NY 10016 (tel. (212) 685-4371; orders tel. (718) 454-2360; fax (718) 454-1391).

# ■ When To Go

Traveling during the off-season is a great way to minimize the damage to your bank account. Airfares drop and domestic travel becomes less congested. What's more, the off-season includes the world-famous "Paris in the Springtime." In spite of the rain, spring is the time to visit. In the summer, the tourists move in and the Parisians move out—on vacation. On the other hand, if you stay away from the Champs-Elysées, Versailles, and the Eiffel Tower, August can be pleasingly calm. On August 15, a national holiday, all of Paris (except the tourist areas) is eerily deserted. For the most authentic Paris, try the city in autumn and winter—it's just as beautiful, and free of the tourists that flood in during the warmer months. Traveling in winter may be tougher on your wallet than you planned; taking refuge from the cold in cafés helps soak up your budget. Paris is a city best appreciated outdoors, wandering through its narrow streets and along the banks of the Seine. Off-season visitors with strong constitutions will, however, reap their share of rewards—pop corks with Parisians on New Year's Eve, avoid long museum lines, and take in a dynamic city that rises above bad weather.

## CLIMATE

Nobody goes to Paris for the climate. No matter when you go, expect it to be cold and rainy. Early and late summer are often quite cool. Evenings can be windy and cold throughout the summer, and hot days (in the 80s, 30°C) don't hit Paris until mid-July. Then you'll discover Paris in the summer, with its high humidity and persistent pollution. Air-conditioning is not as widespread as in America, so the entire city escapes to Deauville in the north when the days begin to swelter. Hottest days are best spent in the city's parks and air-conditioned museums. Winters are mild, averaging about 40°F (5°C) during the day, but the ever-present dampness makes them feel much colder.

# ■ Packing

*Pack light; the rest is commentary.* Lay out everything you think you'll need, pack only half of it, and take more money. Remember that you can buy almost anything you'll need in Paris, and the more luggage you carry, the more alien you'll feel.

Avoid taking electrical appliances, but if you must, remember that electricity in most European countries is 220 volts AC, twice as much as in North America. In France, as in most of Europe, sockets accommodate two-pin round plugs; get an **adapter.** If the appliance is not dual voltage, you'll also need a converter (US$15-18). Both adapters and converters can be purchases in most hardware stores. Otherwise wait until you arrive. For more information, contact **Franzus,** Murtha Industrial Park, P.O. Box 142, Railroad Ave., Beacon Falls, CT 06403 (tel. (203) 723-6664; fax (203) 723-6666), for their free pamphlet, *Foreign Electricity is No Deep Dark Secret.*

If you take expensive **cameras** or equipment abroad, it's best to register everything with customs at the airport before departure. Buy a supply of film before you leave; it's more expensive in France. Unless you're shooting with 1000 ASA or more, airport security x-rays should not harm your pictures. It never hurts, however, to buy a lead pouch, available at any camera store. Either way, pack film in your carry-on, since the x-rays employed on checked baggage are much stronger. If you're bringing a laptop or notebook **computer,** be sure to have both computer and floppy discs hand-inspected, lest stray x-rays wipe out your as-yet-unpublished *chef-d'oeuvre.* Officials may ask you to turn it on, so be sure the batteries are fully loaded. A warning: Lost baggage is common, and not always retrieved. Keep all valuables in your carry-on.

## ■ Specific Concerns

### WOMEN AND TRAVEL

Women exploring any area on their own inevitably face additional safety concerns. In all situations it is best to trust your instincts: if you'd feel better somewhere else, don't hesitate to move on. You may want to consider staying in hostels or *foyers* which offer single rooms which lock from the inside, or religious organizations that offer rooms for women only. Stick to centrally located accommodations and avoid late-night treks or *métro* rides. Remember that hitching is *never* safe for lone women, or even for two women traveling together.

Foreign women in Paris are frequently beset by unwanted and tenacious followers—try to exercise reasonable caution without falling prey to the notion that all French men are best avoided. To escape unwanted attention, follow the example of local women; in many cases, the less you look like a tourist, the better off you'll be. Look as if you know where you're going, and ask women or couples for directions if you're lost or if you feel uncomfortable. Your best answer to verbal harassment may be no answer at all. In crowds, you may be pinched, squeezed, or otherwise molested; wearing a conspicuous wedding band may help prevent such incidents. Seek out a police officer or a female passerby before a crisis erupts, and don't hesitate to scream for help *("Au secours":* oh suh-KOOR). *Always* carry a *télécarte,* change for the phone, and enough extra money for a bus or taxi. Carry a whistle on your keychain, and don't hesitate to use it in an emergency.

**SOS Viol,** the national **rape hotline,** answers calls (in French) from Monday through Friday, 10am to 6pm (tel. 05 05 95 95). A Model Mugging course will not only prepare you for a potential mugging, but will also raise your level of awareness of your surroundings (see Safety and Security). All of these warnings and suggestions should not discourage women from traveling alone—don't take unnecessary risks, but don't lose your spirit of adventure either.

A series of travelogues by women outline their sojourns; check for these and other books: *Nothing to Declare: Memoirs of a Woman Traveling Alone* (Penguin Books); *One Dry Season* (Knopf) by Caroline Alexander; *Tracks* (Pantheon) by Robin Davidson; *The Road Through Miyama* (Random House/Vintage) by Leila Philips.

For additional tips and suggestions, consult *The Handbook for Women Travelers* (£7.99) by Maggie and Gemma Moss, published by Piatkus Books, 5 Windmill St., London W1P 1HF England (tel. (44) (071) 631 0710). *Women Going Places* (US$14) is a new women's travel and resource guide emphasizing women-owned enterprises. Though geared towards lesbians, it offers advice appropriate for all women. This book is available from Inland Book Company, P.O. Box 120261, East Haven, CT 06512 (tel. (203) 467-4257). Wander Women, a travel networking organization for women over 40, puts out a newsletter *Journal 'n Footnotes.* Write to the organization at 136 N. Grand Ave., #237, West Covina, CA 91791. For more specific information about women and travel in Paris, consult *The Virago Women's Travel Guides: Paris* by Catherine Cullen, published by Virago Press/Ulysses Press (US$13.95).

### OLDER TRAVELERS AND SENIOR CITIZENS

The freedom of retirement affords many seniors the opportunity to travel, while an assortment of discounts on transportation and tours helps make it affordable. Proof of senior citizen status is required for many of the discounts listed below. Write the Superintendent of Documents (see Useful Addresses and Publications, above) for a copy of *Travel Tips for Older Americans* (US$1). See Once There—Older Travelers and Senior Citizens for publications and organizations in Paris. The following organizations offer information, assistance, and discounts to seniors.

**AARP (American Association of Retired Persons)**, 601 E. St. N.W., Washington, DC 20049 (tel. (202) 434-2277). U.S. residents over 50 and their spouses receive benefits which include travel programs and discounts for groups and individuals, as well as discounts on lodging, car and RV rental, air arrangements, and sightseeing. US$8 annual fee. Call (800) 927-0111 for information.

**Elderhostel,** 75 Federal St., 3rd Fl., Boston, MA 02110. You must be 60 or over, and may bring a spouse who is over 50. Programs at colleges and universities in over 40 countries focus on varied subjects and generally last 1 week.

**Gateway Books,** P.O. Box 10244, San Rafael, CA 94912. Publishes Gene and Adele Malott's *Get Up and Go: A Guide for the Mature Traveler* (US$10.95, postage US$1.90). Offers recommendations and general hints for the budget-conscious senior. Call (800) 669-0773 for orders.

**National Council of Senior Citizens,** 1331 F St. N.W., Washington, DC 20004 (tel. (202) 347-8800). For US$12 a year or US$150 for a lifetime, an individual or couple of any age can receive hotel and auto rental discounts, a senior citizen newspaper, use of a discount travel agency, and supplemental Medicare insurance.

**Pilot Books,** 103 Cooper St., Babylon, NY 11702 (tel. (516) 422-2225). Publishes *The International Health Guide for Senior Citizens* (US$4.95, postage US$1) and *The Senior Citizens' Guide to Budget Travel in Europe* (US$5.95 postpaid).

# TRAVELERS WITH DISABILITIES

Countries vary in their general accessibility to travelers with disabilities. The following provide general information and guides. For organizations and publications specific to Paris, see Once There—Travelers with Disabilities.

**American Foundation for the Blind,** 15 W. 16th St., New York, NY 10011 (tel. (212) 620-2147). ID cards (US$10); write for an application, or call (800) 829-0500. Also call this number to order AFB catalogs in Braille, print, or on cassette or disk.

**Consumer Information Center,** Dept. 454Z, Pueblo, CO 81009 (tel. (719) 948-3334). Offers *Access Travel: Airports,* which lists designs, facilities, and services at 553 airport terminals worldwide (free). Also *New Horizons for the Air Traveler with a Disability* (US$0.50).

**Directions Unlimited,** 720 N. Bedford Rd., Bedford Hills, NY 10507 (tel. (800) 533-5343 or (914) 241-1700). Specializes in arranging individual and group vacations, tours, and cruises for those with disabilities.

**Disability Press, Ltd.,** Applemarket House, 17 Union St., Kingston-upon-Thames, Surrey KT1 1RP, England (tel.(44) (081) 549 6399). Publishes the *Disabled Traveler's International Phrasebook,* including French (£1.75).

**Evergreen Travel Service,** 4114 198th St. S.W., #13, Lynnwood, WA 98036 (tel. (800) 435-2288 or (206) 776-1184). Arranges wheelchair-accessible tours and individual travel worldwide. Other services include tours for the blind or deaf, as well as tours for those who don't want a fast-paced itinerary.

**The Guided Tour, Inc.** Elkins Park House, #114B, 7900 Old York Road, Elkins Park, PA 19117-2348. (tel. (215) 782-1370 or (800) 738-5843). Year-round travel programs for persons with developmental and physical challenges as well as those geared to the needs of persons requiring renal dialysis. Trips and vacations planned both domestically and internationally. Call or write for a free brochure.

**Mobility International, USA (MIUSA),** P.O. Box 3551, Eugene, OR 97403 (tel. (503) 343-1284 voice and TTD). International headquarters in Britain, 228 Borough High St., London SE1 1JX (tel. (44) (071) 403 5688). Contacts in 30 countries. Information on travel programs, international work camps, accommodations, access guides, and organized tours. Membership costs US$20 per year, newsletter US$10. Sells updated and expanded *A World of Options: A Guide to International Educational Exchange, Community Service, and Travel for Persons with Disabilities* (US$14 for members, US$16 for non-members, postpaid).

**Moss Rehabilitation Hospital Travel Information Service,** 1200 W. Tabor Rd., Philadelphia, PA 19141 (tel. (215) 456-9603). Nominal fee charged for packet of information on tourist sights, accommodations, and transportation.

**Pauline Hephaistos Survey Projects,** 39 Bradley Gardens, West Ealing, London W13 8HE, England. Distributes access guides to London, Israel, Paris, and Jersey (£4 each), researched by people with disabilities.

**Society for the Advancement of Travel for the Handicapped,** 347 Fifth Ave., #610, New York, NY 10016 (tel. (212) 447-7284); fax (212) 725-8253). Publishes quarterly travel newsletter *SATH News* and information booklets (free for members, US$3 each for nonmembers). Advice on trip planning for people with disabilities. Annual membership is US$45, students and seniors US$25.

**Twin Peaks Press,** P.O. Box 129, Vancouver, WA 98666 (tel. (206) 694-2462, orders only (800) 637-2256). *Travel for the Disabled* lists tips and resources for disabled travelers (US$19.95). Also available are the *Directory for Travel Agencies of the Disabled* (US$19.95) and *Wheelchair Vagabond* (US$14.95).

## BISEXUAL, GAY, AND LESBIAN TRAVELERS

The following organizations and periodicals provide general travel information. For more information specific to Paris, see Bisexual, Gay, and Lesbian Paris.

**Are You Two Together?,** published by Random House; available at bookstores (US$18). A new gay and lesbian guide to spots in Europe. Written by a lesbian couple; covers Western European capitals and gay resorts.

**Ferrari Publications,** P.O. Box 37887, Phoenix, AZ 85069 (tel. (602) 863-2408). Publishes *Ferrari's Places of Interest* (US$14.95), *Ferrari's Places for Men* (US$13.95), *Ferrari's Places for Women* (US$12), and *Inn Places: USA and Worldwide Gay Accommodations* (US$14.95). Also available from Giovanni's Room.

**Gay's the Word,** 66 Marchmont St., London WC1N 1AB, England (tel. (071) 278 7654). Tube: Russel Sq. Information for gay and lesbian travelers. Mail-order service available. Open Mon.-Fri. 11am-7pm, Sat. 10am-6pm, Sun. and holidays 2-6pm.

**Giovanni's Room,** 345 S. 12th St., Philadelphia, PA 19107 (tel. (215) 923-2960; fax (215) 923-0813). International feminist and gay bookstore with mail-order service.

**Spartacus International Gay Guide,** (US$29.95). Order from 100 E. Biddle St., Baltimore, MD 21202 (tel. (410) 727-5677) or c/o Bruno Lützowstraße, P.O. Box 301345, D-1000 Berlin 30, Germany (tel. (49) (30) 25 49 82 00); also available from Giovanni's Room and from Renaissance House, P.O. Box 292 Village Station, New York, NY 10014 (tel. (212) 674-0120). Extensive list of gay bars, restaurants, hotels, bookstores, and hotlines throughout the world. Very specifically for men.

## KOSHER AND VEGETARIAN TRAVELERS

National tourist offices often publish lists of kosher and vegetarian restaurants. See the Food Intro and listings under "Kosher" and "Vegetarian" in the restaurant section.

**Jewish Chronicle Publications**, London EC4A 1JT, England. Publishes the Jewish Travel Guide. Available in the U.S. from Sepher-Hermon Press, 1265 46th St., Brooklyn, NY 11219 (tel. (718) 972-9010) for US$11.95, postage US$1.75. In the U.K., order from Jewish Chronicle Publications, 25 Furnival St., London EC4A, England. Lists synagogues, kosher restaurants, and institutions in over 80 countries.

**North American Vegetarian Society**, P.O. Box 72, Dolgeville, NY 13329 (tel. (518) 568-7970). Ask about their publications.

**Vegetarian Society of the U.K.,** Parkdale, Dunham Rd., Altringham, Cheshire WA14 4QG, England (tel. (44) (61) 928 0793). Publishes *The International Vegetarian Travel Guide* (last updated in 1991). Ask about their other publications.

# ■ Alternatives to Tourism

If the often madcap, train-changing, site-switching pace of tourism loses its appeal, consider a longer stay in Paris. Study, work, or volunteering will help you get a better sense of parts of the city that are often hidden to the short-term visitor.

## STUDY

If you choose your program well, study in Paris could be one of the most exciting and cosmopolitan experiences you'll ever have. You'll have to be stubborn about speaking French; it's far too easy to hang out exclusively with other English speakers. Research your options well, as programs vary in expense, academic quality, living conditions, and exposure to French culture and language. Many American undergraduates enroll in programs sponsored by domestic universities, and many colleges give advice and information on study abroad. Ask for the names of recent participants in the programs, and talk to them. Consider enrolling directly in the French universities—by far the cheapest and most authentic (if least organized) way to go.

**American Field Service (AFS),** 313 E. 43rd St., New York, NY 10017 (tel. (800) 237-4636 or (212) 949-4242). High school, summer, and year-long home stay exchange programs. Financial aid available.

**American Institute for Foreign Study/American Council for International Studies,** 102 Greenwich Ave., Greenwich, CT 06830 (tel. (800) 727-2437; for high school students, call (617) 421-9575). Organizes study in various European universities for high school and college students. Government loans recommended.

**Central Bureau for Educational Visits and Exchanges,** Seymour Mews House, Seymour Mews, London W1H 9PE, England (tel. (071) 486 5101). Publishes *Study Holidays* (£7.75) which gives basic information on over 600 language study programs in 25 European countries. Distributed in North America by IIE Books.

**CIEE,** main office at 715 S.W. Morrison, #600, Portland, OR 97205. Helps students secure work visas and find employment through its work-exchange programs. Operates 43 offices throughout the U.S. (See Useful Travel Organizations above.)

**Institute of International Education Books (IIE Books),** 809 United Nations Plaza, New York, NY 10017-3580 (tel. (212) 984-5412; fax (212) 984-5358), puts out several annual reference books on study abroad. *Academic Year Abroad* (US$42.95, US$4 postage) and *Vacation Study Abroad* (US$36.95, postage US$4) detail over 3600 programs offered by U.S. colleges and universities overseas. Offers the free pamphlet *Basic Facts on Foreign Study*. They operate the International Education Information Center at the U.N. Plaza address, open Tues.-Fri. 11am-4pm.

**Unipub Co.,** 4611-F Assembly Dr., Lanham, MD 20706-4391 (tel. (800) 274-4888). Distributes International Agency Publications including UNESCO's *Study Abroad* (US$24, postage US$2.50). International scholarships and courses for students of various ages. Unwieldy but excellent book.

**World Learning, Inc.,** Summer Abroad, P.O. Box 676, Brattleboro, VT 05302 (tel. (802) 257-7751, ext. 3452, or (800) 345-2929). This was founded in 1932 as The Experiment in International Living, but is now titled World Learning, Inc. Positions as tour group leaders are available (see Leading Tours below). For the programs themselves, most U.S. colleges will transfer credit for semester work done abroad. Some financial aid is available.

French educational terminology and equivalencies are radically different from almost anyone elses. For guidance and information, including free pamphlets on various fields of study in France, contact the **Cultural Services of the French Embassy.** The **American Center for Students and Artists** is a student advisory service that provides information on housing, education, and *au pair* and small jobs. Contact the center at 51, rue de Bercy, 12ème, 75592, Paris Cedex 12 (tel. 44 73 77 77).

## Language Schools

Language instruction is a booming business in France; semester and year-abroad programs are run by American universities, independent international or local organizations, and divisions of French universities. The **tourist office** in Paris maintains a list of member language schools.

**Alliance Française, Ecole Internationale de Langue et de Civilisation Française,** 101, bd. Raspail, *6ème*, 75006 Paris Cedex 06 (tel. 45 44 38 28; fax 45 44 89 42). Mo. Notre-Dame-des-Champs, St-Placide, or Rennes. Offers French language courses at all levels, business French, French for the tourism industry, teacher training, and refresher courses for teachers of French.

**Cours de Civilisation Française de la Sorbonne**, 47, rue des Ecoles, 75005 Paris (tel. 40 46 22 11). The Sorbonne has been giving its French civilization course since 1919. Academic-year course can be taken by the semester; 4-, 6-, and 8-week summer programs with civilization lectures and language classes at various levels. The Sorbonne also offers a special course in commercial French during the academic year, and a 3-week session for high-level students during the summer. You can also take the *Cours de Civilisation* through the American Institute for Foreign Study (AIFS), 102 Greenwich Ave., Greenwich, CT 06830 (tel. (800) 727-2437), which also arranges accommodations and meals in Paris for its students.

**Eurocentres,** 101, N. Union St., Alexandria, VA 22314 (tel. (703) 684-1494; fax (703) 684-1495). Another of Council Travel's many associates, with centers worldwide. Long and short intensive courses, holiday courses, and teacher refresher courses at centers in Paris at 13, passage Dauphine, *6ème* (tel. 43 25 81 40; fax 46 34 65 34); in La Rochelle at av. Marillac, 17000 La Rochelle (tel. 46 50 57 33); and in Amboise at 9, Mail Saint-Thomas, BP 214, 37402 Amboise Cedex (tel. 47 23 10 60).

**Institut Catholique de Paris,** 21, rue d'Assas, *6ème,* 75270 Paris Cedex 06 (tel. 44 39 52 00). Mo. St-Placide. Semester-long and summer classes at all levels.

## French Universities

While it is tempting (and comforting) to meet and talk to other Americans, you may regret it later. If your French is already extremely competent, direct enrollment in a French university may be more rewarding than a language or civilization class filled with English-speakers. Enrolling yourself directly can sometimes cost three or four times less than going through an American university's program, but it might be more difficult to receive academic credit at your home university. After 1968, the **Université de Paris** split into ten isolated universities, each occupying different sites and offering a different range of fields. The century-old Sorbonne, now the Université de Paris IV, focuses on a range of traditional fields in the humanities. For a more experimental approach, try one of the more modern universities. Each of them requires at least a *baccalauréat* degree or its equivalents (British A-levels or two years of college in the United States) for admission. For details contact the cultural services office at the nearest French consulate or embassy. Start this way ahead of time and expect to be confused—the bureaucracy of the French educational system is notorious.

As a student registered in a French university, you will be given a student card *(carte d'étudiant)* by your school upon presentation of your residency permit and a receipt for your university fees. In addition to the card's standard student benefits, many additional benefits available to students in Paris are administered by the **Centre Régional des Oeuvres Universitaires et Scolaires (CROUS) de Paris** which has recently started accepting ISIC cards. Founded in 1955 to improve the living and working conditions of students of each academy, this division of the Oeuvres Universitaires welcomes foreign students and can be of great help in answering your (many) questions. The regional center for Paris is at 39, av. Georges-Bernanos, *5ème,* 75231 Paris Cedex 05 (tel. 40 51 36 00; RER Port-Royal). CROUS also publishes the brochure *Le CROUS et Moi*, which lists addresses and information on every aspect of student life in Paris. Pick up the helpful guidebook *Je vais en France* (free), available in French or English, from any French embassy or consulate or in France at the CROUS office at 8, rue Jean Calvin, 5ème (tel. 40 79 91 00).

## WORK

Today's strict regulations can make George Orwell's search for work (described in *Down and Out in London and Paris*) as an unskilled *plongeur* (dishwasher) look like a cakewalk. Because of high unemployment, the French government has become wary of hiring foreigners. Before you can obtain a work permit through normal channels, your employer must convince the Ministry of Labor there is no French citizen capable of filling your position. Even when a foreigner is considered, European Economic Country (EEC) members have priority. Long-term employment is difficult to secure unless you have skills in high-demand areas such as medicine, computer programming, or teaching.

In some cases, friends in Europe can help expedite work permits or arrange informal work-for-accommodations swaps. Many permitless agricultural workers go untroubled by local authorities, who recognize the need for seasonal help. European Community citizens can work in any other EC country without working papers. Students can check with their universities' foreign language departments, which may have official or unofficial connections to job openings abroad.

### Permits

With the exception of *au pair* jobs, it is illegal for foreign students to hold full-time jobs during the school year. Students registered at French universities may get work permits for the summer with a valid visa, a student card from a French university, and proof of a job. After spending one academic year in France, Americans with a valid student *carte de séjour* can find part-time work if they will be enrolled at a French university again in the fall. Check the fact sheet *Employment in France for Students,* put out by **Cultural Services of the French Embassy,** which provides basic information about work in France and also lists the government-approved organizations through which foreign students must secure their jobs.

Work permit programs are run by **CIEE** and its member organizations (see Useful Travel Organizations above). For a US$125 application fee, CIEE can procure three- to six-month work permits (and a handbook to help you find work and housing). You just hop on the plane, land, and start job-hunting. French positions require evidence of language skills. CIEE will provide information on accommodations and job-hunting, but will not place you in a job. Jobs available are mostly short-term, unskilled work in hotels, shops, restaurants, farms, and factories. Wages should cover food, lodging, and basic living expenses. Complete information and an application are enclosed in their *Work Abroad* brochure. Travel CUTS's Canadian program is similar.

### Useful Publications

The number of books listing work-abroad opportunities has ballooned in the past few years. Start with CIEE's free booklet *Work Abroad,* then graduate to the excellent publications put out by **Vacation Work,** 9 Park End St., Oxford OX1 1HJ, England (tel. (44) (0865) 24 19 78). Many of their books are also available in bookstores in the U.S., through Travel CUTS, or from **Peterson's Guides,** 202 Carnegie Center, P.O. Box 2123, Princeton, NJ 08543 (tel. (800) 338-3282 or (609) 243-9111). Peterson's publications include the *1993 Directory of Overseas Summer Jobs* (US$14.95, postage US$6), which lists 50,000 openings worldwide, volunteer and paid. For more detail specific to France, consult CIEE's *Working in France: The Ultimate Guide to Job Hunting and Career Success à la Française* (US$12.95, postage US$1.50).

**World Trade Academy Press,** 50 E. 42nd St., #509, New York, NY 10017 (tel. (212) 697-4999), publishes *Looking for Employment in Foreign Countries*

(US$16.50) which gives information on federal, commercial, and volunteer jobs abroad and advice on resumes and interviews. It also publishes a *Directory of American Firms Operating in Foreign Countries* (look it up in the library—it costs US$195) as well as listings of American firms in specific countries. Remember that many of the organizations listed in books like these have very few jobs available and have very specific requirements. Other guides to check out are *Working Holidays* (US$22.95 from IIE), an annual guide to short-term paid and voluntary work in Britain and around the world, and *Home From Home* (£6.99 plus postage), a guide to international homestays, termstays, and exchanges, available from the Central Bureau for Educational Visits and Exchanges (see Study).

### Finding a Job

Once in Paris, a good place to start your job search is the **American Chamber of Commerce,** 21, av. George V, 8*ème* (tel. 47 23 80 26; Mo. George V or Alma Marceau). The *Membership Directory of the French-American Chamber of Commerce* is available from its Paris office or from its office at 509 Madison Ave., #1900, New York, NY 10022 (tel. (212) 371-4466). It is quite expensive, so go through the directory at the office (library open Tues. and Thurs. 10am-12:30pm; admission 50F). The Chamber also publishes a brochure (50F) for American students who want to have a paid or unpaid internship in France. The **Agence Nationale Pour l'Emploi,** 4, impasse d'Antin, 8*ème* (tel. 42 25 95 57; Mo. Franklin D. Roosevelt), has specific information on employment. You could also visit the **Centre d'Information et de Documentation Jeunesse (CIDJ),** 101, quai Branly, 15*ème* (tel. 44 29 12 00; RER Champ de Mars/Tour Eiffel), a government-run information clearinghouse on French law, camping, touring, sports, employment, careers, and long-term accommodations (open Mon.-Sat. 10am-6pm). Part-time jobs and housing listings are posted at 9am on the bulletin boards outside. Pamphlets available include *Cours d'été pour étrangers en France, Placement au pair en France,* and *Tourisme en France.* The **American Church in Paris,** 65, quai d'Orsay, 7*ème* (tel. 47 05 07 99), posts a full bulletin board of potential job and housing opportunities. Also check help-wanted columns in newspapers, especially *Le Monde, Le Figaro,* and the English-language *International Herald Tribune,* as well as *France-USA Contacts.* Many of these jobs are unofficial, and won't require a work permit. For more under-the-table work, try giving English lessons. Because there are so many foreigners in Paris already offering lessons, don't expect to support yourself on this alone.

The **International Association for the Exchange of Students for Technical Experience (IAESTE)** program, a division of the Association for International Practical Training (AIPT), is an internship exchange program for science, architecture, engineering, agriculture, and math students who have completed at least two years at an accredited four-year institution. There is a non-refundable US$75 fee. Apply to the IAESTE Trainee Program, c/o AIPT, #250, 10400 Little Patuxent Parkway, Columbia, MD 21044 (tel. (410) 997-2200). Applications due by Dec. 10 for summer placement.

### Teaching English

This may be your best chance at a steady salary and a well-paying job. The U.S. State Department **Office of Overseas Schools,** #245 SA-29, 3100 Clarendon Bd., Arlington VA 22201 (tel. (703) 875-7800), maintains a list of elementary and secondary schools abroad, and agencies that arrange placement for Americans to teach abroad. Also, check with your local university's career office. Professional English-teaching positions can be difficult to get; most European schools require at least a bachelor's degree and most often training in teaching English as a foreign language.

**International Schools Services,** 15 Roszel Rd., P.O. Box 5910, Princeton, NJ 08543 (tel. (609) 452-0990), publishes a free newsletter, *NewsLinks;* call or write to get on the mailing list. Their Educational Staffing Department publishes the free brochure *Your Passport to Teaching and Administrative Opportunities Abroad.*

## Leading Tours

Summer positions as tour group leaders are available with **Hostelling International.** Contact the youth hostelling organization in the country in which you would like to travel. **World Learning, Inc.,** P.O. Box 676, Kipling Rd., Brattleboro, VT 05302 (tel. (800) 451-4465 or (802) 257-7751), has positions for group leaders world-wide. Applicants must be at least 24 and have established leadership abilities, language fluency, and in-depth overseas experience for the countries to which they apply. Group leaders have all their expenses paid and receive a US$200 honorarium.

## Au Pair Positions

Au pair positions are reserved primarily for single women aged 18 to 30 with some knowledge of French; a few men are also employed. The au pair cares for the children of a French family and does light housework five or six hours each day while taking courses at a school for foreign students or at a French university. Talking with children can be a great way to improve your French, but looking after them (and ironing their jeans, underwear, etc.) may be extremely strenuous. Make sure you know in advance what the family expects of you. Au pair positions usually last six to 18 months; during the summer the contract can be as short as one to three months, but you may not be able to take courses. You'll receive room, board, and a small monthly stipend (around 1520F).

The **Cultural Services of the French Embassy** offers a detailed information sheet on au pair jobs. Organizations offering placement include **L'Accueil Familial des Jeunes Etrangers,** 23, rue du Cherche-Midi, 75006 Paris (tel. 42 22 50 34; fax 45 44 60 48; Mo. Sèvres-Babylone), and **Centre d'Echanges Culturels Internationaux** (CECI), B.P. 30171, 69406 Lyon Cedex 3 (tel. (16) 78 89 08 36). L'Accueil arranges au pair jobs beginning in September and lasting at least 10 months. **Inter-Exchange Program,** 161 Sixth Ave., New York, NY 10013 (tel. (212) 924-0446), provides information in pamphlet form on international work programs and au pair positions. Au pair jobs can also be arranged through individual connections, but make sure you have a contract detailing hours per week, salary, and living accommodations.

## Volunteering

If you have the financial freedom to forgo a salary, volunteering can provide a wonderful opportunity to meet people and might even secure you room and board in exchange for your work. Also try international firms, museums, art galleries, and non-profit organizations like UNESCO; they may have unpaid internships available.

The following organizations and publications can help you to explore the range of possibilities. Keep in mind: the organizations that arrange placement sometimes charge high application fees in addition to the workcamps' charges for room and board. You can *sometimes* avoid this extra fee by contacting the individual workcamps directly. Listings in Vacation Work's *International Directory of Voluntary Work* (£8.95; see ordering information under Work above) can be helpful.

**Archaeological Institute of America,** 675 Commonwealth Ave., Boston, MA 02215 (tel. (617) 353-9361). The 1994 edition of *Archaeological Fieldwork Opportunities Bulletin* (US$10.50 for non-members) is available from Kendall Hunt Publishers at (800) 338-5578. Lists field projects throughout the world.

**Council on International Educational Exchange (CIEE),** *Volunteer! The Comprehensive Guide to Voluntary Service in the U.S. and Abroad* is published by CIEE. It offers advice on choosing a voluntary service program and lists over 200 organizations in fields ranging from social work to construction. Write to CIEE (US$8.95, postage US$1.50). See Useful Travel Organizations for more information.

**Service Civil International/International Voluntary Service-USA,** Rte. 2, Box 506, Crozet, VA 22932 (tel. (804) 823-1826). Arranges placement in workcamps in European and other countries. You must be 18 to work in European camps.

Registration fees for the placement service in 1992 ranged from US$40-200 depending on the camp location and will most likely go up for 1994.

**Volunteers for Peace,** 43 Tiffany Rd., Belmont, VT 05730 (tel. (802) 259-2759). Arranges placement in over 800 workcamps in 37 countries, primarily in Europe. Gives perhaps the most complete and up-to-date listings in the annual *International Workcamp Directory* (US$10 postpaid). Registration fee US$125.

## LONG-TERM ACCOMMODATIONS

If you plan to stay in Paris for a longer period of time, consider renting an apartment. Rent is high in Paris, and utilities are expensive, but apartments offer convenience, privacy, and a kitchen. Call, fax, write, or visit **Allô Logement Temporaraire,** 4, pl. de la Chapelle, 18ème (tel. 42 09 00 07; fax 46 07 14 41; Mo. Chapelle). This helpful, English-speaking association charges a commission for each month of rental if the rental exceeds 5000F. For less expensive apartments, the maximum commission is 600F. In addition, there is an annual membership fee of 250F. Be sure to leave a phone or fax number where you can be reached easily; vacancies come and go very quickly (open Tues.-Sat. noon-8pm). Consult the French Department at your local university; it may be able to connect you with students abroad who want to sublet. Remember that short-term rentals, usually more expensive per month than longer rentals, can be difficult to procure, especially in winter months.

If possible, stay in a hotel your first week in Paris and find an apartment when you're there. This will allow you to see what you're getting. Try the bulletin boards in the **American Church** and look in any of the English-French newsletters like *Free Voice* or *France-USA Contacts*. **France-USA Contacts** is a free publication found in English bookstores throughout Paris. It is also distributed free in the U.S. (write or fax to 104 W. 14th St., New York, NY 10011-7314; tel. (212) 989-8989; fax (212) 255-5555). This publication gives comprehensive listings of Americans, Anglophones, and Anglophiles offering their apartments for rent or sublet. Renting an apartment—negotiating rent, utilities, and leases—can be difficult for even the most linguistically proficient. Remember that laundromats can be inconvenient and expensive, and as view-obstructing outside clotheslines are illegal in Paris, a dryer may be a plus.

When you do rent an apartment, make sure to sign a contract with your lessor detailing the finances of the transaction. Note that subletting is technically illegal in France. Because of this unofficial status, a subletter cannot depend on the *concierge* to explain how to turn on the pilot light or how to unclog the bathroom sink. Ask the person who usually occupies the apartment *all* your questions before you move in.

# ■■■ GETTING THERE

## ■ From North America

The first challenge in European budget travel is getting there. Call every toll-free number and don't be afraid to ask about discounts. Have a knowledgeable travel agent guide you through the options; better yet, have several knowledgeable travel agents guide you. Students and people under 26 should never need to pay full price for a ticket. Seniors can also get mint deals; many airlines offer senior traveler club deals or airline passes and discounts for seniors' companions as well. Travel sections in Sunday newspapers often list bargain fares from the local airport. Outfox airline reps with the phone-book-sized *Official Airline Guide* (at large libraries); this monthly guide lists all scheduled flights (including prices). George Brown's *The Airline Passenger's Guerilla Handbook* (US$14.95; last published in 1990) is a more renegade resource.

Most airlines maintain a fare structure that peaks between mid-June and early September. Midweek (Mon.-Thurs.) flights run about US$30 cheaper each way than on weekends. Leaving from a travel hub will win you a more competitive fare than from a smaller city; the gains are not as great when departing from travel hubs monopolized by one airline, so call around. Flying to London is usually the cheapest way across the Atlantic, though special fares to other cities can cost even less. It's often cheaper to fly to a nearby city and take a train or ferry to your final destination; check fares for these alternate routes carefully, though, since train tickets are often expensive themselves and might not be worth the aggravation.

Return-date flexibility is usually not an option for the budget traveler. Except on youth fares purchased through the airlines, traveling with an "open return" ticket can be pricier than fixing a return date and paying to change it. Avoid one-way tickets, too: the flight to Europe may be economical, but the return fares can be outrageous. Whenever flying internationally, pick up your ticket in advance of the departure date and arrive at the airport several hours before your flight.

## COMMERCIAL AIRLINES

Even if you pay an airline's lowest published fare, you may be spending hundreds of dollars. The commercial airlines' lowest regular offer is the APEX (Advance Purchase Excursion Fare); specials advertised in newspapers may be cheaper, but have correspondingly more restrictions and fewer available seats. APEX fares provide you with confirmed reservations and allow "open-jaw" tickets (landing in and returning from different cities). Reservations must usually be made at least 21 days in advance, with 7- to 14-day minimum and 60- to 90-day maximum stay limitations, and hefty cancellation and change-of-reservation penalties. For summer travel, book APEX fares early; by May you will have difficulty getting the departure date you want.

Most airlines no longer offer standby fares, once a staple of the budget traveler. Standby has given way to the three-day-advance-purchase youth fare, a cousin of the one-day variety prevalent in Europe. It's available only to those under 25 (sometimes 24) and only within three days of departure—a gamble that often pays off, but could backfire if the airline's all booked up. Return dates are open, but you must come back within a year, and, once again, can book your return seat no more than three days ahead. Youth fares in summer aren't really cheaper than APEX, but off-season prices drop deliciously. Icelandair (tel. (800) 223-5500) is one of the few airlines which offers this three-day fare. Check with a travel agent for details.

A few airlines offer other miscellaneous discounts. Look into flights to relatively less popular destinations or smaller carriers. Call Icelandair or Virgin Atlantic Airways (tel. (800) 862-8621) for information on their last-minute offers. Icelandair offers a "get-up-and-go" fare from New York to Luxembourg (round-trip June-Sept. US$299 weekdays, US$329 weekends; Oct.-May US$268 weekdays, US$288 weekends). Reservations can be made no more than three days before departure. After arrival, Icelandair offers discounts on trains and buses from Luxembourg to other parts of Europe.

## STUDENT TRAVEL AGENCIES

Students and people under 26 with proper ID qualify for reduced airfares. These are rarely available from airlines or travel agents, but are available from student travel agencies like CIEE's Council Travel, STA, Travel CUTS, University Travel Network, and Let's Go Travel. These agencies negotiate special reduced-rate bulk purchases with the airlines, then resell them to the youth market. In 1993, peak season round-trip rates from the east coast of North America to even the offbeat corners of Europe rarely topped US$700, and off-season fares were considerably lower. Return date change fees also tend to be low (around US$50). Most of their flights are on major airlines, though in peak season some seats may be on less reliable chartered aircraft.

## CHARTER FLIGHTS AND TICKET CONSOLIDATORS

Ticket consolidators resell unsold tickets on commercial and charter airlines that might otherwise have gone begging. Look for their tiny ads in weekend papers (in the U.S., the Sunday *New York Times* travel section is best), and start calling them all. There is rarely a maximum age; tickets are also heavily discounted, and may offer extra flexibility or bypass advance purchase requirements, since you are not tangled in airline bureaucracy. But unlike tickets bought through an airline, you won't be able to use your tickets on another flight if you miss yours, and you will have to go back to the consolidator—not the airline—to get a refund. Pay with a credit card; you can't stop a cash payment if you never receive your tickets. Find out everything you can about the agency you're considering, and get a copy of their refund policy *in writing*. Ask about accommodations and car rental discounts; some consolidators have fingers in many pies. Insist on a receipt that gives full details about the tickets, refunds, and restrictions, and if they don't want to give you one, use a different company.

It's best to buy from a major organization that has experience in placing individuals on charter flights. One of the most reputable is the CIEE-affiliated **Council Charter,** 205 E. 42nd St., New York, NY 10017 (tel. (800) 800-8222); their flights can also be booked through Council Travel offices.

Another good organization is **Unitravel** (tel. (800) 325-2222); they offer discounted airfares on major scheduled airlines from the U.S. to over 50 cities in Europe and will hold all payments in a bank escrow until completion of your trip. You should also try **Access International** (tel. (800) 825-3633); **Interworld** (tel. (800) 331-4456, and in Florida (305) 443-4929); **Rebel** (tel. (800) 227-3235); and **Travac** (800) 872-8800).

Consolidators sell a mixture of tickets; some are on scheduled airlines, some on charter flights. The theory behind a charter is that a tour operator contracts with an airline to use their planes to fly extra loads of passengers to peak-season destinations. Charter flights thus fly less frequently than major airlines and have correspondingly more restrictions. They are also almost always fully booked, schedules and itineraries may change at the last moment, and flights may be cancelled. Shoot for a scheduled air ticket if you can, and consider travelers' insurance against trip interruption.

**Airhitch,** 2790 Broadway, #100, New York, NY 10025 (tel. (212) 864-2000), advertises a similar service: you choose a five-day date range in which to travel and a list of preferred European destinations, and they try to place you in a vacant spot on a flight in your date range to one of those destinations. Absolute flexibility—on both sides of the Atlantic—is necessary, but the savings might be worth it: flights cost US\$169 each way when departing from the East Coast of the U.S., US\$269 from the West Coast, and US\$229 from most places in between. Check flight times and departure sites directly with the airline carrier, and read *all* the fine print. The Better Business Bureau of New York received complaints about Airhitch a few years ago; they still don't recommend them, but they don't discourage you from using them, either.

Last minute discount clubs and fare brokers offer members savings on European travel, including charter flights and tour packages. Research your options carefully. **Last Minute Travel Club,** 1249 Boylston St., Boston, MA 02215 (tel. (800) 527-8646 or (617) 267-9800), is one of the few travel clubs which don't require a membership fee. Others include **Discount Travel International** (tel. (800) 324-9294), **Moment's Notice** (tel. (212) 486-0503; US\$25 annual fee), **Traveler's Advantage** (tel. (800) 835-8747; US\$49 annual fee), and **Worldwide Discount Travel Club** (tel. (305) 534-2082; US\$50 annual fee). For US\$25, **Travel Avenue** will search for the lowest international airfare available and then discount it 5-17% (tel. (800) 333-3335.)

## COURIER FLIGHTS

Those who travel light should consider flying to Paris as a courier. The company hiring you will use your checked luggage space for freight; you're left with the carry-on allowance. Restrictions to watch for: most flights are round-trip only with fixed-length stays (usually short), you may not be able to travel with a companion and most flights are from New York (including a scenic visit to the courier office in the 'burbs). Round-trip fares to Western Europe from the U.S. range from US$199-349 (during the off-season) to US$399-549 (during the summer). **Now Voyager,** 74 Varick St., #307, New York, NY 10013 (tel. (212) 431-1616), acts as an agent for many courier flights worldwide from New York, although some flights are available from Houston. They also offer special last-minute deals to such cities as London, Paris, Rome, and Frankfurt, which go for as little as US$299 round-trip. **Halbart Express,** 147-05 176th St., Jamaica, NY 11434 (tel. (718) 656-8279), and **Courier Travel Service,** 530 Central Ave., Cedarhurst, NY 11516 (tel. (516) 374-2299), are other courier agents to try. And if you have travel time to spare, **Ford's Travel Guides,** 19448 Londelius St., Northridge, CA 91324 (tel. (818) 701-7414), lists freighter companies that will take passengers for trans-Atlantic crossings. Ask for their *Freighter Travel Guide and Waterways of the World* (US$14.95, US$2.50 postage if mailed outside the U.S.).

You can also go directly through courier companies in New York, or check your bookstore or library for handbooks such as *The Insider's Guide to Air Courier Bargains* (US$14.95). The *Courier Air Travel Handbook* (US$10.70), which explains the procedure for traveling as an air courier and contains names, telephone numbers, and contact points of courier companies, can be ordered directly from Thunderbird Press, 5930-10 W. Greenway Rd., #112, Glendale, AZ 85306, or by calling (800) 345-0096. Travel Unlimited, P.O. Box 1058, Allston, MA 02134-1058 (no phone), publishes a monthly newsletter that details all options for courier travel (often 50% off discount commercial fares).

## ■ From Europe

### BY PLANE

Unless you're under 25, flying across Europe on regularly scheduled flights will eat up your budget; nearly all airlines cater to business travelers and set prices accordingly. If you are 24 or under, special fares on most European airlines requiring ticket purchase either the day before or the day of departure are a happy exception to this rule. These are often cheaper than the corresponding regular train fare, though not always as cheap as student rail tickets or railpasses. Consult budget travel agents and local newspapers and magazines for more information. The **Air Travel Advisory Bureau,** 41-45 Goswell Road, London EC1V 7DN, England (tel. (071) 636 5000), can put you in touch with discount flights to worldwide destinations, for free. Baggage limitations for intra-European flights (20kg or 32 lbs.) are lower.

### BY TRAIN

You can get to Paris from nearly anywhere on the continent by train. Most European trains are fast, punctual, and convenient. Gas is astronomically expensive in Europe, and the train system is a far more popular mode of transportation than automobiles. Beginning in late 1994 or early 1995, the train system will be expanded: the Channel Tunnel will provide direct autoroute, TGV, and bus travel from the U.K. to France.

Many train stations have different counters for domestic tickets, international tickets, seat reservations, and information; check before lining up. On major lines, reservations are always advisable and often required, even if you have a railpass; make them at least a few hours in advance at the train station (usually less than US$3). France's famed TGV and other fast trains require a special supplement (about US$4-5). Sometimes you can pay for your supplement on board, but it'll cost a little more.

You may be tempted to save on accommodations by taking an overnight train in a regular coach seat, but there are drawbacks; *if* you get to sleep you are sure to wake up exhausted and aching, security problems are rampant, and if you spread yourself over several seats in an empty compartment, someone is sure to come in at 2am and claim one of them. Consider spending extra dollars for a berth in a *couchette* (bunk-bed) car (about US$24; reserve at the station at least several days in advance). Bring some food and a plastic water bottle you can fill at your hostel and take with you on all train trips; the train café can be expensive, and train water can be undrinkable.

## BY FRENCH TRAIN

France has a vast rail network to accommodate its over 15,000 daily departures, and its national rail company, the **Société Nationale de Chemins de Fer (SNCF)** (tel. 45 82 50 50), is wondrously efficient. Off the main lines between cities and large towns, however, service is both less frequent and less convenient. Consequently, be prepared for long waits and obscure timetables. Buses fill in shorter gaps in the system, and recently a few unprofitable SNCF train routes have been replaced with SNCF buses, which also honor railpasses. The **TGV** *(train à grande vitesse)* serves major cities and is faster and more comfortable than normal express trains *("express"* or *"rapide");* it always requires a reservation, even if you have a railpass. Reservations are available from travel agents or from train stations (after a long line) in France.

For domestic travel in France, be sure to validate your ticket in one of the orange ticket punches (with signs marked *"compostez votre billet")* at the entrance to the platforms. This stamps the date on the ticket making it valid for that day of travel. If you break your journey, you must validate your ticket again after the stopover. Always keep your ticket with you, as you may have to present it during your trip.

French timetables are complicated but organized. They consist of three periods, designated by colors, which depend on the expected volume of passenger traffic. Red (peak) periods generally fall on important long weekends; tickets are more costly. Individual days are generally divided into white (peak) and blue (off-peak) hours; again, prices vary accordingly. Every major railroad station in France carries schedules and provides information at computer tellers, via representatives at the station, or most commonly, on poster timetables. You can purchase the complete SNCF timetable at newsstands in the stations. SNCF representatives in the U.S. provide material on France Railpasses and Eurailpasses, as well as a booklet of French and European fares.

## TRAIN DISCOUNTS AND RAILPASSES

For those under 26, **BIJ tickets (Billets Internationaux de Jeunesse),** sold under the Wasteels, Eurotrain, and Route 26 names, are an excellent alternative to railpasses. Available for travel within France, they save an average of 30-45% off regular second-class fares. Tickets are sold from point to point, with free and unlimited stopovers along the way. However, you cannot take longer than two months to complete your trip, and you can stop only at points along the specific direct route of your ticket. You can buy BIJ tickets from **Council Travel, Wasteels** offices, **Eurotrain** outlets, and other student travel agencies. In the U.S., contact Wasteels at (407) 351-2537; in London call (071) 834 7066. In Paris, **Eurotrain** is located at CIT (Compagnie Internationale du Tourisme), a private travel agency, 3, bd. des Capucines, 2*ème* (tel. 44 71 30 00; Mo. Opéra; open Mon.-Fri. 9am-5pm, tel. 9am-noon). Several student travel agencies in Paris also sell BIJ tickets (see Budget Travel Services).

In addition, a number of special discounts can be applied to point-to-point tickets purchased in France. The **Carrissimo,** available for 12- to 25-year-olds traveling alone or with up to three friends all under the age of 26, offers discounts of 50% on blue-period trips for the traveler and three friends or less, or 20% discounts during the white period (valid for 1 year; 4 trips 190F, up to 8 trips 50F). This sounds expensive, but just one trip with the Carrissimo will usually save you enough to more than pay for it. The **Carte Vermeille** (4 trips 130F, a year of unlimited travel 230F) entitles travelers 60 and over to 50% off first- or second-class tickets for trips in blue (off-peak) periods. It also entitles the bearer to additional discounts on museums, sights, and concerts. For senior travelers journeying only in France, the Carte Vermeille is a better bargain than a Eurail Pass. The Carte Vermeille and Carrissimo are sold only in Europe.

If you are planning to rack up many kilometers on French or European trains, you might consider investing in a **railpass** or **Eurailpass** (for more information, see Let's Go: France or Let's Go: Europe).

## BY FERRY

Many ferries link France with England and Ireland. **Sealink Stena Lines** and **P&O European Ferries** offer extensive service across the English Channel. Sealink ferries leave from Dover to Calais, take about 1½ hours, and are the most frequent (at peak times every ½hr.). Alternate routes between England and France include Southampton to Cherbourg (6hr., night service 8hr.) and Newhaven to Dieppe (3-4 per day, 3hr.). **P&O European Ferries** cross in 1½ hours from Dover to Calais (every 45min.). Other convenient Channel crossings include Portsmouth to Le Havre and Cherbourg. Le Havre has the fastest road connections to Paris, and Cherbourg is ideal for a scenic route through Normandy to Brittany. **Brittany Ferries** run from Plymouth or Cork to Roscoff, from Portsmouth to St-Malo/Caen, and from Poole to Cherbourg. From any of these destinations in France, you should be able to catch a train to Paris. **Irish Ferries** offers service between Cherbourg or Le Havre to Rosslare in Ireland, and to Le Havre from Cork. Irish Ferries is rather expensive (price 372-870F, depending on season and discounts), but Eurailpass holders travel free after paying a small tax.

Traveling by **catamaran** is quicker (50min.), but you should book in advance. **Hoverspeed** departs for Calais or Boulogne from Dover. Service is suspended in rough weather, so you may find yourself waiting for a ferry instead. Hoverspeed also offers combination rail/bus and hovercraft service to and from London, Paris, Brussels, Amsterdam, and points in southwestern France. This is often the easiest and cheapest way to get to Paris. Students under 26 travel at youth rates. For information, write Travelloyd, 8 Berkeley Sq., London SW1, or the British Travel Centre, 2-12 Lower Regent St., London SW1Y 4PQ.

# ■ Getting In and Out of Paris

## FROM THE AIRPORTS

### Roissy-Charles de Gaulle

Most transatlantic flights land at **Aéroport Roissy-Charles de Gaulle,** 23km northeast of Paris. As a general rule, Terminal 2 serves Air France (recorded info in French and English tel. 43 20 14 55; arrivals tel. 43 20 12 55; departures tel. 43 20 13 55), and most other carriers operate from Terminal 1 (info tel. 48 62 22 80).

The cheapest and fastest way to get into the city from Roissy-Charles de Gaulle and vice versa is by the **Roissy Rail** (tel. 43 46 14 14) bus-train combination. Take the free shuttle bus from Aérogare 1 arrival level gate 28, Aérogare 2A gate 5, Aérogare 2B gate 6, or Aérogare 2D gate 6, to the Roissy train station. From there, the **RER B3** (one of the Parisian commuter rail lines) will transport you to central Paris. If you are going to transfer to the *métro*, be sure to buy an RER ticket that includes *métro* transfer, and get off at **Gare du Nord** or **Châtelet-Les Halles,** which double as RER and *métro* stops. To go to Roissy-Charles de Gaulle from Paris, take the RER B3 to "Roissy," and change to the shuttle bus (RER 25-35min., bus 10min., 37F with *métro* transfer).

Alternatively, **Air France Buses** run to the Arc de Triomphe (Mo. Charles de Gaulle-Etoile) at av. Carnot (every 15min. 5:40am-11pm, 40min., 48F, group of 3 passengers 112F, group of 4 140F), and the pl. de la Porte de Maillot/Palais des Congrès (Mo. Porte de Maillot), near the *agence* Air France (every 20min. 5:40am-11pm, 40min., same prices). For recorded information about either of these buses, call 42 99 20 18. Air France buses also run to and from a spot near the Gare Montparnasse, 113, bd. du Vaugirard (Mo. Montparnasse-Bienvenue; to the airport hourly 7am-9pm; from the airport hourly 6:30am-7:30pm, 45min., 64F, group of 3 passengers 144F, group of 4 170F). Call 43 23 82 20 for recorded info.

**Taxis** take at least 50 minutes to the center of Paris and cost about 160F during the day, 220F at night.

### Orly

**Aéroport d'Orly** (tel. 49 75 15 15), 12km south of the city, is used by charters and many continental flights. From Orly Sud gate H or Orly Ouest arrival level gate F, take the shuttle bus (every 15min. 5:40am-11:15pm) to the **Pont de Rungis/ Aéroport d'Orly** train stop where you can board the **RER C2** for a number of destinations in Paris (35min., 27F; call RATP at 43 46 14 14 for info).

**Air France Buses** run to and from Montparnasse, 36, rue de Mienne, 6ème (Mo. Montparnasse-Bienvenue), and the downtown Invalides Air France agency (tel. 43 23 82 20 or 43 23 97 10, every 12min., 32F, group of 3 passengers 83F, group of 4 103F). In addition the RATP runs **Orlybus** to and from *métro* and RER stop Denfert-Rochereau. Board at Orly Sud gate H, platform 4 or Orly Ouest level O, door D (every 10-15min. 6am-11pm, 25min., 21F). **Taxis** from Orly to the center cost at least 110F during the day, 140F at night. Allow at least 45 minutes for the trip.

### Le Bourget

Paris's third airport, **Le Bourget** (tel. 48 62 12 12), is notable only because Charles Lindbergh landed there after his historic transatlantic flight. Nowadays, Le Bourget is used for charter flights, generally within France. Should you land at Le Bourget, take **Bus #350** (every 15min. 6:10am-11:50pm, 2 *métro* tickets) to Gare du Nord or Gare de l'Est. **Bus #152** also makes these stops and, for the same price, will take you to Porte de la Villette, where you can catch the *métro* or another bus.

## FROM THE TRAIN STATIONS

Each of Paris's six train stations is a veritable community of its own, with resident street people and police, cafés, *tabacs,* and banks, plus stores selling perfume and tacky Flashdance fashions. Locate the ticket counters *(guichets),* the platforms *(quais),* and the tracks *(voies),* and you will be ready to roll. Each terminal has two divisions: the *banlieue* and the *grandes lignes.* **Grandes lignes** depart for and arrive from distant cities in France and other countries—each of the six stations serves destinations in a particular region of France or Europe. Trains to the **banlieue** serve the suburbs of Paris and make frequent stops. Within a given station, each of these divisions has its own ticket counters, information booths, and timetables; distinguishing between them before you get in line will save you hours of frustration. All train stations are reached by at least two *métro* lines; the *métro* station bears the same name as the train station. For train information, call the SNCF at 45 82 50 50; for reservations call 45 65 60 60 or use the minitel 3615 SNCF (see Communications; reservations and minitel both open daily 8am-8pm). The SNCF line may seem perpetually busy—visiting a local travel agency will let you buy your tickets or make your reservations with more personal attention and little to no fee. There is a free telephone with direct access to the stations on the right-hand side of the Champs-Elysées tourist office.

A word on safety: though full of atmosphere, each terminal also shelters its share of thieves and other undesirables. Gare du Nord, for example, becomes rough at night, when drugs and prostitution take over; Gare d'Austerlitz can be similarly unfriendly. Be cautious in and around stations; the unsuspecting may be invited out for a drink only to be doped up and ripped off. In each train station *métro* stop, you will encounter friendly looking people who will try to sell you a *métro* ticket at exorbitant prices. It is not advisable to buy anything in the stations except at public counters.

Note: the following prices vary according to the time of year, day of the week, and other bureaucratic criteria. Call ahead.

**Gare du Nord:** Trains to northern France, Britain, Belgium, the Netherlands, Scandinavia, the Commonwealth of Independent States, and northern Germany (Cologne, Hamburg). To: Brussels (10/day, 3hr., 221F); Amsterdam (6/day., 6hr., 356F); Cologne (6 direct, 6 indirect/day, 5-6hr., 322F); Boulogne (11/day, 2½hr., 158F); Copenhagen (1 direct, 3 indirect/day, 16hr., 1036F); London (by train and boat, 7hr., return within 5 days 602F, within 2 months 502F).

**Gare de l'Est:** To eastern France (Champagne, Alsace, Lorraine), Luxembourg, parts of Switzerland (Basel, Zürich, Lucerne), southern Germany (Frankfurt, Munich), Austria, and Hungary. To: Zürich (7/day, 6hr., 375F); Munich (4 direct, 4 indirect/day, 9hr. direct, 603F); and Vienna (3/day, 15hr., 923F).

**Gare de Lyon:** To southern and southeastern France (Lyon, Provence, Riviera), parts of Switzerland (Geneva, Lausanne, Berne), Italy, and Greece. To: Geneva (5/day, 3½hr., 397F plus 16-80F TGV reservation); Florence (4/day, 11-12hr., 590F); Rome (3/day, 14-16hr., 678F); Lyon (12/day, 2hr., 275F plus 16-80F TGV reservation); Nice (8/day, 7hr., 450F plus 16-48F TGV reservation); Marseille (10/day, 5hr., 374F plus 16-48F TGV reservation).

**Gare d'Austerlitz:** To the Loire Valley, southwestern France (Bordeaux, Pyrénées), Spain, and Portugal. TGV service to southwestern France leaves from Gare Montparnasse. To Barcelona (3/day, 11-14hr., 575F) and Madrid (5/day, 12-16hr., 561F).

**Gare St-Lazare:** To Normandy. To: Caen (10/day, 2½hr., 160F).

**Gare Montparnasse:** To Brittany, and the TGV to southwestern France. To: Rennes (15/day, 2-2½hr., 246F plus 32-80F TGV reservation).

## FROM THE BUS STATIONS

Most buses to Paris arrive at **Gare Routière Internationale du Paris-Gallieni,** av. du Général de Gaulle, Bagnolet 93170 (tel. 49 72 51 51; Mo. Gallieni; formerly at Porte de la Villette). Some buses, however, have more bizarre ports of call. The **City Sprint** bus (tel. 42 85 44 55), operating in conjunction with Hoverspeed from England, drops its passengers in front of the Hoverspeed offices, three blocks from Gare du Nord at 135, rue Lafayette (Mo. Gare du Nord). For information about buses to other European countries, call **International Express Eurolines Coach Station** at 40 38 93 93.

## HITCHHIKING AND RIDE SHARING

Women, even in a group, should never hitchhike. And anyone who values safety over penny-pinching will take a train or bus out of Paris. Hitchhikers ask around at youth hostels for tips on where to hitch. They don't wait at *portes* (city exits); traffic is too heavy for cars to stop safely. Because of decreased traffic, hitchers find summer a better time to hitchhike. A sign clearly stating the destination, with the letters "S.V.P." *(s'il vous plaît)* helps ingratiate hitchhikers. Hitchhikers sometimes ask customers at gas stations if they are going their way.

For a more formal "hitch," **Allostop-Provoya,** 84, passage Brady, 10ème (in Paris tel. 42 46 00 66; outside Paris tel. 16 (1) 47 70 02 01; Minitel 3615 code PROVOYA; Mo. Strasbourg-St-Denis), will try to match you with a driver going your way. An economical way to go; price varies according to destination. Also available from Allostop is **Eurostop International** membership, valid in 76 cities in Switzerland, Germany, Spain, France, Hungary, Italy, the Netherlands, Belgium, and Canada, which entitles ride-sharers to a 25% reduction on services. If your home country is one of the nine listed above, you must purchase your card there. Ride-sharers can also buy train and bus tickets to points throughout Europe. They sell BIJ/Eurotrain tickets and arrange special weekend tours (open Mon.-Fri. 9am-7:30pm, Sat. 9am-1pm and 2-6pm).

# ■■■ ONCE THERE

## ■ Tourist Offices

Though packed in the summer, the following offices are usually able to keep the wait down to an hour at most. Lines are worst in the afternoon. They all stock the requisite reams of brochures, maps, and pamphlets, as well as information on special seasonal events. Tourist offices will help you find a room in a one-star hotel for 20F, two-star for 25F, three-star for 40F, and hostels for 8F. The Champs-Elysées tourist office will also help you reserve rooms in other parts of the country, though no more than seven days in advance, for a 30F minimum charge. All the offices exchange at decent rates with no commission; they are a sensible option when banks are closed.

**Bureau d'Accueil Central:** 127, av. des Champs-Elysées, 8ème (tel. 49 52 53 54). Mo. Charles-de-Gaulle-Etoile. English-speaking staff. Mobbed in summer. Open daily 9am-8pm. There are 5 smaller *Bureaux d'Accueil,* also operated by the *office de tourisme,* located in the following train stations and at the Eiffel Tower: **Bureau Gare du Nord,** 10ème (tel. 45 26 94 82). Mo. Gare du Nord. Open Mon.-Sat. 8am-9pm; Nov.-Easter daily 8am-8pm. **Bureau Gare de L'Est,** 10ème (tel. 46 07 17 73). Mo. Gare de l'Est. Open Mon.-Sat. 8am-9pm; Nov.-April Mon.-Sat. 8am-8pm. **Bureau Gare de Lyon,** 12ème (tel. 43 43 33 24). Mo. Gare de Lyon. Open Mon.-Sat. 8am-9pm; Nov.-April Mon.-Sat. 8am-8pm. **Bureau Gare d'Austerlitz,** 13ème (tel. 45 84 91 70). Mo. Gare d'Austerlitz. Open Mon.-Sat. 8am-3pm. **Bureau Tour Eiffel,** Champs de Mars, 7ème (tel. 45 51 22 15). Mo. Champs de Mars. Open May-Sept. 11am-6pm.

In addition, both international airports run tourist offices where you can make same-day hotel reservations (with deposit equal to 12% of room rate) and receive information about Paris.

**Orly, Sud:** Near gate H. **Orly, Ouest:** Near gate F (tel. 49 75 01 36). Both open daily 6am-11:45pm.
**Roissy-Charles de Gaulle:** Near gate 36 arrival level (tel. 48 62 27 29). Open daily 7am-9pm.

Also call **Tourist Information** (tel. 49 52 53 56) where a recorded message in English (updated weekly) gives the major events in Paris—call 49 52 53 55 for French.

## ■ Budget Travel Offices

**Accueil des Jeunes en France (AJF):** 119, rue St-Martin, 4ème (tel. 42 77 87 80). Mo. Rambuteau. Across from the pedestrian mall in front of the Pompidou Center. Open Mon.-Sat. 9am-6pm; Oct.-May Mon.-Fri. 9am-5:30pm. Also 16, rue du Pont Louis-Philippe, 4ème (tel. 42 78 04 82), near the Hôtel de Ville. Mo. Hôtel-de-Ville or Pont-Marie. Open Mon.-Fri. 9:30am-6:30pm. Also 139, bd. St-Michel, 5ème (tel. 43 54 95 86), in the *quartier latin*. Mo. Port-Royal. Open Tues.-Sat. 10am-1pm and 1:30-6pm. Another in Gare du Nord arrival hall next to Agence de Voyages SNCF (tel. 42 85 86 19). Open June-Sept. daily 7am-10pm; Oct. and March-May Mon.-Fri. 9:30am-6:30pm. The Gare du Nord office only books accommodations. The other offices will give you free maps, sell ISIC cards (60F), and make room reservations in hotels and youth hostels in Paris (10F) and in *foyers* (72-85F/

night). Reduced-price student train and bus tickets, budget weekend holidays, and meal vouchers for Paris youth hostels. The office across from the Pompidou Center can be used as a mailing address but is so ridiculously crowded that it pays to try one of the other branches—all friendly, centrally located, English-speaking, and very crowded.

**Centre Régional des Oeuvres Universitaires (CROUS):** 39, av. Georges Bernanos, 5ème (tel. 40 51 36 00). Mo. Port-Royal. Next door to the OTU, this helpful university organization has information on student dormitory housing in Paris (min. 2 days stay, max. 1 month) and on the many university restaurants that offer simple but filling meals for rock bottom prices. The **Restaurant Universitaire Bullier** next door is open all year (even during the summer when the university is not in session) for lunch (12F; 11:30am-2:15pm) and for dinner (12F; 6-8pm).

**Council on International Educational Exchange (CIEE) and Centre Franco-Américain Odéon:** main office at 49, rue Pierre Charron, 8ème (tel. 42 59 23 69; fax 42 56 65 27). Also at 1, pl. de l'Odéon, 6ème (tel. 46 34 16 10; fax 43 26 97 45). Mo. Odéon. Both answer questions about work abroad. The branch at place d'Odéon has a comprehensive library with useful information about job offers, travel, and housing opportunities (library open 2-6pm). Open Mon.- Fri. 9am-6pm.

**Council Travel:** 51, rue Dauphine, 6ème (tel. 43 26 79 65). Mo. Odéon. Also at 16, rue de Vaugirard (tel. 46 34 02 90; Mo. Odéon) and at 31, rue St-Augustin, 2ème (tel. 42 66 20 87; Mo. Opéra). English-speaking travel service for young people. Books international flights. Sells student train tickets, guidebooks, and ISIC cards (60F). BIJ/Eurotrain tickets. If you lose your CIEE charter flight ticket, go to the Opéra office and they will telex the U.S. to authorize a substitute; you will pay a penalty depending on your flight. All open Mon.-Fri. 10am-6pm, Sat. 10am-5pm.

**Office de Tourisme Universitaire (OTU):** 39, av. Georges Bernanos, 5ème (tel. 43 36 80 27). Mo. Port-Royal. A French student travel agency. English spoken. The same reduced train and plane tickets for students under 26 that are sold at any travel agent in Paris, but more crowded. Bring an official form of ID. Also sells ISIC (60F) and BIJ tickets. Open Mon. 11am-6:45pm, Tues.-Fri. 10am-6:45pm.

# ■ Embassies and Consulates

If anything serious goes wrong, make your first inquiry to your country's consulate in Paris. The distinction between an embassy and a consulate is significant: an embassy houses the offices of the ambassador and his or her staff; you won't gain access unless you know someone inside. All facilities for dealing with nationals are in the consulate. If your passport gets lost or stolen, your status in France is immediately rendered illegal—go to the consulate *as soon as possible* to get a replacement. A consulate is also able to lend (not give) up to 100F per day (interest free), but you will be forced to prove you are truly desperate with no other source of money. The consulate can give you lists of local lawyers and doctors, notify family members of accidents, and give information on how to proceed with legal problems, but its functions end there. Don't ask the consulate to pay for your hotel or medical bills, investigate crimes, obtain work permits, post bail, or interfere with standard French legal proceedings. If you are arrested during your stay in France, there is little, if anything, that your own government can do to help you.

**U.S.:** 2, av. Gabriel, 8ème (tel. 42 96 12 02 or 42 61 80 75), off pl. de la Concorde. Mo. Concorde. **Consulate** at 2, rue St-Florentin (tel. 42 96 12 02), 3 blocks away. Passports replaced for 325F (under 18 200F). Open Mon.-Fri. 9am-3pm. Closed for both American and French holidays.

**Canada:** 35, av. Montaigne, 8ème (tel. 44 43 29 00). Mo. Franklin-Roosevelt or Alma-Marceau. **Consulate** at same tel. and address. Ask for "consular services." New passport 380F. Open Mon.-Fri. 9-10:30am and 2-3pm.

**U.K.:** 35, rue du Faubourg-St-Honoré, 8ème (tel. 42 66 91 42). Mo. Concorde or Madeleine. New passport 153F. **Consulate** at 9, av. Hoche (tel. 42 66 91 42), near

Parc Marceau. Mo. Charles de Gaulle-Etoile. Open Mon.-Fri. 9am-noon and 2-5pm. Visa bureau open Mon.-Fri. 9am-noon.

**Australia:** Embassy at 4, rue Jean-Rey, 15ème (tel. 40 59 33 00). Mo. Bir-Hakeim. **Consular services:** new passport 380F. Open Mon.-Fri. 9am-noon and 2-5pm.

**New Zealand:** Embassy at 7ter, rue Léonard-de-Vinci, 16ème (tel. 45 00 24 11). Mo. Victor-Hugo. New passport 400F. Open Mon.-Fri. 9am-1pm and 2-5:30pm.

**Ireland:** Embassy at 12, av. Foch, 16ème (tel. 45 00 20 87). Mo. Charles de Gaulle-Etoile. Open Mon.-Fri. 9:30am-5:45pm. **Consular Services** (tel. 45 00 22 16). New passport 380F. Open 9am-1pm.

**South Africa:** Embassy at 59, quai d'Orsay, 7ème (tel. 45 55 92 37).

# ■ Communications

## MAIL

**Post offices** are marked on most maps of Paris by their abstract flying-letter insignia; if you don't have a map, look for the yellow and blue PTT signs. Streets with post offices are usually marked by a cheerful sign at the corner. In general, post offices in Paris are open weekdays until 7pm (they stop changing money at 6pm) and on Saturday mornings. Avoid long lines by purchasing stamps at local *tabacs* or from the yellow coin-operated vending machines outside major post offices.

Air mail between Paris and North America takes five to 10 days and is fairly dependable. Send mail from the largest post office in the area. Surface *(par eau* or *par terre)* mail is by far the cheapest way to send mail, but takes one to three months to cross the Atlantic. It's adequate for getting rid of books or clothing you no longer need; a special book rate makes this option more economical. It is vital to distinguish your airmail from surface mail by labelling it clearly *"par avion."* If you send a parcel air mail *(par avion)*, you must complete a green customs form for any package over 1kg (2kg for letter-post rate). Special delivery is called *avec recommandation,* and express mail *exprès postaux.* Airmailing a 25g (about 1 oz.) letter from France to the U.S. or Canada costs about 4F. Postcards *(cartes postales)* are 3F70. The *aerogramme,* a sheet of fold-up, pre-paid airmail paper, requires no envelope; it costs more (4F50).

If you're writing from home to France and expect a reply (e.g., when making hotel reservations), enclose an **International Reply Coupon** (available at post offices for US$1) for a response by surface mail; send two for airmail.

Postcards and letters sent from the U.S. cost 40¢ and 50¢. The post office also sells aerograms for 45¢. Many U.S. city post offices offer Express Mail service, which sends packages under 8 oz. to major overseas cities in 40 to 72 hours (US$11.50-14). Private mail services provide the fastest, most reliable overseas delivery. **DHL**(US$30), **Federal Express** (US$32), and **Airborne Express** (US$34, max. 8 oz.) can get mail from North America to Paris in 2 days.

If you do not have a specific address in Paris, you can receive mail through the **Poste Restante** system, handled by the 24-hour post office at 52, rue du Louvre, 1er (tel. 40 28 20 00 for urgent telegrams and calls; 42 80 67 89 for postal information; Mo. Châtelet-les-Halles). To ensure the safe arrival of your letter, address it: LAST NAME (in capitals), first name; Poste Restante; R.P. *(Recette Principale);* 52, rue de Louvre, 75001 Paris, FRANCE. You will have to show your passport as identification and pay 2F50 for every letter received.

**American Express** also receives and holds mail for up to 30 days, after which they return it to the sender. If you want to have it held longer, just write "Hold for x days" on the envelope. The envelope should be addressed with your name in capital letters, and "Client Letter Service" should be written below your name. Most big-city American Express offices provide this service free of charge if you have their Traveler's Cheques, but some require that you be an AmEx cardholder. The free booklet *Traveler's Companion* contains the addresses of American Express offices worldwide, and can be obtained from any American Express office or by calling customer service at (800) 528-4800 (allow 6-8 weeks for delivery).

COMMUNICATIONS

## TELEPHONES

Almost all French pay phones accept only **télécartes;** in outlying districts and cafés and bars, some phones are still coin-operated. You may purchase the card in two denominations: 40F for 50 *unités,* and 96F for 120 *unités,* each worth anywhere from six to 18 minutes of conversation, depending on the rate schedule. Local calls cost one *unité* each. The *télécarte* is available at post offices and most *métro* stations and *tabacs.* The best places to call from are phone booths and post offices. If you phone from a café, hotel, or restaurant, you risk paying up to 30% more. Emergency or collect calls do not require coins or a *télécarte.*

A brief **glossary:** A call is *un coup de téléphone* or *un appel;* to dial is *composer;* a collect call is made *en PCV* (pay-say-vay); a person-to-person call is *avec préavis.* A small digital screen on the phone will issue a series of simple commands: *décrochez* means to pick up, *racrochez* to hang up. On some *télécarte* phones, you need to *ferme le volet:* pull down the lever directly above the card slot and wait for a dial tone.

You can make **intercontinental calls** from any phone booth, but it will cost less to have the other person call you back. All European phones receive in-coming calls. The number is posted on a sticker inside the booth, prefaced by *ici le.* To call from the U.S., dial the international access code (011 from the U.S. and Canada, 010 from the U.K., 0011 from Australia, 00 from New Zealand, 09 from South Africa), 33 (France's country code), 1 (Paris's city code), and the eight-digit local number. Calling overseas can cost as little as 5F, and it's much cheaper this way (the French tax calls by as much as 30%). This technique is also cheaper than calling collect or via credit card. Country codes are posted inside most telephone booths. If your credit isn't good at home, the *196 unités télécarte* will serve you well (call to the U.K. 120 units for 20min.; call to the U.S. or Canada 120 units for 12min.). For more information, pick up Telecom's brochure, *Call Home,* available in tourist offices and some post offices.

Another alternative for Americans is **AT&T USA Direct** service, which allows you to be connected instantly to an operator in the U.S. Simply dial 19, wait for the tone, then dial 00 11. Rates run about US$1.75-1.85 for the first minute plus about US$1 per additional minute. Calls must be either collect (US$5.75 surcharge) or billed to an AT&T calling card (US$2.50); the people you are calling need not subscribe to AT&T service. For more information, call AT&T at (800) 874-4000. **Canada Direct, Australia Direct,** and **New Zealand Direct** are similar to USA Direct, though not as extensive. For information call (800) 561-8868 in Canada, 0102 in Australia, or 018 in New Zealand. These services can also be used for international calls within Europe. **MCI's Call USA** program allows its customers to call the U.S. from over 65 countries (US$3.60-5.35 for the 1st minute, US$1-2 per additional minute). MCI offers **WorldReach,** a more expensive program through which you can use a calling card to call from one European country to another. Call MCI at (800) 444-4444 or (800) 444-3333.

**Telephone rates** are reduced Monday through Friday 9:30pm-8am, Saturday 2pm-8am, and Sunday all day for calls to the European Community and Switzerland; Monday through Friday noon-2pm and 8pm-2am, and Sunday afternoon to the U.S. and Canada; Monday through Saturday 9:30pm-8am and Sunday all day to Israel.

A brief **directory:**

**AT&T operator:** tel. 19 00 11.
**Direct international calls:** tel. 19 + country code (listed above and in most phone booths) + area/city code + the number.
**Direct long-distance calls within France:** To call from the Paris region to elsewhere in France, dial 16 + the number. To call the Paris area from elsewhere in France, dial 1 + the number. Within the Paris area, just dial the number; do the same to make a call to a region outside of Paris from a region outside of Paris.
**Directory information** *(Renseignements téléphoniques):* tel. 12.

**International information:** 19 33 12 + country code (Australia 61; Ireland 353; New Zealand 64; U.K. 44; U.S. and Canada 1).
**International Operator:** tel. 19 33 11.
**Operator** *(Téléphoniste):* tel. 10.

## TELEGRAMS AND MORE

To send a **telegram** overseas from the U.S., **Western Union** (tel. (800) 625-6000) charges a base fee of US$8, plus 71¢ per word, including name and address (to Canada 50¢; U.K. 56¢). There is a US$10 surcharge for telegrams not in English or Spanish. Mailgrams, which require one day for delivery, cost US$17.90.

If you're spending a year abroad and want to keep in touch with friends or colleagues in a college or research institution, **electronic mail** ("e-mail") is an attractive option. It takes a minimum of computer knowledge and a little prearranged planning, and it beams messages anywhere for free.

Between May 2 and Octoberfest, EurAide, P.O. Box 2375, Naperville, IL 60567 (tel. (708) 420-2343), offers **Overseas Access,** a service most useful to travelers without a set itinerary. It costs US$15 per week or US$40 per month for an electronic message box. To reach you, people call the "home base" in Munich, Bahnhofplatz 2, 8000 München 2 (tel. (089) 59 38 89), and leave a message; you receive it by calling Munich whenever you wish, which is cheaper than calling overseas. For an additional US$20 per month, EurAide forwards mail sent to Munich to any address you specify.

## MINITEL

Minitel is a computer system which provides telephone numbers, addresses, and professions of French telephone subscribers, as well as newspapers on screen (including the *International Herald Tribune),* shopping, the weather, train schedules, and lots of other information. There are several coin-operated Minitels (2F/min.) for public use at the Bibliothèque Publique Information at the Centre Pompidou (directory information in English: 3614 ED). If you have a listed telephone number, you can lease your very own from the phone company. This is not advisable for anyone on a budget; at 2F a minute, Minitel could break your budget before you're even aware of it. Minitel has a cheaper cousin found in post offices. Use the little yellow machines as phone books to find out numbers and services. There is no charge for use and they are workable with the most rudimentary knowledge of French. In requesting an address, save yourself some trouble and type PARIS for everything short of the name of the business or person you are inquiring about. On the whole, Minitel may not be that useful to visitors: you may want to stick to *Pariscope, Let's Go,* and tourist offices.

## ■ Specific Concerns

### OLDER TRAVELERS AND SENIOR CITIZENS

Although the Tourist Office has no specific publications concerning seniors, most museums, concerts, and sights in Paris offer reduced prices for visitors over 60. Call ahead for *prix réduit* for senior visitors. For additional discounts on sights, special events, and transportation, you may want to invest in the **Carte Vermeille** (see Train Discounts and Railpasses above for details). For travel in Paris, the RATP (Régie Autonome des Transports Parisiens) publishes a free brochure which outlines *métro* and city bus service for senior travelers called *Circuler sans fatigue dans le métro et le RER* (in French only; RATP tel. 43 46 14 14; 6am-9pm).

The Ministère des Anciens Combattants (Ministry of Veteran Affairs), 37, rue de Bellechasse, 7ème (tel. 45 56 50 00) can offer information for veterans abroad.

## TRAVELERS WITH DISABILITIES

The French Tourist Board and the Mairie de Paris provide a number of free publications of interest to travelers with disabilities. The extensive and comprehensive *Touristes Quand Même: Paris* (144 pages) provides useful information in English and French on wheelchair accessibility, closed-caption screenings, sign-language translation, and other services in Parisian hotels, museums, restaurants, and sights. The publication *Paris: Musées, Bibliothèques, Centres et Ateliers culturels... A l'Usage des Personnes Présentant un Handicap* (242 pages) provides information on services for those in wheelchairs or with vision or hearing disabilities. Both publications are distributed free by the Office du Tourisme on the Champs-Elysées (tel. 49 52 53 54).

Many *métro* stations are wheelchair accessible. For a guide to *métro* accessibility, pick up a free copy of the RATP's brochure, *Circuler sans fatigue dans le métro et le RER* (in French), which provides a list of stations equipped with escalators, elevators, and moving walkways. For information, call the RATP (tel. 43 46 14 14; 6am-9pm). The Association Valentin-Hauy provides a map of the Paris *métro* in Braille.

A free *métro* service called *Voyage Accompagné* (Accompanied Travel) allows vision-impaired visitors to be escorted to their destination by a designated guide. This service is offered by the RATP (tel. 46 70 88 74) and is available 8am to 8pm every day of the week on all 13 *métro* lines, RER lines A and B, and over 100 bus routes. Guide dogs are transported free. If you bring a seeing-eye dog into France, you must carry a vaccination certificate for rabies issued in your home country or a certificate showing there have been no cases of rabies in your country for over three years.

Many museums and sights are fully accessible to wheelchairs and some provide guided tours in sign-language. Visitors who are blind may want to contact the Federation de France about touch tours of Parisian museums. Consult *Touristes Quand Même* before you set out—not all museums, hotels, restaurants, and sights are equipped for special needs. Write or telephone, and directly ask restaurants, hotels, railways, and airlines about their facilities: *"Etes-vous accessibles aux chaises roulantes?"* Most places that are wheelchair accessible will understand the question if you ask in English. In general, modern buildings in Paris are wheelchair accessible, as are the more expensive hotels. The majority of the budget hotels in this book do not have elevators; exceptions are noted in the listings. It is wise to call ahead because many of the elevators are too narrow to hold a wheelchair. Check with the following organizations for more information on accessibility and traveling with disabilities in Paris.

**Association des Paralysés de France, Délégation de Paris,** 22, rue du Père Guérin, 13ème (tel. 44 16 83 83). Publishes *Où ferons-nous étape?* (100F), which lists French hotels and motels accessible to persons with disabilities.

**Association Valentin-Hauy,** 5, rue Duroc, 7ème (tel. 47 34 07 90). Houses a cassette and Braille library for vision-impaired tourists and residents of Paris. Also provides a *métro* map in Braille.

**Audio-Vision guides,** at Parisian theaters like the Théâtre National de Chaillot, 1 pl. Trocadéro, 11 Novembre, 16ème (tel. 47 04 86 80), and the Théâtre National de la Colline, 15, rue Malte-Brun, 20ème (tel. 43 66 40 30). Service for people who are blind or visually impaired, which describes the costumes, sets, and theater design of the plays that are currently running.

**Auxiliaire des Aveugles,** (tel. 43 06 39 68). Bilingual staff provides information on services in Paris for people who are visually impaired.

**Comité National Français de Liason pour la Réadaption des Handicapés (CNFLRH),** 38, bd. Raspail, 7ème (tel. 45 48 90 13). Provides a list of hotels with wheelchair access (25F).

**Fédération de France,** 40, av. Hoche, 8ème (tel. 42 25 66 66). Publishes the guide *Des Musées Ouvert à Tous les Sens* (in Braille, French only), a list of museums where visitors with visual disabilities may touch the sculptures in their collections.

**Neuf Orthopedio: Orthopédie, Prothèse, Chaussures,** 9, rue Léopold Bellan, 2ème (tel. 42 33 83 46). Mo. Sentier. This store sells wheelchairs, canes, and other important accessories.

## TRAVELING WITH CHILDREN

Paris is a wonderful place to travel with children, as long as you don't drag them to every possible museum, historic monument, church, and nearby château. Try following them for a change; you'll see the city in a new and very different light. Parks, most of which have playgrounds, fountains, and lots of interesting people-watching, provide an excellent spot for a relaxed, fun, and very Parisian afternoon. Despite the fact that French schoolchildren may seem very well dressed in their miniature Izod shirts and Benetton pullovers, they like to get just as messy as their American counterparts. The **Jardin du Luxembourg** has a *guignol* (puppet show), pony rides, go-carts, a carousel, boats to rent and sail on the ornamental ponds, and swings with attendants who, for a tip, will push the swings while you vanish into a café. In the summer, the carnival at the **Tuileries** has a collection of rides suitable for all ages. Parents will enjoy the ferris wheel—with its outstanding view of central Paris—as much as their kids. **La Villette,** a huge science museum, aquarium, and Omnimax theater complex, offers an entire days worth of innovative entertainment. A climb up the tower of **Notre-Dame,** with its steep, winding stairs, its view of Paris at the top, and—most of all—its leering gargoyles, will liven up any child's tour of the cathedral. The **Jardin des Plantes** (with its new museum La Grande Galérie de l'Evolution) and the Paris **Zoo** are also fun, and even the most clichéd sights, such as the Eiffel Tower and the *bateaux mouches* (tour boats on the Seine), rejuvenate jaded travelers when seen with children. Remember that not all museums in Paris are devoted to traditional art; flip through our Museum section for some more unusual selections. For a surrender to international capitalist homogeneity and children's occasionally unrefined tastes, take the RER out to **Euro Disney® Resort.** You may not like the idea of shaking hands with Mickey on "Main Street USA" while you're in France, but remember that your child put up with you in the Louvre. The **Jardin d'Acclimatation** (tel. 45 01 88 91 or 40 67 97 66) in the **Bois de Boulogne** offers a children's zoo, a hall of mirrors, and a playground, for only 9F. Donkey rides and remote-control speed boats cost extra (7-10F).

In the culinary domain, don't fight the siren song of *le hot dog, le croque monsieur* (a grilled ham-and-cheese sandwich), *les frites* (french fries), or even the dreaded "McDonalds!" If your kids don't take to the subtleties of *haute cuisine,* they aren't any different from French kids, who dismay their parents by insisting on fast food. In general, it's not very common to see kids in restaurants. Head for the less formal cafeterias, *café-restaurants,* and *brasseries.* Not all restaurants have high chairs; you may want to ask first *("Est-ce que vous avez une chaise haute?").*

For bedtime stories before or during your trip, follow the 12 little girls around the sights of Paris in Hugo Bemelmans's *Madeleine* picture books. *Crin blanc* and *Le ballon rouge,* both by Albert La Morisse, are two stories that exemplify a peculiarly French sentimentality regarding early childhood. Kids will enjoy seeing scenes from them come to life on the streets of Paris. Goscinny and Sempé's *Le Petit Nicolas* and *Nicolas en Vacances* recount the antics of the mischievous little Nicolas and friends in rural France. The well-known *Tintin* and *Astérix* comics appeal to a wide range of ages, and the hardbound copies are both travel- and child-proof (well, almost).

For more hints on traveling with children (and on parent-survival) write to **Lonely Planet Publications,** Embarcadero West, Oakland, CA 94607 (tel. (510) 893-8555 or (800) 275-8555), or P.O. Box 617, Hawthorn, Victoria 3122, Australia, for Maureen Wheeler's *Travel with Children* (US$10.95, postage US$1.50 in the U.S.).

## MINORITY TRAVELERS

Tough economic times have exacerbated problems of racism and nationalism in France. The racist, ultra-rightist, ultra-nationalist party called the National Front, led by Jean-Marie Le Pen, emerged in the 1986 legislative elections. Interior minister Charles Pasqua's proposal for "zero immigration" in 1993 (later amended to "zero *illegal* immigration") reflected this unease, as did his proposal that would allow people to be stopped on the basis of *"tout élément permettant de présumer de la qualité d'étranger autre que l'appartenance raciale"* (any evidence that allows one to presume that the person is foreign other than race). The example he gave was of someone reading *The New York Times* on the streets of Paris. Minority travelers should be aware of the current issues. The safety precautions which any traveler takes are particularly important for minority travelers. (See Safety and Security.)

## ■ Emergency, Health, and Help

**Fire:** tel. 18.

**Emergency Medical Assistance: Ambulance (SAMU):** tel. 15. Outside of Paris, call 45 67 50 50.

**Poison Control:** tel. 40 37 04 04.

**Police Emergency:** tel. 17.

**Police:** Each *arrondissement* of Paris has its own *gendarmerie* to which you should take all your non-emergency concerns. Call the operator (tel. 12) and ask where your local branch is.

**Rape Crisis: SOS Viol,** tel. 05 05 95 95. Call from anywhere in France for counseling, medical and legal advice, and referrals. Open Mon.-Fri. 10am-6pm.

**Hospitals:** Hospitals in Paris are numerous and efficient. They will generally treat you whether or not you can pay in advance. Settle with them afterward and don't let your financial concerns interfere with your health care. Unless your French is exceptionally good, you'll have the best luck at one of the anglophone hospitals. **Hôpital Franco-Britannique de Paris:** 3, rue Barbès, in the Parisian suburb of Levallois-Perret (tel. 47 58 13 12). Mo. Anatole-France. Considered a French hospital and bills like one. Has some English-speakers and a good reputation. **Hôpital Américain de Paris:** 63, bd. Victor Hugo, Neuilly (tel. 46 41 25 25). Mo. Port Maillot, then bus #82 to the end of the line. In a suburb of Paris. Employs English-speaking personnel, but much more expensive than French hospitals. You can pay in U.S. dollars. If you have Blue Cross-Blue Shield, your hospitalization is covered as long as you fill out the appropriate forms first. They can also direct you to the nearest English-speaking doctor and provide dental services.

**Late Night Pharmacies: Les Champs Elysées,** in the Galerie des Champs, 84, av. des Champs-Elysées, 8ème (tel. 45 62 02 41). Mo. George V. Open 24 hrs. The only all-night pharmacy in Paris. **Drugstore St-Germain,** 149, bd. St-Germain, 6ème (tel. 42 22 80 00). Mo. St-Germain-des-Prés or Mabillon. Open daily 9am-2am. Every *arrondissement* should have a *pharmacie de garde,* which will open in case of emergencies. The locations change, but your local pharmacy can provide the name of the nearest one.

**AIDS information: AIDES,** Fédération Nationale, 247, rue de Belleville, 19ème (tel. 44 52 00 00). AIDES is one of the oldest and most prolific AIDS public service organizations in France. Roughly equivalent to the AIDS Action Committees found in most major American cities. AIDES runs a hotline that provides information in French and English (tel. 42 70 03 00; daily 9am-7pm).

**Alcoholics Anonymous:** 3, rue Frédéric Sauton, 5ème (tel. 46 34 59 65). Mo. Maubert-Mutualité. A recorded message in English will refer you to several numbers you can call to talk to telephone counselors. Daily meetings. Open 24 hrs. For other 12-step programs call 40 60 61 65.

**Birth Control: Mouvement Français pour le Planning Familial,** 10, rue Vivienne, 2ème (tel. 42 60 93 20). Mo. Bourse. Open Mon. noon-4pm, Tues. 5-7pm, Thurs. noon-3pm. Answers questions and provides information on birth control, pregnancy, and STD prevention.

**Drug Problems: Hôpital Marmottan,** 17-19, rue d'Armaillé, 17ème (tel. 45 74 00 04). Mo. Charles de Gaulle-Etoile. You're not always guaranteed an English speaker. For consultations or treatments, open Mon.-Sat. 9:30am-7pm; Aug. Mon.-Fri. only.

**Emotional Health:** Services and aid for the needy in Paris are provided by a number of organizations. Try calling **SOS Crisis Help Line: Friendship** (tel. 47 23 80 80). English-speaking. Support and information for the depressed and lonely. Open daily 3-11pm. For more personalized counseling (for anything from pregnancy to homesickness), the **American Church,** 65, quai d'Orsay, 7ème (Mo. Invalides or Alma-Marceau) offers 2 services: the **International Counseling Service (ICS)** and the **American Student and Family Service (ASFS).** These 2 groups share the same staff and provide access to psychologists, psychiatrists, social workers, and a clerical counselor. Payment is usually 250-300F per session, but if you are truly in need, the fee is negotiable. The ICS keeps hours in the morning (Mon.-Sat. 9:30am-1pm), the ASFS in the afternoon (Mon.-Fri. 2-7pm). The office is staffed irregularly July-Aug., but will respond if you leave a message on their answering machine. Call for an appointment (tel. 45 50 26 49 for both) at the American Church.

**HIV Testing:** 218, rue de Belleville, 20ème (tel. 47 97 40 49). Mo. Télégraphe. Free and anonymous. Mandatory counseling. Test results take 1 week. Some English spoken. Open Mon.-Fri. 4-7:30pm, Sat. 9:30am-noon. Also at 3-5, rue de Ridder, 14ème (tel. 45 43 83 78). Mo. Plaisance. Open Mon.-Fri. noon-6:30pm, Sat. 9:30am-noon. For more information and counseling, call **SIS (Sida Information Service)** (tel. 05 36 66 36).

**STD Clinic:** 43, rue de Valois, 1er (tel. 42 61 30 04). Mo. Palais-Royal. Testing and treatment for sexually transmitted diseases. Free consultations, blood tests, and injection treatments. Syphilis tests free. Plasma and chlamydia tests usually around 350F each, but free if you are in dire straits. Tests for HIV are free and anonymous, and include mandatory counseling. If you wish to see a doctor, call for a free appointment. English is spoken. Open Mon.-Fri. 9am-7pm.

## OTHER SERVICES

**American Church in Paris:** 65, quai d'Orsay, 7ème (tel. 47 05 07 99). Mo. Invalides or Alma-Marceau. As much a community center as a church. Bulletin boards with notices about jobs, rides, apartments, personals, etc., both in the lobby and downstairs. *Free Voice,* a free English-language monthly specializing in cultural events and classifieds, is published here; submit your ad with 50F by the 20th of the month before. Interdenominational services Sun. at 11am, followed by a ½-hr. coffee break and, during the school year, by a filling, friendly luncheon at 12:30pm (50F, children 40F). International counseling service (tel. 45 50 26 49). Church open Mon.-Sat. 9am-10pm, Sun. 9am-8pm. Free student concerts Oct.-June Sun. at 6pm. Hosts meetings for AA, AL-ANON, ACOA, and FAACTS (workshops for people affected by AIDS, ARC, or HIV-positive status). In October the church sponsors an orientation program for newcomers to Paris. There is a minimal fee. The church also holds a flea market on the 1st and 3rd Sat. of each month (2-5pm).

**Catholic Information Center:** 6, pl. du Parvis Notre-Dame, 4ème (tel. 46 33 01 01). Information about religious activities, prayer, and pilgrimages. Open Mon.-Fri. 9am-noon and 2-6pm.

**Laundromats:** Ask your hotel or hostel for the location of the closest one. The average price is 30F/wash, detergent included, and 2F/6 min. dry. Most laundromats are open 8am-10pm; last wash 9pm.

**Lost Property: Bureau des Objets Trouvés,** 36, rue des Morillons, 15ème (tel. 45 31 14 80). Mo. Convention. You can visit or write to them describing the object and when and where it was lost. No information given by phone. Open Mon.-Fri. 8:30am-5pm; Sept.-June Mon., Wed., and Fri. 8:30am-5pm, Tues. and Thurs. 8:30am-8pm.

**Public Baths:** 8, rue des Deux Ponts, 4ème (tel. 43 54 47 40). Mo. Pont-Marie. Shower 5F, families 2F50, with soap and towel roughly 10F80. For the same price you can also rub-a-dub-dub at 42, rue du Rocher, 8ème (tel. 45 22 15 19; Mo. St-Lazare), and at 40, rue Oberkampf, 11ème (tel. 47 00 57 35; Mo. Oberkampf). They are clean, respectable, and quite popular in summer. All open Thurs. noon-7pm, Fri. 8am-7pm, Sat. 7am-7pm, Sun. 8am-noon.

**Public Libraries: Bibliothèque Publique Information,** in the Centre Pompidou, 4ème (tel. 44 78 12 33). Mo. Rambuteau, Hôtel de Ville, or Châtelet-Les-Halles. Many books in English. Record and video listening room. Novels are arranged alphabetically by century on the 1st floor (entrance to the library on the 2nd floor), so you'll have to hunt for those in translation. Guide books and books about France and Paris abound. Books cannot be checked out. Open Mon.-Fri. noon-10pm, Sat.-Sun. 10am-10pm. If you just need a quiet place to read or write, the historic **Bibliothèque Mazarine,** 23, quai de Conti, 6ème (tel. 44 41 44 06; Mo. Pont-Neuf), provides old volumes and perfect silence. If you plan to visit frequently, apply for a *carte d'entrée*. Open Aug. 16-July 31 Mon.-Fri. 10am-6pm. Free to the public.

**St. Michael's Church:** 5, rue d'Aguesseau, 8ème (tel. 47 42 70 88). Mo. Concorde. Holds Anglican services in English Sun. at 10:30am and 6:30pm. Oct.-May lunchtime services are also held Thurs. at 12:45pm. On the 1st floor, outside the offices, bulletin boards list jobs offered and wanted, accommodations available and sought, as well as information on activities of interest. Office open Mon. 9:30am-12:30pm and 2-5:30pm, Tues. and Thurs.-Fri. 9am-12:30pm and 2-5:30pm. Even if the office is closed, boards and pamphlets should be accessible.

**Synagogue: Union Libéral Israélite de France,** 24, rue Copernic, 16ème (tel. 47 04 37 27). Mo. Victor-Hugo. The multilingual, ever-jovial M. Ogorek presides over a welcoming staff. 1-hr. services Fri. at 6pm and 1½-hr. services Sat. at 10:30am, mostly in Hebrew with a little French. English-speaking rabbi stays after the service to chat. Call for info about the large High Holy Days celebrations and religious groups. Secretariat open Mon.-Fri. 9am-noon and 2-5pm.

**Weather: Allo Météo,** 5-day recorded forecasts. Preferable to call from touch-tone phones. **Paris,** tel. 36 68 02 75; **Ile de France,** tel. 36 68 00 00; **France,** tel. 36 68 01 01; **mountain regions** (choice of northern Alps, southern Alps, Pyrénées, and Massifs), tel. 36 68 04 04; **marine conditions,** tel. 36 68 08 08. All in French. You can also check out a map of the day's predicted weather at the corner of Rapp and Université in the 7ème, posted by **Météorologie nationale.**

# Publications About Paris

On those heartbreaking and rare occasions when *Let's Go* falls just short, consult the following guides. *Le Petit Futé* (65F), *Paris Pas Cher* (109F), and *Paris Combines* (95F) can guide you to the best and cheapest stores, services, restaurants, and a smorgasbord of options especially useful for the long-term traveler. *Connaissance de Vieux Paris* (100F) is a great tome for history buffs. Popular among the French is *Guide du Routard* (69F). Basically a French *Let's Go,* complete with smart-alec comments, it provides useful information on how to live on a budget in Paris. *Gault Millau* is a well-respected guide to Parisian eateries. Patricia Wells's *The Food Lover's Guide to Paris* (US$15, about 100F in France) lists most of the city's greatest and most famous restaurants, cafés, bakeries, cheese shops, *charcuteries,* wine shops, etc. Gourmets may not share all of Wells's opinions (and budget travelers may not be able to verify them), but the guide is generally reliable. Both of the above are available at **Gibert Jeune** and other Parisian bookstores (see Shopping—Bookstores).

Your most important printed resource will invariably be a map (see Maps). The Office du Tourisme publishes a monthly booklet entitled *Paris Sélection* that highlights exhibitions, concerts, suggested walking tours, and other useful information (free). Similarly, the **Mairie de Paris** publishes the monthly *Paris le Journal* (10F) with articles and listings about what's on, touristically and culturally, around the city. It is available at the Mairie's Salon d'Accueil, 29, rue de Rivoli, 4ème (tel. 42 76

42 42; Mo. Hôtel de Ville), and at most *arrondissement mairies.* Some *arrondissements* (like the 16ème) publish their own magazines.

The weeklies *Pariscope* (3F) and *Officiel des Spectacles* (2F; published every Wed.) list current movies, plays, exhibits, festivals, clubs, and bars. *Pariscope* is the most comprehensive—buy one as soon as you arrive to get the rundown on Parisian life. *Pariscope* has recently added (in cooperation with the British entertainment magazine *Time Out*) a new section in English called *Time Out Paris.* The Wednesday edition of *Le Figaro* includes *Figaroscope,* a supplement about what's on in Paris. *Free Voice,* a monthly newspaper published by the Cooperative for Better Living at the American Church, 65, quai d'Orsay, 7ème (Mo. Invalides), is available there and at many student centers for free. *France-USA Contacts* (FUSAC), printed twice monthly and available free from English-speaking establishments (bookstores, restaurants, travel agencies) throughout Paris lists job, housing, and service information for English speakers. For information on gay and lesbian publications, see Bisexual, Gay, and Lesbian Paris.

Although the newspapers in France do have political leanings, they do not necessarily determine who reads them. *Libération* (6F), a socialist newspaper, is carried everywhere by students in search of amusingly written but comprehensive news coverage of world events. Heavy on culture, including theater and concert listings, *Libé* (as it is known in France) has excellent controversial interviews and thought-provoking full-page editorials.

Readers with a penchant for politics will disappear behind a copy of *Le Monde* (6F), decidedly centrist in outlook with a tendency to wax socialist. The equally respectable, solid *Le Figaro* (6F)—a French attempt at *The Wall Street Journal*—leans to the right, with greater emphasis on the financial pages. *Le Parisien* (4F50), *François* (5F), *France Soir* (5F), and *Quotidien* (6F) also write from the right, though their efforts tend toward the more-style-than-quality end of the journalistic spectrum. The Communist Party puts out *L'Humanité* (6F) to present its views. Militants and revolutionaries will want to buy *Lutte Ouvrière,* carried at few newsstands. Look for it in the streets and *métro.* Those homesick for the *Washington Post* and *The New York Times* can get the best of both in the *International Herald Tribune* (8F50). *L'Equipe* (6F), the sports and automobile daily, offers coverage and stats on most sports you can think of and some that you cannot. True hippofanatics will gallop to get *Paris-Turf* (6F50), the horse racing daily.

## ■ Details

### WEIGHTS AND MEASURES

| | |
|---|---|
| 1 millimeter (mm) = 0.04 inch | 1 inch = 25mm |
| 1 meter (m) = 1.09 yards | 1 yard = 0.92m |
| 1 kilometer (km) = 0.62 mile | 1 mile = 1.61km |
| 1 gram (g) = 0.04 ounce | 1 ounce = 25g |
| 1 liter = 1.06 quarts | 1 quart = 0.94 liter |

### TIME

In general, Paris is six hours ahead of North America (Eastern Standard Time) and one hour ahead of the United Kingdom. France springs forward one hour on the last Sunday in March and falls back an hour on the last Saturday in September. Beware: these time changes occur on different weekends than in North America.

## ■■■ ORIENTATION

### ■ Layout

Coursing languidly from east to west, the Seine River forms the heart of modern Paris. Perhaps single-handedly the basis of the city's legendary romance, the river

DETAILS

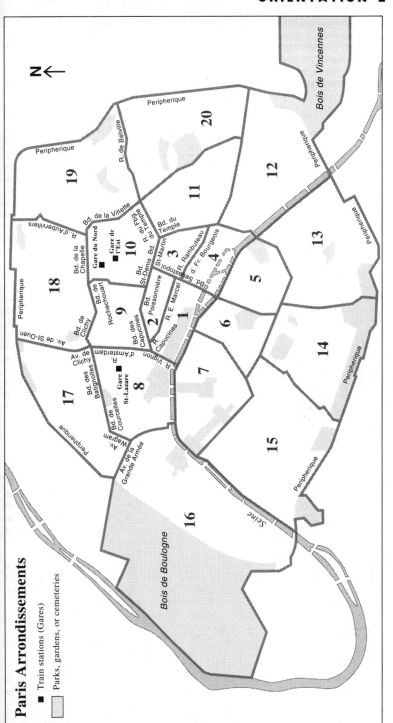

Paris Arrondissements

■ Train stations (Gares)

Parks, gardens, or cemeteries

N

Bois de Vincennes

Bois de Boulogne

Peripherique

Seine

20

12

13

5

4

3

11

19

10 Gare de l'Est

Gare du Nord

18

9

2

1

6

7

8 Gare St-Lazare

17

15

16

14

R. de Belville

Bd. de la Villette

R. d'Aubervilliers

Bd. de la Chapelle

Bd. de Rochechouart

Bd. de Clichy

Av. de St-Ouen

Bd. des Batignolles

Av. de Clichy

R. d'Amsterdam

Bd. de Courcelles

Av. de Wagram

Av. de la Grande Armée

Bd. des Capucines

R. Vignon

R. Capucines

Bd. Poissonnière

R. du Fbg. du Temple

Bd. du Temple

R. St-Martin

Bd. St-Denis

Bd. Sebastopol

R. Rambuteau

R. d. Fr. Bourgeois

R. E. Marcel

played midwife to Paris's birth on an island some 2300 years ago. Today, the Ile de la Cité and neighboring Ile St-Louis remain the geographical center of the city, while the Seine splits Paris into two large expanses—the renowned Left Bank (Rive Gauche) to its south and the Right Bank (Rive Droite) to its north. By the time of Louis XIV, the city had grown to 20 *quartiers*; Haussmann's 19th-century recon-structions shifted their boundaries but kept the number, dividing Paris into 20 *arrondissements* (districts) which spiral clockwise around the Louvre.

The first four *arrondissements*, located on the Right Bank, comprise what has his-torically been central Paris and contain the oldest streets and residences in the city. Across the Seine, the fifth and sixth make up the *quartier latin* (Latin Quarter), site of the Sorbonne and stomping ground of students and urbane culture junkies. The eighth is home to one of the most famous avenues in the world, the Champs-Elysées, which swarms with hordes of tourists. While the Catholic church reigns in the seventh and the BCBG (*bon chic, bon genre:* a type of high-brow French snob) rules the 16ème, much of Paris is a city in the making. In the throes of gentrification and cultural renaissance, the Marais (3ème and 4ème) and the Bastille area (9ème and 11ème) are multi-ethnic areas which rival traditional bastions of Parisian cul-ture, luring students, artists, and their groupies. The 13ème, Paris's Chinatown, bor-ders on the 14ème, a lively area—especially at night when the theaters crowd with Parisians and tourists alike. The 18ème, one of the outer *arrondissements* across the river, crawls with tourists and vendors by day, but is another not-so-safe night spot. The 19ème and 20ème *arrondissements* continue to serve as havens for recent immigrants. For the most part, however, Paris is no longer a city of scrutable districts, compartmentalized into rich, poor, artsy, or strait-laced neighborhoods. Travelers through Paris may easily follow the coil of Paris's geography, moving through the snail-shaped city and observing the shifting architectural, cultural *escar-got* that is Paris.

## MAPS

A map of Paris is essential if you plan to do any serious strolling. By far the best guide to Paris is the *Plan de Paris par Arrondissement,* which includes a detailed map of each *arrondissement,* all the bus lines, a wealth of miscellany, and an essential index of streets and their nearest *métro* stops. Editions L'Indispensable offers a red-or black-covered *plan* at 67F. Don't pay more unless you plan to drive in Paris. All such *plans,* marketed by several different companies, are found at most bookstores, *papeteries* (stationery stores), and kiosks. Unfortunately, the *métro* map in these guides is often out of date. Make sure to pick up a free updated one in any *métro* station: it also includes bus lines and the RER suburban system. If you're lost, keep your eyes out for a *métro* station; every station has a map of the neighborhood, with a street index. The most complete collection of maps you've ever seen can be found at **L'Astrolabe,** 46, rue de Provence, 9ème (tel. 42 85 42 95; Mo. Chaussée d'An-tin), or 14, rue Serpente, 6ème (tel. 46 33 80 06; Mo. Odéon). Both locations stock guidebooks, magazines, and travel literature in almost every language. At the 9ème *arrondissement* location, an entire floor is dedicated just to France (both open Mon.-Sat. 9:30am-7pm).

## ■ Getting Around

### PUBLIC TRANSPORTATION

The **RATP** (Régie Autonome des Transports Parisiens) coordinates an efficient net-work of subways, buses, and commuter trains in and around Paris. For information on the services of RATP, contact their office at 55, quai des Grands-Augustins, 6ème (tel. 40 46 41 41; Mo. St-Michel; open Mon.-Tues. and Thurs.-Fri. 9am-5pm, Wed. 9am-4pm). Or stop by the **Bureau de Tourisme RATP,** pl. de la Madeleine, 8ème (tel. 43 46 14 14; Mo. Madeleine; open Mon.-Sat. 7:30am-7pm, Sun. and holidays 6:30am-6pm). An English-speaking representative is usually available at both offices.

RATP can also be reached round the clock through Minitel: 3615 RATP (see Communications).

If you're only staying in Paris for one day but expect to do a lot of traveling, consider buying a **métro pass.** At 90F for three days and 145F for five, you probably won't get your money's worth with the **Paris Visite** tourist tickets, which are valid for unlimited travel on bus, *métro,* and RER, and which facilitate discounts on sight-seeing trips, bicycle rentals, and more. A more practical saver-pass is the **Formule 1;** for 27F per day, you get unlimited travel on buses, *métro,* and RER within Paris. If you're staying in Paris for more than a few days, get a weekly *(hebdomadaire)* **Coupon Vert** or a monthly *(mensuel)* **Coupon Orange,** which allow unlimited travel (starting on the first day of the week or month) on the *métro* and buses in Paris. Both of these must be accompanied by the ID-style **Carte Orange.** To get your *carte orange,* bring an ID photo (taken by machines in most major stations) to the ticket counter, ask for a *carte orange* with a plastic case, and then purchase your handsome *coupon vert* (59F) or equally swanky *coupon orange* (208F). Finally, the **Carte Hebdomadaire** is a weekly coupon that allows you two rides per day, six days out of seven, starting with the day it was purchased (40F). Write the number of your *carte* on your coupon before you use it. Also remember that these cards have specific start and end dates and may not be worthwhile if bought in the middle or at the end of the month or the week. *All prices quoted here are for passes in zones 1 and 2* (the *métro* and RER in Paris and the immediate suburbs). If you intend to travel to the distant 'burbs, you'll need to buy RER passes for more zones (up to 5). Ask at the ticket windows for details.

## METRO

Inaugurated in 1898, the Paris Métropolitain *(métro)* is one of the world's oldest and most efficient subway systems, able to whisk you within walking distance of nearly any spot in the city. Stations are marked with an "M" or the "Métropolitain" in lettering designed by Art Nouveau pioneer Hector Guimard. Trains run frequently, and connections are easy. The first trains start running at 5am; the last leave the end-of-the-line stations (the *"portes de Paris"*) for the center of the city near 12:15am. One exception is the last train leaving from Porte de Balard; it does not travel the length of the line to Porte de Charenton but goes only as far as République. In the other direction the train runs the whole route from Porte de Charenton to Porte de Balard. For the exact departure times of the last trains from the *portes,* check the poster in the center of each station called *"Principes de Tarification"* (Rate Guidelines).

Free *métro* maps are available in most stations, display maps are posted in all stations, and all have a *plan du quartier.* Connections to other lines are indicated by orange *"correspondance"* signs, and the exits by blue *"sortie"* signs. *Métro* lines are numbered (1 is the oldest), but referred to by their final destination. Transfers to other lines are free if made in the same station, but it is not always possible to reverse direction on the same line without exiting the station and using another ticket.

Each trip on the *métro* requires one ticket. Tickets can be bought individually (6F), but a *carnet* of 10 (36F50) is more practical. *Don't buy tickets from anyone except the people in the ticket booths.* **Hold onto your ticket** until you pass the point marked *Limite de Validité des Billets;* a uniformed RATP *contrôleur* (inspector) may request to see it on any train. If caught without one, you will be forced to pay a hefty fine. Also, any *correspondances* to the RER require you to put your validated (and uncrumpled) ticket into a turnstile. Otherwise you may need to buy a new ticket in order to exit. Keep in mind that a *métro* ticket is valid only within Paris. There is no longer first-class *métro* service; any cars still marked "1" are waiting to be repainted.

Most train lines are well-traveled at night, and Parisian women often travel alone, though their familiarity lends them a confidence you may lack. Violent crime in the *métro* is on the increase; use common sense. Avoid empty cars and corridors. At night, many people choose to ride in the first car, where the conductor is only a door away. Stay away from the most dangerous stations (Barbès-Rochechouart, Pigalle, Châtelet, Trocadéro, and Anvers). Despite the good neighborhoods in which some of these stops are located, they are often frequented by thieves and other troublemakers looking to prey on the tourist or the wealthy. When in doubt, take a taxi.

For information about *métro* services for people in wheelchairs or for people with impaired vision, see Once There—Travelers with Disabilities.

## RER

The **RER** (Réseau Express Régional) is the RATP's local suburban train system, which passes through central Paris. Introduced in 1969, the RER runs through deeper tunnels at higher speeds. Within the city, the RER travels much faster than the *métro*, and for all intents can be regarded as a faster, though more confusing, set of *métro* lines. The main difference is that you need your ticket to exit the station. Within the city, tickets cost the same as the *métro*; to go to the suburbs you'll need to buy a special ticket valid for the entire journey (11-40F depending on destination).

## BUS

Because the *métro* is so efficient and convenient, the Paris bus system is ignored by many visitors and locals alike. Buses, however, offer the distinct advantage of traveling above ground, thereby providing prime sightseeing and a greater familiarity with the city for the cost of one ride. The free bus map *Autobus Paris-Plan du Réseau* is available at the tourist office and some *métro* information booths. The routes of each line are also posted at each stop. The buses no longer take the same tickets as the *métro*; you must buy special tickets that cost exactly the same as *métro* tickets and are available in *métro* stations, *tabacs*, and from the bus drivers themselves. Most trips within the city and nearest suburbs cost one ticket; if your journey takes you out of the city you might need more than one ticket—ask the driver. Enter the bus through the front door and punch your ticket by pushing it into the machine by the driver's seat. If you have a *coupon orange*, flash it at the driver, but **do not** insert the ticket into the machine. *Contrôleurs* may ask to see your ticket; hold onto it until the end of the ride.

Most buses run from about 7am to 8:30pm, although some (marked *Autobus du Soir*) continue until 12:30am, and others *(Noctambus)* run all night. Night buses (3 tickets, 4 if you use 2 buses) start their runs to the *portes* of the city from the Châtelet stop and leave every hour on the half hour from 1:30 to 5:30am. Buses departing from the 'burbs to Châtelet run every hour on the hour 1 to 5am. Buses with three-digit numbers come from or are bound for the suburbs, while buses with two-digit numbers travel exclusively within Paris. Buses with numbers in the 20s come from or are bound for Gare St-Lazare, in the 30s Gare de l'Est, in the 40s Gare du Nord, in the 70s Châtelet/Hôtel de Ville (with exceptions), in the 80s Luxembourg (with exceptions), and in the 90s Gare Montparnasse.

For more detailed diagrams of all bus routes, consult the *Plan de Paris par Arrondissement* (see Maps). The RATP prints a number of useful brochures. Ask for their *Grand Plan de Paris* which includes legible maps with routes of buses which run all hours of the night and on Sundays and holidays. Their pamphlet *Paris Bus Métro RER* lists several bus routes that pass through interesting neighborhoods and by the main sights of Paris (available at *métro* stops). It also lists directions to major museums, churches, and monuments. Some routes pass by enough sights to make them mini-tours in themselves. Buses worth riding from start to finish include:

**Bus #20:** From Gare St-Lazare to the Opéra, Montmartre-Poissonière, République, Bastille (50min.). A trip down the *grands boulevards*. Open platform in back.

**Bus #21:** From Gare St-Lazare to the Opéra, Palais Royal, the Louvre, the Pont Neuf, St-Michel, Gare du Luxembourg, Porte de Gentilly (40min.).

**Bus #29:** From Gare St-Lazare to Porte de Montempoivre (50min.). Intrepid ride through narrow streets of the Marais. Open platform in back.

**Bus #82:** From Gare du Luxembourg to Gare Montparnasse, Ecole-Militaire, Champs-de-Mars, Tour Eiffel, Porte Maillot, Neuilly (45min.).

**Bus #83:** From pl. d'Italie, along bd. Raspail, Gare des Invalides, pl. des Ternes (50min.). Paris's finest real estate and views of the *quais*. Open platform in back.

**Bus #95:** From Tour Montparnasse past St-Germain-des-Prés, the Louvre, Palais Royal, the Opéra, and to Montmartre, near Sacré-Coeur (50min.).

## TAXI

Taxi trips within Paris represent the height of decadence for the budget traveler. Rates vary according to time of day and geographical area, but they're never cheap. Tarif A, the basic rate, is in effect in Paris proper from 7am to 7pm (2F79/km). Tarif B is in effect Mon.-Sat. 7pm to 7am, all day Sunday, and during the day from the airports (4F35/km). Tarif C, the highest, is in effect from the airports from 7pm to 7am (5F87/km). In addition, there is a base fee *(prix en charge)* of 11F, and stationary time (such as at traffic lights and traffic jams) costs 120F per hour. Additional charges (which hover around 5F) are tacked on for luggage weighing over 5kg, a pet in the backseat, a fourth adult in the cab, or for taxis leaving train stations or marked taxi stops. All taxis have lights on top indicating the rate being charged, so you can check to see that the driver is playing it straight. Make sure the meter is on when you start the ride. A 15% tip is customary (round up to the nearest 5F). If you must take a taxi, try picking one up at a train station or waiting at a stand *(arrêt taxis, tête de station),* usually found near bus stops. Calling a radio-cab **(ARTAXI,** tel. 42 41 50 50, **Taxis Radio Etoile** tel. 42 70 41 41, or **Taxis G7** tel. 47 39 47 39) is far more expensive, since you must pay for the distance the cab drives to pick you up. Technically, taxis cannot refuse to take a fare if their roof light is on, but can refuse to take more than three people. Illegal overcrowding of cabs can bring heavy fines upon the driver. If you have a **complaint,** write to Service des Taxis de la Préfecture de Police, 36, rue des Morillons, 75015 (tel. 45 31 14 80). If you expect to file a complaint, ask the driver for a receipt.

## BICYCLE

Bicyclists in Paris may appear to the uninitiated observer as a horde of Mr. Magoos, pedaling obliviously through a chaos of pushy Fiats and bumpy cobblestone streets. If you have never ridden a bike in heavy traffic, don't use central Paris as a testing ground. The Bois de Boulogne and the Bois de Vincennes should be more your speed (see Sports). The *métro* cannot accommodate bikes, but local trains list specific times when they allow bicycles on board for free.

**Mountain Bike Tours,** Three Ducks Hostel, 6, pl. Etienne Pernet, 15*ème* (tel. 48 42 57 87). Mo. Félix Faure. Runs popular 6-hr. guided bike tours (in English) of the Eiffel Tower, the Louvre, and Montparnasse, with a lunch stop in the *quartier latin*. Low impact, less strenuous than walking, and geared for the amateur cyclist 14-65 years old. Groups of 12-17 people. 118F. Or rent a mountain bike for 90F/day. Helmet and insurance included. Open March-Oct. daily 11am-7pm.

**Bicyclub-Roue Libre,** 8, pl. de la Porte-Champerret, 17*ème* (tel. 47 66 55 92; fax 43 80 35 68). Mo. Porte de Champerret. 6 locations, including the Bois de Boulogne (Pré Catelan), the Bois de Vincennes, the Canal de l'Ourcq, and the Forêt de Rambouillet. 3-speed bikes from 25F/hr., 100F/day. 1000F deposit includes insurance that covers you but not the bike. Locks, maps, and baby seats available. Open daily 9am-7pm; Oct.-June Mon.-Fri. 9am-7pm, Sat. 9am-1pm and 2-7pm.

**Paris-Vélo,** 2, rue de Fer-à-Moulin, 5*ème* (tel. 43 37 59 22). Mo. Censier Daubenton. Bikes 90-140F/day (depending on the model) or 1000-2000F/week, with a 1000F deposit (including accident insurance). Try to book in advance and ask for any accessories you'll need. Open Mon.-Sat. 10am-12:30pm and 2-7pm.

Mopeds and motorcycles are no longer leased in the city, but you can rent a scooter from **Mondial Scooter,** 20bis, av. Charles de Gaulle (tel. 46 24 63 64; Mo. Porte Maillot), in Neuilly-sur-Seine from 145F per day or 800F per week, with a 2500F deposit.

## CAR

"Somewhere you have heard a dark apocryphal statistic—that one driver out of every twelve in Paris has killed his man. On foot, the Parisian is as courteous as the citizen of any other city. But mounted, he is merciless." So wrote Irwin Shaw, and he liked Parisians. Parisian drivers are notorious for their *"système D"*—D for *débrouiller* (doing whatever works), which includes driving on the sidewalk in traffic jams, ignoring any lane markings that might exist, and passing in small streets at high speeds. The infamous rotary at the Arc de Triomphe has trapped many an unwary tourist; at rush hour, cars move in any direction they want here. Drivers will even cut in front of ambulances. *Priorité à droite* gives the right of way to the car approaching from the right, regardless of the size of the streets, and Parisian drivers make it an affair of honor to take this right even in the face of grave danger. Drivers may not to honk their horns within city limits unless they are about to hit a pedestrian, but this rule is often broken. The legal way to show discontent is to flash the headlights, so you should be on the lookout in case a law-abiding driver refrains from honking until just before impact. If you don't have a map of Paris marked with one-way streets, the city will be impossible to navigate. Parking is hard to locate (although Parisians park on sidewalks, corners, etc.), and garages are expensive.

Possibly the best excuse for renting a car in Paris is to escape from the city into the provinces. Renting a car for a group of three or four may be even cheaper than buying train tickets. Foreigners need a passport, a license of at least two years, and a credit card to rent in Paris; an international license is not required. None of the agencies in Paris will rent to drivers under 21. The best deal in town is at **ACAR,** 77, rue de Lagny, 20*ème* (tel. 43 79 54 54; Mo. Porte de Vincennes). A Fiat Panda costs 218F per day, first 100km free plus 1F15 per additional km; insurance costs 35F. A weekend with 1000km and insurance included is 710F. A week with unlimited mileage and insurance included is 1820F (open Mon.-Fri. 8am-12:30pm and 2-7pm, Sat. 8am-12:30pm and 2-6pm). **Inter Touring Service,** 117, bd. Auguste Blanqui, 13*ème* (tel. 45 88 52 37; fax 45 80 89 30; Mo. Glacière), rents Renault 4s for 145F per day plus 1F50 per km, insurance included, or 1820F per week, distance and insurance included (open Mon.-Sat. 8:30am-6:30pm). Inter Touring Service also provides vehicles equipped for **drivers with disabilities. Autorent,** 98, rue de la Convention, 15*ème* (tel. 45 54 22 45; fax 45 54 39 69; Mo. Boucicaut), and 3-5, av. Jean Moulin, 14*ème* (tel. 49 92 55 06; Mo. Alésia), rents Fiat Pandas for 199F per day plus 2F40 per km (open Mon.-Fri. 8:30am-7pm, Sat. 8:30am-midnight). Autorent only rents to drivers who have had a license for at least one year.

# Accommodations

There are three basic types of Parisian accommodations suitable to the budget traveler: hotels, hostels, and *foyers*. While hotels are comfortable and give you complete privacy and independence, hostels and *foyers* are the least expensive options. According to the Office du Tourisme, high season in Paris falls around Easter, May-June, and September-October (when trade shows—*salons*—take over the city.) Indeed, many hotels in the 11*ème* and the 12*ème* consider July and August to be off-season. But for hostels and other truly budget accommodations the high season is invariably summer (June-August) and most places are perpetually full. Try to make a reservation in advance, but if you do arrive in Paris without one, don't panic. The **Office du Tourisme** on the Champs-Elysées or one of its other bureaus should be able to find you a room, although the lines may be long and the selections not necessarily among the cheapest in Paris. Unless otherwise noted, we list hostel prices per person; prices elsewhere are per room. It is advisable to check the locks at the establishment where you choose to stay.

**La Centrale de Réservations (FUAJ-HI),** 4, bd. Jules Ferry, 11*ème* (tel. 43 57 02 60; fax 40 21 79 92). Mo. République. The best way to get a bed in a hostel and one of the best to find any budget accommodation in Paris. Near Jules Ferry hostel. Provides same-day reservations in one of their affiliated youth hostels or budget hotels—a total of 10,000 beds in and around the city. The earlier you show up, the better, but they can usually help anyone, any time. Supplementary hostels open up in summer and can sometimes get you hotel rooms for hostel rates. Reservation requires on-the-spot 10F deposit, deducted from your bill. Books beds throughout France and Europe and arranges excursions. Open daily 8am-10pm.

**Accueil des Jeunes en France (AJF),** 119, rue St-Martin, 4*ème* (tel. 42 77 87 80). Mo. Rambuteau; open Mon.-Sat. 9:30am-6pm. Other offices: 139, bd. St-Michel, 5*ème* (tel. 43 54 95 86; Mo. Port-Royal; open Tues.-Sat. 10am-12:30pm and 1:30-6:15pm) and Gare du Nord, 10*ème* (tel. 42 85 86 19; Mo. Gare du Nord; open June 1-Sept. 4 daily 7:30am-10pm). Even in the busiest months, AJF guarantees you "decent and low-cost lodging with immediate reservation" for the same day only. You must pay the full price of the *foyer* room when making your reservation, even before seeing the room. AJF can also help find a hotel room, though not always for full duration of your stay; you may have to use AJF more than once. Individuals must pay a fee of 10F per reservations.

## ■ Hostels and Foyers

Paris's big-city hostels don't bother with many of the restrictions—sleepsheets, curfews, and the like—that characterize most hostels in the world, but they do have maximum stays, though even these are flexible. Accommodations usually consist of bunkbeds in single-sex dormitories. To stay in a **Hostelling International (HI)** hostel, you must be a member. Prospective hostelers should become members of the HI affiliate in their country before they leave. If you show up at an HI hostel without membership, the hostel should issue you a blank membership card with space for six validation stamps. Each night you'll pay a nonmember supplement (19F) and earn one Guest Stamp; get six stamps and you're a member. Membership purchased this way costs 114F. Most student travel agencies sell HI cards on the spot or you can contact one of the national hostel organizations (see Essentials—Useful Addresses and Publications). In summer 1992, the **International Youth Hostel Federation (IYHF)** officially changed its name to **Hostelling International (HI)**, with the result that all signs, membership cards, and other products relating to the association now bear the HI initials and logo, as well as the symbols of the relevant national hosteling association.

HI has recently instituted an **International Booking Network.** To reserve space in high season, obtain an International Booking Voucher from any national youth hostel association (in your home country or Paris) and send it to a participating hostel four to eight weeks in advance, along with US$2 in francs. Pre-booking is wise.

While there are only two official HI hostels in the city (the Jules Ferry and Le D'Artagnan), many other privately run hostels and *foyers* exist all over the city. Normally intended for university students during the academic year, *foyers* offer the security and privacy of a hotel, while providing the lower prices and camaraderie of a youth hostel. Residents live anywhere from one week to three months to an entire year in the *foyer.*

**Centre International de Paris (BVJ).** Relatively luxurious chain of youth hostels; they polish the floors, water the plants, and offer stylish common areas to offset bunkbed uniformity. **Paris Louvre,** 20, rue Jean-Jacques Rousseau, 1er (tel. 42 36 88 18; fax 42 33 40 53). Mo. Louvre. 200 beds. Spacious, dorm-style rooms. Refined courtyard, hung with brass lanterns and strewn with *brasserie* chairs. 2-8 beds/room. Lunch or dinner 50F. Groups pay for 1 meal/day. **Paris Opéra,** 11, rue Thérèse, 1er (tel. 42 60 77 23; fax 42 33 40 53). Mo. Pyramides. 68 beds. Bigger rooms with fewer beds; more subdued than Paris Louvre. **Paris Les Halles,** 5, rue du Pélican, 1er (tel. 40 26 92 45; fax 42 33 40 53). Mo. Palais Royal. 55 beds. Cramped rooms, less common space, toilets and showers on alternate floors. **Paris Quartier Latin,** 44, rue des Bernardins, 5ème (tel. 43 29 34 80; fax 42 33 40 53). Mo. Maubert-Mutualité. 138 beds. Beautiful, spacious, with modern white tile and chrome décor. Spotless, but more densely packed. Photocopier and typewriter. Lockers 10F. All these hostels open 6am-2am. Families not allowed. Rooms available at 2:30 pm. Doubles, triples, and quads 110F per person, breakfast and showers included. Singles (none in Paris Louvre) 120F. Individual reservations not accepted—call or show up the same day, about 8am.

**Auberge de Jeunesse "Jules Ferry" (HI),** 8, bd. Jules Ferry, 11ème (tel. 43 57 55 60). Mo. République. About 100 beds. Wonderfully located. Clean, large rooms. Slightly crowded; noisy party atmosphere. Jovial, multilingual staff. Most spaces full by 10am. If they are full, they'll point you down the block to the Centrale (see above). Adequate kitchen facilities. 4-day max. stay. Open 24 hours. Cleaning lockout 10am-1:30pm but reception staff always present to answer questions or accept membership cards for reservations. No curfew. Single-sex lodging, but can accommodate male/female couples. 2-6 bed rooms 100F per person. Singles 110F. Showers and breakfast (self-serve 7-9:30am) included. Lockers 5F. Sheets 14F or your sleeping bag. Wash plus dry and soap 33F. Basement bike storage.

**Auberge de Jeunesse "Le d'Artagnan" (HI),** 80, rue Vitruve, 20ème (tel. 43 61 08 75; fax 43 61 75 40). Mo. Porte de Bagnolet or Porte de Montreuil. A cross between a hostel and a mall. 411 beds. 7-floor complex with restaurant, bar, and even a small movie theater. Vending machines and free microwaves downstairs. Mostly triples; a few doubles; some 8-bed rooms. Ingeniously designed for maximum space utilization without creating a cramped atmosphere. Groups limited to 150 beds. Friendly English-speaking staff. Wheelchair access. Flexible 3-day max. stay. Open 24 hrs. Lockout 10am-2pm. Triples and dorms 100F per person. Breakfast and sheets included. Doubles 115-125F per person. Lockers 15F. Laundry 15F/wash, 5F/dry; soap 3F. Reservations a must; hostel is packed Feb.-Oct. Individual reservations can be made through HI member hostels: by telefax (*not* the same thing as fax), by HI voucher (ignore the instructions and write one voucher for each day you plan to stay), by HI postcard, or by HI's IBN computerized booking network. From U.S., make reservations by credit card through member hostels in New York City, Washington DC, Miami, San Francisco, and Los Angeles.

**Hôtel des Jeunes (MIJE):** "Le Fauconnier," 11, rue du Fauconnier (tel. 42 74 23 45). Mo. St-Paul or Pont-Marie. "Le Fourcy," 6, rue de Fourcy (tel. 42 74 23 45). Mo. St-Paul or Pont-Marie. "Maubisson," 12, rue des Barres (tel. 42 74 23 45). Mo. Hôtel de Ville or Pont-Marie. All in the 4ème. Star *foyers* located in former aristocratic residences of the Marais, close to sights and to one another. Le Fauconnier is luxury in modern hostelry. Fairly spacious rooms (2, 4, and 8 beds). Le Fourcy surrounds a large courtyard ideal for meeting travelers or for an open-air picnic. In summer, school groups raise cain under evening skies. Light sleepers beware of rooms on the *cour*. Lively Maubisson, smallest of the three has newer, even smaller rooms. All 3 give priority to groups of 10 or more (but no group discounts). For groups, no age specifications or limits to time of stay, but individuals must be 18-30 and can stay no longer than 7 days. Lockout noon-4pm. Curfew 1-6am. 110F per person. Showers and breakfast included (showers in room, toilets down the hall). Lockers 2F. Individuals reserve only in person and by paying in full in advance. Groups can reserve up to 1 year in advance. Within walking distance of all 3 is **Restaurant la Table d'Hôtes,** 16, rue du Pont St-Louis-Philippe. 3-course hosteler special 50F (show up at 12:30, 6:30, or 7:30pm).

**Maisons des Jeunes Rufz de l'Avison,** 18, rue J.-J. Rousseau, 1*er* (tel. 45 08 02 10). Mo. Louvre or Palais-Royal. From Mo. Louvre (not "Musée du Louvre"), take rue du Louvre away from river, turn left on rue St.-Honoré, then turn right on rue J.-J. Rousseau. During academic year, a private residence hall for male university students, but in summer filled with tourists of both sexes. (Some rooms may be open during school year as well.) Absolutely stunning open-air courtyard looks like a king's picnic area. Doubles, triples, and quads; in quads, beds are close together, so it's better to come in a group or book long in advance. 3-day min. stay. Reception open 7am-7pm. No curfew. 95F. Shower and breakfast included. Reserve by mail with 1 night's payment, or arrive early. No credit cards.

**Young and Happy (Y&H) Hostel,** 80, rue Mouffetard, 5*ème* (tel. 45 35 09 53; fax 47 07 22 24). Mo. Censier-Daubenton. Lively hostel with clean, cramped rooms. Ideally located in the heart of the raucous student quarter on rue Mouffetard. Claustrophobes beware the serpentine staircase and incredibly tight hallways. Rooms with 2-6 beds. Lockout 11am-5pm. Curfew 1am. 95F. Breakfast and shower included. Reservations accepted with 1 night's deposit.

**UCJF (Union Chrétienne de Jeunes Filles)** or **YWCA,** 22, rue Naples, 8*ème* (tel. 45 22 23 49). Mo. Europe or Villiers. Extremely organized, well-kept, homey environment. This *foyer* accepts women for 3-day min. stay June-Sept. Spacious, airy rooms, hard wood floors, large beds. Large oak-panelled common room with fireplace, VCR, theater performance space, and family-style dining room with varied daily *menu*. Congenial staff. In summer, singles 148F per day (3 days 444F) and 125F per person to share a double (3 days 375F). Sept.-May, the *foyer* caters to longer stays by women 18-24, breakfast and dinner included in price. 1 week: singles 650F, doubles 567F. 1 month: doubles 2070F. All guests must pay 30F YWCA membership fee and 100F processing fee, so you can at YWCA *foyer*s and *pensiones* worldwide. 200F key deposit returned to you when you leave. Reception open Mon.-Fri. 9am-6:30pm, Sat.-Sun. 9:30am-4:30pm. Curfew 12:30am, negotiable. Reserve space if you can (500F deposit required). Other locations: 65 rue Orfila, 20*ème* (tel. 46 36 82 80; Mo. Gambetta), and 168, rue Blomet, 15*ème* (tel. 45 33 48 21; Mo. Convention). Men should contact the YMCA *foyer* **Union Chrétienne de Jeunes Gens,** 14 rue de Trévise, 9*ème* (tel. 47 70 90 94).

**Foyer International des Etudiantes,** 93, bd. St-Michel, 6*ème* (tel. 43 54 49 63), across from Jardin du Luxembourg. Mo. Luxembourg. Wood floors, large windows, beautiful desks, excellent facilities: this is one of the best. TV lounge, piano, kitchenettes on each floor (bring own equipment), irons, hair dryers, laundry. International students galore; friendly director. Open Sun.-Fri. 6am-1:30am, Sat. all night. Curfew 1:30am. Women only Oct.-June: singles 133F, doubles 82F, breakfast and shower included. Men and women July-Sept.: singles 153F, doubles 102F, shower included. Make written reservations 2 months in advance, 200F deposit if confirmed. Call ahead or arrive around 9:30am to check for no-shows.

**Résidence Bastille (AJF),** 151, av. Ledru-Rollin, 11*ème* (tel. 43 79 53 86). Mo. Voltaire. Recently renovated, with 2-4 wooden bunks per room. 167 beds. Some triples and quads have bathrooms in the room. Doubles use older hall bathrooms. Less crowded and more subdued, but friendly multilingual staff. Ages 18-35 only. Reception open 7am-12:30pm and 2pm-1am. Curfew 1am. 105F. Showers, breakfast, and sheets included. No reservations, so arrive early in the morning.

**Maison Internationale des Jeunes,** 4, rue Titon, 11*ème* (tel. 43 71 99 21; fax 43 71 78 58). Mo. Faidherbe-Chaligny. Well-located, exceptionally clean, airy, and tranquil, with garden in back. Except for 1st floor, not a bunkbed in sight. Mostly bright rooms with 2-8 beds for ages 18-30 (flexible). Especially beautiful new duplexes. Single-sex rooms, but exceptions made for traveling buddies, couples, and consenting groups. Coed bathrooms. Some family housing. 3-day max. stay. If full, they'll find you another place. Reception open 8am-2am. Lockout 10am-5pm. Curfew 2am. Quiet hours 10pm-8am. 110F. Showers and breakfast included. Sheets 15F for entire stay, or bring your own.

**Hôtel Ste-Marguerite,** 10, rue Trousseau, 11*ème* (tel. 47 00 62 00). Mo. Ledru-Rollin. Affiliated with Jules Ferry hostel. 240 beds. Small but airy rooms with real mattresses, atmosphere of happy chaos, and youthful enthusiasm. Most rooms 2-6 beds; those on courtyard especially pleasant. Small showers. Some bathrooms in hall, others in rooms. Safe available for valuables. Room downstairs for eating or just hanging out. Vending machine sells beer for 5F—need we say more? No lockout. 90F per person. Breakfast included. Same-day reservations available through Jules Ferry. Otherwise, show up at 8am to get a room.

**Aloha Hostel,** 1, rue Borromée, 15*ème* (tel. 42 73 03 03), on a tiny side street across from 243, rue de Vaugirard. Mo. Volontaires. Despite the cheesy name, one of the best in the city. Newly renovated, quiet, and centrally located. Young but experienced management full of advice about Paris. Bright rooms with new beds, new mattresses, and freshly painted interiors have space for 2-4 guests. Top floor rooms have slanted roofs and good view of the *quartier*. Brand new kitchen facilities, communal refrigerator, café-style common room. Lockout 11am-5pm. 85F per person. Breakfast 5F. Arrive at 9am or send 1 night's deposit for reservations.

**Three Ducks Hostel,** 6, pl. Etienne Pernet, 15*ème* (tel. 48 42 04 05). Mo. Commerce. On the street to the right of the church. Without a doubt one of the most rowdy and fun hangouts in the city for young vacationing backpackers. Has all the amenities (clean dorm-style rooms with bunkbeds for 2-8 people). Green, ivy-covered central courtyard becomes a loud, fun café hangout at night when a young, mostly Anglo crowd drinks cheap beer from the hostel's watering hole, **Richie's Bar.** Flexible 1-week max. stay. Small kitchen. Lockout 11am-5pm. Curfew 1am. Weekly rate 530F. Reservations accepted with 1 night's deposit. Fabulous **Mountain Bike Trip** (tel. 48 42 57 87) tours of Paris begin here (see Getting Around.)

**FIAP Jean-Monet,** 30, rue Cabanis, 14*ème* (tel. 45 89 89 15; fax 45 81 63 91). Mo. Glacière. From *métro*, go down bd. St-Jacques, turn left at the 1st street (rue Ferrus), then right onto rue Cabanis. An international student center with 507 beds, mostly full with visiting American tour groups in summer. Comfortable, well-furnished rooms are impeccably maintained and equipped with toilet and shower. Offers disco and jazz concerts at night (free), French language classes, and stacks of tourist info, as well as 12 conference rooms, game room, laundry room, and cheap cafeteria (full meal 54F). Some rooms wheelchair accessible. 3-day max. stay. Singles 240F. Doubles 160F per person. Quads 140F per person. 8-bed rooms 120F per person. Open April-Sept. Reservations essential. MC, V.

**Centre International du Séjour de Paris: CISP "Ravel,"** 6, av. Maurice Ravel, 12*ème* (tel. 43 43 19 01; fax 43 44 45 30). Mo. Porte de Vincennes. On the edge of the city. 216 beds. Large and professional in services. Caters primarily to groups. Very imposing and professional reception desk. Large rooms (most with 4 or fewer beds), bar, restaurant, and access to municipal pool next door (50% discount for guests, 15F). Some rooms available for guests with disabilities. Flexible 3-day max. stay. Reception open daily 6:30am-1:30am. Singles 143F, rooms with 2-5 beds 122F, with 8-12 beds 97F. ISIC discount: 132F40, 113F50, 91F respectively. Breakfast included. Make reservations no more than 36 hrs. in advance. Self-serve restaurant open 7:30-9:30am, noon-1:30pm, and 7-8:30pm.

**Association des Foyers de Jeunes: Foyer des Jeunes Filles,** 234, rue de Tolbiac, 13*ème* (tel. 45 89 06 42; fax 45 65 46 20). Mo. Glacière. From *métro,* take a right on rue de Glacière, then a left on rue de Tolbiac. Large, modern foyer for young women (ages 18-25) with excellent facilities—including kitchens on all floors, cable TV, washers, dryers, piano, exercise room, library, cafeteria, and garden. Run by exceptionally friendly, helpful staff. Sunny singles with a sink and closet space and attractive brick walls. Excellent security. Reception open 24 hrs. July-Aug. 100F per night. Showers and breakfast included. Dinner 45F. Sept.-June

2910F per month, plus 30F registration fee; breakfast and dinner included. Mailed reservations accepted, but there are usually vacancies during the summer.

**Maison des Clubs UNESCO,** 43, rue de Glacière, 13ème (tel. 43 36 00 63; fax 45 35 05 96). Mo. Glacière. From *métro*, take a left on rue de la Glacière. Enter through garden on right. Small simple rooms, some newly renovated, run by friendly, multilingual management. Wheelchair access. Flexible 3-day max. stay. Reception open 8am-1am; someone on duty 24 hrs. Singles 150F. Doubles 130F per person. Triples 110F per person. Showers and breakfast included. No individual reservations; call to check for vacancies.

# ■ Hotels

Of the three classes of Parisian budget accommodations, hotels may be the most practical for the majority of travelers. There are no curfews, total privacy, and often concerned managers. Most important, hotels routinely accept reservations. Budget hotels in Paris are not significantly more expensive than their hostel/*foyer* counterparts. Groups of 2, 3, and 4 may actually find it more economical to stay in a hotel. Unlike *foyers,* hotels rent doubles by the room and not by person.

The French government publishes a comprehensive guide that classifies hotels with a star system: 4L (luxury), 4, 3, 2, and 1, depending on the services offered, the percentage of rooms with bath, and other such indicators. Most hotels in *Let's Go* are one-star or unclassified establishments, though two-star establishments offering inexpensive rooms are sometimes included. Most rooms come with double beds. In our listings, double refers to rooms with one double bed; 2-bed double refers to the rare room with two separate single beds. Expect to pay at least 150F for singles. If your room has no shower, you'll usually have to pay extra (12-25F) to get the key to the hall shower. Showers in your room are included in the room charge.

Paris has a number of very nice hotels in the 150-200F range. These hotels are often small, simple, and do not offer the amenities of the Sheraton or the Hilton. But the hotels listed in *Let's Go: Paris* are clean, have well-furnished rooms, and have adequate toilet and shower facilities. Most newly renovated hotels have double-paned glass windows which provide for better insulation against cold and noise.

A few tips about Parisian hotels: Many North Americans are surprised to discover a strange toilet-like apparatus located in all wash-closets called a *bidet.* A *bidet* is a somewhat archaic device intended for the cleansing of the private body parts. Do not use your *bidet* as a toilet. Keep in mind that the French call the ground floor the *rez-de-chaussée,* and start numbering with the first floor *above* the ground floor *(premier étage).* Many hotels serve breakfast for 15-25F. Since local cafés often serve croissants and coffee for less, you may want to eat breakfast out. Remember that there are usually rules against bringing food into your rooms. Parisian law forbids hanging laundry from windows or over balconies to dry. Most hotels in Paris are not wheelchair accessible. It is advisable to call ahead for more information.

## Reservations

Do not reserve for more nights than you might possibly need. If you decide to leave Paris before you intended, or if you want to switch hotels, don't expect to get back all your money. Every year, *Let's Go* receives letters from readers complaining that hotel managers would not refund the nights that went unused. If in doubt, reserve for just one night; you can usually extend your stay once you get to the hotel.

Although most tourists visit Paris in the summer, this is not necessarily the heaviest-booked time, since business travelers take up many rooms in May, June, September, and October. Since the high and low seasons are both complicated and counterintuitive, reserve as soon as you know when you will be in Paris. Make reservations at least two weeks in advance; a number of hotels claim that they are fully booked two months in advance for the summer. To guarantee that you have a room waiting when you arrive, the following process is advised:

1.) Call, write, or fax to the hotel asking for a reservation for a specific date and kind of room (single, double, with bathroom, shower, etc.).

2.) If you write, enclose an International Reply Coupon (sold at post offices), so that the hotel need not bother with postage expenses.

3.) When you receive positive confirmation, send *la caution* (a deposit) for one night. Most hotels will confirm reservations only upon receipt of a check for the first night's rent, although some will accept a credit card number instead. The easiest way to send this deposit is to mail a traveler's check in francs, double signed. This is the equivalent of sending a personal check, and you'll avoid the hefty US$25-30 charge for an international money order. Include an International Reply Coupon (two for air mail) for a prompt reply. Without a deposit, most hotels will not honor a reservation for more than an hour or so, the time it might take to arrive after calling from a pay phone somewhere in Paris.

4.) Call one or two days in advance to confirm (or cancel) and inform the manager of your intended arrival time.

Try your best to honor your reservation. Small budget hotels are of a nearly extinct breed. These small family-run hotels cannot afford to hold a room, turn away potential guests, and then swallow their losses if you decide you don't want it.

## FIRST ARRONDISSEMENT

In the shadow of the Louvre, much of the first remains true to its kingly past. Cartier, Chanel, and the Banque de France set an intimidating mood on the street for the budget traveler. Yet while financiers and ladies-who-lunch may whisk past you, don't let them scare you away. Single travelers who stay near Châtelet-les-Halles should revel in their central, generally safe location, but should consider using a different *métro* station at night.

**Henri IV,** 25, place Dauphine (tel. 43 54 44 53). Mo. Cité. Last outpost of cheap accommodations on Ile de la Cité. Somewhat dilapidated, but clean and average-sized rooms with squishy beds. Friendly management and one of the best locations in Paris. Toilets located outside, accessible only by little staircase that curls around the building. Snug, labyrinthine charm. Singles 100-130F. Doubles 130-190F. Triples with 1 single bed and 1 double bed 185-215F. Quadruples 240F. Reserve 2 months in advance.

**Hôtel de Lille,** 8, rue du Pélican (tel. 42 33 33 42). Mo. Palais-Royal. What it lacks in extras it makes up for in charm. One of the small hotels struggling against pressure to jack up prices and turn budget travelers away. Very good location on a quiet street; close to the Louvre. Coin-operated phone on 1st floor. No breakfast. Singles 170F. Doubles 200-250F. Showers 30F. No credit cards.

**Hôtel Lion d'Or,** 5, rue de la Sourdière (tel. 42 60 79 04; fax 42 60 09 14). Mo. Tuileries or Pyramides. Clean, refurbished rooms are sparse, but carpeted, with colorful bedspreads and double-paned glass. You'll hear the bells toll from l'Eglise St-Roch, but little else. Friendly, English-speaking staff. Singles 180F, with shower 220F. Doubles 220F, with shower 280F, with bath and toilet 360F. Extra bed 60F. Showers 20F. Breakfast 25F. For stays of more than 3 days, 5% discount.

**Hôtel Richelieu-Mazarin,** 51, rue de Richelieu (tel. 42 97 46 20). Mo. Palais-Royal. Industrial carpeting, plastic flowers, and Monet prints make for generic, but nonetheless homey, ambience. Doubles in converted attic are an oasis of taste—muted flowered wallpaper, pine furniture, and skylight (but no view). Otherwise, smallish rooms have radios and a view of bustling thoroughfare. Double-paned glass blocks street noise. Singles 180-200F, with shower or bath and toilet 280-310F. Doubles 220F, with shower or bath and toilet 300-330F. Extra bed 60F. Breakfast 25F, in room 30F. Reserve 3 weeks in advance in summer. No credit cards.

**Hôtel du Palais,** 2, quai de la Mégisserie (tel. 42 36 98 25). Mo. Châtelet. Location by the Seine, at the corner of place du Châtelet and quai de la Mégisserie, gives all rooms (except on top floor) splendid views. Enormous quad (480F) and quint (550F) with 2-sink bathroom and huge windows. On top floor: singles 180F, doubles 230F. Singles with shower 280F, with shower and toilet 320F, with bath and toilet 350F. Doubles with shower 320F, with shower and toilet 350F, with bath and toilet 380F. Triple 420F. Extra bed 70F. Breakfast 30F. Shower included for top-floor, no-frill rooms. Eurocard, MC, V.

**Hôtel Montpensier,** 12, rue de Richelieu (tel. 42 96 28 50; fax 42 86 02 70). Mo. Palais-Royal. From the *métro,* walk around the Palais Royal/Comédie Française buildings until you're on rue Montpensier. Clean, hospitable atmosphere. Elevator. Opt for sunny room with street racket or quieter one with dingy courtyard view. Spruced-up lounge with cheery, stained-glass ceiling. Singles 220F. Doubles 230F. Singles or doubles with toilet 265F, with shower and toilet 365F, with bath and toilet 420F. Extra bed 70F. Shower 25F. Breakfast 30F. Eurocard, MC, V.

**Hôtel de Rouen,** 42, rue Croix des Petits Champs (tel. or fax 42 61 38 21). Mo. Louvre or Palais-Royal. Hotel is across from Banque de France. Steep, narrow staircase leads to small rooms with postage stamp-sized bathrooms. Warm proprietors seek to please. Very much a family affair—you can ask to use the refrigerator. Courtyard triple goes for price of a double. Singles or doubles 180F, with shower 240F, with shower, toilet, and TV 290F. Triple with shower and toilet 290F. Quads with shower and toilet 350F. Breakfast 20F. MC, V.

**Hôtel Saint-Honoré,** 85, rue St-Honoré (tel. 42 36 20 38 or 42 21 46 96; fax 42 21 44 08). Mo. Louvre, Châtelet, or Les Halles. In the throes of all-out renovation during summer '93, sparkling rooms glimmer in the distance. Promising new bathrooms with decorative tile. Friendly, English-speaking staff, and young clientele. Singles or doubles 180-200F, with shower and toilet 280F. Triples or quads with shower and toilet 380-420F. Showers 15F. Breakfast 24F. In summer, confirm reservations by phone or fax the night before, or by telephone upon arrival.

**Hôtel du Centre,** 20, rue de Roule (tel. 42 33 05 18; fax 42 33 74 02). Mo. Pont Neuf, Louvre, Châtelet, or Les Halles. From Mo. Pont Neuf, take rue de la Monnaie towards les Halles straight onto rue du Roule. Recently renovated; shiny modern plumbing. Relatively spacious singles or doubles with shower and toilet 310F. Extra double bed, available only for a few rooms 30% extra. Breakfast 27F. AmEx, Eurocard, MC, V. If arriving after 7pm on 1st night, send 1 night's rent as deposit.

# SECOND ARRONDISSEMENT

Although it is not blessed with many major sights of its own, the second *arrondissement* is within easy walking distance of the Marais, the Centre Pompidou, the Louvre, and more. The southern half, which includes the cobbled pedestrian streets of the rue Montorgueil, rue Tiquetonne, and rue Léopold Bellan is safe and animated; some of Paris's finest food markets reside here. The northern half, which includes the rue St-Denis and the seedy rue d'Aboukir, should be avoided. Nevertheless, the three hotels we list in this area are extremely clean, well-furnished, and make every effort to be safe. Be careful at night, especially on the notorious rue St-Denis.

**Hôtel La Marmotte,** 6, rue Léopold Bellan (tel. 40 26 26 51). Mo. Sentier. On a quiet, safe, cobbled pedestrian street. Pristine rooms with amazingly firm beds. Inexpensive restaurant on 1st floor, run by same cheerful proprietors. Reception desk is connected to bar, but don't be intimidated. TV in every room. Singles 180F, with toilet 200F, with shower and toilet 260F. Doubles 200F, with toilet 220F, with shower and toilet 280F. Extra bed 80F. Breakfast 20F. Shower 15F. Reservations recommended. AmEx, MC, V.

**Hôtel Vivienne,** 40, rue Vivienne (tel. 42 33 13 26; fax 40 41 98 19). Mo. Bourse. Exit *métro,* take right onto rue Vivienne. The most luxurious budget hotel you'll find in Paris. Lush lobby, professional staff, huge rooms. You'll pay a little more, but it won't break your *bourse.* TV in every room. Singles with shower 280F. Doubles with shower 340F, shower and toilet 400F, bath and toilet 430F. 2-bed doubles with bath and toilet 440F. 3rd person under 10 yrs. free, over 10 yrs. 30% extra. Breakfast 40F. Reserve by fax and with credit card deposit. V.

**Hôtel Zora,** 4, rue Léopold Bellan (tel. 45 08 18 75). Mo. Sentier. Not particularly well-lit and somewhat worn, but clean, adequate rooms. Warm family-run hotel on beautiful, safe, quiet pedestrian street. Unlike most Parisian hotels, doesn't require deposit for reservations. Singles 120F, with shower and toilet 150F. Doubles 160F, with shower and toilet 220F. Showers 20F. No credit cards.

**Hôtel Tiquetonne,** 6, rue Tiquetonne (tel. 42 36 94 58). Mo. Etienne-Marcel. Near intersection of rue St-Denis and rue de Turbigo. An open arms hotel this is not, but rooms are clean, and the price is right. Singles 120F, with shower and toilet 190F. Doubles with shower and toilet 220F. Showers 22F. Breakfast 22F. Open Sept.-July.

**Hôtel Chénier,** 1, rue Chénier (tel. 42 33 92 32; fax 45 08 57 73). Mo. Strasbourg-St-Denis. Clean, comfortable, recently renovated. Nice staff who don't speak English. Toilet in every room. No elevator. Singles with shower 220F, with bath 300F. Doubles with shower 250F, with bath 300F, with bath and TV 330F. Triples with shower or bath 450F. Quads with bath 500F, with bath and TV 530F. MC, V.

**Hôtel Bonne Nouvelle,** 17, rue Beauregard (tel. 40 08 42 42, for reservations 45 08 87 71; fax 40 26 05 81). Mo. Strasbourg-St-Denis or Bonne Nouvelle. Cozy hotel with TV in every room. Very clean, modern bathrooms. Singles and doubles with toilet and bath or shower 260-360F. Triples with bath and toilet 390F. One triple/quad with toilet and bath 510F. Breakfast 30F, in room 35F. 1 night's deposit required only if you're arriving after 3pm. MC, V.

**Hôtel Sainte-Marie,** 6, rue de la Ville Neuve (tel. 42 33 21 61; fax 42 33 29 24). Mo. Bonne Nouvelle. This little hotel is simple, clean and distinctly superior to many other hotels in the same price range. The lovely proprietor also runs the Hôtel Sofia in the 18ème. No elevator. Singles 160F, shower and toilet 220F. Doubles 180F, shower and toilet 240F. Triples with shower and toilet 300F. Shower 10F. Breakfast 20F. No credit cards.

## THIRD ARRONDISSEMENT

Much of the third *arrondissement* remains untouched by the gentrification that makes the southern Marais (4ème) a shopper's paradise and budget nightmare. While chic boutiques line rue du Temple and rue des Francs-Bourgeois, on bd. de Sébastopol and rue de Turbigo stores offer their goods wholesale. The streets of this garment district offer two-star accommodations at affordable prices. The historic elegance of this *arrondissement* has been restored over the past three decades; one-time palatial mansions have metamorphosed into exquisite museums. Situated in the midst of it all, the following hotels are budget-friendly, sometimes luxurious home bases from which to explore the new face of Marais chic.

**Grand Hôtel des Arts et Métiers,** 4, rue Borda (tel. 48 87 73 89; fax 48 87 66 58). Mo. Arts et Métiers. The linoleum and chipping paint are simply a consequence of the proprietress's golden rule: keep it cheap and people will come. Central location. Mention *Let's Go* for 20-30F discount. Fridge downstairs. No elevator. Singles with toilet 160F. Doubles with toilet 200F. Singles or doubles with shower 220F, with toilet and shower 280F. Showers 20F. Breakfast 25F. No credit cards.

**Hôtel Picard,** 26, rue de Picardie (tel. 48 87 53 82). Mo. République or Filles du Calvaire. Affordable 2-star hotel, thanks to the generosity of its ever-jovial proprietor and his polyglot daughter. Bring *Let's Go* for a 10% discount. Family actually *likes* American students—the vast majority of their clientele. Charming, clean little rooms. Singles 200F, with shower 250F, with bath and toilet 320F. Doubles 240-260F, with shower 320F, with bath and toilet 390F. Triples 360F. Extra bed 120F. Showers 20F. Breakfast 30F. Eurocard, MC, V.

**Hôtel Bretagne,** 87, rue des Archives (tel. 48 87 83 14). Mo. République, Temple, or Filles du Calvaire. The glitz of the mirrored entryway quickly disappears as you climb the stairs. Light sleepers should ask for rooms on higher floors to avoid street noise. Two small lounges. Wide price range reflects range in room quality: cheaper ones are simple, while more expensive ones have TVs and snazzy new bathroom fixtures. Reception open 24 hrs., but the receptionist before 7pm doesn't speak English. Singles 150F, with bath, toilet, and TV 300F. Doubles 190F, with bath, toilet, and TV 350F. Triples 300F, with 3 separate beds and bath, toilet, and TV 600F. Showers included. Breakfast 30F. No credit cards.

**Hôtel Paris France,** 72, rue de Turbigo (tel. 42 78 00 04, reservations 42 78 64 92; fax 42 71 99 43). Mo. République or Temple. From Mo. République, go down rue de Turbigo; hotel is on left. Fairly clean, well-lit. Elevator. Some rooms invaded by noise from busy rue de Turbigo. Thinking of taking a room with no shower? Be warned—no showers in hall. Singles or doubles 220F, with shower 280F, with bath, toilet, and TV 350F. Extra bed 100F. Breakfast 25F. AmEx, MC, V.

**Hôtel de Roubaix,** 6, rue Greneta (tel. 42 72 89 91; fax 42 72 58 79). Mo. Réamur-Sébastopol or Arts et Métiers. Double-paned glass windows facing street allow for a good night's sleep. Some rooms overlook courtyard and verdant terrace. Flowered wallpaper and 12 rooms with balconies make this a tasteful change from the linoleum universe of many budget establishments. Minitel (1F50/min.) in basement. Modern plumbing and amenities. Elevator. 2 lounges, 1 with TV. All rooms have shower and toilet. Singles 300-330F. Doubles 400F. Triples 500F. Extra bed 40F, only with double. Breakfast 25F. No wheelchair access. Eurocard, MC, V.

**Hôtel Paris-Bruxelles,** 4, rue Meslay (tel. 42 72 71 32). Mo. République or Temple. On a lovely, quiet street off rue de Turbigo, this hotel offers a wide selection of rooms varying in quality but not in price. While rooms on the *cour* have a less-than-scenic view, large rooms facing street on 2nd and 3rd floor feature tall windows and southern exposure. TVs in rooms with bath and toilet. Small elevator (no wheelchair access) stops short of top floor. Singles 150F, with bath and toilet 250F. Doubles with bath and toilet 290F. Triples 375F. Quads 485F.

**Hôtel France-Europe,** 112, bd. de Sébastopol (tel. 42 78 75 33). Mo. Strasbourg-St. Denis. Rooms could use a scrub brush and paint job. TV available on demand for rooms with baths. Get a room high above street to avoid noise. All this may change; the owner hopes to turn the hotel into a 3-star establishment. Singles with shower 220-250F. Doubles with shower 290F. Triples with shower and 2 double beds 370F. 80F per extra person. Breakfast 25F. No credit cards.

# FOURTH ARRONDISSEMENT

**Hôtel Practic,** 9, rue d'Ormesson (tel. 48 87 80 47). Mo. St-Paul or Bastille. Spare but sunny rooms, some with views of place du Marché-Ste-Catherine. Clean as a whistle. If the orange and green spreads don't grab you, the location and price will. Singles with toilet 150F. Doubles with toilet 220F, with shower 260F, with shower, bath, and toilet 320F. Showers 35F. Breakfast 25F.

**Hôtel de la Herse d'Or,** 20, rue St-Antoine (tel. 48 87 84 09). Mo. Bastille or St-Paul. Built around an enclosed courtyard—enjoy the sun without the pigeons. Freshly painted, refurbished rooms. Toilet and shower in rooms. Some parking spaces belong to hotel. No frills. Singles 150F. Doubles 190F, with shower 250F, with shower and toilet 375F.

**Grand Hôtel du Loiret,** 8, rue des Mauvais Garçons (tel. 48 87 77 00; fax 48 04 96 56). Mo. Hôtel de Ville. Décor may be a little frayed around the edges, but you get what you pay for. One of the last real bargains in the Marais. Singles and doubles with toilet 160F, with shower 210F. Shower 15F. Breakfast 15F.

**Le Palais de Fes,** 41, rue du Roi de Sicile (tel. 42 72 03 68). Mo. Saint-Paul or Hôtel de Ville. Large, fairly clean, sparsely decorated rooms. Dingy hallways. Reception is at the bar of the Moroccan restaurant downstairs. Singles 150F, with shower 180F. Doubles 250F, with shower 280F, with shower and toilet 320F. Showers 20F. Breakfast 25F. AmEx, MC, V.

**Hôtel de Nice,** 42bis, rue de Rivoli (tel. 42 78 55 29; fax 42 78 36 07). Mo. Hôtel de Ville. Recently redecorated. A rare find in the world of budget travel. Someone had fun at the wallpaper store: dancing cupids, faux-marble borders, a swish of crimson, a dab of mauve. Sparkling bathrooms, lots of light, a lounge to die for. Singles and doubles with shower or bath and toilet 340-360F. 2-bed doubles with shower and toilet 380F. Triples with bath and toilet 420F. Reserve 3 months in advance for summer. Deposit required (check from French bank, no US$).

**Hôtel Andréa,** 3, rue St-Bon (tel. 42 78 43 93). Mo. Châtelet or Hôtel de Ville. Clean, comfortable rooms with plenty of light. TV in rooms with shower. It's just as well they have an elevator (no wheelchair access), since the common showers are only on 1st floor. Rooms face Pizza Hut or a gray wall. Nevertheless, good location and moderate prices make this a solid base for exploring the *quartier*. Singles 120-180F. Doubles with shower and toilet 310-330F. Cheaper doubles without bathrooms can't be reserved over phone. Showers 15F. Breakfast 25F.

**Hôtel du 7ème Art,** 20, rue St-Paul (tel. 42 77 04 03; fax 42 77 69 10). Mo. St-Paul. To the French, "The 7th Art" is movie-making, and sure enough, this hotel celebrates Hollywood with posters and photos from old movie classics. Décor tips a hat to Art Deco. They even screen the occasional old movie downstairs. Sounds like a tacky gimmick, but it's really quite tastefully done; staff seems to have a genuine (and contagious) love for the hotel's theme. Rooms a bit small, but well-equipped: phone, safe-deposit box, cable TV. Booked 1-2 months in advance. Show up anyway in case someone cancels. Singles 260F, with shower and toilet 380-430F. Doubles with toilet and shower or bath 380-430F. Extra bed 100F. Breakfast 35F. AmEx, MC, V.

**Hôtel Sansonnet,** 48, rue de la Verrerie (tel. 48 87 96 14; fax 48 87 30 46). Mo. Châtelet or Hôtel de Ville. Pastel rooms. Clean, breezy, and near Centre Pompidou and Notre-Dame. Parking nearby on a quiet street off rue de Rivoli. Singles with toilet 230-240F, with shower 270F, with shower and toilet 320-340F. Doubles with toilet and bath or shower 330-350F. Showers 20F. Breakfast 30F.

**Grand Hôtel Jeanne d'Arc,** 3, rue de Jarente (tel. 48 87 62 11; fax 48 87 37 31). Mo. St-Paul or Bastille. Roomy bedrooms with antique-like armoires and big beds. Good location on quiet street. Good for groups of 4-5. Elevator not wheelchair accessible, but 2 rooms on *rez-de-chaussée* are. TV in most rooms. Singles or doubles with toilet and bath or shower 360-425F. Triples with toilet and bath or shower 500F. Quads with toilet and bath or shower 550F. Breakfast 30F. MC, V.

**Hôtel de la Place des Vosges,** 12, rue de Birague (tel. 42 72 60 46; fax 42 72 02 64). Mo. Bastille. Tastefully decorated in what appears to be a late medieval style, but with the best modern standards of cleanliness and comfort. Elevator on 1st floor (no wheelchair access). Usually there is someone who speaks English at reception. Singles with shower and toilet 330F. Doubles with bath and toilet 475F. 2-bed doubles with bath and toilet 495F. Breakfast included.

## FIFTH ARRONDISSEMENT

With the prestigious Sorbonne as its focal point, the 5*ème arrondissement* provides a golden opportunity to mingle with students, professors, and other intellectual types. By day the *quartier latin* surrenders to book-toting students and map-toting tourists, but at night the café-filled *places* and winding streets come alive—the atmosphere is anything but academic. There is no guarantee that just hanging out in the 5*ème* will make you smarter, but several budget hotels in this *arrondissement* will at least make your stay in Paris easier on the wallet.

**Hôtel d'Esmeralda,** 4, rue St-Julien Le Pauvre (tel. 43 54 19 20; fax 40 51 00 68). Mo. St-Michel. Walk along the Seine on quai St-Michel, then turn left at the park. Romantic hotel gives best view of Notre-Dame this side of the Seine. Wooden interior and traditionally furnished rooms with floral wallpaper complement the homey atmosphere and friendly, multilingual staff. Right next door to Shakespeare and Co. Singles 150F, with shower 310-470F. Doubles with shower 410-470F. Triples with shower and toilet 520F. Quads with shower and toilet 580F. Breakfast 40F. Reserve at least 1 month ahead in summer.

**Hôtel St-Jacques,** 35, rue des Ecoles (tel. 43 26 82 53; fax 43 25 65 50). Mo. Cardinal Lemoine or Maubert-Mutualité. Multilingual staff keeps a clean, professional, quiet hotel, with a bit of peeling paint on ceilings. Impressive glass chandelier and red carpet. Singles 140F. Doubles with shower 390F. 2-bed doubles with shower 465F. Triples with shower 515F. Shower 25F. Breakfast 30F. AmEx, MC, V.

**Grand Hôtel Oriental,** 2, rue d'Arras (tel. 43 54 38 12; fax 40 51 86 78), off rue Monge. Mo. Cardinal Lemoine. Run by an amazingly patient, friendly proprietress. Spacious rooms with firm mattresses, large closets. Bonaparte-sized elevator. Singles 230F, with shower and toilet 250F. Doubles with shower and toilet 290F. About 50F more for 2-bed doubles. Shower 12F. Breakfast 30F. AmEx, MC, V.

**Hôtel des Médicis,** 214, rue St-Jacques (tel. 43 54 14 66). Mo. Luxembourg. Don't despair when you see the entrance; the hotel cuts corners to keep the prices down, but rooms are in much better repair than the lobby. Young, energetic clientele. Good-natured management. Conveniently located near cafés and groceries. Singles 75-85F. Doubles 140-160F. Showers 10F.

**Hôtel des Grandes Ecoles,** 75, rue Cardinal Lemoine (tel. 43 26 79 23; fax 43 25 28 15). Mo. Cardinal Lemoine. Contemplating going all-out on a hotel in Paris? This is the place for it. Built around a verdant, flowery garden where guests breakfast in warm weather, this ivy-covered establishment maintains impeccably clean, tastefully decorated rooms to the great pleasure of their faithful guests, many of whom return year after year. Singles 450F, with shower 480. Doubles 530F, with shower 550F. Breakfast 40F. Reserve well in advance, deposit required. MC, V.

**Hôtel des Allies,** 20, rue Berthollet (tel. 43 31 47 52; fax 45 35 13 92), off bd. Port Royal. Mo. Censier Daubenton. Not quite as scenic or centrally located as other hotels in the 5ème, but clean, comfy rooms for next to nothing. Street tends to be a little noisy, the beds a little lumpy, but altogether a fantastic bargain. Singles 130F, with shower 165F. Doubles 200F, with shower and toilet 280F. Showers 15F. Breakfast 27F. Reservations accepted with 1 night's deposit. MC, V.

**Hôtel Gay Lussac,** 29, rue Gay Lussac (tel. 43 54 23 96), at rue St-Jacques. Mo. Luxembourg. Affable owner loves *Let's Go* readers and provides carefully cleaned, sunlit rooms with sculpted plaster ceilings in an old but well-preserved hotel on a noisy street. Renovation now in progress; owner is very proud of his brand-new elevator. Tour groups may limit available space. Doubles 280F, with shower 350-400F. Triples 300F, with shower and toilet 500F. Breakfast included.

**Grand Hôtel du Progrès,** 50, rue Guy Lussac (tel. 43 54 53 18). Mo. Luxembourg. Multilingual proprietors Victoria and Henri welcome guests with open arms. Breakfast room, complete with leafy green plants, piano, and miniature library (for your travel literature needs) makes you feel at home. Clean, bright rooms with great windows, simple décor. Top floors, with charming garrett-like rooms, overlook Panthéon. Singles 168-220F, with shower and toilet 310F. Doubles 240-285F, with shower and toilet 330F. Triples 360F. Shower 15F. Breakfast included.

**Hôtel de Nevers,** 3, rue de l'Abbé de l'Epée (tel. 43 26 81 83), off rue Gay Lussac. Mo. Luxembourg. Run by a sprightly retired couple, this 6-story hotel on a quiet street offers clean rooms, renovated bathrooms, and a view of the Panthéon. Some beds are rather saggy. Singles 150F. Doubles 240F, with shower 270F. Triples 280F, with shower and toilet 350F. Showers 15F. Breakfast 20F. Reservations accepted with 1 night's deposit.

**Hôtel Marignan,** 13, rue du Sommerard (tel. 43 54 63 81). Mo. Maubert-Mutualité. On a quiet street. Spacious rooms, many recently renovated with fresh paint and handmade wood cabinets. In summer, 3-day min. stay. Singles 160F. Doubles 270-290F. Triples 360-390F. Quads 440-490F. Breakfast included. Reservations highly recommended far in advance, but the Californian proprietress tries to save some rooms for unexpected arrivals. Discounts for families, groups in winter.

**Hôtel le Central,** 6 rue Descartes (tel. 46 33 57 93). Mo. Maubert-Mutualité or Cardinal Lemoine. French, Spanish, and Portuguese-speaking clan runs a small, quiet hotel on a café-rich *place* that's party-central at night. Dark rooms; low, squishy beds. Singles 150-160F. Doubles with shower 210-240F. Reservations accepted.

**Hôtel Gerson,** 14, rue de la Sorbonne (tel. 43 54 28 49). Mo. Odéon. Location across from the Sorbonne and bright, clean rooms more than make up for unexciting appearance and woefully mismatched bedspreads, carpet, and curtains. Singles 200F, with bathroom and shower 280F. Doubles 280F, with bathroom and shower 350F. Shower 20F. Breakfast 25F. MC, V.

## SIXTH ARRONDISSEMENT

One of the greatest people-watching arteries in the world, boulevard St-Germain enlivens St-Germain-des-Prés, a lively Left Bank neighborhood that has turned the sidewalk café into an art form. Budget hotels are sparse in this chic neighborhood, stretching from the Seine to the bd. Montparnasse, but the following exceptions provide surprising bargains. Expect crowds of well-dressed Parisians at night, wandering the streets, going to the movies, and relaxing at cafés. This may not be the quietest place to stay in Paris, but it is definitely one of the most exciting.

**Hôtel Nesle,** 7, rue du Nesle (tel. 43 54 62 41), off rue Dauphine. Mo. Odéon. Impeccably clean rooms with wooden rafters (with caricatures depicting the history of Paris), funky Egyptianesque frescoes, the warm, outgoing management, the geese in the rose garden, and an outrageously low price make this charming little hotel in the heart of the 6ème without a doubt the best place to stay on the Left Bank. Turkish bath! Laundry. Singles with breakfast and shower 130F. Doubles 160F, with breakfast and shower 250-300F. Shower 25F. Turkish bath 25F. Breakfast 25F. No reservations; arrive around 11am to see if they can take you.

**Hôtel St-Michel,** 17, rue Git le Coeur (tel. 43 26 98 70), near pl. St-Michel, steps away from the Seine. Mo. St-Michel. Convenient, quiet location. Large, comfy rooms with bright floral prints. Friendly staff. Curfew 1am. Singles 195F, with shower 290F, with shower and toilet 325F. Doubles 220F, with shower 315F, with shower and toilet 350F. 2-bed doubles with shower 350F, with shower and toilet 390F. Shower 12F. Breakfast included. Reservations with 1 night's payment.

**Hôtel Stella,** 41, rue Monsieur le Prince (tel 43 26 43 49; fax 43 54 97 28). Mo. Odéon or Luxembourg. While the office can be a steam bath in summer, wood-trimmed bedrooms are pleasant and breezy. Singles with shower and toilet 188F. Doubles with shower and toilet 258F. Reservations accepted with 1 night's payment, otherwise call in the morning to reserve a room for that evening.

**Dhely's Hotel,** 22, rue de l'Hirlondelle (tel. 43 26 58 25), through the archway and down the steps on the western side of pl. St-Michel. Mo. St-Michel. One step from the Seine. Traditional wood detailing, flower boxes, and modern facilities complement tiny rooms. Singles 120F, with shower 170F. Doubles 250F, with shower 320F. Showers 25F. Breakfast 25F. Reserve with 1 night's payment. MC, V.

**Hôtel St-André des Arts,** 66, rue St-André des Arts (tel. 43 26 96 16; fax 43 29 73 34). Mo. Odéon. Beautiful, unusual fabric is used for walls, curtains, and bedding. Entryway with low ceiling and curving wood staircase adds to hotel's charm. Central location. Manager used to teach philosophy. Singles 210F, with shower 275F. Doubles with shower 400F, with 2 beds and shower 420F. Triples with double bed, single bed, and shower 480F; with 2 double beds and shower 500F. MC, V.

**Hôtel Petit Trianon,** 2, rue de l'Ancienne Comédie (tel. 43 54 94 64). Mo. Odéon. Tiny, clean, whitewashed rooms on a sometimes noisy place. Singles 170F. Doubles with shower 300F, with shower and toilet 350F. Showers 25F. Reserve at least 1 week ahead with 1 night's deposit.

**Hôtel du Dragon,** 36, rue Dragon (tel. 45 48 51 05; fax 42 22 51 62). Mo. St-Germain-des-Prés. The justifiably proud owner of this hotel in the chic-er part of the 6ème personally decorates the recently renovated rooms with very French wallpaper and carefully chosen antique furniture. Singles with shower 275F. Doubles with shower, and toilet 390F; with 2 beds, shower, and toilet 450F. Breakfast 28F. Open Sept.-July. MC, V. AmEx for long stays only.

**Hôtel des Balcons,** 3, rue Casimir Delavigne (tel. 46 34 78 50; fax 46 34 06 27), off the pl. Odéon. Mo. Odéon. Wonderfully decorated, classy exterior and lobby, redone in 1993. Many clean, airy rooms renovated also, though color combos may keep you awake at night. Singles with shower 320-350F. Doubles with shower 410F. Triples with shower 535F. Breakfast 40F. Reservations welcomes. MC, V.

## SEVENTH ARRONDISSEMENT

Numerous hotels cluster around the western edge of the seventh *arrondissement,* all proudly advertising that the Eiffel Tower is indeed visible from their rooms. Hotels in the 7ème tend to be pricier and to cater to business travelers and older couples looking for a quieter, more relaxed atmosphere. You'll pay a little more, but you'll also enjoy the comforts of telephones and TVs in most rooms, breakfast in bed, bathtubs, and the convenience of paying by credit card.

**Hôtel de la Paix,** 19, rue du Gros Caillou (tel. 45 51 86 17). Mo. Ecole Militaire, up av. Bosquet and left on rue de Grenelle. The only true budget accommodations in the *7ème* and it shows. Worn carpets, soft mattresses, peeling paint, but fairly clean and quiet. Noël the manager greets you in fluent French, English, or Japanese. Reception open 9am-9pm. Get key if returning after 10pm. Check-out noon. Singles 135F, with shower 198F. Doubles with shower 250F, with shower and toilet 330F. 2-bed doubles with shower and toilet 290F. Triples with shower and toilet 420F. Shower 15F. Breakfast 30F. Reservations recommended, deposit required depending on time of arrival. Because of Nöel's busy schedule, call ahead to make sure someone is at reception to greet you upon arrival.

**Grand Hôtel Lévêque,** 29, rue Cler (tel. 47 05 49 15; fax 45 50 49 36). Mo. Ecole Militaire. On festive rue Cler, amid *boucheries, charcuteries,* and fruit grocers. Rooms are small, but have beautifully tiled bathrooms and wake-up-call service. Reception open 24hrs. Singles and doubles with sink 195F, with shower 280F, with shower and toilet 305F, with shower, toilet, and a view onto rue Cler 330F. Extra bed 80F. Showers included. Breakfast 25F, served in the salon or in your room 7-11am. Call for reservations, and confirm in writing by letter or fax. MC, V.

**Hôtel Kensington,** 79, av. de la Bourdonnais (tel. 47 05 74 00; fax 47 05 25 81). Mo. Ecole Militaire. A touch of class, and not as expensive as some of the other elegant hotels in the *7ème.* Mahogany reception desk gives lobby a country charm. Well-lit, brightly decorated, compact rooms. Firm mattresses, classy bedspreads, with mirror tile above head of the bed. TV in each room. 1st-floor rooms wheelchair accessible. Singles with shower, TV, and toilet 280F. Doubles with shower, TV, and toilet 350F, with bathtub 390F. Twins with shower, TV, and toilet 360F, with bathtub 450F. Breakfast 27F, served 7:30-11am in dining room or bedroom. Reservations recommended—call first and confirm in writing with 1 night's payment (check or credit card number). AmEx, MC, V.

**Royal Phare Hotel,** 40, av. de la Motte-Picquet (tel. 47 05 57 30; fax 45 51 64 41). Mo. Ecole Militaire. Next to *métro.* Ever-friendly M. Le Rouzic and staff have carefully chosen designer wallpaper, rainbow curtains, and water-drop tile to make their small rooms even more cheerful. Mirrors create airy, bright feel. TV in each room (hair dryer in some). Reception open 24hrs. English spoken. Singles with shower and toilet 300F. Doubles with shower and toilet 320-380F. Breakfast 30F, served 7-10am in room or in lobby. Call for reservations; confirm by letter or fax with credit card number. AmEx, MC, V, or traveler's checks in francs.

**Hôtel du Centre,** 24bis, rue Cler (tel. 47 05 52 33; fax 40 62 95 66). Mo. Ecole Militaire. Across from the Grand Hôtel Lévêque on the festive rue Cler. Dining room full of shiny copper pots is reminiscent of a farmhouse. Dark décor shrinks small rooms further. Clean, if not new. TV room. Check-out noon. Elevator makes many rooms wheelchair accessible. Singles 220F, with shower 280F. Doubles with toilet 220-240F, with shower, toilct, and TV 350-380F. Triples with shower, TV, and toilet 450F. Breakfast 30F. Reservation confirmed in writing with check in French francs or with credit card number. AmEx, MC, V.

**Hôtel du Palais Bourbon,** 49, rue de Bourgogne (tel. 45 51 63 32 or 47 05 29 26; fax 45 55 20 21). Mo. Varenne or Invalides. Near Musée Rodin; down the road from Palais Bourbon. Mme. Claudon has been fostering a family atmosphere here for 23 years. Recent renovations produced ultra-modern, ultra-slick bathrooms. Prices have become as high as the ceilings, but doubles remain more affordable. English spoken. Reception open 24 hrs. Singles with toilet 220F, with toilet and shower 259F, with toilet, shower, and TV 368F. Doubles with toilet 251F, with toilet, TV, and shower 368F. Singles with toilet, tub, TV, minibar, and double bed 435F. Doubles with all of the above 467F. 2-bed doubles with the works 493F. Triples with the works 616F. Showers 12F. Breakfast included. Reservations recommended; call and confirm by letter or fax with credit card number. MC, V.

**Hôtel du Champs de Mars,** 7, rue du Champ de Mars (tel. 45 51 52 30). Mo. Ecole Militaire, off av. Bosquet. Wheelchair accessible once you overcome the 1st step. Singles with toilet and shower 340F, with toilet, shower, and tub 370F. Twins with tub and toilet 400F. Triples with tub and toilet 480F. Breakfast 35F, served in rooms or salon 7-10am. Reservations recommended; call, then confirm in writing with 1 night's deposit. Closed for 15 days (roughly Aug. 10-25). MC, V.

## EIGHTH ARRONDISSEMENT

The luxurious mansions and hotels of the eighth have not been kind to the budget traveler. The number of stars that grace the front doors of 8ème *arrondissement* hotels is second only to the number of stars sipping cappuccino at Fouquet's and shopping in specialty boutiques on the rue du Faubourg St-Honoré.

**Hôtel d'Artois,** 94, rue La Boétie (tel. 43 59 84 12), a stone's throw from the Champs-Elysées. Mo. St-Philippe de Roule. Rugs may be a bit worn, mattresses less than new, but bathrooms are impeccable, the plant-filled lobby an urban greenhouse, and the breakfast room a delight, scented with incense. English spoken. Someone always at desk. Singles 210F, some with shower and toilet. Doubles with shower 340F, with shower and toilet 360F. Showers 20F. Breakfast 25F. Reservations recommended, with deposit for late-night arrivals.

**Hôtel Wilson,** 10, rue de Stockholm (tel. 45 22 10 85). Mo. St-Lazare. Walk up rue de Rome; turn left on rue de Stockholm. No-frills hotel (40 rooms) around the corner from Gare St-Lazare. Soft mattresses, thin, aged carpet, incomplete soundproofing, cracks in wallpaper—but at this price, what did you expect? Bathrooms within rooms are newer and the occasional velvet chair offsets a drab color scheme. Singles 160F, with shower and toilet 220F. Doubles 215F, with shower and toilet 240F. Breakfast included. Phone reservations accepted but not vital.

## NINTH ARRONDISSEMENT

The ninth bridges some of Paris's wealthiest and most heavily touristic quarters—the 2ème and the 8ème—as well as the less tantalizing and less affluent 10ème and 18ème. There are plenty of hotels here, but many in the northern half of the area are used by prostitutes and their customers. Avoid the Anvers, Pigalle, and Barbès-Rochechouart *métro* stops at night; use the Abbesses stop instead. Just a few streets south of bd. de Clichy and rue Pigalle, the neighborhood shifts from red-light district to quaint, quiet, and friendly global village. Pricier hotels, traces of the quarter's elegant past, line the side streets near bd. des Italiens and bd. Montmartre.

**Hôtel des Trois Poussins,** 15, rue Clauzel (tel. 48 74 38 20). Mo. St-Georges. Managed by the Desforges family, this hotel has a lovely courtyard, clean rooms, and editions of *Let's Go* dating from 1982. No children under 15. Singles 140-150F. Doubles with shower 220-230F, with shower and toilet 250F. Showers 15F. Breakfast 25F. Reserve at least 1 week in advance. No credit cards.

**Hôtel d'Espagne,** 9-11, cité Bergère (tel. 42 46 73 30; fax 48 00 95 69). Mo. Montmartre. Not elegant, but clean, with high ceilings and decent beds and lighting. Helpful staff; some English spoken. TVs in some rooms. Singles and doubles 150-180F. Singles and doubles with shower and toilet 300F, with bath and toilet 320F. Triples with shower and toilet 420F. Quads 510F. 1 common shower, 10F. Breakfast 28F. Reserve 2 weeks in advance. Accepts foreign traveler's checks. MC, V.

**Hôtel Beauharnais,** 51, rue de la Victoire (tel. 48 74 71 13). Mo. le Peletier. A *hôtel de charme* and ode to forgotten Paris. Elegant array of beds, *armoires*, and sconces span the centuries and showcase owner's passion for antiques. Run by Mme. Bey and daughters, it brims over with ambient calm, sun, and fresh flowers. Your mother would love it, as you will. Singles and doubles with shower 300F, with shower and toilet 320F. Triples with shower and toilet 465F. Breakfast 25F.

**Hôtel des Arts,** 7, cité Bergère (tel. 42 46 73 30; fax 48 00 94 42). Mo. Montmartre. Two rooms on ground floor decorated with owner's antiques. Recently renovated, sunny, and neat. While somewhat smaller than those on lower floor, top floor rooms have attic charm. All rooms have showers, TV, cable. If you hear someone whistle at you, it's probably the parrot out front. Elevator. Singles with bath 325F. Doubles with bath 350F. Smaller 5th floor singles with shower 300F. 5th floor doubles with shower 325F. Triple 480F. Breakfast 25F. AmEx, MC, V.

**Hôtel Mondial Européen,** 21, rue Notre-Dame-de-Lorette (tel. 48 78 60 47; fax 42 81 95 50.) Mo. Notre-Dame-de-Lorette. Renovated rooms, all very modern. Somewhat uniform study in pastels. Spotless bathrooms; TVs in rooms. Elevator. Lovely breakfast salon, a faithful variation on peach-pink theme. Doubles with shower and toilet 350F-360F. Triples 460-480F. Quads 480F. Breakfast 25F. MC, V.

# TENTH ARRONDISSEMENT

In response to the voluminous traffic that pours through the Gare de l'Est and the Gare du Nord, quite a few inexpensive hotels have set up shop in the tenth. In fact, the supply often exceeds demand, making this crowded corner of Paris a good place to look if you've struck out elsewhere. In this multi-ethnic residential quarter, the current economic downturn has lowered spirits and emptied pockets. The most gloomy and depressed areas are found north of the Gare du Nord, particularly along bd. de Magenta heading towards Mo. Barbès. These hotels are far from the primary sights and nightlife, so you'll have to use taxis once the *métro* stops running.

**Palace Hôtel,** 3, rue Bouchardon (tel. 42 06 59 32). Mo. Strasbourg/St-Denis. A family affair with an assembly of children and pets around reception. Small, cheerful rooms, many facing an attractive, plant-filled courtyard. Recent renovations have yielded lovely new doubles and triples, a host of sunny rooms in light colors with roomy armoires. Quiet back-street location. English spoken. Singles 100F. Doubles 140F, with bath and toilet 250F. Triples 180F, with shower and toilet 280F. Quad 230F, with shower and toilet 350F. Breakfast 20F. No reservations. V.

**Cambrai Hôtel,** 129bis, bd. de Magenta (tel. 48 78 32 13; fax 48 78 43 55). Mo. Gare du Nord. Clean, airy rooms with high ceilings. Beds are wide and firm. Large clean showers. Just steps away from Gare. Some English spoken. Singles 129F, with shower 196F. Doubles 170F, with shower 216F, with shower and toilet 220-240F. Triples 315F, with shower 330F. 2-room suite for 4 with shower 350F. Showers 20F. Breakfast included.

**Hôtel Mêtropole Lafayette,** 204, rue Lafayette (tel. 46 07 72 69). Mo. Louis Blanc. Wildly clashing fabrics and dark rooms, but if you close your eyes, firm mattresses take you away from this world of paisley and plaid. Very clean, with friendly reception. English spoken. Singles 110F, with shower 150F. Doubles 130F, with shower 180F, shower and toilet 200F. Triples with shower 230F, shower and toilet 250F. Showers 25F. Breakfast 15F. AmEx, MC, V.

**Hôtel Sibour,** 4, rue Sibour (tel. 46 07 20 74; fax 46 07 37 17). Mo. Gare de l'Est. Convenient to Gare du Nord and Gare de l'Est, with small, well-lit rooms. TVs in rooms with bath and toilet. Reasonably clean with new wallpaper and streamlined fixtures ordered from the stock-house of budget accommodations. Refurbished breakfast salon is great way to start the day. Elevator. Some English spoken. Singles and doubles 185F, with toilet 200F, with shower and toilet 275F. Triples 250F, with shower 300F, with shower and toilet 345F. Quads 350F. Showers 15F. Breakfast 25F. MC, V.

**Hôtel des Familles,** 216, rue du Faubourg St-Denis (tel. 46 07 76 56). Mo. Gare du Nord. A little dark, a little modest looking, but big beds and clean, hot showers. Singles 130-150F, with shower 200F. Doubles 180F, with shower 220F. Triples 250F, with shower 300F. Quad 300F, with shower and toilet 350F. Showers 17F.

# ELEVENTH ARRONDISSEMENT

The 11ème is a very big *arrondissement*; hotel location is more important than TVs or direct-line service to Australia. Reasonably cheap places to stay line the streets surrounding the place de la République and place de la Bastille. Others dot the interior streets of the *arrondissement*. Many of these hotels consider July and August the off-season; they're very likely to have space should you call once in Paris or even show up unannounced. Five *métro* lines converge on République, three cross over at Bastille. Both *places* are on the western side of the *arrondissement,* neighboring the fourth: the location is excellent, the atmosphere charged with an intriguing mix of youthful vibrance and working-class joviality. If possible, avoid place de la République at night, when prostitutes and pickpockets are ever present.

**Hôtel de Nevers,** 53, rue de Malte (tel. 47 00 56 18; fax 43 57 77 39). Mo. Oberkampf or République. Owners have lived in the U.S. and love Americans; you'll enjoy their renovated rooms. Personalized décor in every room with floral wallpaper that smiles back. Firm mattresses, towels, and face cloths in the bathrooms, and an appealing breakfast to boot. Singles 162F, with shower 232F, with shower and toilet 257F. Doubles 204F, with shower 254F, with shower and toilet 279F. Triples 366F. Quads 466F. Extra bed 50F. Showers 20F. Breakfast included.

**Hôtel Rhetia,** 3, rue du Général Blaise (tel. 47 00 47 18; fax 42 61 23 17). Mo. St-Ambroise, St-Maur, or Voltaire. Well-lit, tastefully decorated rooms overlooking the happy park square Maurice Gardette. A quiet neighborhood, not too far from the Bastille. Reception open Mon.-Fri. 7:30am-10pm, Sat.-Sun. and holidays 8am-10pm. Singles 170F, with shower or bath and toilet 230F. Doubles 190F, with shower or bath and toilet 230F. Triples 240F, with shower or bath and toilet 280F. Showers 10F. Breakfast 10F.

**Plessis Hôtel,** 25, rue du Grand Prieuré (tel. 47 00 13 38; fax 43 57 97 87), off av. de la République. Mo. Oberkampf or République. M. and Mme. Montrazat are authentic *hôteliers* who love their business: they speak English, serve drinks, and have menus and cards from local inexpensive restaurants. Some call it the *hôtel au chien tournant* (hotel of the turning dog). The dog, now in his dotage, moves in circles. Both the mascot and the hotel are charmers. 15 newly renovated rooms come equipped with cable TV and modern bathrooms. You can even tickle the ivories on the piano in the non-smoking lounge. Singles 200F, with shower, toilet, and TV 295F, with bath, toilet, and TV 320F. Doubles 210F, with shower, toilet, and TV 295F-340F, with bath, toilet, and TV 320F. Extra bed 75F. Showers included. Big breakfast 32F. Open Sept.-early July. AmEx, MC, V.

**Hôtel de Belfort,** 37, rue Servan (tel. 47 00 67 33). Mo. Père Lachaise, St-Maur, or Voltaire. Not exactly chic, but the patterned blankets are homey and bathrooms, although worn, are as modern as they come. Breakfast served in a cool *cave;* staff will greet you in multiple languages, including English. Lizard King's tomb is a stone's throw away. Especially attractive for its *Let's Go* traveler special: an excellent 100F per person per night in a double, triple, or quad, with shower, toilet, phone, and TV—a very good deal. None of the listed prices apply—the book is the key. Breakfast 30F, served 7:30-9:30am. AmEx, MC, V.

**Hôtel Baudin,** 113, av. Ledru-Rollin (tel. 47 00 18 91; fax 48 07 04 66). Mo. Ledru-Rollin. A real find: 20 big, recently renovated rooms with patterned bedspreads. Very clean with tranquil décor. Only a few blocks from the Bastille. Check-out noon. Singles 120F. Doubles 170-200F, with shower 230F, with bath and toilet 270F. Extra bed 100F. Showers 20F. Breakfast 25F, served 7-11am. MC, V.

**Hôtel de Vienne,** 43, rue de Malte (tel. 48 05 44 42). Mo. Oberkampf or République. From Mo. Oberkampf, exit at Crussol and take rue de Malte. Peaceful, floral papered rooms with firm mattresses and clean bathrooms. Family atmosphere. No hall shower for those without one in their room. Singles 105F, bigger bed 130F. Doubles 155F, with shower 215F. Breakfast 30F. Open Sept.-July.

**Hôtel de France,** 159, av. Ledru-Rollin (tel. 43 79 53 22). Mo. Voltaire. Good location. Low prices, but facilities to match—worn rug on stairs, shower caulking and plaster in need of redoing, and carpet that doesn't quite fit the rooms. Singles with shower 150F. Doubles with shower 200F, with bath 220F. Triples (with extra bed) with shower or toilet 260F. Breakfast 25F, served 7-9am. Call and confirm reservations in writing. MC, V. Restaurant downstairs (tel. 43 48 11 69) offers 60F lunch or dinner *menu* for guests.

**Hôtel Notre-Dame,** 51, rue de Malte (tel. 47 00 78 76; fax 43 55 32 31). Mo. République. 51 bright rooms—not brand-new, but quite clean. English-speaking staff. TV in more expensive rooms. Check-out noon. Singles 180F, with shower 220F. Doubles 180F, with shower 270F, with shower or bath and toilet 350F. Quads 450F. Extra bed 70F. Showers 20F. Breakfast 30F. MC, V.

**Hôtel Beaumarchais,** 3, rue Oberkampf (tel. 43 38 16 16; fax 43 38 32 86). Mo. Oberkampf or Filles du Calvaire. From Mo. Oberkampf, exit to rue de Malte and turn right on rue Oberkampf. Spanking new, if uniform, décor. TV in each room. Fluent English and German at reception. Wheelchair accessible except for rooms on ground floor. Singles with shower and toilet 300F. Doubles with shower and toilet 340F. Triples with shower and toilet 450F. Breakfast 30F. AmEx, MC, V.

**Pax Hotel,** 12, rue de Charonne (tel. 47 00 40 98; fax 43 38 57 81). Mo. Bastille or Ledru-Rollin. Immaculate rooms off long hallways, with TV and hair dryer, might fool you into believing you're at a Best Western in Kansas. But you're not in Kansas anymore. You're actually near one of the liveliest areas of the Bastille; nightlife, galleries, and budget restaurants are in close reach. Singles with shower 260F, with shower and toilet 280F. Doubles with shower and toilet 310-340F. Quads 520F. Breakfast included. MC, V.

**Hôtel de l'Europe,** 74, rue Sedaine (tel. 47 00 54 38; fax 47 00 75 31). Mo. Voltaire. Spacious, comfortable rooms, firm mattresses, and 2 fairly friendly dogs at reception. Doubles 175F, with shower or bath 200F, with shower and toilet 220F, with bath and toilet 240F. Breakfast 20F.

# TWELFTH ARRONDISSEMENT

Budget hotels cluster in the blocks near the Gare de Lyon, and to the southeast of the Bastille, as well as near place de la Nation. The 12ème is a generally safe *arrondissement* (though be careful around train stations); the streets nearer the Bois de Vincennes offer some of the city's cleanest and most pleasant places to stay, making up somewhat for their distance from the city center. Far from or near the madding crowds of the Bastille, these hotels may have space during the summer months. Hotel managers are less likely to speak English, but they get by.

**Hôtel du Stade,** 111, bd. Poniatowski (tel. 43 43 30 38). Mo. Porte Dorée. On the edge of the city and far from the happening center, but in a relatively safe treelined neighborhood next to the soothing Bois de Vincennes. After a tiring day in the city, you'll feel like you're coming home. 39 small, comfortable rooms with high ceilings, TV, and plenty of afternoon light. Singles and doubles 160F, with TV 180F, with shower 230F, with shower and toilet 260F. 2-bed doubles 190F. Extra bed 70F. Showers 20F. Breakfast 26F, served in rooms 6:45-9:30am. Best to reserve in advance by calling 7am-8pm, but rooms frequently available. MC, V.

**Hôtel de Reims,** 26, rue Hector Malot (tel. 43 07 46 18). Mo. Gare de Lyon. Charming Madame keeps an immaculate hotel, a lobby filled with fresh flowers, and a tree-filled courtyard. Enjoy breakfast in a familial, am-I-really-away-from-home dining room. Singles 170F. Doubles 220F, with shower 250F, with shower and toilet 270F. Triples with shower 320-360F. Showers 25F. Breakfast 30F. Call and confirm in writing to reserve. A good bet if you arrive in the city without reservations, but look respectable when you show up. Open Sept.-July.

**Grand Hôtel Chaligny,** 5, rue Chaligny (tel. 43 43 87 04; fax 43 43 18 47). Mo. Reuilly-Diderot. Classy purple and blue designer bedspreads cover new, solid mattresses; TV and plenty of light (artificial and natural) in each of the 43 rooms. Comment book at reception chronicles years of happy visitors from the world over. Management speaks English and loves its work. Coffee dispenser in lobby. Singles and doubles 200F, with shower and toilet 280F, with bath and toilet 290F. 2-bed doubles with shower and toilet 300F, with bath and toilet 310F. Quads 360F. Extra bed 50F. Showers 25F. Breakfast 25F in salon, 30F in room. MC, V.

**Mistral Hôtel,** 3, rue Chaligny (tel. 46 28 10 20). Mo. Reuilly-Diderot. Comfortable hotel—firm mattresses, TV in each of the 20 rooms, and impeccable bathrooms. Exudes cleanliness—even the aged gray carpet doesn't look remotely stained. Singles and doubles 200F, with shower 245F, with shower and toilet 250F. Triples 300F. Quads 320-340F. Showers included. Breakfast 35F, served in rooms 7-10am. Call 7am-11pm to make reservations and confirm in writing. Often has space July-Aug.

**Hôtel de l'Aveyron,** 5, rue d'Austerlitz (tel. 43 07 86 86). Mo. Gare de Lyon, Quai de la Rapée, or Bastille. Nothing fancy, but small rooms are clean and relaxing. Bathrooms are roomy and filled with plenty of towels. TV lounge downstairs in leather and chrome; bring your leisure suit. Staff speaks English, German, and Danish (yes!) and provides a lively atmosphere. Singles and doubles 160F, with shower and toilet 240F. Triples 190F, with shower and toilet 280F. Quads with shower and toilet 310F. Hall showers included, making this a very good deal. Breakfast 15F. Reservations with deposit recommended. MC, V.

**Nièvre-Hôtel,** 18, rue d'Austerlitz (tel. 43 43 81 51). Mo. Gare de Lyon or Quai de la Rapée. Freshly renovated rooms and a resident feline make this hotel and its 30 small bedrooms a cheery place to stay. High ceilings in some rooms, but no big groups, please. Singles 160-180F. Doubles 200-220F, with shower 260F, with shower and toilet 300F. Showers 20F. Breakfast 20F. Call for reservations and confirm in writing, but space frequently available in summer.

**Modern's Hôtel,** 11, rue d'Austerlitz (tel. 43 43 41 17 or 43 44 51 16). Mo. Gare de Lyon or Quai de la Rapée. A little dingy, but clean; TV in some rooms. Not fancy, but mattresses are up to snuff. Manager Joseph Kouby (make checks out to him) speaks English, Arabic, and Hebrew. Singles 130-140F, with shower 196F, with shower and toilet 210F. Doubles 164-174F, with shower 230F, with shower and toilet 244F. Extra bed 40F. Bath 20F. Showers 15F. Breakfast included. Call 7am-1pm for reservations; confirm in writing at least 1 week in advance, with deposit and arrival time. Usually 10 rooms free daily.

**Hôtel Printania,** 91, av. du Dr. Netter (tel. 43 07 65 13). Mo. Porte de Vincennes. A 2-star hotel starring 25 tastefully decorated rooms with impeccable bathrooms off long brown hallways. Just off the bustling Cours de Vincennes but on the edge of the city. Some English spoken. Doubles 150F, with shower and toilet 210F, with shower, toilet, and TV 250F. Showers 25F. Breakfast 25F, served 7-9am in rooms. Call for reservations.

**Hôtel Jules-Cesar,** 52, av. Ledru-Rollin (tel. 43 43 15 88; fax 43 43 53 60). Mo. Ledru-Rollin or Gare de Lyon. From Mo. Ledru-Rollin, exit onto av. Ledru-Rollin. TV, fancy bedspread, and airy, bright bathrooms with tile halfway up the wall— and you pay for them. Wide range in bathroom size and quality, particularly of doubles; try to see one before settling in. Bedding excellent. Singles with shower and toilet 320F. Doubles with shower and toilet 340F. Extra bed 80F. Breakfast 30F. Reservations taken 24 hrs. in English, among other languages. MC, V.

## FOURTEENTH ARRONDISSEMENT

Renowned for its nightlife, this commercial district just south of the *quartier latin* attracted artists and literati in the 1920s. Picasso and his contemporaries abandoned their traditional haunt of Montmartre for this livelier, more central location. (What would Modigliani, Zadkine, Braque, Chagall, and Klee have to say about that 200m giant, the Tour de Montparnasse? Is it just another misunderstood form of artistic expression?) Today, areas closest to the flashy bd. du Montparnasse maintain their vitality while adjoining neighborhoods, especially those around rue d'Alésia and rue Raymond Losserand, remain residential and sedate. Be prepared for an abundance of sex-shops and sleazy nightlife at the Northern end of av. du Maine (Mo. Gaîté).

**Hôtel de Blois,** 5, rue des Plantes (tel. 45 40 99 48; fax 45 40 45 62). Mo. Mouton-Duvernet. Unquestionably one of the best deals in Paris; these rooms, decked-out with full bathrooms, TVs, telephones, and Laura Ashley décor, would go for twice the price if there were an elevator. Gracious proprietress offers tourist advice and directions to appreciative guests. Doubles 210F, with bath or shower 240F, with shower and toilet 260F, with bath and toilet 310F; 2-bed doubles with bath and toilet 350F. Triples 360F. Shower 15F. Breakfast 25F. AmEx, MC, V.

**Hôtel du Midi,** 4, av. René-Coty (tel. 43 27 23 25; fax 43 21 24 58), off pl. Denfert-Rochereau. Mo. Denfert-Rochereau. A large, professionally run hotel, with rooms that recall a Holiday Inn. The lobby, with its cold tile floor and fake wood accents, gives the visitor the comforting ambiance of a conference-hotel. Knock-off antique headboards doubling as closets frame the queen-size beds. All rooms come with TV and spotlessly clean bathroom. Doubles 208F, with shower and toilet 308F. Breakfast 28F.

**Hôtel Plaisance,** 53, rue de Gergovie (tel. 45 42 11 39). Mo. Pernety. On a quiet street in a somewhat dull neighborhood. Although institutional, it's clean and comfortable. Some rooms have frayed drapes and bedspreads (an unpalatable shade of yellow), but it's difficult to find a cheaper hotel in the 14*ème*. Singles

126F, with shower 180F, with shower and toilet 210F. Doubles 160F, with shower 200F, with shower and toilet 250F. Showers 20F. Breakfast 20F. MC, V.

**Hôtel du Parc,** 6, rue Jolivet (tel. 43 20 95 54; fax 42 79 82 62). Mo. Montparnasse-Bienvenue. Large, modern hotel decked out with marble interior and self-opening doors. Some rooms overlook a tranquil courtyard; others overlook a lively park. Clean, spacious, and bright. You won't feel like a deprived budget traveler at all. Check out *pâtisserie* next door for a delicious treat. Singles 230F. Doubles with shower and toilet 350F. Shower 20F. Breakfast 20F. MC, V.

**Ouest Hôtel,** 27, rue de Gergovie (tel. 45 42 64 99). Mo. Pernety. Thin wood paneling and bland gray carpeting do little for your spirit, but the gold, silver, and mirrored disco-detailing in the lobby will make you want to shake your bootie. Squeaky clean bathrooms. Singles 120F. Doubles 160F, with shower 220F. 2-bed doubles 200F, with shower 230F. Showers 20F. Breakfast 20F. AmEx, MC, V.

**Central Hôtel,** 1bis, rue du Maine (tel. 43 20 69 15). Mo. Montparnasse-Bienvenue. A modern hotel with space-age lobby done in glass and mirrors. Chrome sculpture lining the walls conjures up an image of impaled sea anemones. Rooms are impeccably clean and well-decorated; some look out on a quiet little park that seems to be quite a favorite with local wine-guzzling *clochards*. TV in every room. Singles with bath 320F. Doubles with bath 350F, 2-bed doubles with bath 380F. Triples 410F. Breakfast 25F. MC, V.

# FIFTEENTH ARRONDISSEMENT

Because of the nearby Parc des Expositions, the hotels of the 15*ème* have become a haven for businesspeople who arrive in the winter months for conventions and trade shows. During the summer, when the hall is closed, the hotels go scrambling for business—and you get business-like quality for the price of a discount hotel.

**Hôtel Printania,** 142, bd. de Grenelle (tel. 45 79 23 97; fax 45 78 02 66). Mo. La Motte-Picquet-Grenelle. Centrally located and next to *métro*. Lovely white-marbled hotel is a great choice. Friendly management greets you with fresh flowers in lobby. Red-carpeted hallway leads up a winding staircase to rooms with red bedspreads and modern bathrooms. Singles with toilet 195F, with shower 230F, with shower and toilet 310F, with bath and toilet 350F. Doubles with toilet 240F, with shower 260F, with shower and toilet 350F, with bath and toilet 370F. Breakfast 30F. Reservations accepted with 1 night's deposit. AmEx, MC, V.

**Mondial Hôtel,** 136, bd. de Grenelle (tel. 45 79 73 or 45 79 08 09; fax 45 79 58 65). Mo. La Motte-Picquet-Grenelle. Amid cafés and shops and near the *métro,* this budget haven is run by a friendly proprietor with snow-white *moustaches* and genuine smile. Bright, spacious rooms have slightly saggy beds with knit bedspreads, modern showers, and great view of bd. de Grenelle. Singles with toilet 180F, with shower and breakfast 240F. Doubles with toilet 220F, with shower and breakfast 280F. Triple with toilet 280F, with shower 300F. Otherwise, breakfast 20F. TV 20F. Reservations accepted by fax, with credit card deposit. MC, V.

**Practic Hôtel,** 20, rue de l'Ingénieur R. Keller (tel. 45 77 70 58; fax 40 59 43 75). Mo. Charles Michels. Perhaps the most elegant budget hotel in the 15*ème*. Rooms are extremely modern and clean, with bedspreads worthy of a Sheraton, comfortable mattresses, indirect lighting, vanities, and ultra-modern TVs. Kind, energetic proprietress greets you with efficient service. Doubles with toilet 200F, with shower 310F. Triples with shower and TV 410F. Breakfast 29F. Reservations accepted with 1 night's deposit. AmEx, MC, V.

**Hôtel de l'Ain,** 60, rue Olivier de Serres (tel. 45 32 44 33; fax 45 32 58 95). Mo. Convention. On a quiet residential street. Pleasantly furnished breakfast room, modern lobby. Clean rooms with whitewashed walls and plaid bedspreads upstairs. Singles with sink 140F. Doubles with sink 200F, with shower 240F, with shower and toilet 260F. Twins with bath and toilet 320F. Triples with bath 360F. Breakfast 25F. Reservations accepted with credit card deposit. MC, V.

## SIXTEENTH ARRONDISSEMENT

The chi-chi 16ème will never be the first choice for budget travelers. Sedate and posh, it is better suited to the needs of the multi-star-hotel-seeking voyager, the armies of Paris's young urban professionals (yuppies, or *BCBG* in French lingo), and social-climbing *nouveau riche* Parisians. There are, however, a couple of bargains.

**Hôtel Ribera,** 66, rue La Fontaine (tel. 42 88 29 50; fax 42 24 91 33). Mo. Jasmin. Spotless, bright, modern. In one of the safest neighborhoods in Paris. Single 180F, with shower 210F, with shower, toilet, and TV 260F. Doubles 210F, with shower 240F, with shower, toilet, and TV 300F. 2-bed doubles 230F, with shower 270F, with shower, toilet, and TV 320F. Triples 260F, shower 300F, with shower, toilet, and TV 320F. Breakfast 26F. Call or fax for reservations. AmEx, MC, V.

**Villa d'Auteuil,** 28, rue Poussin (tel. 42 88 30 37; fax 45 20 74 70). Mo. Michel-Ange-Auteuil. *Hôtel de luxe* amazingly has showers, toilets, and TV with both CNN and MTV in *every* room. You'll pay a bit more, but you'll get Mick Jagger, Bill Clinton, and Janet Jackson. Magnificent marble entryway leads into high-ceilinged, airy rooms with floral feel and beautiful bathrooms. Singles 265F, doubles 290F, triples 370F. Reservations advised. MC, V.

**Hôtel Résidence Chalgrin,** 10, rue Chalgrin (tel. 45 00 19 91; fax 45 00 95 41). Mo. Argentine or Mo. Charles de Gaulle-Etoile. Embroidery-covered walls, creative sculpture, and a carriage cab (about as cramped as the cheapest room) lend a homey feel to the hotel lobby. Rooms are a bit dim. Family-style breakfast (25F). Rooms with toilet 150-210F, with bath or shower, toilet, and TV 270-360F, suite 430F. Reservations confirmed in writing recommended, especially for April and Sept. Dogs accepted. V.

## SEVENTEENTH ARRONDISSEMENT

The seventeenth is a curious mix of the elegant flair of its chic western neighbor, Neuilly, and the sordid reputation of its eastern neighbor, Pigalle. While some hotels in the 17ème rent their rooms by the hour to prostitutes, many cater to visiting businesspeople and tourists. We list some hotels in safer enclaves of this neighborhood. They can be wonderful bargains, if you don't mind the clientele next door.

**Hôtel Belidor,** 5, rue Belidor (tel. 45 74 49 91; fax 45 72 54 22). Mo. Porte Maillot. Charmingly polite proprietress shows obvious pride in her well-tended establishment. Flowery courtyard, red carpets, spotless rooms. Singles 150F, with shower 220F, with shower and toilet 270F. Doubles 180F, with shower 250F, with shower and toilet 310F. 2-bed doubles 280F, with shower 340F, with shower and toilet 410F. Breakfast included. Open Sept.-July.

**Hôtel l'Avenir,** 23, rue Jonquière (tel. 46 27 83 41). Mo. Guy Moquet. A real find in this part of town, with cheery flowered wallpaper, clean bathrooms, and rarely a derelict in sight. Singles 100F, with shower 140F, with shower and toilet 160F. Doubles 160F, with shower 210F, with shower and toilet 240F. Breakfast 25F.

**Hôtel des Batignolles,** 26, rue des Batignolles (tel. 43 87 70 40; fax 44 70 01 04). Mo. Place Clichy. Lovely courtyard, brass railings, oak bannisters, and fresh flowers in lobby. So clean and modern, you'll feel like you're in a mini-version of the nearby luxurious Hôtel Meridien. Free maps and info in lobby. English speaking staff. Singles with toilet 190F, with shower and toilet 310F. Doubles with shower and toilet 310F, with shower, toilet, bath, and TV 350F. Breakfast 25F in salon or 35F in room. Reservations recommended; call or fax in advance. Diners, MC, V.

**Hôtel des Deux Avenues,** 38, rue Poncelet (tel. 42 27 44 35; fax 47 63 95 48). Mo. Ternes. A bargain for its location only 10min. from the Champs-Elysées and Arc de Triomphe. Lobby is a modern blue and mirror fantasy. Nondescript rooms are kept clean and tidy. English speaking staff. Singles and doubles 210F, with shower 280F, with shower and bath 350F. Quads with 2 large beds, bath, and toilet 430F. Showers 20F. Breakfast 25F. MC, V.

**Hôtel Riviera,** 55, rue des Acacias (tel. 43 80 45 31; fax 40 54 84 08). Mo. Charles de Gaulle-Etoile. Just minutes from the Arc de Triomphe and Champs-Elysées. Well-furnished, blue and pink interiors. Don't be alarmed by the seemingly simple

lobby—a few words with the lovely proprietor, Mme. Rousseau, and a glance at
her fine rooms will convince you that you're in one of the best locations and most
agreeable spots in Paris. Large comfortable beds. Singles 200F, with shower and
TV 270F, with shower, toilet, and TV 320F. Doubles 270F, with shower, toilet,
and TV 340F. Twins with shower and toilet 350F. Triples with shower and toilet
400F. Breakfast 25F. Reservations accepted by phone or fax. MC, V.

**Hôtel des Deux Acacias,** 28, rue l'Arc de Triomphe (tel. 43 80 01 85; fax 40 53 94
62). Mo. Charles de Gaulle-Etoile. Only seconds from the Arc de Triomphe. Professional management. You have the privilege of paying slightly more than usual
for the spotless but nonetheless run-of-the-mill brown wallpaper, brown bedspread combo. Dogs allowed. Singles 225F. Doubles 310-350F with shower and
toilet, depending on size of the room. Breakfast 25F. MC, V.

# EIGHTEENTH ARRONDISSEMENT

Once a gathering place for artists and intellectuals, the neighborhood between
Pigalle and the top of Montmartre now crawls with tourists. Prices have risen
accordingly, especially as you approach Sacré-Coeur and place du Tertre. In the
other direction, towards the southern border (Mo. Anvers, Pigalle, or Barbès-Rochechouart), the hotels are often brothels—stay away. Use the Abbesses *métro* stop.

**Hôtel Tholozé,** 24, rue Tholozé (tel. 46 06 74 83). Mo. Abbesses. From *métro,*
take a right onto rue Durantin. Small, family-run hotel on a quiet street, away from
the "action" of Pigalle. Rooms are of a reasonable size, unadorned, but clean and
well-lit. Singles 120F, with shower 200F. Doubles 180F, with shower and toilet
240F. Triples with shower and toilet 300F. Breakfast 20F.

**Hôtel André Gill,** 4, rue André Gill (tel. 42 62 48 48; fax 42 62 77 92). Mo. Pigalle
or Abbesses. Found on a quiet, hidden dead-end with eucalyptus and rhododen-
dron trees and a bust of André Gill (1840-1885). Freshly renovated. Funky pastel
stucco walls and modern bathrooms. Elevator. English spoken. Singles 210F, with
shower 300F. Doubles 240F, with shower and toilet 300F, with bath and toilet
330F. Triples with bath and toilet 440F. Showers 25F. Breakfast 25F. MC, V.

**Ideal Hotel,** 3, rue des Trois Frères (tel. 46 06 63 63). Mo. Abbesses. Pleasant,
lively street lined with shops and restaurants, and not at all seedy. Small, bare
rooms, but in good repair and clean. The ornately carved reception desk and the
smell of couscous reveal this impeccable hotel's international side. Singles 120-
130F, with shower 250F. Doubles 160F, with shower 250F. Showers 20F. Reservations accepted by telephone.

**Hôtel Beauséjour,** 1, rue Lepic (tel. 46 06 45 08). Mo. Abbesses. On a noisy, busy
street close to the "hotspots" of Montmartre; a generally safe area, but very
crowded at night. Rooms somewhat small and dark, but definitely livable. Singles
110-130F, with shower 195-225F. Doubles 170F, with shower 195-225F. Triples
300F. Quads 400F. Showers 15F. Breakfast 25F. Reservations accepted.

**Hôtel Sofia,** 21, rue de Sofia (tel. 42 64 55 37; fax 46 06 33 30). Mo. Anvers. Run
by the same friendly proprietor who runs the Hôtel Ste-Marie in the 2ème. Impeccably clean, modern, and efficient. Oak-timbered lobby leads to bright white
rooms with modern bathrooms, new beds, and views of street below. All rooms
have shower and toilet. Singles 190F. Doubles 220F. Triples 270F. Quads 330F.
Breakfast 20F. Call ahead or fax for reservations.

**Tim Hotel Montmartre,** 11, rue Ravignan (tel. 42 55 74 79; fax 42 55 71 01). Mo.
Abbesses. Exit *métro,* take right on rue des Abbesses, and a left on rue Ravignan.
On the secluded, cobblestone *place* Emile Goudeau. This plush hotel may be a bit
pricey, but it's a treat. Spotless rooms, friendly staff, and the most central location
in Montmartre. Singles 215F, shower and toilet 325F. Doubles with toilet and
shower or bath 410F. Breakfast 43F. Reservations accepted by fax. MC, V.

# NINETEENTH ARRONDISSEMENT

The 19ème is by no means central; apart from La Villette, you will have to commute
into the city to do your sight-seeing. You also may find yourself walking significant
distances in order to get a bite to eat. This *arrondissement* is much less hectic than

many others, however, and can provide a quiet place to rest your head after a day of pounding the pavement around the Seine.

**Rhin et Danube,** 3, place Rhin et Danube (tel. 42 45 10 13; fax 42 06 88 82). Mo. Danube. *Métro* leaves you practically at the doorstep. Facing what looks like a village square, this hotel has a country inn feel. Not that it's without modern amenities—TV and kitchenette in every room. Doubles with bath and toilet 300-330F (option of taking up to 2 more people, 50F each). Triples with bath and toilet 380F. Quads with bath and shower 430F. Eurocard, MC, V.

**La Perdrix Rouge,** 5, rue Lassus (tel. 42 06 09 53; fax 42 06 88 70). Mo. Jourdain. Quite plush. All rooms have TV and toilet. Good location next to a pretty church and a *métro* stop. Receptionist may have little or no command of English. Singles with shower 260F. Doubles with shower 290F, with bath 310F. Triples with bath 340F. No extra beds. Breakfast 26F. Dog 20F. AmEx, MC, V.

**Hôtel Polonia,** 3, rue de Chaumont (tel. 42 49 87 15; fax 42 06 32 91). Mo. Jaurès or Bolivar. Friendly Polish immigrants run this modest but clean hotel. Restaurant downstairs is a bit of a Polish hangout. Singles 105F. Doubles 155-170F, with shower 235F. Extra bed 70F. Showers 25F. Breakfast 27F.

**Hôtel du Parc,** 1, pl. Armand Carrel (tel. 42 08 08 37, 42 08 86 89, or 42 08 55 12; fax 42 45 66 91). Mo. Laumière. Good location next to *métro* and the Parc des Buttes Chaumont. Spacious, clean, well-lit rooms; most have TV and view of park or the large square in front of it. Elevator. 5th floor rooms have finest views. Singles with shower 220F. Doubles with shower 250F. 2-bed doubles with shower 295F. Triples with shower 350F. Breakfast 30F, served to your room. Nov.-Feb. prices fall roughly 10%. MC, V.

**Atlas Hôtel,** 12, rue de l'Atlas (tel. 42 08 50 12), off bd. de la Villette. Mo. Belleville or Buttes-Chaumont. Renovated in 1992—new fixtures in all rooms, but furnishings are drab and institutional and the wallpaper has seen better days. Multilingual management. Singles 130F, with shower 140F. Doubles 165F, with shower 205F. 2-bed doubles 172F, with shower 225F. No extra beds. Breakfast not normally provided; guests have access to downstairs kitchen.

**Crimée Hôtel,** 188, rue de Crimée (tel. 40 35 19 57 or 40 36 75 29; fax 40 36 75 29). Mo. Crimée. Near lots of restaurants. Rather upscale—modern rooms, all with soundproofing, hair dryer, TV, radio, and alarm clock. Narrow wheelchair models can fit in elevator. Singles with shower and toilet 280F, with bath and toilet 300-310F. Doubles with shower and toilet 310F, with bath and toilet 320-340F. Triples with shower and toilet 380F. Quads with shower and toilet 420F. Extra bed 50F. Breakfast 30F. AmEx, MC, V.

**Hôtel des Sciences,** 219, rue de Crimée (tel. 40 38 91 00). Mo. Crimée. Near *métro*. Bathrooms and corridors somewhat narrow, but rooms are attractively furnished, comfortable, clean, and equipped with minibar and TV. Double-glazed windows keep out street noise. Elevator. Singles with shower 330F, toilet and shower 380F. Doubles with shower 380F, with shower and toilet 400F. Breakfast 35F. No deposit required for reservation—simply a letter or fax stating your intention to come. AmEx, MC, V.

# TWENTIETH ARRONDISSEMENT

The twentieth often gets a bad rap from Parisians—generally ones who have never been there. While cheap high-rises dot the hillsides and seem to grow at breakneck speed (for Paris), charming streets and open-air markets are no strangers to this quarter. In summer, the slowdown in commercial activity leaves the two-star hotels of this *arrondissement* half empty, which makes them a good bet if you're having trouble finding a place to stay. This quarter is the periphery of the city, so expect a half-hour *métro* ride to the Louvre.

**Hôtel Eden,** 7, rue Jean-Baptiste Dumay (tel. 46 36 64 22). Mo. Pyrénées or Jourdain. Good value. Recently renovated, clean, and equipped with wonderfully firm beds. All rooms have TV, shutters, and double-glazed glass. Some double rooms fairly small, however—it's worth paying the extra 20F for more elbow room.

Salon downstairs stocked with plants and fresh flowers. Elevator, but not wheelchair accessible. Singles 180F. Doubles 220F, with shower and toilet 260-280F. Prices 20F higher Sept.-July. Breakfast 25F. Dogs 30F. MC, V.

**Hôtel Printana,** 355, rue des Pyrénées (tel. 46 36 76 62). Mo. Jourdain. Devoted proprietors, newly refurbished rooms, and a clientele that always comes back. Nice, clean little rooms at very reasonable prices. Elevator is wheelchair accessible. Singles with toilet 120F. Doubles with toilet 180F, with shower and toilet 220F. Triples with shower and toilet 260F. Showers 10F. Breakfast 25F. MC, V.

**Hôtel Dauphine,** 236, rue des Pyrénées (tel. 43 49 47 66; fax 43 36 05 79). Mo. Gambetta. Homey, pastel rooms, though not luxurious on the 2-star hotel spectrum. Sparsely furnished but equipped with TV, and sometimes a minibar. Double-glazing keeps out most noise from bustling vendors on the rue des Pyrénées. Elevator, but no wheelchair access. Singles with shower 200F. Doubles with shower 240-260F, with bath 300F. Extra bed 70F. Breakfast 25F. AmEx, MC, V.

**Hôtel Palma,** 77, av. Gambetta (tel. 46 36 13 65; fax 46 36 03 27). Mo. Gambetta. Fairly plush modern rooms with cable TV and hair dryer. Hallways narrow and a bit dark, however. Lounge downstairs, replete with oriental rug, chintz, and artsy photos. Elevator can't fit wheelchairs, but 2 rooms on ground floor have wheelchair access. Singles with shower and toilet 330F, with bath and toilet 350F. Doubles with shower and toilet 330-360F, with bath and toilet 350-380F. Triples with bath and toilet 435-455F. Breakfast 30F.

**Hôtel Pyrénées-Gambetta,** 12, av. du Père-Lachaise (tel. 47 97 76 57; fax 47 97 17 61). Mo. Gambetta. Modern, well-lit, tastefully decorated. Elevator fits narrow wheelchairs. Some rooms have big, airy bathrooms. Singles with shower and toilet 311F, with shower, toilet, TV, and fridge 324F, with bath, toilet, TV, and fridge 337-350F. Doubles with shower and toilet 337F, with shower, toilet, TV, and fridge 350-376F, with bath, toilet, TV, and fridge 376-402F. Breakfast 26F.

## ◀ Alternative Accommodations

### STUDENT ACCOMMODATIONS

Short-term student housing is available in summer in the dormitories of most French universities. Contact the **Centre Régional des Oeuvres Universitaires (CROUS).**

**Cité Universitaire,** 15, bd. Jourdan, 14ème (tel. 45 89 35 79). Mo. Cité Universitaire. Over 30 different nations maintain dormitories at the Cité Universitaire, where they lodge their citizens who are pursuing higher education in Paris. During summer, dorms lodge anyone (regardless of nationality) on first-come, first-serve basis. Reserved a bed months in advance—at least by April for June and July. To stay in the American House write to Fondation des Etas-Unis, 15, bd. Jourdan, 75690 Paris Cedex 14 (tel. 45 89 35 79), which rents rooms for 3200F/ month (June-July), 2850F/month (Aug.-Sept., when you can phone or show up in person, as there is usually room). Office open Mon.-Fri. 10-11:30am and 4-6pm. For info about other dorms, write to M. le Délégué Général de Cité Universitaire de Paris, 19 bd. Jourdan, 75690 Paris-Cedex 14. No kitchen facilities, but the restaurant in the Maison Internationale offers decent institutional fare at rock-bottom prices. Open Mon-Fri. 11:45am-1:50pm and 5:45-8:20pm. Meal ticket 12F.

### BED AND BREAKFAST

Though B&B is not so common a form in France as it is in, say, England, it is still possible to find rooms in homes. **Bed and Breakfast 1,** 17, rue Campagne Première, 14ème (tel. 43 36 11 26; fax 40 47 69 20; Mo. Raspail) arranges homestays in Paris and its suburbs. Rooms (2-night max. stay) fall into three categories—A (suburbs): singles 250F, doubles 290F; B (Paris proper): 290F, 360F; C (deluxe): from 360F, from 460F. B & B 1 also rents furnished apartments (1 week min.; 350-850F/night). Rent for a month to get a 30% discount on the nightly rate. There is a service charge of 50F per person for arranging the homestay, but mention that you heard about it through *Let's Go* and you'll receive a 50% service reduction for two or more people.

# Food and Drink

"Paris is just like any other city, only people eat better...." Thus the gravelly voice of Maurice Chevalier opens the film *Love in the Afternoon*. That said, neither budget travelers nor most Parisians have the time, appetite, or cash for the Rabelaisian stupor that six-course meals require. Both affordable and eminently French are the breads, cheeses, and pastries that appear as standard fare, with regional modifications, throughout the hexagon and its capital. With a bakery on every corner and dozens of open-air markets, food is a high-profile, high-quality affair. The soup and salad the Parisian makes at home for dinner may not be fancy, but they are made from fresh ingredients carefully selected from specialized food stores, and are prepared with love, respect, and creativity.

## ■ French Cuisine

For a list of French food terms and descriptions of some classic dishes, please consult the Menu Reader at the back of the book.

The aristocratic tradition of extreme richness and elaborate presentation known as **haute cuisine** is actually not French at all; Cathérine de Médicis brought it from Italy along with her cooks, who taught the French to appreciate the finer aspects of sauces and seasonings. In their work and writings, great 19th-century chefs made fine food an essential art of civilized life. To learn about the skills involved—such as preparing base sauces, which are in turn combined with other ingredients to make the classic sauces—leaf through the *Larousse Gastronomique,* a standard reference for chefs, first compiled in the 19th century.

The style made famous in the U.S. by Julia Child is **cuisine bourgeoise,** quality French home-cooking. A glance through her books, *Mastering the Art of French Cooking I & II,* should give you a long list of dishes to try while in France. Both *haute cuisine* and *cuisine bourgeoise* rely heavily on the **cuisine des provinces** (provincial cooking, also called *cuisine campagnarde,* or country cooking), which creates hearty peasant dishes using refined methods. The trendy **nouvelle cuisine,** consisting of tiny portions of delicately cooked, artfully arranged ingredients with light sauces, became popular in the 1970s; since then, its techniques have been integrated with heartier provincial fare. Simple meals such as *steak-frites* (steak and fries) or *poulet rôti* (roasted chicken) can be found for quite reasonable prices on just about every corner in Paris.

French **meat** is not all frogs and snails, though those tasty morsels both make great first courses (frog is reminiscent of both chicken and crab; snails taste like succulent shellfish). It is true that the French tend to eat a wider variety of creatures than do most Anglo-Saxons. *Tripes* (stomach lining of a cow) cooked in herbs is well-loved by many; the sausage version is called *andouille* or *andouillette.* Rabbit is fairly common; pigeon shows up in casseroles and pastry shells. Though not all steaks are *tartare* (raw), most red meat is served quite rare unless you request otherwise. **Fish**-lovers should celebrate seafood specialties of the French southwest and be adept with a blade. Unless clearly marked "filet," the fish will arrive eyes, tail, and all. Smoked salmon is a popular summertime entrée, served with *crème fraîche* and, sometimes, crushed peppercorns. *Tarama,* made with cheap salmon roe and *crème fraîche,* is a Greek import which has become popular of late. Skate is an unusual fish that is sometimes bland and tough but can be delectable *au beurre noir.* Mostly, though, fine French food consists of less exotic fare: saltwater fishes from the Atlantic or Mediterranean, freshwater fish from the Loire, and grilled or sautéed meats, topped with unforgettable sauces—*bordelais, béchamel,* and their kin—and accompanied by potatoes. **Sauce** is a never-ending story, the chef's trademark that makes or breaks evenings. Most are variations on a small family of French classics (for information on specific sauces, consult the Menu Reader).

**Vegetables** may be overcooked by some standards. French asparagus (often served in vinaigrette) is a pale, stumpy version of the matchstick you've come to love. *Haricots verts* (green beans) are a svelte and tastier cousin of the ones your mother made you eat. Americans may be taken aback by the cost of produce. With no immigrant, under-paid, non-unionized sharecroppers to work the land, the farmer, his wife, and their friends charge what they need to and think you can swallow. Restaurants often serve *pommes frites* (french fries) or potato *gratins*, potatoes sliced, doused with cream, butter, and cheese, and baked in an oven. Other starches, such as rice, are pretty good, but stay away from the noodles, which are more of a hellish *al Dante* than a nice and firm *al dente*.

**Bread** is served with every meal. It is perfectly polite to use a piece of bread to wipe your plate. The *baguette* is the long, crisp, archetypal French loaf which, at about 4F, has kept many a budgeteer afloat on treks through Paris. The *bâtard* has a softer crust, the smaller *ficelle* a thicker, harder crust. *Pain de campagne*, made with whole wheat flour, is heavier inside than the baguette. The *pain complet* is a whole grain loaf, and the *pain à six céréales* is made with six grains. Finally, some argue that the best bread in Paris is the *pain Poilâne*, a sourdough blend baked in a wood-burning oven and available from only a few *boulangeries*—ask around. The cheap, government-subsidized bread you buy from a nameless bakery in Paris may well be the best you have ever eaten; don't hesitate to make it your staple.

Tremendously bountiful and various, French **cheeses** fall into three main categories. Cooked cheeses include *beaufort* and *gruyère*. Veined cheeses, such as *bleu* and *roquefort*, gain their sharp taste from the molds that are encouraged to grow on them. Soft cheeses, like brie (the king of cheeses) and Camembert, round out a basic cheese tray. Tangy *fromages de chèvre* (goat cheeses) come in two forms: the soft, fresh *frais* and crumbly, sharp *sec* (dry). Within these broad categories there is much variation. Generally speaking, the criteria by which one judges cheese are the inverse of those for other foods. Runny, moldy, smelly cheeses are the prize of every Parisian; if your wedge of brie appears a near-liquid mass oozing out of its shell, it is probably the best money can buy. Americans have really never had French cheese until they come here; exported versions must be sterilized, killing the bacteria that many believe make the flavor.

Among **charcuterie** (cold meat products), the most renowned is *pâté*, a spread of finely minced liver and meat. Often a house specialty, it comes in hundreds of varieties, some highly seasoned with herbs. *Pâté de campagne* (from pork) is chunky, while *pâté de foie* (liver) is soft and silky. (Technically, a *pâté* is baked in a pastry crust, and the variety without a crust is a *terrine*. In practice, *pâtés* with crusts are rare, and the terms are used interchangeably.) *Rillettes*, rich minced pork, is similar to *pâté*, but more greasy. Both *pâté* and *rillettes* are eaten on or with bread, and often garnished with *cornichons* (gherkins). Though the sausages of France are not as famous as the *Wursts* of Germany or the salamis of Italy, dozens of varieties are quite worth sampling, either as a cold appetizer, or hot, as a main course.

French **pastry** is one of the major arguments in favor of civilization. Breakfast pastries include the delectable *pain au chocolat* (chocolate croissant) and *croissant aux amandes* (almonds). More elaborate choices are fruit tarts and *flans* (open tarts), including the *chausson aux pommes,* a light pastry with apple filling. Many *gâteaux* (cakes) were invented in the 19th century, such as the chocolate-and-espresso *opéra,* the cream-filled-many-layered *mille-feuilles,* and the *forêt-noire,* a rich slice of fudge with a cherry topping. The Paris-Brest cake, another filo dough and cream delight, is the only dessert named for a round-trip on the SNCF. All of these can be eaten in the afternoon with tea, after dinner as a dessert—eat pastry whenever you want to. Also good with tea are crumbly cookies like macaroons and *madeleines.*

And of course, **wine.** In France, wine is not a luxury; it is a necessity. During World War I, French infantry pinned down by heavy shellfire had only iron rations brought to them: bread and wine. And when France sent its first citizen into orbit on a Soviet spacecraft, he took the fruit of the vine with him. Wines are distinguished first by color—white wines are produced by the fermentation of the juice of red grapes. Rosés allow some of the red color from the skin to seep in before the skins are removed, and reds come from the fermentation of the juice, skins, and sometimes stems of black grapes. In general, white wine is served with fish and red wine with everything else, but it is the color of the sauce, not the color of the meat, that really matters. Red wine is preferred with cheese. The wines of Bordeaux break down into three broad categories: *rouge* (red), *blanc sec* (dry white), and *moelleux*, a sweeter white very easy to drink. Different regions, due to soil, climate, types of grapes, and aging processes, produce widely different wines. Connoisseurs know that French wine is best one to three years after an armistice; the years 1921, 1945, and 1947 are celebrated vintages. When buying wine look for the words *Appellation Controlée* surrounding the name of a region. Don't get too self-conscious about not knowing anything about wine. Waiters can give recommendations, and wine bars (see below) let you sample expensive wines by the glass. Or fall back on the *vin ordinaire* (house wine) of the restaurant—it's usually pretty good.

The French frown on hard liquor before meals; it dulls the palate. Lighter *apéritifs* (before-dinner drinks) are preferred. Among the major *apéritifs* are *kir,* made from white wine and *cassis,* a black currant liqueur *(kir royale* substitutes champagne for the wine). *Pastis,* otherwise known as "51" *(cinquante-et-un),* a licorice liqueur diluted with water, is popular with *tabac* owners, gamblers, and the Bastille crowd. *Suze,* fermented *gentiane,* a sweet-smelling mountain flower, yields a wickedly bitter brew; *picon-bière* is beer mixed with a sweet liqueur. It is fairly rare for Parisians to drink these in restaurants; they prefer them at home or, if they are going out, in a bar or café (this is a good way to kill time before restaurants start serving around 7:30pm). Popular *digestifs* (after-dinner drinks) are cognac and various brandies, such as Norman *Calvados.*

Paris's cosmopolitan atmosphere and its colonialist past have provided it with restaurants serving **ethnic cuisine** from all over the globe. Particularly common are North African restaurants, specializing in *couscous. Indo-chinoise* restaurants serving Cambodian and Vietnamese specialties are a reminder of the Eastern empire that collapsed at Dien Bien Phu. Other former colonies in the Caribbean and West Africa do their share. Of course, not all diverse gastronomy is the product of exploitative imperialism. Paris has attracted cooks from India, China, Japan, Italy, and the United States. You can often eat their cuisines for much less than what you'd pay for a comparable French dinner, perhaps because ethnic restaurants are in general less accepted than French restaurants and have to make their food better and cheaper to attract customers.

**Vegetarians** may be dismayed by the dearth of strictly vegetarian restaurants in Paris. And, while you should have little trouble finding tastefully prepared vegetables in Paris, they are often cooked with salt, butter, sugar, or meat stock. Furthermore, vegetarians will have trouble eating cheaply in restaurants, since *menus à prix fixe* almost always feature meat or fish. Ordering a salad may prove cheaper (be careful, however, of green salads with eggs, ham, tuna, or chicken in them). A *salade verte* is a green salad with lettuce only; a *salade de tomates* is a delicious tomato topped with vinaigrette. Served with a healthy basket of French bread, both make an inexpensive and surprisingly satisfying meal at a café or *brasserie. Viande* refers only to red meat. If you don't eat pork, chicken, fish, eggs, or dairy products, you should make this clear to the server. Ethnic cuisine, especially Vietnamese and North African, often provides excellent vegetarian options. Look for health food stores *(diététiques* or *maisons de régime).* Health food products are sometimes referred to as *produits à santé* and are often available in supermarkets. *Biologique* refers to organically grown food (see Essentials—Specific Concerns for more information).

**Kosher** travelers and anyone else looking for a good deli should stroll through the Jewish neighborhood around rue des Rosiers, in the fourth *arrondissement,* where you'll find an assortment of delicious bakeries, groceries, and kosher restaurants. You might also ask at a synagogue for tips. Given the large North African community that has settled in Paris, **halal** food should also be readily available, particularly in the 5ème, 19ème, and 20ème *arrondissements.*

**Breakfast** *(petit déjeuner)* is usually light, consisting of bread and sometimes *croissants* or *brioches* and *café crème* (espresso with hot milk) or hot chocolate. Many people still eat **lunch** *(déjeuner),* the largest meal of the day, between noon and 2pm. Most shops, businesses, and government agencies close for two hours during this time; Paris has four rush hours—morning, evening, and two in the middle of the day as people hurry home and back. But this tradition is slowly giving way as more working Parisians choose to take their two-hour lunches in restaurants with friends and colleagues.

**Dinner** *(dîner)* begins quite late, and goes on for hours as revelers extend their meals into the early morning. Traditionally, the complete French dinner includes an *apéritif, entrée* (appetizer), *plat* (main course), salad, cheese, desserts, fruit, coffee, and a *digestif.* The French generally take wine with their meals, but mineral water is an almost acceptable substitute. Order sparkling water *(eau pétillante* or *gazeuse)* or flat mineral water *(eau plate).* Ice cubes *(glaçons)* are rare. To order tap water, ask for *une carafe d'eau.* Finish the meal with espresso, which comes in lethal little cups. Of course, few Parisians indulge in the entire ritual frequently (or even sometimes); most eat an abbreviated version in a restaurant.

French etiquette dictates keeping the hands above the table, not in the lap. As many a high school French teacher will attest, if you put your hands out of view, your companions may ask what you're doing with them. Elbows shouldn't rest on the table, but they often do. If you want to try eating in true French manner, hold your fork in your left hand, your knife in the right, and scoop food onto your fork with the sharp edge of the knife (not with the dull edge—that's British). A last word: don't say *"Je suis plein,"* meaning "I'm full." This phrase is used for cows, and means they're pregnant. A more polite way of refusing food: *"Je n'ai plus faim."* (I'm not hungry anymore.)

With a little practicality, and lots of *savoir-faire*, it's possible to eat like an emperor in Paris, on a peasant's budget. At breakfast-time, head to the nearest *boulangerie* for croissants of all varieties, often still warm from the oven. *Boulangeries* also sell delicious sandwiches (12-25F) throughout the day, an excellent option for a cheap lunch. For the classic sandwich, ask for *jambon et gruyère* (ham and cheese); if you're starved for vegetables, the *crudités* sandwich is a delectable lettuce, tomato, and hard-boiled egg concoction. Although these are traditionally made with a fresh-baked *demi-baguette,* a few sandwiches with sliced *pain americain* are often available for the philistines who prefer Wonder Bread to French panache. If you can't speak French, just point.

And, of course, if you get hungry at any point during the day, the *boulangeries* and *pâtisseries* have lots of options for heavenly snacking (see Pastries, above). For a more nutritional snack, stop at a fruit stand or buy some bread and cheese. Bread remains the cheapest bet. Plan on splurging once a day on a real sit-down meal for your health and sanity. Many elegant restaurants offer lunch *menus* for 60-80F, often one-third the cost of dinner à la carte; consider following the French example and having a long mid-day meal followed by a heavenly afternoon siesta.

University restaurants are often crowded with students, thus providing a good opportunity to meet some local friends. Anyone with a student ID can buy meal tickets here from 11:30am to 1:30pm and from 6 to 8pm (tickets 18F40, *carnet* of 10 100F). For more information, including summer and weekend schedules, stop at **CROUS,** 30, av. Georges Bernanos, 5ème (tel. 40 51 36 00; Mo. Port-Royal). The following University Restaurants are most convenient, but the list is not nearly exhaustive. In addition, all the following, except Citeaux, Grand Palais, and C.H.U. Necker, are also *brasseries,* open between lunch and dinner for sandwiches and drinks: **Bullier,** 39, av. Georges Bernanos, 5*ème* (Mo. Port-Royal); **Cuvier-Jussieu,** 8bis, rue Cuvier, 5*ème* (Mo. Cuvier-Jussieu); **Censier,** 31, rue Geoffroy St-Hilaire, 5*ème* (Mo. Censier Daubenton; closed for dinner); **Châtelet,** 10, rue Jean Calvin, 5*ème* (Mo. Censier Daubenton); **Mazet,** 5, rue Mazet, 6*ème* (Mo. Odéon); **Assas,** 92, rue d'Assas, 6*ème* (Mo. Port-Royal or Notre-Dame-des-Champs; closed for dinner); **Mabillon,** 3, rue Mabillon, 6*ème* (Mo. Mabillon); **Grand Palais,** cours la Reine, 8*ème* (Mo. Champs-Elysées Clemenceau); **Citeaux,** 45, bd. Diderot, 12*ème* (Mo. Gare de Lyon); **C.H.U. Pitié-Salpe-Trière,** 105, bd. de l'Hôpital, 13*ème* (Mo. St-Marcel); **Dareau,** 13-17, rue Dareau, 14*ème* (Mo. St-Jacques); **C.H.U. Necker,** 156, rue de Vaugirard, 15*ème* (Mo. Pasteur); **Dauphine,** av. de Pologne, 16*ème* (Mo. Porte Dauphine).

## ■ Restaurants

The world's first restaurant was born in Paris over 200 years ago. Ironically, its purpose was not to indulge its clientele with delicious foods and wines, but rather to restore (from the French verb *restaurer)* over-fed party-goers to a state of physical health. Restaurants were a social respite from the high-calorie world of soirées, balls, and private dinner parties. Here one could be in a social atmosphere and eat nothing. Today, on the contrary, you are encouraged by the French to eat shamelessly the proverbial cake; Marie-Antoinette herself has given you permission to gorge on all the *gâteaux* and *pâtisseries* you want.

Do not approach French dining with the equation that chic equals *cher.* Recent economic hard times have led many of the BCBG snobs (French yuppies) to experiment with bistros, more informal, intimate, family-run (and less expensive) restaurants. Even more casual and hearty are *brasseries;* they are usually oriented towards beer and Alsatian specialties—lots of *choucroute,* a sauerkraut and sausage meal. Usually crowded and lively, *brasseries* are best for large groups and high spirits. The least expensive option is usually a *crêperie,* a restaurant specializing in the thin Breton pancakes filled with various meats, cheeses, chocolates, fruits, and condiments; surprisingly, you can often eat at one for the same price as at McDonald's. Restaurants with stars have been awarded such an honor because of innovative and high quality cuisine. They are usually more formal and more expensive.

Clearly, the best way to pick a restaurant is by what you *want,* since quality runs the gamut in both formality and price. Avoid the telltale signs of an unsatisfying meal, such as an advertised "tourist special," a menu in any language but French, or any place that offers you raw vegetable *crudités*—often just a mound of carrot shreds—as an entrée on a *prix fixe menu.* Should you tire of French food, there are scads of other ethnic options, from the Marais's Mexican and Kosher scene to the many Thai and Chinese delights of the 13*ème,* to the vast selection of Japanese, Moroccan, and West African restaurants throughout the city.

There are several gastronomic cautions. Dinner is generally served later than in the U.S. (7pm on) and is composed of smaller, multiple courses. An *entrée* is an appetizer, the *plât* is the main course. Service or the tip is usually *compris,* included in the price. The check *(l'addition)* may be a long time in coming—spending two hours in a restaurant is not unusual. If you are particularly pleased with the service, feel free to leave a small cash tip as a sign of your gratitude (anywhere from a few francs to 5% of the check) but don't feel obligated. The initials BC mean *boisson compris,* drink included; BNC, or *boisson non-compris,* means the opposite.

If you are on a tight budget, be sure to ask for a *carafe d'eau* (a pitcher of tap water). If you simply order "water" *(de l'eau),* you will end up paying for a 25F bottle of Evian. Although wine can be lovely with your meal, you might consider skipping it because unless it is included *(vin compris)* you will pay too much. To enjoy wine inexpensively, buy it for lunch at any supermarket. You will have an extensive choice for 8-35F, and most fine vintages will cost no more that 15-20F. Also, consider ordering the fixed *menu* or *formule,* a *prix fixe* lunch or dinner usually composed of three or four courses and a choice of several appetizers, main courses, and desserts. Ordering à la carte can be much more expensive, especially at dinner.

The restaurants are arranged both by type and by location. Restaurants—By Type provides a list of restaurants cross-referenced by food and features (including price, hours, and ambience). The "Splurge" category consists of restaurants where the dinner *prix fixe menu* costs over 85F. Every restaurant listed in this section is followed by an *arrondissement* label; turn to Restaurants—By Location for the full write-up.

# ■ Restaurants—By Type

## All-You-Can-Eat
Restaurant L'Escapade, 5*ème*
Sangria Restaurant, 17*ème*

## American
The Front Page, 1*er*
Hard Rock Café, 9*ème*
Hayne's Bar, 9*ème*
Hollywood Canteen, chains
The Rib Joint, 5*ème*
Slice, 6*ème*
Le Taxi Jaune, 3*ème*

## Australian
Café Oz, 5*ème*

## Beer and Wine
Café Oz, 5*ème*
Le Château Poivre, 14*ème*
Léon de Bruxelles, chains
Le Monsegur, 5*ème*
La Taverne, 3*ème*
Le Temps des Cérises, 4*ème*

## Belgian
Léon de Bruxelles, chains
La Taverne, 3*ème*

## Bistro
Au Lyonnais, 2*ème*
Au Petit Keller, 11*ème*
Les Bacchantes, 9*ème*
Bistro Bourdelle, 15*ème*
Bistro Romain, chains
Bistro Romain, 16*ème*
Le Mazet, 6*ème*
La Palette, 11*ème*
La Poule au Pot, 7*ème*
Restaurant Brissemoret, 2*ème*
Restaurant Perraudin, 5*ème*
La Route du Château, 14*ème*

## Cambodian, Thai, and Vietnamese
Cap St-Jacques, 13*ème*
Dynastie Thai, 8*ème*
Lao Thai, 13*ème*

Phetburi, 15*ème*
Phuong Hoang, 13*ème*
Tricotin, 13*ème*

## Caribbean
Babylone-Tropiques, 2*ème*
La Papaye, 20*ème*
Le Rocher du Diamant, 12*ème*

## Chinese
Aux Délices de Széchuen, 7*ème*
Château de Choisy, 13*ème*
Laurier de Chine, 17*ème*
Man Lung, 16*ème*
L'Oiseau de Paradi, 13*ème*
Le Palais de l'Est, 10*ème*
Tai-Yien, 19*ème*

## Crêperie
Le Bouquet de Grenelle, 15*ème*
Crêperie Le Biniou, 14*ème*
Crêperie Ferme Ste-Suzanne, 5*ème*
Crêperie Saint Germain, 6*ème*
Crêperie St-Malo, 14*ème*
La Pie Gourmande, 7*ème*

## Deli
Chez Jo Goldenberg, 4*ème*
Finkelsztajn's, 4*ème*

## Eastern European
Chez Marianne, 4*ème*
Finkelsztajn's, 4*ème*
Restaurant Le Beautrellis, 4*ème*
Restaurant Maroussia, 6*ème*

## French (Traditional)
See any *arrondissement* for one of Paris's abundant French restaurants.

## Greek
Café Le Volcan, 5*ème*
Donys, 2*ème*
Le Tahar, 15*ème*

## Indian
Anarkali, 9*ème*
Thamouline, 10*ème*

BY TYPE

### Italian

Le Carpaccio, 1er
De Graziano, 18ème
Le Jardin des Pâtes, 5ème
Scossa, 16ème
Spago, 3ème

### Japanese

Kiotori, 6ème
Restaurant Japonais Robata, 2ème

### Kosher

Chez Jo Goldenberg, 4ème

### Lebanese

Café le Volcan, 5ème
Samaya, 15ème
Sannine, 9ème

### Marxist

Sampiere Corsu, 15ème

### Middle Eastern

Chez Marianne, 4ème
Specialités Turques, 17ème

### North African

Au Clair de Lune, 2ème
L'Ebouillanté, 4ème
Paris-Dakar, 10ème
Restaurant Le Berbère, 14ème

### Nouvelle Cuisine

Au Petit Prince, 6ème

### Open Late

Au Paradis du Fruit, chains
Babylone-Tropiques, 2ème
Les Bacchantes, 9ème
Le Bouquet de Grenelle, 15ème
Brasserie Flo, 10ème
Chez Les Fondues, 18ème
Chez Paul, 11ème
Crêperie Saint Germain, 6ème
Donys, 2ème
Le Mazet, 6ème
Le Monsegur, 5ème
Le Palais de l'Est, 10ème
Pizza Pino, 6ème

### Organic

Aquarius Café, 14ème
Crêperie Saint Germain, 6ème
Le Grenier de Notre Dame, 5ème
Le Jardin des Pâtes, 5ème

### Outdoor Dining

A la Courtille, 20ème
L'Amanguier, 2ème
Anarkali, 9ème
Aux Délices de Széchuen, 7ème
Le Chartier, 9ème
Chez Lena et Mimille, 5ème
De Graziano, 18ème
L'Ebouillanté, 4ème
Fontaine de Mars, 7ème
Le Fouquet's, 8ème
L'Incroyable, 1er
L'Oiseau de Paradi, 13ème
La Poule au Pot, 7ème
Scossa, 16ème

### Pizza

Pizza Pino, 6ème
Slice, 6ème

### Portuguese

Chez Didier, 16ème

### Provençale

Au Boeuf Bourgignon, 9ème
Le Divin, 4ème
Fontaine de Mars, 7ème

### Regional Cuisines

Aquarius, 4ème
Au Limonaire, 12ème
Au Sancerrois, 20ème
Aux Arts et Sciences Réunis, 19ème
Le Brouet, 10ème
Chez Francis, 18ème
La Croque au Sel, 7ème
La France-Comté, 9ème
Joël's, 12ème
Occitanie, 11ème
Le Petit Chose, 18ème

### Sandwich Shops

Le Boulanger, 1er
Le Bouquet de Grenelle, 15ème
Cosi, 6ème
CROQ 100WICH, 7ème
Donys, 2ème
Le Monsegur, 5ème
Spago, 3ème
Specialités Turques, 17ème

### Seafood

Brasserie Flo, 10ème
La Criée, chains
Léon de Bruxelles, chains

### Spanish

Les Jardins d'Aranjuez, 3ème

## Splurge

L'Auberge Nicolas Flamel, 3ème
Auberge de la Reine Blanche, St-Louis
Au Gourmet de l'Isle, St-Louis
Au Lyonnais, 2ème
Au Pierre de la Butte, 18ème
Au Sancerrois, 20ème
Aux Délices de Széchuen, 7ème
Brasserie Flo, 10ème
Chez Claude et Claudine, 18ème
Chez Francis, 18ème
Chez Lena et Mimille, 5ème
Le Club des Poètes, 7ème
Le Colvert, 14ème
La Criée, chains
De Graziano, 18ème
Dynastie Thai, 8ème
Le Fouquet's, 8ème
La France-Comté, 9ème
Le Hangar, 3ème
Les Jardins d'Aranjuez, 3ème
Joël's, 12ème
La Maison du Valais, 8ème
L'Oiseau de Paradi, 13ème
Le Petit Chose, 18ème
Restaurant Brissemoret, 2ème
Restaurant Montecristo, St-Louis
Le Rocher du Diamant, 12ème
Scossa, 16ème

## Swiss

Chez Les Fondues, 18ème
La Maison du Valais, 8ème
La Taverne Suisse, 8ème

## Take-Out

Le Boulanger, 1er
Chez Jo Goldenberg, 4ème
Finkelsztajn's, 4ème
Hollywood Canteen, chains
Le Palais de l'Est, 10ème

## Tex-Mex

Ay, Caramba!, 19ème
Grill Churrasco, 17ème
Texas Blues, 10ème

## Vegetarian

Aquarius, 4ème
Aquarius Café, 14ème
Au Paradis du Fruit, chains
Le Chant de la Terre, 10ème
Country Life, 2ème
L'Epicerie Verte, 17ème
Le Grenier de Notre Dame, 5ème
Joy in Food, 17ème
Naturesto, 8ème
Piccolo Teatro, 4ème

## West African

A la Banane Ivoirienne, 11ème
N'Zadette-M'foua, 14ème

# ■ Restaurants—By Location

## RESTAURANT CHAINS

Unlike those well-known American burger, fries, and pizza chains, these restaurant chains serve French cuisine at an affordable price and convenient location near you.

**Au Paradis du Fruit,** 1, rue des Tournelles, 4ème (tel. 40 27 94 79). Mo. Bastille. Paradis St-Michel, 27-29, quai des Grands Augustins, 6ème (tel. 43 54 51 42). Mo. St-Michel. Creative health food café with orientalist murals that match the sorbet. Fresh juices 18F. "Paradise salads" 55-69F. Mostly light fare, but in cold weather they have stews called *"marmites."* Open daily 11am-2am; last service at 1am.

**Bistro Romain** has over 40 locations around Paris including 103, bd. Montparnasse, 6ème (tel. 44 07 22 97), 9, bd. des Italiens, 2ème (tel. 42 60 22 78), and 6, av. Jean Moulin, 14ème (tel. 40 44 03 63). Chain or no, the combination of plush benches, tapestry-covered walls, and reasonably priced food is tough to beat—reliable if not exceptional. At lunch, their 65F *Les Express menu* gives a choice of filling dishes; *menu* at 80F is appropriate for dinner. In summer, the 90F *menu* full of fruit and fish lightens up the day. Dinner à la carte is around 130F. Desserts are the Bistro's specialty—they offer a choice of 35. Chocolate addicts will die for the *Colisée,* alternating layers of bitter chocolate mousse and white chocolate mousse with a layer of milk chocolate shavings (32F). Usually open daily 11:30am-1am, but times sometimes vary from location to location. Credit cards accepted.

**La Criée,** 15, rue Lagrange, 5ème (tel. 43 54 23 57). Mo. Maubert-Mutualité. 31, bd. Bonne Nouvelle, 2ème (tel. 42 33 32 99). Mo. Bonne Nouvelle. 54, bd. Montparnasse (tel. 42 22 01 81). Mo. Montparnasse-Bienvenue. One of the few places in Paris where you'll be able to afford eating anything that came out of the sea. The deep blue interior and nautical memorabilia stick to the theme without going overboard. Prices are good considering the quality of the food. 2-course *menu* (main course plus appetizer or dessert) 79F. 95F buys you all three plus wine. Open daily noon-2:30pm and 7-11:30pm. MC, V.

**Hollywood Canteen,** 4, rue Pierre Lescot, 1*er* (tel. 42 33 66 30). Mo. Châtelet-Les-Halles. 8, rue de Berri, 8*ème* (tel. 45 62 35 97). Mo. Georges V or Etoile. 53, rue de la Harpe, 5*ème* (tel. 46 33 89 33). Mo. St-Michel. 18, bd Montmartre, 9*ème* (tel. 42 46 46 45). Mo. Montmartre. 25, rue de la Roquette, 11*ème* (tel. 47 00 18 28). Mo. Bastille. They also have their own *boutique traiteur* (food shop) at 29, rue de Charenton, 12*ème* (tel. 40 02 09 42). Mo. Bastille. More American than America. Neon-illuminated 1950s-style diner grills decent burgers named after American movie stars (22-45F) and serves 'em up with a miniature stars and stripes in the top. 59F *menu* features salad, steak, and a choice of wine or Coke. Huge brownies drowned in ice cream and chocolate sauce (25F). Open daily 8:30am-1am.

**Léon de Bruxelles,** 8, pl. de la République, 11*ème* (tel. 43 38 28 69). Mo. République. Also on the Champs Elysées, 8*ème* (tel.42 25 96 16), in Les Halles, 1*er* (tel. 42 36 18 50), at the Bastille, 11*ème* (tel. 42 71 15 55), and in Pigalle, 18*ème* (tel. 42 80 28 33). Léon started selling his mussels in Brussels in 1893; his Paris versions are popular with the local crowd. Heaps of mussels—fried, with snails, with all kinds of sauces (45-75F)—served up in classy surroundings. Mussels and fries from 59F. The *complet*—appetizer, beer, mussels, and fries—will finish you off (98F). Belgian beer is a specialty. Wonderfully located in the eventful pl. de la République (but beware of pickpockets at night). Open daily 11:45am-12:30am.

## ILE ST-LOUIS

The restaurants on Ile-St-Louis are everything you'd expect: expensive, romantic, and full of charming half-timbered rooms. Come here for classic French cuisine and look for the bargain *menu* that just might make it affordable.

**Auberge de la Reine Blanche,** 30, rue St-Louis-en-l'Ile (tel. 46 33 07 87). Mo. Pont Marie. A small, charming restaurant, full of the delicious aromas of French cuisine. Covers all the bases of traditional French cooking, with lots of veal, lamb, and beef served with heavy sauces. The walls are a light peach, covered with hand-carved dollhouse furniture; the clientèle is a pleasant mixture of families and middle-aged couples. *Menus* of 85F and 130F provide an option for the budget traveler. Open daily noon-11:30pm. Reservations recommended for dinner. AmEx, V.

**Au Gourmet de l'Isle,** 42, rue St-Louis-en-l'Ile (tel. 43 26 79 27). Mo. Pont Marie. A dark, cozy restaurant, with walls covered by wooden grills and wine bottles. Traditional French cuisine with a specialty of *pavé de saumon à l'estragon* (salmon steak with tarragon). Clientele and *Maître* are local. Dinner à la carte is expensive, but a 125F *menu* is reasonable, given the food and the location. Open Wed.-Sun. noon-2pm and 7-10pm. Dinner reservations recommended. MC, V.

**Restaurant Montecristo,** 81, rue St-Louis-en-l'Ile (tel. 46 33 35 46). Mo. Pont Marie. A truly delightful gourmet Italian restaurant that is long, narrow, and stylishly decorated with plants and Art Nouveau lamps. The specialties are pasta, veal, and sorbets. Dinner *menus* at 98F and 128F. This place fills up early, so it's best to reserve ahead. Open daily 1-11:30pm. MC, V.

**Les Fous de l'Isle,** 33, rue des Deux-Ponts (tel. 43 25 76 67). Mo. Pont Marie. Come here for the flip-side of Ile St-Louis—a neighborhood cantina for a neighborhood crowd. Friendly proprietor has traveled the globe, and if he's not home, his spirit reigns. The light snacks and lovely tarts here go well with a book or conversation. Appetizers 25-35F; check the blackboards for daily specials. Salads 28-85F, starting with *cabreze* and ending with the *scandinave* mixed platter of smoked salmon and trout, tarama, and toast. Hot entrées 60-85F, featuring pastas and steak. The pastries win the prize at the *salon de thé*—try the brownies, cheesecake, or carrot cake (30F). Sunday brunch served Sept. 15-April 15. Open Tues.-Sun. noon-3pm and 7-10:30pm; *salon de thé* open 3-7pm.

# FIRST ARRONDISSEMENT

The small streets around Palais-Royal teem with small, traditional restaurants, each one worth a special visit. For faster meals and a younger crowd, head toward Les Halles, where you'll find everything from fast food to four-course Italian and American follies. The earthy delights of rue St-Denis may put off first-time visitors. Sex shops and thoroughly respectable restaurants coexist *face-à-face* in the stretch that lines Les Halles. During daylight hours, travelers may consider these eateries welcome bargains, despite being part of a street scene which may be unwelcome.

**Au Petit Ramoneur,** 74, rue St-Denis (tel. 42 36 39 24). Mo. Les Halles. Exceptional value for your money. 64F *menu* includes appetizer, main course, and ½L of wine. The food is hearty, the price is right, and the word is out. Crammed during lunch hour, this is a place to eat—and eat well—but not to relax. The restaurant's location is convenient if you're visiting St-Eustache or Les Halles. Open Mon.-Sat. 11:30am-2:30pm and 6:30pm-9:30pm, Sun. 11:30am-2:30pm.

**Le Boulanger,** 80, rue St-Denis (tel. 42 36 53 58). Mo. Les Halles. A self-service spot to eat breakfast or lunch in a breezy cafeteria setting. Take out a salad (15-30F) or sit and eat for a few francs more (24-34F). *Plats du jour* hover around 40F. Quiche 17F. *Café crème* 5F50-7F50. Open daily 7am-8pm.

**Le Carpaccio,** 6, rue Pierre Lescot (tel. 45 08 44 80). Mo. Les Halles. Conveniently located for visits to Les Halles or the Centre Pompidou, this restaurant offers outstanding Italian food at affordable prices. A variety of 2-course *menus* (54-90F). Don't think it's a 4-course *menu* that you're getting—the menu is confusing on this point. Try the namesake *carpaccio:* wafer-thin slices of beef (58F), tuna, or salmon (90F). If you feel like celebrating, the pastries, as well as the *apéritif* "Bellini" (peach liqueur and wine), are memorable. Open daily noon-12:30am.

**L'Emile,** 76, rue J.J.-Rousseau (tel. 42 36 58 58). Mo. Les Halles. Even Jean-Jacques and his nature child, after whom the restaurant is named, would feel at home here. Sophisticated but unpretentious atmosphere. If only they could all be like this. 3-course lunch *menu* 78F. A la carte, veal with green lemon 88F, beef with onion preserves 78F. The menu changes with the seasons, so à la carte items may vary. Open Mon.-Fri. noon-2:30pm and 8pm-midnight, Sat. 8pm-midnight.

**L'Epi d'Or,** 25, rue J.-J. Rousseau (tel. 42 36 38 12). Mo. Les Halles. The elegant interior complements spirited cuisine. 105F 2-course *menu* of simple food, prepared properly. Dine among pitchers of flowers, majolica, and a journalistic crowd. Exquisite *entrecôte Bordelaise. Menu* served until 9pm. Open Mon.-Fri. noon-2:30pm and 7:30pm-2am, Sat. 7:30pm-2am.

**The Front Page,** 56-58, rue St-Denis. Mo. Châtelet-Les Halles. The menu declares "I must be suffering from a mental disease" to choose American over French cuisine. Nonetheless such follies have arisen in the past and are likely to recur. Choose from 3 *menus* featuring hamburger with chili and fries, grilled chicken with BBQ sauce or *entrecôte.* 3 courses for 59F. Elaborate burgers for 56F and up. Open daily 11:30am-5am.

**L'Incroyable,** 26, rue de Richelieu or 23, rue de Montpensier, (tel. 42 96 24 64). Mo. Palais-Royal. Certainly incredible, this intimate restaurant serves up a 3-course *menu* at an *incroyable* 60F (in the evening 70F). Steak and grilled pork are among its simple but honest *plats;* 10F extra for veal or chicken cutlet, and 8F extra for a slice of the delectable *tartes maison. Foie de veau* 55F. Terrace and quaintly decorated interior. Open Tues.-Fri. 11:45am-2:15pm and 6:30-9pm, Sat. and Mon. 11:45am-2:15pm. Closed late Dec. and for the first 3 weeks of Jan.

**Lescure,** 7, rue de Mondovi (tel. 42 60 18 91). Mo. Concorde. Lively ambience has accompanied hearty French cuisine for over 70 years in this popular restaurant. 98F *menu* (includes 3 courses and wine) offers a wide selection and huge servings. Open Mon.-Fri. noon-2:15pm and 7-10pm, Sat. noon-2:15pm. Closed Aug.

**La Mangerie,** 17, rue des Petits Champs, not to be confused with rue Croix des Petits Champs (tel. 42 97 51 01). Mo. Bourse. Casual, understated refinement in a little restaurant with a view of the Palais-Royal and its gardens. *Plat du jour* 60F, *entrecôte* 65F. Save room for exquisite, homey pastry. Fruit tart 22F, *crème cara-*

*mel* 18F. The room in the back has the view; sit in the front room if you're in a hurry. It's worth making reservations. Open Mon.-Fri. noon-2pm.

**La Moisanderie,** 52, rue de Richelieu or 47, rue Montpensier (tel. 42 96 92 93 or 42 96 93 98). Mo. Palais-Royal. A 2-level restaurant serving a wonderful 3-course *menu* for 75F. The décor is charming: the rue de Richelieu level has wood paneling and copies of medieval tapestries, while the rue Montpensier level has stone walls like a castle. Open Mon.-Sat. noon-3pm and 7-10pm. AmEx, Diner's, V.

**Le Vieil Ecu,** 166, rue St-Honoré (tel. 42 60 20 14). Mo. Palais-Royal. Checkered tablecloths, soft light, and exposed beams set the tone for a 62F *menu* of traditional French food. Not a quiche in sight. Feast on *foie gras, onglet à l'échalottes* (flank steak with shallots), and *tarte tatin* with a glass of wine, beer, or mineral water. Vegetarian entrées available. Open Mon.-Sat. 12:15-7pm.

## SECOND ARRONDISSEMENT

If you're down near the Louvre and can't find anything cheap, consider walking a few blocks north for better values. There are a number of inexpensive restaurants in the *2ème*, especially in the festive pedestrian streets of rue Montorgueil, rue Léopold Bellan, and rue Bachaumont (Mo. Sentier). The long rue Montorgueil is lined with excellent *pâtissiers, marchés, fromagers,* and *chocolatiers* as well as the affordable Codec supermarket at no. 69. **Passage des Panoramas** off rue St-Marc (Mo. Bourse) is a colorful inside atrium walkway, packed with various national food counters. The two chic hang-outs in the *2ème* are the cafés, **Segaffredo Expresso Café** and **Le Centre Ville,** both on rue Montorgueil, at the corner of rue Mandar.

**L'Amanguier,** 110, rue de Richelieu (tel. 42 96 37 79). Mo. Bourse. This elegant restaurant near the Bourse is nestled in a receded courtyard. This place, *sous-titré* as a *"restaurant de charme,"* lives up to its name. The *menu séduisant* features a main course and an appetizer or dessert for 85F. Main dishes include *pavé de saumon aux herbes* and *coquilles St-Jacques.* Open daily noon-midnight.

**Au Clair de Lune,** 27, rue Tiquetonne (tel. 42 33 59 10). Mo. Etienne-Marcel. A small corner restaurant. Friendly service and very large helpings of good French or Algerian food at moderate prices. Couscous 44-58F. *Entrecôte* 52F. 3-course *menu* 62F. Try one of the Algerian wines, a *Royal Smahah* or a *Sidi Brahim* (56F). Paëlla is served on Fri. (70F). Open daily noon-3pm and 7:30-11pm.

**Au Lyonnais,** 32, rue St-Marc (tel. 42 96 65 04; fax 42 97 42 95). Mo. Richelieu-Drouot or Bourse. One of the best restaurants in the *2ème.* The dining room is done in floral porcelain tile and victorian lamps. An oak-bannistered staircase leads you to the upstairs dining hall and downstairs the tables are draped with white linen. *Caille rôtie* (roast quail) or *lapin aux échalotes* (rabbit with shallots) 70F. 2-course *menu* 87F. Open Mon.-Fri. 11:30am-2:45pm or 6:30pm-midnight, Sat. 6:30pm-midnight. Reservations a must for dinner.

**Babylone-Tropiques,** 34, rue Tiquetonne (tel. 42 33 48 35). Mo. Etienne-Marcel. Revelers streaming out of discos after midnight pour into this Afro-Caribbean restaurant for dishes from the Antilles like *gombo* and *maffé.* Banana leaves, bamboo, and drums hang from the ceiling, and the walls are adorned with zebra-skin wallpaper and African carvings. Caribbean dance music blares over the speaker system. Prices are fairly high: main course 70-100F. Desserts feature tantalizing banana delicacies such as *Aloko* (fried bananas 35F) and *saisai.* Apéritifs 35-65F, punch 40F, cocktails 50F. Open nightly 9pm-7am, Fri.-Sat. 9pm-9am.

**Country Life,** 6, rue Daunou (tel. 42 97 48 51). Mo. Opéra. Vegetarian *haute cuisine* in a charming, wooded health food store. 66F buffet includes soups and salads as well as hot and cold entrees. Open Mon.-Fri. 11:30am-2:30pm. Store open Mon.-Thurs. 10am-6:30pm, Fri. 10am-3pm.

**Donys,** 8, rue Etienne Marcel (tel. 42 36 28 30), on the corner of rue St-Denis. Mo. Etienne-Marcel. This Greek diner serves up huge, greasy, and great-tasting Greek sandwiches for 22F. To avoid the grease, try the tuna sandwich (12F), chicken sandwich (20F), or incredibly cheap *pizza turc* (7F). Sandwiches served on Greek pocket bread made before your very eyes. Open 10am-2pm and 4pm-7am.

**La Perdrix,** 6, rue Mandar (tel. 42 36 83 21). Mo. Sentier. The inside looks like a warm, medieval banquet hall. The décor is rustic—wood paneling and a boar's head—but the crowd is urban office workers. Great food at reasonable prices. The 57F *menu* includes 3 courses and a drink. A la carte: *entrecôte* 55F, *cassoulet au confit de canard* 75F. Succulent homemade desserts. 80F lunch *menu* features salmon or *canard à l'orange.* Also a more sumptuous 100F *menu.* Open Mon.-Fri. 11:30am-3pm and 6:30-10pm, Sat. 6:30-10pm.

**Restaurant Brissemoret,** 5, rue St-Marc (tel. 42 36 91 72). Mo. Bourse. A hidden bistro the likes of which you've only dreamed about. Tiled floors, zinc bar, and fresh roses on each table. This intimate bistro is run by the accomplished Claude Brissemoret. *Salade chèvre frais sur toast* (40F) and *foie gras maison* (85F) are musts. *Magret de canard* 85F. *Gâteau au chocolat* (40F) or a crispy *tarte tatin* (38F) to finish. Open Mon.-Fri. noon-2pm and 7-10:30pm.

**Restaurant Japonais Robata,** 60, rue Montorgueil (tel. 42 33 49 61). Mo. Sentier. Except for its all-Western clientele and location on a Paris street, this restaurant might as well be in Tokyo. From the bar, you see a cook with a Japanese sweat-band slaving over a charcoal grill; what he produces is certainly worth the sweat. Several *menus* with soup, rice, and grilled meat or fish. The *koumoda menu* (52F) features soup, 4 *brochettes de canard,* and rice; the *goydou menu* (80F) has soup, rice, and a beef dish. Open Mon.-Sat. noon-2:30pm and 7-10:45pm.

# THIRD ARRONDISSEMENT

Chinese, Indian, Middle Eastern, and East European cuisines abound along the *grands boulevards* and back alleyways of the third *arrondissement,* but the area is best known for offering affordable classic Parisian fare in intimate, conversation-fostering surroundings. Take-out sandwiches and *plats* are perfect for picnics in the Square du Temple or strolls past the *grands hôtels* of the *quartier*'s southern half.

**Les Arquebusiers**, 12, rue des Arquebusiers (tel. 48 87 94 12). Mo. Sebastian-Froissart. A neighborhood corner bar whose clientele is a Marais cross-section; artists, merchants, and young plain-folk escape the tourist hordes and head for wood paneling, soft lighting, and great prices. The upright piano in the corner caters to a young crowd that has had a few drinks. Temporary art expositions rotate monthly. Lunch-time fare includes daily specials (55F). Coffee 6F. Open Tues.-Fri. 11am-3:30pm and 7pm-1:30am, Sat. 7pm-1:30am, Sun.-Mon. 11am-3:30pm.

**L'Auberge Nicolas Flamel,** 51, rue Montmorency (tel. 42 71 77 78). Mo. Rambuteau. Occupying what is believed to be the second oldest residential building in Paris, this *auberge* has a history spanning 5 centuries. In the 15th century, Nicolas Flamel, alchemist and wacky idealist, used this address as a soup kitchen and shelter for transients, asking only *Ave Marias* in return. In its current state, the *auberge* feeds a less needy crowd. Unupholstered Louis XVI furniture, gilt mirrors, and whimsical Chagallian figures attached to walls and window frames serve as the backdrop for adventurous regional cuisine. A la carte prices will send penny-pinchers reeling, but the 72F midday special recalls the *auberge*'s charitable origins. The 3-course *menu* changes with the seasons, but usually includes Lyon sausage prepared with lentils, chicken *fricassée à l'ancienne,* and chocolate cake. A la carte will cost around 180F without wine. Try a glass of Haut-Médoc for 55F. Open Mon.-Fri. 12:15-2:15pm and 8:15-11:15pm, Sat.-Sun. 8:15-11:15pm.

**Le Hangar,** impasse Berthaud. Mo. Rambuteau. Le Hangar is the kind of place you often hear of but never find, where "it doesn't look like much but the food's outta this world." Tucked away from the Pompidou's nearby world of *pizzettes* and street mimes, this stopping place is a haven for weary museum visitors and locals alike. Try the salmon quiche with salad (54F) or the vast asparagus salad with green beans, *jambon de pomme,* and fresh *chèvre* for 78F. Those looking to splurge could try the *boeuf aux marilles* for a hefty 104F. Order coffee and get a varied tray of miniature *gâteaux.* Open Mon. 7pm-midnight, Tues.-Sat. noon-midnight. They serve tea and cakes but no meals 3:30-7pm.

**Les Jardins d'Aranjuez**, 9, rue de Picardie (tel 42 74 21 41). Mo. Temple. Stucco walls and foliage set the mood in this Spanish eatery. Pricey evening meals (à la carte only), but a bargain lunch (60F) welcomes the budgeteer. The 3-course lunch *menu* offers a tasty assortment of Iberian cuisine. Ask about the house *croquettes* and *flan*. The take-out *paella* (Spanish rice and seafood) for 98F is large enough to split with a friend. If you choose to spring for the pricier evening fare, try *tapas* (25-40F a pop) and listen to live flamenco guitar. Open Mon.-Sat.

**Spago,** 2, rue St-Gilles (tel. 48 87 24 09). Mo. Chemin-Vert. This Italian *charcuterie* and sandwich shop near Beaubourg is *the* place to buy homemade pasta, sandwiches stuffed to the hilt, or antipasto by the gram. Dodge the museum crowd and its profiteers; grab a sandwich, and picnic in the nearby green spot on rue du Parc-Royale. Sandwiches 18-27F. If you eat in Spago, expect higher prices: *antipasti variés* 38F, *cabreze* 32F. Open daily 10:30am-2:30pm and 4:30-9:30pm.

**La Taverne,** 5, place de la République (tel. 42 78 50 86). Mo. République. If you are a beer fan in search of something exotic, this place is for you. The menu features mussels cooked in beer (54F, plus 20F if you take a side order of *pommes frites)* and beer fondue. This is not a frat-party joke—the tavern is deadly serious about providing Belgian cuisine, which happens to rely heavily on Belgium's distinctive beers, *gueuze* and *kriek*. The prices are fairly high (set *menu* 105F), but portions are generous. Seating is available in back and in the basement, in case you want to avoid the noise and pollution on the terrace. Open daily 9am-2am.

**Le Taxi Jaune,** 13, rue Chapou (tel. 42 78 92 24). Mo. Arts et Métiers or Rambuteau. Gulp down 3-course meals amidst conviviality and kitsch Americana. Close to both the Pompidou and Arts et Métiers, the Taxi Jaune may be a perfect spot to drop anchor while exploring the Marais. The 62F lunch *menu* offers entrée, *plat*, dessert, and wine or soda. Try the curried chicken and apple pie, sip a glass of wine, and check out cartoons of cabs and folksy ads in all shades of yellow. 89F will get you 3-courses with more variety—they serve a delicious duck in raspberry vinegar and *charlotte aux fraises*. Open Mon.-Fri. lunch and dinner (until 11pm), Sat. dinner only. Carte Bleu, Eurocard, MC, V.

# FOURTH ARRONDISSEMENT

Budget travelers be warned: the fourth *arrondissement* is on its way to becoming a museum. A landmark on every corner, a gallery for every *tabac*, this chic-er half of the Marais is not the *quartier* it once was. Even with prices on the rise, budget restaurants are holding their ground. On rue des Rosiers, the pulse of the Marais's Jewish quarter, you'll find delis and felafel stands that will fill your stomach without hanging you out to dry. Avoid the pricey *croques-monsieurs* on the rue de Rivoli.

**Aquarius,** 54, rue Ste-Croix-de-la-Bretonnerie (tel. 48 87 48 71). Mo. Hôtel de Ville. 40, rue de Gergovie 14*ème* (tel. 45 41 36 88). Serves fresh and wholesome vegetarian food in a non-smoking setting somewhere between a cafeteria and a waiting-room for the harmonic convergence. *Plats* tip a *chapeau* to the regions of France. *Galettéa chevalier* with egg and cheese 27F. *Menu* at 53F includes yogurt and veggie daily special. Try the *assiette paysanne* (50F), a combo platter of *chèvre chaud,* garlic bread, and roasted mushrooms and potatoes (dinner only). Open Mon.-Thurs. noon-10pm., Fri.-Sat. noon-10:30pm. *Plats du jour,* cereals, and hot vegetable dishes are served only noon-2pm and 7-10pm. Open Sept.-July.

**L'Arbre Aux Sabots,** 3, rue Simon Leclerc (tel. 42 71 10 24). Mo. Rambuteau. The decoration (a lot of Klimt, some temporary art exhibits), and good location near the Centre Pompidou may explain why this restaurant attracts such an artsy crowd. The 65F *menu* includes *roquefort* salad, steak or chicken fricasée, and a choice of sorbet, chocolate mousse, or vanilla cream. Salads 28F, *plats du jour* 38F. Open Mon.-Fri. noon-midnight. AmEx, MC, V.

**Chez Jo Goldenberg,** 7, rue des Rosiers. Mo. St-Paul. In the heart of the Marais's Jewish quarter, Goldenberg's has become something of a landmark. Because of its nature as a curiosity and pilgrimage site, Goldenberg's is a little expensive. A slice of the old world almost, but not quite. A deli and restaurant since 1920, it suffered a 1985 terrorist attack which took the life of the owner's son. *Plat du jour* (70F), soups (50F), and pastries galore. Take-out section where you can buy borscht, sauerkraut, pickles, pastries, and other traditional foods. Deli open daily 8:30am-11pm; dining room open daily noon-midnight.

**Chez Marianne,** 2, rue des Hôspitalières St-Gervais (tel. 42 72 18 86). Mo. St-Paul. Nearly every Israeli specialty and many Eastern European ones. Best known for the felafel (30F), blini, pirogi, and *vatrouchka,* a *gâteau de fromage,* rather different from what Americans call cheesecake. Sit in a cozy dining room and order 4, 5, or 6 specialties (50F, 60F, or 70F) from options such as chopped liver, tabouli, and hummus. Take-out available. Open Sat.-Thurs. 11am-midnight.

**La Dame Tartine,** 2, rue Bisemiche (tel. 42 77 32 22). Mo. Rambuteau. From the ample terrace, you can watch the sculptures in the Stravinsky fountain bobbing about. The restaurant itself has an atmosphere almost as lively as the fountain. A mostly young crowd. Main courses 20-36F. Open daily noon-11:30pm.

**Le Divin,** 41, rue de la Croix de la Bretonnerie (tel. 42 77 10 20). Mo. Hôtel de Ville or Rambuteau. A taste of Provence in a rustic stucco-and-beam setting, Large portions of food for a low price. 3-course lunch *menu* 69F. Lighter fare includes *assiettes* with salads, blini, and cheeses (around 70F). *Coeur de Rumsteack à la crème d'oursin* is part of a 3-course dinner (89F). Open Tues.-Sun. AmEx, MC, V.

**L'Ebouillanté,** 6, rue des Barres (tel. 42 78 48 62). Mo. St-Paul or Pont Marie. A restaurant and *salon de thé,* L'Ebouillanté offers light snacks as well as entrées. In summer months, sit in the quiet cobblestone courtyard and watch as the gallery crowd and monks from St-Gervais mingle here, just steps from the bustle of cars and *bouquinistes* along the Seine. House specialities include "Bricks"—Tunisian crêpes—with varied fillings (41-56F). Try them with salmon and *fromage blanc* or cheese, eggs, and tomatoes. Salads (53F). Open Tues.-Sun. noon-9pm.

**Finkelsztajn's,** 27, rue des Rosiers (tel. 42 72 78 91). 24, rue des Ecouffes (tel. 48 87 92 85). (See Groceries.)

**Piccolo Teatro,** 6, rue des Ecouffes (tel. 42 72 17 79). Mo. St-Paul. Vegetarian cuisine served in the heart of the Jewish quarter. Woodsy, soothing interior complements the food. Midday *menu* at 53F includes soup or appetizer (try the miso soup), a *gratin de légumes,* and dessert of *fromage blanc.* Various platters offer a savory, filling mélange of grains and vegetables. Nighttime *menu* hovers around 90F. Open Wed.-Sun. noon-3pm and 7-11pm.

**Restaurant le Beautrellis,** (tel. 42 72 36 04). Mo. Bastille. Jim Morrison fans will want to stop by this restaurant, located across from the address where he died. Or did he? Ask Vieran, the proprietor, who dons a leather vest and chains during daylight hours to blend with the groupies. 3 volumes of comment books are a fascinating read over goulash (house specialty). Lunch *menu* for 53F highlights Slavic cuisine. Dinner à la carte will cost 200F and includes musical entertainment—an accordionist who may have once played for Ceaucescu. Open Sept.-July.

**Le Temps des Cérises,** 31, rue de la Cériseraie (tel. 42 72 08 63). Mo. Bastille or Sully-Morland. Photos of yesteryear and a young, neighborhood crowd give this restaurant the relaxed feel of a familiar, local hangout with elbow-to-elbow familiarity. Hearty 3-course lunch *menu* goes for 60F; includes veal sauté or ratatouille with fries. Turns into a bar at night. Open for lunch Mon.-Fri.

# FIFTH ARRONDISSEMENT

Foraging for food in the 5*ème* poses no problem at all. Rue Mouffetard indisputably constitutes the main culinary artery of this lively arrondissement. Traditional French and ethnic (mainly Greek and Lebanese) restaurants line "the Mouff" as it extends to rue Descartes, all the way down to bd. St-Germain. On tiny rue du Pot-de-Fer, a pedestrian passage crossing rue Mouffetard, side-by-side restaurants with competitive *menus* foster a village atmosphere. If you want to create your own lunch or dinner, it's easy to find treats at one of the morning open-air markets (See Markets).

**L'Apostrophe,** 34, rue de la Montagne Ste-Geneviève (tel. 43 54 10 93). Mo. Maubert-Mutualité. Tiny, unpretentious French restaurant on a lovely street that winds its way down the hill from the Panthéon. Somewhat garishly decorated with huge candles. This restaurant offers an excellent bargain. 3 *menus:* 49F served until 8pm, 59F until 9pm, and 75F all night. Open Tues.-Sat. noon-2pm and 7-10pm.

**Café Oz,** 184, rue St-Jacques (tel. 43 54 30 48). Mo. Luxembourg. The crew at this newly opened café/bar swears it's "the only Australian thing in continental Europe." Boomerang-shaped ashtrays, Aussie knick knacks tacked to the walls, and rustic wood furnishings. If you're nice to the guy behind the bar, he may even let you play the *didgeridoo,* the aboriginal wind instrument hanging above his head. Ever-changing menu includes fresh fruit juices, meat and vegetable pies, chocolate and banana cake, and daily specials. Huge and increasing beer menu. Cans, bottles, and draught 20-35F. Australian wine a little steep at 25-45F.

**Café Le Volcan,** 10, rue Thouin (tel. 46 33 38 33). Mo. Cardinal Lemoine. A boisterous restaurant that gets hopping at night with a young clientele at home in the plain brick-floored interior. Posters of Bogart, Chaplin, and Dexter Gordon stare at you from the walls. Specializes in moussaka and other Greek dishes. The 55F *menu* includes appetizer, main dish, and dessert; at lunch a glass of wine as well. Dinner *menus* at 80-100F. Open daily noon-2pm and 7-11:30pm. MC, V.

**Cepage,** 26, rue de la Mont Ste-Geneviève (tel. 43 54 17 65). Mo. Maubert-Mutualité. Sophisticated yet unintimidating restaurant specializing in such classics as *canard* and *grillade de gigot d'agneau*. Black tables with white tablecloths, traditional stone walls, and wooden beams. Soft jazz plays in the background. *Menus* at 78 and 115F. Open at 11:30am for lunch and 7pm for dinner.

**Chez Lena et Mimille,** 32, rue Tournefort (tel. 47 07 72 47). Mo. Censier Daubenton. Everything you imagine a classic French restaurant to be, and more. Truly traditional cuisine served in an elegant setting of pink and burgundy. In summer months, dine on the flowered terrace overlooking a leafy *place*. Lunch menu at 98F. Dinner with complimentary cocktail, *entrée, plat*, dessert, wine, and coffee 185F. Open Wed.-Mon. noon-2pm and 7:30-11pm. Reservations accepted. MC, V.

**Crêperie Ferme Ste-Suzanne,** 4, rue des Fossés St-Jacques (tel. 43 54 90 02). Mo. Luxembourg. Although the painting of Elvis and the Harley Davidson woodcuts on the walls of this tiny *crêperie* make a puzzling statement in contrast with the muted pink walls and marble tables, it's the perfect place to grab a light lunch or dinner. Choice of *crêpe* or salad with appetizer or dessert 45F. Salad, *crêpe*, dessert, and drink for 59F. MC, V.

**L' Estrapade,** 15, rue de l Estrapade (tel. 43 25 72 58). Mo. Luxembourg or place Monge. This tiny bistro, decorated in non-traditional tones of salmon and green, specializes in such exquisitely prepared traditional French cuisine as *poulet de pot* and *soupe à l'oignon*. Old-fashioned caricatures of French celebrities and statesmen on the wall. Lunch *menu* quite affordable at 80F. Dinner à la carte runs 70-90F. Open Wed.-Mon. noon-2:30pm and 7-11pm. MC, V.

**Le Grenier de Notre Dame,** 18, rue de la Bûcherie (tel. 43 29 98 29). Mo. St-Michel. Macrobiotics' and soybean-freaks' delight. A restaurant that ladles up vegetarian *cassoulet*, a stew of beans, tofu and soy sausages, along with an appetizer and dessert, all for 75F. How about *la spéciale protéines*: granola, mixed veggies, tofu, beans, lettuce, cabbage, and potatoes? Pricier at 85F, but with a protein kick like that you may be set for the rest of your stay in Paris. Carnivores may want to look elsewhere. Open daily noon-2:30 and 7:30-11pm. MC, V.

**Le Jardin des Pâtes,** 4, rue Lacépède (tel. 43 31 50 71). Mo. Jussieu. Gourmet pasta made from organically grown grains and served in a variety of recipes ranging from sesame butter to duck and *crème fraîche*. Locals suggest the *pâtés de seigle* (54F) with ham, white wine, and *comté* cheese. Many vegetarian offerings. 8 tables unassumingly set with paper tablecloths. Main course 48-70F. Open Tues.-Sun. noon-2:30pm and 7-10:30pm.

**Le Monsegur,** 34, rue du Cardinal Lemoine (tel. 43 26 36 08). Mo. Cardinal Lemoine. This place has become an institution with the late-night party crowd. Pierre (Peter to his close personal friends) serves up a vast array of sandwiches (25-36F) and boasts that his *grillade avec omelet* is made with 5 eggs while his competitors skimp with only 2. Food and alcohol flow freely all night. Open noon-7am.

**Restaurant L'Escapade,** 11, rue de la Mont Ste-Geneviève (tel. 46 33 23 85). Mo. Maubert-Mutualité. All-you-can-eat meets Paris chic. For 90F you can buy an *hors d'oeuvre*, buffet of cold salads and *pâté* (heap those plates high!), an *entrée*, dessert, and wine (serve yourself from the keg). For atmosphere, eat in the cool, dark *cave* downstairs. Reservations accepted. Open 6:30pm-2am.

**Restaurant Perraudin,** 157, rue St-Jacques (tel. 46 33 15 75). Mo. Luxembourg or Maubert-Mutualité. At this family-style bistro, rub elbows with the locals and relax in the burgundy and dark wood décor. Gamble on *le plat du jour selon l'humeur du chef* (daily special according to the chef's mood), or try old favorites like *sautée d'agneau aux flageolets* (sautéed lamb with white beans, 55F). Come early; this place gets crowded. Lunch *menu* at 60F. Appetizers 25F. Main dishes 50-60F. Open Tues.-Fri. noon-2:15pm and 7:30-10:15pm, Mon. and Sat. 7:30-10:15pm.

**The Rib Joint,** 14, rue Thouin (tel. 43 26 37 09). Mo. Cardinal Lemoine. The perfect answer to your BBQ cravings. Funky joint with checkered tablecloths and exhibitions of contemporary photos lining the walls (featuring mostly American artists). The 95F *menu* is pricey, but when you gotta have it, you gotta have it. Fill up on your choice of Southern BBQ pork ribs or chicken (Louisiana style), macaroni salad, potato salad, coleslaw, beans, and a brownie with *crème fraîche.* A la carte, vegetarian plates, and pecan pie. Open 7:30pm-2am.

## SIXTH ARRONDISSEMENT

Tiny restaurants with rock-bottom *prix-fixe menus* jostle each other for space and customers in the area bound by bd. St-Germain, bd. St-Michel, and the Seine, making it an excellent area to wander around looking for a filling meal. The streets around the rue de Buci offer many bargain restaurants as well as a rambling daily street market, where you can pick up anything from a whole roasted chicken and fries to fresh yogurts and cheeses. The rue Gregoire de Tours has the highest density of cheap restaurants, and makes a great place to start if you feel like doing a little menu browsing. Farther west toward the St-Germain-des-Prés area and closer to the seventh *arrondissement,* affordable eateries fade fast and are replaced by elegant but expensive restaurants where the crowd comes to see and be seen.

**Au Petit Prince,** 3, rue Monsieur le Prince (tel. 43 29 74 92), just off the pl. Odéon. Mo. Odéon. St-Exupéry fans will love this sophisticated restaurant that offers a taste of delicate but rarely filling *nouvelle cuisine* with creations such as grilled sole in orange butter. Subtly decorated with a tiny airplane in the window and watercolors on ceramic of *Le Petit Prince* himself. The 125F *menu* includes 3 courses but no wine. Open Mon.-Sat. noon-2:30 and 7:30-11pm.

**La Cambeuse,** 8, rue Casimir Delavigne (tel. 43 26 48 84), off pl. Odéon. Mo. Odéon. Specializing in *cuisine traditionnelle,* this simple restaurant will satisfy your craving for *soupe à l'oignon, boeuf bourgignon,* or *coq au vin.* Hearty servings. 3-course *menu* 80F. Open Mon.-Sat. noon-2pm and 5-11pm. AmEx, MC, V.

**Cosi,** 54, rue de Seine (tel. 46 33 35 36), off rue de Buci. Mo. Odéon. Strains of *Così Fan Tutte* emanate from this totally hip little sandwich shop where you can have a sandwich made to order from tantalizing ingredients such as curried turkey, goat cheese, and tomato and basil salad, stuffed between two slices of piping hot, freshly baked *focaccia* bread (33-48F). It may sound expensive for just a sandwich, but this isn't just a sandwich. Respectable wines (14F/glass) complement the gargantuan creations, making a satisfying meal. Open daily noon-midnight.

**Crêperie Saint Germain,** 33 rue St-André des Arts (tel. 43 54 24 41). Mo. Odéon. This place promises 60 varieties in *une ambiance décontractée* (a laid-back atmosphere) and they're not kidding. Mosaic insets on the tabletops, strategically placed kitschy statuettes, and blue-sky-and-clouds ceiling. Specializes in *crêpes noirs,* made from all-natural wheat flour. Try a *rasta* (cucumbers, red beans, and corn) or an *agora* (salmon paste with a shot of ouzo on the side). Most 30-45F. Sinful dessert *crêpes.* Wash it all down with a mildly alcoholic *cidre* (13F50). Open Mon.-Fri. noon-1am, Sat.-Sun. until 2am. AmEx, MC, V.

**Kiotori,** 61, rue Monsieur le Prince (tel. 43 54 48 44). Mo. Odéon or Luxembourg. A young, energetic, international crowd packs into this Japanese restaurant to gorge on the succulent skewers of grilled beef, chicken, and shrimp, or to relish the visually stunning plates of sushi and maki. A large variety of amazingly cheap *menus,* ranging from 48-90F. All *menus* include a bowl of soup and *crudités* salad along with the main dish. Open Mon.-Sat. noon-2:30pm and 7-11pm.

**Le Mazet,** 61, rue St-André des Arts (tel. 43 54 68 81). Mo. Odéon. This no-nonsense café/bar serves up generous portions of *poulet frites* (39F), *steak frites* (40F), and *saucisse frites* (35F) in a casual atmosphere. Exceptionally fast service. 14 beers on tap (14F/glass). Open daily noon-2am.

**Oh! Poivrier,** 143 bd. Raspail (tel. 43 26 98 27). Mo. Notre-Dame des Champs. 25, quai des Grands Augustins (tel. 43 29 41 77). Mo. St-Michel. This chain's *grandes assiettes gourmandes* make a great light lunch, snack, or quick dinner. Snazzy gray, black, and glass interior. Plates come with an assortment of salads, smoked fish, duck, roast beef, fresh fruit, coleslaw, and cheese (48-70F). All come with toasted *pain levain* (unleavened bread). Open daily 11:30am-midnight.

**Orestias,** 4, rue Gregoire de Tours (tel. 43 54 62 01), off bd. St-Germain. Mo. Odéon. Their *menu* is an inspired bargain with copious first and second courses as well as cheese or dessert for only 44F, lunch *and* dinner. Both the food and dark wood-paneled ambience run toward middle-of-the-road French, with lots of grilled meats (the lamb skewers are the best offering) accompanied by fries and green beans. You can't eat more for the price anywhere in the area. Open Mon.-Sat. noon-2:30pm and 6-11:30pm.

**Le Petit Vatel,** 5, rue Lobineau (tel. 43 54 28 49). Mo. Odéon or Mabillon. This tiny restaurant offers little in ambience—plastic tables adorned with simple bouquets of daisies—but provides delicious, inexpensive meals. Choose a main dish plus an appetizer or dessert from the 59F *menu* scribbled on the chalkboard, including rotating daily specialties like *poivrons farcis, gratin d'épinards au jambon,* and vegetarian stews. Take-out available. Open Mon.-Fri. noon-3pm and 7pm-midnight, Sat. noon-1am, Sun. 7pm-midnight. Closed 1 week in Aug.

**Pizza Pino,** 57, bd. Montparnasse (tel. 45 48 94 77). Mo. Montparnasse. An Italian pizzeria that bakes its pies in genuine wood-burning ovens. An excellent choice for a magisterial Italian Thanksgiving dinner. The incredible hours are this restaurant's biggest appeal; it stays open from 11am-5am, 7 days a week.

**Restaurant Des Beaux Arts,** 11, rue Bonaparte (tel. 43 26 92 64), across from the Ecole des Beaux Arts. Mo. St-Germain-des-Prés. Extremely popular with the locals, this place features friendly service, a simple décor, and festive frescoed walls. The 72F *menu* includes eccentric choices like *maquereau aux pommes à l'huile* (mackerel with apples in oil) and a daily vegetarian dish. Generous salads 25-35F. Open daily noon-2:30pm and 7-10:45pm.

**Restaurant Maroussia,** 9, rue de l'Eperon (tel. 43 54 87 50). Mo.Odéon. This tiny restaurant specializes in classic Russian dishes and hearty peasant fare. Dried flowers, rustic wooden tables, and heavy red print drapes recreate the feeling of the countryside. Come at lunch for an affordable 75F *menu,* which includes 2 courses and wine. Dinner specialties like the filling *chicken kiev* or smoked salmon, herring, and blinis beckon at prices ranging around 70F. Dinner *menu* 150F. Open Tues.-Fri. noon-2:30pm and 7:30-11pm, Mon. and Sat. 7:30-11pm.

**Slice,** 62, rue Monsieur le Prince (tel. 43 54 18 18). Mo. Odéon or Luxembourg. Bakes huge New-York-style pizzas dripping with toppings of your choice. Whole pies (serves 4) 90-130F, half-pies (serves 2) 60-85F. Finish off with a brownie (18F) or chocolate chip cookies (18F for 3). Open daily 10am-11:30pm.

## SEVENTH ARRONDISSEMENT

Although Empress Josephine loved to host sumptuous feasts, her austere and regimented husband never allowed himself more than 20 minutes to dine. Now that Napoleon has been laid to rest, you can spend hours dining in the 7*ème's* pricey, but often excellent restaurants. This *arrondissement* is a good place to indulge in that 100F+ menu meal that you promised to do at least once in Paris. There are low-budget options; don't expect great variety, but the standards are well executed.

**Au Babylone,** 13, rue de Babylone (tel. 45 48 72 13). Mo. Sèvres-Babylone. The kind proprietor in pince-nez glasses has been serving simple, but affordable dishes for over 30 years. A faithful clientele enjoys coming back to this restaurant again and again. 80F *menu* includes appetizer, steak or *plat du jour,* and drink or dessert. A la carte appetizers 12-20F. Main dishes 45-60F (*poulet rôti* 45F, *boeuf tomate* 48F). Desserts 15-18F. Open Sept.-July Mon.-Sat. 11:30am-2:30pm.

**Aux Délices de Széchuen,** 40, av. Duquesne, on the corner of av. Duquesne and av. Breteuil behind l'Eglise St-François-Xavier. Mo. St-François-Xavier. Run by a charming proprietress and her family, this elegant Chinese restaurant serves up the most refined Chinese dishes you will ever taste. The extensive, interesting menu includes both French and Szechuan delicacies such as *salade de méduse* (jellyfish salad) or *poulet sauté champignon noir*. Large shaded outdoor terrace in summer. 96F *menu*. Open Tues.-Sun. noon-2:30pm and 7-10:30pm.

**Le Club des Poètes,** 30, rue de Bourgogne (tel. 47 05 06 03). Mo. Varenne. The small, timbered dining room is a great setting for dinner and the nightly poetry readings which begin at 8pm and includes delicious entrées like *grenadin de veau à la crème* (90F) and a 96F *menu* of veal, beef, or lamb with an appetizer, cheese course, and dessert. The proprietor, Jean-Pierre Rosnay also directs the 24-hr. poetry hotline called *Allo Poésie* (tel. 45 50 32 33). (See Entertainment—Highbrow Diversions, for more information.)

**CROQ 100WICH,** 23bis, av. de la Motte Picquet. This deli/sandwich shop can offer you a quick bite at the lunch counter or to go: filling sandwiches with fancy names. "Le Méditeranée" tuna sandwich (21F). "Le Parisien" ham and cheese sandwich (16F). *Salade paysanne* (25F) is full of potatoes, chicken, bacon, and olives. Vegetarian options. Open Mon.-Fri. 9am-8pm, Sat. 9am-5pm.

**La Croque au Sel,** 131, rue St-Dominique (tel. 47 05 23 53), off av. Bosquet next to la Fontaine de Mars. Mo. Ecole Militaire. Country cuisine in a charming restaurant with brightly painted windows and ceramic lamps. The restaurant offers two *menus* (56 and 98F) with seemingly endless choices. The 56F *menu* offers entrées like *pavé de boeuf émincé* smothered in *sauce croque au sel* (the house specialty) and *quart de poule rôti aux herbes de Provence,* among countless others. The difference between the 56F and the 98F *menus* is, as the waiter explains, more choice and 42F. Open Mon.-Fri. noon-2pm and 7-10:30pm, Sat. 7-10:30pm.

**Fontaine de Mars,** 129, rue St-Dominique (tel. 47 05 46 44), off av. Bosquet. Mo. Ecole Militaire. Wonderful restaurant with lace curtains, pine wood interior, red checkered tablecloths, and brass instruments. Optional terrace seating overlooking the fountain whose name the restaurant celebrates. One of the best places in the 7*ème* for a generous sampling of traditional French *provinçale* cuisine. House specialties include *saumon au chèvre frais* (65F) or *salade canard* (65F). Or try the less interesting, but filling 85F *menu* of *steak tartare, pommes de terre, salade verte,* and dessert. Also good (and more adventuresome) is the *andouillette au chablis pomme* (85F). Open Mon.-Sat. noon-2:30pm and 7:30-11pm.

**La Pie Gourmande,** 30, rue de Bourgogne (tel. 45 51 32 48). Mo. Varenne or Chambre des Députés. Families and jeans-clad friends mix happily in this comfortable *crêperie*. Sit at the oak and brass counter or one of the floral-clothed tables. Sizzling *galettes* (35-55F). *Crêpes* (for dessert, 20-40F). A salad for starters (20-40F) rounds out a filling meal. Open Mon.-Fri. 11:30am-3pm.

**La Poule au Pot,** 121, rue de l'Université (tel. 47 05 16 36), near the corner of rue Surcouf. Mo. Invalides or Pont de l'Alma. Join the suits on the small terrace under the faded striped awning or venture inside to the soothing green décor. The feel of a 1930s *bistro* from a George Brassaï photograph. Try the *poule au pot farcie* (stuffed chicken stew, 85F), the signature dish. Appetizers 28-46F. Main dishes 72-106F. Dessert 22-36F. 110F *menu*. Open Mon.-Sat. 12:30-3pm and 7-11pm.

# EIGHTH ARRONDISSEMENT

Despite the large concentration of *restaurants de luxe* and other salons of *haute couture* in the eighth, there are a number of affordable restaurants. Swiss restaurants—that don't require you to have a Swiss bank account to have a good meal—cluster on the side streets around the rue La Boétie just off the Champs-Elysées.

**L'Aubergade,** 122, rue La Boétie (tel. 42 25 10 60). Mo. Franklin D. Roosevelt. Chaos may reign a few steps away on rue La Boétie, but you'll find peace through the stained-glass doors. Enticing lacy tablecloths, arched mirrors, and luscious dessert table. 65F lunch *menu:* filling salad and meat or fish dish. Old leather-bound menu (in English and French) offers more elaborate *menus* at 75F and 120F. House duck 75F. Open Mon.-Fri. 10am-3pm and 6-11pm, Sat. 6-11pm.

**Dynastie Thai,** 101, rue La Boétie. Mo. St-Philippe du Roule. Acknowledged top choice among Paris's Asian restaurants. One of the most elegant and appetizing places in the city. Bargain weekday *menu* (90F) lists exquisitely prepared Thai cuisine in an ambience *de luxe.* Chicken sautéed in basil, Thai beef sautéed in pepper, and chicken Thai lemon soup. Open daily noon-2:30pm and 7-11:30pm.

**Le Fouquet's,** 99, av. des Champs-Elysées (tel. 47 23 70 60). Mo. George V. "Created" in 1899 and located in the shadow of the Arc de Triomphe, this is the premier gathering place for Parisian *vedettes* (stars) of radio, television, and cinema. Tourists, oblivious to celebrities drinking inside, bask on the *terrasse.* James Joyce dined here with relish. Bank-breaking coffee and a chance to be seen 35F. Entrees from 92F. Open daily 8am-midnight; food served noon-3pm and 1pm-midnight.

**La Maison du Valais,** 20, rue Royale (tel. 42 60 22 72). Mo. Madeleine. This Swiss restaurant has great view of the Madeleine, but you might prefer to eat inside the wooden-beamed chalet interior with cowhide-upholstered chairs. Fondue, salmon tartare, and raclette from 90F. Open Mon.-Sat. 12:15-2:30pm and 7-11pm.

**Naturesto,** 66, av. des Champs-Elysées, in the Galerie Point Show, no. 67 (tel. 42 56 49 01). Mo. Franklin D. Roosevelt. *"Mangez juste!"* is this vegetarian eatery's motto. Vitamin and protein shakes and fruity cocktails will "pump you up" without deflating your pocket, as will the tasty dishes (37-47F). Try the "Caroline"— lettuce, carrots, sprouts, apples, raisins, tomatoes, cheese, and sunflower seeds. Green salads 22F. "Salade Capri" with tomatoes, celery, mushrooms, and carrots 25F. Fruit tartes (apple and berries) 23F. Open Mon.-Fri. noon-3pm.

**Le Roi de Pot-au-Feu,** 40, rue de Ponthieu (tel. 43 59 41 62), off rue de la Boétie. Mo. Franklin D. Roosevelt. Small restaurant with red and white checkered table-cloths, dark wood interior, and black and white silver screen photos. Filling *pot-au-feu* (beef and vegetable stew; 85F). Open Mon.-Sat. noon-3pm and 7-11pm.

**La Taverne Suisse,** 48, rue de Ponthieu (tel. 42 56 01 67), near Le Roi de Pot-au-Feu. Mo. Franklin D. Roosevelt. Intimate Swiss restaurant with a central oak and brass bar. 68F *Formule Suisse menu* features French and Swiss specialties like *fondue savoyard* and *raclette du valais.* 75F *menu* is more elaborate, but not as traditionally Swiss. Open Mon.-Fri. noon-3pm and 7-11:30pm, Sat. 7-11:30pm.

## NINTH ARRONDISSEMENT

Except for a few gems, meals close to the heavily touristed Opéra area can be quite expensive; for truly cheap deals, head farther north. Displaced by the projectile force of the city's skyrocketing prices, much of ethnic Paris has found itself here, providing visitors to the ninth with wondrous delicacies from former French colonies. Non-French cuisine goes for lower prices, reflecting its lack of acceptance.

**Anarkali,** 4, place Gustave Toudouze (tel. 48 78 11 48). Mo. St-Georges. On a lovely secluded square. Serves up a familiar assortment of spicy South Indian fare. Relax on the terrace under wide, colorful umbrellas, cut from the cloth of the owner's native land. Appetizers 20F, entrées 30-50F. Chutneys cost an extra 6-8F. Open Tues.-Sat. noon-2:30pm and 7pm-12:30am. Open Sun. in summer.

**Au Boeuf Bourguignon,** 21, rue de Douai (tel. 42 82 08 79). Mo. Pigalle. Pearl of the neighborhood, sharing only a *métro* stop with the sleazy hangouts that line streets nearby. Close to record stores and sound studios hiding behind bd. de Clichy. Checkered tablecloths and movie posters contribute to the subdued bohemian atmosphere. Cheerful French family presents 3-course 60F and 92F *menus.* The 92F *menu* offers more variety and a complimentary *kir.* The *boeuf bourguignon* comes highly recommended. Open Mon.-Sat. noon-3pm and 6:30-10:30pm.

**Les Bacchantes,** 21, rue de Caumartin (tel. 42 65 25 35). Mo. Havre-Caumartin. Hearty portions of perennial French favorites and wine. This *bistrot à vins* offers an extensive wine list and cheap food despite its proximity to the Madeleine. *Andouillette* (58F) is the house specialty. *Assiette de campagne* (40F) is a sampler of *rillette,* pâté, and sausage. Salads 40F. An oasis of cheer through the night. Open Sept.-July daily 11:30am-6am; Aug. Mon.-Sat. 11:30am-6am.

**Le Chartier,** 7, rue du Faubourg-Montmartre (tel. 47 70 86 29). Mo. Montmartre. On a little courtyard, this huge restaurant is really in the grand old French style, with chandeliers and wooden booths. The waiters here are older and very jovial; the clientele is mainly an older, local crowd. Specialties include beef in a house tomato sauce, *pot au feu* (stew), and roast veal. Portions are huge. A full meal will cost about 90F. Open daily 11am-3pm and 6:30-9:30pm. MC, V.

**La Franche-Comté,** 2, bd. de la Madeleine (tel. 47 42 86 52; reservations 49 24 99 09). Mo. Madeleine. Half-restaurant, half-tourist office about this eastern French province, this place offers tantalizing regional specialties. Wild mushrooms, trout, and pâté make frequent appearances, keeping prices a little high. *Menus* at 82F, 110F, and 175F. Brochures free. Open Mon.-Sat. noon-10:30pm. AmEx, MC, V.

**Hard Rock Café,** 14, bd. Montmartre (tel. 42 46 10 00). Mo. Richelieu Druot. Loud music, burgers, and guitars on the wall. Seen it all before? Burgers, ribs, steaks— you know, American stuff. 69F lunch *menu* includes guacamole, cheesesteak, and beer or California wine. Happy hour 4-6:30pm. Good gig on July 4. You can buy t-shirts next door. Please don't. Open daily noon-2am. Credit cards accepted.

**Hayne's Bar,** 3, rue Clauzel (tel. 48 78 40 63). Mo. St-Georges. This restaurant bar specializes in downhome New Orleans cooking. Come here for some good old fried chicken, New Orleans-style red beans, BBQ chicken, and the like. Portions are very generous and dinner comes out to less than 100F. On Fri. nights, a pianist plays New Orleans jazz. Hot tamales 90F. Gumbo with shrimp, chicken, okra, and rice 90F. Sister Lena's BBQ spare ribs 70F. Open Tues.-Sat. 7:30pm-1am.

**Le Palmier de Lorette,** 19, rue de Châteaudun (tel. 48 78 34 41). Mo. Notre-Dame-de-Lorette. Across from the church. In the *grand brasserie* style, a roomy, red plush interior owned by a genial couple who take pride in their cuisine and hospitality; Monsieur does the cooking. Evening *menu* offers exciting French classics made with ingredients so fresh you'll think you're back on the farm. Open Mon.-Fri. 7am-1am; open for meals noon-3pm and 7-11:30pm. MC, V.

**Sannine,** 32, rue du Faubourg-Montmartre (tel. 48 24 01 32). Mo. Montmartre. A small, family affair specializing in Middle Eastern basics: kebabs, marinated beef, felafel, and tabouli. Red tablecloths and painted murals of the Lebanon that once was. Dinner à la carte for around 90F; *menu* for 49F (lunch) and 62F (dinner). Open daily noon-3pm and 6pm-midnight. Take-out available.

# TENTH ARRONDISSEMENT

While many tourists may see no more of the tenth than their two-hour layover at the Gare du Nord allows, those who venture out will find French, Indian, and African food to make any gourmand smile. Catering to locals rather than tourists, these restaurants permit short and long-term visitors alike the chance to soak up a Paris that doesn't revolve around the Eiffel Tower or the Louvre. Passage Brady is filled with Indian eateries and a festival of the palate for rock-bottom prices. Try **Mouroganc,** 87-93, passage Brady (tel. 42 46 06 06), a specialty store brimming over with Indian delicacies; a full meal here may cost you less than coffee and a magazine at the *gare.*

**Brasserie Flo,** 7, cour des Petites-Ecuries (tel. 47 70 13 59). Mo. Château d'Eau. Beautiful dining room, with dark wood paneling and mirrors. A chic chain, specializing in seafood, with every imaginable type of oyster. Dinner à la carte can be somewhat expensive at 200F, but a 94F *menu* is a great buy. Reservations recommended. Open 7pm-2am. Credit cards accepted.

**Le Brouet,** 14, rue de la Fidélité (tel. 45 23 26 26). Mo. Gare du Nord. Emphasis is on wine, rather than food. Entrées are simple, but good and very French *(pâté,* medallions of veal and duck, etc.). Of course, all this is secondary to the primary attraction: good wine at good prices. Specializes in wines from Franche Comté, Savoie, Jura, and Alsace. 29cl glass 9F, 45cl glass 18F. Dinner à la carte runs 120F. Open Mon.-Fri. 12:30-3pm and 7:30pm-1:30am, Sat.-Sun. 7:30pm-1:30am.

**Le Chant de la Terre,** 29, rue du Château d'Eau (tel. 42 49 39 08). Mo. Château d'Eau or J. Bonsergent. A vegetarian, smoke-free restaurant, located in a courtyard. Lunchtime self-service is a good bet for the healthful budgeteer fleeing from the bustle of the *gare* or place de la République. Daily specials 35F. 3-course *menu* 60F. Open Mon.-Fri. noon-2:30pm. Open Sept.-July.

**Le Dogon,** 30, rue René Boulanger (tel. 42 41 95 85). Mo. République. Elegant African restaurant steps away from place de la République. White walls, dark wood, and batiks serve as the backdrop for sumptuous cuisine made affordable by a 55F lunch *menu*. Otherwise about 160F à la carte. Open Sun.-Fri. 11:30am-2:30pm and 7pm-1am, Sat. 11:30am-2:30pm.

**Le Palais de l'Est,** 186, rue du Faubourg St-Martin (tel. 46 07 09 99; fax 42 09 34 69). Mo. Château Landon. This exotically decorated place specializes in Chinese and Vietnamese cuisine. More expensive than many of its counterparts, it serves up big plates of light, tasty food, including a wide variety of *dim sum*. Good late-night option for hungry itinerants, located one *métro* stop north of Gare de l'Est. Karaoke gets the crowd on its feet. Dinner à la carte for around 170F; lunch *menu* 48F, dinner 68F and 78F. Open daily noon-3pm and 7pm-5am. Take-out available.

**Paris-Dakar,** 95, rue du Faubourg St-Martin (tel. 42 08 16 64). Mo. Gare de l'Est. Run by a Senegalese family, this place is extremely popular among Parisians who keep coming back to what is heralded as "the most African of all African restaurants." Brochettes and curries abound; *Tiep Bou Dieone*—the "national dish of Senegal"—is recommended. Prepare to feast. Dinner à la carte costs up to 150F. 59F lunch *menu* is more economical. Waiters walk you through the menu. Open daily noon-4pm and 7pm-midnight. Credit cards accepted, except AmEx.

**Restaurant de Bourgogne,** 26, rue des Vinaigriers (tel. 46 07 07 91). Mo. Château d'Eau, J. Bonsergent, or Gare de l'Est. Calico curtains, hearty traditional food, and service with a smile. 3-course lunch *menu* 55F (60F at night) includes old reliables: roast pork, ham omelettes, and grilled *andouillette*. 75cl house red 30F. Open Mon.-Fri. noon-2:30pm and 7-10:30pm, Sat. noon-2:30pm. Open Sept.-July.

**Texas Blues,** 54, rue René Boulanger (tel. 42 08 60 20). Mo. République. A laidback Tex-Mex shrine to food you never tire of and bikes you love to ride. Slick photos of even slicker Harleys complement the 80F 3-course *menu*. The *assiette dégustation* is a filling choice, with chili, tacos, pork, guacamole, and red beans. American and Mexican beer 25F per bottle. Beer on tap 15F. Blues or rock 'n roll Fri.-Sat. at 10pm. Open Mon.-Fri. noon-2pm and 7-11pm, Sat.-Sun. noon-2pm.

**Thamouline,** 12, rue Arthur Grossier (tel. 42 49 31 11). Mo. Goncourt. An inviting, refined restaurant, more expensive and *métro* stops away from passage Brady. Waitresses in saris invite you to sample spicy Sri Lankan and Indian cuisine. Cream-colored interior lined with kitschy murals. 3-course 45F lunch *menu*, 85F in evening; mention *Let's Go* and get free drink with meal. Take-out available. Beef or lamb *masala* 45F. *Kottu Roti*, Sri Lankan *galette* with eggs, vegetables, or roasted meat 39-45F. Open Mon.-Sat. 11:30am-3pm and 7-11pm, Sun. 7-11pm.

## ELEVENTH ARRONDISSEMENT

The eleventh is not the Paris of *hôtel particuliers* or strolls through the park with a parasol. This is post-museum, post-rock-'n-roll chic. The only things retro are the fashions, the prices, and the traditional, home-cooked food. Restaurants cater to the *arrondissement*'s youthful appetites and budgets.

**A la Banane Ivoirienne,** 10, rue de la Forge-Royale (tel. 43 70 49 90). Mo. Faidherbe-Chaligny. Run by a gregarious Ivoirian emigré—he wrote his doctoral thesis on his country's banana industry. Cheerful place. Delicious West African specialties, such as *attieke*, made from cassava, and *aloko*, from bananas. Stuffed *crabs à l'Abgidinaise* 30F. Entrées 49-80F. *Menu* 89F. Open Tues.-Sat. 7pm-midnight.

**Au Petit Keller,** 13, rue Keller (tel. 47 00 12 97). Mo. Ledru-Rollin. Traditional bistro in the heart of the vibrant Bastille district. Filling, wholesome food, extremely popular with locals of all backgrounds—everyone looks like a regular. 60F *menu* includes beer or wine. *Gâteau de riz* (rice cake) is the house specialty. Open Mon.-Fri. noon-2:30pm and 7-11pm.

**Au Trou Normand,** 9, rue Jean-Pierre Timbaud (tel. 48 05 80 23). Mo. Oberkampf. More than the hole in the wall that the name indicates. Indeed, a veritable neighborhood institution, with orange tablecloths and unbelievably low-priced no-fuss French food. Youthful lunch crowd of regulars. The *onglet rocquefort* and *frites* (30F) is a favorite. Have the banana tart or Mme. may be insulted. Appetizers 9-13F, *plats du jour* 29-39F, tasty desserts 9-13F. Open Mon.-Fri. noon-2:30pm and 7:30-11pm, Sat. 7:30-11pm. Open Sept.-July.

**Chez Justine,** 96, rue Oberkampf (tel. 43 57 44 03). Mo. St-Maur. Log-cabin interior ushers in mostly tourists for food like *grand-mère* used to make. 2nd floor dining room good for parties of 12-20. Lunch (68F) and dinner (95F) *menus* include fabulous appetizer spreads on the *table d'hôte*. Other appetizers 45-60F, *plats* 58-100F. Open Mon.-Sat. noon-2:30pm and 7-10:30pm. Open mid-Aug. to mid-July.

**Chez Paul,** 13, rue de Charonne (tel. 47 00 34 57). Mo. Charonne, Ledru-Rollin, or Bastille. You have to see the late-night crowds to believe people can have so much fun eating. Friendly staff serves perfectly prepared heaps of traditional fare. Don't come for intimacy. This place never stops serving up the fun to a deliriously happy Parisian crowd. Appetizers 30-50F. Entrees 60-80F. Open Mon.-Sat. noon-2:30pm and 7:15pm-2am, food served until 12:30am. Open Sept.-July.

**La Courtille,** 16, rue Guillaume Bertrand (tel. 48 06 48 34). Mo. St-Maur. Peach surroundings for a chic yuppie crowd. Named for the hamlet of Courtille to which 18th-century Belleville residents fled to replenish themselves during Ash Wednesday celebrations. Lunch *menu* 72F; 118F at night. Appetizers 34-50F, *plats* 66-82F, dessert 32F. Open Mon.-Fri. noon-2pm and 7:45-10pm, Sat. 7:45-10pm.

**Occitanie,** 96, rue Oberkampf (tel. 48 06 46 98). Mo. St-Maur. Rough weave material over wooden tables provides perfect setting to indulge in specialties from the south of France. 3-course Midday *formule* at 50F gets you the ever-delectable *pâté de campagne*, wine, and coffee. Entrées 30-50F, *plats* 45-92F. Open Mon.-Fri. noon-2pm and 7-10:30pm, Sat. 7-10:30pm. Open mid-Aug. to mid-July.

**La Palette,** 116, av. Ledru-Rollin (tel. 47 00 34 39). Mo. Ledru-Rollin or Bastille. Built in 1900, this bistro is a lively neighborhood haunt and Art Nouveau period piece. National landmark and corner hangout. Dine on light fare amid carved wood arabesques and fleshy murals. Omelettes 20-32F. Salads 30-50F. *Confit de canard* with sautéed apples 69F. Night owls with Wilde enthusiasm keep bistro up late. Open Mon.-Sat. noon-2am, food served until midnight, Sun. noon-9:30pm.

**Le Passage,** 18, passage de la Bonne-Graine (tel. 47 00 73 30). Mo. Ledru-Rollin. A hidden Bastille restaurant for connoisseurs of wine. Assorted *andouillettes* and hitherto-unknown entrées: try the *pieds Janet*, pigs feet cooked in *fois gras*. Daily specials on chalkboard are cheaper than main dishes on menu; specials 60F, entrées otherwise about 70F. Wine by the glass of the week's chosen vintage; hard-core oenophiles should inquire about regular wine-tasting events. Open Mon.-Fri. noon-3:30pm and 7:30-11:30pm, Sat. 7:30-11:30pm.

**Le Val de Loire,** 149, rue Amelot (tel. 47 00 34 11). Mo. Filles du Calvaire or Oberkampf. Locals share tables with tourists from nearby hotels. Nondescript décor and standard French fare: 57F *menu* includes a *kir* and a phenomenal buffet of appetizers. *Menu* at 105F adds an opening *terrine*. Open Mon.-Sat. noon-2:30pm and 6:45-10pm. Open Sept.-July.

# TWELFTH ARRONDISSEMENT

**Au Limonaire,** 88, rue de Charenton (tel. 43 43 49 14). Mo. Ledru-Rollin or Gare de Lyon. Light bulbs strung outside match the festive feeling inside this bistro/folk music venue. This place was founded in 1890 as Au Pissenlair, and has changed hands several times since. Well-used chairs and nifty pictures add to the ambience created by tasty regional cuisine and fine wines from the Rhône Valley. Appetizer and main dish *menu* 55F. Dessert 23-28F. Wed.-Sat. from 10-11pm, when folk musicians perform live on accordion, violin, and guitar; repertoire runs from Brel to burlesque. Reservations encouraged. Drop by to pick up monthly schedule. Open daily noon-3pm and 6pm-midnight; Aug. Tues.-Sat. same hours.

**Joël's,** 22, rue de Cotte (tel. 43 43 88 20). Mo. Ledru-Rollin. A restaurant decked out in blue and yellow, bringing specialties from the southwestern province of Tarn to young Parisian crowds. All the *foie gras* you could want. 60F lunch *menu* includes appetizer, entrée, and dessert picked from the *ardoise* (chalkboard). 3-

course 86F dinner *menu* features pâté, trout, and the house *crème caramel*. For those long on funds and appetite, the 4-course 155F *menu gastronomique* stars a fabulous *pavé de boeuf à la mousse de foie gras*. A la carte, try the *magret de canard aux pêches* (82F) or *foie gras* for 2 (140F). Open Mon.-Thurs. noon-2:30pm and 7-11pm, Fri. noon-2:30pm and 7pm-midnight, Sat. 7pm-midnight.

**Le Parrot,** 5, rue Parrot (tel. 43 43 05 64). Mo. Gare de Lyon. High-ceilinged, wood-paneled, mirrored dining room welcomes a local crowd for good French food at good French prices. 54F *menu* includes appetizer, *plat*, and dessert. Open Mon.-Sat. 11:30am-2:45pm and 7-10pm, Sun. 7-10pm.

**Le Rocher du Diamant,** 284, rue de Charenton (tel. 40 19 08 78). Mo. Dugommier or Daumesnil. A burst of chic on the Paris outskirts with cuisine from Antilles and a décor that takes you there—palms and paintings of seasides set the scene for seafood specials. A la carte will set you back, but 92F 2-course lunch *menu* includes a choice of *colombos* (otherwise 80F). Try the *marmites des Caraïbes* (240F), a savory and much touted assortment of seafood. Appetizers 35-50F, entrées 80-100F, desserts 40-45F. Open daily 11am-3pm and 7pm-1am.

## THIRTEENTH ARRONDISSEMENT

It's Chinatown, but if you've got your heart set on a pu-pu platter, fortune cookies, or free tea, take the first flight out to New York or San Francisco. Because of the ethnic mix south of place d'Italie, it's probably even erroneous to call this *arrondissement* Chinatown. In the thirteenth, Chinese, Cambodians, Vietnamese, Thai, Laotians, and Taiwanese have brought together centuries of their family recipes and the result is eclectic, inexpensive, and delicious. *Pâtisseries* in this area carry such delights as *biscuits aux amandes* (almond cookies) and *beignets sesames* (fried dough covered in sesame seeds and filled with nuts and honey). *Dim sum*, known as *cuisine à la vapeur,* is a delicacy. Head to Asian supermarkets like Tang Frères to put together an exotic, atypical picnic (see Groceries).

**Cap St-Jacques,** 105, av. d'Ivry (tel. 45 86 06 72). Mo. Tolbiac. This new establishment, tastefully decorated in tones of salmon and gray instead of the usual red glitz, serves up the best authentic Vietnamese food in Paris. Spicy soup specialties like their beautifully prepared rice noodles with beef and vegetables (32F). Maybe the best restaurant in the 13*ème*. Open Tues.-Sun. 11:30am-3pm and 6:30-11pm.

**Château de Choisy,** 44-46, av. de Choisy (tel. 45 82 40 60). Mo. Porte de Choisy. Not the utmost in gourmet Chinese food, this restaurant relies on its specialty, an all-you-can-eat buffet (55F lunch, 72F dinner), to attract the hordes of customers that pack in here. Their offerings include spring rolls, beef lo mein, tangy salads, and chicken with lychees nuts. Open daily noon-2:30pm and 6:30-11pm.

**Lao Thai,** 128, rue Tolbiac (tel. 43 31 98 10). Mo. Tolbiac. A small Thai restaurant that fills up quickly with hordes of faithful Thai and French customers. Their 46F50 *menu* (lunch only) includes appetizer, main dish, rice, and dessert or coffee. Dinner *menus* 184-198F (for 2 people). Open Thurs.-Tues. noon-2:30pm and 7-11:15pm. MC, V.

**L'Oiseau de Paradi,** 44-46, rue du Javelot (tel. 45 83 46 17), in the cement pagoda structure set back from the street at 101, rue Tolbiac (go up the escalator and walk straight ahead). Mo. Tolbiac. A gourmet Chinese restaurant where you can dine outside in warm weather on fantastic creations like stuffed crab claws (60F). It's more expensive than some of the other restaurants in the area, but the food is worth it. Open Mon.-Sat. noon-3pm and 6-11:30pm. AmEx, MC, V.

**Phuong Hoang,** 52, rue du Javelot (tel. 45 84 75 07). Mo. Tolbiac. Vietnamese and Thai specialties in a subdued, almost elegant setting without the high prices. Dine upstairs for a better view of the aluminum pagoda-esque building and the cement skyscrapers across the way. Satisfying lunch *menus* 50-70F including wine. Dinner à la carte gets a little pricey. AmEx, MC, V.

**Tricotin,** 15, av. de Choisy (tel. 45 84 74 44), in the building labeled "le Kiosque de Choisy." Mo. Porte-de-Choisy. Whatever you're craving, the two branches of this restaurant have it. They face each other, serving Cambodian, Vietnamese, and Thai cuisine between them. Their décor bears a haunting resemblance to an Asian

Denny's, but you'll forget the comparison as you sit side-by-side with other happy customers at long tables, slurping up noodles (30-40F) and feasting on *dim sum* (starting at 30F), rumored to be the best around. One side open Wed.-Mon. 11am-2:30pm and 6:30-11:30pm, the other 9:30am-11:30pm. AmEx, MC, V.

## FOURTEENTH ARRONDISSEMENT

The budget traveler is forever indebted to the Bretons, the French from the northwest whose exodus to Paris at the turn of the century carried them to Montparnasse. The *crêpes* and *galettes* (a larger, buckwheat version) which they brought with them are easy to find, easy to eat, and even easier on the wallet. Don't be tempted to settle for an overcooked *biftek* and limp *frites* at one of the hundreds of utterly forgettable restaurants that cluster around the Tour de Montparnasse.

**Aquarius Café,** 40, rue de Gergovie (tel. 45 41 36 88). Mo. Pernety. Serene vegetarian restaurant, where wood tables and an exceptionally friendly staff enhance a politically correct meal. The famous "mixed grill" includes tofu sausages, cereal sausages, wheat pancakes, wheat germ, brown rice and vegetables in a mushroom sauce for 65F. Or get your vitamins via an Aquarius salad (55F) with *chèvre*, avocado, egg, vegetable pâté, potato salad, *crudités,* and vinaigrette. 3-course lunch *menu* 60F. Open Mon.-Sat. noon-2:30pm and 7-10:30pm. AmEx, MC, V.

**Le Château Poivre,** 145, rue du Château (tel. 43 22 03 68). Mo. Pernety. The proud owner takes his food very seriously, and the generous portions, enhanced by 80 varieties of wine, will encourage you to do the same. 89F *menu* (lunch and dinner) features *escargots, truite belle manière, gigot d'agneau, crème caramel,* and *mousse au chocolat.* Open Mon.-Sat. noon-3pm and 7-11pm. MC, V.

**Le Colvert,** 129, rue du Château (tel. 43 27 95 19). Mo. Penerty. This tiny restaurant, frequented by locals in the know, is covered with ducks—they're on the walls, on the plates, and sitting (ceramic, of course) on the shelves. Even a quacking duck telephone. Beautifully presented, large portions of classic French fare. You will waddle out of here satisfied. Lunch *menu* 60F (wine included). Dinner *menus* 90-143F. Open Mon.-Fri. 11:30am-2:30pm and 7-11pm, Sat. 7-11pm.

**Crêperie Le Biniou,** 3, av. du Général Leclerc (tel. 43 27 20 40). Mo. Denfert-Rochereau. Decorated in the starkest tones of yellow, blue, and white, but its twist on the traditional *crêpe* is far from minimalist. Unusual combinations of calamari or mussels with curry, or more mainstream cheese, egg, and ham. Top off your dinner with a killer pear, chocolate, and chantilly *crêpe.* Main course and dessert *crêpes* at 22-35F. Open Tues.-Sat. 11:45am-2:30pm and 6:45-10pm.

**Crêperie St-Malo,** 53, rue de Montparnasse (tel. 43 20 87 19). Mo. Edgar Quinet. Your mouth will water as you head down this street which boasts perhaps a higher concentration of *crêpes* and *galettes* than in all of Brittany. This restaurant offers the most promising *menu*—*galette*, dessert *crêpe,* hard cider and coffee 49F. Open Mon.-Fri. noon-3pm and 6pm-1am, Sat.-Sun. noon-midnight.

**Le Jerobam**, 72, rue Didot (tel. 45 39 39 13), off rue d'Alésia. Mo. Plaisance. Authentic, comfortable French restaurant serving superb traditional fare at unbeatable prices. Frescoed pastoral scenes on the ceiling give this place a homey touch. Lunch *menu* at 65F includes delectable dishes such as *Tarine de Poisson aux olives et citron confit* (a fish stew with preserved lemons and olives). Dinner *menu* 95F. Open Tues.-Sat. noon-2pm and 7-10pm, Mon. noon-2pm. MC, V.

**N'Zadette-M'foua,** 152, route du Château (tel. 43 22 00 16). Mo. Pernety. A well-received break from traditional French fare can be had at this lively restaurant specializing in Congolese cuisine. You'll be smiling after a "Sourire Congolais," a fish, tomato, pineapple, and cucumber concoction (42F). The daring will want to sample a *maboke*, meat or fish cooked in a wrapper of banana leaves. African relics and woven wall hangings will take your mind to sunnier climates, far from that infernal Parisian drizzle. *Menu* at 85F. Open daily noon-3pm and 8pm-midnight.

**Restaurant Le Berbère,** 50, rue de Gergovie (tel. 45 42 10 29). Mo. Pernety. A serious selection of Moroccan specialties, including hearty couscous with chicken or beef for just 50F. Save room to attack the glorious dessert tray, which supports an amazing array of fantastic sugar creations, such as the honey-laden baklava (20F). Open Mon.-Sat. noon-2:30pm and 7-10:30pm. AmEx, MC, V.

**Restaurant au Rendez-Vous des Camionneurs,** 34, rue des Plantes (tel. 45 40 43 36), off rue d'Alésia. Mo. Alésia. A low-key establishment with more emphasis on food than on décor (plain chairs and checkered tablecloths), but honest traditional fare at unbeatable prices. The 65F *menu* includes stuffed grape leaves, sausage in garlic, leg of lamb, and *civet de lapin* (rabbit stew). House wine starts at 6F50 a glass. Open Mon.-Fri. 12:45-2:45pm and 6-9:30pm.

**La Route du Château,** 123, rue du Château (tel. 43 20 09 59). Mo. Pernety. This tiny bistro more than makes up for what its location lacks in ambience. Classy, authentic décor with food to match. Specialties include *langue de boeuf* and rabbit sautéed with cider. *Menu* 80F, and definitely worth it. Open Mon. 7:30pm-2am., Tues.-Sat. noon-2pm and 7:30pm-2am. AmEx, MC, V.

## FIFTEENTH ARRONDISSEMENT

Eateries in this *arrondissement* remain treasured local establishments, where owners personally welcome their regulars to their usual tables and then lovingly detail the specials of the day. Traditional bistros, complete with oak and brass bars and mirrored walls dot the area around bd. de Grenelle and the rue du Commerce. The food tends to be rich, heavy in chicken and beef dishes in thick gravy sauces.

**Bistro Bourdelle,** 12, rue Bourdelle (tel. 45 48 57 01). Mo. Montparnasse-Bienvenue. A traditional small, dark bistro where many dignified old men come to pass lunch hour drinking decent house wine and feasting on the impeccably prepared dishes of meat and fish. 90F *menu* includes such house specialties as *salade de choux et champignons* (warm salad with cabbage and mushrooms) and *quenelles de brochet* (*crêpe* with fish). Open Mon.-Fri. noon-2:30pm, 7-10:30pm.

**Le Bouquet de Grenelle,** 78, av. de la Motte-Picquet (tel. 47 34 30 01). Mo. La Motte-Picquet-Grenelle. This corner *brasserie* is one of the best places to hang out and watch the bustle of provincial life in the 15*ème*. It also has an affordable *brasserie* menu of *crêpes* (18-36F), omelettes (25-45F), and sandwiches (18-32F). Coffee 10F. *Café au lait* 19F. Open daily 8am-2am.

**Café Aux Artistes,** 63, rue Falguière, (tel. 43 22 05 39). Mo. Falguière. Cheap restaurant with an extensive menu, where you can eat with your compatriots (whether they be Canadian, Australian, British, German, or American), while perusing posters of Ronald Reagan in his younger, better days. The low prices and late hours attract less discriminating palates; gourmets may want to keep looking. Lunch menu 54F, dinner 72F. Open Mon.-Fri. noon-2pm and 7pm-1am.

**Café du Commerce,** 51, rue du Commerce (tel. 45 75 03 27). Mo. La Motte-Picquet-Grenelle. This venerable Paris institution has been around for over 30 years, offering great food at decent prices. The 3-level interior surrounds a central atrium courtyard with overflowing vines and flowers. Bright, airy, and surprisingly full, this café-restaurant has an 88F *menu* (2 courses) and a 114F *menu* (3 courses) which feature *éscalope de saumon, cuisse du porc à l'ancienne,* and *mousse au chocolat.* Open daily noon-midnight.

**Phetburi,** 31, bd. de Grenelle (tel. 48 58 14 88). Mo. Motte Picquet-Grenelle. The place to go if you're suffering from Thai food withdrawal. Not the place to go if you're averse to lemon grass—specialties include lemon grass fish soup, lemon grass squid salad, lemon grass beef.... Lunch *menu* (68F), dinner *menu* (89F). Open Mon.-Sat. noon-2:30pm and 7-10:45pm.

**Restaurant Les Listines,** 24, rue Falguière (tel. 45 38 57 40). Mo. Falguière or Pasteur. A pink and green interior and a delicious menu of *saumon aux herbes, cuisses de canard, boeuf à la moutarde ancienne,* and other French delights. The 70F *menu* gives you a main course and appetizer or dessert. 130F *menu* offers all 3 courses. Open Mon.-Sat. noon-2:30pm and 7-10:30pm.

**Samaya,** 31, bd. de Grenelle (tel. 45 77 44 44). Mo. Dupleix. A small eatery specializing in Lebanese cuisine. Tasteful peach interior with dried flowers. 62F *menu* and 85F *menu* feature *taboulé, labaa concombre* (yogurt with cucumber), hummus, and lamb delicacies. Mint tea (10F) and a wide range of Middle Eastern desserts such as *baklava* (24F) and *Maihalabien* (a flan flavored with orange, 20F). Open Mon. and Thurs. 7pm-midnight, Tues.-Wed. and Fri.-Sun. noon-midnight.

**Sampieru Corsu,** 12, rue de l'Amiral Roussin. Mo. Cambronne. Run by a Marxist Corsican separatist, as you can see from articles and posters on the walls. Simple tables which you might share with other visitors. Pay according to your means, though the suggested price for the simple, but copious, 3-course *menu* is 40F (beer or wine included). On some nights there is entertainment, and you should give a little extra for the artist. Open Mon.-Fri. noon-2pm and 7-9:30pm.

**Le Tahar,** 166, bd. de Grenelle (tel. 43 06 44 65). Mo. La Motte-Picquet-Grenelle. The simple décor and print curtains of this Mediterranean restaurant belie the wonderful menu. The 69F *formule méditerranéenne* features *sardine grillées, tomates basilic,* and *chèvre* with *escalope de volaille roquefort* and *poêle de gigot d'agneau aux poivres et olives.* House specialty *sole fondu de plaisir* 79F. Open daily 9am-3pm and 7pm-1am.

## SIXTEENTH ARRONDISSEMENT

The 16*ème arrondissement* is not the place to go for a cheap meal. You can buy food for a feast at the European supermarket chain, **Leader Price,** on the western end of rue Lauriston. Otherwise, check out the *menus* at these restaurants, many of which are located on the beautiful, illuminated place Victor Hugo.

**Bistro Romain,** 6, pl. Victor Hugo (tel. 45 00 65 03). Mo. Victor Hugo. This Italian bistro features 4 *menus* at 60F, 76F, 89F, and 130F. The 76F *menu* includes a *terrine de saumon maison, foie gras de canard,* or *carpaccio de boeuf à basilic.* The 89F *menu St. Tropez* features a stout glass of port, a refreshing melon and grapefruit salad, and *langoustines fraîche au mayonnaise.* Open Mon.-Fri. noon-2:30pm and 7-10:30pm, Sat.-Sun. noon-2:30pm and 7pm-midnight.

**Les Chauffeurs,** 8, chaussée de la Muette (tel. 42 88 50 05). Mo. La Muette. The checkered tablecloths will make you feel at home no matter where you're from, but the scenes of Paris sketched on the wall will remind you of where you actually are. The local professional crowd packs in at lunch for the 65F *menu* and 20F bottles of wine. Open daily 5:30am-10pm or midnight; call ahead.

**Chez Didier,** 18, pl. Victor Hugo (tel. 45 01 76 95). Mo. Victor Hugo. Delicious food in an elegant Portuguese and French restaurant, run by M. Didier Veloso, a French-Portuguese Gide and Pessoa scholar. Décor and the food are very *BCBG* and very 16*ème.* Try *pasta carbonara, glace mystère,* and a glass of Portuguese *porto.* 65F, 85F, and 110F *menus.* Open Mon.-Sat. noon-2:30pm and 7-11pm.

**Man Lung,** 10, bd. Delessert (tel. 45 20 47 17). Mo. Passy. Quality Pekinese dishes served at long wood tables inside and on the terrace. A favorite of Yves Montand and Peter Ustinov, it can be yours too, for the price is right: 69F *menu* includes a starter, a main meal, dessert, and drink. Anything with duck is especially worth trying. English spoken. French isn't. Open daily noon-3pm and 7-11pm.

**Scossa,** 8, pl. Victor Hugo (tel. 45 01 73 67). Mo. Victor Hugo. A bit expensive, but elegant and luxurious, this Italian restaurant is one of the 16*ème's* finest. Sit outside on the spacious veranda overlooking the place. The 175F is a stretch but worth it for the gazpacho, *saumon grillé sauce béarnaise,* and *tarte aux pommes,* with a ½ pitcher of *rosé.* Open Mon.-Sat. noon-2:30pm and 7-11:30pm.

**Le Victor Hugo,** 4, pl. Victor Hugo (tel. 45 00 87 55). Mo. Victor Hugo. This neighborhood *brasserie* is the cheapest deal in the 16*ème.* The zinc bar and café tables are basic and bare, but you can find salads for 46-52F, sandwiches for 58-60F, and a large variety of sundaes for 32-48F. Other specialties include *poulet fermier et frites* (62F), *coquilles St-Jacques à la crème, riz créole* (88F), and *grenadine de veau jurasienne* (78F). Open Mon.-Fri. 10am-10pm, Sat.-Sun. 10am-midnight.

## SEVENTEENTH ARRONDISSEMENT

The 17*ème* offers a number of restaurants from varied regions of the world, especially on bd. Pereire (Mo. Porte Maillot), across from the Palais des Congrès.

**L'Epicerie Verte,** 5, rue Saussier Leroy (tel. 47 64 19 68). Mo. Ternes. This literally green grocery sells vegetarian food and runs an excellent lunch counter. Even unyielding carnivores may want to try their salads (20-35F) and quiche (45F). 2 warm dishes served daily. Order to go or grab one of the 9 spots at the long table. Save even more money by making your own lunch from the market's vegetables. Open Mon.-Sat. 9:45am-8pm; food served Mon.-Sat noon-7pm. Open Sept.-July.

**Grill Churrasco,** 277, bd. Pereire (tel. 40 55 92 00), across from the Palais des Congrès. Mo. Porte Maillot. Lively and festive Mexican restaurant which features 3 *menus*. The 77F *menu* "Idée Churrasco" consists of gazpacho soup and *noix d'entrecôte grillé;* the 88F "Idée Cavaliero" serves *moules churrasco* and *brochette de rumsteack;* and the 99F "Idée Gringo" offers *empanada de queso* with *bife de chorizo grillé.* Bar serves sangria (20F), piña coladas (30F), and margueritas (32F). Open Sun.-Thurs. 11:45am-midnight, Fri.-Sat. 11:45am-1am.

**Joy in Food,** 2, rue Truffaut (tel. 43 87 96 79), on the corner of rue des Dames. Mo. Place de Clichy. A vegetarian restaurant dedicated not only to taking care of your body—with quiches and brown rice (30-50F)—but also your mind: their card reads *"Chaque incarnation humaine est la continuation de l'historie inachevée de Dieu."* (Every human incarnation is the continuation of God's incomplete history.) A small interior and open kitchen area let you watch the chef whip up salads, omelettes, milkshakes, herbal teas, and fruit *tartes.* Lunch *menu* (43F) includes a steamed-vegetable appetizer, ratatouille, and an omelette. Larger 69F *menu* includes an appetizer, a main course, and dessert. Weekly meditation session Wed. at 8pm. Open Mon.-Fri. noon-3pm, Tues. and Fri.-Sat. 7-10:30pm.

**Laurier de Chine,** 278, bd. Pereire (tel. 45 74 33 32), near the Palais des Congrès. Mo. Porte Maillot. Elegant Chinese restaurant with white linen tablecloths and carved red cherry wood chairs serving an 80F *menu* of *poulet citron* or *boeuf aux ciguans chinoises,* with a peking ravioli appetizer, rice, and dessert. Entrées such as *canard chinoi*s 59-75F. Open Mon.-Sat. noon-2:30pm and 7-10:45pm.

**Restaurant Natacha,** 35, rue Guersant (tel. 45 74 23 86). Mo. Porte Maillot. Another restaurant offering an extraordinary lunch *menu* with an hors d'œuvres buffet (mostly raw vegetables), a filling second course of fish or a *grillade,* as well as dessert for only 78F. Dinner 95F. Open Mon. 7-11:30pm, Tues.-Fri. noon-2:30pm and 7:30-11:30pm, Sat. 7:30-11:30pm. Call ahead for reservations.

**Sangria Restaurant,** 13bis, rue Vernier (tel. 45 74 78 74). Mo. Porte de Champerret. A budget traveler's dream of a restaurant, with a self-serve hors d'œuvres buffet, truly copious and mouth-watering main dishes—including juicy steaks and char-grilled swordfish—as much wine as you want (lunch only), and desserts like chocolate mousse to top it off, all for only 75F at lunch, 85F at dinner. Open Mon.-Fri. noon-2pm and 7-11pm, Sat. 7-11pm.

**Spécialités Turques,** 76, av. Clichy. Mo. Place de Clichy. Actually, this isn't the name of the place, but this tiny Middle Eastern stand complete with a couple of tables in the back doesn't have a name, so you'll have to identify it by what's emblazoned on the awning. The owner/cook bakes fresh bread for his huge *shwarma* submarine sandwiches, which come with fries, hot sauce, tomatoes, and onions. Together with a drink, this will cost you only 27F (and you'll have enough left over for your next two meals). Open Mon.-Sat. 11am-10pm.

## EIGHTEENTH ARRONDISSEMENT

Although the cafés and restaurants of the place du Tertre tend to be pricey because of their popular tourist-draw, they make a great place to sit and have an inexpensive *café crème* or a *kir.* But if you're looking for a place to eat, walk down the *butte* towards the cheaper eateries that dot the hillside's winding streets.

**Au Pierre de la Butte,** 41, rue Caulaincourt (tel. 46 06 06 97). Mo. Lamarck-Caulaincourt. This restaurant which overlooks a garden serves great French food at reasonable prices. Popular with a local French crowd. *Artichauts au saumon à la crème fraîche, brochette de boeuf,* and a refreshing sorbet for 150F. Also a 70F lunch *menu* and a 90F dinner *menu.* Reservations recommended—this is a popular, though hidden, place. Open Mon.-Sat. noon-2pm and 7:30-11:30pm.

**Chez Claude et Claudine,** 94, rue des Martyrs (tel. 46 06 50 73). Mo. Abbesses. Grape-trellised, this intimate restaurant on a steep side street just below Sacré-Coeur has a small baby grand piano whose keys rarely remain idle. Feast on *côte de veau, saumon aux herbes,* or *magret de canard,* on the 100F, 120F, or 180F *menus.* There's also a 69F lunch *menu* with *soupe à l'oignon, boeuf bourguignon,* cheese, and dessert. Open daily 6-11:30pm.

**Chez Francis,** 122, rue Caulaincourt (tel. 42 64 60 62). Mo. Lamarck-Caulaincourt. Perched on the corner of a pleasant street, this restaurant commands a panoramic view of the city below and winding streets toward the Sacré-Coeur above. Indoor and outdoor seating. The house cuisine is from southwestern France, with such specialties as filet mignon, filet of sole, lamb, *jambon de Bayonne,* and *salade landaise* (a green salad with chunks of *foie gras* in it), and a 110F *menu.* Dinner à la carte about 250F. Reservations for dinner recommended. Open Thurs.-Mon. noon-3pm and 7pm-midnight, Wed. 7pm-midnight. Credit cards accepted.

**Chez les Fondues,** 17, rue des Trois Frères (tel. 42 55 22 65). Mo. Abbesses. Not the widest selection of food; in fact there are only two main dishes: *fondue bourguignonne* (meat fondue) and *fondue savoyarde* (cheese fondue). A small place—fun and crowded at night. The 80F *menu* includes appetizer, fondue, desserts (e.g. *ananas au kirsch*), and half *pichet* (jug) of wine. Open daily 5pm-2am.

**De Graziano,** 83, rue Lepic (tel. 46 06 84 77). Mo. Blanche. Some of the best Italian food in Paris in a restaurant tucked behind an iron gate in a pleasant garden, overshadowed by the Moulin de la Galette. Northern Italian food, with specialties of veal, seafood, and pasta. Lunch *menu* 70F; dinner *menu* 195F. A la carte about 350F (including wine, dessert, and coffee). Reservations recommended for dinner. Open daily noon-3pm and 7:30pm-midnight. Credit cards accepted.

**Le Petit Chose,** 41, rue des Trois Frères (tel. 42 64 49 15). Mo. Abbesses. This little restaurant, whose name means "whatchamacallit," is located in a former artist's studio. The atmosphere is warm and familiar, and the phonograph plays hits from the 1920s. Specializes in southwestern French cuisine, especially fish. 95F and 190F *menus* include *escargot de truite de mer, escargots de bourgogne, confit de canard,* and *fondue au chocolat.* Dinner à la carte runs 200F. Reservations recommended for dinner. Open Mon.-Sat. noon-2pm and 7-11:30pm.

# NINETEENTH ARRONDISSEMENT

Despite the ethnic diversity in the 19*ème,* it has not translated into an abundance of notable restaurants. In fact, due to the proliferation of high-rise housing and office buildings, eateries are few and far between. Along main drags such as rue de Crimée, corner cafés do abound. The eastern half of rue de Belleville harbors a string of *pâtisseries, épiceries,* and *boucheries,* while the western end leads into an Asian enclave with Chinese, Vietnamese, Thai, and Malaysian restaurants and groceries.

**Aux Arts et Sciences Réunis,** 161, av. Jean-Jaurès (tel. 42 40 53 18). Mo. Ourcq. The neighborhood clientele provides a very French atmosphere. The food comes quickly and is outstanding, traditional fare from southwestern France (try *foie gras* or *canard*). 3-course *menu* with wine only 57F. Open Sept.-June Mon.-Fri. 6am-9pm, Sat. 8am-pm (in July until 2pm).

**Ay, Caramba!,** 59, rue de Mouzaïa (tel. 42 41 23 80). Mo. Botzaris. Tex-Mex food has become quite fashionable among young Parisians, with the unfortunate consequence that it is almost always overpriced. Not so at this lively restaurant whose brightly colored walls make it visible from a mile away. Good food, fiesta atmosphere. Margueritas 37F. *Nachos caramba* (chips, cheese, *pico de gallo*, guacamole, and choice of beef, chicken, or *chile con carne*) 39F. Fajitas 79F. *Menus* 120-140F. Open Mon.-Thurs. 7:30-11pm, Fri.-Sun. noon-2:30pm and 7:30-11pm.

**Tai-Yien,** 5, rue de Belleville, 19*ème* (tel. 42 41 44 16). Mo. Belleville. The large size and simple decoration of this Chinese restaurant give it the atmosphere of an eating factory, but the excellent food compensates. Often packed, with a high proportion of Asian customers. Sautéed crab claws 58F. Rice is an extra 7F. 3-course *menu* 60F. Take-out available. Open daily 10am-2am. AmEx, MC, V.

## TWENTIETH ARRONDISSEMENT

**A la Courtille,** 1, rue des Envierges (tel. 46 36 51 59). Mo. Pyrénées. Traditional French cuisine (with a yuppie flavor) served on a charming terrace on a cobblestone square. From the edge of the square, look past the uninspiring modern architecture to the lovely slopes of the Parc de Belleville. Lunch *menus* at 70F and 100F available Mon.-Sat. A la carte appetizers 35-60F, entrées 70-85F, desserts 35-40F. Open daily 11am-11pm, although lunch service doesn't begin until noon.

**Au Sancerrois,** 39, rue Pelleport (tel. 43 61 49 19). Mo. Porte de Bagnolet. A merry crowd of old faithfuls salute the cuisine of Michel Zolli, the proprietor and cook, the finest chef in the *20ème arrondissement*. That, at least, is the opinion of the Confrérie Gastronomique de la Marmite d'Or, a society of food connoisseurs that has existed since the time of Richelieu. Nonetheless, the restaurant retains an unpretentious, familial air. *Menus* at 85F and 140F feature specialties from the French southwest. A la carte: *manchons de canard* 50F, *rognons de veau* 120F. Open Mon. noon-3pm, Tues.-Fri. noon-3pm and 7:30-10:30pm, Sat. noon-3pm and 7:30-11pm. Closed for 3 weeks in Aug.

**La Papaye,** 71, rue des Rigoles (tel. 43 66 65 24). Mo. Jourdain. Owner/chef has traveled the world over, serving an adventurous mix of Caribbean and South American specialties. *Menus* at 61F, 100F, and 149F feature a range of *colombos* (Caribbean curry dishes), grilled fish, and a delicious and light coconut cake, which hails from Brazil. A la carte entrées about 70F. Open Mon-Tues. and Thurs.-Fri. noon-2pm and 7pm until last customer, Sat.-Sun. open at 7pm. Groups of 10 or more may reserve for lunch on weekends.

# ■ Cafés

It may seem like there are more cafés in Paris than there are paintings in the Louvre. While this is obviously not true, you will find a café on almost every corner of the city. Their diverse styles range from the posh Art Deco hangout of film stars, clothing designers, and literati, to the hip outdoor meeting spot for students on the Left Bank, to the quiet neighborhood haunt where locals stop for a drink and some conversation before heading home from work. Despite what everyone says about the "fine art" of café sitting, you don't need to be a writer, a student, or a Parisian to enjoy the quiet retreat or boisterous carnival of Paris's cafés. Sitting in an outdoor café can be one of the best ways to see Paris. You can watch students debating Rousseau, French bus drivers contemplating a strike, lovers holding each other, and fine old ladies out for an afternoon tea. Cafés are also an excellent place simply to relax during a busy sight-seeing schedule or an visually trying day at the Louvre.

Cafés entered Parisian society in 1675 when **Le Procope** opened its doors to an eager coffee-drinking, cigarette-smoking crowd that included such luminaries as Montesquieu, Diderot, and Rousseau. Ever since Voltaire wrote some of his greatest works to the tune of 40 cups of coffee a day at Le Procope, the café has been an integral force in French political, social, cultural, academic, and literary life. Although they make their money selling drinks, their real function has been to provide a dry, comfortable place to write, think, meet friends, or plot revolutions in a city that has traditionally housed much of its population in dark, cramped apartments. In other words, it is perfectly acceptable to spend three hours in a café without concern that the management wants you to move on. While the world-famous cafés listed here were hangouts for the fashionable and the literati, hundreds of cafés across the city have catered to a widely varied clientele and often have widely varying prices. Cafés near monuments charge monumental prices for minimal atmosphere. The best seats in the theater of Parisian culture are the cafés on fashionable thoroughfares, such as the Champs-Elysées, bd. St-Germain, bd. Montparnasse, or rue de la Paix. They charge exorbitant prices (coffee 14-25F), but an intriguing crowd passes the sidewalk tables, providing hours of entertainment for the price of one cup.

More casual crowds frequent the more dilapidated, hidden spots where coffee is only 8F and the use of *argot* (slang) makes eavesdropping an educational challenge. Make sure the prices posted outside correspond to your budget. Prices in cafés are two-tiered, cheaper at the counter (*comptoir* or *zinc*) than in the seating area (*salle*). Both these prices should be posted. Coffee, beer, and wine are the staple café drinks, but there are other refreshing options. A *citron pressé* is a sour drink of freshly squeezed lemons (with sugar on the side); a *limonade* is a soda. Cafés also offer Coke, but be prepared to pay twice what you would in the U.S. You can also order a wide range of spring, mineral, and soda waters.

If you order a *café,* you will get a *demitasse* (a small cup) of very strong espresso with sugar on the side. While this is the popular choice of many Parisians who are interested in the *goût* (taste) and the perk that an espresso and a cigarette gives them, you might be disappointed. If you'd prefer a more familiar brew, order a *café crème,* which is coffee with milk (and not cream) plus sugar on the side. Some cafés still call this kind of coffee a *café au lait,* or a *café americain,* but in general *café crème* is more widely understood and acceptable. Realize, however, that even a *café crème* comes in a fairly small cup. If you'd prefer a large cup of coffee with milk and sugar (i.e. something you'd have in a New York coffee shop), order a *grand crème.* You'll pay more, but you may be more satisfied.

If you order a *demi* or a *pression* of beer, you'll get a pale lager on tap. You can also order bottled imported beer: Heineken and Tuborg are popular in Paris. A glass of red is the cheapest wine in a café (4-6F); white costs about twice as much.

Cafés are not suited to cheap meals, but snacks are usually quite economical. A *croque monsieur* (grilled ham-and-cheese sandwich), a *croque madame* (the same with a fried egg), and assorted omelettes cost about 15F. A more popular choice is a salad. Try the *salade niçoise,* the French version of a chef's salad, or a *chèvre chaud,* a salad with warm goat cheese. Cheaper varieties are the *salade verte* (read: lettuce) and *salade de tomates.* Check the posted menu before you sit down; some cafés (particularly the ones near the big monuments) will charge you 50F for a salad.

Also a note on courtesy. Contrary to popular belief, it is *not* appropriate to call a waiter *garçon.* Café waiters in Paris, unlike part-time teenage waiters and waitresses in the U.S., are in professional, career positions and take their job very seriously. They should be politely addressed as Monsieur or Madame.

**Café Beaubourg,** 100, rue St-Martin, 4ème (tel. 48 87 63 96). Mo. Rambuteau. Like its neighbor, Café Costes, the Beaubourg is an extremely chic place to hang out. Designed in black and gray marble, the Beaubourg has a huge outdoor terrace as well as two floors inside, providing an L.A.-style salon for drinking and talking. Excellent place to watch the carnival of outdoor musicians, dancers, and performers in front of the Centre Pompidou. Coffee 14F, tea (5 kinds) 25F, hot chocolate or cappuccino 30F, Vittel 30F. Open Mon.-Fri. 8am-1am, Sat.-Sun. 8am-2am.

**La Closerie des Lilas,** 171, bd. du Montparnasse, 6ème. Mo. Vavin. Exit the *métro* and walk 9 blocks down bd. du Montparnasse. This lovely flower-ridden café was the one-time favorite of Hemingway (a scene in *The Sun Also Rises* takes place here), and the Dadaïsts and Surrealists before him. Picasso came here weekly to hear Paul Fort recite poetry. Exquisite décor and a *terrasse* in summer. Gorgeous dark interior with baby grand piano and a huge vase of fresh wild flowers on it. A wildly expensive *menu,* but affordable drinks and desserts. Coffee 14F, red wine 26F, *marquise au chocolat* 50F. Open daily 11am-1:30am.

**Café Cosmos,** 101, bd. du Montparnasse, 6ème (tel. 43 26 74 36). Mo. Vavin. While this café is much newer and less famous than its neighbors, this place is fast becoming the nouveau Procope or Séléct. Its ultra-modern interior features blue neon hidden lighting, black tables, and slick black leather chairs. An elegant cabaret staircase will take you to the second floor tables. If you sit under the huge yellow awning and umbrellas on the street, you just might see a French producer or film mogul. This place is out of this world, and it's become a hot spot. Coffee 14F, *café crème* 23F, teas 22F, hot chocolate 22F. Menus at 59F, 89F, and 87F feature gazpacho, barbecued chicken, and some Tex-Mex options. Open daily 23 hrs.

**Café Costes,** 4-6, rue Berger, pl. des Innocents, 1er (tel. 45 08 54 39). Mo. Les Halles. Opened in 1905, Philippe Starck's strikingly modern café is a fashionable people-watching spot between Les Halles and Beaubourg. Right in front of the busy Fontaine des Innocents, this hip café has gray marble tables and steel Art Deco chairs. Coffee 16F, Heineken 24F, Coke 26F, Vittel 24F, sandwiches (i.e. ham and cheese) 26-30F. Open daily 8am-2am.

**La Coupole,** 102, bd. du Montparnasse, 14ème (tel. 43 20 14 20). Mo. Vavin. This enormous Art Deco café decorated in mirrors, modern sculpture, wooden chairs, and elegantly tiled floor is part café and part 1930s emporia restaurant. This café has seen the likes of Lenin, Stravinsky, Hemingway, and Einstein at its tables. The *menus* are outrageously expensive, but you can still afford a coffee (10F). *Café crème* 20F, beer 20-27F, sandwiches 15-25F. Open daily noon-2am.

**Café Danton,** 103, bd. St-Germain, 6ème (tel. 43 54 65 38). Mo. Odéon. Across the street from the Relais Odéon, and just as centrally located to the cinemas of l'Odéon, this student-filled Left Bank café is surprisingly less expensive than its neighbor across the boulevard. A special favorite of American students. Coffee 10F, *café crème* 16F, *grand crème* 19F, soda 21F, mineral water 17F, salads 22-50F, sandwiches 15-25F. Open Mon.-Fri. 8am-2am, Sat.-Sun. open 24 hrs.

**Les Deux Magots,** 6, pl. St-Germain-des-Prés, 6ème. Mo. St-Germain-des-Prés. Sartre's second choice and Simone de Beauvoir's first—the two first spotted each other here. Home to Parisian literati since its opening in 1875, this place is now a favorite of Parisian youth. Named after two Chinese porcelain figures *(magots),* this café has beautiful high ceilings, gilt mirrors, and 1930s Art Deco café décor. *Café Deux Magots* 21F, *café crème* 23F, *chocolat des Deux Magots* (a house specialty) 28F, beer 25-30F, ham sandwich 34F. Desserts such as *gâteau au chocolat amer* 40F, *tarte tatin chaude* 40F, assorted pastries 38F. Before you go, buy your Roland Barthes and Derrida at **La Lune,** the *hyper-chic* bookstore across the street, and brood over it as you drink your espresso. Café open daily 7am-1:30am.

**Le Dôme,** 108, bd. du Montparnasse, 14ème (tel. 43 35 25 81). Mo. Vavin. This illustrious café shares all the literati history and fame of its neighbors, but its smaller interior and elegant 1920s décor make it the best café on the boulevard. The swank interior boasts yellow marble tables, black and white photos from the 1920s and 30s, gilded mirrors with engravings of 1920s flappers, and stained-glass Victorian windows behind the bar. Hanging lamps are draped in bohemian sheer cloth and weighted with glass amulets. Coffee 12F, beer 18-28F, Vittel 18F, ham and cheese sandwiches 18F. Open Tues.-Sun. 8am-1:30am. Closed Sun. in Aug.

**Le Flore,** 172, bd. St-Germain, 6ème, next door to Les Deux Magots. It was here, in his favorite hangout, that Jean-Paul Sartre composed *L'être et le néant (Being and Nothingness).* Apollinaire, Picasso, André Breton, and even James Thurber also sipped their brew in this light and happy atmosphere. Coffee 22F, *café espresso spécial Flore* 21F, *café crème* 25F, Coke 32F, beers 38-40F, sandwiches (such as *jambon et gruyère*) 44F. Open daily 7am-1:30am.

**Le Fouquet's,** 99, av. des Champs-Elysées, 8ème (tel.47 23 70 60). Mo. George V. "Created" in 1899 and located in the shadow of the Arc de Triomphe, this is the premier gathering place for the Parisian *vedettes* (stars) of radio, television, and cinema. Tourists, oblivious to the celebrities drinking inside, bask on the *terrasse.* James Joyce dined here with relish. Bank-breaking coffee and a chance to be seen 35F. Entrées from 92F. Open daily 8am-midnight; food served noon-3pm and 1pm-midnight.

**Café de la Paix,** 2ème (tel. 40 07 30 12), at the corner of av. de l'Opéra and rue de la Paix. Mo. Opéra. This institution on the rue de la Paix (the most expensive piece of property on French Monopoly) has served a wealthy clientele ever since its founding in 1862. The elegant café occupies the terrace; inside, in the same building, are two restaurants owned by the same people. You probably don't have enough money to eat at the restaurants, but you may decide that 26F isn't too bad for a Coke on the terrace. The waiters are really friendly—a sign of true class. Coffee 19F, desserts such as *tarte aux fraises, gâteaux maison,* and assorted *glaces* 40-50F. Open daily 10am-1am.

**Le Procope,** 13, rue de l'Ancienne Comédie, 6ème (tel. 43 26 99 20). Mo. Odéon. This quiet café/restaurant was once frequented by the famous philosophers and writers whose figurines line its back wall. Founded in 1686 as the first café in the world, le Procope has been the stage for such weighty moments as Voltaire drinking 40 cups of coffee per day while drafting *Candide* and Marat expounding revolutionary strategy. But history has a price—a 299F *menu*. Frugal diners might choose the café, where less expensive *menus* are served. The 72F *menu* features a main course and a choice of appetizer or dessert; the 99F *menu* offers 3 courses and a choice of entrées such as *coquille de crevettes* or *steak tartare,* and desserts such as *panache de sorbets.* Coffee 14F, beer 21-28F. Open daily 11am-1am.

**La Rôtonde,** 105, bd. du Montparnasse, 6ème (tel. 43 26 48 26). Mo. Vavin. Busy and funky, this café greatly resembles its bd. du Montparnasse neighbors. The café serves a lovely breakfast (50F) that consists of tea, coffee, or hot chocolate, croissants, *confiture,* butter, and freshly squeezed orange juice. A great way to start your day. Coffee 10F, *le chocolat a l'ancienne* 24F (house specialty), *café au lait* 20F, teas 22F. Also a 159F lunch and diner *menu.* Open daily 8am-4am.

**Le Séléct,** 99, bd. du Montparnasse, 6ème (tel. 45 48 38 24). Mo. Vavin. Across the street from Le Coupole, this swank bistro-like café has seen a select few go on to international political, scientific, literary, and artistic fame, including Trotsky, Satie, Breton, Cocteau, and Picasso, who all hung out here regularly. Coffee 10F (in the morning), 14F (in the afternoon and evening), *café au lait* 22F, teas 20-24F, *kir* 16F, red wine (Bordeaux) 25F, beer 22-50F, *limonade* 24F, iced coffee 30F, ice cream and huge sundaes 48F. Open daily 8am-2:30am.

# ■ Salons de Thé

Less crowded and less famous than cafés, *salons de thé* are just as much a ritual of the Parisian *savoir vivre.* Here, sample a fresher, more extensive offering of light meals and exquisite pastries, and of course, the friendly pot of tea. For the panic-stricken traveler, *salons de thé* provide a multitude of relaxing *infusions* (herbal teas); try *menthe* (mint) or *verveine* (vervain).

**Angelina's,** 226, rue de Rivoli, 1er (tel. 42 96 47 10). Mo. Concorde or Tuileries. Two floors of mirrored luxury. Rumored to have the best chocolate in Paris, Angelina's reputation extends to its pastry (20-35F). Take tea (22-30F) in this holdover from the era when everyone knew how to hold a *demitasse* and remembered who poured. Try the Black Forest *millefeuille* or the *Opéra* (28F). Open Mon.-Fri. 9:30-7pm, Sat.-Sun. 9:30-7:30pm.

**A Priori Thé,** 35-37, Galerie Vivienne, 2ème (tel. 42 97 48 75). Mo. Bourse or Palais-Royal. Classy place to have a meal or just sip tea. Shielded from the city noise because it's tucked away in a pleasant *galerie* (see Sights—2ème). You can get to the *galerie* from 6, rue Vivienne, 4, rue des Petits Champs, or 5, rue de la Banque. Best to visit on weekdays. Desserts nod to both Europe and the U.S. Brownies here are a delicious treat. 1-course meals 75-85F range. Tea 22F. Open Mon.-Sat. noon-7pm, Sun. 1-7pm. Tea service starts at 3pm.

**L'Arbre à Canelle,** 57, Passage de Panoramas, 2ème (tel. 45 08 55 87). Mo. Rue Montmartre or Bourse. Pastry (26-29F), and 13 varieties of tea (18F) served in a refurbished 19th-century *galerie.* Try the apple crumble (28F). Salads 39-54F. Open Mon.-Sat. 10:30am-6:30pm.

**Dalloyau,** 2, pl. Edmond Rostand, 6ème (tel. 43 29 31 10). Mo. Luxembourg. Also at 99-101, Faubourg Saint-Honoré, 8ème, and other locations. This chic *pâtisserie* serves up light salads and lunches, but is known for its tantalizing array of hand-crafted dessert pastries (18-20F). Get them to go and nibble in the Jardin du Luxembourg. Young crowd on the terrace, 30+ upstairs. Open daily 8:30am-7:30pm.

**L'Ebouillanté,** 6, rue des Barres, 4ème (tel. 42 78 48 62). Mo. Pont Marie or St-Paul. One of the loveliest courtyards around makes for a dream of a terrace in summer. Take tea in this cobblestone alleyway and watch hours (and the monks from St-Gervais) go by. Salads (55F), *crêpes,* and blini are a cut above. Tea (20F), flavored coffees (33F). Homemade tarts and cakes (30F). Open Tues.-Sun. noon-8pm.

**Les Enfants Gâtés,** 43, rue des Francs-Bourgeois, 4ème (tel. 42 77 07 63). Mo. St-Paul or Chemin Vert. A *salon de thé* reinterpreted by the young and hip Marais crowd. Take tea (25F) or a lunch of blini or salad (50F). Champagne brunch is an event not to be missed if you have the cash (100-200F). Pastry 30F, *café crème* 22F. Brunch Sat.-Sun. Reservations recommended. Open Tues.-Sun. noon-8pm.

**Ladurée,** 16, rue Royale, 8ème (tel. 42 60 21 79). Mo. Concorde. The perfect spot for a sandwich (11F50-13F80) or an éclair (12F), under the painted ceiling in this bustling tea room. Famous for its macaroons (16F) and almond croissants (7F), Ladurée endures as *the* chic *salon de thé* near La Madeleine. Lunch served Mon.-Sat. 11:30am-3pm. Open Sept.-July Mon.-Sat. 8:30am-7pm.

**Le Loir Dans la Théière,** 3, rue des Rosiers, 4ème (tel. 42 72 90 61). Mo. St-Paul. The name means "the dormouse in the teapot," an allusion to *Alice in Wonderland.* Furnished with 1930s armchairs and tables assembled haphazardly from garage sales, "Le Loir"'s atmosphere lies somewhere between an upper-crust *salon* and bohemian student lodgings. Tea 20F. Coffee 10-12F. Homemade cakes 35-45F. Breakfast and brunch on Sun.—breakfast of fresh juice, tea, chocolate, or coffee, croissants and toast is 60F; brunch with all of breakfast plus a savory tart is 100F. Open Mon.-Sat. noon-11pm, Sun. 11am-11pm.

**Marriage Frères,** 30, rue du Bourg Tibourg, 4ème (tel. 42 72 28 11). Mo. Hôtel de Ville. Also at 13, rue des Grands Augustins, 6ème (tel. 40 51 82 50). An elegant rattan salon which takes tea oh-so-seriously. 400 varieties sold in the aromatic boutique. An upstairs *musée de thé* for enthusiasts. Open daily 10:30am-7:30pm.

**Pény,** 3, pl. de la Madeleine, 8ème (tel. 42 65 06 75). Mo. Madeleine. For afternoon tea, *chocolat,* or *café viennois* (28F), sit with the older couples and feel *très raffiné* (and pretend you're rich). Stay on the covered terrace to watch the waitresses surveying the comings and goings in the *place.* Open daily 8am-8pm.

**René Saint-Ouen's salon de thé,** 111, bd. Haussmann, 8ème (tel. 42 65 06 25), corner of rue d'Argenson. Mo. Miromesnil. Specializes in bread sculptures—bikes, horses, dogs, ducks, etc. Grab an edible Eiffel Tower for 45F. Open 8am-7pm. Open Sept.-July.

**La Tarte Tempion,** 195, bd. Voltaire, 11ème. Mo. Rue des Boulets. Beautiful pastries, chocolates, and sandwiches—made with American-style sliced bread. Try *Le Voltaire,* a delight of layered chocolate and cake with candied fruit in the middle and divine powdered chocolate on top. Sit on the terrace that juts into the busy roads out front. Open Fri.-Wed. 8am-8pm.

**Thé-Troc,** corner of rue de Nemours and rue de Jean-Pierre Timbaud, 11ème. Mo. Parmentier. Call it the alternative *salon de thé*—non-smoking, environmentally conscious, with windows chock full o' teas, spices, and Asian figurines, as well as records, comics, and T-shirts, all on sale inside. Natural and perfumed teas 13-18F. Open Mon.-Fri. 9am-noon and 2-8pm, Sat. 10am-1pm and 4-8pm.

## ■ Wine Bars

Although wine bistros have existed since the early 19th century, the modern wine bar emerged only a few years ago with the invention of a machine that pumps nitrogen into the open bottle, protecting wine from oxidation. Rare, expensive wines, exorbitant by the bottle, have become somewhat affordable by the glass, but this is still not the place for pinching pennies. Expect to pay 20-80F for a glass of high-quality wine. Add to that the requisite *tartine* and several more glasses of wine, and you'll find yourself on the streets, drunk and penniless. Keep in mind that Parisians frequent these places to socialize and sample; wine bars are *not* the destination to do any serious partying. In the afternoon you will see groups of men and women in work attire doing a business lunch or relaxing before heading back to the office, as well as people taking a break from shopping, loaded down with bags from chic boutiques. In the evening the crowd mellows to couples staring soulfully into each other's eyes, or small groups of friends having a drink before a night on the town.

Try to go with a friend who knows wine, a helpful guide book, or an open mind and inquisitive tongue. The owners personally and carefully select the wines which constitute their *caves* (cellars) and are usually available to help out less knowledgeable patrons. Over 100-strong, the wine shops in the **Nicolas** chain are reputed for having the world's most inexpensive cellars, though Nicolas himself owns the fashionable and expensive wine bar **Jeroboam,** 8, rue Monsigny, 2ème (tel. 42 61 21 71; Mo. Opéra). Enjoy your bottle or glass with a full meal or a *tartine* (cheese and/or *charcuteries*—French equivalent of cold cuts—served on *pain Poilâne* or *pain de*

*ampagne)*. Don't hesitate to ask the waiters for advice on which wine best com-
•lements your order; most are more than happy to oblige.

**Au Sauvignon,** 80, rue des Sts-Pères, 7*ème* (tel. 45 48 49 02). Mo. Sèvres-Babylone.
This wine bar offers a sublime sampling of Beaujolais (especially in early Nov.)
and Alsatian wines. Caricatures praising the owner and his wines coat the walls,
and they are merited; the wines have won many national awards. Wine from 25F
a glass. Open Sept.-July Mon.-Sat. 9am-11pm.
**Le Bar du Caveau,** 17, pl. Dauphine, 1*er* (tel. 43 26 81 84), facing the front steps
of the Palais de Justice. Mo. Cité. Stylishly dressed Parisians make a point of meeting for lunch at this traditional brass and wood saloon where they can sample
glasses from the vast selection of heavenly wines (14-35F) over a plate of grilled
*chèvre* and Poilâne bread (40F). It's worth every *sou*. Open Mon.-Sat. 10am-8pm.
**Chez Bailly,** 174 rue St-Jacques, 5*ème* (tel. 43 26 80 74). RER Luxembourg. This
neighborhood favorite has served as a *cave* for 65 years, and in mid-1991 started
serving wine by the glass. Proprietors Jean (a Frenchman) and Gary (an American/
Irishman) will be happy to direct you to the perfect accompaniment to your
*salade, fromage,* or *charcuterie* (42-65F), served in a casual, intimate setting, surrounded by wall-to-wall wines from all over France. Their wines by the glass are
quite affordable (from 22F) because they do much of their own bottling. Walk
away with a bottle of the house *cuvée bailly* (22F) or an 1873 cognac (25,000F).
Open Tues.-Sat. 8pm-midnight. Wine sold 11:30am-2:30pm and 6pm-midnight.
**L'Ecluse,** 120, rue Rambuteau, 1*er* (tel. 40 41 08 73). Mo. Les Halles. 13, rue de la
Roquette, 11*ème*. Mo. Bastille. 15, quai des Grand-Augustins, 6*ème*. Mo. St-
Michel. 15, pl. de la Madeleine, 8*ème*. Mo. Madeleine. 64, rue Francois 1*er*, 8*ème*.
Mo. Georges V. Possibly the best and certainly the most famous of Parisian wine
bar chains. The food is prepared not in a kitchen but in a "laboratory." Elegant
and trendy, this small chain defies the assumption that what is mass-owned must
be conformist. Seafood stew 57F, *foie gras* 110F. L'Ecluse specializes in wines
from Bordeaux, starting at a healthy 85F per bottle. Open Mon.-Sat. noon-1am.
**Jacques Mélac,** 42, rue Léon Frot, 11*ème* (tel. 43 70 59 27). Mo. Charonne. *The*
Parisian family-owned wine bar and bistro, frequented by a friendly crowd. In
Sept. owner Mélac harvests his own vines and convinces some women to crush
them with their feet. *Tartines* from 16F, wine from 15F per glass. Open Aug. 16-
July 14 Mon., Wed., and Fri. 9am-7pm, Tues. and Thurs. 9am-10pm.

# ▌ Sweets

Iow sweet it is. Indulge your fickle foreign sweet-teeth on some real ice cream with
•ne of Paris's renowned *glaces,* which are lighter, wetter, and less creamy than their
▲merican counterparts, or work off all those cardio-funk exercise classes with a sin-
ully exquisite French pastry at any number of *pâtisseries.* Paris is also filled with
*hocolatiers,* where ornately sculpted chocolates are made on the premises.

**The Baker's Dozen,** 3, pl. de la Sorbonne, 5*ème* (tel. 44 07 08 09). Mo. Luxem-
bourg. Real live fudge brownies (10F) and chocolate chip cookies (4F50) are the
specialty of this micro-bakery. Open Mon.-Fri. 8am-6pm
**Berthillon,** 31, rue St-Louis-en-l'Ile, 4*ème* (tel. 43 54 31 61), on the Ile-St-Louis. Mo.
Cité or Pont Marie. Berthillon reputedly has the best ice cream and sorbet in Paris.
The ice cream comes in every imaginable flavor, from varieties of chocolate to
*cassis* (black currant). Lines can be long in mid-summer, but the wait is worth it.
Or try one of the many cafés on Ile St-Louis which also sell Berthillon ice cream—
the *glace* is the same, lines are often shorter, and they're open in August, when
the main Berthillon is closed. Unfortunately, Berthillon's ice cream is not only
Paris's best, but also its most expensive. Open Sept.-July Tues.-Sun. 10am-8pm.
**Christian Constant,** 26, rue du Bac, 7*ème* (tel. 47 03 30 00). Mo. Rue du Bac. On
one of the tastiest streets in Paris, Christian Constant offers over 30 flavors of tea
as well as 5 varieties of sugar. Modern chic rather than elegant refinement, but the

desserts and chocolate transcend mere prose (*Opéra* 18F). Fresh jams and jellies line the windows. Open Mon.-Sat. 8am-8pm.

**Debauve et Gallais,** 33, rue Vivienne, 2ème (tel. 45 48 54 67). Mo. Bourse. Founded in 1800, this *chocolatier* is the oldest in Paris. One of the founders, Sulpice Debauve, was the official royal *chocolatier* to Louis XVI, Louis XVIII, Charles X, and Louis-Philippe. 40 different kinds of chocolates from the largest single chocolate in Paris (weighing in at a hefty 400g) to the darkest chocolate in the city. If nothing else, just come in and look. Open Mon.-Sat. 10am-7pm.

**Maison du Chocolat,** 4, bd. de la Madeleine, 9ème (tel. 47 42 86 52). Mo. Madeleine. Every imaginable kind of chocolate: bonbons, blocks, milk chocolate, dark chocolate. Plus delicious ice cream and sorbets. A place *not* to be missed. Open Mon.-Sat. 9:30am-7pm.

**Mandarine,** 6, pl. du Marché Ste-Catherine, 4ème (tel. 42 74 01 14). Mo. St-Paul. On a cobblestone square in the Marais, this café sells superb ice cream from Berthillon. On the terrace, 2 (large) scoops for 32F. Take-out service: 2 (smaller) scoops 18F. Open Fri.-Wed. 11am-midnight; in bad weather 3pm-midnight.

**Le Nôtre** hawks wonderful pastries all around the city. Join the local children pointing out their chosen treat to *maman* at one of the counters. Place your order, pay your bill at the *caisse,* and then return to the same counter to pick it up. Quiche 16-19F, buttery croissants 4F70. Open daily 9am-9pm.

**Peltier,** 66, rue de Sèvres, 7ème (tel. 47 83 66 12 or 47 34 06 62). Mo. Vaneau or Duroc. Also at 6, rue St-Dominique, 7ème (tel. 47 05 50 02). Mo. Solférino. Also in Japan. This delectable sweet-tooth haven shows that *pâtisseries* too can have slogans: *Les gâteaux Peltier, un défi vers un goût nouveau* (Peltier cakes, a challenge toward a new taste). Sample their specialty, *tarte au chocolat,* not overly rich but oh-so-gooey (16F). Sit at the tastefully decorated chairs in the *salon de thé* area, or order, pay at the *caisse,* and pick up your treat to go. Open Mon.-Sat. 8:15am-7:45pm, Sun. 8:15am-7pm.

# ■ Groceries

When cooking or assembling a picnic, buy supplies at the specialty shops found in most neighborhoods. *Crémeries* (selling dairy products), *fromageries* (cheese shops), *charcuteries* (meats, sausages, *pâtés,* and *plats cuisinés*—prepared meals by the kilo), and *épiceries* (groceries, with cold salads by the kilo) are open in the morning until noon and then again from 2 or 3 to 7 or 8pm. *Epiceries* also carry staples, wine, produce, and a bit of everything else. *Boulangeries* sell several varieties of bread; get there in the morning, when the goods are still hot. *Pâtisseries* sell pastries, and a *confiserie* stocks candy and ice cream (though the border between these two kinds of stores is often unclear). You can buy your produce at a *primeur.* *Boucheries* sell all kinds of meat and poultry, as well as roast chicken. Look for small neighborhood stores to unearth some truly incredible deals. Your hotel manager or any local can point you to the neighborhood *fromagerie, charcuterie, boucherie,* and *boulangerie.* Warning: French store owners are incredibly touchy about people touching their fruits and vegetables; unless there's a sign outside your corner store that says "*libre service,*" ask inside before you start grabbing stuff outside.

**Supermarkets** (*supermarchés*) are found in every neighborhood. Avoid the evening scramble, lest you be trampled by homemakers trying to get the last loaf of bread. Also take note that in many *supermarchés* it is up to you to weigh your produce, bag it, and label it. If you're in the mood for a five-and-dime complete with a supermarket, go to any of the **Monoprix, Prisunics, Franprix** or **Uniprix** that litter the city. Also look for the small foodstore chains such as **Casino** and **Félix Potin.** Starving students and travelers-in-the-know swear by the ubiquitous **Ed l'Epicier.** Buy in bulk and watch the pile of francs you save grow; it's possible to end up paying 30-50% less than you would at other stores. Two of Ed's drawbacks: you can't find some brand names (alas, no Nutella) and some stores do not carry produce.

Open-air markets, held at least once a week in most *arrondissements,* remain the best places to buy fresh fruit, vegetables, fish, and meat. Competition here is fierce,

nd prices low (see Markets). The **Nicolas** chain sells wines at inexpensive prices,
ut doesn't always carry the widest selections. No luck finding that special ingredi-
nt? Try the following:

**Alleosse,** 13, rue Poncelet, 17*ème* (tel. 46 22 50 45). Mo. Ternes. An immense and
exquisite selection of cheeses.

**Au Bon Marché,** 3, rue de Babylone, 7*ème* (tel. 45 49 21 22). Mo. Sèvres-Babylone.
Here, at Bon Marché's ever-popular food annex La Grande Epicerie, you'll find all
the necessities for *haute cuisine*, as well as lots of "gourmet" American fare. Well-
wrapped chocolates and *bonbons* make mouth-watering souvenirs. Open Mon.-
Fri. 9:30am-6:30pm, Sat. 9:30am-7pm.

**Charcuterie Coesnon,** 30, rue Dauphine, 6*ème* (tel. 43 54 35 80). Mo. Odéon.
Traditional homemade sausage and prepared foods. Open Tues.-Sat. 8:30am-8pm.

**Fauchon,** 26, pl. de la Madeleine, 8*ème* (tel. 47 42 60 11). Mo. Madeleine. The
supermarket to end all supermarkets. You can savor the scent from the *pâtisserie*
at least a block away. But do not dare to pick your expensive tea off the shelf
yourself—turn to the brown-clad salespeople with the ornate F on their breast to
do the dirty work for you. The cafeteria downstairs serves hot dishes for 30-50F
and desserts for 17-30F (and beyond). Indulge. Open Mon.-Sat. 9:40am-7pm.

**Finkelsztajn's,** 27, rue des Rosiers, 4*ème* (tel. 42 72 78 91). 24, rue des Ecouffes,
4*ème* (tel. 48 87 92 85). Grab a bagel or *piroghi* on your gambol through the
Marais. Serving East European Jewish delicacies since 1946, this is the place to go
for everything from strudel to chopped liver. Be warned: *pickel* is intestines and if
you've never had it before, stick to *cornichons* (pickles). Store on rue des Rosiers:
open Wed.-Sun. 10am-1:30pm and 3-7:30pm. On rue des Ecouffes: Mon. and
Thurs.-Sun. 10am-2pm and 3-7pm.

**Hédiard,** 21, pl. de la Madeleine, 8*ème* (tel. 42 66 44 36). Mo. Madeleine. A store
of spices and exotic products, founded in 1854. Their neighboring *cave* offers a
fine selection of wines. Open Mon.-Sat. 9:30am-9pm.

**Paul,** 4, rue Poncelet, 17*ème* (tel. 42 27 80 25). Mo. Ternes. Parisians from all over
the 17*ème* float in through the door of this bakery, following the overpowering
scent that wafts from its crusty loaves, baked throughout the day in their wood-
fired ovens. Open Mon. and Wed.-Sat. 6:30am-7:30pm, Sun. 6:30am-1pm.

**Peanut Shoppe,** 37, rue Dauphine, 6*ème.* Mo. Odéon. A gorgeous little Indian
spice shop stocked with all those ingredients you'd almost given up on finding:
cumin, cardamom, coriander, and curry powders, all in a sparklingly clean gem of
a shop. Spices sold loose by weight. Open Mon.-Sat. 10:30am-7:30pm.

**Poilâne,** 8, rue du Cherche Midi, 6*ème* (tel. 45 48 61 61), off bd. Raspail. Mo.
Sèvres Babylone. This tiny, rather sparse shop services a huge bakery which
makes the city's most famous bread: fragrant, crusty sourdough loaves baked
throughout the day in wood-fired ovens. Menus in the city's finest restaurants
proudly declare that they serve *only* Pain Poilâne. Unlike the faithful baguette,
these circular loaves don't come cheap (up to 40F for a whole loaf). If you want a
taste, just ask for a *quart* (a quarter), for about 10F. It's probably enough; they're
extraordinarily filling. Try them with cheese. Open Mon.-Sat. 7:15am-8:15pm.

**Tang Frères,** 48, av. d'Ivry, 13*ème* (tel. 45 70 80 00). Mo. pl. d'Italie. In the heart
of Chinatown, this grocery carries an exotic selection of rice products, sauces,
spices, and Asian fare to go. Fresh produce, a porcelain market, and an Asian
bookstore as well. If you don't read French, don't worry—all of the signs by the
checkout counter are printed in Chinese, too. Open Tues.-Fri. 9am-7:30pm, Sat.-
Sun. 8:30am-7:30pm.

**Thanksgiving,** 13, rue Beautreillis, 4*ème* (tel. 42 77 68 29). Mo. Sully-Morland or
Bastille. Homemade American delights including cheesecake and pecan pie, plus
plenty of groceries like nacho chips, brownie mix, peanut butter, and ketchup.
Prices are pretty high. Brownies 10F, cookies 5F, bagel with cream cheese 18F.
They also have take-out dishes: chili 100F per kg, barbecue ribs 40F for 5 pieces.
Open Mon.-Sat. 11am-8pm, Sun. 11am-6pm.

## ■ Markets and Noteworthy Streets

In the 5th century, the ancient Roman settlement of Lutèce held the first market on what is now Ile de la Cité. More than a millennium later, markets are not a novelty but an integral part of daily life. Both open-air and covered markets can be found around almost every corner, in every *arrondissement*. For a complete list of food and other markets, along with hours and days open, pick up *Les Marchés de Paris* at the tourist office or your local *mairie*.

**Marché Montorgeuil,** 2*ème*. Mo. Etienne Marcel. An old-fashioned market that extends from rue Réaumur to rue Etienne Marcel, along rue des Petits Carreau and rue Montorgeuil. Come here to buy bread, wine, cheese, or any other French specialty. Lots of meat, fish, and fruit. Crowded after office hours on weekdays. Many shops and stalls open until the early evening and on weekends.

**Rue Mouffetard,** towards the intersection of bd. du Port-Royal, 5*ème*. A rather chaotic scene, crammed onto narrow streets. Wonderful produce, fish, cheese, and meats. You may ask yourself how all of the tables loaded down with shoes, cheap chic, and housewares are squeezed in. Open daily 9am-1pm, 4-7pm.

**Marché Biologique,** on bd. Raspail between rue Cherche-Midi and Rennes, 6*ème*. Mo. Rennes. French hippies peddle everything from organic produce to 7-grain bread, and tofu patties. A great place to buy natural facial products, stock up on some homeopathic drugs, or just people-watch. Open Sun. 7am-1:30pm.

**Rue Cler,** between rue de Grenelle and av. de la Motte-Picquet, 7*ème*. Mo. Ecole Militaire. *Fromagers, boulangers,* and *bouchers* sell their tasty wares side-by-side; fruit and vegetable stands abound.

**Marché Europe,** 1, rue Corvetto, 8*ème*. Covered food-market. Open Mon.-Sat. 8am-1:30pm and 4-7pm, Sun. 8am-1pm.

**Marché St-Quentin,** 85bis, bd. de Magenta, 10*ème*. Mo. Gare de l'Est. This market is a massive, elegant construction of iron and glass, built in 1866 with a glorious glass ceiling. Inside you'll find an enormous variety of goods, including flowers and fresh produce. Open Tues.-Sat. 8am-1pm and 3:30pm-7:30pm, Sun. 8am-1pm.

**Rue du Convention,** at the intersection of rue de Vaugirard, 15*ème*. Mo. Convention. A bewildering array of fruits, vegetables, meat, fish, cheese and pastries every Tues. and Sun. 7am-1pm.

# Sights

You're not the first person to be fascinated by Paris. Over the centuries people have sung her praises, penned her history, acted out her trials and tribulations, painted her portrait, and immortalized her façades in film and photographs. What is it about this city that creates such mystique and evokes such attraction? For one, an historic monument on every corner and in every *place*. For another, an aesthetic quality enhanced by the eclectic mélange of architectural styles and the graceful curves of the Seine. With map in hand, comfortable shoes on feet, and adventurous spirit, you are ready to discover what makes Paris tick.

Try to resist the temptation to pack every famous edifice and museum into your itinerary, whatever the length. Be realistic about what you can see in a day: Romanesque fades to Byzantine fades to Impressionism fades to Cubism in a whirl-wind tour. Take a moment between monument-hopping to sit down in a café or on a bench to get a second wind and plot your next move. You don't need to drag yourself to a major, much-celebrated something-or-other just because you feel you should. You could spend a lifetime in Paris just doing what passionately interests you. Pick out your high points, concentrate on what you do see (as opposed to what you miss), and have no regrets.

Although Paris is inarguably one of the world's most expensive cities, you don't have to be rolling in dough to have a good time. Once you've smiled back at Mona, oohed and ahhed over the rose window in Notre-Dame, nearly been blown off the Eiffel Tower, and made the requisite pilgrimage to Père Lachaise to see Jim Morrison's grave, take time out to soak up the day-to-day facets of city life that make Paris so uniquely Parisian. A "sight" need not be a monument with several weighty tomes of historical documentation. A sight is whatever gives you that thrill, that feeling of "Aha! So this is Paris": a colorful market that you stumble upon just as your stomach is growling for lunch, a tiny, anonymous alleyway whose window boxes are garnished with flowers that perfume the air, strains of Edith Piaf wafting down from a top floor apartment to the street below. Perhaps the most authentic part of Paris are the Parisians themselves: the jovial *charcutier,* the schoolchildren clutching their *pain au chocolat,* the elderly woman with her yappy little dog, and the models pouting in trendy cafés. Try to look at the city through their eyes. If anything, respect them for having the good fortune to live in one of the most exciting cities in the world. And above all, keep your sense of humor.

## ■ Seine Islands

### ILE DE LA CITÉ

If any one location could be called the sentimental and physical heart of Paris, it is this slip in the river. Ile de la Cité sits in the very center of Paris, and indeed at the very center of the Ile de France; all distance points in France are measured from the *kilomètre zéro,* a circular sundial on the ground in front of Notre-Dame. The island was first inhabited by a Gallic tribe of hunters, sailors, and fisherfolk called the Parisii, who immigrated to the island in the 3rd century BC in search of an easily fortifiable outpost to defend themselves against the Romans. The first certifiable record left by this tribe was, sadly, their defeat by Caesar's legions in the year 52 BC. The island became the center of the Lutèce colony, languishing for four centuries under the crumbling Roman empire. In the early 6th century, Clovis crowned himself king of the Franks and adopted the embattled island as the center of his domain. No kingdom being complete without an adequately glorious church, work was begun on St-Etienne, the island's first Christian church. The basilica, built into the wall which still surrounded the island-fortress, was finished in the late 6th century under Clovis's son, Childebert I, but completely destroyed only two centuries later by Norman invaders. It was rebuilt, but razed again to make room for Notre-Dame.

During the Middle Ages, the island began to acquire the features for which it is best known and loved today. In the 12th century work commenced on Notre-Dame and Ste-Chapelle under the direction of Bishop Maurice Sully. The cathedral, completed in the 14th century, was the product of five generations, 200 years, and millions of hours of work and is one of the most beautiful, and most famous, examples of medieval architecture.

## Notre-Dame

In 1163, Pope Alexander III laid the cornerstone for the **Cathédrale de Notre-Dame-de-Paris** (tel. 43 26 07 39; Mo. Cité) over the remains of a Roman temple. The most famous and most trafficked of the Cité's sights, this massive structure was not completed until 1361. The exterior was gaily painted, making the now-somber cathedral as showy as any Italian church. During the Revolution, it was renamed the *Temple du Raison* and dedicated to the Cult of Reason. The Gothic arches were hidden behind plaster façades of virtuous, Neoclassical design. Although reconsecrated after the Revolution, the building fell into disrepair and was even used to shelter livestock. But Victor Hugo's 1831 novel, *Notre-Dame-de-Paris (The Hunchback of Notre Dame)*, inspired King Louis-Philippe and thousands of citizens to push for restoration. The modifications by Eugène Viollet-le-Duc (including the addition of the spire, the gargoyles, and a statue of himself admiring his own work) remain highly controversial. Is Notre-Dame as we see it today a medieval building, or a product of the 19th century? After the restoration, the cathedral became a valued symbol of civic unity. In 1870 and 1940 thousands of Parisians attended masses to pray for deliverance from the invading Germans—both times without immediate success. But the faithful do not demand results; on August 26, 1944, Charles de Gaulle braved sniper fire to give thanks for his victory. All of this turmoil seems to have left the cathedral unmarked; as do the hordes of tourists who invade its sacred portals every day. In the words of e.e. cummings: "The Cathedral of Notre-Dame does not budge an inch for all the idiocies of this world." Victor Hugo expressed the same sentiment 100 years earlier: "Time is blind, humanity stupid."

Today, thousands of visitors float in torrents past the doors of the cathedral, depriving themselves of one the most glorious aspects of the structure: the **façade.** "Few architectural pages," Hugo proclaimed, "are as beautiful as this façade...a vast symphony in stone." Although it was begun in the 12th century, the façade was not completed even in the 17th, when artists were still adding Baroque statues of dubious artistic value. Highly symbolic, the carvings were designed to instill a fear of God and desire for righteousness in a population of which less than 10% were literate. Revolutionaries, not exactly your regular churchgoers, wreaked havoc on the façade of the church during the ecstasies of the 1790s; not content to decapitate Louis XVI, they attacked the stone images of his ancestors above the doors. The heads were found in the basement of the Banque Française du Commerce in 1977, and were installed in the Musée de Cluny (see Museums). Chips of paint on the heads led to a surprising discovery: Notre-Dame was once painted in bright and garish colors. Replicas of the heads (unpainted) now crown the royal bodies.

The cathedral's interior focuses on soaring light and the seeming weightlessness of the walls. Spidery flying buttresses support the vaults of the ceiling from outside, allowing the walls to be opened up to stained glass. The effect is increased by a series of subtle optical illusions, including the use of smaller pillars to surround the bigger ones, diminishing their apparent size. The most spectacular feature of the interior are the enormous stained-glass **rose windows** that dominate the transept's north and south ends. Originally, similarly masterful artistry adorned the windows on the ground level. But "Sun King" Louis XIV, trying to live up to his nickname, ordered all the windows on the ground level to be smashed. Louis's clear windows have since been replaced by mediocre stained glass.

Free **guided tours** of the cathedral are an excellent way to discover its history and architecture; inquire at the information booth to the right as you enter. A rousing tour in English is led by Irving Levine, "the only non-Roman Catholic to give tours at Notre-Dame." A 60-year-old psychiatrist from New York, he has been living in Paris for the last 26 years (tours in English Wed. noon, in French Mon.-Fri. noon, Sat.-Sun. 2pm; free). The cathedral's **treasury,** south of the choir, contains a rather humdrum assortment of robes and sacramental cutlery from the stately period of 1949 (open Mon.-Sat. 10am-6pm, Sun. 2-6pm; admission 15F, students 10F, under 17 5F).

Outside again, don't miss the opportunity to visit the haunt of the cathedral's most famous fictional resident, the Hunchback of Notre-Dame, with a hair-raising climb into the two **towers.** The perilous and claustrophobic staircase emerges onto a spectacular perch, where a bevy of gargoyles survey a stunning view of the heart of the city. The climb generally deters the bus-load tourists, and you may even have the towers relatively to yourself if you come early. Although this is not the highest view of Paris, it affords you a detailed view of both the festive *quartier latin* on the Left Bank in the 6*ème,* and the Marais on the Right Bank in the 4*ème.* Continue on to the south tower, where a tiny door gives access to the 13-ton bell, which even Quasimodo couldn't ring, since it requires the force of eight full-grown men to move. (Towers open daily 9:30am-6pm. Admission 36F, seniors and students 20F, under 17 6F. Cathedral open Mon.-Fri. 8am-5:15pm, Sat.-Sun. 8am-7:30pm.) Roman Catholic masses are held here daily and on Sunday (high mass with music at 11am) and you can make your confession here in eight different languages.

For a view of Notre-Dame's magnificent backside, cross pont St-Louis (behind the cathedral) to Ile St-Louis and turn right on quai d'Orléans. At night, the buttresses are lit up, and the view from here is breathtaking. Follow the *quais* to pont de Sully, at the far side of Ile St-Louis, for an equally striking view of the cathedral.

## Other Sights

The **Mémorial de la Déportation,** behind the cathedral, across from place Jean XXIII, and down a narrow flight of steps, is a haunting memorial erected for the French victims of Nazi concentration camps. 200,000 flickering lights represent the dead, and an eternal flame burns over the tomb of an unknown deportee. The names of all the concentration camps glow in gold triangles which recall the design of the patch that French prisoners were forced to wear for identification purposes. A series of quotations is engraved into the stone walls—most striking of these is the motto *"Pardonne; N'Oublie Pas"* (Forgive; Do Not Forget) engraved over the exit. The old men who frequently visit the museum may act as voluntary guides. You may hear one of these men chanting the chillingly beautiful *Kadish,* the Jewish prayer for the dead.

Far below the cathedral towers, in a cool and dark excavation beneath the pavement of the square in front of the cathedral, the **Archeological Museum,** pl. du Parvis du Notre-Dame (tel. 43 29 83 51), houses a remarkably preserved archeological dig of the Roman village that once covered the island. The museum provides a self-guided tour through the dig, wandering through the old *quais,* baths, and houses, as well as an exhaustive display of the history of Ile de la Cité (open daily 10am-6pm; admission 25F, seniors and students 17F, under 17 6F).

If you're hungry when you emerge again into the sunlight, buy a sandwich and wander into the garden of the **Hôtel Dieu,** a hospital located along the north side of the Parvis, whose original mission was the aid of foundlings. The hospital dates back to the Middle Ages, though then it was more a place to confine the sick than to cure them; guards were posted at the doors to keep the patients from getting out and infecting the city. Pasteur did much of his pioneering research inside. In 1871, the hospital's proximity to Notre-Dame saved the cathedral; the defeated *Communards* were only dissuaded from burning the latter by the fear that the flames could engulf their hospitalized wounded. Across the street is the **Préfecture de Police,** where at

7am on August 19, 1944, members of the Paris police force began the insurrection against the Germans that lasted until the Allies liberated the city six days later.

The **Palais de Justice** (tel. 44 32 51 51), spanning the western side of the island, harbors the infamous **Conciergerie,** prison of the Revolution, the ethereal **Ste-Chapelle,** St-Louis's private chapel, and numerous tribunals where you can still see the law in action. Since 52 BC, the French judiciary has been housed in a building on this site. Since the 13th century, the structures here have contained the district courts for Paris. All trials are open to the public, but don't expect a *France v. Dreyfus* every day. *Chambre 1* of the *Cour d'Appel* witnessed Pétain's convictions after WWII. Even if your French is not up to legal jargon, the cool sobriety of the interior, along with the lawyers archaic black robes, makes a quick visit worthwhile, especially since it's free (trials usually Mon.-Fri. at 1:30pm around 5pm). Criminal cases are the most interesting (criminal courtrooms open Mon.-Fri. 1:30-4pm).

At the heart of the Palais, **Ste-Chapelle** (tel. 43 54 30 09) remains one of the foremost examples of 13th-century French architecture. Because the church is crowded into an interior courtyard, its beautiful exterior is lost to view; the random passerby sees no more than the iron steeple, a 19th-century addition. The church was begun in 1241 to house the most precious of King Louis IX's possessions, the crown of thorns from Christ's Passion. Bought from the Emperor of Constantinople in 1239 along with a section of the Cross for an ungodly sum of 135,000 livres, the crown required an equally princely chapel. Although the crown—minus a few thorns which St-Louis gave away as political favors—has been moved to Notre-Dame, Ste-Chapelle still remains a masterpiece—"the pearl among them all," as Marcel Proust called it. A blissfully dark and serene interior and domed roof mark a room of golds, reds, and blues in the lower chapel. In the upstairs chapel, reserved for royalty and their court, stained glass windows provide a miracle of color and lace-like delicacy; their melding of blues and reds lights the church with a hue of fine wine, giving rise to the saying "wine the color of Sainte Chapelle's windows." The windows are the oldest stained glass in Paris, tastefully restored in 1845; the glass you see is for the most part the same under which St-Louis prayed to his holy relic. Check weekly publications for occasional concerts here, or ask at the information booth; tickets run 75-155F (open daily 9:30am-6pm; admission 25F, students and seniors 17F, under 17 6F; combined ticket for the Chapelle and the Conciergerie 40F).

The **Conciergerie** (tel. 43 54 30 06), around the corner of the Palais from the entrance to the Chapelle, lurks ominously, jealously brooding over the memories of the prisoners who died here during the Revolution. The northern façade is that of a gloomy medieval fortress. At the farthest corner on the right, a stepped parapet marks the oldest tower, the Tour Bonbec, which once housed the prison's torture chambers. The modern entrance lies between the Tour d'Argent, stronghold of the royal treasury, and the Tour de César, which housed the revolutionary tribunal. As you enter, notice the 16th-century face of Paris's first public clock.

Don't pause too long at the guard room at the entrance, but instead flee along the *"Rue de Paris"*—the corridor leading from the entrance, so named for the prisoners' destination, *"M. Paris,"* the executioner. At the end is the Great Hall, an enormous Gothic hall. Past the hall, stairs lead to facsimiles of prisoners cells, now inhabited by glum-looking mannequins, especially in the *pailleux* cell, where prisoners who weren't rich enough to bribe their jailers were forced to sleep on straw. Next door, the wealthier mannequins, the *pistoliers,* sleep two to a cell in relative comfort. Farther down the hall is a cell where Maximilien de Robespierre awaited his death. It has been converted into a display of his letters, as well as a guillotine from 1836. Engraved on the wall are Robespierre's famous last words: *Je vous laisse ma Mémoire. Elle vous sera chère, et vous la défendrez.* (I leave you my memory. It will be dear to you, and you will defend it.) Beyond Robespierre's cell lies a small room dedicated to the memory of those who died in the Revolution, containing walls covered with the thousands of names and occupations of the executed. A surprising number of bakers, servants, and other commoners are represented, testifying to the frenzy of death into which the Revolution degenerated during its final chapter. Marie-Antoinette's cell has been converted to a chapel, but a rather unsatisfying replica can be found upstairs. In the center of the Conciergerie is the desolate Cour des Femmes, the only place where men and women prisoners were allowed to talk freely, and where prisoners chosen for the guillotine were allowed to say their goodbyes. The Conciergerie is still used as a temporary prison for those awaiting trial in the Palais de Justice. (Open daily 9:30am-6pm; Oct.-March 10am-5pm. Admission including guided tour in French 25F, seniors and students 17F, under 17 6F. Combined ticket to the Conciergerie and Ste-Chapelle 40F.)

**Place Dauphine,** behind the Conciergerie, was a delightful oasis in 1607, when Henri IV ordered its construction. Throughout the 18th century, art exhibitions were held here on Corpus Christi, allowing many of France's young artists to gain recognition for the first time. But renovations in 1874 largely destroyed the symmetry of the square, leaving the park as just a patch of dirt for happy poodles. Surrealist André Breton called it "one of the most profoundly withdrawn places that I know, one of the worst wastelands that exists in Paris. Every time I am there, I feel myself abandon little by little the wish to go anywhere else." Even if you can't sympathize with Breton's fondness for devastation, the square offers a uniquely peaceful respite from the chaos of the *île* and a positive jewel of a wine bar. Behind the place Dauphine, at the very tip of the Ile de la Cité, sits a park called the square du Vert Galant. As you leave Ile de la Cité from here, you'll walk over the oldest bridge in Paris, ironically named **Pont-Neuf,** "New Bridge." Completed in 1607, the bridge's radical design lacked the usual domestic residences lining its sides. Before the construction of the Champs-Elysées, the bridge was the most popular thoroughfare, attracting peddlers, performers, thieves, and even street physicians. Although not of particular architectural interest, the bridge does have individual gargoyle capitals on its supports, which can be viewed by hanging your head over the edge, or better yet, from a *bateau-mouche* (see Entertainment). Christo, the Bulgarian performance artist, once wrapped up the entire bridge in 44,000 square meters of nylon.

## ILE ST-LOUIS

A short walk across the Pont St-Louis will take you to the elegant neighborhood of **Ile St-Louis.** Originally two small islands (the Ile de Vâches and Ile de Notre-Dame), it was considered suitable for duels, cows, and little else throughout the Middle Ages. The eccentric King Louis loved to sit and read in its seclusion, decked out in his preferred habit of white peacock feathers. The good king took up gauntlet and cross for the Tunisian crusade here in 1267, leaving only his name behind. The island became habitable in the 17th century due to the collaboration of Henri IV with the bridge entrepreneur Christophe Marie, after whom the Pont Marie is named. Despite Marie's efforts, the island proved an uncompromising loner; the original bridges collapsed within 50 years of completion due to fire and high tides.

Today's Ile St-Louis looks much as it did 300 years ago, housing an elite which includes the Rothschilds and Pompidou's widow. The charming streets hide houses in which such luminaries as Voltaire, Mme. de Châtelet, Daumier, Ingres, Baudelaire, and Cézanne resided. Floating somewhere between small village and chic address, the island retains a certain remoteness from the rest of Paris. Older residents say *"Je vais à Paris"* (I go to Paris) when stepping onto one of the four bridges between Ile St-Louis and the mainland. In a rare burst of activist vigor, inhabitants declared the island an independent republic in the thirties.

While you may not be able to afford the rent, you can afford the view. Many a literary personage has watched the passage of *bateaux-mouches* down this stretch of the Seine. Leave Ile de la Cité by the pont St-Louis and follow the quai de Bourbon. To your right, catty-corner to the quai and rue des Deux Ponts, sits the **Cabaret du Franc-Pirot,** whose wrought-iron and grilled façade is almost as old as the island. The grapes that punctuate the ironwork gave the cabaret its name; the *pirot* is a grape from Burgundy. Closed in 1716 after authorities found a basement stash of anti-government tracts, the cabaret would re-emerge as a notorious address during the Revolution. The infamous Cécile Renault, daughter of the cabaret's proprietor, mounted an unsuccessful attempt on Robespierre's life in 1794. The young coquette and admirer of Charlotte Corday climbed the scaffold the following year.

The **Quai d'Anjou,** between Pont Marie and Pont de Sully, houses some of the island's most beautiful *hôtels*. No. 29 once housed Ford Madox Ford's **Transatlantic Review,** *the* expatriate lit mag, to which Hemingway frequently contributed. No. 17, the **Hôtel Lauzun,** built in 1657 by Le Vau, may only be seen by guided tour. Check the "Conférences" section of *Pariscope* or stop by the Caisse Nationale des Monuments Historiques, 62, rue St-Antoine (tel. 44 61 00 00). In the 1840s, the *hôtel* became the club house for the Hachischins, a bohemian salon. Charles Baudelaire and Théophile Gautier reclined with a houkah at many a soirée. Jeanne Duval, Baudelaire's mulatto mistress—the famous "hemisphere in a head of hair"—lived nearby at no. 6 rue Legrattier. No. 9, quai d'Anjou marks the house where Honoré Daumier, realist painter and caricaturist, lived from 1846-1863.

Loop around the end of the quai and walk down **rue St-Louis-en-l'Ile.** This is the "main drag" of Ile St-Louis, filled with gift shops, art galleries, and traditional French restaurants, as well as the famous **Berthillon** *glacerie* (see Sweets, Restaurants, and Shopping sections). The **Hôtel Lambert,** at No. 2, designed by Le Vau and built in 1640 for Lambert le Riche, has housed such luminaries as Voltaire and Mme. de Châtelet. **Eglise St-Louis-en-l'Ile,** at the corner of rue St-Louis-en-l'Ile and rue Poulletier was also designed by Le Vau. Built between 1664 and 1726, the church is covered with a thick coat of soot which makes it look more like a prison than a house of worship. The dark exterior, however, hides the airiest of Rococo interiors, magnificently decorated with gold leaf, marble, and graceful statuettes (open to the public Mon.-Sat. 9am-noon and 3-7pm). Legendary for its acoustics, the church holds a yearly music festival in July (check with FNAC for details). On either side of rue St-Louis-en-l'Ile, residential streets lead to the *quais*. Follow rue Budé to 6, quai d'Orléans, for the **Musée Adam Mickiewicz,** full of memorabilia from this 19th-century Polish poet and his compatriots (see Museums). Proust fans should remember that Swann lived on quai d'Orléans. And while Marcel's *tante* Léonie may have found the island "a neighborhood most degrading," Parisians seem to have skipped that page.

## ■ First Arrondissement

The spectre of the Ancien Régime walks proudest through the first *arrondissement*. Hugging the Seine, the Louvre—world-famous art museum and former residence of kings—occupies about one seventh of the *arrondissement* (for a full description of the museum and its treasures, see Museums). The Jardin des Tuileries, a large formal garden attached to the Louvre, looks just as it did in the days of Cathérine de Médicis. Next to the Louvre but on a smaller scale is the Palais-Royal, a palace that Cardinal Richelieu built for himself in 1632. This is the France of rising absolutism; sharp-cornered buildings and stone promenades built in the 16th and 17th centuries dwarf the passerby. The section of the 1*er* west of the rue du Louvre is one of elegance on a massive scale, a far cry from the cozy, meandering streets of the Marais which recall the village that was Paris. The projects mounted by Louis XIV (notably the place Vendôme) are grand, humbling, and seem to miss their king. To the other side of the rue du Louvre, the city takes on a more humble demeanor and provides a startling blend of the medieval and here-and-now; Les Halles, a subterranean shopping mall, buzzes beneath a park which abuts the Eglise St-Eustache, the 16th-century church where Richelieu was baptized and the Sun King took his first communion. On the grounds of what was once the most feared and septic cemetery of Paris—la Cimetière des Sts-Innocents—skateboarders, bongo players, and guitar-strumming riff-raff entertain tourists heading to the Pompidou. To the east and to the west of the Louvre, the 1*er* moves to the beat of very different drums.

The **Jardin des Tuileries,** at the western foot of the Louvre, celebrates the victory of geometry over nature. The views from the elevated terrace by the river and along the central path of the park are spectacular. From the terrace you can see the Louvre, the gardens, the Eiffel Tower, and the Musée d'Orsay (right across the river). From the central path, gaze upon the obelisk of Luxor (in place de la Concorde), the Arc de Triomphe, and (on a clear day) the Arche de la Défense in the distance; turn around to see the Arc de Triomphe du Carrousel and the Cour Napoléon of the Louvre. Sculptures are sprinkled throughout the park, including 18 bronze nudes by Auguste Maillol. Cathérine de Médicis, missing the public promenades of her native Italy, had the gardens built in 1564; in 1649 André Le Notre (designer of the gardens at Versailles) imposed his preference for straight lines and sculptured trees upon the landscape of the Tuileries. The gardens were made public and have since become one of the most popular open spaces in Paris. Flanking the pathway through the gardens are the Jeu de Paume (thus named because it was built on a tennis court in 1851) and the Musée de l'Orangerie (see Museums). Along with the gardens, Cathérine ordered the **Palais des Tuileries,** which stretched along the west end of the Jardin du Carrousel, forming the western wall of the Louvre. Long after most of the Louvre had been converted into an art museum, the Tuileries remained the royal residence. Louis XVI and Marie-Antoinette attempted to flee from here in 1791. Napoleon lived here prior to his exile; Louis XVIII was chased out of here upon Napoleon's return in 1814. Louis-Philippe fled in similar haste in 1848, and in 1870, the Empress Eugénie scrambled out as the mob crashed in the main entrance. She then successfully escaped Paris with the help of her American dentist. Nine months later, as forces streamed into the city to crush the Commune, a Communard official packed the palace with gunpowder, tar, and oil and the building erupted into flames. The burnt-out ruins of the Tuileries survived until 1882, when the Republican Municipal Council, unwilling to restore a symbol of the monarchy, had them flattened. Today, only the Pavillion de Flore and the Pavillion de Marsan remain.

In recent years, the government has allowed an amusement park to spring up seasonally. If you're with kids or simply want to nourish your inner child, come for the rides between the first weekend of December and the first weekend of January, or between the last Sunday of June and the first Sunday after August 15. At night, the huge Ferris wheel offers a magnificent view of nocturnal Paris. There are also some more traditional amusements for children, which operate year- round (except for a few weeks in winter). The park opens at 7am on weekdays, and on weekends and holidays at 7:30am. From the last Sunday of March to the Saturday preceding the last Sunday of September, closing time is 10pm; for the rest of the year it is 8pm.

The **place Vendôme,** three blocks north along the rue de Castiglione from the Tuileries, was begun in 1687 according to plans by Jules Hardouin-Mansart, who convinced Louis XIV and a group of five financiers to invest in the ensemble of private mansions and public institutions. The project ran out of funds almost immediately; for several decades, before it was finished in 1720, the theatrical and ostentatious place Vendôme remained no more than a series of empty façades. Many of the buildings were gutted in the 1930s; again, their uniformly dignified façades were protected. Place Vendôme, as it exists today, is a series of 17th-century façades masking 20th-century offices. In 1972, a huge underground carpark was installed, another major change that did not vary the outside appearance of the square. The recently renovated *place* is one of the few in Paris safe for high heels, and looks today like the perfect spot to practice the box-step after dark under the iron lampposts past Chanel and Cartier. Waltz over to the Ritz (no.15) where Hemingway drank, and drank, and is duly remembered: they named the bar after him. After riding into Paris with the U.S. Army, Hemingway gathered some Resistance troops and went off to liberate the Ritz. Greeted by his old chum, the assistant manager, Hemingway ordered 73 dry martinis. Raise a glass in his memory at **Hemingway,** 36, rue Cambon (tel. 42 60 38 30), and pay through the nose for a glimpse of this shrine to Papa (open daily 7pm-1am). Chopin died at no. 12; no. 11 and no. 13 house the Ministry of Justice. To the left of the entrance is The Meter, the mother of all rulers. Nowadays meters are defined using krypton 86 radiation, but this 1848 unit is a pretty reliable source. Today, the entire *place* shimmers with opulence. Well-known bankers, perfumers and jewelers sprinkle the area; savor the moment with a 50,000F watch from Cartier.

Napoleon presides over the square from atop the central **column,** looking down on the Ministry of Justice and the Bank of Spain. Originally, the square held a 7m statue of Louis XIV in Roman costume. The statue was destroyed on August 10, 1792, and the square was renamed place des Piques. *(Piques* were long spears used in the Revolution to carry guillotined heads.) In 1805, Napoleon erected a central column modeled after Trajan's column in Rome. Cast from Austrian and Russian bronze cannons captured in battle, surrounding a core of stone, the bas reliefs of the column showed a series of military heroes; the emperor at the top was represented in the Roman toga that once covered Louis XIV. Nine years later the statue of Napoleon was deposed—not without difficulty. (In order to remove it, the Royalist government had to arrest the maker of the statue and force him, on penalty of execution, to figure out how to get rid of it.) Soon after, the return of Napoleon from Elba brought the original statue back to its proud stance. Over the next sixty years it would be replaced by the white flag of the ancient monarchy, by a renewed Napoleon in military garb and by a classical Napoleon modeled after the original. During the Commune, a group led by Gustave Courbet toppled the entire column, planning to replace it with a monument to the "Federation of Nations and the Universal Republic." Later, in Napoleon's final victory, the original column was recreated. New bronze reliefs were made from the original molds and the undamaged Emperor returned to the top where he still holds sway over the gracious square.

Nearby, at 328, rue St-Honoré, is the former site of the **Jacobin convent,** a Dominican convent which furnished a meeting-place for Robespierre, who lodged at no. 398-400. The **Feuillants Monastery,** nearby, arranged for an apartment house to be built between 229 and 235, rue St-Honoré, where the Feuillants club, a group of moderates such as Lavoisier, met in 1791, in close proximity to their opposition, the Jacobins. The monastery extended as far as the Tuileries riding school, known as the **Manége**. The National Assembly met here from 1789 to 1793, and in 1792 the Convention condemned Louis XVI to death here by a majority of only one vote.

The **Palais-Royal** lies across rue de Rivoli from the Louvre. Constructed in 1639 by Jacques Lemercier as Cardinal Richelieu's Palais Cardinal, it became a Palais Royal when Anne of Austria, regent for Louis XIV, set up house there, as did his mistress, Louise de Vallière. Louis-Philippe d'Orléans, the Duc de Chartres whose son became King Louis-Philippe, inherited the palace in 1780. Strapped for cash, in 1784 he built and rented out the elegant buildings that enclose the palace's formal garden, turning the complex into the 18th century's version of a shopping mall. It had boutiques, restaurants, prostitutes, and—in lieu of a multi-screen cinema—theaters, wax museums, and puppet shows. On July 12, 1789, 26-year-old Camille Desmoulins leaped on a café table and urged his fellow citizens to arm themselves, shouting "I would rather die than submit to servitude." The crowd filed out, and was soon skirmishing with cavalry in the Tuileries garden. The revolutions of 1830 and 1848 also began with angry crowds in these gardens. In the second half of the 19th century, the Palais recovered as a center of luxury commerce, preserving a serene aristocracy amid the "commercialism" of Haussmann's boulevards and modern department stores.

Today, the galleries of the venerable buildings contain small shops and a few cafés, with a splendid view of the palace fountain and flower beds, both of which were re-landscaped in 1992. The levels above the cafés and shops, as well as the older parts of the palace, are occupied by government offices (including the Ministry of Culture). A popular place to kiss for couples with a large height disparity are the *colonnes de Buren*—a set of black and white striped pillars and stumps that completely fill the *cour d'honneur* (the main courtyard). Planted there in 1986, Daniel Buren's columns created a storm of controversy comparable to the one that greeted the Louvre pyramid. Separating this courtyard from the gardens are more staid columns, built in the early 19th century. On the southwestern corner of the

Palais-Royal, facing the Louvre, the **Comédie Française,** formerly the Théâtre Français, is home to France's leading dramatic group. The theater was built in 1790 by architect Victor Louis. The entrance displays a number of busts of famous actors, including Mirabeau by Rodin, Talma by David, d'Anges and Voltaire by Houdon. Molière, the company's founder, died here on stage; ironically, he was playing the role of the "Imaginary Invalid." The chair onto which he collapsed can still be seen. A monument to the great playwright rises not far from here at the corner of rue Molière and rue Richelieu, a few steps away from no. 40, where he died. The Fontaine de Molière, designed by Visconti, splashes nearby.

Stretching north from the Comédie into the second and ninth *arrondissements* is the glittering **Avenue de l'Opéra.** Haussmann leveled the butte de Moulins and many old homes to connect the old symbol of royalty, the Louvre, to the new symbol of imperial grandeur, the Opéra. The grand creation was intended to bear the mightiest name of all—avenue Napoléon—but the Franco-Prussian war interrupted this scheme, and when finished, the avenue was named for its terminus instead.

The **Bourse du Commerce** is the large round building between the rue du Louvre and the Forum des Halles. Not to be confused with the stock exchange (the "bourse des valeurs" or the "bourse"), the Bourse du Commerce is a commodities exchange where deals on agricultural produce are made. It's worth stepping inside to admire the iron-and-glass cupola and the paintings that surround it (open Mon.-Fri. 8:30am-7pm). In the Middle Ages, a convent of repented sinners occupied the site. Cathérine de Médicis threw out the penitent women in 1572, when a horoscope convinced her that she should abandon construction of the Tuileries and build her palace here instead. Cathérine's palace was demolished in 1748, leaving only the observation tower of her personal astrologer (a huge stone pillar that stands right next to the wall of the Bourse du Commerce) as a memorial to her superstition. Louis XV replaced the structure with a grain market on the site; it was transformed into a commodities market in 1889, when the current building was built.

**St-Eustache** (Mo. Les Halles, Châtelet les Halles) is the large Gothic/Renaissance church visible from all over Les Halles, right next to the Turbigo exit of the Les Halles *métro*. In front of the church is a large cobblestoned area with fountains and a distinctive sculpture of a huge human head and hand. Come to this area with a frisbee on a summer evening and you'll be sure to meet plenty of local youths and foreign backpackers who want to play. Eustatius was a Roman general who is said to have converted to Christianity upon seeing the sign of a cross between the antlers of a deer. As punishment, he and his family were locked into a brass bull which was then placed over a fire until it became white-hot. Construction of the church in his honor began in 1532, and dragged on for over a century. In 1754 the unfinished façade was knocked down and replaced with the Roman façade that it has today—incongruous with the rest of the building, but appropriate for the saint in question. You can get a good view of the older parts of the church if you go down the stairs of the Porte St-Eustache. To visit the interior you can just look around, or take a guided tour (in French only). See Colvert's tomb and Pigalle's exquisite statue of the Madonna. Perhaps the best way of taking in the architecture and the stained glass is to attend one of the **organ concerts** organized in June and July. The organ is one of the best in Paris; classical music lovers will not want to miss the experience of its thrilling baritone. Berlioz heard his *Te Deum* at St-Eustache for the first time; Liszt conducted his *Messiah* here in 1886. For information on the organ festival, check *Pariscope,* call 45 22 28 74, or read the posters in front of the church. (Organ festival tickets 120F, students 80F. Church open Mon.-Sat. 8:30am-7pm, Sun. 8:15am-12:30pm and 3-7pm. Guided tours 3pm on Sun.; June-July daily 2pm. Mass Mon.-Fri. 10am and 6pm, Sat. 6pm, Sun. 8:30am, 9:45am, 11am, and 6pm. On Sun., the 11am mass is with choir and organ; the 6pm mass is with organ.) The statue in front of the church was created in 1986 by sculptor Henri de Miller. Its apt title is *The Listener*.

**Les Halles** (Mo. Les Halles, Châtelet-Les Halles) was called *"le ventre de Paris"* (Paris's belly) by Emile Zola. Since 1135, when King Louis VI built two wooden buildings here to house a bazaar, Les Halles was the site of the largest food market in Paris. The Les Halles Zola described received a much-needed facelift in the 1850s and 60s, with the construction of large iron and glass pavilions that sheltered the vendors stalls. Designed by Baltard, the pavilions resembled the one that still stands over the small market at the Carreau du Temple in the third *arrondissement*. In the 60s, the market had again slipped into disrepair. This time, however, the authorities decided to solve the problem simply by sending the vendors to a suburb near Orly.

After moving the old market in 1970, politicians and city planners debated how to fill *le trou des Halles* (the gap at Les Halles), 106 open acres which presented Paris with the largest urban redesign opportunity since Hausmannization. Most of the city adored the elegant pavilions and wanted to see them preserved. But planners insisted that only by destroying the pavilions could they create a needed transfer point between the *métro* and the new RER; demolition began in 1971. The city retained architects Claude Vasconi and Georges Penreach to replace the pavilions with a subterranean shopping mall, the **Forum des Halles.** Two hundred boutiques (the most fashionable of which have floated to the uppermost levels) are crammed into the complex, along with a swimming pool and several museums: the Musée Grevin, the Musée d'Holographie, and the Les Martyrs de Paris/Rock 'n' Roll Hall of Fame complex (see Museums). There is a small Vidéothèque de Paris which offers consultations on video and screenings of videos concerning Paris (tel. 40 26 34 30; open Tues.-Sun. 12:30-9pm; admission 20F). By putting the mall underground it allowed the vast Les Halles quadrangle to be landscaped with greenery, statues, and fountains. Watch your wallet inside Les Halles, and stay above ground at night.

Getting around the Forum can be quite confusing; computerized maps, scattered throughout the complex, tell you what's available and how to get there. The computers will communicate with you in English—if you see a French screen, keep pressing the words *sommaire* or *fin* until you get to a display which features a button marked "change language." The Forum has wheelchair-accessible elevators.

South of the forum, along the rue St-Honoré, is the **rue de la Ferronnerie.** In 1610, as he passed no. 11, Henri IV met his death at the hands of a man named Ravaillac, who leapt into the king's carriage and stabbed him mortally. Ravaillac, who was upset that Henri was not persecuting the Protestants, was later seared with red-hot pincers and scalded with boiling lead in an effort to uncover his accomplices; finally, the torturers concluded that Ravaillac acted alone. He was then torn to pieces and burned by an angry mob. Later, this street became the center of the metal trade in the city. The nearby **Fontaine des Innocents,** built in 1548, is the last trace of the church and cemetery that once stood there, **L'Eglise** and **Cimetière des Sts-Innocents,** which once bordered and overlapped with Les Halles. Until demolition in the 1780s, the cemetery provided the macabre setting for many a merchant who sold his wares amidst tombstones and the smell of rotting corpses. The cemetery was closed during the era of Enlightenment hygienic reform; the corpses were relocated to the city's catacombs. The fountain, once attached to the church, now attracts punks and the overflow lunch-time crowd from McDonald's.

Tucked behind the Louvre, near the Pont Neuf, is the Gothic church **St-Germain l'Auxerrois.** On August 24, 1572, the church's bell functioned as the signal for the St. Bartholomew's Day Massacre. Huguenots were rounded up by the troops of the Duc de Guise and slaughtered in the streets, while King Charles IX shot at the survivors out the palace window. **Pont Neuf** itself, the oldest and most famous of the Seine bridges, connects the first *arrondissement* to the Ile de la Cité (see Sights—Seine Islands). At its left, **Samaritaine** is one of the oldest department stores in Paris. Founded in 1869, and named after the Samaritaine pump of Henri IV, it ushered in the modern age of consumption. The building you see today began as a delicate iron and steel construction in 1906 and was revamped in the Art Deco style of 1928.

# ■ Second Arrondissement

Since the 19th century, the *2ème* has centered around the work of buying and selling— in the *quartier*'s many indoor, glass-covered shopping arcades called *galeries* or *passages*, at the national stock market called the *bourse*, and on the streets, where prostitutes exchange sex for money.

**Galerie Colbert** and **Galerie Vivienne,** near the Palais Royal, are the finest remaining examples of Parisian *galeries,* pedestrian streets inside city blocks, lined with cafés, restaurants, and quaint boutiques. Both arcades, recently restored, date from the early 19th century, when developers searched for new opportunities in the dense central district. Later, the indoor arcades provided a perfect showcase for the art of *flânerie*—strolling aimlessly in the crowd—invented by Bohemians like Gérard de Nerval and Baudelaire. Their marbled colonnades, lined with elegant shops, brought the busy street indoors. These two galleries, like the nearby Palais Royal (see 1*er),* demonstrate the desperate folly of past ages as they groped through the darkness of ignorance before achieving the Nirvana of the shopping mall.

An entrance at 4, rue des Petits Champs reveals Galerie Colbert, an elegant passageway with a long row of seemingly marble columns; actually, the columns are made of wood—yet another example of mid-19th-century superficiality. At the end of this passage is a rotunda with a bronze statue from 1822. Turn right twice at the rotunda, making a U-turn into the Galerie Vivienne. Here again you'll find a pleasant Neoclassical décor and plenty of little boutiques; in addition, a number of large windows feature displays from the Bibliothèque Nationale, which uses this building as an annex. Another beautiful *galerie,* the **Passage des Panoramas** off of the rue St-Marc, features a fully intact 19th-century glass and tile atrium roof that allows the sun to pour in over the many Algerian, French, and Italian food stands and shops. Other *galeries* include the **Passage du Grand-Cerf** (off rue St-Denis's lower end), the **Galerie Véro-Dodat** (off rue Croix-des-Petits-Champs), **Passage Jouffroy** (off bd. Montmartre), and the **Passage Verdeau** (off rue de la Grange-Batelière).

The **Bibliothèque Nationale,** 58, rue de Richelieu (tel. 47 03 81 26), competes with the British Library for the title of largest library in Western Europe. Its collection of 12 million volumes includes two Gutenberg Bibles, countless first editions from the 15th century to the present, and unmatchable resources on Bohemian Paris. The private collections of the kings of France provided the embryo, and the library has been growing ever since. Ever since 1642, the law has stipulated that every book published in France must be archived in the Bibliothèque Nationale; not surprisingly, the place is bursting at the seams. Annexes have been built nearby to house the ever-rising volume of books, notably the Annexe Vivienne. In the late 80s, however, the government decided that it could no longer expand the Bibliothèque Nationale and resolved to build a new library, the Bibliothèque de France (see 13*ème).* The collections of the Bibliothèque Nationale will be moved into their new home over several months, starting in late 1994; when this process is complete, the old Bibliothèque Nationale will become the Bibliothèque Nationale des Arts.

Foreigners are not allowed into the library's reading room, unless they can prove they're doing research that calls for publications unavailable elsewhere in Paris. Normally, they must be studying at a graduate level or higher to qualify. If you can get a letter from a university, publisher, or publication, call 47 03 81 02 for approval, or stop by at the library's main office (open Mon.-Sat. 9am-4pm). Even for plebes who can't get into the stacks, the library is worth visiting. Temporary exhibitions highlight different portions of the library's priceless collection; if your French is up to it, call 47 03 81 10 to ask what's being shown (opening hours vary). There is also a Musée des Médailles, displaying a wide mix of coins and medallions from various cultures and centuries (open daily 10am-8pm; admission 30F, reduced 20F).

While you may not be able to see the ancient manuscripts at the *bibliothèque,* you might try your hand at bidding on one at the **Hôtel Drouot,** 9, rue Drouot (Mo. Richelieu-Drouot), Paris's foremost auction house of fine art and antiques. Like at Christie's or Sotheby's, you can bid on a Picasso sketch, a Fabergé egg, or an 1814

Château Neuf de Pape if you have enough points on your Gold Card. Auctions are usually listed in *Pariscope*; you can view the goods from 11am to 6pm the day before an auction or 11am to noon on the day of the auction.

Bidding of another sort occurs daily at the **Bourse des Valeurs** (stock exchange), 4, place de la Bourse (tel. 42 33 99 83, 40 41 10 00, or 49 27 10 00; Mo. Bourse). Despite being housed in a sober building with an unmistakably financial air, the generic Neoclassical building might as well be a church, a bank, or, as Hugo continued the list in *Notre-Dame de Paris*, "a royal palace, a house of commons, a town hall, a college, a riding school, an academy, a trade market, a tribunal, a museum, a barracks, a sepulchre, a temple, a theater." Massive Corinthian colonnades create a reassuring impression of stability, reinforced by four stone women in classical garb.

The exchange was founded in 1724, long after those of Lyon, Toulouse, and Rouen. Through it flowed the ever more worthless bonds of the old regime, as the debts of the last, extravagant Bourbons multiplied to finance their debauchery and wars. It was closed briefly during the Terror, due to Jacobin suspicion of profiteering traders, but it recovered under the regime of Napoleon, who first limited the number of seats. Construction of the present edifice began in 1808, according to plans laid by Alexandre Brogniart. Progress was slow and stopped entirely between 1814 and 1821 for lack of funds; only in 1826 were the stockbrokers able to move in from their temporary home on rue Feydeau (a workshop for opera props). Almost immediately, with the growth of stock trading, Brogniart's palace became too small. As a stopgap measure, various parts of the market were moved elsewhere in Paris. Eventually, someone realized this could not go on forever; between 1902 and 1907, the wings to the left and right of the façade were added. The only way to visit the interior is by taking one of the **guided tours** offered at least twice a day (be ready to show your passport as you enter). You get a little lecture about stock markets, complete with audio-visuals, then a look at the trader's pit (which is tame compared to London or New York). Unless markets fascinate you, this probably isn't worth the 10F or the 60 to 75 minutes (visits usually at 2 and 2:30pm, but call ahead or check the sign by the entrance to confirm).

To the east of the Bourse, the **rue de Cléry** and the parallel **rue d'Aboukir** mark the line of the old rampart of Charles V. The buildings between the two streets were constructed after the destruction of the wall in the 17th century, and they illustrate the adaptation of the fanciest Italianate forms to more inexpensive dwellings. Lintels and plaster were used instead of arches and stone, making handsome, serviceable abodes. They now form a backdrop for the prostitutes who work the streets.

In the mid 70s, the city's prostitutes occupied churches, monuments, and public spaces demanding unionization. They marched down their place of business, the **rue St-Denis,** demanding equal rights and protections under French law. They won these rights and are today a unionized trade. Prostitution is legal in France, and censorship of sexual material in store displays is very lax. In 1993, the police mobilized an enormous effort to rid the Bois de Boulogne of the prostitutes who frequented the area at night. The police were successful at returning the Bois to its 19th-century respectability, but the Bois's sex workers simply migrated to rue St-Denis in the *2ème*. The sidewalks are constantly patrolled by cops, so it is not particularly dangerous, but it can be intimidating, especially for a woman walking alone.

## ■ Third Arrondissement: The Marais

The third *arrondissement,* together with the fourth, is called the Marais ("the swamp") because of its distinguishing quality of dampness before 13th-century monks drained it. With Henri IV's construction of the place des Vosges (see *4ème arrondissement)* at the beginning of the 17th century, the area became the center of fashionable living. Leading architects and sculptors were kept busy building the *hôtels particuliers* that still dot the Marais—discreetly elegant mansions nestled between large courtyards in front and gardens in the rear. Under Louis XV, the center of Paris life moved out of the Marais to the faubourgs St-Honoré and St-Germain, and construction of *hôtels* in the Marais slackened considerably.

The 19th and early 20th centuries were not kind to the old Marais. Many *hôtels* were destroyed or allowed to fall into disrepair. Narrow, medieval streets were widened at great architectural cost. Nineteenth-century planners who didn't want to widen a whole street at once tried to do it piecemeal; new laws specified that any new building had to be built some meters back from the curb. This has resulted in streets with sawtoothed sides. (Given the longevity of some buildings, widening a street in this manner would take several hundred years. The idea was given up in 1974.) Recently the government has shown a greater interest in conservation: in 1964, part of the Marais was declared a historic neighborhood and protected from further destruction. In addition, museums such as the Musée de la Chasse, the Musée Picasso, and the Musée Cognacq-Jay have moved into and restored old *hôtels*.

But there is more to see than these handful of *hôtels*. Stroll down side streets, wander around Beaubourg, and catch the traces of medieval Paris—a bustling village of storefronts and inns that have, over time, begun to sway with gravity, to shift with the tilt of the earth. The oldest buildings in the city are to be found here on the rue de Montmorency and rue Bolta, dating from the 14th and 13th centuries respectively. Look around; much of what the third has to offer doesn't charge admission.

**Les Archives Nationaux (National Archives)** lie in the center of the architecturally rich southern part of the third. Many of the most important documents from French history are housed in the Hôtel de Soubise, the Hôtel de Rohan, and the few other old residences that happen to be on the same city block. The archives display the original sources of the tragedies and triumphs of the last centuries; hidden here are letters from Benjamin Franklin and George Washington, the Treaty of Westphalia, the Edict of Nantes and its Revocation, the Declaration of the Rights of Man, a will from 627, the wills of Louis XVI and Napoleon, and Marie-Antoinette's touching last letter. Here too is kept Louis XVI's famous diary, with the one word "rien" (nothing) scrawled for the day July 14, 1789; it had been a bad day for hunting. You can see the most intriguing of these documents at the **Musée de l'Histoire de France** (see Museums), housed at the Hôtel de Soubise. The **Hôtel de Soubise** was built between 1705 and 1709 under the direction of Delamair, the same architect who designed the Hôtel de Rohan. The majestic courtyard is a classic example of 18th-century aristocratic architecture. The very rich—some would even say gaudy—interior decorations (executed between 1730 and 1745) still adorn the museum.

A little farther on at 58, rue des Archives, the towered gate is the only surviving portion of a mansion, the **Hôtel de Clisson,** that was built in 1380. The unusual angle between the gate and the road was chosen to facilitate the entrance of litters and carriages. On the other side of the street from the entrance to the Hôtel de Soubise, notice the crack between nos. 57 and 59. The stone base of the red brick building in the background is a vestige of Philippe-Auguste's city wall, built from 1180 to 1220. One of the oldest medieval residences, former home of Jacques Coeur, Charles VII's Chancellor of the Exchequer, can be admired at 40, rue des Archives. Off the rue de Bretagne, the restful park that is now the square du Temple has a tumultuous past. Just beyond the grounds where children play was the **Quartier du Temple**, the late 12th-century headquarters for the Knights of the Templar. In the 14th century, the palace, ultimately demolished under Napoleon, came under the jurisdiction of the Order of St-Jean-de-Jerusalem and subsequently the Order of the Malta. Under the direction of the prince de Conti, the Grand Prior, the palace became the site for social gatherings of the wealthy; Rousseau lived here in 1765. After the revolution, from 1792-1808, it was turned into a prison of the state and housed members of the royal family in their last years; Louis XVI was taken directly from here to the guillotine. The young Louis XVII died here in 1795.

**Hôtel de Rohan,** one of the most famous *hôtels* in the Marais, stands at no. 87, rue Vieille-du-Temple. It was built between 1705 and 1708 for Armand-Gaston de Rohan, Bishop of Strasbourg, and housed many of his descendants. Cardinal Rohan

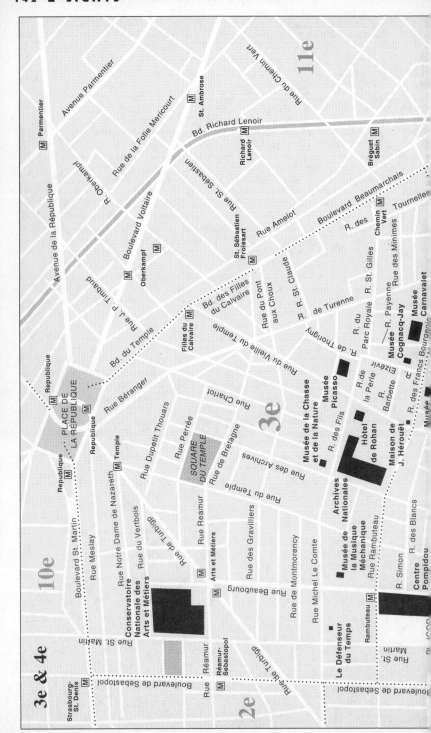

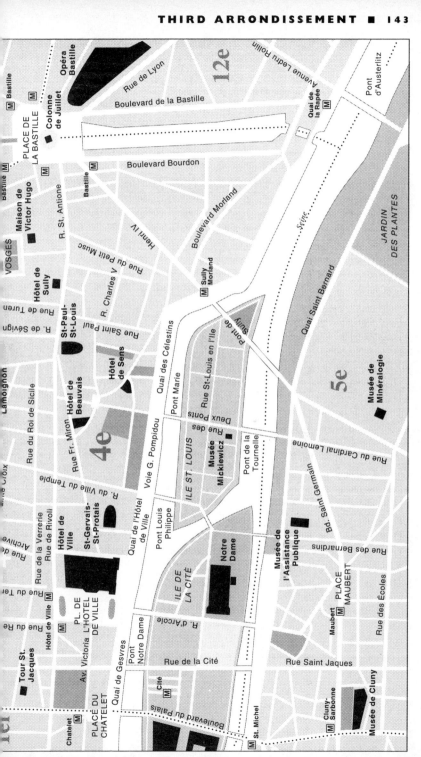

was arrested here as a result of the infamous *affaire du collier* (affair of the necklace). The Cardinal tried to court Marie-Antoinette's favor by offering her a rather expensive gift; the Comtesse de la Motte ruined his plans. During temporary exhibitions, you can visit the palace's sumptuous interior—if you pay about 10F for the temporary exhibit, often housed in the Cabinet des Singes; otherwise, just tour the impressive courtyard.

Across the rue des Quatre Fils from the archives is the **Hôtel Guénégaud,** built by Mansart in the 17th century and home of the Musée de la Chasse (see Museums). Nos. 16 and 18, rue des Quatre Fils, illustrate the city's piecemeal efforts to widen the streets in the Marais. The 17th-century gate of no. 16 used to stand forward of where it is now. The *hôtel* was destroyed, and the gate moved backward and was stuck onto a newer building. At no. 18, a modern building with three arches occupies part of the courtyard of a 17th-century *hôtel.* Behind it, you can see the inner façade of the older building, which was spared by the street-widening policy. Straight ahead, at 1, rue de la Perle, the **Hôtel Libéral-Bruant** houses the five room Musée de la Serrurerie (see Museums). The recently restored *hôtel* was built in the 17th century by the architect of the Invalides for his personal use.

The **rue Vieille-du-Temple,** which runs along the east side of the Hôtel de Rohan, is lined with stately residences. The tower at the corner of the rue des Francs-Bourgeois belongs to the **Hôtel Hérouêt,** built in 1528 for Louis XII's treasurer. Hérouêt had to get special permission to add the bold angle turret to his home; normally such extravagances were reserved for royalty. Farther down at no. 75 is the 18th-century **Hôtel de la Tour du Pin.** No. 64 includes the remains of the façade of a 17th-century *hôtel.* Between rue des Coutures and rue de la Perle is the entrance to a park—a great place to have a picnic.

The park adjoins the garden of the **Hôtel Salé,** once the Hôtel de Juigné and currently home of the Musée Picasso (see Museums). Built for a salt merchant and profiteer of the hated *gabelle* (salt tax), the *hôtel* has served many different functions during its transition from *parvenu* residence to Picasso museum. In 1793, it served as Dépôt Nationale Littéraire, a warehouse for books sequestered by Revolutionary censors. Balzac lived here while it was a 19th-century *pension* for artists and students. Now the Picasso collection whimsically, even irreverently, fits the ornate interiors. His sculpture and paintings thumb jagged noses and raise one, long eyebrow at the *putti* on the ceiling and the sphinx which guard the building. Sculptures and light fixtures by Giacometti share this incongruous setting.

**Rue de Sévigné** (Mo. Chemin Vert) is a small street worth passing through on your way to the place des Vosges or the Eglise St-Paul-St-Louis. Near the top of the street, on the rue St-Gilles, is a pink *hôtel* from 1620. On the left side, at no. 52, an imposing gate is all that's left of the Hôtel de Flesselles, built in the 18th century and demolished in 1908. No. 48, the building with the French flag, houses an elementary school. The woman doing the breast-feeding is Charity, as sculpted by Fortin in 1806. On the right side of the street (no. 23), in the *hôtel* that once housed the Marquise de Sévigné, the **Hôtel Carnavalet** houses an enlightening museum of Parisian history (see Museums). Even if you don't visit the museum, it's worth looking at the building's gate and courtyard, built in the 1540s and 50s for Jacques des Ligneris, the ambitious president of the Parlement of Paris. The statue in the middle of the courtyard is Louis XIV; it used to be in front of the Hôtel de Ville. To maintain architectural unity, the walls to your left and right, added in 1655, were given similar bas-reliefs: to the left are the four elements and to the right, the four winds. In the 1860s, architects tried to restore the building to its original appearance. Unfortunately, they mistook a 17th-century proposal to remodel the building for the original plans, and ended up carrying out the remodeling two centuries late.

From the Hôtel Carnavalet, head back to rue des Francs-Bourgeois and take a right onto rue Beaubourg. At no. 51 on the side street Montmorency sits the **Auberge Nicolas Flanel,** built in 1407. The French alchemist Flanel ran a chanty house here, providing medieval workers and homeless free food and lodging. A chic restaurant, with an affordable midday *menu,* now occupies this address (see Restaurants—3ème). Nearby, on the other side of Beaubourg, the building on rue du Grenier-St-Lazare without an address, a door, or a light switch, provides whimsy with a hard edge for Marais visitors. Art collaborative and commune, the building is a junk collage; you can hang out here—if that's your scene and you have a spare cigarette.

Travel farther north on Beaubourg, turn right on rue de Réamur and left on rue Volta. At no. 3 sits the oldest residential building in Paris, a four-story structure dating from 1300. The building in its day towered over its rue Volta fellows, an equally impressive collection of medieval shops and homes, where, as in this dark low-ceilinged *rez-de-chaussée,* many an artisan worked, ate and slept. Look carefully: rue Volta provides a taste of the past sliced but not demolished by Haussmania.

## ■ Fourth Arrondissement: The Marais (Lower Half)

Relatively undisturbed by Haussmann's reconstruction, the fourth *arrondissement* encourages visitors to wander past decaying edifices once inhabited by kings and their mistresses, through cobblestone streets lined with *galeries* and felafel stands, and into parks and *places* in which the well-heeled mix with the unshod. The 4ème should be seen as a miracle of urban development; once a swamp, now a gentrified package of seasoned Parisians and newer arrivals, the Marais is a *quartier* built for the *flâneur* who sets a languid pace and loose course through its maze. From place des Vosges on the north and Ile St-Louis on the south, to the Hôtel de Ville on the west and the boulevard Henri IV on the east, the 4ème offers a panoply of elegant historic monuments, market streets, and sudden, fanciful extravagance, bisected by the busy rue de Rivoli and rue St-Antoine. You can't help bumping into history; royals and literary greats as well as a centuries-old and still thriving Jewish community have left their mark here. Politically opposed groups also live side by side in this self-contradictory *quartier;* both ultra-conservative *garde républicaine* Jean-Marie Le Pen supporters and an active and growing gay population call the fourth home.

The **Hôtel de Lamoignon,** 24, rue Pavée (Mo. St-Paul), directly south of the Hôtel Carnavalet (see 3ème), is one of the finest *hôtels particuliers* in the Marais, built in 1584 for Diane de France, daughter of Henri II. The noble façade, with its two-story Corinthian pilasters, is the first example in Paris of the "colossal" style of decoration later to appear in the Louvre. In the staid 16th century, these ground-to-roof pilasters were quite daring, but no one was going to tell that to the princess. The left wing, which blends rather clumsily into the original building, was added a generation later by Diane's heir, Charles de Valois. The buildings of the small courtyard to the right date from 1968; added to make room for the library that moved here that year, they provide a surprisingly graceful counterpoint to the left wing. The unfortunate modern construction visible farther to the right dates from 1992. Through a door in the courtyard you can enter the **Bibliothèque Historique de la Ville de Paris** (tel. 42 74 44 44). This noncirculating library of Parisian history lends its 500,000 volumes to anyone who can present a valid ID. This is not a tourist attraction; visit only if you want information. (Open Mon.-Sat. 9:30am-6pm.) To see the gardens of the *hôtel,* which are closed to the public, exit onto rue Pavée (thus named because it was the first street in the city to be paved) and turn right on rue des Francs Bourgeois. Next door you can still see traces of the prison de la Force, where more than 150 citizens were massacred in 1792.

**Place des Vosges** (Mo. Chemin Vert or St-Paul), Paris's oldest remaining public square and perhaps its most charming, provides one of the city's most refreshing strolls. The central square, now the site of a park, is surrounded by 17th-century townhouses built at the height of French Renaissance style. Several kings lived in mansions occupying this lot, until Cathérine de Médicis ordered the royal Palais de Tournelles destroyed after the accidental death of her husband Henri II in a jousting tournament. In a drastic transformation from its formal royal glory, the newly vacant space became the site of a horse market. Yet the area was brought to a new glory in 1605, when Henri IV expelled the market and decreed the construction of a new public square to be known as the place Royale. Wishing to promenade himself in courtly opulence, he wanted a *place* large and central enough to accommodate leisurely strolls. Each of the 36 buildings have arcades on the street level, topped by two stories decorated with pink brick capped by a steep, slate-covered roof. The "brick" on most of the façades is just a layer of mortar; this money-saving measure is most evident on the south side of the square (near the rue St-Antoine and the Seine), where the mortar has wrinkled and cracked. The largest townhouse, forming the *place*'s main entrance on the south side, was the majestic King's pavilion; directly opposite, forming a smaller but equally gracious exit, is the pavilion of the Queen.

Assassinated in 1610, Henri died two years before the place Royale's completion. The marriage of his successor, Louis XIII, to Anne d'Autriche would inaugurate the square as a place of kingly regalia. The event drew a crowd of 10,000 spectators and 150 buglers. Although Henri intended the *place* as a home and workplace for merchants (hence the arcades), the king's design restrictions made the *place* an address only gentlefolk could afford. Mme. de Sévigné (born at 1bis) and Cardinal Richelieu number among the illustrious few. Another character who occupied and then got bounced from the *place* was Marion Délorme, renowned for her beauty and number of lovers. As a friend of Richelieu, Marion would visit his home in the guise of a man. Her house repossessed in 1648, Marion died at (and of) middle age, a pauper.

Molière, Racine, and Voltaire filled the grand parlors with their *bon mots*. Mozart played a concert here at the age of seven. Even when the majority of the city's nobility moved across the river to the faubourg St-Germain, the place Royale remained among the most elegant spots in Paris. Then, during the Revolution, the 1639 Louis XIII statue in the center of the park was destroyed (the statue there now is a copy erected by the restored monarchy in 1818) and the park renamed place des Vosges after the first department in France to pay its taxes (1800). Since then, successive liberal and right-wing regimes changed the name back and forth from "Vosges" to "Royale" until 1870 and the Third Republic, when "Vosges" finally won out.

Follow the arcades around the edge of place des Vosges for an elegant promenade and some delightful window-shopping. Look for plaques that mark the habitations of famous residents. Théophile Gautier and Alphonse Daudet lived at no. 8; Rachel, the 19th century's most famous tragedian, lived at no. 9. Victor Hugo lived at no. 6, now an excellent museum with displays on his life, work, and contemporaries (see Museums). During summer weekends, these arcades fill with an array of talented musicians who play and sing a variety of mostly classical music, from harp medleys to Mozart arias. For some first-class relaxation, stop at one of the many cafés for coffee. Or, if you are able to avoid the park *gardiens*, sit on the grass in the central park. Inside, under the shade of the tall trees and next to the fountains, visitors are entirely isolated from the traffic noises and fumes of central Paris. Come here at dusk for a romantic stroll, when the illuminated iron lamps and gracious silhouettes of the townhouses will put you in the middle of a 19th-century drama. The most scenic way of escaping the place des Vosges is through the little corner door at the right of the south face (near no. 5), which leads into the garden of the Hôtel Sully.

The **Hôtel Sully**, 62, rue St-Antoine (Mo. St-Paul), is the most congenial of all the Marais *hôtels* for a relaxing summer afternoon. The small inner courtyard, with its elegant formal garden, offers all that a tired tourist could want: several stone benches, a classy (if pricey) café, and even a few trees. What's more, if you're lucky, you'll come upon one of their frequent concerts—either the official, often free chamber music performances or the unofficial student musicians who sing for extra money. The main building in the courtyard, adorned with allegorical statues of the four elements and the four seasons, was built in 1624 and acquired by the Duc de Sully, minister to Henri IV. Sully, often cuckolded by his young wife, would say when giving her money, "*voici tant pour la maison, tant pour vous, [et] tant pour vos amants*" (here's some for the house, some for you, and some for your lovers), asking only that she keep her paramours off the property. Today young couples steal a kiss on the stone benches in the *cour*. At the other side of the garden, now home to the café, is an extension known as the "Petit-Sully," added in the 1630s. The *hôtel* is occupied in part by the **Caisse Nationale des Monuments Historiques** (tel. 44 61 20 00), a government agency dedicated to preserving historic monuments. At the information office, you can pick up brochures about their English-language guided tours of Paris monuments (40F, including the Hôtel de Sully). It you tire of relaxation, culture, and people-watching, cross through the gardens to the **rue St-Antoine,** the major thoroughfare of the *4ème arrondissement,* on the other side. Along this boulevard, you'll find a variety of cafés, fruit and vegetable stands, *fromageries,* and boutiques, together with the more prosaic Monoprix supermarket. Buy food here for a picnic lunch in the Hôtel Sully or place des Vosges.

The **Eglise St-Paul-St-Louis,** 99, rue St-Antoine (Mo. St-Paul), dates from 1627 and is one of the earliest examples of the Jesuit style in Paris. Its large dome—one of the trademarks of Jesuit architecture—is visible from afar, but hidden at close range by ornamentation on the façade. The church, where the Jesuit Bossuet preached, retains a rich Baroque interior, complete with three 17th-century paintings representing the life of St-Louis. There used to be four, but one was lost and replaced by Eugène Delacroix's equally dramatic *Christ in the Garden of Olives* (1826). The two large stoups (holy water vessels) were a gift from Victor Hugo. (Open Mon.-Sat. 9:30am-7:30pm, Sun. 9:30am-12:30pm. Masses Sat. 6pm, Sun. 10am and 11:15am.)

The **Hôtel de Sens,** 1, rue du Figuier (Mo. Pont Marie), is one of the city's three surviving examples of medieval residential architecture. (The others are the Hôtel de Cluny in the *quartier latin* and Jacques Coeur's House in the *3ème.*) Built in 1474 for Tristan de Salazar, the archbishop of Sens, its military features reflect both Salazar's life as a soldier and the violence of the day. The turrets on rue du Figuier and rue de l'Hôtel de Ville were designed to survey the streets outside, while the square tower at the far left corner of the courtyard served as a dungeon. An enormous Gothic arch for the entrance—complete with chutes for pouring boiling water on invaders—and steep chimneys and spires contribute to the mansion's intimidating air.

The former residence of Queen Margot, whom Henri IV divorced because of her illustrious sexual appetite, this magnificent edifice has witnessed some of Paris's most daring romantic escapades. One Sunday in 1606, the 55-year-old "Queen Venus" drove up to the door of her home, in front of which her two current lovers were arguing. One of them strode to open the lady's carriage door, and the other shot him dead. Unfazed, the queen demanded the execution of the other, which she watched from a window the next day. The same tempestuous queen had a fig tree that encumbered her carriage immediately removed from the street; this episode gave rue du Figuier its name. (Tours on the second Thurs. of every month; call 42 78 14 60 for information.) The *hôtel* now houses the **Bibliothèque Forney** (tel. 42 78 14 60), a library that focuses on fine arts, decorative arts, graphic arts, and artisanry. The collection includes 200,000 books, 15,000 posters, and 1,000,000 postcards. Anyone with an ID can consult works in the library, but to check out books you must live in the Paris area. (Open Tues.-Fri. 1:30-8:30pm, Sat. 10am-8:30pm.)

Since the 13th century, when King Philippe-Auguste forced the Jewish population living in front of Notre-Dame to move to the Marais (then outside of city limits), this quarter has been the Jewish center of Paris. The area around rue des Rosiers and rue des Ecouffes still forms the spine of the Jewish community, with two synagogues (at 10, rue Pavée and 25, rue des Rosiers), one oratory (18, rue des Ecouffes), and dozens of kosher restaurants and delis. Down toward the river, at 17, rue Geoffroy de l'Asnier, the solemn 1956 **Mémorial du Martyr Juif Inconnu** (Memorial to the Unknown Jewish Martyr; Mo. St-Paul), commemorates European Jews who died at the hands of the Nazis and their collaborators. Due to a 1983 terrorist shooting, the center now asks that visitors pass through a metal detector. The crypt downstairs contains ashes brought back from concentration camps and from the Warsaw ghetto. Comment books at the base of the stairwell provide a moving narrative by survivors, partisans, and other visitors worldwide of their reflections upon this monument (open Sun.-Thurs. 10am-1pm and 2-6pm, Fri. 10am-1pm and 2-5pm; free). Upstairs, the **Centre de Documentation Juive Contemporaine** (Jewish Contemporary Documentation Center; tel. 42 72 44 72) has a small Holocaust museum (admission 15F), a library with more than 400,000 documents relating to the Nazi era, and frequent temporary exhibits (open Mon.-Thurs. 2-5:30pm).

Two streets and centuries away at 68, rue François-Miron stands the **Hôtel de Beauvais,** built in 1655 for Pierre de Beauvais and his wife Catherine Bellier. The fortune used to build the *hôtel* was given to Catherine, Anne d'Autriche's chambermaid, because of Catherine's tryst with 15-year-old Louis XIV. As the story goes, Anne was actually overjoyed to learn that her son would please his future wife more than Anne's impotent husband Louis XIII had pleased her. From the balcony of the hôtel, Anne d'Autriche and Cardinal Mazarin watched the entry of Louis XIV and Marie-Thérèse into Paris. A century later, as a guest of the Bavarian ambassador, Mozart played his first piano recital here.

The **Hôtel de Ville** (Mo. Hôtel de Ville), Paris's grandiose city hall, dominates a large square with refreshing fountains and Victorian-style lampposts. The present edifice is little more than a century old, a 19th-century creation which replaced the medieval structure built originally as a meeting hall for the *hause,* the cartel which controlled traffic on the Seine. In 1533, under King François I, the old building was destroyed and construction of a more spacious version which would house Paris's municipal government was begun on the same spot. The newer building, designed by Boccadoro, recalled the Renaissance style of the châteaux along the Loire.

On May 24, 1871, *communards* doused the building with petrol and set it afire. Lasting a full eight days, the blaze spared nothing but the frame. The Third Republic built a virtually identical structure on the ruins—the few changes made are worthy of mention. The republican Gambetta regime integrated statues of its own heroes into the façade. Michelet, rhapsodic historian of the Revolution, flanks the right side of the building. Look for Eugène Sue, author of *Les Mystères de Paris,* a novel about the city's underbelly. This melodramatist of the boulevard can now be seen forever surveying the rue de Rivoli which he made (in)famous. In addition to updating the façade's cast of *Grands Hommes,* the Third Republic added a group of bronze knights to the roof. All dressed up and nowhere to go, the knights share much with the officials that commissioned them.

The Third Republic spared not a *centime* for the finest of crystal chandeliers and gilded every possible interior surface, even creating a Hall of Mirrors in conscious emulation of the one at Versailles. In choosing painters, the officials in charge were suspicious of the new-fangled Impressionists; when Manet, Monet, Renoir, and Cézanne offered their services, they were all turned down in favor of heavy, didactic art. Bare-breasted women act out *Philosophy* (in the Salon des Lettres), *The Triumph of Art* (in the Salon des Arts), and *Light Guiding the Sciences in the Heavens* (in the Salon des Sciences). To be fair, a few of the paintings are not so bad, and the opulent decoration can be quite impressive. Rodin's bronze bust of the Republic (in the Salon Laurens) is one work of note.

Foreign heads of state are welcomed with receptions at the Hôtel de Ville, but for most people the only way to visit the interior of the building is to take a guided tour. (in French; Mon. except public holidays at 10:30am). Tours leave from the Information Office on 29, rue de Rivoli (tel. 42 76 40 40, open Mon.-Sat. 9am-6pm). Thanks to an elevator, these visits are entirely accessible to people in wheelchairs. The Information Office also holds temporary exhibits in its lobby.

In front of the Hôtel de Ville, the **place Hôtel de Ville,** formerly the place de Grève, took its name from the Right Bank's medieval topography. A marshy embankment (*grève*) of the Seine, the *place* would serve as a meeting ground for angry workers throughout the Middle Ages, giving France the phrase *en grève* (on strike). In the late 18th and 19th centuries, the place de Grève became a theater of

# LET'S GO® Travel

## 1994 CATALOG

We give you the world
at a discount!

•Discount Flights •Eurails •Travel Gear

# LET'S PACK IT UP

## Let's Go Supreme

Innovative hideaway suspension with parallel stay internal frame turns backpack into carry-on suitcase. Includes lumbar support pad, torso and waist adjustment, leather trim, and detachable daypack. Waterproof Cordura nylon, lifetime guarantee, 4400 cu. in. Navy, Green or Black.

**A** ・・・・・・・・・・・・・ **$175**

## Let's Go Backpack/Suitcase

Hideaway suspension with internal frame turns backpack into carry-on suitcase. Detachable daypack makes it 3 bags in 1. Waterproof Cordura nylon, lifetime guarantee, 3750 cu. in. Navy, Green or Black.

**B** ・・・・・・・・・・・・・・・ **$130**

## Let's Go Backcountry

Full size, slim profile expedition pack designed for the serious trekker. New Airflex suspension. X-frame pack with advanced composite tube suspension. Velcro height adjustment, side compression straps. Detachable hood converts into a fanny pack. Waterproof Cordura nylon, lifetime guarantee. Main compartment 6530 cu. in. extends to 7130 cu. in.

**C** ・・・・・・・・ **$210**

## Undercover NeckPouch

Ripstop nylon with soft Cambrelle back. 3 pockets. 6 x 7". Lifetime guarantee. Black or Tan.

**D** ・・・・・・・・・・・・・・・ **$9.95**

## Undercover WaistPouch

Ripstop nylon with soft Cambrelle back. 2 pockets. 12 x 5" with adjustable waistband. Lifetime guarantee. Black or Tan.

**E** ・・・・・・・・・・・・・・ **$9.95**

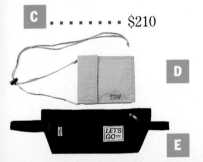

# LET'S GO BY TRAIN

**Eurail Passes**

Convenient way to travel Europe.
Save up to 70% over cost of individual tickets.

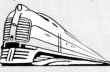

### EURAILPASS
FIRST CLASS

| | |
|---|---|
| 15 days · · · · · · · · · · | $498 |
| 21 days · · · · · · · · · · | $648 |
| 1 month · · · · · · · · · | $798 |
| 2 months · · · · · · · · | $1098 |
| 3 months · · · · · · · · | $1398 |

### EURAIL FLEXIPASS
FIRST CLASS

| | |
|---|---|
| Any 5 days in 2 months · · · · · | $348 |
| Any 10 days in 2 months · · · · | $560 |
| Any 15 days in 2 months · · · · | $740 |

### EURAIL SAVERPASS**
FIRST CLASS

| | |
|---|---|
| 15 days · · · · · · · · · · | $430 |
| 21 days · · · · · · · · · · | $550 |
| 1 month · · · · · · · · · | $678 |

**Price per person for 2 or more people travelling together. 3 people required between April 1 - September 3.

### EURAIL YOUTHPASS*
SECOND CLASS

| | |
|---|---|
| 15 days · · · · · · · · · · · | $398 |
| 1 month · · · · · · · · · · · | $578 |
| 2 months · · · · · · · · · | $768 |

*Valid only if passenger is under 26 on first date of travel.

### EURAIL YOUTH FLEXIPASS*
SECOND CLASS

| | |
|---|---|
| Any 5 days in 2 months · · · · · | $255 |
| Any 10 days in 2 months · · · · | $398 |
| Any 15 days in 2 months · · · · | $540 |

*Valid only if passenger is under 26 on first date of travel.

# LET'S GO BY PLANE

**Discounted Flights**

Over 150 destinations including:

## LONDON

## MADRID

## PARIS

## ATHENS

## ROME

Domestic fares too!
For prices & reservations
**call 1-800-5-LETS-GO**

### EURAIL COUNTRY PASSES

**POLAND HUNGARY
AUSTRIA FRANCE
SCANDINAVIA
FINLAND
LUXEMBOURG
GREECE SPAIN
CZECHOSLOVAKIA
GERMANY PORTUGAL
NETHERLANDS
BRITAIN SPAIN**

Call for prices, rail n' drive
or rail n' fly options.
Flexotel passes too!

# LET'S GO HOSTELING
## 1994-95 Youth Hostel Card

Required by most international hostels.
Must be a U.S. resident.

**F1** Adult (ages 18-55) ...... $25

**F2** Youth (under 18) ....... $10

## Sleepsack

Required at all hostels. Washable durable
poly/cotton. 18" pillow pocket. Folds into
pouch size.

**G** ........... $13.95

## 1993-94 Youth Hostel Guide (IYHG)

Essential information about 4000 hostels in
Europe and the Mediterranean.

**H** ........... $10.95

# LET'S GET STARTED
### Please print or type. Incomplete applications will be returned

| Last Name | First Name | Date of Birth |
|---|---|---|

| Street | *We do not ship to P.O. Boxes. U.S. addresses only.* | |
|---|---|---|

| City | State | Zip Code |
|---|---|---|

| Phone | Date Trip Begins | |
|---|---|---|

| Item Code | Description, Size & Color | Quantity | Unit Price | Total Price |
|---|---|---|---|---|
| | | | | |
| | | | | |
| | | | | |
| | | | | |
| | | | | |

| **Shipping & Handling** | | |
|---|---|---|
| | Total Merchandise Price | |
| If order totals: ..... Add | Shipping & Handling (See box at left) | |
| Up to $30.00 ..... $4.00 | | |
| 30.01-100.00 ..... $6.00 | For Rush Handling Add $10 for continental U.S., $12 for AK & HI | |
| Over 100.00 ..... $7.00 | MA Residents (Add 5% sales tax on gear & books) | |
| | **Total** | |

Mastercard/Visa Order

**Cardholder name**_____

**Card number**_____

**Expiration date**_____

Allow 2-3 weeks for delivery. Rush
orders delivered within one week of
our receipt.

Enclose check or money order
payable to:
Harvard Student Agencies, Inc.
53a Church St. Cambridge, MA 0

Prices subject to change without notice

political conflagration and metamorphosis. The first Paris Commune declared itself there in 1789; later the July Monarchy and Second Republic followed suit. Now, however, the only hordes demanding bread are the flocks of plump, swaggering, aggressive pigeons.

Cross quai de l'Hôtel de Ville to the backside of the city hall to the **Eglise St-Gervais-St-Protais,** one of the city's most beautiful examples of 16th- and 17th-century ecclesiastical architecture. The exterior is Neoclassical; the interior, with its intricate vaulting and stained glass, is flamboyant Gothic. Look for the Baroque wooden Christ by Préault, the less dramatic 16th-century Flemish Passion painted on wood, the beautiful 16th-century stained glass in the choir, and the strange Boschian misericords in the 16th-century choir stalls of the nave. François Couperin (1688-1733), together with eight other members of his family (spanning two hundred years of the church's history), was the main organist here; the organ on which they played is the same used in services today. St-Gervais-St-Protais is part of a working monastery, and if you come at the right time (check posted services) you will hear the nave filled with Gregorian chant and sung passages of the Bible.

Two blocks west of this area, the **Tour St-Jacques** (between 39 and 41, rue de Rivoli) stands alone in the center of its own park. The flamboyant Gothic tower is the only remnant of the 16th-century Eglise St-Jacques-la-Boucherie which once stood here. (The rest of the church was destroyed in 1802.) The 52m-high tower has a meteorological station at its top, continuing a long, scientific tradition that began with Pascal's experiments on the weight of air performed here in 1648; the statue of Pascal at the base of the tower commemorates this event. The tower marks the grand intersection of the rue de Rivoli and the boulevard Sébastopol, Haussmann's treasured *grand croisée* (great crossing). Here was the intersection of the builder's new east-west and north-south axes for the city, only meters from where the Roman roads had crossed two thousand years earlier.

In the northwest corner of the fourth, the **Centre Pompidou** (also referred to as the Palais Beaubourg) looms like an oversized engine abandoned next to the Seine. An anti-Hôtel de Ville, the Palais Beaubourg flaunts a 'what-you-see-is-what-you-get' inside-out architecture, which has been looking down on the surrounding buildings of the *quartier* since 1977. The center sits on the former site of a slum whose high rate of tuberculosis gained it the classification of an *îlot insalubre* (unhealthy block) and demolition in the 1930s. The lot remained vacant for many years, and two decades after the building's construction, some Parisians wish it still were. (For a fuller description of the center, see Museums).

In afternoon and early evening, the vast cobblestone *place* in front of the center is extraordinarily animated. A great place to people-watch, the *place* in front of the colorful museum gathers a mixture of wanna-be artists, street performers, and curious passersby. Pickpockets also frequent this area. In this chaotic scene, talent does not seem to matter; the police are quite tolerant just as long as you don't make too much noise. This is a classic performance area for Paris's street mimes; but watch out, they may pick you as their next victim from the crowd. Consult the big numerical display that counts the seconds until the year 2000; if you want a precise record of your visit, buy a postcard which will tell you the date and time to the millisecond (30F). Late at night when the tourists have left, the square can get fairly dangerous due to the plethora of drunk men who hang around and occasionally pick fights.

The **Fontaine Stravinski,** adjacent to the museum, complements the Beaubourg crowd of minstrels and eccentrics with its cartoon-like kinetic sculptures. Like a motorized water park of the absurd, the fountain's dancing g-clef, spinning *chapeaux,* and multi-colored menagerie spit water on passing crowds. A collaborative effort between Jean Tinguely and Niki St-Phalle, the work does justice to the memory of Igor Stravinsky, whose atonal music offended the tender ears of audiences 80 years ago. Tinguely created the iron works, St-Phalle the animals.

Next to the fountain, the **Eglise St-Merri** conceals some impressive Renaissance painted-glass windows behind its flamboyant Gothic exterior. Ravaged during the

Revolution, this church was known as the "Temple of Commerce" from 1796-1801, a sly reference to the flesh trade that has dominated this area since the 14th century. Free concerts are often held here (Sat. 9pm, Sun. 4pm, except Aug.). After the concert on the first and third Sunday of each month, there is a guided tour of the church (in French). Another clue to the widespread trade in this *arrondissement* can be found in the name of the rue du Petit Musc, which originated from *Pute y muse* (the prostitute idles here). One street away, in a house on the rue Beautreillis, pop culture icon Jim Morrison died, allegedly of a heart-attack, while in his bathtub. His grave can be found at Père Lachaise cemetery (see Sights—20*éme*).

## ■ Fifth Arrondissement: The Quartier Latin

Only one part of the Left Bank deserves a Bohemian reputation: the *quartier latin* (Latin Quarter). The Romans built some of the area's ancient streets, but the *latin* in the *quartier's* name refers to the language of scholarship and daily speech heard here until 1798. Home since the 13th century to the famed Sorbonne, the *quartier* symbolizes the romantic myth of the starving, shabby scholar, who skips meals to save money to buy books. In fact, for most of the 19th century it was something of a slum, and any student who could spent as much time as possible on the Right Bank.

In the early 1960s, dissent began brewing among the student population over certain characteristics of the French university system: an impenetrable, unapproachable bureaucracy, overcrowded classrooms, elitism in the matriculation process, and the growing strength of conservative elements who wanted to preserve traditional teaching methods. The crisis reached a boiling point in 1968 when student protest at the **Sorbonne** became violent. During the infamous **jours de mai** of the *quartier latin*, impassioned students forged human barricades, rioted in the streets, and occupied many university facilities. They also desecrated the statues of Hugo and Pasteur in the Sorbonne courtyard. Charged altercations with the police led to firebombing, looting, and brutality which left none dead but 400 wounded. As the situation spun further and further out of control, the students lost a sense of the legitimacy of their initial agenda. It was perhaps this conspicuous lack of real ideology that began to erode the faith of their supporters, notably the workers of the Comité Général du Travail (CGT), precluding any real political strength vis-à-vis de Gaulle and his government.

The result: a rush of public support for de Gaulle, and decentralization of the University of Paris into 13 autonomous campuses of which the Sorbonne is number four. With this decentralization, the *quartier latin* lost many of its youthful and scholarly inhabitants in one blow. In the 25 years since then, a tidal wave of tourist gold has swept over the area and drowned many of its small booksellers and cafés. Much of the area now resembles any other Parisian commercial center, except for the tell-tale used book shops and repertory cinemas.

The 5*ème arrondissement*—bounded by the Seine to the north, the Jardin des Plantes to the east, bd. St-Michel to the west, and the bd. de Port Royal and bd. St-Marcel to the south—still swarms with students of the University of Paris at the Sorbonne and the *grandes écoles,* prestigious exam-entry schools such as the Ecole Normale Supérieure and the Ecole Nationale des Sciences Politiques. While artists and hipper intellectuals are migrating to the Bastille, the *quartier latin* maintains an eternally youthful air. Untouched medieval streets twist their way through cafés, restaurants, and neighborhood *pâtisseries* and *charcuteries.* The many dead-end streets ending in walls testify to Haussmann's demolition of the hills that used to roll through the neighborhood. A few hills still remain; the tiny rue Rollin (Mo. Monge) drops down to rue Monge, a major thoroughfare.

The **boulevard St-Michel,** with its fashionable cafés, restaurants, bookstores, and movie theaters, is the pulsing center of life in the *quartier*. **Place St-Michel,** at the northern tip of this grand avenue, offers a microcosm of the entire *quartier*—complete with tourists, students, and drunken *clochards*. The majestic fountain dates from 1860, but includes a memorial to the liberation of France after World War II (the *place* was the scene of student fighting against the Germans in August, 1944). At the intersection of bd. St-Germain and bd. St-Michel at 6, pl. Paul-Painlevé, the **Hôtel de Cluny** (Paris's second-oldest residential building still standing) is now home to the **Musée de Cluny,** one of the world's finest collections of medieval art, jewelry, architecture, and tapestry (see Museums).

Farther south on bd. St-Michel, the **place de la Sorbonne** (Mo. Cluny-La Sorbonne, RER Luxembourg), a square lined with cafés, lounging students, and bookstores, is the focus of student life in the *quartier latin*. **Librairie J. Vrin,** 6, pl. Sorbonne (tel. 43 54 03 47), is France's premier bookstore for philosophical dissertation. At the eastern end of the square stands the **Sorbonne,** 45-7, rue des Ecoles, Europe's oldest university. Founded in 1253 by Robert de Sorbon as a dormitory for 17 theology students, the Sorbonne soon became the administrative quarters for the University of Paris. Its scholars were treated as nobility; they could wear swords and were not subject to arrest while on campus. In 1469, Louis XI established the first printing house here. One of the Sorbonne's many famous students was 15th-century poet and criminal, François Villon. Later, Roger Bacon haltingly developed the scientific method, and Pierre Lombard assembled an early encyclopedia. As it grew in power and size, the Sorbonne often contradicted the authority of the French throne. During the Hundred Years War, it even had the gall to side with England over France.

All the original buildings have been destroyed and rebuilt, the last time in 1885, except for **Ste-Ursule de la Sorbonne** (the main building), commissioned in 1642 by Cardinal Richelieu. The Cardinal, himself a *sorbonnard,* lies buried inside, his hat suspended above him by a few threads hanging from the ceiling. Legend has it that when Richelieu is freed from Purgatory, the threads will snap and the hat will tumble down. The public is allowed only in the chapel, which occasionally hosts art exhibits (open Mon.-Fri. 9am-5pm). Behind the Sorbonne is the less exclusive **Collège de France,** an institution created by François I in 1530 to contest the university's supreme authority. Outstanding courses, given over the years by such luminaries as Henri Bergson, Paul Valéry, and Milan Kundera, are free and open to all. Check the schedules that appear by the door in September. (Courses run Sept.-May. For more information, call 43 29 12 11.) Just south of the *collège* lies the **Lycée Louis-le-Grand,** where Molière, Robespierre, Victor Hugo, Baudelaire, and Pompidou spent part of their student years. Sartre taught there as well. If you're hooked on academic sight-seeing, the **Ecole Normale Supérieur,** France's leading liberal arts college and home to deconstructionist Jacques Derrida, is located southeast of the Sorbonne, on rue d'Ulm.

The **Panthéon,** its proud dome visible from any point in the *quartier latin,* towers over the highest point of the Left Bank (tel. 43 54 34 52; Mo. Cardinal Lemoine). The Panthéon is only the latest church to be built on this hill, the Montagne Ste-Geneviève. The Romans used it for a temple to Mercury, and Clovis built a shrine to the saints Peter and Paul. The people of Paris, however, were faithful to their patron saint, Ste-Geneviève, whose prayers had deflected Atilla's hordes to Orléans, and soon renamed the church and surrounding hill in her honor. (Oddly enough, the Orléannais prefer Jeanne d'Arc, as saints go.) After being destroyed by Norman invasions in the late 9th century, the church was rebuilt and remained basically untouched until 1754, when it was requisitioned by Louis XV. As a sign of his gratitude to Ste-Geneviève for helping him recover from a grave illness in 1744, the king created this enormous, somber structure. Jacques-Germain Soufflot's design challenged the conventions of church architecture of the period, launching the Greek revival in France. The church took 40 years to build, reaching completion on the eve of revolution.

The Revolution converted the church into a mausoleum of heroes, designed to rival the royal crypt at St-Denis. On April 4, 1791, the great parliamentarian Mirabeau was interred, only to have his ashes expelled the next year when his correspondence with Louis XVI was revealed. Voltaire's body was moved here, amid great ceremony, to the new Temple of Reason and Science. Dubbed the Panthéon in this epoch, the building underwent minor decentralizing alterations under the direction of Quatremere du Quincy, a renowned design theorist of his day. With nearly all its windows sealed to showcase light emanating from the dome, the necropolis took on the tomb-like aspect we see today. In addition, Quincy had a statue of liberty placed atop the dome to replace the cross. Over the next few centuries, the purpose of the Panthéon bounced between church and mausoleum, reflecting the history of France in its journey. In 1885, it became a national necropolis forever. Whoever the next trumpeted may be will enjoy immortality among an illustrious few: in the **crypt** you'll find Voltaire, Rousseau, Hugo, Zola, Jean Jaurès, Louis Braille, and Jean Moulin. Léon Daudet, in his *Souvenirs littéraires,* recalled the pomp and circumstance of Hugo's interment here in 1885, when two million mourners, marching to the tune of Chopin's *Marche funèbre,* followed the coffin to its final resting place: "A cold crypt, where glory is represented by an echo which the *gardien* will make you admire. A room full of the leftovers of republican and revolutionary immortality. It's freezing in there, even in the summer, and the symbolic torch held up by a hand from Rousseau's tomb has the air of a cruel joke, as if the author of the *Confessions* could not even light a cigarette for the author of *Les Misérables.*"

From the crypt, a twisting staircase winds upward to the roof and dome, where you can get an upclose view of a garish set of Neoclassical frescoes proclaiming the glory and justice of France. While you can walk around the outside of the roof, the building is not high enough to afford anything but a view of nearby rooftops. The dome's interior is an extreme example of Neoclassical architecture, replete with grand, austere Corinthian columns and expansive heights (open daily 10am-5:30pm; admission 25F, students 13F, children 17F).

While you're at the Panthéon, don't miss the fanciful **Eglise St-Etienne du Mont** next door. St-Etienne was built between 1492 and 1626—the resulting edifice is a mix of flamboyant Gothic and gingerbread castle. The façade mixes aesthetic forms: delicate rose windows are outlined by broken Renaissance pediments, topped off by a clock tower that belongs more to a parish church in the Alps. Moving inside, feast your eyes on the huge 17th-century **rood screen,** a structure used in the abbey churches of Western Europe to separate the chancel occupied by monks from the nave where the congregation sat. This is the last place in Paris where you can still be preached at from on high (once a common custom). On the right side of the nave, you will find epitaphs for Pascal and Racine, both of whom are buried farther down at the opening of the choir. Also on your right is the sanctuary of Ste-Geneviève, a chapel and reliquary of gilt copper built in the 19th century. Ste-Geneviève's actual remains were burnt during the Revolution—the reliquary holds a piece of her original tombstone together with a few bones and other scraps. A blank book placed in front allows you to render homage to these fragments, as well as to ask for a few choice favors. As you explore the church, notice the lovely 16th- and 17th-century stained glass, particularly the cloister (accessible through the back of the choir).

From St-Etienne du Mont, head south on rue Descartes, past the Lycée Henri IV, to the picturesque **place de la Contrescarpe.** The geographical center of the 5ème, this *place* has the feel of a tiny medieval village. The streets leading to it date back even farther; many (like rue Mouffetard) served as ancient Roman causeways. A festive atmosphere and cheap rent brought Hemingway here during his first years in Paris. John Dos Passos and Samuel Beckett were also former residents. Gone are those days; residents watch as the renovated buildings are snapped up by French yuppies (*Mon Dieu*—there goes the neighborhood!).

True Hemingway fans will want to make a pilgrimage to two of his former haunts around Contrescarpe: the studio he rented at 39, rue Descartes, and the home he shared with his wife Hadley at 74, rue du Cardinal Lemoine. To the left of this unassuming brown door is the former site of Bal du Printemps, a dance hall that Hemingway used as a raucous setting for parts of *A Movable Feast* and *The Sun Also Rises.* At No. 67 on the same street, Pascal died in 1662.

If you get hungry, head down rue Mouffetard towards **boulevard de Port-Royal**. Here you'll find one of the liveliest street markets in Paris (daily 9am-1pm and 4-7pm). Wade through tables piled high with lingerie, shoes, and random housewares to reach the *charcuterie, fromage,* and fruits and vegetables that taste even better than they look. Also on rue Mouffetard, notice the old, picturesque houses; in 1938 a hoard of 3500 gold coins was discovered at No. 53, presumably hidden more than 150 years earlier by the Royal Counselor to Louis XV.

East of the Panthéon, at the intersection of rue de Navarre and rue des Arènes, rest the remains of the **Arènes de Lutèce,** a 100 by 130m oval Roman amphitheater, built to accommodate 15,000 spectators (far surpassing the needs of the still-tiny colony of Lutetia). The ruins were unearthed during the construction of rue Monge and were restored in the 1910s; all the seats are reconstructions. Benches on winding paths above the arena offer an oasis of calm and provide the setting for a serene picnic supper.

People looking to kill a Sunday afternoon, but bored by the run-of-the-mill walk in the park, will love the **Jardin des Plantes** (tel. 40 79 37 00; Mo. Jussieu; main entrance at place Valhubert, off quai St-Bernard). The 45,000 square meter park, opened in 1640 by Guy de la Brosse, personal doctor to Louis XIII, was originally intended for the sole purpose of growing medicinal plants to promote his Majesty's health. Later it became a general garden for botanical research. Thomas Jefferson, an avid naturalist, loved this place. The garden has since been converted into a group of museums, including a natural history museum, a mineral museum, an insect gallery, a hedge maze, an arboretum, greenhouses, and a full-fledged zoo. Watch the leopards, bears, and 4m pythons stalk and slither, then head over to admire 5cm-long diamonds and meter-high quartz formations. While attractions such as the arboretum—a series of rare trees labeled with metal nameplates, scattered throughout the park—and the hedge maze, located at the northeastern end of the park, are free, all of the museums have separate tickets and hours (see Museums). Ask at the entrance gate for a free park map. The Jardin des Plantes also has two exhibitions devoted to botanical fascinations, including the **Jardin Alpin** and **Serres,** both greenhouses full of rare flowers and plants, the first from the Alpine domain and the second from tropical and desert regions (open Wed.-Mon. 1-5pm; admission 12F, students 8F). An interesting addition to the already extensive array of exhibits is the **Grande Galerie de l'Evolution**, due to open in fall of 1993. A renovation of the old *galerie de zoologie* which has been closed since 1965, this *galerie*—the first of its kind in the world—will have temporary exhibits, a cultural center, and a conference hall.

The **Ménagerie,** also found in the Jardin des Plantes, surprises those who did not expect to find live jaguars roaming in downtown Paris. The cages are painfully small, the weather is damp, and the general countenance of the animals is downtrodden and miserable. There are a few pleasant exceptions. The reptile house shelters boa constrictors as well as an assortment of lethal pythons, cobras, and rattlesnakes, all of which spend their time sleeping peacefully in their tree displays—entirely oblivious to the crowds of admiring visitors. During the siege of Paris in 1870, the zoo was raided for meat. Elephant became a great delicacy, but no one was brave enough to try slaughtering the lions. (Open in summer 9am-6pm, in winter 9am-5pm; admission 25F, students and ages 6-16 13F.)

Behind the Jardin des Plantes, visit la **Mosquée de Paris,** a Muslim place of worship constructed in 1922 by French architects to honor the role played by the countries of North Africa in World War I. Admire the graceful ivory and aqua tower, then enter the sculpted archways to tour the courtyard with its soothing fountain, carved wooden doors and ceilings, and ornate detailing. To really indulge, visit the *hammam* for a wonderful steam bath (59F) and enjoy a cup of mint tea in the *salon de repos* at 39, rue Geoffroy St-Hilaire (tel. 43 31 18 14; Mo. Jussieu). (Mosque open Sat.-Thurs. 9am-noon and 2-6pm. Guided tour 15F, students 10F. *Hammam* open to men Fri. 11am-8pm, Sun. 10am-8pm. Open to women Mon.-Tues.11am-8pm, Thurs. 11am-9pm, Sat. 10am-8pm.)

Walking west along the Seine back toward pl. St-Michel, stop to rest in the beautiful **Jardin des Sculptures en Plein Air,** quai St-Bernard, a lovely collection of modern sculpture on a long stretch of green along the Seine, with works by such artists as Zadkine, Brancusi, and Schéffer. Although this is a great place to catch some sun during the day, avoid this area at night. Across the street is the **Institut du Monde Arabe** (see Museums). Just next door to the institute, **La Tour d'Argent,** 15, quai de la Tournelle (Mo. Maubert), is one of Paris's most prestigious, most expensive restaurants. Also in the area, on the small rue de Bièvre off the ancient pl. Maubert, note Mitterand's home; the president created quite a stir by preferring to reside here rather than at the Elysée.

Farther west along the Seine, square René Viviani (Mo. St-Michel) sequesters the oldest tree in Paris (a false acacia dating from 1693), one of the best views of Notre-Dame, and the **Eglise de St-Julien-le-Pauvre.** Though not the most beautiful in the city, this church, built in 1165, is the oldest in Paris, finished even before Notre-Dame. Some parts of St-Germain-des-Prés predate St-Julien-le-Pauvre, but that was back when St-Germain was a suburb of Paris.

## ■ Sixth Arrondissement: St-Germain-des-Prés

Less frenzied and more sophisticated than its neighbors, the sixth *arrondissement* combines the vibrancy of the *quartier latin* (Latin Quarter) to the east with the fashionable cafés, restaurants, and movie theaters of Montparnasse to the south. This area has long been the focus of literary and artistic Paris, and it remains less ravaged by tourists than other, more monumental quarters. Join the locals at one of the famous cafés on the bd. St-Germain, former haunts of the likes of Picasso, Sartre, de Beauvoir, Prévert, Apollinaire, and Hemingway, and watch the hordes of well-dressed Parisians watch each other.

"There is nothing more charming, which invites one more enticingly to idleness, reverie, and young love, than a soft spring morning or a beautiful summer dusk at the **Jardin du Luxembourg**" wrote Léon Daudet in 1928 (RER: Luxembourg). Parisians appreciate this park in all its facets—every chance they get, they are here, sunbathing, contemplating, writing, romancing, strolling, or just gazing at the beautiful rose gardens and the still surface of the central basin. A mammoth task force of gardeners keeps this most beloved of Parisian gardens looking like paradise on earth: every year, they plant or transplant 350,000 flowers and move the 150 palm and orange trees back outside from winter storage. Thanks to the Parisians who defended this park against Haussmann's intentions to carve a street through it, you can sail a toy boat, ride a pony, attend the *grand guignol* (puppet show—see Entertainment), shoot hoops, play *boules* with the groups of old men, or simply soak up Paris.

The **Palais du Luxembourg,** within the park, was commissioned in 1615 by Marie de Médicis, who asked for an Italianate palace to remind her of her native Tuscany. The palace was completed in a mere five years, gaining a symmetry and uniformity rare to the buildings of Paris. Marie installed herself in the palace in 1625, but her days here were numbered as she opposed the powerful **Cardinal Richelieu.** Her son, Louis XIII, promised to dismiss the cardinal, but revoked his promise the next day and in 1630 Marie was banished to Cologne, where she died penniless. After housing various members of the royalty and high nobility—including the infamous Duchesse de Montpensier, better known as La Grande Mademoiselle because of her large figure—the Palais served as a prison during The Terror, then as a prison for the proponents of The Terror. Jacobin artist **Jacques-Louis David** used his time confined here to paint the haunting self-portrait now displayed in the Louvre. Future Empress Joséphine was imprisoned in the palace together with her republican husband, Beauharnais. Half a decade later, Joséphine returned with her second husband, the new Consul Bonaparte, to the palace, then their official residence. The Chamber of Peers met here under the Restoration and July Monarchy, when it judged many notorious trials of various traitors and assassins such as Camille Desmoulins, Maréchal Ney and Louis-Napoleon Bonaparte. The palace first served its current function as the meeting place for the *sénat,* the French upper house, in 1852. The *sénat*, despite its large and increasing number of members, is a fairly ineffectual body which can be overruled by the Parliament. The president of the *sénat* lives in **Petit Luxembourg,** a gift from Marie de Médicis to her nemesis, Cardinal Richelieu. The **Musée du Luxembourg** (tel. 42 34 20 00), next to the palace on rue de Vaugirard, often shows free exhibitions of contemporary art.

Entering from bd. St-Michel and the Luxembourg RER station, you will be faced with the lovely gold-embossed wrought iron gates—closing off the busy city from Marie de Médicis's garden of Paradise. Bring a book and relax in one of the folding chairs rimming the basin in front of the Palais du Luxembourg. It is also an excellent vantage point from which to observe passersby. Follow the paths leading in each direction, moving past the statues of the queens to the garden's many secluded glens, each with monuments to different poets and heroes of French history.

The bust of Henry Murger, author of the 1851 bestselling *Scenes of Bohemian Life,* was set up in 1895, amidst a storm of controversy. An official banquet to cost 5F was planned for the Café Voltaire, on the Right Bank. An alternative group—"True Bohemia"—accused the committee of possessing bourgeois values and arranged an alternate unveiling and a 2F banquet at the Café Procope, to be held a day *earlier* than the official ceremony. Finally, a third group organized a third banquet to be held at the Cabaret de la Bohème, with a super-non-bourgeois 70 centimes meal made up of sausage, fried potatoes, and (for dessert) toothpicks. A newspaper accused the mostly-Catholic Murger enthusiasts of anti-Semitism, and the unveiling of the bust turned into a violent riot that had little to do with Murger's literature and even less to do with the merry, starving artists and musicians he had described.

The **Fontaine Médici** is a tranquil spot in the northeast corner, at the end of a long alleyway and reflecting pool. Tall shade trees line the alley, giving the spot the shade of an enchanted bower. A row of chairs along the reflecting pool provides a traditional spot for daydreaming. Unfortunately, the fountain cannot always be seen in all its glory; in summer it often runs dry. Here, you may notice a phenomenon that one Parisian man of letters expressed in his 1852 description of the Jardin: "The soul still feels an involuntary impulse of sadness, a something melancholy and subdued in the air you breathe there. One does not move, as in the Tuileries, with completely unfettered spirits; one feels oneself pursued by the ghosts of the past."

South of the Luxembourg stretch its elegant, linear annexes, the Jardin R. Cavelier-de-la-Salle and the Jardin Marco Polo, both forming the northern half of the **avenue de l'Observatoire.** The elaborate **fontaine de l'Observatoire** (1875) marks the halfway point between the observatory and the Jardin du Luxembourg; its rearing horses provide a fittingly sumptuous perspective on the grand avenue that stretches at either side. At the extreme southeastern corner of the *6ème,* proudly stands Rude's statue of **Maréchal Ney,** *"le plus brave des braves,"* one of Napoleon's marshals. After a lifetime as a soldier, the courageous marshal gave his last command to the firing squad lined up in front of him: "Comrades, fire on me, and aim well."

At the nearby **Closerie des Lilas** café, such notables as Baudelaire, Verlaine, Breton, Picasso, and Hemingway listened to poetry and discussed their latest works (see Cafés). Hemingway described it as "one of the best cafés in Paris. It was warm inside in the winter and in the spring and fall it was fine outside..." Other expatriate watering holes extend farther down the bd. Montparnasse: La Rotonde at no. 103,

Le Séléct at no. 99 (Jake Barnes and Brett Ashley head here in a taxi in *The Sun Als* *Rises*), and La Coupole at no. 102-104. French artists sought refuge in this neighbor hood as well. Picasso, along with Matisse, found encouragement and financial sup port at 27, rue de Fleurus, off bd. Raspail west of the *jardin*, where Gertrude Stei and her brother Leo lined the walls with paintings they had bought from some c the century's greatest artists. Branching off bd. Raspail and curving down to Mont parnasse is rue Notre-Dame-des-Champs. American artist James MacNeill Whistle had a studio at no. 86, and Ezra Pound lived in a rear garden apartment at no. 70.

Branching off from the avenue de l'Observatoire and moving back along the edg of the Jardin du Luxembourg, the **boulevard Saint-Michel**—central axis of the *qua tier latin*—marks the eastern boundary of the 6ème. Follow bd. St-Michel to th place Edmond Rostand, where a small fountain marks the end of the rue Soufflo From this busy intersection, you'll have a majestic view (especially good at night) u the hill to the Panthéon—and the ever-popular McDonald's.

Follow the arcades of the rue de Médicis around the edge of the Jardin du Luxem bourg to Paris's oldest and largest theater—the **Théâtre Odéon,** founded in 1770 hovering majestically over the place d'Odéon, the nexus of six streets (Mo. Odéon) The Odéon company has competed with the rival Comédie-Française across the riv er (see1er *arrondissement)* for centuries, sometimes in the political arena. Beau marchais' *Marriage of Figaro,* after being nearly banned by the king, premiere here in 1784; aristocrats laughed wildly at the very jokes which ridiculed them an fist fights broke out on the street outside as people of all social classes struggled t get the last remaining tickets. In 1789, the actor Talma staged a performance of Vo taire's *Brutus* in which he imitated the pose of the hero in David's painting (see Lou vre). The rest of theater did not follow his leftist inclinations; the company wa imprisoned for monarchist sympathies during the Revolution, and Talma fled acros the river to the more liberal Comédie Française. The theater itself burned dow twice in its early years; the present Greco-Roman incarnation dates from 1818 an was restored to its former glory under the advice of David. The theater was built i the garden of the demolished Hôtel de Condé, where the infamous Marquis de Sad was born. During the 19th century, the Odéon earned the title of *théâtre maud* (cursed theater) after a chain of failures left it nearly bankrupt. All this changed i the 20th century, when the Odéon, under the direction of Jean-Louis Barrault an Madeleine Renaud, turned to contemporary playwrights and became *the* place t see modern drama. Leaders of the student revolt seized the building on May 17 1968 and destroyed much of the interior. Although it was given up as one of the strong points, the theater has never recovered; it is currently run by the state.

Nearby, off rue de Vaugirard at 5, rue de Tournon, resided Marie Lenormand, th *voyante* (fortune-teller) to Napoleon and others in desperate need of her service Two blocks west of the theater, the awe-inspiring 17th-century **Eglise St-Sulpic** (Mo. St-Sulpice) contains Delacroix frescoes in the first chapel on the right, a stu ning *Virgin and Child* by Jean-Baptiste Pigalle in one of the rear chapels, and enormous Chalgrin organ, among the world's largest and most famous with 658 pipes. In the transept of the church a copper band is inlaid in the floor running fro north to south, crossing from a plaque in the south arm to an obelisk in the nort arm. A ray of sunshine passes through a hole in the upper window of the south tran sept during the winter solstice, striking marked points on the obelisk at exactly mi day. The sunlight falls on the copper plaque during the spring and autumn equino (Open daily 7:30am-7:30pm.) From St-Sulpice, move north to the **boulevard Sain Germain.** This area, jam-packed with cafés, restaurants, cinemas, and expensiv boutiques, is always crowded, noisy, and exciting.

Begin exploring this area with a stroll through the **Cour du Commerce St-An dré,** a historic pedestrian passageway one street west of rue de l'Ancienne Coméd off bd. St-Germain (look for the name of the *cour* arching over the entryway). A you pass under the arch, to your immediate right is a turn-of-the-century bistro, th **Relais Odéon.** Its stylishly painted exterior, complete with floral mosaics and ol fashioned hanging sign, gives you an idea of what Paris was like during La Belle Epoque. The proprietor of the Odéon swears that during the Revolution the space now occupied by his outdoor tables was devoted to a more gruesome activity—the Jacobins parked a guillotine here, practicing on sheep to make sure the blade was sharp enough. Another version of the story has it that the first guillotine was designed at *atelier* no. 9 by a doctor Guillotin who wanted to find a more humane way of killing sheep. The doctor, greatly dismayed at the subsequent use of his contraption, tried desperately to have the name changed. The Assemblée, always logical and ever so artistically inclined, decided guillotine rhymed too melodically with machine to merit changing the name. Have a seat, nurse a *café crème* (20F), and try not to think about it. Or poke your head inside the café to admire the carved wood designs on the walls, beautiful lamps, and classic bistro mirrors. Farther down this passageway, on the top floor of the building on your left, was the site of a Revolutionary-era clandestine press which published Marat's *L'Ami du Peuple*. Marat was assassinated in his bath at a now demolished house where the *cour* meets the rue de l'Ancienne Comédie. The famous 19th-century poet Baudelaire was born on another of the small streets off the place St. André-des-Arts, at 15, rue Hautefeuille.

Along with bd. Montparnasse, bd. St-Germain has also played host to the literary and artistic crowd through the centuries. **Les Deux Magots**, at 6, pl. St-Germain des Prés, is named after a store that sold Chinese silk and imports at this spot in the 1800s. It was converted into a café in 1875, and by 1885 became a favorite hangout for Verlaine, Rimbaud, and Mallarmé. Forty years later, it attracted the Surrealists: Breton, Desnos, Artaud, and company. Picasso and St-Exupéry were also regular patrons. Also worth a visit is **Café de Flore,** 172, bd. St-Germain. Established in 1890, this café was made famous in the 40s and 50s by Sartre, Camus, and Jacques Prévert. Although they may have been convinced of the futility of life, they did enjoy a good cup of coffee (see Cafés). Across from these cafés sits the **Brasserie Lipp**, a former haunt of the famous and well-dressed in search of a beer and *choucroute garnie*.

The **Eglise St-Germain-des-Prés** (Mo. St-Germain-des-Prés) watches benevolently over all this excitement. The first church on this site was founded in the fields outside Paris by King Childebert I in order to hold relics he had brought back from the Holy Land; it was finished in 558 and consecrated by Saint Germain, Bishop of Paris, on the very day of the king's death (conveniently, since he was to be buried inside the church's walls). Sacked by the Normans and rebuilt three times, St-Germain-des-Prés remained for a long time a heavily fortified abbey outside of Paris. Parts of the modern-day church date from 1163, making it officially the oldest standing church in what is now Paris, yet the building you see is a mix of eclectic architectural styles; each generation added to the church its own version of the "modern," and the result is a mixture of Romanesque, Gothic, and Baroque features. The last remains of the old abbey walls and gates were destroyed when Haussmann extended the rue de Rennes in front of the church and created the place St-Germain-des-Prés in front.

During the Revolution, the church was desanctified and even had a brief sojourn at the end of the 18th century as a saltpeter mill, which, of course, did wonders for the already badly deteriorating structure. In 1794, just after St-Germain-des-Prés was restored to its original function as a church, a major fire consumed its remaining collection of artwork and treasures. Yet the church as you see it today has an air of sanctity that bears its battle scars well. The magnificent, painted interior, in shades of terra cotta and deep green with gold, was restored in the 19th century. In 1993, the city of Paris commissioned a team to study the effects of these restorations, as well as the eroding effects of rain, leaky plumbing, and capillary action from the soil. Wander around looking for the details—the Romanesque capitals on some of the pillars, the hidden stonework in the side chapels, the medieval shrines, the 17th-century vaulting—that attest to this building's near-millennium of history. In the second chapel on the right inside the church you'll find a stone marking the interred heart of Descartes and an altar dedicated to the victims of the September 1793 massacre, in which 186 Parisians were slaughtered by *sans-culottes* in the courtyard.

Pick up one of the free maps of the church, with information in English on St-Germain's history and its artifacts. (Information office open Mon. 2:30-6:45pm, Tues. and Thurs. 10:30am-6:45pm; Wed., Fri., and Sat. 10am-noon and 2:30-6:45pm.) Come here for one of their frequent concerts. As in most medieval churches, built to accommodate an age without microphones, the acoustics are wonderful. (Prices range from 60F to 160F. Church open daily 9am-7:30pm.)

Moving north from St-Germain toward the Seine, you'll find some of the most tangled streets in central Paris. Haussmann retired before he could figure out a way to extend his rue de Rennes to the riverbank and across a bridge, to meet up with the rue de Louvre. For years the impassable quarter presented a tempting morsel to urban designers wishing to improve circulation. But before they could decide on a plan, a new aesthetic of preservation kicked in; the neighborhood has been left as a largely unreconstructed maze. Don't even try to figure it out; if you lose yourself in this *quartier* you'll only have more time to ogle the goods in the art galleries that line every street. The rue de Seine, rue Mazarine, and rue Dauphine are prime routes for window shopping. The art you will find is as diverse as Paris itself: modern mixed-media works, sculpture, engravings, and classic oil paintings. Specialty stores carry eclectic decorative arts, elegant home furnishings, and collections of books on everything from English gardening to anthropology. To see what local art students are up to, walk around the **Ecole Nationale Supérieure des Beaux Arts (ENSBA),** 14, rue Bonaparte (tel. 42 60 34 57; Mo. St-Germain-des-Prés), at quai Malaquais. France's most acclaimed art school, the *école* was founded officially by Napoleon in 1811 and soon became the bastion of French academic painting and sculpture. The current building for ENSBA was finished in 1838 in a gracious style much like that of the nearby Institut de France. The school remains a springboard, as it has been since its founding, for young artists to launch themselves into a fiercely competitive field. To check out some of the best talent, stop by the Galérie CROUS, 11, rue des Beaux-Arts (tel. 43 54 10 99), where students, most of whom have just received their degree, show their work individually or in pairs (open Mon.-Sat. 10am-7pm; free).

Just one block to the east on the *quais,* the **Palais de l' Institut de France,** pl. de l'Institut (Mo. Pont-Neuf), broods over the Seine beneath its famous *coupole,* the black- and gold-topped dome. This one-time school (1688-1793) and prison (1793-1805) was designed by Le Vau to house the college established in Cardinal Mazarin's will. The glorious building has housed the Institut de France since 1806. Founded in 1795, the *institut* was intended to be a storehouse for the nation's knowledge and a meeting place for France's greatest scholars. During the Restoration, appointment to the *institut* was more dependent on one's political position than one's talent, but since 1830 the process has been slightly more meritocratic.

One of the *institut*'s branches is the prestigious **Académie Française,** which, since its founding by Richelieu in 1635, has assumed the task of compiling the official French dictionary and purging the sacred French language of dastardly foreign influence. Already having registered its disapproval of *le weekend, le parking,* and other "Franglais" nonsense, the Academy recently triumphed with the passing of a constitutional amendment that French is indeed the official language of France. For years the academy has been gearing up for a battle with those government-sponsored infidels who want to eliminate the circumflex, that pointed hat of an accent capping words like *tête* and *crêpe.* It is so difficult to become elected to this arcane society, limited to 40 members, that Molière, Balzac, and Proust never made it, and only in 1981 was a woman, Marguerite Yourcenar, granted membership.

Next door, the **Hôtel des Monnaies,** once the mint for all French coins, still proudly displays its austere 17th-century façade to the heart of the Left Bank. Today it mints only honorary medals. You can still tour its foundry and its significant coin collection by entering the **Musée de la Monnaie de Paris** (see Museums). The **Pont des Arts,** the footbridge across from the *institut,* is celebrated by poets and artists for its delicate ironwork, its beautiful views of the Seine, and its spiritual locus at the heart of France's most prestigious Academy of Arts and Letters. Built as a toll bridge in 1803, the *pont* was unique on two counts: it was the first bridge to be made of iron, and it was for pedestrians only. On the day it opened, 65,000 Parisians paid to walk across it. Today it's just a cheap thrill. Come here at dusk to watch the sun go down against the silhouette of Paris's most famous monuments.

## ■ Seventh Arrondissement: The Faubourg St-Germain

The elegant avenues, monuments, ministerial offices, and parks of the seventh *arrondissement* have made this part of Paris one of the most fashionable places to live since the 18th century. Home to the French National Assembly, the elegant Musée Rodin, the Musée d'Orsay, the infamous Eiffel Tower, UNESCO headquarters, and the grandiose Invalides, the *7ème arrondissement* is a microcosm of France's contributions to politics, art, European history, western architecture, and international diplomacy. Don't be alarmed by the large amount of policemen and soldiers in the *7ème;* they're guarding the *7ème*'s many famous residences. Once owned by Talleyrand and Mme. Adelaide, Louis-Philippe's sister, the Hôtel Matignon, at 57, rue de Varenne, is now the official residence of the French Prime Minister. But unless Edouard Balladur invites you in, it's off-limits.

The neighboring **Hôtel Biron,** at no. 77, was built by Gabriel in 1728. The state made it an artists' residence in 1904; sculptor Auguste Rodin rented a studio on its ground floor in 1908. When the Ministry of Education and Fine Arts evicted all tenants in 1910, Rodin offered to donate all of his works to make a museum—on the condition that he could spend his last years at Biron, where the museum was to be founded. Despite fierce debate, the state agreed to accept Rodin's gift, today called the **Musée Rodin** (see Museums).

Turning right along rue de Grenelle and then up rue de Bellechasse you arrive at the elegant Hôtel de Salm, built in 1786 by Pierre Rousseau for the Prince of Salm-Kyrbourg. The *hôtel*, which at one time hosted Mme. de Staël's outrageous parties, now houses the **Palais de la Légion d'Honneur** (founded by Napoleon in 1802); it also provides a rare opportunity to go inside a *hôtel*, in this case to visit the Musée National de la Légion d'Honneur at 2, rue de Bellechasse (see Museums). Across the street stands the now more famous rue de Bellechasse resident, the **Musée d'Orsay** (see Museums). The Gare d'Orsay, the train station housing the museum, takes its name from the nearby *quai.* The façade borrows from the monumental grandeur of the Louvre, but the glass and metal roof heralded the arrival of the modern era.

Next door, the **Caisse des Dépôts et Consignations,** 3, quai Anatole France, operates on the site of the Count of Belle-Isle's 1730 mansion. Destroyed by Commune fires in 1871, the *hôtel* was rebuilt between 1872 and 1875. The Caisse moved into the building in 1858 and today continues to live up to its motto of "public trust" by letting people into its lovely courtyard and bustling lobby.

You can continue up to 75, rue de Lille where Montesquieu, Marivaux and others frequented the literary salon of Mme. de Tencin. Or, exit at 56, rue de Lille (passing Mérimée's former home at no. 52), turn left and then right onto rue du Bac. In the 18th century, this street marked the boundary between town and country. Now it is lined with stores displaying mouth-watering delicacies. Satiate chocolate cravings at **Christian Constant,** 26, rue du Bac and the ever-exquisite **Le Nôtre,** 44, rue du Bac (see Sweets).

**Eglise St-Thomas-d'Aquin** (tel. 42 22 59 74), off rue du Bac on rue de Gribeauval, was originally dedicated to Saint Dominique when it was built in the 17th century. Ironically, in this *quartier* of military heroes, the church was made into a Temple of Peace during the Revolution. Although under renovation, the 17th- and 18th-century paintings are still impressive and the central half dome is awesomely ornate. (Church open Mon.-Sat. 9am-noon and 4-7pm, Sun. 9:30am-6:30pm.)

Just off to the left from rue du Bac, at 55-57 rue de Grenelle, the **Fontaine des Quatres Saisons** (Fountain of Four Seasons) celebrates the city of Paris (the seated

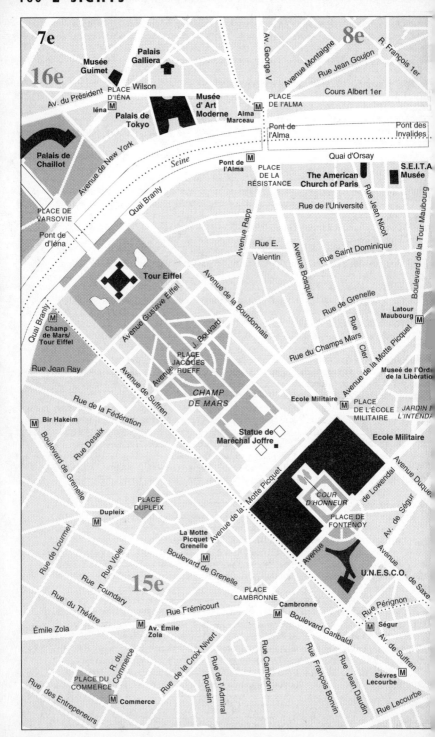

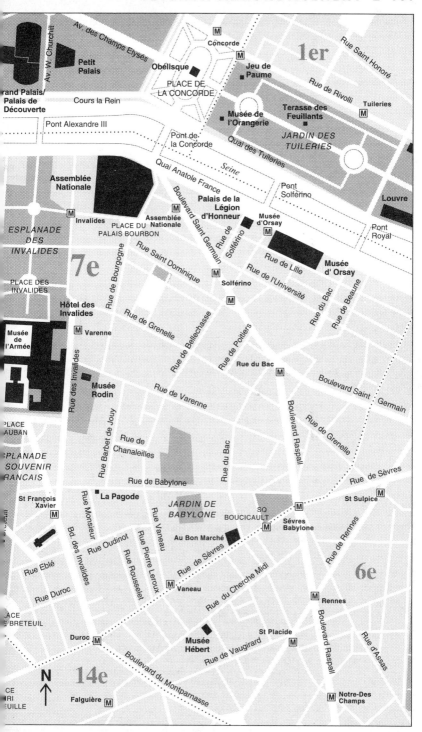

figure), who in turn controls the reclining Seine and Marne. Bouchardon sculpted the fountain between 1739 and 1745 to provide water to this part of Paris during all four seasons of the year. A little out of the way—a short walk up the bd. St-Germain at no. 202—the brilliant poet Guillaume Apollinaire lived and died. **Square Boucicart,** on the corner of bd. Raspail and rue de Babylone, has plenty of benches for adults and sand, slides, and a playhouse for children.

Past the Caserne de la Garde Républicaine (the yellow brick and funny hats give it away), stumble on **la Pagode** (corner of rue Babylone and rue Monsieur). In 1895 M. Morin of the Bon Marché fortune had it built for his wife as a testament to his love and the 19th-century orientalist craze in France. After Mme. Morin left him for a colleague's son, the building became the scene of Sino-Japanese soirées during the pre-WWI years, a period of tension between the two lands. The Chinese Embassy, located nearby, thought of renting the elegant building but never did. In 1931, la Pagode opened its doors to the public, becoming a cinema and fashionable address where the likes of Gloria Swanson, silent screen star and Joe Kennedy Sr.'s mistress, were known to lift a glass. After the period of German occupation and film censorship, the theater closed, only to be reopened by Frederic Rossif in 1945 in new resplendence. Today, preserved as a historic monument, it livens up the architectural tedium of ministries and *conseils,* and offers a range of excellent movies, old and new (see Entertainment—Cinema). Walk down rue Monsieur, turn left on rue Oudinot, and take rue Rousselet down to **rue de Sèvres.** Restaurants line the streets of this busy road, also full of *boucheries, marchés, pâtisseries,* and the like.

The **Palais Bourbon,** 33, quai d'Orsay, challenges the Madeleine across the river for colonnaded supremacy of the place de la Concorde axis. Napoleon erected the present façade in 1807, but the *hôtel* itself was built in 1722 for the Duchess of Bourbon, daughter of Louis XIV and Mme. de Montespan. From 1940-44, the Germans occupied the *Palais*; during the liberation parts of it were damaged, including a large number of books. Allegorical sculpture festoons the palace, but the high iron gates and machine-gun-laden police planted every few meters tend to be distracting. They're guarding the **Assemblée Nationale,** the French legislature, from a replay of the 1934 attempt by a mob to overthrow the government. French-speakers and government majors may want to observe the assembly in session (if you are neither you won't understand and you won't care). A security check that lasts as least one hour must be run on all foreigners who want to enter the chamber—show up with your passport well in advance of the start of the day's sitting. Appropriate dress is required. If you are a foreign national and want to attend a session of the National Assembly, you need to write in advance for permission to 33, quai d'Orsay 75007 Paris (tel. 40 63 64 80). (Sessions Oct.-Dec. and April-June, weekday afternoons.

If you would simply like a tour of the Assemblée Nationale, the process is much easier (and free). Just show up at 33, quai d'Orsay (tel. 40 63 63 08) on Saturday afternoon at 10am, 2pm, or 3pm for a tour (in French, but pamphlet in English available). The tour includes a visit to the Salon Delacroix and the library (both spectacularly painted by Eugène Delacroix), which, along with 700,000 books and documents contains the transcripts of Jeanne d'Arc's trial. The tour continues to the Assembly Chamber itself, called the **Salle de Séances.** A red semi-circle with colonnaded gallery, the chamber is presided over by the *Président du conseil,* who sits in an ornate chair decorated by Lemot and Michallon. Behind him, a framed tapestry of Raphael's *School of Athens* presents an ideal of the republic of philosopher-kings. The representatives from the political right and the political left sit appropriately to the right or left of the president's seat. (From the gallery, you are actually seeing the reverse, since the right and the left are defined from the president's point of view.) Free tours are offered all year. Kiosque de l'Assemblée Nationale, 4, rue Aristide-Briand (tel. 40 63 61 21) has information about the Assemblée Nationale, as well as the standard collection of souvenirs. (Open Mon.-Fri. 9:30am-7pm, Sat. 9:30am-5pm.)

The large, green, tree-lined space of the **Esplanade des Invalides** stretches from Pont Alexandre III, lined with ornate late 19th-century gilded lampposts, to the gold-leaf dome of the **Hôtel des Invalides,** 2, av. de Tourville (Mo. Invalides). In 1670, Louis XIV decided to "construct a royal home, grand and spacious enough to receive all old or wounded officers and soldiers." The first stone was laid November 30, 1671; architect Libéral Burand's building accepted its first wounded in 1674, and veterans still live in the Invalides today. Jules Hardouin-Mansart was responsible for finishing the **Eglise St-Louis,** the chapel of the Invalides, and, in 1706, the imposing dome. The Church of the Dome received Napoleon's body for funeral services in 1840, but Visconti's ostentatious tomb was not ready for occupation until April 2, 1861. According to legend, when Napoleon's coffin was opened 19 years after his death (the day the British finally allowed it to leave St. Helena); his body was still perfectly preserved. You can tour the Tomb, as well as the Musée de l'Armée, Musée d'Histoire Contemporaine, and Musée de l'Ordre de Libération, all housed within the complex (see Invalides Museums). Enter the complex either from place des Invalides to the north or place Vauban and avenue de Tourville to the south. Around the "back," to the left of the Tourville entrance, the **Jardin de l'Intendant** provides shade and benches in an ornamental setting, albeit next to a busy street. The ditch, lined with foreign cannon captured in various wars, used to be a moat, and it still makes it impossible to leave by any but the official entrance.

A pleasant riverside walk awaits you to the east of the Invalides, on the quai d'Orsay. The **SEITA** (Société pour l'Exploitation Industrielle des Tabacs et Allumettes), on the corner of rue Surcouf and quai d'Orsay stands as a testament to the paradoxical approach of France to government—tobacco is state-run, state-promoted product that is sticking the state-run, state-promoted health system with increasingly large bills. Don't miss the nearby **Musée-Galerie de la Seita** (see Museums).

The **American Church in Paris,** 65, quai d'Orsay (tel. 47 05 07 99), bustles with English speakers in search of accommodations, jobs, counseling, cultural programs, and other services for Americans abroad (see Practical Information). Appropriately named, the leafy av. Bosquet (Thicket Avenue) borders an area to the east rich in restaurants, hotels, and food stores. Rue Cler can satisfy any and all culinary needs. Or you can join the sewer rats at the **Musée des Egouts de Paris** (Museum of the Paris Sewers), entrance near pl. de la Résistance (see Museums).

And now, for the *pièce de résistance...*

At the opening of his impressive iron monument in 1889, Gustave Eiffel scrawled on the fan of an adoring spectator, "France is the only country in the world with a 300m flagpole." Still flying the tricolor, the skyline-piercing **Tour Eiffel (Eiffel Tower)** (tel. 45 50 34 56; Mo. Bir-Hakeim) is a globally admired symbol of Paris. The tower's design, actually conceived by engineers Emile Nouguier and Maurice Koechlin (who worked for Eiffel's bridge building company), was the winning entry in an 1885 contest. Judges chose the plans that bore Eiffel's name for the centerpiece of the 1889 World's Fair, which was held to celebrate the centennial of the French Revolution. Shockwaves of dismay reverberated around the city before the construction site at the end of the Champs-de-Mars even opened. Architects whined throughout 1886; one month into construction, in February of 1887, the artistic establishment published a scathing letter in *Le Temps.* Writers Guy de Maupassant, Alexandre Dumas *fils,* Charles Garnier, architect of the Opéra, and the composer Gounod joined countless other artists in condemning the erection "in the heart of our capital, of the useless and monstrous Eiffel Tower."" Maupassant spoke of it elsewhere as a "giant and disgraceful skeleton;" after it was built he allegedly ate his lunch in the one-hectare expanse beneath it because it was the only place in Paris where he could avoid seeing the thing. It was even labeled with that most damning of epithets: "American." The condemnation was not altogether surprising. With its metal girders and boldly modern look, the tower was a triumph of engineering, seemingly cementing the split between science and art. Eiffel patiently responded to his critics by saying that his engineer's sense of beauty was delighted primarily by design that served a purpose, and that the grand curves of the tower would possess the beauty of wind resistance. The tallest structure in the world would be a monument to modern engineering and industry, comparable to the pyramids of Egypt.

Inaugurated March 31, 1889, the tower opened for visitors May 15, 1889 to great popular acclaim: nearly two million people went up in the tower during the fair. Numbers dwindled by comparison during the following decades and the entrepreneurial Eiffel began to confront the unpleasant prospect of tearing his masterpiece down: the lease on the property from the City of Paris expired on Dec. 31, 1909 and it was expected that the tower, like the other world fair buildings on the Champs de Mars, would be destroyed. But the so-called Tower of Babel survived because of its importance as a science and communications installation, which Eiffel had cultivated carefully in the 1890s. The radiotelegraphic center established on the top of the tower worked full-time during World War I, intercepting enemy messages, among them the ones which resulted in the arrest and execution of Mata Hari.

With another world exposition in 1937 and a new Trocadéro Palace built across the river in its honor, the Eiffel Tower again became a showpiece, firmly established as the ultimate symbol of Paris. Eventually, even Eiffel was forced to bow before his own creation, sighing, "I ought to be jealous of that tower. She is more famous than I am." Loving centennial renovations have made the tower look sparkling-new and Parisians and tourists alike have reclaimed the monument. Sadly, the image of the tower, emblazoned on everything from postcards to t-shirts to lampshades and umbrellas has come to be seen as the height of kitsch. As a result, many visitors shun the tower and miss out on one of the most satisfying experiences in Paris. The Eiffel Tower is not as tacky as its countless imitations; do as Paul Fort urged in 1872, *"Va, prends l'ascenseur, mon enfant, ma soeur. Et qu'il rest en bas ce pauvre idiot, chignant contre un poste de radio."* (Go, take the elevator, my child, my sister...)

Seeing the Eiffel Tower, even for the umpteenth time, is inevitably breathtaking. The tower is huge and literally towers over its surroundings. It's also a soft brown, not the metallic steel gray that most visitors anticipate. And despite the 18,000 pieces of iron, 2,500,000 rivets, and 9,100,000 kilograms of sheer weight that compose the Eiffel Tower, many of the girders take on a spidery, web-like elegance. This is especially true at night, when lines of light follow the delicate skeleton, turning it into a brilliant lace-like apparition—a modern counterpart to the heaven-reaching spires of Notre-Dame.

The Tour Eiffel offers a range of services. Buy exorbitantly priced souvenirs in the stores, eat good food at high cost in the restaurants, and even send mail with the "only-available-here" Eiffel Tower postmark. The *Cinemax,* a fun and relaxing stop midway through the climb on the first floor, shows documentaries about the tower. Informative posters about bizarre moments in the tower's history are everywhere—take the time to read them; you'll appreciate the opportunity to rest your distended calves. The cheapest way to get up the tower is to walk up the first two floors (8F). This method also gives you an unbeatable, step-by-step tour of the tower's complex structure. But you can't go to the Eiffel Tower and not go all the way. The third floor/summit/tippy-top is accessible only by elevator. Tickets can be bought from the *caisse,* when open, or from the coin-operated dispenser in the east corner. Excellent aerial photographs point out significant landmarks, and accompanying blurbs, in English, fill in the history. (Tower open daily July-Aug. 9:30am-midnight, including holidays. Sept.-June 9:30am-11pm. Elevator to: 1st floor admission 18F, 2nd floor 25F, 3rd floor 52F. Under 12 and over 60 1st floor 8F, 2nd floor 17F, 3rd floor 24F. Under 4 free. Wheelchair accessible.)

Across the river (and the Pont d'Iléna) from the Eiffel Tower is the **Trocadéro** and the **Palais de Chaillot.** Constructed by Napoleon for his son, the Palais de Chaillot's elegant and expansive terrace, gardens, and fountains are a perfect place to view the Eiffel Tower from afar. Save your pictures for here. (See Sights—16ème.)

For an area dedicated to the God of War, the **Champ de Mars** teems with a remarkable amount of peace and happiness. In its 220 year existence, the Champ de Mars stands as a hopeful glimpse of a pacifist, non-violent world, dedicated to leisure and children's play amidst all the monuments to war in the 7ème. A green, flower-embroidered carpet stretching from the Ecole Militaire to the Eiffel Tower, the park is a veritable kid's heaven: jungle gyms, monkey bars and wood trains line the southwest side. The park's name comes from its original function as a drill ground for the neighboring Ecole Militaire. During the Revolution and the First Empire, it hosted several ceremonies of great patriotic import and political demonstrations. It was here that Robespierre proclaimed his doctrine of Supreme Being. Still, peaceful activities did take place; in 1780 Charles Montgolfier launched the first hydrogen balloon (with no basket attached) from here. The Champs de Mars was again tainted, this time with Alfred Dreyfus' public humiliation in 1894. Later, during the 19th and 20th centuries, the park served as a fairground site; it was the site for the 1889 World's Fair that gave Paris the Eiffel Tower. After the 1900 Exhibition, the Municipal Council seriously considered parceling off the Champ de Mars for development, but was persuaded that the dense city needed all the open space it had.

The **Ecole Militaire** was created by Louis XV at the urging of his mistress, Mme. de Pompadour, who wanted to transform "poor gentlemen" into educated officers. Jacques-Ange Gabriel's building accepted 500 students only after funds raised from a lottery and a tax on playing cards allowed for its completion in 1773. In 1784, a 15-year-old Corsican named Napoléone Buonaparte arrived and within weeks presented the school's administrators with a comprehensive plan for its reorganization.

The Ecole's architectural and spiritual antithesis, **UNESCO (United Nations Educational, Scientific, and Cultural Organization)** (tel. 45 68 17 13 or 45 68 17 18; Mo. Ségur) stands in the shape of a Y across the street at 7, pl. de Fontenoy. Established to foster science and culture throughout the world, the agency developed a reputation for waste, cronyism, and Marxist propaganda, which prompted the United States, the United Kingdom, and Singapore to withdraw in 1984, taking with them 30% of the agency's budget. The new head, Federico Mayor Zaragoza, is trying to persuade the U.S. to come back, especially now that the Soviet Union can't bankroll his organization. But recent criticism of UNESCO by international diplomats has only further tarnished its reputation. Nine appropriately international pieces of art decorate the building and garden: ceramics by Miró and Artigas, a nameless painting by Picasso, a Japanese garden, and an angel from the façade of a Nagasaki church destroyed by the bomb, among others. UNESCO frequently mounts temporary exhibitions of photography as well as exhibits on international art, science, and culture—anything from Japanese wood-carving to Ugandan irrigation projects. The library is open only to accredited researchers, but the bookstore is full of UNESCO publications. Bring your passport and call about conferences or lectures, when the place bustles with representatives from its 158 member countries. During especially important conferences when security needs are highest, you may have trouble getting in. (Open Mon.-Sat. 9am-6pm. Bookstore open Mon.-Fri. 9:15am-12:45pm and 2:15-5:45pm. Variable times for temporary exhibits. Free.)

## ■ Eighth Arrondissement: The Champs-Elysées

> To the Arc de Triomphe de l'Etoile:/ raise yourself all the way to the
> heavens, portal of victory/ That the giant of our glory/ Might pass without
> bending down.
>
> —Victor Hugo

Almost as elegant as its neighbor to the southwest, the 16ème, the eighth is home to Haussmann's wide sidewalks and tree-lined *grands boulevards,* including the famous **avenue des Champs-Elysées.** Well-known salons and boutiques of *haute couture* pepper fashionable streets like rue du Faubourg St-Honoré. Embassies crowd around the Palais de l'Elysée, the state residence of the French president. Already attractive to the bourgeoisie of the early 19th century, the neighborhood took off with the construction of boulevards Haussmann, Malesherbes, Victor Hugo, Foch, Kléber, and the others that shoot out from the Arc de Triomphe in a star-like formation known as l'Etoile (the star). The whole area bustles, and it should; within a very few blocks, the 8ème provides the resources necessary to dine exquisitely, dress impeccably, and accessorize magnificently. Moreover, you can indulge your esoteric musical tastes, satisfy your *penchant* for sweets, and buy the ticket for your winter flight to Rio with the greatest amount of ease (and money). Most importantly, the wide open spaces of the 8ème provide you with the chance to show it all off. But be forewarned. In the 8ème, you may feel underdressed and overwhelmed. This is the Paris you've seen in *Vogue* and in *Cosmo*, where the scarf is always Hermès, the watch is pure Cartier, and everyone has had a busy day at the boutique.

The **Arc de Triomphe** (tel. 43 80 31 31; Mo. Charles-de-Gaulle-Etoile), looming gloriously above the Champs-Elysées at place Charles de Gaulle, commemorates France's military victories as well as its long obsession with military history. The world's largest triumphal arch and an internationally recognized symbol of France, this behemoth was commissioned by Napoleon in 1806. When construction began, the Etoile marked the western entrance to the city through the *fermiers généraux* wall. Napoleon was exiled before the monument was completed, but Louis XVIII ordered resumption of work in 1823 and dedication of the arch to the war in Spain and to its commander, the Duc d'Angoulême. The Arc, designed by Chalgrin, was finally consecrated in 1836, 21 years after the defeat of the great army of *"Le Petit Corporal."* There was no consensus on what symbolic figures could cap the monument, and it has retained its simple unfinished form. The names of Napoleon's generals and battles are engraved inside; those generals underlined died in battle. The most famous of the Arc's allegorical sculpture groups depicting the military history of France is François Rude's *Departure of the Volunteers of 1792,* commonly known as *La Marseillaise,* to the right facing the arch from the Champs-Elysées.

Primarily, the Arc is a military symbol. As such, the horseshoe-shaped colossus has proved a magnet to various triumphal armies. The victorious Prussians marched through in 1871, inspiring the mortified Parisians to purify the ground with fire. On July 14, 1919, however, the Arc provided the backdrop for an Allied celebration parade headed by Maréchal Foch whose memory is now honored by the boulevard that bears his name, stretching out from the west side of the Arc into the 16ème. In 1940, Parisians were brought to tears as the Nazis goose-stepped through the Arc and down the Champs-Elysées. After four years of Nazi occupation, France was liberated by British, American, and French troops who marched through the Arc on August 26, 1944 to the roaring cheers of thousands of grateful Parisians. The Tomb of the Unknown Soldier has rested under the Arc since November 11, 1920; the eternal flame is rekindled every evening at 6:30pm, when veterans and small children lay wreaths decorated with blue, white, and red. De Gaulle's famous cry for *Résistance* is inscribed on a brass plaque in the pavement under the Arc.

The Arc sits in the center of the **Etoile,** which in 1907 became the world's first traffic circle. Rather than risk an early death by crossing the traffic to reach the Arc, use the underpasses on the even-numbered sides of both the Champs-Elysées and av. de la Grande-Armée. Inside the Arc, climb 205 steps up a winding staircase to the *entresol* and then dig deep for the 29 more that take you to the *musée* or tackle the lines at the elevator for a muscle-pull-free ride. The museum recounts the Arc's architectural and ceremonial history in French, complete with drawings and appropriately tacky souvenirs. The real spectacle lies just 46 steps higher—the *terrasse* at the top of the Arc provides a terrific view of the gorgeous avenue Foch (see 16ème) and the sprawling city. (Observation deck open daily 9am-6pm. Admission 31F, students 18-25 and ages 60 and older 20F, ages 7-17 6F, under 7 free. Lockers underneath the Arc for 5F a day. Phones available. Expect lines even on weekdays and buy your ticket before going up to the ground level.)

The **avenue des Champs-Elysées** is the most famous of the twelve symmetrical avenues radiating from the huge rotary of place Charles de Gaulle; it may even be the most famous avenue in the world. In a popular children's song, French youth are taught that you can do all you want on the Champs-Elysées. While this may not be entirely true, no one can deny that this 10-lane wonder, flanked by exquisite cafés and luxury shops and crowned by the world's most famous arch, deserves its reputation. Le Nôtre planted trees here in 1667 to extend the Tuileries vista, completing the work begun under Marie de Médicis in 1616. In 1709, the area was renamed the "Elysian Fields" because of the shade provided by the trees. During the 19th century, the Champs (as many Parisians call it) developed into a fashionable residential district. Mansions sprang up along its banks, then apartments and smart boutiques, making this strip of pavement the place to see and be seen in Paris. Balls, café-concerts, restaurants, and even circuses drew enormous crowds; the *bal Mabille* opened in 1840 at no. 51, and, at no. 25, in a somewhat more subdued setting, the charming hostess and spy Marquise de Païva entertained her famous guests.

Today, you can escape the crowds and watch the modern-day circus of tourists walk by while seated at **Fouquet's,** an outrageously expensive and famous café/restaurant near the Arc de Triomphe where French film stars hang out. Paris's answer to Hollywood's Sunset Strip, this stretch of the Champs-Elysées bears golden plaques with the names of favorite French entertainers who have won the coveted César award (the French equivalent to the Oscar). Among the winners whose names are emblazoned here are Isabelle Adjani (*Camille Claudel*), Catherine Deneuve, and Louis Malle, the director of *Au Revoir Les Enfants* and husband of Candice Bergen. Street performers move in at night all along the Champs-Elysées, moving to an industrial beat. During the day, anyone can enjoy the potpourri of restaurants and overpriced stores, planted next to airlines and commercial offices.

Six big avenues radiate from the Rond Point des Champs-Elysées. Av. Montaigne runs southwest from the point and shelters the houses of *haute couture* of Christian Dior, Chanel (no. 42), Valentino (no. 17 and 19). St-Laurent, Nina Ricci, and Pierre Cardin (pl. François 1*er)* hold sway nearby. You may not be able to afford even the smallest bottle of Chanel, but it's fun to look. Nearby, 15, av. Montaigne is home of the **Théâtre des Champs-Elysées,** built by the Perret brothers in 1912. The three large *salles* still host performances, but the theater is best known for staging the first performance of Stravinsky's *Le Sacre du Printemps,* an event which caused an uproar in the staid music world of the day. Around the corner from the *théâtre*, the long-time cabaret, the Crazy Horse Saloon, still entertains a mostly Parisian clientele.

Next to Cartier's (no. 51), at 49, rue Pierre Charron, stands Pershing Hall, a 113-year-old, five-story piece of America. Given to the U.S. federal government, the building has allegedly been used as a brothel, a brawling bar, a gambling house, and a black- market money exchange. Since refurbished, it now provides office space for respectable businesses like Council Travel and CIEE.

At the foot of the Champs-Elysées, the **Grand Palais** and the **Petit Palais** face one another on av. Winston Churchill. Built for the 1900 World's Fair, both *palais* are prime examples of Art Nouveau architecture; the glass over steel and stone composition of the Grand Palais makes its top look like a giant greenhouse. The Petit and Grand Palais house exhibitions on architecture, painting, sculpture, and French history; the Grand Palais also houses the Palais de la Découverte (see Museums). Built at the same time as the palaces, the first stone of Pont Alexandre III was placed by the tsar's son, Nicholas II. It made a stir as the first bridge to cross the Seine in a single span. Today this is considered the most beautiful bridge across the Seine, providing a noble axis with the Invalides (see Sights—7*ème).* The statues on pilasters facing the Right Bank represent Medieval France and Modern France; facing the Left Bank, they show Renaissance France and France of the Belle Epoque.

The guards pacing around the house at the corner of avenue de Marigny and rue du Faubourg St-Honoré are protecting the **Palais de l'Elysée.** The palace was built in 1718 but was embellished to its present glory as the residence of the Marquis de Marigny, brother of Madame de Pompadour. During the Restoration, July Monarchy, and Second Empire, the Elysée was used to house royal guests. Since 1870, it has

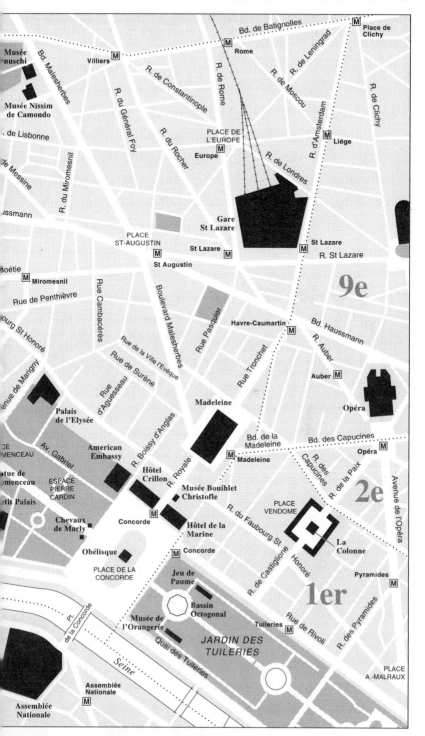

served as state residence of the French president. Socialist or not, President Mitterrand lives in style. Or ought to—in recent years Mitterand has been criticized by the French for living in his own residence instead of the grandiose state palace. Although entrance requires a personal invitation, the persistent visitor can catch a glimpse of the luscious gardens (Mo. Champs-Elysées-Clemenceau). The Union Jack flying overhead at no. 35, rue du Faubourg-St-Honoré marks the British embassy. At 2 av. Gabriel, an equally large building flies the Stars and Stripes.

The **place de la Concorde** (Mo. Concorde), Paris's largest and most infamous public square, forms the eastern terminus of the Champs-Elysées. Like many sights in Paris, this immense *place* was built from pride—constructed between 1757 and 1777 to provide a home for a monument to Louis XV. Fittingly, as punishment for this royal hubris, the vast area soon became the place de la Revolution, the site of the guillotine which severed 1,343 necks. On Sunday, January 21, 1793, Louis XVI was beheaded by guillotine on a site near where the Brest statue now stands. In 1993, hundreds of French (and the American ambassador) honored this event with flowers placed on the very spot. The celebrated heads of Louis XVI, Marie-Antoinette, Charlotte Corday (Marat's assassin), Lavoisier, Robespierre (the brutal merchant of death), and others rolled into baskets here and were held up to the cheering crowds who packed the pavement. After the Reign of Terror, the square was optimistically renamed place de la Concorde, and now stands as reminder of a bloody revolution.

Standing at the center of the place de la Concorde, the **Obélisque de Louxor** was one of those king-pleasing gifts offered by Mehemet Ali, Viceroy of Egypt, to Charles X in 1829. Getting the obelisk from Egypt to the center of Paris was no simple task; a canal to the Nile had to be dug, the monolith had to be transported by sea, and a special boat built to transport it up the Seine. Finally erected in 1836, Paris's oldest monument dates back to the 13th century BC and recalls the deeds of Ramses II. On July 14th, a marvelous fireworks display lights up the sky over the place de la Concorde. Every other night, the obelisk, fountains, and turn-of-the-century cast-iron lamps are illuminated, creating a romantic glow from the *place's* otherwise dark and dismal past. Don't be surprised if you see a commercial being shot on location here—and why not? What better way to create demand for your favorite product?

Flanking the Champs-Elysées at the place de la Concorde stand the **Cheveaux de Marly** (Africans Mastering the Numidian Horses), 18th century creations of Guillaume Coustou who originally designed them for Marly, Louis XIV's château near Versailles. Although the originals are now in the Louvre to protect them from the devastating effects of city pollution, perfect replicas still boldly hold their places. Eight large statues representing the major French cities also grace the *place*; Juliette Drouet allegedly posed for the town of Strasbourg.

Directly north of the *place,* like two sentries guarding the gate to the Madeleine, stand the **Hôtel Crillon** (on your left) and the **Hôtel de la Marine** (on your right). Architect Jacques-Ange Gabriel built the impressive colonnaded façades between 1757 and 1770. Chateaubriand lived in the Hôtel Crillon between 1805 and 1807. On February 16, 1778, the Franco-American treaties were signed here, making France the first European nation to recognize the independence of the U.S. Today it is one of the most expensive and elegant hotels in Paris. If you're dressed for the occasion, step inside and have an espresso in the plush salon to the accompaniment of soft chamber music. Coffee will run you 40F, but you'll be able to experience Parisian life in a different form. The businesses along rue Royale boast their own proud history. Christofle has been producing works in gold and crystal since 1830. (Call 49 33 43 00 to make an appointment to see their museum, or save yourself the hassle and just gawk at the store.) World-renowned Maxim's restaurant, 3, rue Royale, won't even allow you a peep into what was once Richelieu's home.

The **Madeleine,** formally called Eglise Ste-Marie-Madeleine (Mary Magdalene), is the commanding building ahead at the end of rue Royale. Screened for the present behind a construction barrier tastefully painted to resemble the façade, the church is nevertheless impressive.It was begun in 1764 at the command of Louis XV and modeled after a Greek temple. Construction was halted during the Revolution, when the Cult of Reason proposed making the generically monumental building into a bank, a theater, or a courthouse. Completed in 1842, the structure stands alone in the medley of Parisian churches, distinguished by its four ceiling domes, which light the interior in lieu of windows, 52 exterior Corinthian columns, and the lack of even one cross. An immense sculpture of the ascension of Ste-Marie-Madeleine adorns the altar (open Mon.-Sat. 7:30am-7pm, Sun. 7:30am-1:30pm and 3:30-7pm; occasional organ and chamber concerts, look for posters.) Marcel Proust spent most of his childhood at 9, bd. Malesherbes, which runs northwest from the place de la Madeleine. At the end of the Madeleine's rue Royale, the high-fashion, and high-priced **rue du Faubourg St-Honoré** stretches out like a jeweled Cartier necklace. You could spend hours window-shopping at the lavish, colorfully outrageous, and oh-so French decorated windows of Hermès (no. 24), Yves St-Laurent, Guy Laroche, and others. You'll find no number 13, rue du Faubourg St-Honoré; the superstitious Empress Josephine banned the number during the reign of Napoleon.

**Square Louis XVI,** on rue Pasquier below bd. Haussmann, include the improbably large **Chapelle Expiatoire** and a park whose many benches make it a popular spot for lunch. The intriguing Chapelle holds monuments of Marie-Antoinette and Louis XVI. A cemetery, affiliated with the Madeleine, was opened on the site in 1722; during the Revolution victims of the guillotine, Louis and Marie among them, were dumped here. Although Louis XVIII had his brother's and sister-in-law's remains removed to St-Denis in 1815, Charlotte Corday (Marat's assassin) and Philppe-Egalité (Louis XVI's cousin, who voted for the king's death, only to be beheaded himself) are buried on either side of the staircase. Statues of the expiatory ex-king and queen, displaced crowns at their feet, stand inside the Chapelle. Their last letters are engraved in French on the statue bases. (Open April-Sept. 10am-6pm; Nov.-Jan. 10am-4pm; Oct. and Feb.-March 10am-5pm.)

A few blocks north squats the **Gare St-Lazare,** whose platforms and iron-vaulted canopy are not to be missed by train riders and fans of Monet and Emile Zola. To the north of the *gare* is the place de Dublin, the setting for Caillebotte's famous painting, *A Rainy Day in Paris,* which hangs in the Art Institute of Chicago.

The **Parc Monceau,** a bizarre preserve guarded by gold-tipped, wrought iron gates, borders the elegant bd. de Courcelles. Whereas the Jardin du Luxembourg emphasizes show over relaxation, the Parc Monceau serves as a pastoral setting for kids to play and parents to unwind in the shade—all in a series of false ruins and strange grottoes built in the best of the Romantic tradition. The painter Carmontelle designed the park for the duc d'Orléans; it was brought to its present form in 1862 by Haussmann. The Rotonde de Monceau is a remnant of the Farmers-General wall of the 1780s. Designed to enforce customs duties rather than to keep out invaders, the wall and its fortifications reflected their creator's tastes in ornament more than the latest advances in military engineering. An array of architectural follies—a pyramid, covered bridge, pagoda, Dutch windmills, and picturesque Roman ruins—make this one of Paris's most pleasant spots for a *déjeuner sur* bench. Here, as elsewhere in Paris parks, frolicking on the grass is forbidden. Unlike most Parisian parks, however, this rule is not always strictly enforced. (Open 7am-10pm; Nov.-March 7am-8pm. Gates close 15min. earlier; Mo. Marceau.) For more release from Paris's architectural uniformity, skip down the rue Rembrandt to the place du Pérou, where a Chinese pagoda holds the Galerie C.T. Loo.

In the days of pre-revolutionary Russia, many Russian aristocrats owned vacation houses in France. Paris still retains a sizable Russian community. Paris's onion-domed **Eglise Russe,** also known as **Cathédrale Alexandre-Nevski,** 12, rue Daru tel. 42 01 10 23; Mo. Termes), built in 1860, is an attractive church that continues to serve the quarter's Russian residents. The gold domes, spectacular from the outside, are equally beautiful on the inside; they were intricately painted by artists from

NINTH ARRONDISSEMENT

St. Petersburg. The church holds a spectacular procession with music at Easter—call for more details. (Open 10am-7pm.)

# ■ Ninth Arrondissement: Opéra

The ninth *arrondissement* goes by the name *"Opéra;"* the Opéra Garnier and the boulevards nearby form this area's central core. The Opéra lies on the southernmos border of the 9*ème*, and this area is definitely the most prosperous and the most vis ited by tourists. Along the boulevards des Capucines, des Italiens, and Montmartre many pleasant restaurants serve mouth-watering delicacies and cater to the post-the ater and post-cinema crowd. This area also contains quite a few major movie house showing big American and European box office hits. Near the Opéra, many large banks and chic boutiques greet their affluent clientele. Perhaps the busiest site o the 9*ème*, however, is the American Express office, where hordes of tourists g each day to change their Traveler's Cheques commission-free.

Most tourists, willy-nilly, begin their tour with the Opéra Garnier. Emerging from the underground den of the Opéra *métro* station, feast your eyes on Charles Garn er's grandiose **Opéra** (tel. 40 17 33 33; 40 17 35 35 for recorded program and sched ule information), built under Napoleon III in the showy eclecticism of the Secon Empire. This is Haussmann's most extravagant creation: an outpouring of opulenc and meaningless allegory, not actually opened until 1875, five years after th Empire's collapse. Towering high above the *grands boulevards* of the souther 9*ème*, the Opéra epitomizes both the Second Empire's obsession with canonize ostentation and its rootlessness; a mix of styles and odd details tie it to no formal tra dition, other than late 19th-century modernism. Queried by the Empress Eugénie a to whether his building was in the style of Louis XIV, Louis XV, or Louis XVI, Garn ier responded that his creation belonged to Napoleon III. The interior of the Opér demonstrates the fabric of 19th-century bourgeois social life, with its grand stai case, enormous golden foyer, vestibule, and five-tiered auditorium—all designed s that the audience could watch each other as much as the action on stage.

Garnier's elaborate design beat out hundreds of competing plans in an 1861 con petition, outshining even the entry of the "Pope of Architects," Viollet-le-Duc. A that time, Garnier was a virtual unknown; the Opéra made him famous. The magni icent and eclectic interior is adorned by Gobelin tapestries, gilded mosaics, a 196 Chagall ceiling (with a whimsical, Chagallian view of Paris), and the six-ton chande lier, which fell on the audience in 1896. Since 1989, when the new Opéra de Bastille was inaugurated, most operas occur at the newer hall and Garnier's opera i used mainly for ballets. Ballet these days tends to perform its own elegy, staging re rospectives on the work of 20th-century greats; summer 1993 featured the work Balanchine and Jerome Robbins. In 1992, Rudolf Nureyev made his last publi appearance here shortly before his death after a long battle with AIDS. Schedules fo performances are available in the entrance hall at the opera (see Entertainment).

Visits cost a hefty 33F, 20F for ages 10-16, and they include all public parts of th theater, except for the auditorium on performance days. The library and museur hold documents about costumes and objects tracing the history of opera and danc They focus particularly on the *ballet russe*, Diaghilev's innovative troupe which lil erated classical dance from fluffy Romanticism, and launched 20th-century exper mentation with such works as Stravinsky's *Firebird*. Take a peek at Picasso costumes and sets for this work at the library. To arrange for private tours, call 44 6 21 66 or 69. (The Opéra is open for visits Mon.-Sat. 10am-4:30pm. Library ope Mon.-Sat. 10am-5pm. Tickets for the ballet start at 30F; for the opera 50F; for th movies 60F. Rush tickets at reduced prices available at the box office 15 min. befor each performance. To reserve seats, call 7-14 days ahead at 47 42 53 71 noon-6pm.

Directly across from the Opéra is the **Café de la Paix,** a famous café from the 19t century, catering to the after-theater crowd and anyone else who doesn't mind pa ing 30F for coffee (see Cafés). Rue de la Paix, originally called rue Napoléon, is th most expensive piece on French monopoly and lives up to its reputation for luxur

Cartier is located at no. 11. Behind the Opéra, at 9, rue Scribe, tourists line up at the American Express office; it's probably not worth a special trip. All around this area, change bureaus advertise "No commission." Unless you're trying to change traveler's checks already in francs, they aren't lying, and rates aren't bad. Of more historic interest, a bit farther down the bd. des Capucines, is the **Olympia** music hall, where Edith Piaf achieved her fame, along with Jacques Brel, Yves Montand, and many others. Popular artists still perform here; check posters for concerts. Following bd. des Capucines, you will arrive at bd. des Italiens and bd. Montmartre. These three *grands boulevards* represent one of the busiest areas in the *quartier,* crowded with popular restaurant/cafés (pricey, but perfect for people-watching), cinemas, and shops. Thomas Jefferson, in Paris in the 1780s as the American ambassador, lived near what is now the intersection of bd. Haussmann and rue du Helder. At no. 10, bd. Montmartre stands the carnivalesque **Musée Grevin** (see Museums).

West from this area along bd. Haussmann, toward Mo. Chaussée d'Antin and Trinité, you'll find the largest clothes shopping area in Paris. Two of Paris's largest department stores, **Au Printemps** and **Galeries Lafayette,** are located on the bd. Haussmann, and the streets around here are littered with stores selling clothes and shoes (see Shopping). At the northern end of the rue de la Chaussée (Mo. Trinité), is the **Eglise de la Sainte-Trinité.** This church, built at the end of the 19th century in Italian Renaissance style, has beautiful, painted vaults. It is surrounded by a pleasant park with a fountain and tree-shaded benches. The quixotic **Musée Gustave Moreau** is also in this area, up the rue de La Rochefoucauld (see Museums). The museum is located in the painter's house and studio, on a quiet residential street.

A short walk west from here, on the place Kossuth, at Mo. Notre-Dame-de-Lorette, is the church **Notre-Dame-de-Lorette,** built in 1836 to "the glory of the Virgin Mary." This Neoclassical church is full of statues of the saints and frescoes of scenes from the life of Mary. The street of the same name, constructed in 1840, quickly became the site of low-rent apartments of ill repute, stomping ground for Emile Zola's Nana (whose name has made its way into French *argot*—slang for girl, on par with "chick"). The term *lorette* came to refer to the quarter's crop of young *demoiselles* of easy virtue—post-adolescent adventuresses who came to the city from the provinces, their reputations forever tarnished. The mere mention of Notre-Dame-de-Lorette made men look away and good girls blush. As home to illicit bars, hotels, and restaurants for a crowd which rented by the hour, the rue des Martyrs enjoyed an equally bad reputation. Now filled with fruit stands, cheese shops, and multi-ethnic *épiceries*, the street no longer advertises delicacies of a different ilk. History has left few footprints on these picturesque narrow streets. Continuing up rue Notre-Dame-de-Lorette, you reach the **place St-Georges,** one of the most pleasant parks in Paris, with benches, tall shade trees, and well-kept flower beds.

North of the rue Châteaudun is a quiet, mostly residential area with a large student population and many small, well-priced, ethnic restaurants. The streets are narrow and quiet, full of small shops, *tabacs,* little hotels and modest private residences. The **Musée Renan-Scheffer,** or Musée de la Vie Romantique, is up one of these charming narrow streets, the rue Chaptal, off the rue Fontaine (see Museums). The interior courtyard and garden of the house are representative of the layout of most of the residences on these streets. Farther north, at the border of the 18*ème,* is the area called **Pigalle,** which Marcel Proust characterized as "almost another Paris in the heart of Paris itself." The area where Colette and her lover the marquise frequented women-only establishments in the early 20th century is now a Xanadu for men looking to get laid on a tight budget. Pigalle is famous the world over, not only as home to the **Moulin Rouge** cabaret and popular discotheques (see Entertainment), but also as the center of much of the city's prostitution. Toulouse-Lautrec immortalized Pigalle in its *fin-de-siècle* resplendence as a hub of cabarets and lesbian life. Impressionistic sketches have given way to sexploitation flicks. Tourists, especially women, should never walk around here alone at night and should be wary of

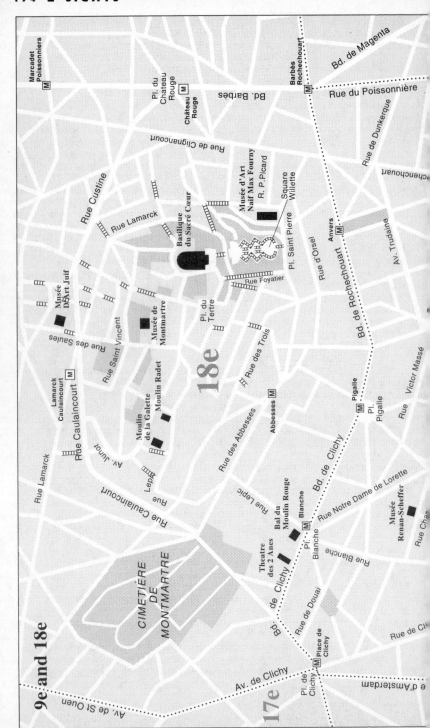

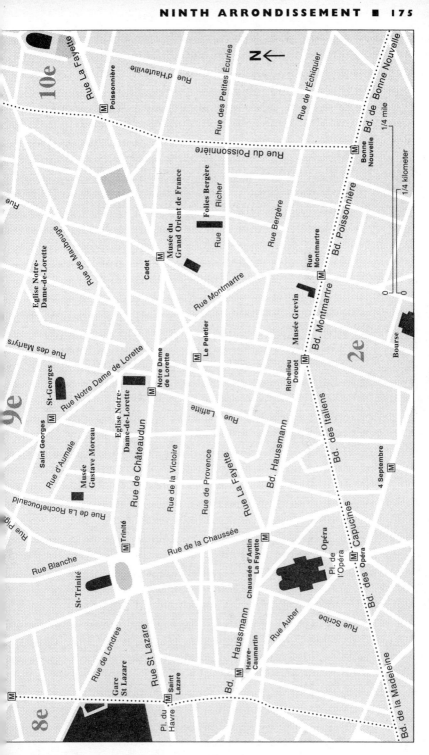

pickpockets. Like humanity itself, which in the words of Dimitri Karamazov, spans from the insect to the divine, the 9ème spans from the most chic to the most sordid.

# ■ Tenth Arrondissement

"I live between two train stations, at the edge of a canal, in one of the *arrondissements* of Paris most rich in prisons, hideouts, pleasures, and hospitals. It is a rather vague *arrondissement*...much like one of those animal-molecules that can both expand and be cut in half. Half-worm, half-butterfly, one never knows which is the head and which the tail, and it is permanently caught at the mid-point of creation, straddling flight on the one side, abjectly crawling on the other." So wrote a resident of the tenth *arrondissement* in the 1920s, in terms still accurate today. Far from the normal tourist route, and not the safest or most well-kept of areas, the tenth offers a few gems of its own to the adventurous soul. In the southern portion, along the faubourg St-Denis, a curious and bustling market area offers ethnic foods and spices. The rue de Paradis in the western section is home to some of the world's finest china and crystal. Travelers looking to stretch their legs on a layover at the Gare de l'Est or Nord should head for the tree-lined Canal St-Martin and relax in the shade of trees, away from the noise and bustle of downtown Paris. Still waters and moss-covered drawbridges make this a pleasant jog close to the *gares*.

Besides these interesting walks, the 10ème is a slightly rundown area which now houses a good portion of the city's minorities. There is some crime in areas around the place de la République; it is prudent not to walk the small side streets alone at night, and single women should avoid this area entirely after dusk. Though it lacks the tourist gloss of central Paris and the nightlife of the adjacent eleventh, the tenth is known for two things important to the budget traveler—trains and food.

The **Gare du Nord** (Mo. Gare du Nord) is generally encountered out of necessity rather than curiosity, but it merits a look. Jacques-Ignace Hittorf created the enormous station in 1863, in the midst of the great re-building of Paris. The grandiose Neoclassical exterior is topped by statues representing the great cities of France. Inside, the platforms are covered by a vast *parapluie* (umbrella), as Napoleon III called the glass and steel heaven which creates the giant vault of the train station. Across from the station a fringe of *brasseries* and cafés caters to the thousands of travelers who go through here every day.

Facing away from the Gare du Nord and walking one block down the rue de Compiègne takes you to the rue de Belzunce and the **Eglise St-Vincent de Paul,** a Neoclassical structure built in the early 19th century by architects Hittorf and Jean-Baptiste Lepère. The entrance, in the shape of a temple, is topped with a dramatic frieze sculpted by Leboeuf-Nanteuil. It stands on a flight of steps bordered by terraced gardens, offering a welcome rest and a pleasant view down the rue d'Hauteville. (Church open to the public Mon.-Sat. 7:30am-noon and 2-7pm; Sun. 7:30am-12:30pm and 3:30-7:30pm. A mass with Gregorian chant Sun. at 9:30am.)

Returning down rue de Belzunce to the bd. de Magenta, you will arrive at the **Marché St-Quentin,** 85, bd. de Magenta. This market is a massive, elegant construction of iron and glass, built in 1866 with a glass ceiling as glorious, if smaller, as that of Gare du Nord. Inside you can find an enormous variety of goods, from flowers to fresh produce and skinned rabbits for your delectable *lapin à la moutarde d'Irène* (open Tues.-Sat. 8am-1pm and 3:30-7:30pm; Sun. 8am-1pm). From the Marché St-Quentin cross bd. de Magenta and follow rue du 8 Mai 1945 until it arrives at the **Gare de l'Est.** More functional than beautiful, this train station is on a smaller scale than its neighbor Gare du Nord, but conforms to the same Neoclassical style. Directly across from the train station, the place du 11 Nov. 1918 opens into the bd. de Strasbourg, a hopping thoroughfare, crowded with cafés, shops, and fruit stands.

Close by, the small **rue de Paradis** offers a quaint little area bordered by shops displaying fine china and crystal. The beautiful (and expensive) objects mark the road to the **Baccarat Co.** headquarters and the **Cristalleries Baccarat,** housed in an 18th-century building at 30-32, rue de Paradis (see Museums). Farther up the street, at 18,

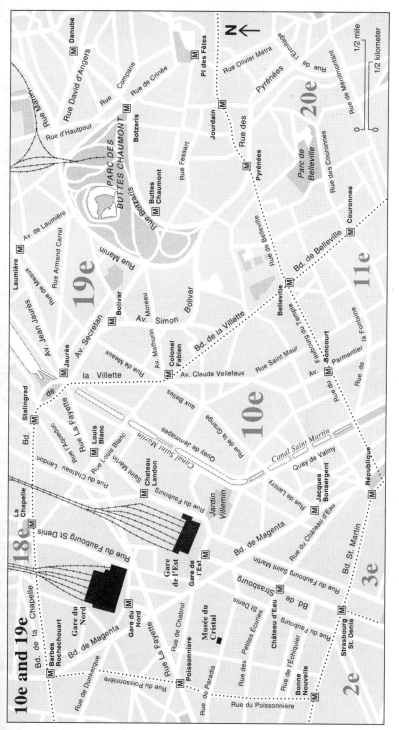

**10e and 19e**

rue de Paradis, the art gallery **Le Monde de l'Art** displays a variety of exhibits; it is housed in what was once the headquarters of the Boulanger china company (see Museums). Turn the corner from rue de Paradis onto rue du Faubourg St-Denis and look out for **Passage du Désir,** a perhaps inauspicious causeway with an erotic name, marked in fading block letters on the arch above the entrance. Following the Revolutionary vogue of renaming things, residents of the quarter voted in 1789 to rechristen the passage, formerly known as Passage du Puits (hole in the ground).

Going south on the **rue du Faubourg St-Denis,** you will walk through crowds of Parisians buying dinner ingredients in a very active market area. Individual stores, many owned by African, Arab, and Indian vendors, specialize in seafood, cheese, bread, or produce, rebuking supermarkets everywhere with the quality and selection they offer. **Passage Brady,** which intersects with bd. de Strasbourg and rue du Faubourg St-Martin, is lined with South Asian stores that are stocked with exotic foodstuffs and prepared delicacies that the budget traveler can afford.

At the end of rue Faubourg St-Denis, the majestic **Porte St-Denis** (Mo. Strasbourg/ St-Denis) welcomes the visitor into the inner city. Built in 1672 to celebrate the victories of Louis XIV in the Rhineland and Flanders, it is an imitation of the Arch of Titus in Rome. In the Middle Ages, this was the site of a gate in the city walls, but the present arch, characterized by André Breton as *très belle et très inutile* (very beautiful and quite useless) served only as a ceremonial marker and a royal entrance on the old road to St-Denis. On July 28, 1830, it was the scene of intense fighting; revolutionaries scrambled to the top of the old Bourbon icon and rained cobblestones on the monarchist troops below. At its side, two blocks down the bd. St-Denis, the **Porte St-Martin** is a smaller copy, built in 1674 to celebrate yet another victory. On the façade, look for Louis XIV represented as Hercules (nude, except for the wig).

The stretch from Porte St-Martin to place de la République, along rue René Boulanger and bd. St-Martin, served as a lively theater district in the 19th century and has recently begun to retrieve some of its former sparkle. Newly refurbished, the **Théâtre de la Renaissance,** with a sculpted façade of griffins and arabesques, has breathed new life into neighboring streets. A handful of mid-priced, fashionable establishments hail from this Bohemian enclave (see Bars and Restaurants).

Going east from here along the bd. St-Martin, you arrive at the **place de la République** (Mo. République), the meeting point of the tenth, the third and the eleventh *arrondissements.* This is a good place to avoid at night, when prostitutes and swindlers abound. In the center a monument to the Republic of France celebrates the victories of the 23 years of intermittent republican rule between 1789 and the monument's erection in 1880. The statue of *La République* by Morice stands on a base by Dalou, with bronze reliefs representing various revolutions in French history.

A bit farther east lies the **Canal St-Martin,** 4.5km long and connecting the Canal de l'Ourcq to the Seine. The canal has several locks, which can be traveled by boat on one of the **canauxrama** trips (see Entertainment). You can also walk along the tree-lined banks. Again, it is probably a good idea to be careful in this area after dark. East of the canal, follow rue Bichat to the entrance of **hôpital St-Louis,** one of the oldest hospitals in Paris. Built by Henri IV as a sanctuary/prison for victims of the plague, it was located across a marsh from the city, and downwind of both the smelly mess at Buttes-Chaumont (see 19*ème)* and a gallows. Its distance from any source of fresh water confirms that it was intended more to protect the city from contamination than to help the unfortunates inside. The hospital is designed in two quadrilaterals: the inner one for victims, the outer one for functionaries, who communicated with the diseased through a tower in one of the pavilions. A cemetery inside the hospital walls made the complex entirely self-sufficient. Today, hôpital St-Louis specializes in dermatology, and offers a peaceful Renaissance courtyard to those willing to brave any plague bacilli that might have survived the centuries.

Just north of hôpital St-Louis, in the area between the canal, rue des Ecluses St-Martin, rue Louis Blanc, and rue de la Grange aux Belles, once stood the **Montfaucon gallows**—famous for its hanging capacity of 60, an efficiency unrivalled until the invention of the guillotine several centuries later. In the early 14th century, the initial wooden structure was replaced by a two-story stone framework, designed by Pierre Rémy, treasurer to Charles IV. (Rémy had a chance to test his creation in 1328, when he was hanged with great pomp and circumstance.) By the 17th century, the Montfaucon gallows had fallen into disuse, and today only memories linger. But in 1954, workers building the garage at 53, rue de la Grange aux Belles uncovered an eerie reminder of this area's former use: two of the original pillars, along with several human bones.

# ■ Eleventh Arrondissement

As it courses eastward, rue de Rivoli changes into rue St-Antoine, which runs to the **place de la Bastille** at the union of the third, eleventh, and twelfth *arrondissements*. Here squatted the **Bastille**, the famous fortress and prison built in the 14th century by Charles V at the eastern entrance to his new city walls. The Bastille served to defend this entrance and to imprison some of the most prestigious enemies of the state: religious heretics and political prisoners, many of them arrested on an arbitrary *lettre de cachet* and confined for years without trials. The fortress, a treasury vault under Henry IV, was first liberated of its contents by Catherine de Médicis, who spent state funds with abandon, nearly liquidating her son and his realm.

Under Louis XIII, the fortress became a state prison; internment there followed specific orders from the king. The man of the iron mask—the stuff that films are made of—sat out his days in the Bastille at the behest of Louis XIV. In the last years of the Ancien Régime, the prison turned from draconian nightmare into a rather deluxe prison. Its subversive and illustrious clientele furnished their suites, brought their servants, and received guests. The Cardinal de Rohan held a dinner party for 20 in his cell. Fresh linen came courtesy of the warden. Notable inmates included Mirabeau, Voltaire, and Fouquet, Louis XIV's unfortunate finance minister. The Marquis de Sade, no doubt nostalgic for the prison's chamber-of-horrors past, left with revolutionary insurgents on July 14, 1789. Sade, four forgers, and two lunatics were the last prisoners to be held at the Bastille.

On that great revolutionary *journée,* about the only thing in abundance at the fortress was gunpowder. After raiding the arsenal at Invalides, the hordes set out to sack the prison for munitions. Surrounded by the well-armed rabble, short on food, and unsure of the loyalty of his small garrison of Swiss mercenaries and pensioned veterans, the prison's governor agreed to surrender after a battle that left almost 100 revolutionary corpses scattered outside the walls. As he was escorted to the Hôtel de Ville, the mob overpowered his captors and hacked off his head with a pocket-knife, only to stick it on a pike and parade it around as a symbol of success. Symbolic function quickly supplanted practical need in the Revolution's romance with itself. The need for liberty, not gunpowder, was said to have moved the crowds.

The storming of the Bastille has come to signal a victory of popular power over the monarchy. Its first anniversary was the occasion of a great celebration, and since the late 19th century, July 14th has been celebrated as the national holiday of the French Republic. Within a day of the Bastille's capture, ardent revolutionaries began the destruction of the hated edifice. By October 1792, they had completely demolished the prison. Some of its stones are now incorporated into the Pont de la Concorde. Others are stacked up in a memorial in the square Henri Galli, a few blocks down the bd. Henri IV from the place de la Bastille. A certain Citizen Palloy, the main contractor for the destruction, used other stones to construct 83 models of the prison, which he sent to the provinces outside Paris to remind them of "the horror of despotism." Only the ground plan of the prison remains on its original site, marked by a line of stones. In 1831, King Louis-Philippe laid the cornerstone for the **July column,** in the center of the *place,* as a memorial to the dead of the Revolution of 1789 and the Revolution of 1830, which had brought him to power. In its vault, 504 martyrs of 1830 are buried, along with two Egyptian pharaohs (mummies) formerly in the Louvre who had started to decompose.

ELEVENTH ARRONDISSEMENT

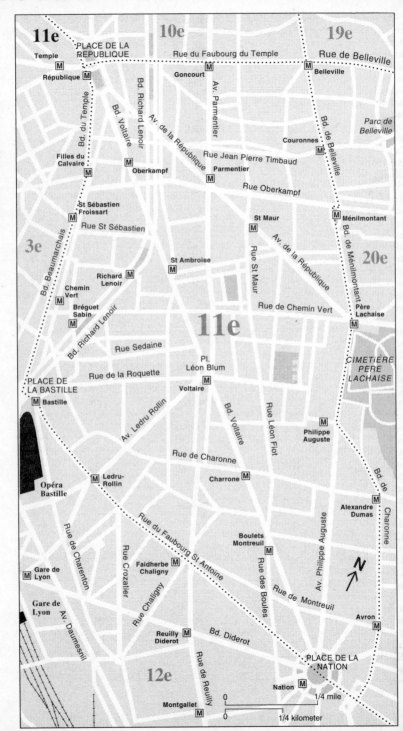

The **Opéra Bastille,** a space-age study in plexiglass, now sits in the *place* amidst jeers from passersby. Commissioned by François Mitterand, this "People's Opera House" is one more of the president's *grands projets,* poised to assume its true function in the new intergalactic order. Designed by Canadian architect Carlos Ott, the building is second only to Euro Disney® in the minds of many Parisians as an example of North American barbarism. If nothing else, it is a conversation piece. The Opéra has been described as a huge *toilette,* a version no doubt of the coin-operated facilities in the streets of Paris. Many complain that the acoustics of the much-vaunted hall leave much to be desired. Tickets are pricey, not the stuff of a People's Opera House. Tours (20F, students 10F; 1-2 per day at 1 or 5pm) are the only way to see the interior unless you attend a performance. The schedule frequently changes. Call 40 01 19 17 for performance information; stop in the box office for a free brochure describing the season's events. (Discount tickets sold 15 min. in advance. Office open Aug. 26-July 19. See Entertainment—Opera for more information.)

The flocks of students lounging on the steps in front of the Opéra are tugging the youthful, artistic center of Paris away from the *quartier latin* and into this up-and-coming neighborhood; the Bastille has become, as had Montmartre, Montparnasse, and the *quartier latin* before it, the hip quarter of Paris, the new bohemia, the new hangout of the young and the eclectic. Don't count on the *BCBG* glamor of the steadfast fifth or sixth; styles here change as quickly as new galleries open and close. Today's Beautiful People sport tattered miniskirts, bell-bottoms, platform shoes, and false eyelashes for both men and women. But tomorrow they might drape themselves in anything from monk's habits to Jean-Paul Gautier's creations. Thankfully, the area has not entirely lost its former proletarian personality; some of Paris's more garrulous and crotchety old inhabitants maintain a strong and refreshing presence.

The streets which surround and radiate from Opéra Bastille sing elegies to the Revolution, its profiteers, and its victims. Nos. 157-161, rue de Charonne once housed the infamous Docteur Belhomme whose **Maison de Retraite et de Santé** sheltered condemned aristocrats and other notables with ready cash during the Terror (1792-1795). For 1000 *livres* a month, Dr. Belhomme would let a room in his sham sanatorium and certify his clients as too ill to brave the scaffold. Arrested himself after word got out, Dr. Belhomme holed up in a like establishment on the rue de Picpus (12*ème*). Thrown in jail under the Directory for uncivicism, he died peacefully at home at the age of 87.

Off rue de Charonne, **Eglise Ste-Marguerite** was built in 1627 to save parishioners the commute to St-Paul in the Marais (see Sights—4*ème*). The Chapelle des Ames du Purgatoire, added to the church in 1764 by architect Louis, is of particular note. The *trompe l'oeil* paintings are by Brunetti; the pietà behind the altar is by Girardon. During the Revolution, Ste-Marguerite continued to act as a place of worship despite the sweep of anticlericism throughout the nation. Its vicar was among the first priests to get married. (Open daily 9am-noon, 5-7pm.)

Next to the church, **Cimetière Ste-Marguerite** is another stop on the Revolution's trail of blood and trivial pursuit. At least 73 victims of the guillotine from June 1794 fertilized these grounds. The most enigmatic headstone to be found here remains that of "the child dead in the dungeon of the Temple"—the headstone of Louis XVII, located near the outside wall of the Chapelle des Ames du Purgatoire Ornot. Nineteenth-century forensic tests confirmed that the body had been a boy aged 18 to 20. The stone reads, "L...XVII 1785-1795."

Back on the rue de Charonne toward the Bastille, turn left onto **rue de Lappe** for a showcase of 17th- and 18th-century quotidian life and architecture. In this heart of Bastille chic, the streets are lined with cafés, galleries, old passageways, and gardens. This is the 11*ème* at its most accessible and most charming. Michelet, the great 19th-century historian of the Revolution, lived at no. 49. His statue may be seen on the Hôtel de Ville (see Sights—4*ème*). The one *grande maison* on the side street is at no. 71; the late 18th-century whorehouse serves to remind tourists and solitary walkers that, despite political tumult, life in the *boudoir* was business as usual. The house's proximity to the Bastille and Faubourg St-Antoine suggests that more than one young ideologue on his way to or from the Revolutionary theater visited the *demoiselles* at this address. Turn right from rue de Lappe onto rue de la Roquette for a glimpse of another 17th-century byway. The house and gardens from no. 1 to 17 once belonged to La Compagnie Royale des Chevaliers de l'Arbalète et de l'Arque-buse, a knightly brotherhood formed under Louis le Gros to protect the city. The chevaliers, their number fixed at 280 persons in 1690, proved too small a police force to render service to the king. Now galleries and black jeans fill the street. Next door to the knightly cabal at no. 17 lived the poet Verlaine, famous for his writings and infamous for shooting the poet Rimbaud in a lover's quarrel.

Farther east along la Roquette, past its intersection with the rue Voltaire, sits a park where a prison once stood. This bucolic spread all but effaces the reminder of la Petite Roquette, a death-row waiting zone until its demolition in 1899. History has, however, left its traces—five flat stones at the street's juncture with rue de la Croix Faubin lie where a guillotine once stood. Communard soldiers decapitated numerous abbots and curés here in 1871.

## ■ Twelfth Arrondissement

The area east of the Bastille, on both sides of the *arrondissement* line, was, until its incorporation into Paris, the **faubourg St-Antoine.** Home of poor artisans in the 18th century, it was exempted by royal decree from certain duties and regulations. Hard hit by food shortages in the last years of the Ancien Régime, *faubourg* residents would come to provide the muscle behind the Revolution's demagogues. Constituting what has come to be known as the "red belt" around Paris, the *faubourg* rose up in 1830 and 1848. In the 20th century, the region has proved a bastion of both left- and right-leaning unrest. Residents numbered importantly among the pre-1944 resistance movement; plaques to this effect, conspicuously absent in central Paris, are sprinkled throughout eastern Paris. On May 28, 1958, over 150,000 people marched to protest the expected takeover of the government by the armed forces. They followed what historian Jean Lacouture has called "the traditional left-wing route from the place de la Nation to the place de la République."

The 12ème, made up mostly of businesses and quiet tree-lined boulevards, is pleasant but unexciting. The **Ministère des Finances** (Ministry of Finances) on the quai de Bercy is the product of two of Mitterrand's *grands projets.* After a century of cohabiting the Louvre, the finance ministry and museum found they needed elbow room. The swelling French bureaucracy sought walkways and computers; the museum sought a facelift and receiving room. Both parties have been more or less accommodated (see Museums—Louvre). Chemetov and Huidobro's prefab centipede which yawns across the Seine is the only of Mitterrand's *Grands Projets* accessible by both dinghy and parachute; employees drive speed boats from here to the Assemblée Nationale (3min.). Topped with a helicopter landing pad, the Ministry has a certain Jetsonian appeal.

Head east toward the Bois de Vincennes for an afternoon of zoos and greenery. On the way, **place de la Nation** (Mo. Nation), at the convergence of nine streets and on the boundary between the 11ème and the 12ème, sports a classy statue of the *Triomphe de la République* by Dalou (1899). This square was known formerly as place du Trône, in honor of the throne placed here in 1660 when Louis XIV returned to Paris with his new bride, Marie-Thérèse. During the Revolution, the throne was replaced by a guillotine that proudly chopped off over 1300 heads, and the square was renamed place du Trône-Renversé (Square of the Toppled Throne), a name which it held until July 14, 1880 when the place of the throne and the guillotine became the place of the nation. Just east of the *place,* twin tollhouses—part of Ledoux's 18th-century city walls—herald the Cours de Vincennes, the grand avenue toward the Château de Vincennes and the great park that surrounds it.

## ■ Thirteenth Arrondissement

A mostly residential *arrondissement,* the thirteenth feels like a small town despite the location of many of Paris's taller apartment buildings and office towers here (built before the imposition of the current height restrictions). Due to the presence of the **Bièvre**, a weak stream whose waters had been diverted into aqueducts and whose bed had been clogged with refuse from the dyeing and bleaching done at the many tanneries that lined the river, this *arrondissement* used to be one of the most evil-smelling areas in France. It was also one of the most impoverished *quartiers* in Paris—little coincidence that Victor Hugo used parts of the 13ème as a setting for *Les Misérables.* By 1910, the environmentalists won a decisive victory—the tanneries and paper factories were relocated and the Bièvre was filled in. Despite this drastic improvement, the 13ème doesn't offer much for even the most dedicated tourist, except perhaps a dinner-foray into Chinatown, or a fascinating tour of the still-functioning Gobelins factory (and, of course, the trains that depart non-stop from Gare d'Austerlitz to exotic destinations like Barcelona and Lisbon). However, this *arrondissement* does harbor some interesting surprises—you just have to look a little harder than you do in some of the 13ème's flashier neighbors.

The **Butte aux Cailles district** is, ironically, one of Paris's oldest yet least-frequented and least known parts of the city. As you stroll around its winding streets, you'll feel like you're in the provinces. La Butte may not enjoy its secluded status much longer—trendy Parisian party-goers have begun to frequent bars in the area, and on weekends the section of la Butte aux Cailles that intersects rue des Cinq Diamants becomes quite animated.

Just south of la Butte aux Cailles, you will notice a striking church in Romano-Byzantine style. The **Eglise Sainte-Anne de la Maison Blanche** (rue Tolbiac) was built from 1894 to 1912. After a dearth of funds caused construction to halt in 1898, building resumed with the assistance of donations from the wealthy Lombart family, tried-and-true inhabitants of the 13ème, who wished only that by the 1900 World Expo in Paris Ste-Anne de la Maison Blanche would at least "bear some resemblance to a church." Their generous donation allowed for completion of the façade, which has kept the name *la façade chocolat* after the Lombart's family business: they ran a chocolate shop on av. de Choisy. Although Ste-Anne's pointed twin towers and rose-shaped clock make it impressive from the outside, it is dark and plain inside, the light blocked by heavy columns and small windows. If you venture inside, look up—the ornate design on the inside of the large cupola is breathtaking.

To the northeast, the streets around the **place d'Italie** reveal a sad story of urban renewal. In the early 1960s, sociologist Henri Coing studied this area and found that despite the poor housing conditions, the residents of the neighborhood regarded this corner of Paris as their world, and could not conceive of living anywhere else. But planners saw only slums without running water. The old buildings and their working-class tenants were swept away, replaced with sterile apartment buildings filled with the middle classes. One interesting exception is the ultramodern Gaumont movie theater (home to the largest screen in France) and office building at 30, pl. d'Italie designed by Japanese architect Kenzo Tange. Rectangular glass panels lead up to an odd-looking tower topped with colored steel mesh shapes. Some are beam-like, hanging from wire, giving the entire creation the effect of a work in progress—you may wonder if Tange plans to come back and finish it. If you can smooth your way past the receptionists at the entrance, a ride up and down in the glass elevator is a cheap thrill.

Also located in the place d'Italie area, running down avenue de Choisy and avenue d'Ivry, **Chinatown** is populated not only by thousands of Chinese, Vietnamese, and Cambodians, but hundreds of Asian restaurants and grocery stores. Like Chinatowns the world over, this one offers delicious Asian cuisine for about half the price of elsewhere in the city.

The **Manufacture des Gobelins,** 42, av. des Gobelins (tel. 43 37 12 60; Mo. Gobelins), is the workshop time forgot, where artisans, after being apprenticed by the factory for more than ten years, slave meticulously over complex tapestry weavings. Taken over by Louis XIV's finance minister, Colbert, in 1663, the Gobelins became a prison-like establishment, where whole families lived to produce tapestries the likes of which can now be found in the Cluny museum and in many of the châteaux near Paris. Still an adjunct of the state, the factory produces commission work for France's ministries and foreign embassies. Carefully chosen artists spend as much as one year weaving one square meter of colorful tapestry. Traditional, 17th-century weaving methods are still in use today; the colors are selected from the factory's range of 14,000 different tones. Guided tours, the only way to get inside the factory, explain the intricate techniques that go into the weaving process. The two-hour tour is given in French only, but a free English-language handout translates the essential points of the tour and details the history of the Gobelins factory. (Tours Tues.-Thurs. 2 and 3pm. Admission 22F, ages 18-25 12F, under 18 5F.)

If city planners, government officials, and the mayor of the 13ème have their way, the biggest attraction is yet to come. The 13ème is host to a massive urban renewal project called **ZAC (zone d'aménagement concerte) Seine-Rive Gauche.** Its crowning glory will be the installation of the new **Bibliothèque de France,** designed to replace the Bibliothèque Nationale in 1996 (for more on the old Bibliothèque, see Sights—2ème). The library, designed by architect Dominique Perrault, is a seven-billion-franc endeavor that will encompass 288,000 square meters along the Seine across from the Ministry of Finance. The design has faced much opposition. Librarians' associations, as well as ad-hoc committees of intellectuals (including such big names as Claude Lévi-Strauss) have written open letters to François Mitterrand urging a radical redesign of the Bibliothèque. Critics claim that the four L-shaped towers (designed to look like open books from above), one on each corner of the plot, would be difficult for researchers who needed one book from the 15th story of tower A and another from the 16th story of tower B across the way. Others worry that the light streaming through the large glass "walls" will damage the cover and contents of rare volumes. There has also been much debate about the division of floors between the general public and certified researchers, a necessary task, yet one which runs contrary to the fundamental concept of the library. Created on allegedly socialist principles, the library's goal is to provide access to everyone.

New resolutions have called for the height of the towers to be shortened to 80m, for materials other than glass to be used for some construction, and for truly fragile volumes to be placed in the underground levels. With these concessions, much of the controversy has subsided and emphasis is being placed on specifics—the cataloguing and arranging of 400,000 volumes for free public access, the cultivating of over 10,000 square meters of green space in the area enclosed by the towers, and the development of a sophisticated system that will search and retrieve a book from the off-limits stacks in under 20 minutes, a huge improvement on the current four-day wait. A detailed exhibit of the plans for the library (scale models, printed information, and a film in French) can be found at the **Bureau d'Accueil Cité Chantier,** 139, quai de la Gare (tel. 44 23 03 70; open Mon.-Sat. 10am-5pm, Sun. 10am-6pm).

The Bibliothèque de France is just one piece of the urban renewal puzzle—the ZAC Seine-Rive Gauche (comprising the areas from the Gare d'Austerlitz to the Masséna *métro* stop) will also mean a university, five schools, public daycare, a sports complex, and a public garden for the *arrondissement*. The creation of a new *métro* line (Méteor) and a RER-SNCF station may bring the 13ème out of its isolation and relative second-class citizenship, making it a new hub of culture, leisure, and learning. As of 1993, the hottest issue was the naming of the ZAC's new streets; imagine the difficulty in coming up with a name not already used by some other street in Paris. For the street running along the Seine in an area hoped to become a dominant cultural center, the name "l'Allée Arthur Rimbaud" seemed fitting. And for the new, wide avenue that splits the new development in half? Avenue de France, *bien sûr.*

South of the library, at 12, rue Cantagrel, is Le Corbusier's **Cité de Refuge,** a Salvation Army shelter he designed in 1931. It is a daring, Modernist structure. How did the staid Salvation Army choose so innovative and iconoclastic an architect? The fact that the chief donor of the project, the Princesse de Polignac, was a patron of the avant garde and a friend of Le Corbusier seems to have had something to do with it.

## ■ Fourteenth Arrondissement: Montparnasse

At first glance, the fourteenth *arrondissement* may appear to have nothing more to offer the tourist than the much-acclaimed cafés along the bd. Montparnasse and the eight-level commercial center, a true shopping mecca that serves as a base for the architecturally tragic Tour de Montparnasse. Deeper into the *arrondissement,* however, hidden sights abound. Still, quaint this *quartier* is not—you may have to save your search for postcard Paris for another day.

Montparnasse has served as a magnet for an impressive array of residents since the turn of the century. The first to arrive were the Bretons, fleeing their failed crops, pouring out of the Gare de Montparnasse, and anchoring themselves around the station for easy access back to the north should the agricultural horizon brighten. Vestiges of Breton culture—*crêperies,* stores selling traditional Breton crafts and books, and even Breton cultural associations—remain strong in this area. Montparnasse then became a center for the avant garde of art and thought, marking a veritable golden age of Bohemia. Artists including Modigliani, Utrillo, Soutine, Chagall, and Léger migrated from the lamentably less hip Montmartre, forming the base of the artistic movement called the Paris School. Political exiles, notably Lenin and Trotsky, spent evenings planning strategies over vodka in cafés.

After WWI, Montparnasse's reputation as a place for intellectual freedom drew in other artists (along with wanna-bes and general hangers-on), especially Americans who wanted to escape prohibition and profit from a favorable exchange rate. Man Ray transformed an apartment into a photolab; Calder worked on his first sculptures; Hemingway did some of his most serious writing and drinking; and Henry Miller created the shocking, steamy *Tropic of Cancer* at Seurat's villa with the encouragement of Anaïs Nin and Lawrence Durrell. It was all fun and games until the outbreak of the Spanish Civil War, then WWII, which put a final, resolute damper on the Bohemian community in Montparnasse. The *quartier* is now predominantly Parisian. Denfer-Rochereau, Plaisance, and Penerty remain admittedly unattractive and residential, and the Cité Universitaire is a French Animal House for the university set. Only the area around the *tour* teems with commercialism and caters to tourists.

Although officially in the 15*ème,* the **Tour de Montparnasse** merits a word of discussion as your eye is involuntarily, inexplicably drawn to it from any point in the 14*ème.* Yes, it is as tall and unattractive as you've heard—all 209m of it. Rising from the intersection of the 6*ème, 14ème,* and 15*ème arrondissements* like a rook in a game of urban renewal of monumental proportions, the *tour* casts a black pall on anything unlucky enough to fall in its shadow. (See Sights—15*ème.*)

The **Cimetière Montparnasse,** 3, bd. Edgar Quinet (tel. 44 10 36 50; Mo. Edgar Quinet) is less than romantic. Shrouded by the shadow of the Tour Montparnasse, crisscrossed by avenues, too crowded with tombs for grass, and occupied by cats and chattering grounds keepers who appear to be doing their best not to disturb the final resting places of heaps of beer and mineral water bottles, the Cimetière Montparnasse is better left to the dead. Armed with a free *Index des Célébrités* (the detailed map available just left of the main entrance), determined sightseers thread their way through the unknown to pay their respects to writers like Guy de Maupassant, Samuel Beckett, Jean-Paul Sartre and Simone de Beauvoir (who share a grave), car manufacturer André Citroën, composer Camille Saint-Saëns, sculptor Ossip Zadkine, editor Pierre Larousse (of dictionary fame), artist Man Ray, and loyal Frenchman Alfred Dreyfus. Don't miss the tomb of Charles Baudelaire who, in his *Fleurs du Mal,* six years before he died, greeted Death willingly: "O Death, old captain, it is

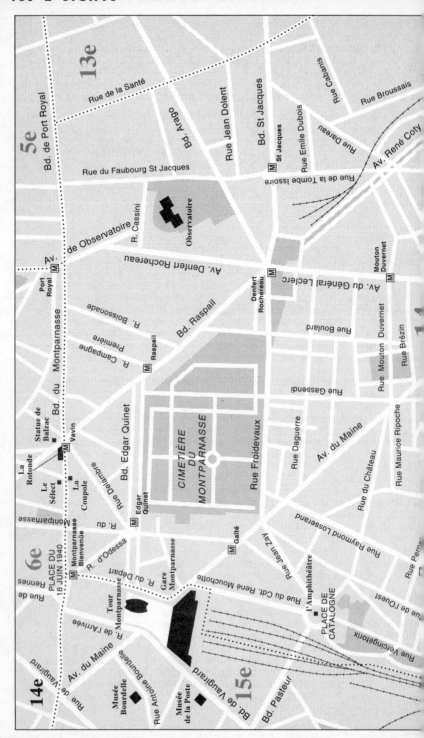

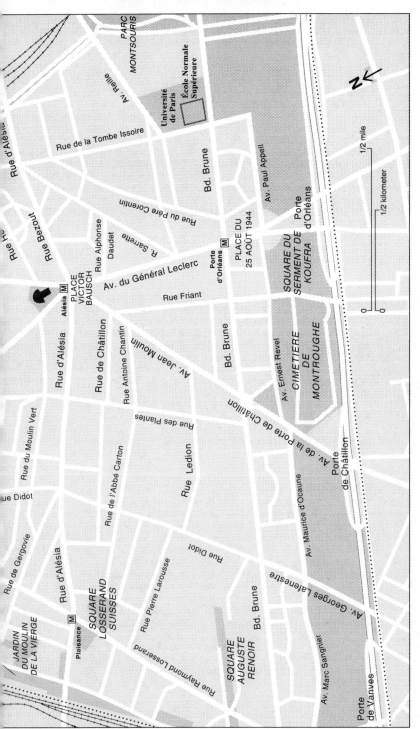

time! Lift the anchor! We wish, so much this fire consumes our brains, to plunge
into the abyss, Heaven or Hell, what matters? To the very edge of knowledge in
order to find something *new!*" (Open Mon.-Fri. 7:30am-6pm, Sat. 8:30am-6pm, Sun.
9am-6pm; Nov. 6-March 15 closes 5:30pm. Free.) **Place Denfert-Rochereau** is pre
sided over by a magnificent lion sculpted by **Bartholdi,** the creator of the Statue of
Liberty (the lion and Lady Liberty even share that same funny green color...).

**Les Catacombs,** 1, pl. Denfert-Rochereau (tel. 43 22 47 63; Mo. Denfert-Roch
ereau) are subterranean tunnels which were originally excavated to provide stone
for building the city. By the 1770s, much of the Left Bank was in danger of caving in
and digging stopped. The former quarry was then converted to a mass grave, to
relieve the unbearable stench emanating from cemeteries around Paris. Near the
entrance to the ossuary reads the ominous caution, "Stop! Beyond Here Is the
Empire of Death." Many have ignored the sign. In 1793, a Parisian got lost and was
not found for nine years, at which point, he'd become, so to speak, one with the
pile of bones. During World War II, this place was actually full of life—the resistance
set up headquarters among these old and loyal Parisian bones.

In the depths of the ossuary, you will find yourself in an underground city (note
the "street" names on the walls) with bones for bricks and marrow for mortar. Nav
igate your way through tunnels lined with femurs stacked on top of fibulas
anchored by craniums. Although verging on ghoulish, the arrangement is tidy, prac
tical, and often quite artistic. Beware the low ceilings and unidentifiable liquid seep
ing from the walls—don't even stop to ponder what it could be. Some rooms spor
cheery sayings to make the journey more interesting—*"Pensez le matin que vou.
n'irez peut être pas jusques au soir et au soir que vous n'irez pas jusques au
matin."* (Think each morning that you may not be alive in the evening, and each
evening that you may not be alive in the morning.) The stacks of bones are often
labeled, indicating which cemetery they came from, but they all look alike—who
would notice if something were out of order? Bring a sweater, a flashlight, and a
friend for support. Not recommended for the faint of heart or leg; the 85 steep step:
you climb on the way out will provide you with a day's worth of exercise. No
wheelchair accessible. (Open Tues.-Fri. 2-4pm, Sat.-Sun. 9-11am and 2-4pm. Admis
sion 27F, students 15F, under 6 free.)

**Parc Montsouris** offers a sunny return to the land of the living. Begun in 1867 by
the Baron Haussmann, this park doubles as an arboretum, offering sanctuary to hun
dreds of rare and unusual trees, all well-labeled and cared for. An amazing variety of
birds, ducks, and geese splash contentedly in the artificial lake at one end of the
park. (The designer of this lake killed himself after the water mysteriously drained
during the park's opening ceremony.) Sunbathers, children, and *clochards* are ever
allowed to stretch out on a 50m x 50m strip of grass along the street side of the lake
Don't give into the temptation to pet a lesser snow goose, Australian rajah shelduck
or a fulvous whistling duck—all of these hiss a warning, then deliver a nasty bite.

Across the bd. Jourdan, thousands of students rage the night away in the **Cite
Universitaire,** a 40-hectare rompus park brimming with students from no less than
122 countries worldwide in more than 30 different dormitories, two of them by Le
Corbusier. The "vertical slab" called the **Pavilion Suisse** (1932) is adored by archi
tects as a monument of his early career. With its *pilotis* (stilts) underneath and its
garden on the roof, the building reflects the architect's dream of a vertical city, with
life lived on several levels. During the German occupation, the roof garden housed
a battery of anti-aircraft guns. Le Corbusier returned in 1959 with the **Maison de
Brasil.** South and west of the dorms, the expansive greenery flaunts Parisian park
customs, as hundreds of joggers, frisbee throwers, bikers, and boom-box player:
totally disregard the signs to keep off the grass.

North of the Parc Montsouris is the **Hôpital Ste-Anne,** 15, rue Cabanis, a psychi
atric hospital with an interesting history. It first opened its doors to the nervous citi
zens of Paris in 1221 but did not begin to thrive until Louis XIV took the throne
when state funds, mostly earmarked for the imprisonment of "wanton girls and

women," poured in. After a series of fires, the hospital went through several incarnations, including a dairy farm in the 18th century with a full complement of 140 cows and 700 pigs, before being finally restored to its original life as a clinic by Napoleon III in 1863. Although access to most of the buildings is restricted to the medical staff and patients (neither of which you really want to visit), a tour of the grounds affords a quick respite from the bustle of the streets (open daily 7am-9pm). In a bizarre, and perhaps planned, coincidence, all of the neighboring streets are named after people like Camille Claudel and Vincent Van Gogh, many of whom were out of their minds.

## ■ Fifteenth Arrondissement

Although the museums, the shopping districts, and the famous concert halls and opera houses all belong to other *arrondissements,* the 15*ème* possesses the most important sight of them all, the true Paris, where people go about their daily lives, isolated from tourist invasions and busy traffic. Just breathing the air, drinking in a café among dedicated patrons, and watching children play in a nearby park is the kind of irreplaceable Parisian experience you can't find on the Champs Elysées. *Coiffures,* drugstores, grocers, *boulangeries,* cafés, and *boucheries*, reminiscent of the calmer bourgeois life of smaller towns outside of Paris, line the streets of the 15*ème*. You'll see lots of older Parisians walking the dog or shopping in the market, and younger Parisians on their way home from school. Neither anachronistically antique nor oppressively modern, the architecture of the 15*ème* mirrors its inhabitants; solid, staid, slightly uptight, and built about 80 years ago.

The bd. de Grenelle stretches through most of the brighter cafés, stores, and specialty shops of the 15*ème*. The festive rue du Commerce overflows with flower-shops, markets, and inexpensive houseware shops. But perhaps the best introduction to the 15*ème* is the *métro* ride that brings you to the heart of the *arrondissement* itself. Get on Métro 6—one of the only *métro* lines in Paris that has an elevated track with a view—at Trocadéro and ride to the 15*ème*'s central stop, **La Motte-Picquet-Grenelle.** From your *métro* car, you'll have a lovely view of the Seine, the Eiffel Tower, and the rooftops of the 16*ème* and the 15*ème*—all for the low cost of a *métro* ticket.

For coffee and a front-row view of this vibrant Parisian neighborhood, get off at the La Motte-Picquet-Grenelle stop and relax at the **Café Bouquet de Grenelle** next door. Or take a walk through the colorful markets of the rue du Commerce. For more people-watching, pop out of the Convention *métro* stop, where perfect cafés occupy each corner of the intersection between rue de la Convention and rue de Vaugirard. If you're still interested in seeing the city's sights from afar, take the elevator to the top of the towering Tour Montparnasse.

The **Tour Montparnasse** (tel. 45 38 52 56; Mo. Montparnasse-Bienvenue) dominates the *quartier's* northeast corner. Standing 56 stories tall, this controversial building looks somewhat out of place amidst the older architecture of Montparnasse. Some argue that the *tour,* completed in 1973, looks like a bit of Manhattan protruding awkwardly in the middle of Paris. But the group of French architects who designed the tower believed that it would revolutionize the Paris skyline. It has, but not without the disapproval of many Parisians. Shortly after it was completed, the city of Paris passed an ordinance forbidding any further structures to be built within Paris proper, designating La Défense as the only possible home of future structures like the Tour Montparnasse. The *tour,* which houses a huge underground shopping mall and train station, used to hold the European record for the tallest office building. Take advantage of this fact by riding to the top, where a fabulous view of the unobstructed Paris skyline awaits (open daily 9:30am-11:30pm, Oct.-March 9:30am-10:30pm; admission 39F, students and seniors 22F).

In front of the Tour Montparnasse, the **place du 18 juin** commemorates two important events from World War II. The name recalls the June 18, 1940 radio broadcast from London by General de Gaulle in which he called on his fellow citizens to resist the occupying Nazi forces and the Vichy collaborationist *régime* of

Maréchal Pétain. And it was on this *place* that General Leclerc, the leader of the French forces, accepted the surrender of General von Choltitz, the Nazi commander of the Paris occupation, on August 25, 1944. It is due to his love of the city that the Tour Montparnasse is not Paris's only monument. Despite continual orders from Hitler to destroy Paris ("Is Paris burning?") and retreat, von Choltitz disobeyed, thus saving countless landmarks of Parisian history and architecture.

**La Ruche,** 52, rue Dantzig (Mo. Convention), is a round brick building designed as a wine pavilion by Gustave Eiffel for the exposition of 1900, a decade after its more famous sibling came into existence. During the early 1900s the building, whose name means "the beehive," was bought by the private charitable foundation La Ruche Seydoux, and used to house struggling artists (among them Chagall and Soutine). Today the foundation still assists artists by providing grants, studios, and housing. The garden surrounding the building is studded with sculpture, the work of the house's residents. As La Ruche is a private foundation, visitors must call ahead to gain entry to the garden, though some people just wander in when the gate is open.

**L'Institut Pasteur,** 28, rue du Dr. Roux (tel. 45 68 80 00; Mo. Pasteur), founded by the French scientist Louis Pasteur in 1887, is now an international center for biochemical research, development, and treatment facilities. It was here that Pasteur, a champion of germ theory in the 17th century, developed his famous technique for purifying milk products. Today, some of the most interesting research on HIV is conducted here. In 1983, the *institut* gained notoriety for Dr. Luc Montaigner's isolation of HIV, the virus that causes AIDS. For years, Montaigner was embroiled in an international legal and scientific dispute with Dr. Robert Gallo of the American Centers for Disease Control over who had first isolated the HIV virus. Now less interested in such debates over "fame," Montaigner continues his work here on HIV.

The Institute houses an extensive museum on Pasteur and his work. The museum offers an exhaustive run-down of Pasteur's medical and artistic projects, a tour of his lab equipment and preserved living quarters, and a visit to the crypt which houses the scientist's corpse. Pasteur's son designed the symbolic fantasyland on the ceiling, a mosaic recalling Pasteur *père's* work with wine casks, rabid dogs, sheep, and of course, lots of happy cows. Tours are in French with photocopied English translations (open Mon.-Fri. 2-5:30pm; admission 15F, students 8F). Should Pasteur's life spur you to perform some selfless act, a blood donation center is across the street.

Also in the 15ème is the surprisingly interesting **Musée de la Poste** (Postal Museum), and the **Musée Bourdelle,** a well-stocked collection of the works of the French sculptor Emile-Antoine Bourdelle (see Museums).

# ■ Sixteenth Arrondissement

Welcome to the 16ème, where Gucci rubs elbows with Hermès, and Mercedes pull ahead of BMWs. This is the world of the French *nouveau riche* yuppie class, affectionately known in French as *BCBG* (*bon chic bon genre*). Despite the abundance of old money in the 16ème, it is not very *NAP* (the appellation given to those residents of the old-money suburbs of Neuilly, Auteuilly, and Passy), partly because many of the area's former residents have moved to other parts of Paris. And the *BCBG* who do live here are *NAP*-wanna-bees who will probably move out to the provinces and the country club once they move up a few more income brackets. Here you'll find young investment analysts and consultants, *boulangers* that are too chic to sell baguettes (focaccia bread only, please), newly graduated students from France's Ivy-League institutions like Hautes Etudes Commerciales and Ecole Normale Supérieure, and ministerial aids rushing home to prepare briefs for the Assemblée Nationale's morning session. Magnificent buildings of the style found all over Paris stand majestically in the 16ème: façades clean, balcony grilles intricate, and flower baskets bursting with color. An abundance of ladies (for they are definitely ladies) pass serenely above the urban fray, devotedly exercising their compact dogs.

The 16ème was created on January 1, 1860, when the villages of Auteuil, Passy, and Chaillot banded together and joined Paris. History continues to loom large in this area, a result of the few old aristocratic families who have held on to their heritage. Some of these families refuse to allow their children to sing *La Marseillaise* in the home because it was to this same tune that their ancestors were beheaded during the Revolution. Not surprisingly, this sumptuous neighborhood remains the nucleus of the city's conservative politics, fashion, and culture. Much social life here revolves around a uniquely French institution called a *rallye,* an exclusive group of children and young adults whose parents pay for the privilege of having their children *sortent* (go out) with other grand families of their class. Other less wealthy families crowd into small apartments to establish the residency that will allow them to send their children to the city's finest schools.

Lining the Right Bank from avenue de la Grande-Armée in the north to Porte St-Cloud in the south, the opulent 16ème spreads east from the immense Bois de Boulogne (annexed in 1929) to the nearly equally luxuriant 8ème and the less plush 17ème north and east. Excellent museums abound; almost half of Paris's museums are located in this *quartier* of grand avenues and huge mansions.

**Avenue Foch,** one of Haussmann's finest creations, runs from the Arc de Triomphe to the Bois de Boulogne. It was originally named for Napoleon III's consort, l'Impératrice, but was given the more neutral title, avenue du Bois de Boulogne, after her downfall. This is one of Paris's grandest boulevards, the 16ème's widest, and reputedly the richest of them all. Not all mansions are created equal, however—those on the south side are even more expensive because they receive better sun. To the north of av. Foch sits a quiet, narrow-street residential area, where you can sit in the **Parc-Etoile Foch,** located near a number of the 64 embassies in the 16ème.

Avenue Victor Hugo cuts southwest from the Arc and serves as one of the main places to shop in the 16ème. You will know you've hit the **place Victor Hugo** when you see the line snaking out of the Häagen-Dazs store. Guarded by the dignified **Eglise St-Honoré d'Eylau,** place Victor Hugo is the center from which most of this part of the *quartier's* roads radiate. The *place's* lovely fountain stands to remind the residents of the 16ème that they are descended from the folks at Versailles. At 24, rue Copernic, the **Union Libéral Israélite de France** synagogue remains a symbol of Jewish strength, in spite of the 1980 bombing that killed four people. **Rue Bugeaud,** leading out in the opposite direction from the *place,* runs through the beautiful **place du Chancelier Adenauer.** South of Bugeaud, old and new meet comfortably; a row of old classic Parisian buildings on one side of rue Spontini faces its reflections in the glass FRADIM building across the street. Next to it all—old and crumbling, old and classy, new and chic—squats the terribly posh Saint James Paris driving club.

**Eglise St-Pierre de Chaillot,** between av. Marceau and rue de Chaillot, while not intended for tourists, has a striking sculpture by Henri Bouchard over its front three arches and brilliantly lit stained glass. It is also a good place to find out about foreign language religious services around Paris.

Across from the *place* stands the **Palais Galliera,** built for the Duchess of Galliera by Louis Ginain between 1878 and 1888, in Italian Renaissance style. It now houses the **Musée de Mode et Costume.** In the Palais's back garden, off av. du Prés. Wilson, kids frolic under the gazes of *Painting, Architecture,* and *Sculpture,* allegorical figures framed by Romanesque arches. The **Palais de Tokyo,** home to the **Musée d'Art Moderne de la Ville de Paris** and numerous visual exhibitions, was built for the International Expo in 1937 and was named after the quai de Tokyo that separated it from the Seine. The *quai's* politically incorrect name was a WWII casualty—it became the quai de New York—but the Palais has endured. Farther along av. du Prés. Wilson, in the place d'Iéna, you will find the **Musée Guimet.** (See Museums.)

The **Palais de Chaillot** is the final product of a series of attempts to build a palace on the heights of Chaillot. Cathérine de Médicis had a château here. Napoleon wanted to erect a residence for his son, but was interrupted by that bother called Waterloo. In the 1820s, the duc d'Angoulême built a fortress-like memorial to his victory at Trocadéro in Spain. In 1878, this was replaced by the Palais du Trocadéro (affectionately known as the "Trock" or "Troca"), which in turn yielded to the

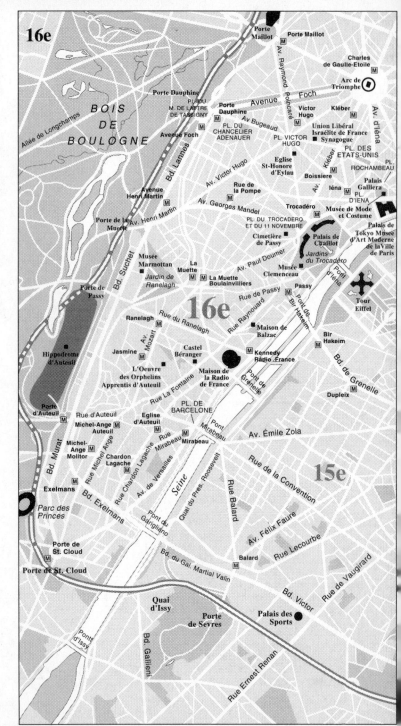

present structure prior to the 1937 World's Fair. Architect Jacques Carlu's radical design features two curved wings with a gap where a central hall might be expected. Today the Palais houses the **Musées du Cinéma Henri-Langlois, de l'Homme, de Marine, et National des Monuments Français** (see Museums) as well as the **Théâtre National de Chaillot** and the **Cinémathèque Française** (see Entertainment). The large terrace welcomes tourists, sun worshipers, souvenir vendors, roller-skating street dancers, and political demonstrators, and is watched over by the 1.5m-tall bronze Apollo by Henri Bouchard. It also provides the best view of the Eiffel Tower and the Champ de Mars, right across the Seine.

The **Jardins du Trocadéro** bask beneath the palace, with cooling fountains (no bathing allowed) and much green grass. Toss a frisbee, lie on the grass, or spin on the carousel in the place de Varsovie (10F, kid or adult). Watch out for the maniacal roller skaters who jump over barriers and slalom on one foot around the fountains.

**Passy** (or **La Muette**), the area to the immediate south and southwest of the Trocadéro, has been known historically for its restorative waters, châteaux, and grand houses. The marks of its famous residents linger. You can visit the homes of a famed novelist and of a revered statesman by entering the **Maison de Balzac** and the **Musée Clemenceau** (see Museums). Jean-Jacques Rousseau lived on rue Raynouard, and Benjamin Franklin lived in the area for several years and built France's first lightning rod nearby. Manet and Debussy, among others, are buried in the **Cimetière de Passy.**

**Rue de Passy** in modern-day Paris is another upscale shopping street—window-shop until it becomes Chaussée de la Muette. Northwest of the La Muette *métro* stop lies the former site of the Château de la Muette, where Louis XV went for his mistress-trysts. In 1783, Pilâtre de Rozier and the Marquis d'Arlandes became the first two humans to escape gravity as they lifted off from the château's lawn in a Montgolfier balloon, landing 20 minutes later in what is now the 13ème. Walk through the **Jardin de Ranelagh,** where kids will enjoy the old-style carousel. On the other side of the park, the **Musée Marmottan** offers an exquisite collection of Impressionist paintings and medieval illuminations (see Museums).

The southernmost part of the 16ème, **Auteuil** was once the meeting spot for poets and philosophers like Racine, Molière, and Boileau. Less oppressively ostentatious than its neighbors to the north, Auteuil's charm is linked in part to its Art Nouveau architecture. Who needs New York? A smaller replica of the **Statue of Liberty** can be found off Pont de Grenelle on Allée des Cygnes. Impossible to miss on av. du Prés. Kennedy is the circular **Maison de la Radio-France,** the largest building in France and headquarters of the French national media. Besides touring its Musée (see Museums), you can also attend one of Radio-France's concerts or appear in a studio audience, listening to a group of literati debate such classic French topics as *"Qu'est-ce que c'est qu'un intellectuel?"* ("What is an intellectual?"). Call 42 30 33 83 for details; shows rotate monthly. Show up 30 minutes before to gain free admission.

**Rue La Fontaine** is one of a number of streets to showcase the Art Nouveau style of Hector Guimard. At 14, rue La Fontaine stands the famous **Castel Béranger** (1898) whose curving lines (called "noodle style" by one skeptical *hôtelier)* on balconies, staircases, and rooftops work to achieve the harmony of the building's elements. Guimard designed numerous buildings around Paris at the end of the 19th century and beginning of the 20th, as well as the green *Métropolitain* stations (Dauphine is a particularly good example). Guimard lived for a while in the Castel Béranger, then moved to 122, av. Mozart, another of his creations. Several Le Corbusier structures lurk in the architecturally rich 16ème; the mairie can provide a list.

**L'Oeuvre des Orphelins Apprentis d'Auteuil** (Society of Apprenticed Orphans), 40, rue La Fontaine, testifies to the faith of two men. Abbé Roussel founded the society in 1866, to provide a home and a future for local orphans. Despite financial obstacles, Roussel kept his organization going until his death in 1897. When the group seemed headed for disaster in 1923, Father Daniel Brottier (beatified by the Pope in 1984—the first step toward sainthood) became director. Today's orphans can perform apprenticeships in 30 occupations (the Auteuil "campus" does printing), and are an important part of the Auteuil community, as they are in communities all over France. Visit one of the churches or enjoy the gardens—carefully tended by apprentice gardeners.

## ■ Seventeenth Arrondissement

*La pauvre 17ème!* The seventeenth suffers from its schizophrenic identity as part chic, part kitsch. Like its wealthy and snobbish western and southern neighbors in Neuilly, Passy, the 8ème, and the 16ème, the 17ème can take on the aristocratic feel of old money. But like its seedy eastern neighbors in Pigalle, the 17ème has also been known to harbor prostitutes and heroin dealers. The Dr. Jekyll and Mr. Hyde syndrome is taken to the extreme here; the 17ème's daytime personality near the Arc de Triomphe epitomizes bourgeois respectability, while its nighttime personality, based around the place de Clichy, wades in a seamy underside of heroin, crime, and prostitution. Finding little but boredom on the one hand, or just a little too much adventure on the other, most visitors to Paris just avoid both sides of the 17ème. The wealthier half of the *arrondissement*, extending west from the bd. Malesherbes and south to the Arc de Triomphe, encompasses largely residential neighborhoods, as well as a number of pricey hotels that cash in on their location near the place Charles de Gaulle. To the east, the place de Clichy overflows with the *zonards:* junkies chased out of the place Pigalle by police intent on making the latter safe for busloads of tourists in for a little bare-breasted entertainment.

The most interesting and safe sections of the 17ème are the eastern and southern halves. The lovely **place des Ternes,** on the border of the 8ème, has a number of lively cafés and a daily flower market that brings color to the drab 17ème. **Parc Monceau,** technically located in the 8ème, provides an open space and a number of architectural marvels (see Sights—8ème). From *métro* station Monceau the nearest entrance to the gilded iron gates of the park is from the bd. de Courcelles. (Open 7am-10pm; Nov.-March 7am-8pm. Gates begin closing 15 min. earlier.)

Frankly, there isn't much else to see. While barricades were erected and novels written in the heart of the city, Les Batignolles was, until the mid-19th century, little more than farmers' fields. Though it has since been urbanized, it does not merit a special excursion for the sole purpose of tourism. If you happen to be staying in the area, though, don't miss the **Musée Jean-Jacques Henner,** 43, av. de Villiers, a museum dedicated to this late 19th-century painter (see Museums). Near the museum, at 1, place Général Catroux, a building belonging to the **Banque de France** (tel. 42 27 78 14) dominates a small garden with its huge mosaic brickwork. Built in 1884 as the residence of the bank's regent, the house features gargoyle capitals leering from the façade and serpentine iron drainpipes which slither down the building's sides. The interior, open to the public, contains a lobby with vaulted ceilings rising to impossible heights (open Mon.-Fri. 8:45am-noon and 1:45-3:30pm).

The enormous and ultra-modern **Palais des Congrès** stands at the very farthest western end of the 17ème and of Paris (Mo. Porte Maillot). The high-rising glass-towered shopping galleries and conference halls are used as a convention center year-round. For a free view of the sprawling Bois de Boulogne to the south, go up to the terraces on the fifth and seventh floors. The Palais also houses restaurants, a disco, and a cinema. The conference hall hosts conferences and music and theater performances, and is considered one of the most modern and acoustically effective performance spaces in Europe. (For more info on performances call 40 68 25 11.)

The **Cimetière des Batignolles** (tel. 47 37 25 44; Mo. Porte de Clichy), in the northwest corner of the 17ème, contains the graves of both André Breton and Paul Verlaine. Nearby, the less famous and somewhat comic, though touching, **Cimetière des Chiens** is the final resting spot of countless Parisians' beloved pets. Names like Fifi, Jean-Pierre, Jack, and Chérie mark small stones and tiny graves for all these beloved pups (open Wed.-Sun. 10am-noon and 3-5pm).

The far-ranging flavor of the 17*ème* is perhaps best exemplified by a number of streets with widely diverse atmospheres. Rue des Batignolles is considered the center of the **Village Batignolles,** a chic and quiet village of shops and residences near the place Félix-Lobligeois and the Eglise de Ste-Marie des Batignolles. Rue Lemercier has a daily covered market filled with meat, cheese, flowers, produce, and old bourgeois women who've shopped on this street since before World War II. Rue de la Jonquière (Mo. Guy Môquet), lined with shops and restaurants, forms the focus of an active North African community. And looking like it was taken directly from a Balzac novel, Cité des Fleurs boasts a row of exquisite private homes and gardens.

# ■ Eighteenth Arrondissement: Montmartre

Built high above the rest of Paris on a steep *butte* (knoll), Montmartre was once a fertile farming area, covered with vineyards and wheat fields. The last of these vineyards, behind the Musée du Vieux Montmartre (rue Cortot), is still operational. Wheat was processed in Montmartre's famous windmills, of which the Moulin de la Galette is one of the last remaining examples. But this hilly area gets its name from its more ancient history of Roman occupation and Christian martyrdom. A bishop named Dionysus, now known as St-Denis, came to this hill to introduce Christianity to the Gauls. The Romans, unappreciative of his efforts, cut off his head in 272. Legend has it that he and two other martyred bishops picked up their heads and carried them north to their final resting point, 7km away, where the Eglise St-Denis now stands—thus the name *Montmartre* (Hill of the Martyrs), which this area has borne ever since. In the 12th century, Louis VI brought a group of Benedictine nuns here to set up an Abbey—the origin of the area called "Abbesses" (around Mo. Abbesses).

Montmartre gained particular attention during the siege of Paris of 1870 and the Commune of 1871. It was here, from the highest point in the city, that Minister of the Interior Léon Gambetta ascended in a flimsy balloon, floating over the Prussian lines to the unoccupied provinces, where he mustered a new army in a desperate attempt to save Paris. In 1871, a bloody battle in which radical Guards and citizens of Montmartre fought Adolphe Thiers's Republican troops sparked a series of uprisings all over Paris. By the end of the day, the government had fled for Versailles; 10 days later the Paris Commune was proclaimed. On May 23, the Commune came to a bloody end; many captured *communards* were shot without trial by the victorious Republicans and buried in mass graves in the Montmartre Cemetery.

Revolution in the 19th century gave way to 20th-century art, music, and literature. Many 20th-century artists chose Montmartre for their home primarily because of its low-cost rent. Untouched by Haussmann's demolitions, its narrow streets and sharp corners attracted such notable Bohemians as Gustave Charpentier, Toulouse-Lautrec, and Eric Satie, and performers like "La Goulue" and Aristide Bruant. Toulouse-Lautrec, in particular, immortalized Montmartre through his paintings of life in cabaret-concerts like the Moulin Rouge and the Lapin Agile. A generation later, in its last moment of glory before the devastation of World War I, Montmartre welcomed Picasso, Modigliani, Utrillo, and Apollinaire into its artistic circle.

Montmartre's heyday has since passed. Once lively places are merely shells for tourists to gape at and photograph. But there is still something magical about the *butte*. Perhaps it is the images from such classic films as *Le Balon Rouge* or *Les 400 Coups* of the stairways up its hillside and the façades of its half-crumbling houses. Maybe it is the dramatic views of the rooftops of Paris at one's feet, the musicians and peddlers who gather in front of Sacré-Coeur at night, or the artists who sell their sketches of the *butte's* streets and corners. Even with hordes of tourists, this place has its charm. Together with Mont. Ste-Geneviève (see 5*ème*), this is the only hill of Paris left intact by Haussmann's plan. Come at dusk to watch the lights of Paris turn on below, and the famous gas lamps trace the line of the steps up the hillside.

One does not merely visit Montmartre; one ascends it. Enter this *quartier* at *métro* stops Barbès-Rochechouart, Anvers, Pigalle, Blanche, or Clichy, all along its southern boundary. At nighttime, it is best to use Mo. Abbesses instead; what's

EIGHTEENTH ARRONDISSEMENT

more, you'll enjoy the colorful frescoes that decorate one of its staircases. You can take the direct route from Anvers up rue de Steinkerque through sweaty, noisy crowds of tourists, and "sex-shop" owners inviting one in for a voyeuristic orgy. Or avoid these less desirable aspects of Montmartre altogether by taking more round-about routes such as the rue Caulaincourt and the rue Lepic. Both are quiet, scenic streets, lined with trees, restaurants, bookstores, and antique stores, and both offer dramatic views of the city below and the Basilique du Sacré-Coeur above.

For the classic approach to Sacré-Coeur, climb up the switchbacked stairs leading up from the **square Willette.** At night, crowds of students and tourists mingle in the square to play guitar music, sing, smoke, and drink wine. The **Musée d'Art Naïf Max Fourny,** to the east of the square, is housed in a marketplace, an excellent example of late 19th-century iron and glass architecture (see Museums). Or, take the glass-covered *funiculaire* from the base of the rue Tardieu (from Mo. Anvers, walk up rue Steinkerque and take a left on rue Tardieu to the very top of the *butte*). This *funiculaire,* reminiscent of a ski lift or a San Francisco cable car, is operated by the *métro* service and can be used with a normal *métro* ticket (6F). In 45 seconds, you are miraculously whisked up an impressive 45 degree gradient. Turn around and watch how the city below comes almost immediately and spectacularly into sight.

The **Basilique du Sacré-Coeur (Basilica of the Sacred Heart),** 35, rue du Cheva-lier de la Barre (tel. 42 51 17 02; Mo. Anvers, Abbesses, or Château-Rouge), crowns the very top of the *butte* Montmartre like an enormous, white meringue. In 1873, the Assemblée Nationale selected the birthplace of the Commune to build Sacré-Coeur "in witness of repentance and as a symbol of hope." Politician Eugène Spuller called it "a monument to civil war." The basilica was not completed until 1914, after a massive fundraiser. It was consecrated in 1919, at the end of World War I. The style is pseudo Romanesque-Byzantine, a hybrid of onion domes and arches. Ever since its consecration, there has been a perpetual prayer vigil for peace that has con-tinued without interruption for 74 years. The mosaics in the basilica's interior are stunning, especially the enormous mosaic of Christ on the ceiling interior of the dome, and the expressive mosaics of the Passion of Christ (the "stations of the cross") around the back of the altar. Before you leave, read the gray slate plaque that hangs to the right of the basilica's main doors. It explains how, in an act of divine intervention, the basilica was spared from vicious German bombardment of the *butte* in 1943. Unfortunately, much of the stained glass was blown out by bombers in World War II and replaced afterward. Climb the 112m bell tower for the highest point in Paris and a view that stretches as far as 50km on clear days. The crypt is open (for a price) and contains a relic of what many believe is a piece of the sacred heart of Christ. (Basilica open daily 7am-11pm; free. Dome and crypt open daily 9am-7pm; in winter 9am-6pm. Admission to dome 15F, *tarif réduit* 8F; to crypt 10F, *tarif réduit* 5F.) When you exit the basilica, take a right on to the winding rue du Mont, which leads to the lovely place du Tertre. Crowded with cafés, restaurants, and artists, this is one of the loveliest spots for a *café* or a *kir*. Many of the oil paint-ers and sketch artists here are ambitious painters who need to sell their less interest-ing and more typical paintings and sketches of Paris landscapes in order to eat. At 21, place du Tertre, the **tourist office** (tel. 42 62 21 21) gives free annotated maps and information about the area (open daily 10am-10pm; Oct.-April daily 10am-7pm). Nearby, the **Musée Montmartre, Musée du Vieux Montmartre,** and **Musée Salva-dor Dalí** highlight a variety of artistic and historical displays (see Museums).

Moving away from the crowded place du Tertre you'll find narrow, winding streets, hidden walled gardens, sharp corners, and whimsical clues to the way life used to be when Montmartre was a center of Bohemian life. The area west of the *place,* including the rue des Abbesses, rue des Trois Frères, and rue Lepic, is crowded with pleasant restaurants, antique stores, and *boulangeries.* Cobblestone roads twist around, moving down the hill; many of the 18th-century residences hide charming gardens behind their iron gates. Above the rue Lepic stands the **Moulin de la Galette,** one of the last remaining windmills from the days when Montmartre was covered with fields. Farther west, the **Cimetière Montmartre,** 20 av. Rachel (tel. 43 87 64 24; Mo. La Fourche), makes for a nice stroll—don't miss the last resting place of Emile Zola, Edgar Degas, Hector Berlioz, Vaslav Nijinsky, Stendhal, and Pierre Trudeau. In 1871, this cemetery was the site of huge mass graves from the Siege and Commune (open Mon.-Fri. 8am-5:30pm, Sat. 8am-8pm, Sun. 8am-9pm).

Along the boulevard de la Rochechouart, you'll find many of the cabarets and nightclubs that were the definitive hangouts of the Belle Epoque: the **Moulin Rouge,** for example, immortalized by the paintings of Toulouse-Lautrec and the music of Offenbach. After World War I, the literati crowd mostly returned to the Left Bank, leaving behind what turned into a seedy red-light district centered around **place de Pigalle** (see 9ème). The Moulin Rouge, at place Blanche, still offers its risqué *revues,* but at a ridiculously high price. During the Belle Epoque, Paris's (otherwise respectable) upper bourgeoisie came here to play at being Bohemian; nowadays, the crowd is made up mostly of (otherwise respectable) tourists, out for a taste of Paris's flashiest experience (see Entertainment—Cabarets). Pigalle also has some *discothèques,* trendy nightspots for Parisian and foreign youth (see Entertainment—Discos). Other than that, it is the home of a large portion of Paris's seedy "sex-shop" industry, where one can see just about any sexual art either on screen or live. During World War II, American servicemen appropriately called Pigalle, "Pig-alley." No one should walk around this area alone at night. Farther down bd. de Clichy, at the edge of the 17ème, the place de Clichy is filled with popular restaurants and cinemas, but also functions as a haven for drugs and crime.

# ■ Nineteenth Arrondissement

Apart from La Villette (see Museums), the 19ème *arrondissement* has little to offer the ordinary pleasure-seeking tourist. Instead of historical monuments, it flaunts unaesthetic tower blocks that serve as *habitations à loyer modéré* (HLM), subsidized, low-cost housing. Taking on a somewhat suburban air, the 19ème is where many middle and working class Parisians live, raise their families, work, and socialize. An ethnically and culturally diverse *arrondissement,* the 19ème is also home to many immigrants, notably from Africa, India, and East Asia. It is common to see native dress in the streets, or unique combinations of traditional and Western styles.

The **Parc des Buttes-Chaumont** (Mo. Buttes-Chaumont) occupies the southern part of the 19ème. Now a fascinating mix of artificial scenery and transplanted vegetation, from the 13th century until the Revolution it was home to a gibbet, an iron cage in which the rotting corpses of criminals were displayed on high in an effort to deter further crime. After the Revolution it was used as a garbage dump, then as a dumping-ground for dead horses. After a stint as a commercial breeding-ground for worms (sold as bait), it became a gypsum quarry, the source of "plaster of Paris." Then Napoleon III ascended to the throne. As a young man, he had been exiled in England, where he had been impressed by London's large public parks. As emperor, he decided to imitate them, creating four large public parks: the Bois de Boulogne, the Bois de Vincennes, the Parc Montsouris, and the Parc des Buttes-Chaumont.

Making a park out of this mess took four years and 1000 workers. In order for trees to grow, all of the soil had to be replaced. Furthermore, designer Adolphe Alphand ordered the heavily quarried remains of a hill be built up with new rock to create fake cliffs surrounding a lake. Workers made a fake waterfall and a fake cave with fake stalactites. A pioneering suspension bridge leads to a fake Roman temple on top of the mountain. From this little temple, you have a view of the whole park and of the skyscrapers that surround it. If all this sounds rather ridiculous, remember that the urban proletariat in the 1860s had very little access to travel or greenery; the park provided the next best thing to seeing a real waterfall or Roman temple. Despite the kitsch, this low-tech Disneyworld makes for pleasant strolls and people-watching. The park is well-policed at night (open 7am-11pm; Oct.-April 7am-9pm).

TWENTIETH ARRONDISSEMENT

## ■ Twentieth Arrondissement: Belleville and Ménilmontant

As Haussmann's rebuilding expelled many of Paris's workers from the central city, thousands migrated east to Belleville (the northern part of the *arrondissement)* and Ménilmontant (the southern). By the late Second Empire, the 20ème was known as a "Red" *arrondissement,* solidly proletarian and radical. In January 1871, just before the lifting of the siege, members of Belleville's National Guard stormed a prison to demand the release of some leftist political leaders—an omen of the civil war to come. Some of the heaviest fighting during the suppression of the Commune took place in these streets, as the *communards* made desperate last stands on their home turf. Caught between the *Versaillais* troops to the west and the Prussian lines outside the city walls, the Commune fortified the Parc des Buttes-Chaumont and Père-Lachaise cemetery, but soon ran out of ammunition. On May 28, 1871, the *communards* abandoned their last barricade and surrendered.

After the Commune, the 20ème continued on as the fairly isolated home of those workers who survived the massacres. As historian Eugen Weber has written, "Many a workman's child grew to adolescence before World War I without getting out of Ménilmontant or Belleville." Today, locals freely admit that the only thing to see in the area is Père Lachaise. The neighborhood is fairly safe, but avoid the area around the Belleville *métro* stop at night.

The **Cimetière Père Lachaise,** bd. de Ménilmontant (tel. 43 70 70 33; Mo. Père-Lachaise), encloses the decaying remains of Balzac, Colette, Corot, Danton, David, Delacroix, La Fontaine, Haussmann, Molière, and Proust within its winding paths and elaborate sarcophagi. Nor is this, the most illustrious of Parisian cemeteries (named after Louis XIV's confessor), restricted to the French; foreigners inhumed here include Chopin, Jim Morrison, Gertrude Stein, and Oscar Wilde. Although so many famous people are buried in Père Lachaise, it was never meant to be an all-star resting place like Westminster Abbey. Indeed, the land for Père Lachaise was bought in 1803 by Napoleon's government to create a "modern and hygienic necropolis" that would relieve the overcrowding of city cemeteries.

As seen today, the cemetery is a landscaped grove which celebrates perpetual remembrance; many of the tombs here display sculptures and inscriptions reminding visitors of the dead's many worldly accomplishments. The grave of Géricault wears a bronzed reproduction of *The Raft of the Medusa;* on Chopin's tomb sits his tressed muse with a lyre in her hand. Père Lachaise is the antithesis of the church cemetery; a tribute to this world and not to the next, this cemetery is a 19th-century garden party for the dead. Hero-worship and idyllic strolls are the order of the day.

At first, Parisians were reluctant to bury their dead in a site which, at the time, was far from the city. To increase the cemetery's popularity, the resourceful Napoleon ordered that the remains of a few famous figures be dug up and reburied in Père Lachaise. Thus arrived the remains of Molière, Héloïse and Abélard, La Fontaine, and several other pre-19th century figures. Since then, over one million people have been buried here. Yet there are only 100,000 tombs. The discrepancy is primarily because poor people used to be buried in unmarked mass graves and that old graves are usually dug up after a while to make room for new generations of the dead. This process of digging up graves, although it sounds grisly, is necessary in a densely pop-ulated city like Paris. The 44 hectares of Père Lachaise are filled to bursting, so the government makes room by digging up any grave which has not been visited in a certain number of years. (In other words, if this likely event seems unattractive to the soon-to-be-dead, it's best to hire an official "mourner," much as wealthy patrons used to hire church choirs to sing their masses every year after their death.)

How did Jim Morrison and Oscar Wilde end up here? Simply by dying in Paris. Anybody who was born in or who died in Paris has the right to burial in a Parisian cemetery. Because of overcrowding, however, city policy now requires a family to pay a hefty fee for a departed member to be inhumed in a popular cemetery like

# Père Lachaise Cemetery

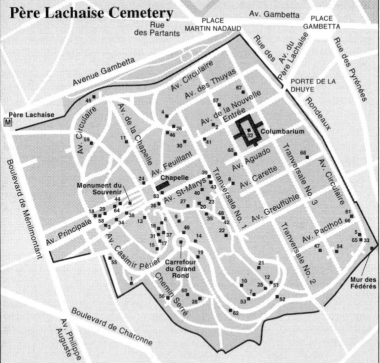

1 Abélard and Héloïse
2 Guillaume Apollinaire
3 Arago
4 Honoré de Balzac
5 Henri Barbusse
6 Vincenzo Bellini
7 Beaumarchais
8 Sarah Bernhardt
9 C. Bernard
10 Anna Bibesco
11 Georges Bizet
12 Caroline Bonaparte
13 Eduoard Branly
14 Jean Champollion
15 Gustave Charpentier
16 Luigi Cherubini
17 Frédéric Chopin
18 Colette
19 Auguste Comte
20 Camille Corot
21 David d'Angers
22 Alphonse Daudet
23 Honoré Daumier
24 Jacques-Louis David
25 Maréchal Davout
26 Eugène Delacroix
27 Gustave Doré
28 Ferdinand de Lesseps
29 Alfred de Musset
30 Gérard de Nerval
31 Bernardin de St-Pierre

32 Isadora Duncan
33 Paul Éluard
34 Félix Faure
35 Joseph Gay-Lussac
36 Thédore Gericault
37 André Grétry
38 Baron Haussmann
39 Jean Auguste Ingres
40 General Junot
41 Allan Kardec
42 Jean La Fontaine
43 René Lalique
44 General Lecomte
25 Maréchal Lefebvre
25 Maréchal Masséna
45 Georges Méliès
46 Michelet
47 Modigliani
48 Molière
49 Monge
50 Jim Morrison
51 Prince Murat
52 Nadar
53 Maréchal Ney
54 Edith Piaf
55 Camille Pissarro
56 Francis Poulenc
57 Marcel Proust
58 Rossini
59 Georges Seurat
60 Simone Signoret

61 Gertrude Stein
62 Talleyrand
63 Adolphe Thiers
64 Général Thomas
65 Maurice Thorez
66 Alice B. Toklas
67 Général Trujillo
68 Oscar Wilde

Père Lachaise. Cheaper, less desirable cemeteries are farther away from the city center. Still, if you're looking for a unique gift for that special someone, a gravesite near a path is only 38,395F, one away from a path only 23,595F. If these prices are beyond your reach, but you still want your remains to be near those of Jim Morrison, your family can rent shelf space for your cremated ashes in the columbarium: 50 years 9000F, 30 years 6000F, 10 years 2000F.

Remembered by inauspicious plaques in the columbarium are Isadora Duncan and Richard Wright, whose monument, hidden behind a stairwell, is hard to find. Fans of his will necessarily be disappointed. The columbarium, a landscape of memorials to the cremated, is located beyond the entrance from the place Gambetta. The plaques of Maria Callas and Max Ernst may also be purchased there.

As thousands of tourists discover every year, Père Lachaise (with its variety of tombs, from the pompous and ornate to the charming and fanciful) makes for a pleasant, strangely surreal stroll. The cemetery is beautifully landscaped with winding paths and abundant trees. As for the graves, they are crowded with ornate funerary monuments vying with each other for attention. Among the most beautiful is that of Chopin, with a marble statue of a young girl, bedecked with fresh flowers; among the most interesting is that of Oscar Wilde, a whimsical, gravity-defying bronze creation. Others seem abandoned and broken down. The most adored grave has to be that of **Jim Morrison** (lead singer of The Doors). Morrison-lovers' graffiti fills the cemetery. In summer, dozens of young people hang out at this cult tomb. Many of them bring offerings of flowers, joints, beer, poetry, or general Doors paraphernalia to leave on Jim's grave. A few smoke joints quite openly. You're allowed to take photographs, but there's a rule against filming Morrison's grave.

Père Lachaise's other big pilgrimage site is the **Mur des Fédérés (Wall of the Federals).** Nobody actually hangs out at this small wall (found on the upper right hand corner of the map), but most French people have heard of it and will at least have a look. In May 1871 a group of frustrated *communards* murdered the Archbishop of Paris, who had been taken hostage at the beginning of the Commune. They dragged his mutilated corpse to their stronghold of Père Lachaise, where they tossed it in a ditch. Four days later the victorious *Versaillais* found the body. In retaliation, they lined up 147 *Fédérés* against the eastern wall of the cemetery, shot them, and buried them on the spot. Ironically, Republicn Adolphe Thiers shares the same cemetery with them; he died of natural causes in 1877. Since 1871, the Mur des Fédérés has been a rallying point for the French Left, which recalls the massacre's anniversary every Pentecost. Near the wall, a number of monuments containing human remains from concentration camps commemorate the victims of the Nazis. (Père Lachaise is open Mon.-Fri. 7:30am-6pm, Sat. 8:30am-6pm, Sun. and holidays 9am-6pm; in winter Mon.-Fri. 8am-5:30pm, Sat., Sun., and holidays 9am-5:30pm.)

# ■ Bois de Boulogne

Spreading its leafy umbrella over 846 hectares at the western edge of Paris, the Bois de Boulogne (Mo. Porte Maillot, Sablons, Pont de Neuilly, Porte Dauphine, or Porte d'Auteuil) is a popular place for walks, jogs, and picnics. Formerly a royal hunting ground, the Bois was given to the city of Paris by Napoleon III in 1852. The Emperor had become a dilettante landscape-architect during his exile in England and wanted Paris to have something comparable to Hyde Park. Baron Haussmann did a fair job of imitating the famous London park, filling in sand-pits and giving the Bois artificial lakes and winding paths through thickly wooded areas. This attempt to copy nature marked a radical break with the tradition of French formal gardens established by Le Nôtre (rectilinear paths framed by strictly disciplined lines of shrubs and flowerbeds). The carefully landscaped "wilderness" is, of course, utterly artificial, yet it expressed a new urge to escape from Paris into a world of nature "outside the city"—the same urge captured by the Impressionists in their *plein air* painting.

When Auteuil was annexed to the city in 1860, the park, though outside the city walls, became part of the 16ème. In 1871, it was the site of yet another massacre of

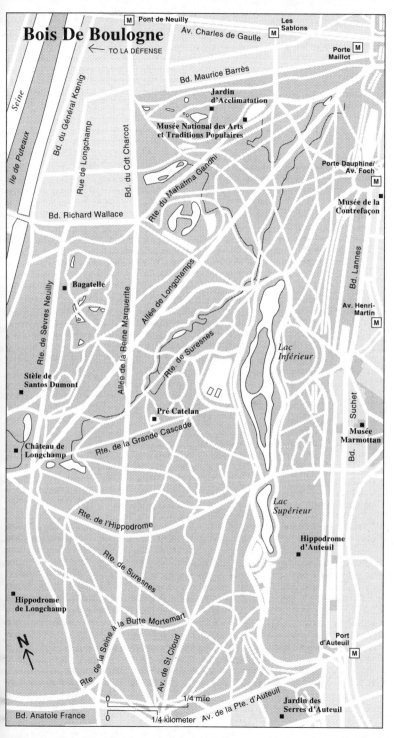

**Bois De Boulogne**

← TO LA DÉFENSE

M Pont de Neuilly

Av. Charles de Gaulle

Les Sablons M

Porte Maillot M

Bd. Maurice Barrès

Seine

Île de Puteaux

Bd. du Général Kœnig

Rue de Longchamp

Bd. du Cdt Charcot

Rte. du Mahatma Gandhi

Jardin d'Acclimatation

Musée National des Arts et Traditions Populaires

Porte Dauphine/ Av. Foch M

Musée de la Contrefaçon

Bd. Richard Wallace

Bagatelle

Allée de Longchamps

Allée de la Reine Marguerite

Rte. de Sèvres Neuilly

Rte. de Suresnes

Bd. Lannes

Av. Henri-Martin M

Lac Inférieur

Stèle de Santos Dumont

Pré Catelan

Rte. de la Grande Cascade

Château de Longchamp

Suchet

Bd.

Musée Marmottan

Lac Supérieur

Rte. de l'Hippodrome

Rte. de Suresnes

Hippodrome d'Auteuil

Hippodrome de Longchamp

N

Rte. de la Seine à la Butte Mortemart

Av. de St. Cloud

Port d'Auteuil M

Bd. Anatole France

0 — 1/4 mile

0 — 1/4 kilometer

Av. de la Pte. d'Auteuil

Jardin des Serres d'Auteuil

*communards,* as General Gallifet performed a Mengele-like selection on the column of prisoners bound for Versailles. The hundreds he pointed out—men with gray hair, with watches, with "intelligent faces"—were shot that night. But bloodstains can be washed away, and during the Belle Epoque the park regained its status as a fashionable locale for carriage rides and horse-racing. The running of the Grand Prix at Longchamp in June was one of the premier events of the social calendar. The park became *the* place to see and be seen, and no family was fashionable unless they went to the Bois de Boulogne for their "Sunday afternoon in the country."

Although the park continues to fill its original purpose as a place for afternoon strolls, successive governments have added to its list of diversions. The Bois now has a number of stadiums, the most famous of which are Longchamp and Auteuil (horse racing), Parc des Princes (mostly soccer), and the home of the French Open tennis tournament, Stade Roland Garros (see Sports). In addition, the Bois contains several separate parks, and boathouses that rent rowboats. For a more exciting, albeit vicarious, ride, try renting the remote-control boats that zoom across the lakes in all varieties—from the classic tug boat to a fine replica of George Bush's cigarette boat.

There are some amusements, however, that the government has tried to discourage. Until a couple of years ago, the Bois by night was a bazaar for sex and drugs, where transvestite prostitutes would stand along the roads, and violent crime was quite common. Since 1991, however, the police have calmed things down considerably, closing the roads at night and stepping up patrols. Nonetheless, it's a bad idea to come here for a moonlight stroll. In 1991, a flood of newly liberated Eastern Europeans visiting Paris camped out in the park, in an odd imitation of the Cossacks who bivouacked here after Waterloo. The lawn-crashers have since been nudged out.

The **Jardin d'Acclimatation** (tel. 40 67 90 82), an amusement park at the northern end of the Bois (Mo. Sablons), lacks big, scary roller-coasters, but has plenty of stuff designed to appeal to kids. There's a small zoo, a mini-golf course, a carousel, and even a racetrack where kids can ride tiny motorcycles around in circles. And, for a little culture, try the **Musée en Herbe** (tel. 40 67 97 66), an art museum designed for children. The Jardin has a certain old-fashioned charm. (Open Sept.-July daily 10am-6pm. Ticket office closes 5:15pm. Admission 16F, *tarif réduit* 11F, under 3 free. Admission to the Musée en Herbe is an extra 10F, under 3 free.) To get to the Jardin from the Porte Maillot *métro,* go to the big house marked l'Orée du Bois and follow the brown signs that point to the right of the building. Or you can go to the left of the building and take a cutesy little train. (Trains run Wed., Sat.-Sun., and public holidays, daily during school vacations, every 10min., 1:30-6pm. 5F, under 3 free.)

You can hear a pin drop at **Bowling de Paris** (tel. 40 67 94 00), near the rte. Mahatma Gandhi entrance of the Jardin d'Acclimatation (see Sports). On the edge of the Jardin, the **Musée des Arts et Traditions** (tel. 44 17 60 00; Mo. Sablons) displays exhibits of tools and everyday artifacts illustrating French rural life before the Industrial Revolution. Enter from the Jardin or from rte. Mahatma Gandhi. (Museum open Wed.-Mon. 10am-5pm. Admission 20F, under 25 and over 60 10F, Sun. 10F.)

**Pré Catelan** is a manicured park whose paths wind through neatly clipped grass and lovely old trees. The huge purple beech tree on the central lawn is almost 200 years old. You can sit on the grass, except where there are *pelouse interdite* signs. Inside the Pré Catelan, the **Jardin de Shakespeare** (created 1952-53) features plants mentioned by the bard, grouped by play—there is a collection of Scottish highland vegetation in the *Macbeth* area, a Mediterranean section for *The Tempest,* etc. In the center, a lovely open-air theater, the **Théâtre de Verdure du Jardin Shakespeare** (tel. 42 76 47 72), gives popular performances of Shakespeare's plays (in French) in the summer (see Entertainment—Theater). The park also hosts marionette shows for children (Mon.-Sat. at 3 and 4pm). Take the *métro* to Porte Maillot, then take bus #244 to Bagatelle-Pré-Catelan. (Pré Catelan open 10am-6pm. Jardin de Shakespeare open daily 3-5pm; admission 3F, under 10 3F.)

The **Parc de la Bagatelle** (tel. 40 67 97 00; same bus stop as Pré Catelan) was once a private estate within the Bois; Bagatelle did not become a public park until

1905. The Count of Artois, the future Charles X, built the little Château de la Baga-telle in 64 days in 1777, because of a wager with Marie-Antoinette, his sister-in-law. The garden is famous for its June rose exhibition and for its water lilies, which the gardener added in tribute to Monet. It frequently plays host to art exhibits. Do *not* walk on the grass. They really care about this—enough to put up signs in English shouting "Grass Prohibited." Guided French tours of the castle at 3, 4, and 5pm (25F) and of the castle and park at 4pm (35F) run from March 15 through October on weekends and public holidays. Meet at the castle. Call 40 71 75 23 to check these times. (Admission to park 6F, ages 6-10 3F. Open Jan. 16-31 9am-5:30pm; Feb. 1-15 and Oct. 16-Nov. 30 9am-6pm; Feb. 16-28 and Oct. 1-15 9am-6:30pm; March 1-15 and Sept. 8:30am-7pm; March 16-April 30 and Aug. 8:30am-7:30pm; May 1-15 8:30am-8pm; May 16-July 31 8:30am-8:30pm; Dec. 1-Jan. 15 9am-5pm. No, we don't know why they made it this complicated. Maybe it's because they're French.)

The two **artificial lakes** stretching down the eastern edge of the Bois make for a delightful stroll. Come on a weekday to avoid the crowds; come on a weekend to watch them. The manicured islands of the **Lac Inférieur** (Mo. Porte Dauphine) can be reached by rented rowboat only. (Boathouses open late Feb.-early Nov. Mon.-Fri. 9am-6pm, Sat.-Sun. 9am-7pm. Daily and annual schedules depend on weather; in good weather they rent boats longer, in bad weather they close earlier. Rentals 50F/hr., 400F deposit; with insurance against damage to boat 50F/hr., 200F deposit.)

Dedicated horticulturists may want to stroll through the **Jardin des Serres d'Au-teuil** (Greenhouse Garden), full of greenhouses, labeled trees, and semi-sickly flow-ers (open daily spring-summer 10am-6pm; autumn-winter 10am-5pm; admission 3F). Free, and prettier, although somewhat of a make-out spot (and what French gar-den is not?), is the neighboring **Jardin des Poètes.** Each cluster of flowers has an accompanying quote. Feeling saccharine? You can easily leave the poetry behind by attending a hard-fought and ardently cheered soccer or rugby match at the **Parc aux Princes,** one of several stadiums in the Porte d'Auteuil area.

**Bicycles,** a delightful way to get around the park, can be rented at two locations: across the street from the boathouse at the northern end of the Lac Inférieur and in front of the entrance to the Jardin d'Acclimatation. (Open Mon.-Fri. 1-6:30pm, Sat.-Sun. 9:30am-7pm; Sept.-June Wed. 1-6:30pm and Sat.-Sun. 9:30am-7pm. 32F/hr., passport or driver's license deposit.)

# ■ Bois de Vincennes

Like the Bois de Boulogne, the Bois de Vincennes (Mo. Château de Vincennes or Porte Dorée) was once a royal hunting forest, walled in to keep the exotic game from escaping. Outside the city limits, it was also a favorite ground for dueling. Alex-andre Dumas, *père* was frustrated here in his duel with a collaborator who claimed to have written the *Tour de Nesle.* Dumas's pistol misfired, and the author had to content himself with using the experience as the basis for a scene in *The Corsican Brothers.* Along with its fellow *bois,* the Vincennes forest was given to Paris by Napoleon III to be transformed into an English-style garden. Not surprisingly, Hauss-mann oversaw the planning of lakes and pathways. Annexed to a much poorer sec-tion of Paris than the Bois de Boulogne, Vincennes was never quite as fashionable or as formal. As one *fin-de-siècle* observer wrote, "At Vincennes, excursionists do not stand on ceremony, and if the weather is sultry, men may be seen lounging in their shirt sleeves, and taking, in other respects, an ease which the inhabitants of the Bou-levards, who resort to the Bois de Boulogne, would contemplate with horror." Today's Bois, officially part of the 12*ème,* is less swanky and less well-known than the Bois de Boulogne, making it arguably the more peaceful park to visit.

The **Parc Zoologique de Paris,** 53, av. de St-Maurice (tel. 44 75 20 10; Mo. Porte Dorée), is considered the best zoo in France. Unlike their kin in the Jardin des Plan-tes, the animals strut around in relatively natural surroundings. Indeed, the zoo was something of a novelty when it opened in 1934 because it was designed to give the animals space to roam outside. While it's still disturbing to see waterbucks prance

BOIS DE VINCENNES

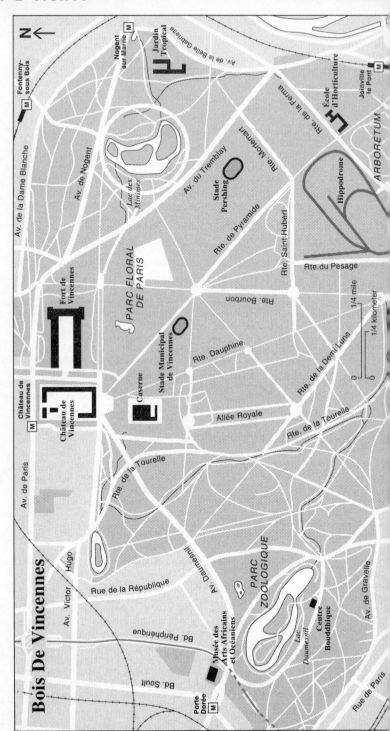

**Bois De Vincennes**

on hard, dry ground when the sign says their natural habitat is swampy, the zoo has been working hard to improve the animal's environment. The *phoques* (yes, it's pronounced just like you think it is)—seals—are fed with great spectacle daily at 4:30pm. Don't feed the animals; the food stands and café are far too expensive for that. (Open Mon.-Sat. 9am-6pm, Sun. 9am-6:30pm; winter Mon.-Sat. 9am-5pm, Sun. 9am-5:30pm. Ticket office closes ½hr. before zoo. Admission 35F; ages 6-16, students 16-25, and over 60 20F; under 6 and disabled free. Wheelchair accessible. Train tour leaves from restaurant: 10F, under 10 8F.)

Joggers, cyclists, and park bench sitters happily share the turf around **Lac Daumesnil.** People actually dare to sit on the grass. Discover the lake in a rented rowboat. (Boat rental May-Nov. 15 daily 10:30am-5:30pm. 1-2 people 41F/hr., 3-4 people 47F/hr., 50F deposit, plus tip.) Penetrate farther into the park for good running and cycling paths. The **Vélodrome Jacques Anquetil,** the **Hippodrome de Vincennes,** and many other sports facilities lie within the sizable *bois* (see Sports).

The **Château de Vincennes,** on the northern edge of the park, is called "the Versailles of the Middle Ages" (Mo. Château de Vincennes). French kings held court here as early as the 13th century. Although the Louvre was royalty's principal home, every French monarch from Charles V to Henri IV spent at least part of his time at Vincennes. Charles V built up a true medieval fortress on the site his ancestor Philippe-Auguste chose for a royal hunting residence. Henri III found it a useful refuge during the Wars of Religion, and Mazarin and the court found its defenses useful in the wake of the Fronde. Château lovers will recognize the inimitable hand of Louis Le Vau in the buildings farthest from the entry; the Queen's palace and the King's palace, built for Louis XIV, face each other across the courtyard, bounded by an arch-filled wall. In the 18th century, Vincennes became a country-club prison for well-known enemies of the state. Mirabeau spent 3½ years here, killing time by writing lecherous letters to his (married) mistress. Diderot was imprisoned in the château; Rousseau enjoyed the walk through the forest necessary to visit his friend.

In the 19th century, the complex resumed its military functions, serving as fortress, arsenal, and artillery park. In 1917, the infamous Mata Hari, convicted of spying for the Germans, faced the firing squad within its walls. In 1940, the château served as headquarters for General Maurice Gamelin, Supreme Commander of French Land Forces. De Gaulle later criticized Gamelin for holing himself up in the *Thébaïde*—ivory tower—of Vincennes, without even a radio tower to connect him with the front. Today, the Services Historiques des Armées and other military historical institutes are headquartered at the château.

The **donjon** (keep) was built between 1360 and 1370. At a height of 52m, it is a striking piece of medieval architecture and an impressive hide-out for any king. The **Sainte-Chapelle** was founded as a church in 1379 but the building was not inaugurated until 1552. Dainty in its décor and especially beautiful at the end of the day with the sun shining through the rose window, the Sainte-Chapelle is looking even better these days after restoration of the exterior. (Open daily 9:30am-7pm; Oct.-April 10am-5pm. Guided visits of the Sainte-Chapelle and *donjon* daily at 10:15am, 11am, 12:30pm, 1:30, 2:45, 3, 3:45, 4:30, 5:15, and 6pm are the only way to get inside. Tours are in French, but guides have written English translations. Admission 25F, students under 26 and seniors 14F.) Have a look at the archeological digs in the main courtyard. Wander around the ramparts, for a pleasant, if unexciting, view of the surrounding area. If you go on the appropriate day, drop by the **Musée des Chasseurs,** dedicated to the art of hunting (open Wed. 10am-5pm, Sat. 9am-3pm).

One of the gems of the Bois de Vincennes is the **Parc Floral de Paris,** esplanade du Château (tel. 43 43 92 95; Mo. Château de Vincennes), reached by walking down rue de la Pyramide from the castle. Aside from fine horticultural displays, the park has miniature golf and all kinds of games (10 that cost, 60 that don't) for kids. Picnic areas, restaurants, and open-air concerts make it a center of summer entertainment (open daily 9:30am-8pm; shorter winter hours; admission 10F, children 5F).

# ■ La Défense

Located just outside the city limits, La Défense is the comic-book city of the future come to life. As the skyscraper's rebuttal to Paris's *hôtels particuliers* and nostalgia for Henri IV, this office complex and beacon of the new world order makes first-time visitors feel like time travelers. Clustered around the Grande Arche (a 35-story office block in the shape of a hollowed cube), shops, galleries, trees, and a sprinkling of sculptures make the pedestrian esplanade a pleasant place for a stroll. The artwork to be found here—by such European notables as Miró, Calder, and César—are for the most part open-air sculptures built to harmonize with the techno theme park that surrounds them. Concrete, steel, and glass are the preferred working materials here for architects and sculptors alike.

La Défense is the current endpoint of the famous *axe historique de Paris* (the historical axis of Paris), also known as the v*oie triomphale* (the triumphal way). This magnificent corridor began in 1664 as an extension of the path through the Tuileries garden, designed by Le Nôtre and lined by a gracious row of elms. Its purpose was to make it easier for the court to get from the Louvre to the hunting-grounds of St-Germain-en-Laye. In 1772, the construction of the Pont de Neuilly extended the path across the Seine to a hill called the Montagne du Chante-Coq. Back in Paris, the route became more and more elaborate. In 1808, the Louvre end saw the completion of a little arch, the Arc de Triomphe du Carrousel, built to commemorate Napoleon's victories in 1805. Then in 1836, the larger Arc de Triomphe d'Etoile was completed, aligned perfectly with the Arc de Carrousel. Forty years later, planners selected Chante-Coq for a memorial to the defenders of Paris during the Siege of 1870. The resulting statue, called La Défense, gave the area its current name.

The proliferation of office towers in the area began in 1956, as part of a scheme to provide office space for Paris without drastically altering the city center. Not that this growth has been unregulated—since 1958, a government agency known as EPAD has directed the development of La Défense. (Today, La Défense boasts headquarters of 14 of France's top 20 corporations, each trying to outdo the other with its sleek modern architecture.) Originally the planners intended to limit buildings to certain heights and styles to create a unified complex. By the late 1960s and early 70s, companies were allowed to build distinctive *gratte-ciels* (skyscrapers), "Manhattan-style." But this haphazard building threatened the grandeur of the *axe historique*. La Défense needed something more than a random assortment of office towers if it were to maintain the monumentality of the line stretching down the avenue Charles de Gaulle, the avenue de la Grand Armée, the avenue des Champs Elysées, and the place de la Concorde all the way to the Louvre.

In 1969, Ioh Ming Pei suggested the first plan for a monument to anchor the end of the axis. French Presidents Pompidou, Giscard d'Estaing, and Mitterrand all sponsored international contests for such a monument, though only Mitterrand acted on the results. Of 424 projects entered, four were presented anonymously to the president, who chose the plan of previously unknown Danish architect Otto von Spreckelsen for its "purity and strength." Spreckelsen backed out of the project before completion, disheartened by red tape and by his own design, which he deemed a monument without a soul. Others, however, have celebrated the arch as a "window to the world" whose slight asymmetry gives the empty cube a dash of humanity. Spreckelsen died of cancer in 1987 and never saw the monument's completion.

The **Grande Arche de la Défense,** inaugurated on the French Republic's bicentennial, July 14, 1989, now towers over the *métro*/RER stop bearing its name. The roof of this unconventional office building covers 2.5 acres—Notre-Dame cathedral could fit within its hollow core. The plan is remarkably ingenious, and the walls are covered with white marble that shines blindingly in the sunlight. Most of all, its modern design blends into the centuries-old architectural context of the *axe historique;* though unlike the smaller arches, this one is aligned 6 degrees off the axis. The addition of this third arch, coherent within the older row of monuments, makes the assertion that La Défense is *part of* Paris, not just a new-fangled project on the horizon. Encouraged by this success, EPAD plans to extend the *axe historique* further by building up the area behind the Grande Arche; most of the work should be finished by 1995. As for I. M. Pei, who first proposed a monument at the western end of the *voie triomphale,* he was instead commissioned to redesign the eastern terminus: the courtyard of the Louvre.

As you approach the Grand Arche and walk around its perimeter, it shifts from a two-dimensional paper-cut-out arch to a starkly three-dimensional cube. An unparalleled view and an entirely modernist aesthetic experience await at the top. But first go to the **Info Défense booth** (tel. 47 74 84 24), located near the arch in front of the CNIT building. If you are interested in sculpture, ask for the *Guide to Works of Art in the La Défense District,* available in English. Tickets for the roof are sold at a booth near the elevator shaft. (Open Sun.-Thurs. 9am-8pm, Fri.-Sat. 9am-9pm; roof closes 1 hr. after ticket office. Admission 32F, under 18 25F. Wheelchair accessible.)

Even if you don't want to go through the roof, it's worth climbing up the steps of the big white cube and admiring the view of the Arc de Triomphe across the river. Notice, on your left, the odd shape of the **Bull Tower,** which looks as if it's had a piece cut out of it. As you walk down toward Paris, the **CNIT building,** the oldest building at La Défense, a survivor from 1958, is on the left. To the right sits the **Colline de l'Automobile** (tel. 46 92 46 00), a slick showcase for cars past and present. **L'Espace Marques** promotes itself as the "premier permanent auto display in the world." Resist the urge to test drive a Toyota, and head to the adjoining **Musée de l'Automobile**—of interest to anyone who needs a breather from the Minis and Fiats which clog the streets of central Paris. Car-related accessories and 110 vintage *voitures* are gathered here (open daily 10am-7pm; admission 45F, reduced 35F).

Just a few steps away to the right of L'Espace Marques, the globe-shaped hi-tech cinema **Dôme IMAX** (tel. 46 92 45 45) offers programs in-the-round which compensate for lack of plot, substance, or taste with their immediacy (see Entertainment—Cinema). Upstairs, the Spider cafeteria offers a good lunch deal at 50F, which includes quiche, salad, a *petit pain,* dessert, and coffee (open 10am-4pm).

Near here, plans are underway to construct the **Tour sans fin** (tower without end)—a 400m structure that will be Europe's highest skyscraper. The brightly colored sculpture at pl. de La Défense is by **Joan Miró,** and looks remarkably like one of his anthropomorphic paintings come to life. Across the *place,* **Alexander Calder's** linear, spidery red steel sculpture provides a fitting counterpart. Calder seems to have thought Miró's work resembled a popsicle: when he first saw a model of it, he asked, "Is that good to lick?"

Just past the little lawn in front of you is a white tube called the **galerie art 4** (tel. 46 98 94 98; open Wed.-Mon. noon-7pm; call to find out about temporary exhibits and tours of La Défense, in French only, 20F). To the right, standing on a high pedestal, is the bronze statue after which La Défense was named (formerly the area was known as Courbevoie). Louis-Ernest Barrias's statue beat 100 other proposals, including one by Auguste Rodin. It was moved while the district was constructed, then returned to its original place in 1983. The name "La Défense," by the way, has engendered some serious confusions. An official whose title was "Managing Director of La Défense" was not allowed off a plane in Egypt, because that country did not welcome military personnel during wartime.

To the left of the brightly colored fountain behind the statue, the 1964 Esso building is being replaced by the Coeur-Défense complex, to be completed in 1995. Built in 1964, the Esso building came to be something of an embarrassment for the company, dwarfed as it was by the Fiat and Elf headquarters nearby. Esso executives, mortified that other businessmen had bigger towers, crawled off to Reuil in 1992. The planned Coeur-Défense will provide acres of office space and a modern art museum. A staircase in front of the construction site leads to another art gallery, the **Galerie de l'esplanade** (open for temporary exhibits daily noon-7pm). A tree-lined path takes you the rest of the way to the Esplanade de la Défense *métro* stop. The low buildings on either side are apartment blocks. At the end of the path, the stark steel lamps rising out of water are the work of the Greek artist Takis.

If you want to eat or shop in La Défense, the best place to go is the huge **4 Temps shopping center**—one of the largest shopping malls in Europe. Enter from the Grande Arche *métro* stop, from doors behind the Miró sculpture, or from next to the Colline de l'Automobile. The multilingual information desk on the first floor near the escalator to and from the *métro* distributes maps of the complex. (Shops open Mon.-Sat. 10am-8pm. Supermarkets—*hypermarchés*—open Mon.-Sat. 9am-10pm.) A good bet among the mall's restaurants is **Le Bistrot d'Edmond** (tel. 47 73 73 88). Located at pl. de la Patinoire, level 1, it's a large place with a vaguely rural feel. (2-course *menu* 76F90F. A la carte entrées 62F. Open Mon.-Sat. 7:30am-10pm.)

The **La Défense park,** accessible one stop farther west on the RER (Nanterre-Préfecture), offers a pleasant area in which to picnic and rest up after your visit to the modernist metropolis. This is the largest park built in or near Paris in the 20th century, and includes botanical gardens, numerous basins, and sand boxes for the little kids. Other than rolling hills and a *gazon remarquable* (remarkable lawn), it is also home to the **Ecole de Danse de l'Opéra de Paris** (Opéra Ballet Dance School) and the experimental **Théâtre des Amandiers.**

To get to La Défense from Paris you can take the *métro* or RER. Older maps do not show the La Défense *métro* stop (opened in 1992). The RER is faster, but the *métro* is cheaper—La Défense is zone 2 for the *métro* but zone 3 for the RER. If you do take the RER, buy the more expensive ticket before going through the turnstile—a normal *métro* ticket may get you into the RER station in Paris, but it won't get you out at La Défense. Though the deserted La Défense is eerily impressive at night, you really need a car to appreciate it, and a taxi would be quite expensive.

# Museums

Since Charles de Gaulle appointed France's first minister of culture in 1956, thousands of hours and millions of francs have been spent shaking the dust off the reputation of the museum. Paris's national museums are multi-purpose, user-friendly machines shaped by public interest and state funds. Serving as forums for lectures, art films, concerts, and the occasional play, the museums here—most prominently the Louvre, Orsay, and Pompidou—broadcast Paris, past and present.

Catering to an international public, Paris's *grands musées* are mobbed, particularly in summer months. Take advantage of evening hours and be forewarned: the Mona Lisa may be obscured by raised cameras and clamoring schoolchildren. If you tire of dangling from chandeliers for a better view, look at Paris's smaller museums, which display specialized collections often comparable in content to wings of their larger cousins. Fans of Impressionism will find no shortage of alternatives to the Orsay's train-station bustle. As for the rest of Paris's myriad collections, it may seem like people threw together whatever didn't fit in the U-Haul, called it a "museum," and now sit hoping someone will take it seriously. Some of these one-roomers work, some of them don't. Houses of the now-dead rich, famous, and talented often make the most enjoyable museums, with a homey setting and friendly staff.

For listings of temporary exhibits, consult the bimonthly *Le Bulletin des Musées et Monuments Historiques,* available at the central tourist office at 127, av. des Champs-Elysées. *Paris Museums and Monuments* provides not only phone numbers, addresses, and hours, but also describes the museums (including wheelchair access) and lists them by *arrondissement. Pariscope* and *l'Officiel des Spectacles* also list museums with hours and temporary exhibits.

Frequent museum-goers may want to invest in a **Carte Musées et Monuments.** This pass covers admission to any of 65 museums in the Paris area *without waiting in line*—an important consideration in the summer, when lines to museums like the Louvre are often more than half an hour long. The card is available at all major museums and *métro* stations (1 day 60F, 3 consecutive days 120F, 5 consecutive days 170F; for more information, call **Association InterMusées,** 25, rue du Renard, 4ème, tel. 44 78 45 81). It is only economical for die-hard museum goers who do not qualify for student or senior discounts, which are nearly omnipresent. Indeed, many museums (including the Louvre, Orsay, and Pompidou) are free for those under 18. In accordance with a policy set by the Ministry of Culture, the number of such museums should increase in the next few years.

Larger museums often offer group tours in various languages. Prices are typically around 500F for a group of adults, 250F for students and seniors. Seniors means 60 and over unless otherwise stated. Over the last several years, many of the Parisian museums have turned their attention toward a national audience, foregoing regularly scheduled English-language tours for more extensive programs in French, often catering to local school groups. This is particularly the case in Paris's smaller museums with major collections. Relatively inexpensive anglophone pamphlets can usually be found at bookstores within these museums.

**Galleries** are an art lover's quick fix when *en route* to the cinema or a bar. Pick up the indispensable *L'Officiel des Galleries* (35F), a reader-friendly monthly publication available at newsstands and *librairies* in the chic-er areas of town and at the Pompidou bookstore. Inside you'll find complete listings of temporary expositions at both museums and galleries throughout town. The back section lists exhibitions by artist, so if you've been dying to check out Niki St-Phalle, you'll get a complete listing of locations near you.

Most of the city's 200 galleries specialize in one type of art, such as naive painting, modern sculpture, prints, or sketches of Parisian scenes. The eighth *arrondissement* is loaded with galleries of a more canonical sort; those near Mo. Franklin

Roosevelt on the Champs-Elysées (av. Matignon, rue du Faubourg St-Honoré, and rue de Miromesnil) offer collections which focus on Impressionism and post-Impressionism. Thanks to the new opera house, the Bastille area has become a haven for artists and galleries with an *épater-les-bourgeois* (shock-the-bourgeoisie) spin. The highest concentration of galleries is in the Marais; during a casual stroll through the third and fourth *arrondissements*, you're sure to pass by several. The St-Germain-des-Prés area also contains an assembly of small, enticing galleries. Walk right in and don't feel intimidated; you're not necessarily expected to buy.

# ■ Musée du Louvre

Built on the site of a medieval castle, constructed by a team of French architects to house the king's court, restructured by a 20th-century Socialist politician and a Chinese-American architect, and filled with priceless objects from the tombs of ancient Egyptian pharaohs, the halls of Roman emperors, the castles of Dutch princes, the studios of French painters, and the walls of Italian churches, the Louvre is an enormous intersection of time, space, and national boundaries. And you thought museums were boring. Just think of how many thousands of years (5000, to be specific), how many millions of lives, and how many traditions are represented in the building and collection of the Louvre. There are paintings that were painted to seduce monarchs, and sarcophagi that hold the remains of emperors who ruled over all the Middle East. Even the hordes of visitors add a final impressive touch; just imagine, yours are perhaps the 53 millionth pair of eyes that have gazed into the Mona Lisa's.

## THE BUILDING

Construction of the Louvre began in 1200, and still isn't finished. Every ruler who has left a major mark on Paris has also reshaped the Louvre. Like the city itself, it is a living edifice that belongs to no single era or architectural style. The Louvre's history has been one of slow but steady westward expansion. The original Louvre was a fortress built by King Philippe-Auguste just outside his new city walls, meant to protect Paris while the king was off on a Crusade. A century and a half later, Charles V extended the city walls to what is now the Jardin des Tuileries, and the fortress sat useless in the middle of the city. Not one to let a good castle go to waste, Charles converted the austere defensive structure into a residential château. Later monarchs destroyed his palace out of a wish for more modern and more grandiose structures, and all that remains of the old Louvre are its foundations. Unearthed in the early stages of Mitterrand's ongoing renovation, they can be seen in an underground exhibit called "le Louvre Médiéval" (admission included in the museum ticket).

Philippe-Auguste's fortress sat in the southwestern quarter of what is now the **Cour Carrée,** or Square Courtyard. The western wall of this court is part of the **Renaissance wing,** begun by François I in 1546. Early in his reign, François tried to avoid the Louvre, which was narrow, dank, and rat-infested. For a long time, he lived in elegant countryside mansions, particularly Fontainebleau. In 1527, however, he returned to the Louvre in an attempt to flatter the Parisian bourgeoisie, whom he hoped to distract from their raised taxes. As soon as he could afford it, François rebuilt the medieval palace in the open style of the Renaissance.

Except for the west wall, finished by Louis XIII, the Cour Carrée owes its ponderous classicism to Louis XIV, who reconstructed its interior façades in the hopes of transforming the Louvre into the grandest palace in Europe. At first, he commissioned Bernini, the greatest of Baroque architects, to coordinate this mammoth job. Bernini's plan, however, began with destroying the existing palace, and Louis XIV turned instead to a domestic trio: Le Vau, Le Brun, and Claude Perrault. These architects destroyed what was left of the medieval palace, yet left François's gracious addition untouched. With typical subtlety, Louis XIV's addition changed the palace's main entrance to the eastern side, so that, like the great medieval cathedrals, it would face the rising sun. Louis eventually abandoned the Louvre in favor of Versailles, and the grandiose transformation did not get past the Cour Carrée.

Through the passage in the Renaissance wing is the much larger courtyard known as the **Cour Napoléon,** begun conceptually by Cathérine de Médicis and completed by Napoleon III over 200 years later. The two wings stretching into the distance were once connected by the Palais des Tuileries, a royal residence that was begun in 1563 in order to make a separate château for Cathérine de Médicis. Henri IV completed the Tuileries and embarked on what he called the Grand Design—a project to link the Louvre and the Tuileries with two large wings like the ones you see today. He only managed to build a fraction of the project before he died in 1610.

With the departure of the court to Versailles, the buildings around the Cour Carrée (the **Sully** wing) fell into disrepair. Indigent artists, prostitutes, and soldiers occupied much of the palace, but some chambers were maintained as a storage center for the royal art collections. In 1725, the Academy of Painting inaugurated annual *salons* in the halls to show the work of its members. For over a century, French painting would revolve around the *salons.* In 1793, the Revolution made the exhibit permanent, creating the first Musée du Louvre. The galleries filled with artists, copying the works of the masters, their air of reverence forming a strange counterpart to the squalor of beggars and prostitutes that had taken over the rest of the palace.

The museum's fortune took a turn for the better when Napoleon I evicted the squatters and filled the Louvre with plundered art from all over Continental Europe. With the defeat at Waterloo, however, most of this art had to be returned to the countries from which it was "borrowed." More durably, Napoleon built the **Arc de Triomphe du Carrousel,** a copy of the Arch of Septimus Severus in Rome, to commemorate the victories of 1805. It was originally surmounted by four world-famous bronze horses, which had been taken from St. Mark's in Venice; but these were duly returned in 1815 to their place of outlook over the Venetian bay.

In 1857, Napoleon III finally instituted Henri IV's Grand Design, extending the two wings of the Louvre to meet the Tuileries palace. In order to give architectural unity to the newly dubbed Cour Napoléon, Napoleon ordered his architects to redo the façades of all the older buildings. The result is that the François I wing gained a new façade on its west side while retaining its original design on the Cour Carrée side. Only 14 years after the completion of the Grand Design, the Tuileries palace was burned to the ground by the Paris Commune. Ever since, the Louvre has had two large wings **(Denon and Richelieu)** that reach out to grasp only empty space.

The glass **pyramid** in the middle of the courtyard made its dazzling appearance in 1989. The new entrance to the Musée du Louvre, the pyramid was the crucial step in Mitterrand's campaign to make the Louvre into a museum that welcomes visitors instead of sending them away cursing the French. Previous entrances were hobbled by huge lines and utter disorganization. I. M. Pei, designer of the sleek East Wing of the National Gallery of Art in Washington, came up with the proposal to create one underground entrance at the center of the Cour Napoléon. At first, Pei's proposal met with intense disapproval, and many still lament its stark contrast with the courtyard's Baroque façades. Others, however, consider Pei's pyramid a stroke of genius. An enlarged reception area has solved the problem of an unstructured welcoming service, and escalators provide ready access to each of the palace's wings. Equipped with a bookstore, a cafeteria, and even an auditorium, this **Hall Napoléon** glows in the sunlight streaming through the glass pyramid, cleaned (at great expense) by robots of its grime and pigeon droppings. Legend has it there are exactly 666 panes of glass on the Pyramid; we haven't counted them.

The second major step of Mitterrand's Grand Louvre project, scheduled to be completed in 1994, will be the incorporation of the Richelieu (north) wing into the museum. The Ministry of Finance, which had "temporarily" occupied this space since 1871, has already moved to new offices in Bercy (see Sights—12ème *arrondissement).* The Louvre will double its display area. The curators plan to display only 20% more works (taken out of storage); the extra space will alleviate the overcrowding of art on the Louvre's walls. It should also reduce the overcrowding of tourists. In the process the collection will be undergoing moves and changes.

Sometime late in 1994, a new parking lot and shopping center will open under the Arc de Triomphe du Carrousel, linked to the Hall Napoléon and the *métro*. The subterranean mall will include restaurants, specialty boutiques, and a cinema. When everything is completed, the Louvre's first 800 years of renovations will have been the longest single construction job in French history—that should give Mona something to smile about.

## THE MUSEUM

The last stage of the Grand Louvre project, currently underway, will be tough on tourists. The curators plan to move 80% of the museum's art to new positions by the end of the project in 1997; at any given time over the next four years, a few rooms will be closed because of this work. More importantly, all of this juggling means that no guidebook can give you an adequate walking tour of the museum. For the current scheme, pick up an updated map (available in several languages) in the entrance hall or take one of the guided tours of the museum. Alternatively, make use of the racks of information sheets that stand in corners of many of the Louvre's chambers. These sheets, which most visitors seem not to notice, provide intelligent commentaries on the works nearby (usually available in English).

Though best known for its European paintings, the Louvre contains seven departments. **Oriental Antiquities** has nothing to do with East Asia, and everything to do with ancient Mesopotamia. Its collection includes the world's oldest legal document, a basalt slab from the 18th century BC on which is inscribed the code of King Hammurabi—the first written set of laws. The **Egyptian Antiquities** section is stocked with statues of jeweled cats and interesting tools, and keeps several mummies under wraps. Only a tiny fraction of the **Graphic Arts Collection** is displayed at one time. The 140,000 pieces are rotated through a series of exhibits in the Pavillon de Flore. **"Objets d'Art"** refers to a grab-bag of furniture, jewelry, and porcelain.

The **Greco-Roman Antiquities** department includes two of the Museum's most famous pieces: the *Venus de Milo* and the *Winged Victory (Nike) of Samothrace*. The *Venus de Milo* was discovered in fragments by a Greek peasant on April 19, 1820, 500 steps from the theater of Mélos (Milo), and subsequently bought by the Comte de Marcellus and given to Louis XVIII for the Louvre. A 2nd-century BC piece copied from a 4th-century BC statue, Venus's harmonious proportions and sensuous curves quickly became world-famous as the ideal of classical female beauty. *Winged Victory,* standing aloft atop a flight of stairs, was sculpted around 190 BC. Nike—Greek goddess of victory—presides over the Louvre with the same majesty with which she once presided over the bow of a stone ship, set in a fountain.

The **Sculpture** department picks up where the Romans left off, and runs until the 19th century. The undisputed stars of the collection are two of **Michelangelo's** *Slaves,* originally planned for the tomb of Pope Julius II. Michelangelo—a workaholic notorious for sleeping in his boots—said that he attempted to free each of his sculptures from the marble block in which it was imprisoned; his tormented *Slaves* are the physical embodiment of this sentiment. Given to Henri II in 1560, the *Slaves* were subsequently awarded to the valorous Constable de Montmorency, who moved them to his château at Ecouen. With Montmorency's death, the noble statues passed through Richelieu's soiled hands before ending up back in the Louvre.

## PAINTINGS

Having lost some of its former glory to the Musée d'Orsay and the Centre Pompidou, the Louvre's painting collection begins in the Middle Ages and stops in the early 19th century. But there's plenty within that interval, to say the least.

The **French works** are intimidating by their sheer numbers. Hundreds of portraits, still-life paintings, genre paintings, and allegories are crammed together on the walls. Don't linger on each one; just try to pick out a few that strike your fancy. The reign of Louis XIV and the high Baroque are almost synonymous. **Nicolas Poussin's** highly structured "classical" theories of painting, are exemplified in his *Et in Arca-*

*dia Ego.* Meanwhile, portraits of Louis XIV and other notables show nothing but undiluted power. The decadent court of Louis XV abandoned the Baroque in favor of the pastel colors and cloying cupids of the Rococo. **Antoine Watteau, Jean-Honoré Fragonard,** and **François Boucher** delighted the aristocracy with their tender, delicate visions of festivals, Venuses, and garden flirtations. The delicate colors and soft lines of Boucher—first painter of the academy and a close friend of Louis's mistress, Mme. de Pompadour—appealed to courtiers. Enlightenment leaders like Diderot gravitated to the serious scenes of daily life by **Jean-Baptiste Greuze.** But Greuze disgraced himself when he sought prestige by painting Romans. His clumsily drawn *Septimus Severus* (1769) made him the laughingstock of the Academy.

**Jacques-Louis David** (1748-1825) was more successful. No matter how lost you get in the Louvre, you are unlikely to miss the wall-sized canvases of the greatest Neoclassical painter. As a young man, David rejected the Rococo fluff of Boucher (his cousin and one-time instructor), seeking to illustrate moments of classical history in an austere fashion. In 1785, the young artist electrified Paris with the *Oath of the Horatii,* which shows three Roman brothers swearing loyalty to their father, each other, and most of all, the *patrie.* Such paintings jibed perfectly with the republican ideals brewing on the eve of the Revolution.

When the Revolution did come, David was in the thick of it, as a prominent member of the Jacobin club. He served the regime with his art, arranging extravagant festivals and replacing the Romans of his earlier days with heroes of the Revolution. He became administrator of the Louvre, living in the palace and controlling the museum's budget. Arrested in Thermidor, as part of the aftermath of the Terror, he vowed to give up politics. *The Intervention of the Sabine Women* (1799) was both a wish for peace and a means by which David could replenish his fortune—he admitted thousands of people to see it at 1F80 a head. The chastened David mostly gave himself to painting portraits, but like so many others, David soon fell under the charismatic spell of General Bonaparte, a spell that would culminate in his colossal *Sacre* (Coronation), which depicts in detail the Corsican's self-crowning. The beautiful Empress Josephine kneels before the Emperor in luxurious robes, surrounded by her ladies in waiting. Each face in this room-sized scene is a specific person; David himself can be seen sketching in the gallery.

David's followers are well represented. **Antoine-Jean Gros's** portraits of the emperor are even more adoring; look for Napoleon curing a plague victim with a touch of the imperial hand. **Jean-Auguste Ingres,** one of David's students, abandoned his mentor's devotion to classical physiques in favor of a more sensuous line. **Théodore Géricault's** *Raft of the Medusa* (1819) used David's classical physiques and formal composition, but the story it tells is one of disaster and brutality, not moral heroism. After a French frigate ran aground, 150 of its passengers lashed together a raft. Over the next 13 days, the castaways on the raft fought each other with sabers, stole provisions, and, by the third day, resorted to cannibalism. Géricault spent eight months on the painting, keeping his head shaven so he wouldn't be tempted to leave the studio. **Eugène Delacroix,** one of the models for Géricault's work, was one of the last French painters to successfully carry off a big canvas showing a heroic action; his *Liberty Leading the People* expresses the heroism of violent uprising. Louis-Philippe thought the painting so dangerous that he immediately bought it and kept it from view for the duration of his reign. Rather than imitating the severe colors and polished drafting of David, Delacroix founded the Romantic School, with an emphasis on dramatic movement, flashy colors, and swirling lines.

**Hieronymous Bosch**'s small *Ship of Fools,* hidden away in the **Flemish** art galleries, provides a surreal allegory of greed and folly. **Jan Van Eyck's** *Madonna and Chancellor Rolin* is one of the finest products of the late Gothic period—all three figures rendered with the same attention to naturalistic detail. Moving ahead several centuries, the soft light and human interaction of **Rembrandt's** *Supper at Emmaus* vie Nike in flawlessness. Meanwhile, the height of Baroque spectacle, **Peter Paul Rubens'** *Medici Cycle* (1621-5), unfolds in its very own room. Returning from exile

PRACTICAL INFORMATION

imposed by her son, Louis XIII, Marie de Médicis hired Rubens to retell her personal history to the world (or at least to the treacherous French court).

The **Italian Renaissance** collection is rivalled only by the Uffizi in Florence. For the height of Renaissance portraiture, turn to **Raphael's** *Portrait of Balthazar Castiglione* and **Titian's** *Man with a Glove,* held up as a model by the great portraitists of the Baroque era. Titian's *Fête Champêtre* presents a quietly atmospheric feast of the Gods, later reinterpreted scandalously by Manet's *Déjeuner sur l'Herbe* (see Musée d'Orsay). Veronese's gigantic *Marriage of Cana* occupies an entire wall. It was the center of much controversy recently when, in the process of restoration, it was unintentionally dropped, causing a meter-long tear in the canvas. The tear has since been repaired and the painting hangs again, showing off its stunning colors.

And, of course, the most famous painting among the Italian Renaissance works is perhaps the most famous painting in the world. **Leonardo da Vinci's Mona Lisa** (a.k.a. La Gioconda, 1503), bought by François I in order to hang over his bathtub, smiles mysteriously at millions of guests each year. Actually, she's fortunate to be here at all. Louvre curators discovered her missing one morning in 1911. Guillaume Apollinaire warned his friend Pablo Picasso, who owned two statues stolen from the Louvre, that a search for the *Mona Lisa* might uncover the contraband sculptures. The pair panicked, and at midnight struck out into the darkness with the statues packed into a suitcase, intending to dump them in the Seine. Near the *quais* they suspected they were being followed and decided instead to leave the statues anonymously with a local newspaper. But the police soon tracked down and jailed Apollinaire as a suspect in the *Mona Lisa* heist. After two days of intense questioning, Apollinaire's resolve broke—the loyal friend accused Picasso of stealing the painting. In spite of this treachery, Picasso cleared his name with a convincing plea. Only through the efforts of local artists, who attested to the fine quality of Apollinaire's character, was the poet released. The *Mona Lisa* turned up two years later in the possession of a former Louvre employee, who had snuck it out of the museum under his overcoat, leaving behind only the frame and a fine impression of his left thumb. Unfortunately, the museum recorded only its employees' right thumbprints. The joyful, albeit embarrassed, museum directors returned the smiling lady to her proper place, where it now resides securely within a glass enclosure. Look at the *Mona Lisa*, but don't forget to look at her remarkable neighbors as well. Leonardo's *Virgin of the Rocks* is unquestionably one of his most beautiful paintings, illustrating the rocky landscapes and *sfumato* (smoky) technique for which he is famous.

## PRACTICAL INFORMATION

Before its most recent renovations, the Louvre was an organizational nightmare. But now the Louvre (tel. 40 20 50 50; Mo. Palais-Royal/Musée du Louvre) is easy. Entrance to the entire museum (the Sully, Denon, and—to be opened in 1994— Richelieu wings) is through the center pyramid, where an escalator descends into a huge sun-filled marble lobby, the **Hall Napoléon.** Buy your ticket to the museum at any one of 15 ticket booths. Don't be intimidated by long lines; they move quickly (usually no more than a 20-minute wait). If you are buying full-priced tickets, save time by using coins or a credit card in one of the automatic ticket machines. Pick up an updated map at the circular information desk in the center of the Hall Napoléon.

Decide on what you'd like to see and don't be too ambitious; more than three or four hours is already pushing the limits of what the human mind and eye can hold. The Louvre is simply too big for anyone's intellectual stamina, especially when (as on summer afternoons) it's crowded and hot. Try to take in a few galleries over the course of several days. The extra admission charges are a small price to pay for the satisfaction. To avoid heat and crowds, visit on weekday afternoons or Wednesday evenings, when the museum stays open until 9:30pm. If you can't afford to spend more than one day at the Louvre, at least give yourself a couple of breaks; your ticket is valid for the whole day, and entitles you to leave the museum and come back. Holders of a **Carte Musée** can skip the line by entering the Louvre from the

Rivoli entrance, normally reserved for journalists, art students, and VIPs. (The Rivoli entrance is on the passage connecting the Cour Napoléon to the rue de Rivoli. For Carte Musée prices, see the introduction to Museums.)

There are two places to eat in the Louvre, a café on the second floor of the Hall Napoléon that serves sandwiches for 25-35F, and a pricier restaurant on the first floor, directly below the café. You might consider bringing a picnic lunch and eating it in the courtyard upstairs or in the green Tuileries gardens in front.

The Louvre is now fully **wheelchair accessible.** You may borrow a wheelchair for free at the central information desk if you leave your passport as deposit. The Louvre has begun a series of **workshops for children** in English (selected Mon. and Fri. at 2:15pm). Check at the information desk in the Hall Napoléon for more information and an updated schedule of events. The Hall Napoléon has an **auditorium** that hosts concerts, films, lectures, and colloquia. For information on lectures and colloquia, call 40 20 51 12. (For films and concerts, see Entertainment.) The **bookstore** sells a wide range of postcards and posters of the museum's collection, as well as various guides (open 9:30am-10pm).

Special **guided tours** are conducted in English at 10am, 10:30am, 11:30am, 2pm, 2:30pm, and 3:30pm (30F—in addition to your original admission ticket). **Cassette tours,** available at the top of both Denon and Sully escalators, focus on a list of highlights. The tapes are more-or-less attuned to the changes in the location of works, since they are re-recorded every few months. The commentary lasts 50 minutes, but the tour takes about 2 hours when you include walking time (25F; 500F, driver's license, or passport deposit). Temporary expositions are housed in the **Hall Napoléon,** the **Pavillon de Flore,** and the **Salle des Etats** (additional admission 36F, under 26 and over 60 23F, under 13 free; ticket to both the regular collection and the temporary expositions 50F, under 26 and over 60 30F, under 13 free). Tours last 90 minutes and meet at the "Accueil Groupes" desk.

(The museum is open Mon. and Thurs.-Sun. 9am-5:30pm, Wed. 9am-9:30pm. Last entry 45 min. before closing, but they start asking people to leave the museum 30 min. before closing. Admission 35F, under 26 and over 60 20F, under 18 free with proper ID—i.e. passport or ISIC.)

# ■ Musée d'Orsay

The **Musée d'Orsay (M'O),** 1, rue de Bellechasse, 7ème (tel. 40 49 48 14, recorded information tel. 45 49 11 11; RER Musée d'Orsay; Mo. Solférino) offers visitors the Paris they dreamed of but couldn't find or afford—evenings in the *café-concerts* and Sundays in the park with Renoir. Covering the period from1848 to 1914, the museum showcases avant-garde iconoclasts of the 19th-century art world. Works by Monet, Dégas, Pissarro, and others have established the Musée d'Orsay as the "impressionist museum" despite an equally illustrious collection of paintings and sculpture from before and after this period. Many of the great Impressionist works were originally in the Jeu de Paume (see Sights—*6ème arrondissement*). The Orsay is devoted to sculpture as well; the museum's collection is a parade that begins with reclining Napoleons and ends at Rodin's *Gates of Hell.* Statues on modest pedestals displayed in the lower-level courtyard meet passing crowds at eye-level. In contrast to the aloof hallways of the Louvre, this is art at its most accessible.

The steel, glass, and stucco Musée d'Orsay is itself a period piece from the epoch it celebrates; a former train station built in time for the 1900 Universal Exposition, Victor Laloux's design marries elegance to industry. This building recalls for modern viewers the period when how you dressed mattered as much as when you got there. For several decades, it was the main departure point for trains to the Southwest, but newer trains were too long for its platforms and it closed in 1939. During World War II, the Gare d'Orsay served as the most important French repatriation center, receiving thousands of concentration camp survivors.

The current museum has, since its opening in 1986, retained more than the ceiling of its former self. The much acclaimed collection of Impressionist work has created a traffic frenzy; tourists check their watches and run to catch Dégas before heading to the Louvre. The Musée d'Orsay's multi-tiered exhibitions and maze of escalators may remind you of the *métro* you took to get there. Yet for all its size and complexity, Orsay may be the friendliest museum of its size that you'll ever encounter. It's crowded, it's noisy, but it is designed to help you. A slew of maps and English language pamphlets are available at the information desk, just past the ticket booths. The museum wants visitors to learn a little history—to see the big picture—and many a guide book has been compiled for this purpose. The best one is the *Guide to the Musée d'Orsay* by Caroline Mathieu, the museum's curator—more than worth the 110F price. For 15F, you can buy the practical, if rushed, *Guide to the Visitor in a Hurry*. Multilingual **Audioguides** provide analysis of 30 masterpieces throughout the museum. The tape lasts 50 minutes, but you need at least 90 minutes to do the path (28F, driver's license or passport deposit; tapes must be returned by 6pm). (See below for information on guided tours.) Underneath the main staircase, the display L'Ouverture sur l'Histoire takes you on a tour of the period of the building's existence through newspapers, photos, and posters. An adjoining room explains the history of the station and the museum.

In addition to the permanent collection, seven temporary ("dossier") exhibitions are dispersed throughout the building. They tackle themes with a multi-disciplinary approach. In the 1993-94 season, the Orsay will display the Barnes collection.

## GROUND FLOOR: FROM CLASSICISM TO THE PROTO-IMPRESSIONISTS

Academic and eclectic painting from the Second Empire adorn the rooms along the right-hand side of the ground floor. *Venus at Paphos* (1852-3) shows the soft, rounded curves, and crisp lines that defined Ingres's "Classical" style. Representing the opposite and highly controversial "Romantic" school, Eugène Delacroix focused on brilliant colors, swift movement, and dramatic landscapes. More conventional artists achieved great success and appropriation by the Salon by following in Ingres's footsteps, best symbolized by Alexandre Cabanel's *Birth of Venus* (1863), bought by Napoleon III. The result, to the eyes of contemporaries like Manet and Courbet, was not only artificial but utterly absurd.

The paintings by Jean-François Millet, Jean-Baptiste-Camille Corot, and Théodore Rousseau illustrate the spirit of the Barbizon school of painting, named for the village on the edge of the Fontainebleau forest to which they retreated in 1849.

Gustave Courbet began a school of Realist painting, rooted in socialist-utopian ideas. Courbet's monumental *Burial at Ornans,* displayed in the Salon of 1850-1851, caught flak for its unflattering depiction of 50 people from his village attending a funeral. Courbet's equally grandiose *Allegory of an Artist's Studio* (1855) was refused by the Salon; in defiance Courbet set up a separate "Pavilion of Realism" outside the Salon grounds. The face at the far right is Baudelaire.

For the most controversial of paintings—and the artist whom many consider to be the first modern painter—look to Edouard Manet. His *Olympia* (1863) caused an uproarious scandal when exhibited at the 1865 salon. Manet had taken the format of Titian's *Venus of Urbino* (1538), the standard for female nudes in Western art, and transformed it to the contemporary age of Realism and objectivity. As his model, he used a high-salaried prostitute whose compact body, olive skin, and tied-back hair put her as far as possible from the classical standard of female beauty. Viewers objected to Olympia's fuzzy slippers and the ridiculously awake black cat (taking the place of the sleeping dog in Titian's painting). Caricatures of the painting covered the pages of Paris's newspapers and art journals; Manet was met with insults as he walked down the street. Whereas the *Venuses* of both Titian and Cabanel seem entirely passive and vulnerable to the spectator's gaze, *Olympia* stares boldly back, comfortable with her nudity, rebuffing the bourgeois observer who might, after all, be her next client. This was pornography, cried the critics, not art. (Sound familiar?)

Manet himself was bewildered by the scandal; the ever-optimistic Baudelaire told him by way of support, "you are only the first in the decrepitude of your art."

# UPPER LEVEL: IMPRESSIONISM AND POST-IMPRESSIONISM

Upstairs, the Impressionist celebration begins in earnest. The location is ideal; soft light, filtered through the glass ceiling, illuminates the paintings to highlight the colors and the spontaneity of brushstrokes without producing a glare off the canvases.

Manet's *Déjeuner sur l'Herbe* (Luncheon on the Grass, 1863) caused yet another brouhaha. Once again (actually, two years before *Olympia)*, Manet took an icon of Western art, Titian's *Fête Champêtre* (see Louvre), and brought it scandalously into the everyday, contemporary world. *Why,* critics asked, were two perfectly respectable bourgeois gentlemen (the artist's brother and future brother-in-law) picnicking with a nude female? In a mythological context this situation was entirely acceptable; in the context of modern-day Paris, and an afternoon picnic at the Bois de Boulogne...Never! *Déjeuner* was refused by the official Salon and subsequently shown in the famous *"Salon des Refusés"* (Salon of the Rejected), where Manet and contemporary "rejected" artists proudly showed their work, independent of the Academy.

Paintings like Claude Monet's *Gare St-Lazare* (1877) and Renoir's *Le bal du Moulin de la Galette* (1876) capture modern-day Paris—the iron train stations, the huge, crowded boulevards, and balls. Paintings by Alfred Sisley, Camille Pissarro, and Berthe Morisot provide a tranquil expression of daily life, especially in the countryside around Paris. Monet indulged in an almost scientific endeavor to capture the changing effects of light, as in his stunning series on the Rouen cathedral (1892-3), which demonstrates how intensities of light can overwhelm a classic structure.

Edgar Degas represents an alternative side of Impressionism, focusing on lines, patterns, and simple human expressions. His sculptures and paintings of ballet dancers are set not on stage, but in rehearsal or backstage. The dancers in *La classe de danse* (1874) scratch their backs, massage their tense necks, and cross their arms while vaguely listening to the ballet master. Paintings like *l'Absinthe* highlight the loneliness and isolation of life in the city, especially among the female working class.

Pushing on through the museum and through history, you arrive at the Post-Impressionists. Everyone inevitably crowds around Vincent Van Gogh's tormented *Portrait of the Artist* (1889). The bold colors and distorted perspective of *The Room of Van Gogh at Arles* (1889) were planned "to be suggestive of *repose* or of sleep in general." The stunning *Doctor Paul Gachet* and *Eglise d'Auvers-sur-Oise* are two of the last works Van Gogh painted. Meanwhile, Paul Cézanne painted his famous still-lifes, portraits, and landscapes, experimenting with the soft colors and broken-down geometric planes that would open the door to cubism.

As you're leaving this area, don't miss the pastels displayed in a special, darkly lit room. Inside, the strange creations of Odilon Redon represent a unique strain of mysticism among his more conventional contemporaries. His *Bouquet of Wildflowers* (1912) glows against the brown paper on which it is drawn.

Moving into the north wing, you arrive at the chaos of the late 19th-century avant-garde. Pointillists like Paul Signac and Georges Seurat strayed from their Impressionist beginnings to a theory of painting based on tiny dots—a proto-version of the TV-screen. Henri de Toulouse-Lautrec left his aristocratic family background behind to paint the dancers and prostitutes who alone accepted his physical deformity. Paul Gauguin's *chef d'oeuvre, La belle Angèle* (1889) pictures the title figure—a Breton peasant woman—in a circle reminiscent of Japanese art.

# MIDDLE LEVEL: BELLE EPOQUE AND ART NOUVEAU

After taking you through the ornate Neo-Rococo Salle des Fêtes, once the elegant ballroom of the Hôtel d'Orsay, the middle level displays late 19th-century sculpture, painting, and decorative arts. A display on Salon painting from 1880-1900 shows what was going on in the official world, while Impressionists were gaining their separate victories away from the Academy. (Most of the world's art museums display only the Impressionists and not their traditionalist rivals, depriving viewers of the chance to see why the Impressionists were so revolutionary.) Naturalism that carried an almost photographic realism, as in Jules Bastien-Lapage's *The Hay* (1877), was one of the most favored forms of art under the Third Republic.

Even if you're exhausted, don't miss a walk through the furniture, lamps, and general extravaganza of the whimsical *art nouveau* displays—an elegant exhibit of desks, vases, and sofas with wavy lines and arabesques which sought to give 'function' new prominence in design. Walk forward into the 20th century, with brilliantly colored works by the Nabis artists, as well as paintings by Henri Matisse (1861-1954) and Gustav Klimt (1862-1918). And, providing perhaps the clearest tie to our own age, end your tour with the fascinating "Birth of Cinema" display.

## PRACTICAL INFORMATION

Feeling exhausted? Experiencing complete sensory overload? Try going to the museum early, leaving to explore the area, and coming back later in the afternoon (keep your ticket stub and they'll let you right in). Otherwise, the museum is best visited on Thursday evenings when it is open late (until 9pm, 9:30pm in summer). For a break while you're inside, unwind in the **Café des Hauteurs,** situated artistically behind one of the train station's huge iron clocks. The adjoining balcony offers a beautiful view of the Seine and Right Bank. Climbing the stairs leads to the **Salle de consultation** (documentation room). Usually uncrowded, the *salle* has books about many of the featured artists and the official guide book on hand for consultation. Remarkable computer terminals provide on-line access to information about any artist or painting, complete with video replica. Downstairs, browse in the **bookstore,** which offers reproductions, postcards, and every 19th-century art book imaginable (open Tues.-Wed. and Fri.-Sun. 9:30am-6:30pm; Thurs. 9:30am-9:30pm).

Don't miss a look at the **Restaurant du Palais d'Orsay** on the middle floor. A stylish artifact of the Belle Epoque designed by Gabriel Ferrier (1877-1914), the restaurant offers a view of the Seine, a gilt ceiling, and plenty of chandeliers. Despite appearances, you *can* afford to eat here. *Formule rapide* at 72F provides all-you-can-eat access to the bottomless buffet table and a dessert. (Open Tues.-Sun. 11:30am-2:30pm, Thurs. 7-9:30pm; open Tues.-Sun. as a *salon de thé* 4-5:30pm.)

**Guided tours,** which leave from the group reception desk, highlight the major artistic currents, and discuss certain paintings in more detail. (Tues.-Sat. 11:30am, Thurs. also at 7pm; in summer additional tour at 2pm; 90min.; 35F.) Inquire at the information desk for all details. Other tours are offered exclusively in French. The booklet *Nouvelles du Musée d'Orsay,* available free from the information desk, gives details about current tours, conferences, concerts, and temporary exhibits.

The **museum** is open June 20-Sept. 20 Tues.-Wed. and Fri.-Sun. 9am-6pm, Thurs. 9am-9:30pm; Sept. 21-June19 Tues.-Wed. and Fri.-Sat. 10am-6pm, Thurs. 10am-9:45pm, Sun. 9am-6pm. Last tickets sold 5:15pm, Thurs. 9pm. Admission 32F; ages 18-25, over 60, and all on Sun. 17F; under 18 free. Wheelchair accessible.

## ■ Centre Pompidou

Often referred to as the Palais Beaubourg, the Centre National d'Art et de Culture Georges-Pompidou, 4*ème* (tel. 44 78 12 33; 42 77 12 33 for recorded information in French on the week's events) has inspired architectural controversy ever since its inauguration in 1977. (Mo. Rambuteau, Hôtel de Ville, or Châtelet-Les Halles. Wheelchair accessible: enter through the back on rue Beaubourg.) Chosen from 681 competing designs, Richard Rogers and Renzo Piano's dazzlingly shameless building-turned-inside-out bares its circulatory system to all passersby. Piping and ventilation ducts in various colors run up, down, and sideways along the outside (blue for air, green for water, yellow for electricity, red for heating). Framing the structure like a cage are the huge steel bars supporting all of the building's weight. Apart from its aesthetic shock value, this inside-out architecture has the advantage of creating enormous flexibility of interior design: each floor is a plateau of 7500 square meters, unencumbered by any need for supporting walls or circulatory ducts.

The Centre Pompidou attracts more visitors per year than any other museum or monument in France—more than Versailles, and more than the Louvre and the Eiffel Tower combined. And, of course, that's the point. Aimed at reaching the masses, the Pompidou, part of a Socialist vision of art, offers up its art as an accessible form of culture. The museum also eats up eighty percent of the Ministry of Culture's budget, causing people to wonder about the price of accessibility.

**The Musée National d'Art Moderne,** the center's main attraction, houses a rich selection of 20th-century art, from the Fauves and Cubists to Pop and conceptual art. The captioning (in French) leaves something to be desired. The sun and the museum's own harsh track lighting create unappealing glares and reflections on many of the works. Check your lipstick and move on. This is a state museum, with all the drawbacks; curators may be able to fit everything, but not gracefully. The various rooms are organized according to historical period and color scheme. Many works were contributed by the artists themselves or by their estates; Joan Miró and Kandinsky's wife number among the Pompidou's founding members.

The entrance to the museum is on the fourth floor, which is particularly strong on modernism: Matisse, Derain, Picasso, Magritte, Braque, and Kandinsky. Three terraces display sculptures by Miró, Tinguely, Ernst, and Calder. The lower level of the museum (which can only be reached by a small escalator from the floor above) houses works from 1960 to the present. In addition to the permanent collections of the Musée National d'Art Moderne, the Centre Pompidou has temporary display areas on the *rez-de-chaussée,* the mezzanine and the fifth floor. (Open Mon. and Wed.-Fri. noon-10pm, Sat.-Sun. 10am-10pm. Admission 30F, under 26 20F, under 18 free, Sun. 10am-2pm free. Prices for temporary exhibits vary with show. Buy your tickets downstairs; they are not available at the museum entrance.)

Displaying art is only one of the four functions of the Centre Pompidou. The **Bibliothèque Publique d'Information** (tel. 42 77 12 33), a free, non-circulating library, is open to anyone who walks in (entrance on the second floor). The computerized card catalog and large holdings (including many English books) make this a place where you can do serious research. There are video and microfiche facilities, a computer room, a lounge with newspapers from around the world, a stereo center, and a language lab. Creative use is made of the little rooms scattered through the library: you may be able to catch a debate on women's issues, or see a video about La Traviata. Twenty photocopiers are available, charging 50 centimes per copy. To avoid crowds, come before 2pm or after 7pm. (Open Mon. and Wed.-Fri. noon-10pm, Sat.-Sun. 10am-10pm.) The **Centre de Creation Industrielle (CCI),** studies the relationships between humanity, architecture, and technology. Although the resources of the center are closed to the public, its gallery is open to visitors for 16F. Finally, the **Institut de la Recherche et de la Coordination Acoustique/Musique (IRCAM),** until recently directed by composer/conductor Pierre Boulez, is an institute of musical research housed next to the Stravinsky fountain. Except in summer, the institute organizes concerts (for inquiries, call 44 78 48 16; for reservations call 42 74 43 19). Concert repertories fall somewhere between out and way-out: the 1993-94 season includes multi-media events which combine film, theater, and contemporary music.

While you're there, move up to the fifth floor for coffee or a meal. The Pompidou restaurant offers two courses plus drink and a dazzling view for 110F, coffee for 12F. The cafeteria has lighter fare: a sandwich, soft drink, and coffee for 33F50. (Both open Mon., Wed.-Thurs., and Sun. noon-3pm, Fri.-Sat. noon-3pm and 7-11:30pm. Tea service available in the restaurant Wed.-Mon. noon-6:30pm.) Also, look for the self-service part of the restaurant, to the left of the cafeteria counter (open Mon.-Fri. 1:30-2:40pm and 6:20-9pm, Sat.-Sun. 1-3pm and 6:20-9pm).

■ **Musée Rodin**

The Musée Rodin, 77, rue de Varenne, 7ème (tel. 47 05 01 34; Mo. Varenne), located both inside and outside the elegant 18th-century Hôtel Biron (see Sights—7ème), highlights the work of France's greatest sculptor. During his lifetime, Auguste Rodin (1840-1917) was among the country's most controversial artists, classified by many as sculpture's Impressionist (Monet was a close friend and admirer). Today, almost all acknowledge him as the father of modern sculpture. Born in a working-class district of Paris, Rodin began study at the Petite Ecole, a trade school, of sorts, for technical drawing. He tried three times to get into the famous Ecole des Beaux-Arts, and failed each time. Frequenting the Louvre to study Classical sculpture, he later began work as an ornamental carver, eventually setting up a small studio of his own. His travels away from Paris allowed him to articulate a definitive, powerful style, completely unlike the flowery academic style then in vogue. One of his first major pieces, *The Age of Bronze* (1875), was so anatomically perfect that he was accused of molding it directly from the body.

The museum houses many of Rodin's better known sculptures in plaster, bronze, and marble such as *The Hand of God* (1902) which depicts a rough-hewn hand holding a man and woman embracing, and *The Kiss* (1888-98) which portrays a woman kissing her seated lover. But don't just look at the famous sculptures. Take time to appreciate lesser-known but no less powerful pieces on the second floor.

As you wind through the *hôtel,* take advantage of the placement of the statues to study them from all sides. Rodin's training in drawing is evident everywhere: as he said, "my sculpture is but drawing in three dimensions." On the first floor one room is dedicated to a rotating display of Rodin's drawings and sketches/studies. In addition to temporary exhibits, the museum has several expressive works by Camille Claudel, Rodin's muse, collaborator, and lover. Her *Chatterers* shows a scene in which even the benches on which the figures are seated lean in to hear the gossip.

The *hôtel*'s expansive garden, newly landscaped in 1993, is a museum unto itself. Flowers, trees, and fountains provide a lovely backdrop for outdoor sculptures, scattered throughout the gardens. If you're short on time or money, consider paying the smaller admission fee for the grounds only. You won't miss the stars of the collection: just inside the gates sits Rodin's most famous work, *The Thinker* (1880-1904).

*Balzac* (1891-1897), behind *The Thinker*, was commissioned in 1891 by the Société des Gens de Lettres, but a battle over Rodin's design and his inability to meet their deadlines raged for years. (At one point the Société demanded, rather ridiculously, that Rodin deliver the statue within 24 hours.) Unlike the portrait the Société expected, the finished product shows a dramatic, haunted artist with hollow eyes—a personification of genius. The plasticity of the body and the distortion of the author's well-known face enraged countless artists and non-artists. Rodin cancelled the commission and kept the statue for himself, claiming proudly, "I have the formal wish to remain the sole owner of my work." Later in his life, he noted, "Nothing which I made satisfied me as much, because nothing had cost me as much; nothing else sums up so profoundly that which I believe to be the secret law of my art."

On the other side of the garden, the stunning *Burghers of Calais* (1884-1895) somberly recreates a moment in the Hundred Years War, recorded in Froissart's Chronicles. Beyond stands Rodin's largest and most intricate sculpture, *The Gates of Hell* (1880-90). What you see is actually a preparatory model, planned as the portal to the then-soon-to-be-built Musée des Arts Decoratifs. The statue was never completed in its planned immensity; the planned site for the museum was used instead for the Gare d'Orsay—which, ironically, has become today the Musée d'Orsay.

A small **café** is tucked away in a leafy and shaded part of the garden to the right as you enter the gardens behind the Hôtel Biron. The café, a superb place for lunch, offers an extensive salad bar (30F), desserts (7-20F), and a daily 50F *menu.*

Before you leave the museum grounds, check out the temporary exhibit space in the chapel (to your right as you enter). Entrance is included in the price of your admission to the museum. (Open Tues.-Sun. 10am-5:45pm; Oct.-March Tues.-Sun.

10am-5pm. Last admission 30min. before closing. Admission 26F; students, seniors, and under 18 17F; admission to park alone 4F. Cafeteria open same hours, but April-Oct. only.) Persons who are blind or visually-impaired may get permission to touch the sculptures, but they must obtain an okay before they begin their visit.

For more on Rodin and his sculpture, go out to the smaller Musée Rodin, 19, av. Auguste Rodin (tel. 45 34 13 09), in Meudon. The "country" house where Rodin spent the final years of his life now contains most of his minor works and the plaster models for *The Thinker, The Gates of Hell,* and his other major bronze casts. In the garden, *The Thinker* sits contemplatively above the tombs of Rodin and his wife, Rose Beurat, whom he married the year of her death—after 53 years of cohabitation. (Open Sat.-Sun. 1:30-6pm. Admission 9F, students 5F.) Take RER line C to Meudon-val-Fleury. Be sure to take a train that stops at all stations; some express trains zoom right by. When you exit the train station, take your first right, then your next right onto av. A. Rodin. The museum is on the left-hand side (15min. walk). Or take the #192 bus, destination "Hôpital Percy." Ask the driver to let you off at the museum.

## ■ The Invalides Museums

The Invalides complex guards a series of museums, revolving around French history and above all, France's martial glory (Mo. Invalides; also see Sights—7*ème*).

Lying under the massive gilded dome constructed by Jules Hardouin-Mansart is **Napoleon's Tomb.** A painting of God giving St. Louis the sword to slay the infidels adorns the inside of the dome. Six chapels dedicated to different saints lie off the main room, sheltering the tombs of famous French Marshals.

Finished in 1861, Napoleon's tomb itself is actually six concentric coffins, made of materials ranging from mahogany to lead. As if that weren't enough, the tomb is placed on the lower level and viewed first from a round balcony above, forcing everyone who visits to bow down to the emperor even in his death. This delighted Adolf Hitler on his visit to Paris in 1940. You can actually approach the sacred sarcophagus by descending the stairs beside the baldacchino, an impressive copy of the Bernini masterpiece in the Vatican. Over the entryway, an inscription records the last line of Napoleon's will: "I wish that my ashes repose on the shores of the Seine, in the midst of the French people whom I have so loved." Names of significant battles are engraved in the marble surrounding the coffins—note Waterloo's absence. Ten bas-reliefs recall the institutional reforms of law, education, and the like under Napoleon, who is depicted wearing that most typical of French attire: a toga and laurels. The Roi de Rome, Napoleon's son, is buried at his feet. Bring a 5F coin to the Tomb for a 5-minute recorded explanation in English.

On your way out, peer across the glass partition into the **Eglise St-Louis des Invalides,** also known as the Eglise des Soldats. Berlioz's *Requiem* was first played on this organ and in 1837 the first performance of Berlioz's *Grande Messe des Morts* echoed in chorus with a battery of artillery on the *esplanade*. The colorful, yet ominous banners that hang from the ceiling of the church are both trophies to French victories and war booty. (Tomb open daily 10am-7pm; Oct.-March 10am-5pm; April-Dec. 10am-6pm. Admission 32F; students, seniors, and under 18 22F; under 7 free. Ticket entitles you entrance to Musée de l'Armée and Musée des Plans-Relief.)

More war trophies are housed inside the **Musée de l'Armée** (tel. 44 42 37 72 or 44 42 37 64), which celebrates centuries of French military history. The museum is housed in two wings on opposite sides of the Invalides's cobblestoned Cour d'Honneur (main courtyard). The East Wing houses war paraphernalia from the 17th, 18th, and 19th centuries and culminates in the First Empire exhibit on the second floor. See Napoleon's death mask, his charger Le Vizir (stuffed and branded with an N), a recreation of his death room, and the big files that he kept on enemy armies, whose accompanying tiny pieces eerily resemble those in the board game Risk.

If Napoleon reigns over the East Wing, it is his successor, Charles de Gaulle, who looms large over the west side's 20th-century exhibits. Electronic maps trace troop movements during the First and Second World Wars. The General's *képi* and letters join an elaborate model of one of the D-Day beaches. The incongruity of peppy martial music floating over numerous swastikas and pictures of work camps can be nauseating, but somehow powerful and chilling. Escape by going upstairs to the temporary location of the **Musée des Plans-Reliefs,** a collection of a hundred models of fortified cities. Spanning the period from 1668 to 1870, the exhibit is one-of-a-kind, of interest to architects and urban planners. Most of the descriptions in the museum are in French. Pick up the English brochure (free) at the coat room on the ground floor of the East Wing. (Museum open daily 10am-6pm; Oct.-March 10am-5pm. Admission included in price for Napoleon's Tomb. No wheelchair access.)

Independent from its warring neighbors, but housed in a gallery off of the Invalides's Cour d'Honneur is the **Musée de l'Histoire Contemporain** (tel. 44 42 38 35). M. et Mme. Henri Leblanc decided in 1914 to create a library and museum to hold documents about the history of the unfolding world war. The three-room museum mounts two temporary exhibits per year (March-June and Oct.-Dec.), using posters, magazines, pictures, and other documents from the library to probe recent history. Most of the posters and all of the labels are in French, but the visual nature of the exhibits helps transcend the language barrier, as does the enthusiasm of the staff. "Images et Colonies," an exhibition on the nature, discourse, and iconography of African representation and French colonialism from 1920 to Independence opened in October of 1993. An exhibit on the Dreyfus Affair will open in March of 1994. (Open March-June and Oct.-Dec. Tues.-Sat. 10am-1pm and 2-5:30pm, Sun. 2-5:30pm. Admission 20F, students and seniors 10F.)

One of the least celebrated, but most worthwhile parts of the Invalides is the **Musée de l'Ordre de la Libération,** 51bis, bd. de Latour-Maubourg (tel. 47 05 04 10). This museum conveys the pathos of World War II just as surely as the Musée de l'Armée fails to do so. Charles de Gaulle founded the order in November1940 to recognize civilian and military organizations and individuals, as well as cities that had distinguished themselves in the liberation of France and its Empire. Quiet and uncrowded, the museum tells the story of those who fought for the liberation of France. Linger over well-labeled cases of the General's letters and speeches, among them his response to an arrest notice from the French government. Beyond the room full of his medals and possessions, lie tributes to the fighters of Free France. Samples of machinery sabotaged by the Resistance stand chillingly close to Nazi diagrams depicting, so far as they knew, Resistance organization. Scrawlings believed to be Hitler's notes from a meeting with Chamberlain, next to the ever-popular swastika cookie-cutter, recall an all-too-real past. Many of the objects in the museum are accompanied by letters from the donors, creating a personal, as well as a national, context. The staircase and upstairs gallery, dealing with deportation, present by far the most devastating message. *"N'oubliez jamais!"* (Never forget) cries the newspaper article next to the heartbreaking picture of a five-year-old girl, in concentration camp uniform. The exhibit juxtaposes forbidden journals and prisoner drawings with camp uniforms and instruments of torture, in an attempt to capture the mental and physical horror endured by so many. Though the museum is housed in the Invalides complex, it is independent; you cannot gain access to it from the Cour d'Honneur, but must exit and walk around to the bd. de Latour-Maubourg (open Mon.-Sat. 2-5pm; admission 10F; seniors, students, and under 18 5F).

## ■ Musée De Cluny

The **Hôtel de Cluny,** 6, pl. Paul-Painlevé, 5*ème* (tel. 43 25 62 00; Mo. Cluny-La Sorbonne), not only houses one of the world's finest collections of medieval art, jewelry, and tapestries, but is itself a perfectly preserved medieval manor, built on top of restored Roman ruins. Excavations by Paul-Marie Duval after World War II unearthed a multi-chamber complex of *Thermae* (baths), which were then incorporated into the Abbot of Cluny's 15th-century mansion that had been built on the spot. Visitors may now pass through the flamboyant Gothic museum entry, replete with pointed arches and a cobblestone courtyard, into a time when Paris was not

Paris but Lutèce, the Gallo-Roman city which emerged in the first century AD. Most of the building actually dates from the 1480s and 90s, when it was built for the Order of Cluny, a religious order then led by the powerful Amboise family, whose fondness for Italian forms is evident in their home. The house was converted to the National Museum of the Middle Ages by the state in 1843, cleverly combining these two impressive relics of Paris's past.

The best-preserved room of this ancient health club once served a function that even the abbot would applaud: 3rd-century Gauls gathered in the *frigidarium* to take cold showers. First they worked out in the *palestre,* then took a hot bath in the *caldarium* and a cold one in the *frigidarium.* The shock of this transition was eased by a dip in the *tepidarium,* or lukewarm bath. Only the *frigidarium* and swimming pool remain intact and open to the visitor. Call the museum for details about guided tours of the hallways and rooms that comprise the rest of the *thermae*.

The museum houses one of Europe's most impressive collections of tapestries, most of which come from northern France and date from the 15th and 16th century. Particularly pleasing to the eye are those of the *mille fleurs* variety, so named because of the incredible variety of plants and flowers that adorn the background. Among the museum's many treasures, the **la Dame et la Licorne tapestries** (Lady and the Unicorn) may be the triumph, due to its rich red base, intricate work, and interesting symbolism. The series chronicles what appears to be an idyllic flirtation between a woman, a lion, and a unicorn. It culminates with *A mon seul désir* (my only desire) in which the animals get a peak inside her outstretched jewelry box. Critics believe that this last frame illustrates the lady's repudiation of the passions. Removing the necklace she has worn in the previous frames, she will lock it away forever. Romantic tale or spiritual allegory? You be the judge. While art historians agree that five of the tapestries each depict one of the senses, the unicorn—part goat, part horse, part labrador—continues to baffle historians. Jean Le Viste, a merchant aspiring to knighthood, commissioned the works; they are sprinkled with his would-be three-crescent coat of arms.

Upstairs you'll find an entire room (Room XVI) devoted to medieval royal jewelry and crowns. The gold rush continues down the corridor with an enormously rare and valuable gold altarpiece, a finely worked ornament from Basel, Switzerland (Room XIX). Those longing for the bygone years of knighthood and chivalry will love Room XXV, packed with sets of armor, shields, and swords; the rare display of iron chastity belts once proudly exhibited by the museum has, unfortunately, been removed. Downstairs, the **Galerie des Rois** (Room VII) proudly displays a set of 21 stone heads of Judean and Israelite kings, dating from 1210 to 1230. These heads (attached to statues) sat atop Notre-Dame's portals until the revolutionaries of 1793 severed them from their bodies, mistaking them for statues of the French kings.

Down the hall, Room VI glows with colored light from its eye-level display of medieval stained glass, including some of the original windows that adorned Ste-Chapelle. In this otherwise dark room, back-lit windows set against black walls depict the legends of saints and the story of Joseph, and pay homage to that ever-present medieval theme: *cherchez-la-femme* (look-for-the-woman). (Museum open Wed.-Mon. 9:30am-5:15pm. Admission 26F; under 25, over 60 and Sun. 17F; under 18 free.) The museum also sponsors **concerts** of medieval chamber music performed on original instruments. (Fri.-Sat. 12:30pm—call ahead to confirm the time. 60F with admission to the museum.) A free lecture series entitled *Une heure, une oeuvre* takes place (in French) at 12:30pm on the first Wednesday of every month.

# ■ La Villette

La Villette, 19ème (Mo. Porte de la Villette or Porte de Pantin), is a highly successful urban renewal project in the northeastern corner of Paris. Its 55 hectares enclose a huge science museum, a landscaped park, an Omnimax cinema, a music conservatory, an exhibition hall, and a concert arena. The area had previously been home to a nationalized meat market-*cum*-slaughterhouse compound that provided most of

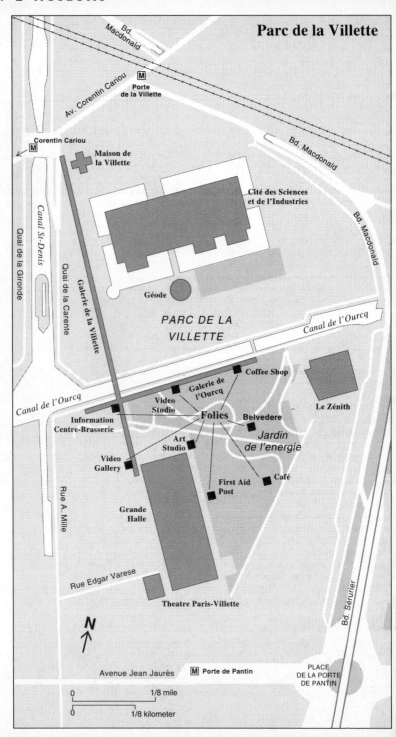

LA VILLETTE

Parc de la Villette

Paris's beef. With the advent of refrigerated transport in 1969, it became more economical to kill cattle in the countryside and deliver the meat directly to butchers; the government closed down the La Villette slaughterhouse and market in 1974. In 1979, plans began for the new and modern La Villette that you can visit today.

**The Cité des Sciences et de l'Industrie** (tel. 40 05 80 00) perches on the northern end of La Villette, next to the Porte de la Villette *métro* stop. Inaugurated in 1985, this establishment is dedicated to making science more accessible to lay people. It is housed in a vast building originally intended as an auction hall. The star attraction, located on the top two stories, is the **Explora** science museum, packed with interactive exhibits that can fill almost anyone with a sense of wonder. Even when you know the scientific principles behind a particular display, you'll be surprised by the ingenious way it is presented. One highlight of the museum is its sophisticated optical illusions, in Sténopé (1st floor) and Jeux de Lumière (2nd floor). There are quite a few English translations throughout the museum. The Cité-Pass ticket allows you to enter the **planetarium** (2nd floor) as well as temporary exhibitions, the 3-D movies in the Cinéma Louis-Lumière (floor 0, tel. 40 35 79 40), and the modest aquarium (floor S2). Floor S1 houses the *médiathèque*—a multimedia, open-stack library with more than 300,000 scientific and technical works.

If you're traveling with children, you may wish to leave them in the care of the Cité's innovative **children's programs.** The Inventorium (for ages 3-6) costs 20F for a 90-minute session (free for 1 or 2 accompanying adults per family). The Cité des Enfants (ages 5-12) costs 20F for a 90-minute session (no adults admitted). They also offer hands-on classes that delve deeper into scientific concepts (90 min., 30F). All programs are in French, but are suitable for kids of all languages. Or take the kids with you to the Explora museum; many exhibits will fascinate the whole family. The *vestiare* (level 0) rents strollers and wheelchairs; the entire Cité is wheelchair-accessible. To guide you around the Cité and La Géode (below), headsets with commentaries on each major attraction (in English) can be rented in the Cité on Level 0 (museum open Tues.-Sun. 10am-6pm; *Médiathèque* open Tues.-Sun. noon-8pm).

**La Géode** (tel. 40 05 80 00), the huge mirrored sphere mounted on a water basin in front of the Cité des Sciences, will remind you of an enormous extraterrestrial golf ball caught in a tiny water trap. The exterior is coated with 6433 polished stainless-steel triangles, which reflect every detail of the surroundings. Inside, Omnimax movies are shown on a 1000 square-meter hemispheric screen, "the largest in the world" (or so they say). Come here for exciting 3-D documentaries on such topics as Niagara Falls or volcanoes. (Showings Tues.-Sun. on the hour 10am-9pm. Also Mon. during French school holidays; last showing 7pm. Get tickets early; they sell out.)

Between the Canal St-Denis and the west side of the Cité is a little marvel called the **Cinaxe** (tel. 42 09 34 00). Watch one of several 10-minute movies representing what you would see if you were in a Formula 1 car, in a rocket, in an airplane flying low over mountains, etc., while sophisticated hydraulic pumps jerk and spin the movie theater, so that you feel the curves and bumps as you see them. (Open Tues.-Sun. 11am-7pm; shows every 20min. Forbidden to those under 6; not recommended for pregnant women or people with heart disorders.)

A one-day "Cité-Pass" covers entrance to all exhibits of the museum, including the planetarium and the *Argonaute* (passes 45F, under 25 35F, under 7 free; tickets to *Argonaute* only 25F, ages 3-7 free). Buy tickets for Géode shows at the Géode entrance (admission 55F, students and under 18 37F; no reduced-price tickets 1-7pm weekends or holidays). (Cinaxe tickets 32F, students and under 18 27F; combined tickets: Géode, museum, and Cinaxe 117F, *tarif réduit* 99F; Géode and museum 90F, *tarif réduit* 72F); Géode and Cinaxe 82F, *tarif réduit* 64F.)

At the opposite end of La Villette from the Cité des Sciences is the **Cité de la Musique** (tel. 40 03 75 00; Mo. Porte de Pantin). At the moment only the conservatory is open, but by January 1995 the whole project will be completed—featuring a concert hall, housing for music students, and a museum displaying 4500 musical instruments from the 16th century to the present.

The **Parc de la Villette** is a vast open area separating the two Cités, cut in the middle by the Canal de l'Ourcq and bordering the Canal St-Denis. Bernard Tschumi, the park's designer, rejected the 19th-century notion of a park as an oasis of nature, attempting instead to achieve a 20th-century urban park, "based on cultural invention, education, and entertainment." Unifying this space, a set of roughly cubical red metal structures form a grid of squares 120m x 120m. Known as *folies,* they serve a variety of purposes. One houses a fast-food restaurant, three are day-care centers, and one, right on Canal l'Ourcq, next to the Canal St-Denis, is an **information office** (open daily 10am-7pm). Also in the park, the steel-and-glass **Grande Halle** (tel. 40 03 75 75), constructed in 1867 as the La Villette beef building, has become a cultural Jack-of-All-Trades, with frequent plays, concerts, temporary exhibitions, and films. Next to the Canal de l'Ourcq is the **Zénith** (tel. 42 40 60 00 or 42 08 60 00), a concert hall whose high-tech acoustics and 6400-person capacity make it a favorite among such artists as Tina Turner, Ziggy Marley, and Bon Jovi. Originally intended as a stopgap until a permanent concert-space was built, the Zénith is essentially an enormous domed tent; the roof is made out of fabric and supported by peripheral columns, so that no internal supports block the view of the stage.

Finally, the park encompasses a number of thematic **gardens,** which you are likely to miss unless you follow the winding path known as the *promenade cinématique* (the map in the information office helps). Of particular interest, the Mirror Garden uses an array of mirrors to create optical illusions, while the Garden of Childhood Fears takes you through a little wooded grove resonant with spooky sounds. At night the *promenade cinématique* is lit up, and makes for an interesting walk (reasonably safe, too, because the park has plenty of security guards).

## ■ Other Major Art Collections

**Musée Marmottan,** 2, rue Louis-Boilly, 16*ème* (tel. 42 24 07 02). Mo. Muette. Collector Jules Marmottan purchased this hunting lodge in 1882; his son Paul, fascinated by the art and history of the Napoleonic period, turned it into a mansion and bequeathed both buildings and collections to the Académie des Beaux-Arts. Miniatures from around Europe, Empire furniture, and Italian Renaissance works abound, but the Claude Monet sign outside the Musée is not there for nothing. The lower level of the museum displays roughly 100 Monet canvases. Of course, Mssrs. Renoir, Pissarro, and Gaugin also figure prominently. *Impression: Soleil Levant* (Impression: Sunrise) is a must-see. Displayed in 1874 with eight other paintings, it led one critic to refer derisively to those *impressionistes,* a name Monet and his colleagues enthusiastically embraced. It was stolen in 1985, but was recently recovered in Corsica together with eight others stolen at the same time. Open Tues.-Sun. 10am-5:30pm. Admission 35F, *tarif réduit* 15F.

**Musée National des Arts Asiatiques (Musée Guimet),** 6, pl. d'Iéna, 16*ème* (tel. 47 23 61 65). Mo. Iéna. The largest collection of Asian art in the western world. Named for erudite industrialist Emile Guimet (1839-1918), traveler and collector of Japanese art, it is also one of the best organized and most peaceful of the 16*ème*'s museums: the benevolent smiles of Buddha, Jina, and Vishnu welcome visitors. Admire the detail of the 19th-century model of a Burmese monastery, made out of teak wood, and the sheer breadth of Khmer art. *Midi l'Asie* (Asia Noon) is an informative conference in French focusing on some aspect of Asian culture. Open Wed.-Mon. 9:45am-6pm. Admission 26F, students and seniors 17F. When temporary exposition is showing 33F, students and seniors 24F, grants admission to everything. Inquire about group visits, workshops, and concerts— activities, some free, abound. A few steps away is the Musée Guimet's annex, the **Hôtel Heidelbach-Guimet,** 19, av. d'Iéna. Devoted to Buddhist pieces from China and Japan, some of them 14 centuries old, the *hôtel* also offers a tranquil Japanese garden. Open same hours as Musée Guimet. Admission to one ensures entry to the other. Both museums are wheelchair accessible, but call ahead.

**Musée d'Art Moderne de la Ville de Paris,** 11, av. du Président Wilson, 16*ème* (tel. 47 23 61 27 or 40 70 11 10). Mo. Iéna. One of the world's foremost collections of 20th-century art. Permanent exhibit includes works by Matisse *(La Danse)* and Picasso. Temporary exhibits display avant-garde concoctions. Less complete and less accessible to novices than the Pompidou Center, this museum may not be the best place for an introduction to modern art. Open Tues.-Fri. noon-7pm, Sat.-Sun. 10am-7pm. Admission to permanent collection and temporary exhibits 35F, *tarif réduit* 25F; to permanent collection 26F, *tarif réduit* 14.

**Musée de l'Orangerie**, 1er (tel. 42 97 48 16). Mo. Concorde. Nestled in the southwest corner of the Tuileries, the Orangerie welcomes visitors to its small collection of Impressionist painting. Though less spectacular than the Orsay, this museum is also less crowded, so you can admire the Cézannes, Renoirs, Matisses, Picassos, and other greats in comfort. Claude Monet's *Les Nymphéas* (The Water Lilies) occupies 2 rooms of the underground level. Each is paneled with 4 large curved murals that were created for these chambers. It was on the day of the Armistice that Monet decided to give to France, like a bouquet of flowers, these paintings of the lilies in his garden at Giverny. He spent the rest of his life working on them, finishing in the year of his death (1926). The museum also hosts temporary exhibitions. Through Jan. of 1994 visitors may view "Les Arts à Paris chez Paul Guillaume," an ensemble of Dérains, Modiglianis, and Picassos. Open Wed.-Mon. 9:45am-5:15pm. Admission 26F; ages 18-25, over 60, and Sun. 17F.

# ■ From Art Africain to Zadkine

**Musée des Arts Africains et Océaniens**, 293, av. Daumesnil, 12ème (tel. 43 43 14 54), on the western edge of the Bois de Vincennes. Mo. Porte Dorée. One of Paris's best non-Western museums, housing several millennia of African and Pacific art. Particularly beautiful are the wedding dresses, jewelry, and decorated tile from the Maghrib—Morocco, Tunisia, and Algeria. Displays show that Tunisians knew about platform soles long before Edie Sedgwick. Explanations are in French. The tropical fish aquarium downstairs is immensely popular with Parisian families and school children. Open Mon.-Fri. 10am-noon and 1:30-5:20pm, Sat.-Sun. 12:30-5:50pm. Last entry 30min. before closing. Aquarium and superb temporary exhibits open daily 10am-5:20pm. Admission to museum and aquarium 17F, students and seniors 9F, under 18 free. Combined admission with temporary exhibit 23F, students and seniors 15F, under 18 free.

**Musée des Arts Décoratives**, 107, rue de Rivoli, 1er (tel. 42 60 32 14). Mo. Palais-Royal. Enter through a side door of the Louvre building. The definitive collection of interior décor. Tapestries, china, paintings, and furniture from the late Middle Ages to the avant-garde fill 5 stories. Come here for the true meaning of "changing fashions." Under construction in 1993, but due to reopen in 1994. Admission 25F, under 25 16F, under 5 free. Open Wed.-Sat. 12:30-6pm, Sun. noon-6pm.

**Musée d'Art Juif**, 42, rue des Saules, 18ème (tel. 42 57 84 15). Mo. Lamarck Caumartin. Housed on the 3rd floor of the Jewish Center. Founded after the war, the collection includes objects used during Jewish rituals, as well as an enormous model of Jerusalem. The library displays a variety of beautifully illustrated Jewish texts and a collection of works by popular artists from North Africa and Eastern Europe. Open Sun.-Thurs. 3-6pm. Closed on Jewish holidays. Admission 30F, students and groups 20F, children 10F. Open Sept.-July.

**Cristalleries Baccarat**, 30-32, rue de Paradis, 10ème (tel. 47 70 64 30). Mo. Gare de l'Est. The impressive building, built under the Directory between 1798 and 1799, houses both the Baccarat crystal company headquarters and the Baccarat museum (on the 2nd floor). Since its founding in 1764, Baccarat has become one of the most prestigious and expensive of crystal makers, patronized by kings, czars, and shahs. The museum houses an array of every imaginable crystal object, including a life-size chandelier-woman at the entrance. Open Mon.-Fri. 9am-6pm and Sat. 10am-noon and 2pm-5pm. Free.

**Maison de Balzac**, 47, rue Raynouard, 16ème (tel. 42 24 56 38). Mo. Passy. Honoré de Balzac (1799-1850), one of France's greatest novelists, lived here from 1840-47, penning the last part of *la Comédie Humaine.* He was a quirky man, who denied himself the pleasure of orgasm during sex for fear that the loss of sperm would diminish his capacity to write. (After accidentally going too far one day, he exclaimed, "I lost a book this morning!") The house gives a feel for Balzac's entire life with portraits, samples of his work, and caricatures of him amid fellow 19th-century literati. Open Tues.-Sun. 10am-5:40pm. Admission 17F, students and big families 9F, seniors free; temporary exhibitions 25F, *tarif réduit* 18F.

**Musée Henri Bouchard,** 25, rue de l'Yvette, 16ème (tel. 46 47 63 46). Mo. Jasmin. The cluttered workshop of Henri Bouchard (1875-1960), sculptor of the Palais de Chaillot's 7.5m bronze Apollo, illustrates not only his range of media (copper, plaster, clay, stone) and subjects (monuments, religious decoration, portraits), but also the complex technique involved in sculpture. Temporary 3-month exhibits in the front hallway bring out Bouchard's fascination for the ordinary, his attention to detail, and his skill at portraying human effort. Bouchard's son (who speaks English) and daughter-in-law act as knowledgable curators. On the first Sat. of each month at 3pm, Mme. Bouchard conducts a tour (free with admission). Open June 30-Sept. 15 and Sept. 30-June 15 Wed. and Sat. 2-7pm. Admission 25F, students and seniors 15F. Call about conferences on sculpting technique.

**Musée Bourdelle,** 18, rue Antoine Bourdelle, 15ème (tel. 45 48 67 27). Mo. Fal-guière. Even people who don't yet appreciate the raw aggressive style of Antoine Bourdelle (1861-1929) will become fans after spending the afternoon wandering the rooms of Bourdelle's studio-turned-museum. Room after room packed with statues overwhelms the casual visitor with the sheer productivity and genius of the sculptor, a longtime friend and artistic contemporary of Rodin. Open Tues.-Sun. 10am-5:40pm. Last entry 5:15pm. Admission 17F, students 9F.

**Musée Nissim de Camondo,** 63, rue Monceau, 8ème (tel. 45 63 26 32). Mo. Villi-ers or Monceau. This building tells the story not only of 18th-century decorative arts but of a family that met tragedy. Comte Moïse de Camondo built this *hôtel particulier* from 1911-1914, on the model of the Petit Trianon at Versailles, to house his exquisite collection of 18th-century furniture, paintings, tapestries, and porcelain. Camondo's will left the house to the Union des Arts Décoratifs, dedicated to the memory of his son, Nissim, who died in aerial combat in 1917. The rest of the family died at Auschwitz. On a visit in 1990, Barbara Bush—overcome by the combination of Savonnerie carpets, Sèvres porcelain, and a ravishing 1780 mahogany roll-top desk—in a rare burst of strong language exclaimed, "Isn't this the darnedest place you ever saw?" Take one of the 45-min. audio-guides (25F, 35F for 2, available in English) or buy a 20F general brochure (more detailed guide 60F) to supplement the otherwise meager explanations. Open Wed.-Sun. 10am-noon and 2-5pm. Admission 20F, students under 25 and seniors 14F.

**Musée Carnavalet,** 23, rue de Sévigné, 3ème (tel. 42 72 21 13). Mo. Rivoli or Carnavalet. Housed in a 16th-century *hôtel,* this is Paris's main display of its own history. Beginning with bones and stones from prehistoric Paris, it continues with a series of paintings and other memorabilia, arranged chronologically. While individual works of art may not display virtuosity, history paintings parade the changing faces of Paris before the viewer. The reconstructed Bijouterie Fouquet may be the star of the show for Art Nouveau junkies—a witty interior designed by poster artist Alphonse Mucha plays with a peacock motif as a symbol of vanity well-suited for a jewelry store. French decorative art fans will also appreciate the period rooms. The museum is popular with large groups of French schoolchildren and their teachers. Offers free lectures and guided visits, in French, on Tues. and Sat. at 2:30pm. Pick up schedule at front desk. See Sights—3ème for comments on the museum's courtyard. Wheelchair access. Open Tues.-Sun. 10am-5:30pm. Admission 20F, Sun. free. Temporary exhibits extra.

**Musée Cernuschi,** 7, av. Velasquez, 8ème (tel. 45 63 50 75), outside the gates of Parc Monceau. Mo. Villiers or Monceau. A magnificent, charmingly personable collection of Asian art is housed in a villa that belonged to Henri Cernuschi (1820-1896), a financier of Milanese descent who took off on a trans-world tour after being "affected" by the Commune. Second to the Guimet as an Asian art museum, the Cernuschi nevertheless contains some very impressive pieces including an 18th-century Japanese 3-ton, 3.5m-high bronze Buddha. Wheelchair access. Open Tues.-Sun. 10am-5:40pm. Admission to permanent collection 17F, reduced 9F; to both permanent and temporary exhibits 20F, reduced 15F.

**Musée de la Chasse (Museum of Hunting),** 60, rue des Archives, 3ème (tel. 42 72 86 43). Mo. Rambuteau. A delightful, bloodthirsty little museum about hunting, featuring exotic animal heads alongside hunting weapons. Paintings by Brueghel, Rubens, Velcours, and Monet serve as backdrop to the animal trophies and *objets d'art.* Open Wed.-Mon. 10am-12:30pm and 1:30-5:30pm. Admission 25F, students 12F50, children 5F. Permission to take photos 10F.

**Musée du Cinéma Henri-Langlois,** in the Palais de Chaillot, 16ème (tel. 45 53 74 39). Mo. Trocadéro. The history of sound and light in film starting with magic lanterns and shadow theaters. Sets, costumes, scripts, and posters tell the tale of modern cinema. You can only see the museum by 1-hr. tour conducted in French. Open Wed.-Mon. for tours at 10am, 11am, 2pm, 3pm, and 4pm. Tours canceled if fewer than 8 people. Admission 22F, *tarif réduit* 15F. Open Sept.-July.

**Musée Clemenceau,** 8, rue B. Franklin, 16ème (tel. 45 20 53 41), through a small courtyard. Mo. Passy. The 4 rooms in which Georges Clemenceau (1841-1929), the mayor of Montmartre, Prime Minister, *Président du Conseil,* Minister of War (1917-20), expert duellist, accomplished journalist, and hero to the French people, lived for 35 years has not been changed since his death: the yellowed calendars are all hauntingly torn off at November 24, 1929. Explanation sheets in French or the bilingual guide point out details like the painting *Le Bloc,* done for Clemenceau by his friend Monet, or the withered bouquet of flowers given to him by a soldier at the front, the other half of which lies in his coffin, at his personal request. Open Tues., Thurs., Sat.-Sun., and holidays 2-5pm. Admission 20F, students and seniors 14F. Open Sept.-July.

**Musée Cognacq-Jay,** 8, rue Elzévir, 3ème (tel. 42 74 33 66). Mo. St-Paul, Chemin Vert, or Rambuteau. The city of Paris acquired this collection of Enlightenment art, which belonged to department store mogul Ernest Cognacq and his wife, Marie-Louise Jay, upon the death of M. Cognacq in 1929. Highlights include works by Watteau, Canaletto, Rembrandt, Greuze, and Fragonard. The museum is a showcase of the Ancien Régime as it would like to be remembered; lute-strumming nobles at *fête galantes* and wind-blown coquettes set the tone. Works are grouped together in a natural manner, combining furniture and paintings to produce a "total" picture of a rich 18th-century household. The museum occasionally hosts 18th-century plays. Two works by Diderot Nov. 1993-Feb. 1994. Call 40 27 07 21 for more information. Open Tues.-Sun. 10am-5:40pm. Admission 12F.

**Musée de Contrefaçon (the Counterfeit Museum),** 8, rue de la Faisanderie, 16ème (tel. 45 01 51 11). Mo. Porte Dauphine. I can't see the difference. Can you see the difference? Is there a difference? You will ask these questions about the assembled bottles, logos, hand bags, and their illegal counterfeits for about 2 minutes. Then you'll ask: Who cares? Absence of brochures and insufficient labeling turns what could have been a novel presentation into a trivial look-but-don't-buy garage sale. Open Mon.-Tues. 2-4:30pm, Fri. 9am-noon. Free.

**Musée Salvador Dalí (Espace Montmartre),** 11, rue Poulbot, 18ème (tel. 42 64 40 10). Mo. Anvers, Blanche, or Pigalle. Right off pl. du Tertre, this space dedicated to the "Phantasmic World of Salvador Dalí" is chock full of drawings and sculptures by the Spanish surrealist. Don't miss the bronze sculptures of the famous droopy clocks. Other works include several sculptural versions of the *Cabinet Anthropomosphique,* or the human body as a collection of empty half-open drawers. The museum is well laid out, with interesting lighting and slightly ridiculous "space-music" in the background. Open daily April-Sept. 10am-10pm, Oct-March 10am-7pm. Admission 35F, students 25F.

**Musée Delacroix,** 6, rue Furstenberg, 6ème (tel. 43 54 04 87). Mo. St-Germain-des-Prés. Behind the Eglise St-Germain off rue de l'Abbaye. This small museum, located in Eugène Delacroix's house and studio, contains works spanning the duration of the painter's productive career. The intimate tone is enhanced by the shady courtyard and old-fashioned square. Delacroix (1799-1863) was one of the leaders of French Romanticism—the fine arts counterpart of Victor Hugo. Some works by Delacroix's friend and contemporary Pierre Guerin are also displayed, though Guerin's heavy-handed Neoclassicism possibly detracts from this otherwise delightful museum. Open Sat. 9:45am-5:15pm, last entry 4:45pm. Admission 12F, ages 18-25 and over 60 8F, under 18 free.

**Musée des Egouts de Paris (Museum of the Sewers of Paris),** actually inside the sewers, at the corner of the quai d'Orsay and pl. de la Résistance, 7ème (tel. 47 05 10 29). Mo. Pont de l'Alma. This unique museum details the history of the city's fascinating subterranean avenues. In *Les Misérables*, Victor Hugo wrote, "Paris has beneath it another Paris, a Paris of sewers, which has its own streets, squares, lanes, arteries, and circulation." More than 2000km of gravitational galleries, all visitable, wind beneath the city. The actual museum exhibit filters through Parisian sewage from the days of Lutetia to 1989. In English, French, German, and Spanish, the display tells of the advances made after Napoleon asked a doctor what he could do for Paris and was told *"Donnez-lui de l'eau"* (Give her water). Thorough historical panels explain the sewer sights well, but a guided tour with a real live *égoutier* (sewer worker) brings the place to life. These are organized informally throughout the year—if enough people are present, a tour is started. Although the tours are not as gross as one might imagine, the odor is quite powerful. Ask at the *caisse* about guided visits or call ahead. Not wheelchair accessible. Open Sat.-Wed. 11am-6pm; winter Sat.-Wed. 11am-5pm. Last ticket sold 1hr. before closing. Admission 24F, students and under 10 19F. Closed for 3 weeks in Jan. for maintenance.

**Musée d'Ennery,** 59, av. Foch, 16ème (tel. 45 53 57 96). Mo. Porte Dauphine. This collection of Chinese and Japanese decorative art, numbering close to 7000 pieces, was assembled under the Second Empire by author and librettist Adolphe d'Ennery (1811-1899). Free. On the 1st floor of the same building, you'll find the interesting **Musée Arménien** (tel. 45 56 15 88), which displays jewelry, paintings, and religious decoration of the past and the present, from Armenia. Both open Thurs. and Sun. 2-6pm. Free. Open Sept.-July.

**Galerie d'Entomologie (Insect Museum),** in the Jardin des Plantes, 5ème. (tel. 40 79 34 00). Mo. Censier Daubenton or Gare d'Austerlitz. Most of the 1-room gallery is dedicated to various specimens, in different colors and sizes, of this beetle, with a small concession to butterflies, displayed in 2 cases. Open Wed.-Mon. 2-5pm. Admission 12F, students 8F.

**Musée du Grand Orient de France et de la Franc-Maçonnerie,** 16, rue Cadet, 9ème (tel. 45 23 20 92). Mo. Cadet. Housed in a masonic lodge, this 1-room museum tells the story of the masons from early Scottish brotherhood to their peak in the 18th and 19th centuries. Folksy captioning, hand-written in French, accompanies one-of-a-kind pamphlets, medals, portraits, and busts of renowned freemasons, including Voltaire and Talleyrand. The museum is housed in the Hôtel Cadet, built in 1852 and designed as the headquarters for French freemasonry. During World War II, Vichy officials used it to identify and persecute masons. Open Mon.-Sat. 2-6pm. Free.

**Grand Palais,** 3, av. du Général Eisenhower, 8ème (tel. 44 13 17 17). Mo. Champs-Elysées-Clemenceau. Most of the building houses the Palais de la Découverte (see above), but the other 2 entrances lead the way to temporary exhibitions. Call to see what's on. Open, when an exhibit is there, Thurs.-Mon. 10am-8pm, Wed. 10am-10pm. Last entry 45 min. before closing. Admission varies with the exhibit, but anticipate something like 42F, *tarif réduit* and Mon. 29F, under 13 free.

**Musée Grevin,** 10, bd. Montmartre, 9ème (tel. 42 46 13 26). Mo. Rue Montmartre. This wax museum is rather light fun, but it's definitely worth a visit, if you don't mind the screaming and running of hundreds of over-enthusiastic French kids on field days or the disturbing stares of life-like figures. The super-ornate halls are filled with illustrious personages from the present and past. Marie-Antoinette awaits her execution in the Conciergerie; the cannibals from Géricault's painting *The Raft of the Medusa* reach out for the rescue ship on the horizon. Open daily 1-7pm, last entry 6pm. Admission 48F, ages 6-14 34F. The smaller subsidiary at level "-1" of **Forum des Halles,** near the Porte Berger, 1er (tel. 40 26 28 50; Mo. Châtelet-Les Halles), presents a fascinating spectacle of Paris in its "Belle Epoque" (1885-1900). A terrific sound and light show recreates the turn of the century. If you don't speak French, however, you'll miss most of the action. Open Mon.-Sat. 10:30am-6:45pm, Sun. and holidays 1-6:30pm. Ticket office closes 45 min. before museum. Admission 42F, ages 6-14 32F, under 6 free.

**Musée Jean-Jacques Henner,** 43, av. Villiers, 17ème (tel. 47 63 42 73). Mo. Malsherbes. This small museum displays the paintings of Jean-Jacques Henner (1829-1903), who developed his own uniquely non-partisan style. Especially noteworthy are the haunting series of nymphs. Henner's carefully studied portraits, on the ground floor, honestly portray their bourgeois subjects. Open Tues.-Sun. 10am-noon and 2-5pm. Admission 14F, students 8F.

**Musée de l'Histoire de France,** 60, rue des Francs-Bourgeois, 3ème (tel. 40 27 60 96). Mo. Hôtel de Ville or Rambuteau. Housed in the Hôtel de Soubise, this museum overflows with important French documents—Napoleon's will, a letter by Jeanne d'Arc, and *the* Edict of Nantes. Labels are in French only. For more information on content and history of the Hôtel Soubise, see Sights—*3ème arrondissement*. Open Wed.-Mon. 1:45-5:45pm. Admission 12F, students 8F.

**Musée d'Histoire Naturelle (Museum of Natural History),** in the Jardin des Plantes, 5ème (tel. 40 79 30 00). Mo. Gare d'Austerlitz. Schoolchildren, teachers in tow, romp through the collection of dinosaurs, which includes the skeleton of a massive 7m iguanodon, as well as the more modern mastodon. The rest of the museum is devoted to more mundane though equally large skeletons, such as elephants, and whales. Open Wed.-Mon. 10am-5pm. Admission 25F, students 15F.

**Musée de l'Holographie,** level "-1" of Forum des Halles, between porte Berger and porte Lescot, 1er (tel. 40 39 96 83). Mo. Châtelet-Les Halles. A small, moderately interesting set of holograms. A woman blows a kiss at you and winks as you walk by. Open Mon.-Sat. 10am-7pm, Sun. 1-7pm. Admission 30F, students 25F.

**Musée de l'Homme (the Museum of Man),** in the Palais de Chaillot, 16ème (tel. 44 05 72 72). Mo. Trocadéro. A painted cart from Sicily, a Turkish store, and the requisite polar bear leading into the Inuit display....The museum's multi-media presentation begins in pre-historic times and branches out into the different customs of the world. Current renovations will update the layout by 1995. Labels are in French only, but exhibits are often self-explanatory. Special exhibition *"Tous parents, tous différents"* on human biological diversity open through spring 1994. Open Wed.-Mon. 9:45am-5:15pm. Admission 25F, reduced 15F, people with disabilities and children under 6 free. Films Sat.-Sun. 2:30.

**Maison de Victor Hugo,** 6, pl. des Vosges, 4ème (tel. 42 72 16 65). Mo. Chemin Vert. A small museum, dedicated to the "father of the French Romantics," and housed in the building where he lived from 1832 to 1848. The museum offers an assortment of Hugo memorabilia, including his own highly expressive graphic art. In addition, relics/icons attest to the cult of the poet that persisted in France long after his death. Victor Hugo playing cards and 5F notes pitch to fans with a penchant for kitsch remembrance. You'll also find works by Rodin, Delacroix, and Bonnat. Francophones can read his elegant love letters. Open Tues.-Sun. 10am-5:40pm. Admission 17F, students 9F.

**Musée Jacquemart-André,** 158, bd. Haussmann, 8ème (tel. 45 62 39 94). Mo. St-Philippe-du-Roule. A terrific museum, closed for renovation in 1993 but expected to reopen Jan. 1994. Works from the Italian Renaissance (Donatello, Della Robbia) and the French 18th century (Fragonard, Watteau) join pieces by Rembrandt and Rubens under Tiepolo's fresco. Collections belonged to the Jacquemart family, the *hôtel particulier* to 19th-century collector Edouard André; hence the name. Open Sept.-July Wed.-Sun. 1:30-5:30pm; closed holidays. Admission 10F.

**Musée du Jeu de Paume,** 1er (tel. 47 03 12 50). Mo. Concorde. The Jeu de Paume (tennis court), in the northeast corner of the Tuileries, was originally constructed under Napoleon III as a court on which to play *jeu de paume*, an ancestor of tennis. In 1909, it was converted into a display area, mostly for art exhibits. When the Nazis took over Paris, they sent plundered art here, where much of it was labelled "degenerate" and burned. Between 1947 and 1986, the building housed an Impressionist collection which has been transferred to the Musée d'Orsay. Since June 1991, the museum has been a showcase for contemporary art. For exhibit info, call 42 60 69 69 (answering machine, in French), or just go there and take a look. Open, when exhibits are on, Tues. noon-9:30pm, Wed.-Fri. noon-7pm, Sat.-Sun. 10am-7pm. Admission 35F students, reduced 25F, under 13 free.

**Kwok On Museum,** 41, rue de Francs-Bourgeois, 4ème (tel. 42 72 99 42). Mo. St-Paul. A private collector of Chinese Opera costumes, M. Kwok On left his collection to the city of Paris in 1971. Since then, the museum has acquired masks, marionettes, and garments from many other Asian countries. Displays are rotated every year. Ask about their extensive collection of documentation on Asian theatrical traditions. Open Mon.-Fri. 10am-5:30pm. Admission 10F, students 5F.

**Musée National de la Légion d'Honneur et des Ordres de Chevalerie,** 2, rue de Bellechasse, 7*ème* (tel. 45 55 95 16). Mo. Solférino. Housed in an 18th-century mansion built for the German Prince of Salm-Kyrbourg, this museum displays innumerable medals, ribbons, and dress costumes associated with the French Legion of Honor, created by Napoleon in 1802 to reward civilian and military virtue. Unless Jerome Bonaparte's wedding reception glass or such foreign orders as the Laotian Order of a Million Elephants is guaranteed to thrill you, consider admiring the architectural view from across the street at the Musée d'Orsay. Open Tues.-Sun. 2-5pm. Admission 10F, students and seniors 5F.

**Musée des Lunettes et Lorgnettes (Spectacles Museum),** 2, av. Mozart, 16*ème* (tel. 45 27 21 05). Mo. La Muette. Fittingly, the display is squeezed into the office of Pierre Marly, *opticien*, because it was Marly himself, eyeglass designer to the King of Morocco and the Dalai Lama, whose private collection of historical eye pieces gave birth to the museum. Exhibits show the development of eye gear in all forms and from all cultures, from the 17th century to the present. Dog glasses, suspiciously resembling Snoopy's WWI flying ace helmet, and glasses of the rich and famous help to make this museum fun. Open Tues.-Sat. 9:30am-7pm. Free.

**Musée de la Marine (Museum of the Navy),** in the Palais de Chaillot, 16*ème* (tel. 45 53 31 70). Mo. Trocadéro. The collection of model ships has been growing since 1748, when Navy Inspector General Louis Henri Duhamel du Monceau placed his private holdings in the Louvre for study by students at the new school of naval architecture. The museum moved to the Palais in 1943. While torpedoes, paintings, and the ornate *Canot de l'Empereur* in which Napoleon inspected Antwerp can be impressive, explanations are brief and chronology loosely traced. A semi-informative brochure is available in English at the ticket counter. Open Wed.-Mon. 10am-6pm and on holidays. Tickets issued until 5:30pm. Admission 31F, seniors, ages 5-12, and big families 16F, under 5 free. No student discount.

**Les Martyrs de Paris,** porte du Louvre of the Forum des Halles, 1*er* (tel. 40 28 08 13). Mo. Les Halles. A macabre museum of torture, with a heavy emphasis on the medieval. Realistic waxwork representations of people being branded, burned, and abused, while signs in English and French explain the historical details. Heavy Metal fans will be delighted to see a model of the "Iron Maiden" torture machine from Nuremberg Castle. All of it is most appropriate for the city that brought you the Bastille, the Guillotine, and the St. Bartholemew's Day Massacre. Admission 43F, students 32F. Martyrs of Paris and Rock 'n Roll Hall of Fame, 66F, students 48F, groups of more than 10 adults 48F per person. Open daily 10:30am-6:30pm.

**Centre de la Mer et des Eaux,** 195, rue St-Jacques, 5*ème*. (tel. 46 33 08 61). Mo. Luxembourg. Opened in 1993 after extensive renovation, this museum presents more than just the requisite tanks of corals and tropical fish. There is a "hands-on" learning area: push buttons and pull handles to educate yourself about such topics as fish disguises and algae life cycles. An entire room entitled "The Mysterious Voyage of Eels." Films and changing exhibitions as well. Open Tues.-Fri. 10am-12:30pm and 1:15-5:30pm, Sat.-Sun. 10am-5:30pm. Admission 25F, students 15F.

**Musée Adam Mickiewicz,** 6, quai d'Orléans, 4*ème* (tel. 43 54 35 61), on the Ile-St-Louis. Mo. Pont Marie. During the 19th century, this *hôtel* was a meeting place for Polish exiles and the residence of Adam Mickiewicz, one of Poland's greatest poets (1798-1835). Left as it was during the poet's lifetime, the museum is bursting with memorabilia about Mickiewicz and compatriots like Chopin. Displays highlight the poet's correspondence with other writers of the Romantic period. The building also houses a large Polish library. Open Thurs. 3-6pm. Free.

**Musée de Minéralogie (Museum of Mineralogy),** Jardin des Plantes, 5*ème*. Mo. Gare d'Austerlitz. Precious minerals—diamonds, rubies, and sapphires—are eclipsed by the *objets d 'art* created with these minerals, including 2 Renaissance Florentine marble tables, inlaid with lapis lazuli, amethyst, and other semi-precious stones. What the minerals in the upstairs gallery lack in value per gram, they make up in sheer size. Open Tues.-Sun. 10am-5pm. Admission 25F, students 16F.

**La Musée de la Monnaie de Paris,** 11, quai de Conti, *6ème* (tel. 40 46 55 33), on the Rive Gauche between Pont Neuf and Pont des Arts. Mo. Pont-Neuf. Housed in the Hôtel des Monnaies, once the mint of all money in France, this high-tech museum displays an impressive array of French coins from the 9th century to the present. Today, the Monnaie manufactures medals of special honor, some of which are for sale on the ground floor. Tues. and Thurs. at 2 and 2:45pm, a guided tour of the workshops takes you past artisans at work. Reservations 1 month in advance (tel. 40 46 55 35). The bulk of the coins are exhibited on the 1st floor, all accompanied by small video or slide shows explaining their history (in French). Open Tues.-Sun. 1-6pm. Admission 20F, students 15F, children free.

**Musée de la Mode et du Costume (Museum of Fashion and Clothing),** in the Palais Galliera, 10, av. Pierre 1er-de-Serbie, 16ème (tel. 47 20 85 23). Mo. Iéna. With over 12,000 ensembles in its possession, this museum mounts temporary exhibitions showcasing fashion throughout the past 3 centuries. Van Cleef, Arpels, and Givenchy have all been the foci of recent expositions. Although the museum itself is small, you can still revel in the splendor of yet another domain of Parisian pre-eminence. Open Tues.-Sun. 10am-5:40pm, when an exhibition is on. Admission 30F, students and seniors 20F.

**Institut du Monde Arabe (Institute of the Arab World),** 23, quai St-Bernard, 5ème (tel. 40 51 38 38). Mo. Jussieu. One of Paris's newest museums (opened in 1987), a cooperative project between 27 Arab nations and the French government to promote education about Arab history, art, culture and language. The riverside façade is shaped like a boat, representing the migration of Arabs to France. Notable for its displays of Arabic rugs and ceramics, the museum compares the art from the 3 Arab regions of Maghrib/Spain, the Near East, and the Middle East from the 3rd through the 18th centuries. Level 4 is devoted entirely to contemporary Arab artists. An extensive library contains works of Arabic literature in Arabic, French, and English, as well as periodicals, all of which are open to the public. At night, the auditorium provides a space for Arab movies (subtitled in English and French; 22F, students 18F) and theater (free). Call for a schedule of events. On Level 9, a delightful cafeteria cooks up 3-course lunches (60F), including many Arab specialities. Take your tray to the rooftop terrace outside for one of the best views of the Seine. Museum and Library open Tues.-Sun 10am-6pm. Museum admission 25F, students 20F, under 12 free. A 90-min. guided tour of the museum on Mon.-Fri.at 2 and 4pm and Sat.-Sun. 3pm is 40F. Institute open Tues.-Sat. 8am-8pm. Cafeteria open Tues.-Sun. 11:30am-6pm.

**Galerie Le Monde de l'Art,** 18, rue de Paradis, 10ème (tel. 42 46 43 44). Mo. Gare de l'Est. The airy and light-filled interior of this gallery is decorated with tiles, holdovers from the days when the building was headquarters for the Boulanger China Company. Tiles of every possible style and color, arranged in a variety of motifs, from African designs to Portuguese frescoes and Art Nouveau landscapes. Exhibits rotate every few months and often highlight work of young up-and-comings of the non-Western world. Definitely a very cool place. And, unless you're planning to buy some artwork, it's free. Open Mon. 2-7pm, Tues.-Sat. 1-7pm.

**Musée National des Monuments Français (National Museum of French Monuments),** 1, pl. du Trocadéro and pl. du 11 novembre, in the Palais de Chaillot, 16ème (tel. 45 53 21 93 or 44 05 39 10). Mo. Trocadéro. Almost everything in this warehouse-like structure is a copy of something else. Cavernous ceilings stretch above moldings of monumental religious French sculpture and reproductions of French murals. Only a few labels (in French) and no brochures. Open Thurs.-Mon. 10:30am-7pm, Wed. 10:30am-9pm. Admission 27F, students 18-25, seniors, and Sun. 20F. Conferences free with admission Wed. at 1 and 3pm.

**Musée Gustave Moreau,** 14, rue de La Rochefoucauld, 9ème (tel. 48 74 38 50). Mo. Trinité. This museum is a gem; located in the house of the 19th-century symbolist painter Gustave Moreau, it contains thousands of his drawings and paintings. The house itself is charming, and the rooms are lined with works in all stages of completion, from sketches and half-painted canvases to fully complete works, including the celebrated painting of Salomé dancing before the severed head of John the Baptist. Open Mon. and Wed. 11am-5:15pm, Thurs.-Sun. 10am-12:45pm and 2-5:15pm. Admission 17F; students, children, and Sun. 9F.

**Musée Naïf Max Fourny** (Halle St-Pierre), 2, rue Ronsard, 18ème (tel. 42 58 72 89). Mo. Anvers. Housed in a large turn-of-the-century iron structure that was once a marketplace, this museum displays "naive" paintings from the Caribbean, South America, and Europe, mostly imaginary and childlike visions of cities. The collection is interesting, but won't astound you. More a warehouse than an art gallery. Open Tues. and Thurs.-Sat. 10am-10pm, Wed. and Sun. 10am-6pm. Admission 22F, students 16F.

**Palais de la Découverte (Palace of Discovery),** in the Grand Palais, entrance on av. Franklin D. Roosevelt, 8ème (tel. 43 59 18 21 answering machine or 40 74 80 00). Mo. Franklin Roosevelt. More central, less flashy than the Cité des Sciences. Within one enormous section of the Art Nouveau Palais, interactive exhibits run the gamut of scientific subjects and run it remarkably well. Kids will (and do) tear around at a manic pace to turn wheels that teach about complementary colors, press buttons that start comets on their celestial trajectories, spin on seats to investigate angular motion, and glare at all kinds of cleverly camouflaged creepy-crawlies. Open Tues.-Sat. 9:30am-6pm, Sun. 10am-7pm. Admission 22F, students, seniors, and under 18 11F. Planetarium show 15F extra, students, seniors, and under 18 10F extra. Planetarium shows Tues.-Fri. 2, 3:15, and 4:30pm, Sat.-Sun. and holidays 11:30am, 2pm, 3:15pm, 4:30pm, and 5:45pm. Film at 2:30 and 4pm.

**Palais de Tokyo,** 13, av. du Président Wilson, 16ème (tel. 47 23 36 53). Mo. Iéna. Closed for renovations until 1995 when it will become **Palais de l'Image,** an enormous film library. Open Wed.-Mon. 10am-5pm, last entry 4:30. Admission to exhibitions varies, generally 25-30F, students 12-22F.

**Petit Palais,** also called the Palais des Beaux-Arts de la Ville de Paris, av. Winston Churchill, 8ème (tel. 42 65 12 73). Mo. Champs-Elysées-Clemenceau. A comfortable museum with displays of gems from ancient art through 19th- and 20th-century painting and sculpture. Each of the rooms of the permanent collection has a theme: 17th-century Flemish and Dutch painting or canvases depicting the French Revolution. Houses Jean-Baptiste Carpeaux's *Young Fisher with the Shell,* Camille Claudel's bust of Rodin, Monet's *Sunset at Lavacourt,* as well as the occasional Rubens, Rembrandt, Cézanne, Pissarro, and Renoir. Wheelchair accessible by the door at 1, av. Dutuit—call ahead. Open Tues.-Sun. 10am-5:40pm. Admission to permanent collection 26F, *tarif réduit* 14F. Admission to temporary exhibits roughly 40F, *tarif réduit* 30F. Conference visits (1-1½hr.), focusing on a special theme, held in French in the afternoon; admission 24F.

**Musée Picasso,** 5, rue de Thorigny, 3ème (tel. 42 71 25 21). Mo. Chemin Vert. In France there is a hefty tax on inherited wealth. When the great cubist Pablo Picasso died in 1973, his heirs opted to pay this tax in artwork rather than money, which is why the French government owns this museum's collection. (The 17th-century Hôtel Salé which houses this collection did not, however, belong to Picasso. See Sights—*3ème arrondissement* for more information.) Many works are of minor significance, but the collection as a whole is fascinating, thanks to the museum's tasteful and informative layout. It illustrates the artist's development through his career, grouping works together by period. Alongside Picasso's pieces are works by artists who influenced him, including Braque, Cézanne, and anonymous African and Oceanian sculptors. In addition, photos of Picasso's illustrious friends—Marie Laurencin, Braque, and Cocteau among others—taken in his studio provide a who's who of the early 20th-century avant-garde. Works by Giacometti decorate the stairwell. Open Wed.-Mon. 9:30am-6pm; Oct. 1-March 31 9:30am-5:20pm. Admission 33F, reduced 24F. Wheelchair access.

**Musée des Collections Historiques de la Préfecture de la Police,** 1bis, rue des Carmes, 2nd floor, 5ème (tel. 43 29 21 57). Mo. Maubert-Mutualité. Founded in 1909, this 1-room gallery is devoted to the preservation of police paraphernalia. Guarded by a group of life-like wax *flics* (slang for cops), the cases protect wholly uninteresting writs and warrants, police awards, and metals. More interesting are the 2 cases of exotic weaponry. Near the weapons the museum proudly displays a Revolutionary-era guillotine, along with a 15cm stuffed doll tied and prepared to undergo the treatment. You can also peruse bounteous cuffs, including a ghastly 2kg iron neck-and-handcuff combination. While the museum is mostly a favorite with retired officers visiting Paris from the provinces, it can be an amusing diversion for anyone, especially since it's free. Open Mon.-Fri. 9:30am-4:30pm.

**Musée de La Poste,** 34, bd. de Vaugirard, 15*ème* (tel. 42 79 23 45). Mo. Montparnasse-Bienvenue. Most impressive here are the several thousand stamps which adorn the walls of an entire floor. Also of note are various mailbox designs on display, including a conceptionally original hollow cannonball, which was stuffed with letters and then floated downstream to Parisians during the Prussian siege of 1870. Nascent bureaucrats thrill to a scale replica of a post office window; everyone else suffers mysterious waves of impatient anxiety. Tours Tues. and Thurs. 5pm, Sat. 3pm; 35F. Open Mon.-Sat. 10am-6pm. Admission 25F, students 12F.

**Musée de la Maison de la Radio-France,** 116, av. du Prés. Kennedy, 16*ème* (tel. 42 30 21 80). Mo. Passy or Mirabeau, RER (C) Av. du Pt. Kennedy/Maison de la Radio France. A whirlwind tour through communications history. The museum can be visited only by guided tour in French, which hastily covers the history of the Maison, of radio, and of TV, with appropriate bias toward the French contribution to all three. Childhood radio builders will enjoy the chance to look at classic specimens. Open Mon.-Sat. Tours at 10:30am, 11:30am, 2:30pm, 3:30pm, and 4:30pm. Admission 14F, students and seniors 7F.

**Rock 'n Roll Hall of Fame,** porte du Louvre of the Forum des Halles, 1*er* (tel. 40 28 08 13). Mo. Les Halles. The Hall is much less interesting than its neighbor the Martyrs of Paris. Wax dummies of stars like Madonna and the Beatles; video clips and piped-in music. If you think that can't be any more exciting than staying at home and watching MTV, well...you're right. Admission 40F, students 29F. Martyrs of Paris and Hall of Fame 66F, students 48F. Open daily 10:30am-6:30pm.

**Musée Renan-Scheffer,** also called the **Musée de la Vie Romantique,** 16, rue Chaptal, 9*ème* (tel. 48 74 95 38). Mo. St-Georges. This small museum is housed in the former residence of 19th-century painter and *salonnier* Ary Scheffer, a friend of George Sand. Busts, portraits, letters, and personal belongings (rings, locks of hair) recall Scheffer, Sand, Franz Liszt, and many others who belonged to this salon. The house is lovely—down a tree-lined lane and surrounded by a garden—and never crowded. Open Tues.-Sun. 10am-5:40pm. Admission 20F, students 10F.

**Musée-Galerie de la Seita (Société d'Exploitation Industrielle des Tabacs et Alumettes),** 12, rue Surcouf, 7*ème* (tel. 45 56 60 17 or 45 56 60 18). Mo. Invalides or Latour-Maubourg. Tobacco and cigarettes are state-managed commodities in France and the propaganda center is here, right next to corporate headquarters. This very politically incorrect museum tells the story of tobacco from Jean Nicot's 1561 presentation of its medicinal qualities to the court, through Napoleon's 1810 imposition of a state monopoly, and up to the present-day. Temporary exhibits come and go, one devoted to tobacco, the other to something unrelated. Open Mon.-Sat. 11am-6pm. Free, usually: some exhibitions may require a fee (around 25F, 15F *tarif réduit*). Nice free bathrooms too.

**Musée de la Serrurerie,** 1, rue de la Perle, 3*ème* (tel. 42 77 79 62). Mo. Chemin Vert or St-Sébastien Froissart. Housed in the Hôtel Libéral-Bruant, this museum holds an odd but interesting collection of locks. 5 lavishly decorated small rooms display an assortment of padlocks, slide-bolts, hammers, clasps, and latches. Original iron-work adds an artistic touch. Open Mon.-Fri. 2-5pm. Open Sept.-July.

**Musée des Techniques,** 292, rue St-Martin, 3*ème* (tel. 40 27 23 31). Mo. Réaumur-Sébastopol or Arts et Métiers. In 1794, French revolutionaries decided to create a national collection of new technology to be housed in the 12th-century priory, St-Martin-des-Champs. Here you can find Volta's original battery, wooden telescopes, and brass models of the solar system, as well as a roomful of 18th-century automata—activated on the first Wed. of each month at 2:30pm. Two billion francs are earmarked for renovating the museum in time for its 200th anniversary (Oct. 1994), but in its present condition it has a certain flea-market charm. Open Tues.-Sun. 10am-5:30pm; closed public holidays. Admission 20F, Sun. 10F.

**Musée du Vieux Montmartre,** 12, rue Cortot, 18*ème* (tel. 46 06 61 11). Mo. Lamarck-Caulaincourt. A museum dedicated to the political, artistic, cultural, and religious past of the *butte* Montmartre. The beautiful 17th-century house, overlooking a pleasant garden and Montmartre's only vineyard, once housed one of Molière's actors and, in more recent times, has been the residence of such artistic luminaries as Renoir and Utrillo. The museum's collection includes old maps, paintings, photographs, and a wooden model of the *quartier*. One room recreates the ambience of a turn-of-the-century café owned by M. Buillot. Open Tues. Sun. 11am-5:30pm. Admission 25F, *tarif réduit* 15F.

**Musée du Vin,** rue des Eaux or 5-7 sq. Charles Dickens, 16ème (tel. 45 25 63 26). Mo. Passy. Located in the cool, damp, vaulted cellars of the 14th-century Abbey of Passy, this museum tries to explain the process of wine production through wax dummies, old tools, and many barrels. Of interest, perhaps, only to the oenologists among you, it's at its most compelling when offering tasty tidbits of trivia—you should only fill a wine glass to its widest point so as to better release the vintage's bouquet. Don't miss your free tasting. Short guide sheet is available in primitive English. Open daily noon-6pm. Admission 28F, seniors 22F, students 20F.

**Musée Zadkine,** 100bis, rue d'Assas, 6ème (tel. 43 26 91 90), just south of the Jardin du Luxembourg. Mo. Notre-Dame-des-Champs. This reasonably sized museum is the perfect antidote to Parisian aesthetic overload. Installed in 1982 in the house and studio where he worked from 1928 until his death, the museum highlights the work of master sculptor Ossip Zadkine (1890-1967). Zadkine's work spans the major developments in modern sculpture, moving from the extremes of Cubism to a renewed Classicism, and using a wide variety of mediums, including granite, bronze, lava, and wood. Even if you don't want to pay the admission to the museum, a visit to the garden is both free and worthwhile; a good selection of the artist's most important works, including his two-faced *Woman with the Bird*, reside there and you can relax on the benches in peace while you contemplate Zadkine's work. Open Tues.-Sun. 10am-5:30pm. Admission 17F, students 9F.

# Entertainment

Long after the museums have been closed and the sun has set (which in summer isn't until around 11pm), Paris continues to pulse with dancing, jazz, music, theater, and nightlife. Paris teems with constantly changing *boîtes* (nightclubs), cabarets, discos, and smoky jazz clubs. You'll find every type of cinema from the silver screen to the latest American and European releases; modern, jazz, and ballet dance; avant-garde and traditional theater; opera; and rock and classical concerts galore. For those who'd like to spend a nice relaxing evening observing all the madness around them, Paris's innumerable cafés provide front row seats for only the price of a *kir*.

For a complete list of films, theater performances, opera, dance, poetry-slams, disco, and cabaret nightlife, consult the two bibles of Paris entertainment: the magazine **Pariscope** and the **Officiel des Spectacles,** both on sale weekly at any newsstand for 3F. Even if you don't understand French, you should be able to decipher the listings of times and locations. Or, contact **Info-Loisirs,** a recording that keeps tabs on what's on in Paris (in English tel. 49 52 53 56; in French tel. 49 52 53 55).

The city has much to offer, but don't expect the whole shebang of glamorous options to fall into your lap. The hottest spots in town change at the whim and fancy of elite Parisian party-goers. "In" spots are usually hard to find and frequented by a moderately exclusive crowd that will not go out of its way to accommodate newcomers. Meeting a local may be your only chance to enter a highly private culture that loves to stomp, shimmy, sing, or mellow out until dawn.

The Parisian music scene provides some of the best jazz in the world, much of it imported from the United States. The Parisians have also imported West African beats, Caribbean calypso, Latin American salsa, North African raï music, and rap. Classical concerts play in both expensive concert halls and more affordable churches, especially during the summer. To get more information and to buy tickets for rock, jazz, or classical concerts, check out **FNAC Musique,** 24, bd. des Italiens, *9ème* (tel. 48 01 02 03) or 1, rue de Charenton, *12ème* (tel. 43 42 04 04).

Some things do stay the same. The famous cabarets of Montmartre still offer their topless extravaganzas. A number of cabarets, such as the comedy-oriented *café-théâtres* and the music-oriented *chansonniers,* are offering alternative and intimate entertainment reminiscent of the 1930s Paris cabarets of Edith Piaf and Jacques Brel.

Fortunately, the most traditional Parisian entertainment—*la flânerie,* strolling and observing other passersby—is free. Hit the streets, walk around, and seek out your own adventures. Weave your way through the *quartier latin*—and join the many Parisians doing so already. The area around Beaubourg (the Centre Pompidou) fills with fire-eaters, Chilean guitar bands, and other performers. Around place St-Germain, you'll find throngs of people parading by in the latest fashions and a few bars where unlimited jazz comes with the price of one drink.

To see a movie or linger in the more fashionable cafés, wander around Montparnasse, the touristy Champs-Elysées, the Marais and the streets radiating from bd. St-Michel, bd. St-Germain, and bd. Sébastopol in the *6ème*. Parisians are as addicted to cinema as they are to people-watching and, unlike in the U.S., you will find anything from Bergman to Spielberg to Louis Malle playing at any one time in the city.

Many of these activities can actually be enhanced by nightfall. Every evening from sunset until midnight (1am in the summer), Paris literally becomes the City of Lights as bright lights flood the Arc de Triomphe, Notre-Dame, the Tour Eiffel, the Bastille, and other great and famous sights. Walk around to experience the unique magic this phenomenal electric display brings to the centuries-old monuments.

A few words of caution. Keep in mind that several sections of Paris have developed entertainment businesses of a different sort. The areas around Pigalle, Gare St-Lazare, and Beaubourg fill nightly with prostitutes and drug dealers, and everyone,

CINEMA

should avoid Bois de Boulogne after dark. The *métro* stops running at 1am, but you should take the last train at around 12:30am if you have to make a connection.

# ■ Cinema

Paris is famous the world over for a movie scene that rivals—some say, surpasses—that of New York. Sitting in the dark need not be a vacation from the Parisian experience. After all, cinema was invented here, by the Lumière brothers, Auguste and Louis. The first moving picture flickered to life in 1895, in the basement of the Grand Café at 14, bd. des Capucines. Although proud of his movie, Louis claimed that "the cinema is an invention without a future;" obviously, he was wrong.

While an evening at the movies in the U.S. has become a vat of popcorn and, all too often, a trip to the megaplex, film-going in Paris remains something of an evening on the town. Cafés, bars, and restaurants cohabit with projector rooms in some of the city's smaller theaters. The **fête du Cinéma,** a three-day, all-day, city-wide celebration transforms Paris into a community of film fans young and old (see Festivals for more info). Also keep in mind that the VCR and the video store have not really caught on yet in Paris, so most movies are still played on the big screen.

Proof of Paris's movie enthusiasm are the mile-long lines for anything from Robert Mitchum to Bambi. Beating the crowds requires some know-how. The two big theater chains—Gaumont and UGC—offer *cartes privilèges* for frequent customers. At 150F for five entries, the *carte Gaumont* allows bearers to skip past lines and reserve seats in advance. UGC offers a like deal: 120F for 4 entries, 180F for 6. Cards are active for two months, at all shows and all franchise locations. As the system was only started recently, watch out for changes. In any case, don't worry, the Parisians are as confused as you are. Most theaters require you to wait in two lines—one line to buy your ticket and then a second line for the movie you want; as a result it is advisable to buy your ticket in advance and then return to the theater later.

Movie buffs on tight budgets should not despair at high-priced tickets; on Mondays and Wednesdays prices drop about 10F. Check *Pariscope* for details—days and reductions vary with the theater. The confederation of independent cinemas, a bulwark of little-guys competing with Gaumont and UGC, offers reduced tickets for all on both days. Interestingly enough, *chomeurs* (the unemployed) get discount rates.

The entertainment weeklies list show times and theaters. Film festivals are listed separately. The notation "V.O." (*version originale*) after a non-French movie listing means that the film is being shown in its original language with French subtitles; watching an English-language film with French subtitles is a great way to pick up new (and sometimes very interesting) vocabulary. "V.F." (*version française*) means that it has been dubbed—an increasingly rare and entirely avoidable phenomenon. If you're in Paris during its annual (short) hot spell, make sure the movie theater advertises *"climatisé."* If not, you'll regret it: although air-conditioning is becoming more customary, many theaters preserve a traditional, overpowering heat.

Film is at the center of France's romance with the U.S. While Hollywood studios have tended to option and remake French films (*Trois Hommes et un Berceau* became *Three Men and a Baby, Le Retour de Martin Guerre* became *Sommersby*), Parisians celebrate U.S. exports as they find them. The five-o'clock-shadow chain-smokers of westerns and thrillers live on in the hearts of local audiences. In the 1940s, French critics discovered the wonderful crime films being made in Hollywood and elevated them to an art form with the title, *film noir*. Ever since the New Wave crested in the early 1970s and Jean-Paul Belmondo began imitating Bogart, French interest in U.S. movies has been phenomenal, making the career of many an American star. When Clint Eastwood took his first Oscar in 1993, he thanked the French heartily. Enthusiasts of the genre that made him great may want to check out the western festival (July 15-Aug. 7) at Parc de la Villette, 19ème (tel. 40 28 40 33).

Throughout the city, and particularly on the Left Bank, you'll find more old Hollywood movies—from Hitchcock to Lubïtch—than you ever knew existed. Many American movies that never make it to the big American theaters are shown here don't be surprised to find a "blockbuster" hit that never played in your home town. Mickey Rourke is an icon here—a chinless take on the unwashed American tough guy. Rosanna Arquette, and, of course, master *auteur* Jerry Lewis have also reached stardom. French audiences show far more respect for film directors than their American counterparts. Feature films play in the grand theaters on the Champs-Elysées, bd. St-Germain, bd. Montparnasse, and bd. St-Michel. Artsier flicks roll in the little theaters on the side streets of the Left Bank.

Before the feature comes the *séance*—a series of commercials and previews that roll for as much as a half hour. Don't be surprised if a sultry, skin-filled perfume-type commercial turns out to be a coffee ad. After all, a recent study shows that coffee-drinking prolongs one's sexual drive. Also amusing are the cigarette ads, which by law aren't allowed to show anyone smoking. Hmm... Make sure you tip the person who points you to your seat (about 2F). An old law assuring service workers 12-15% inadvertently bypassed ushers and taxi drivers. Most foreigners are not aware they are expected to tip ushers and often encounter hostility when they fail to do so.

Many theaters in Paris specialize in *art-et-essai* programs featuring the great European *auteurs,* current independent film, and U.S. classics. *Art-et-essai* is the umbrella term for this particular mix of old and new, but always edifying, cinema.

The options below are some of the most interesting, most unusual, and most popular theaters in Paris.

**Action Christine,** 4, rue Christine, 6*ème,* off rue Dauphine (tel. 43 29 11 30). Mo. Odéon. A revival cinema for American classics. Admission 38F; students, Mon., and Wed. 28F. Some rooms wheelchair accessible.

**L'Arlequin,** 76, rue de Rennes, 6*ème* (tel. 45 44 28 80). Mo. St-Sulpice. A revival *art-et-essai* cinema with occasional visits from European *auteurs* and preview showings. Admission 40F, students 30F (Mon.-Fri. only), Mon. and Wed. general admission 30F. Full price for all on festival opening nights. Buy tickets in advance.

**Centre Georges Pompidou, Salle Garance,** rue St-Merri, 4*ème* (tel. 42 78 37 29). Mo. Rambuteau. Multi-cultural film series provide the missing link in the U.S.-heavy Parisian film scene. Recent series on Georgian and Armenian cinema. Korean film fest Oct. 20, 1993-Jan. 24, 1994. Admission 25F, student 20F.

**Cinémathèque Française,** at the Musée du Cinéma in the Palais de Chaillot, on av. Albert de Mun at av. Président Wilson, 16*ème* (tel. 47 04 24 24). Mo. Trocadéro. Answering machine lists all shows. A must for serious film buffs. This government-supported theater shows 1-2 films per day, many of them classics, near-classics, or soon-to-be classics. Foreign films almost always shown with French subtitles. Expect long lines. Open Tues.-Sun. Last show 9pm. Admission 24F.

**Dôme IMAX,** La Défense (tel. 46 92 45 45), to the right of L'Espace Marques. Programs in-the-round which compensate for lack of plot, substance, or taste with their immediacy; past features include *The Fires of Kuwait* and *In Space.* Admission (for 2 films) 55F during the day, 75F at night. Students 45F, 65F at night. Upstairs, the Spider cafeteria offers a good lunch deal at 50F. Open 10am-4pm.

**L'Entrepôt,** 7-9, rue Francis de Pressensé, 14*ème* (tel. 45 43 41 63). Mo. Pernety. Organizes a wide variety of week-long festivals, sometimes with director debates. Indy cinema from across the globe gets a fair shake. Adjoining bookstore **L'Atmosphère** (tel. 45 42 29 26) offers a selection of technical manuals, picture books, and biographies of auteurs. Open Mon.-Sat. 2-8pm. Delightful bar/restaurant (tel. 45 40 60 70) at same address with secluded garden terrace. 58F menu at lunchtime. Beer 15-22F. Restaurant open Mon.-Sat. 12:30-11pm, Sun. 12:30-3pm. Bar open daily 2pm-1am. Two branches project high-quality independent, classic, and foreign films. **Les Trois Luxembourg,** 67, rue Monsieur-le-Prince, 6*ème* (tel. 46 33 97 77). Mo. Odéon. **Le St-Germain-des-Prés,** pl. St-Germain-des-Prés, 6*ème* (tel. 42 22 87 23). Mo. St-Germain-des-Prés. A big, beautiful theater. Open noon-midnight. Admission 35F, students and Mon. 25F.

**La Géode,** 26, av. Corentin-Cariou, 19*ème* (tel. 40 05 80 00). Mo. Corentin-Cariou, in La Villette. Mostly scientific documentaries on this huge hemispherical screen.

A 3-D sound, light, and comfortable chair extravaganza. Shows daily on the hour 10am-9pm. Admission 55F, students Mon.-Fri. 37F. Wheelchair accessible.

**Le Grand Rex,** 1, bd. Poissonnière, *2ème* (tel. 42 36 83 93). Mo. Bonne-Nouvelle. This 2800-seat behemoth is the largest theater in Paris. Well worth a visit just to experience the phenomenon of "privatized" viewing amid thousands. Primarily first-runs, but the atmosphere is unique. Last show around 9:30pm. Admission 42F, students and Mon. 34F. A UGC affiliate.

**Musée du Louvre,** 1*er* (tel. 40 20 52 99). Mo. Palais Royal/Musée du Louvre. Hosts cutting-edge series that defy the museum's classical ambience. Movies 22F. Call 40 20 54 55 for schedule. Auditorium open Sept.-June.

**La Pagode,** 57bis, rue de Babylone, 7*ème* (tel. 47 05 12 15). Mo. St-François-Xavier. No tremendous screen, and not even Dolby sound, but the intimate *salle japonaise* and the oriental architecture make this Paris's most charming cinema. Specializing in contemporary films of the artsy-though-accessible ilk, La Pagode also houses a lovely *salon de thé* whose terrace spills into the Japanese garden. (See Sights—7*ème arrondissement* for historical information.) Teas 20F, tarts and brownies 22F. *Salon de thé* open Mon.-Sat. 4-9:45pm, Sun. and holidays 2-8pm. 3-5 screenings per day. A well-disguised outpost of Gaumont—the *carte Gaumont* is serviceable here. Admission 42F, students and Wed. 34F.

**Passage du Nord Ouest,** 13, rue du Faubourg Montmartre, 9*ème* (tel. 47 70 81 47). Mo. Rue Montmartre. A descent into cutting-edge multi-media productions. The chameleon-like *café-ciné-concert* adapts its interior to the mood of the festival. Outlandish, progressive, and bemused, the Passage Nord-Ouest is an experiment and something to behold. Also a concert space for blues, reggae, Irish music, and whatever else comes into town. Prices vary with the soirée.

## ■ Theater

Theater in Paris is not limited to Molière, Corneille, or Racine. The classics are there if you want them, but so are modern masterworks by Beckett and Genet, Broadway-type comedies and musicals, experimental plays, and political satires. Aside from the intimate *café-théâtres, cafés chansonniers,* and the Las Vegas-style *revues,* theater in Paris takes two main forms: the national theaters, such as the Comédie Française, and the private theaters, which concentrate on newer and more experimental works. Although intended for children, the famous *guignols* (traditional puppet shows) may offer the most comprehensible text for Anglophones.

Theater tickets can run as high as 200F, but students can often pay lower prices. Some of the *café-théâtres* and *chansonniers* sell standby tickets a half-hour before the performance. Most theaters close at least for the month of August. *Pariscope* and *l'Officiel des Spectacles* print complete listings of current shows. Try one of the following discount ticket organizations:

**Kiosque-Théâtre,** 15, pl. de la Madeleine, 8*ème*. Mo. Madeleine. Far and away the best place to get reduced tickets. This splendid kiosk sells tickets at half-price the day of the show. Open Tues.-Sat. 12:30-8pm, Sun. 12:30-4pm. Also at *métro* level of Châtelet-les-Halles. Open Tues.-Sat. 12:30-7pm.

**COPAR** (Service des Activités Culturelles), 39, av. Georges Bernanos, 5*ème* (tel. 40 51 37 13). Mo. Port-Royal. Sells discounted tickets and publishes a monthly list of plays for which these tickets are available. Also sells reduced-price concert tickets, even in summer. Accepts any student ID. Open Sept.-July Mon.-Fri. 9:30am-4:30pm; July-Aug. Mon.-Fri. 9:30am-noon and 2-4:30pm.

**Alpha FNAC: Spectacles,** 136, rue de Rennes, 6*ème* (tel. 49 54 30 00). Mo. Montparnasse-Bienvenue. Also at Forum des Halles, 1-7, rue Porte Lescot, 1*er* (Mo Châtelet-Les Halles); 26-30, av. des Ternes, (tel. 44 09 18 00; Mo. Ternes); and 71 bd. St-Germain, 5*ème* (tel. 44 41 31 50). Sells tickets for theater and a variety of concerts and festivals. Carte FNAC (150F for 3 years, students 100F) gets you discounts of up to 40% on music and theater tickets. Open Mon.-Sat. 10am-7pm.

**Virgin Megastore,** 52, av. des Champs-Elysées, 8*ème* (tel. 40 74 06 48 or 42 89 87 27). Mo. George V. Look for the ticket office below the first floor.

## NATIONAL THEATERS

Supported by the French government, the national theaters are the brightest stars of Parisian theater. With the advantages of giant auditoriums, superb acoustics, veteran actors, and, in some cases, several centuries of history, these companies stage superlative and extremely popular productions. Although modern pieces appear occasionally, expect Molière, Racine, Goethe, and Shakespeare (all in French). Unless you're trying to get last-minute rush tickets, make reservations 14 days in advance.

**La Comédie Française,** 2, rue de Richelieu, 1er (tel. 40 15 00 15). Mo. Palais Royal. Founded by Molière, this is the granddaddy of all French theaters. Guaranteed pomp and prestige, with red velvet and chandeliers. Expect over-acted slapstick farce in the typical and much parodied *"style Comédie Française."* You don't need to speak French to understand the jokes. 892 seats. Open Sept. 15-July. Box office open daily 11am-6pm. Admission 20-160F, under 25 55F. 20F rush tickets available ½ hr. before show; come 1½ hr. ahead to wait in line.

**Odéon Théâtre de l'Europe,** 1, pl. Odéon, 6ème (tel. 44 41 36 36). Mo. Odéon. Eclectic programs running the gamut from classics to avant-garde. 1042 seats. Also **Petit Odéon,** 82 seats. Open Sept.-July. Box office open Mon.-Sat. 11am-6:30pm. Admission 30-150F; Petit Odéon 50-70F, under 26 and rush tickets 50F.

**Théâtre National de Chaillot,** in the Palais de Chaillot, pl. du Trocadéro, 16ème (tel. 47 27 81 15). Mo. Trocadéro. Mostly plays but occasional musicals as well. 2 *salles* with 1000 and 400 seats. Special arrangements for disabled visitors. Box office open Mon.-Sat. 11am-7pm, Sun. 11am-5pm. Admission 140F, under 25 and over 60 100F. Student standby tickets 70F.

**Théâtre Nationale de la Colline,** 15, rue Malte-Brun, 20ème (tel. 43 66 43 60). Mo. Gambetta. 760 seats. Also **Petit Théâtre,** 200 seats. Open Sept.-July. Box office open daily 11am-7pm. Admission 140F, under 25 and over 60 110F.

## PRIVATE THEATERS

Although private theaters don't carry the reputations or historical baggage of the national theaters, some stage outstanding productions. Poor showings are much more common than in the national theaters; check the reviews in newspapers and entertainment weeklies before investing in a seat.

**Athénée-Louis Jouvet,** 4, sq. de l'Opéra, 9ème (tel. 47 42 67 27). Mo. Opéra or Auber. 687 seats. Hard-to-find, with an unremarkable exterior, but a magnificent 18th-century interior and outstanding classical productions. Open Oct.-May. Box office open Mon.-Sat. 11:30am-6pm. Admission 80-110F.

**Experimental Theater Wing Studio,** 14, rue Letellier, 15ème. Mo. Emile Zola. Six-year-old extension of New York University's theater program. Interesting and unusual productions in English. Prices vary with performance.

**Jardin Shakespeare du Pré Catelan,** at the end of the Bois de Boulogne (tel. 42 71 44 06). Take bus #244 from Porte Maillot. 500 seats. Summertime Shakespeare in French. Tickets at the door or at FNAC. Shows Fri.-Sat. 7:30pm, Sun. 5pm. Buses won't be running after the show, and but don't try walking. Take a taxi to Porte Maillot; some find rides among audience members. Admission 60-100F.

**Lucernaire Centre National d'Art et d'Essai,** 53, rue Notre-Dame-des-Champs, 6ème (tel. 45 44 57 34). Mo. Vavin or Notre-Dame-des-Champs. 130 seats. Plays by classic authors like Chekhov, Tennessee Williams, St-Exupéry. Box office open 2-7pm or call for reservations 9am-5pm. Admission 118F, reduced price 84F.

**The Sweeney,** 18, rue Laplace, 5ème (tel. 47 26 87 77). Mo. Maubert-Mutualité. This Irish pub hosts the Gare St-Lazare players, an English-speaking, Chicago-based theater company under the direction of Bob Mayer. Admission 60F, students 50F, children 40F. Call for more information.

**Théâtre de la Huchette,** 23, rue de la Huchette, 5ème (tel. 43 26 38 99). Mo. St-Michel. 100 seats. Tiny theater whose productions of Ionesco's *La Cantatrice Chauve (The Bald Soprano)* and *La Leçon (The Lesson)* are still popular—after 33 years. Shows Mon.-Sat. Box office open Mon.-Sat. 5-9:30pm. Admission 100F, students 70F; for both shows 130F, students 90F. No discounts Sat.

**Théâtre Mogador,** 25, rue de Mogador, 9ème (tel. 48 78 04 04). Mo. Trinité. With 1792 seats, one of the largest theaters in Paris. Grandiose comedies and musicals on a colossal stage. Open Oct.-May. Box office open daily 11am-7pm. Admission 80-200F. Ask about student discounts.

**Théâtre Renaud-Barrault,** 2bis, av. Franklin D. Roosevelt, 8ème (tel. 44 95 98 00). Mo. Franklin D. Roosevelt. 920 seats. Also **Petite Salle** (tel. 42 56 08 80). 150 seats. Large stage allows for some outlandish musicals and comedies. Open Sept.-July. Box office open Tues.-Sat. 11am-6pm, Sun. noon-5pm. Admission 110-140F, students and seniors 100F. Petite salle 120F, reduced to 80 and 60F.

**Théâtre de la Ville,** 2, pl. Châtelet, 1er (tel. 42 74 22 77). Mo. Châtelet. 1000 seats. Excellent productions of all sorts, with a heavy emphasis on the musical. Fully wheelchair accessible. Box office open Sun.-Mon. 11am-6pm. Admission 70-120F, students 60-85F.

## CAFÉ-THEÂTRES

Continuing the European showtime tradition, *café-théâtres* deliver caustic, often political satire through skits and short plays. Puns and double-entendres galore: those who aren't up on French slang and politics may miss most of the fun. Despite the name, not all *café-théâtres* have tables with waiter service.

**Au Bec Fin,** 6, rue Thérèse, 1er (tel. 42 96 29 35). Mo. Palais Royal. Usually 2 different shows per night in this tiny place (60 seats). Dinner and 1 show from 220F. Dinner and 2 shows from 300F. Shows at 7, 8:30, and 10:15pm. Auditions sometimes open to the public (45F). Admission 80F, students 65F.

**Café de la Gare,** 41, rue du Temple, 4ème (tel. 42 78 52 51). Mo. Hôtel-de-Ville. Where the infamous Coluche got his start. Comedy and satire about social and political issues. Reservations daily 3-7pm. Shows start at 8 and 9:15pm. Admission 80-100F, students 60F.

**Le Point Virgule,** 7, rue Ste-Croix-de-la-Bretonnerie, 4ème (tel. 42 78 67 03). Mo. Hôtel-de-Ville. Often features works of special interest to gays and lesbians. Reservations suggested, available 24 hrs. Mon.-Fri. 2 shows 130F; 3 shows 150F. Admission 80F, students 60F. Open 3pm-midnight.

## CHANSONNIERS

The *chansonnier* is the musical cousin of the *café-théâtre*. In the spirit of old Paris, the audience is invited to sing along to French folk songs. The better your French, the better you'll follow the proceedings. Admission usually includes one drink.

**Au Lapin Agile,** 22, rue des Saules, 18ème (tel. 46 06 85 87). Mo. Lamarck-Coulaincourt. Picasso, Verlaine, Clemenceau, Renoir, Apollinaire, and Max Jacob used to hang out here during the heyday of Montmartre. Arrive before 7pm for a good seat. Usually crowded with tourists. Shows at 9pm. Admission and first drink 110F, students 80F. Subsequent drinks 35F. Open Tues.-Sun. until 2am.

**Caveau des Oubliettes,** 11, rue St-Julien-le-Pauvre, 5ème (tel. 43 54 94 97). Mo. St-Michel. Located in what were once the bowels of the Petit-Châtelet Prison. The dark wood paneling and *"musée avec guillotine,"* together with the old French folk songs, give this place a medieval feel. Drinks 140F. Open Mon.-Sat. 9pm-2am.

**Caveau de la République,** 1, bd. St-Martin, 3ème (tel. 42 78 44 45). Mo. République. A mostly Parisian crowd fills the 482 seats. Tickets sold 6 days in advance from 11am. Shows Tues.-Sat. 9pm, Sun. 3:30pm. Admission 160F, students 95F.

**Deux Anes,** 100, bd. de Clichy, 18ème (tel. 46 06 10 26). Mo. Blanche. 300 seats. Shows Mon.-Sat. 9pm. Reservations by phone 11am-7pm, 2 weeks in advance. Admission 120F, students 95F. Open Sept.-June.

## GUIGNOLS

These renowned traditional puppet shows entertain adults as much as children. Go to them for your badly needed dose of slapstick humor—a veritable (and uniquely French) cartoon in wood. The puppets speak French, but you'll have no problem understanding their outrageous antics. Even if you miss the joke, seeing rows of schoolchildren roar with laughter is as amusing as the show itself. Almost all parks have *guignols* and look in *Pariscope* for others that change their location weekly.

**Marionettes des Champs-Elysées,** Rond Point de Champs-Elysées, 8*ème* (tel. 42 57 43 34), at the intersection of av. Matignon and Gabriel. Mo. Champs-Elysées-Clemenceau. The classic adventures of the Guignol character. Wed. and Sat.-Sun. 3, 4, and 5pm. Admission 12F50.

**Marionettes du Luxembourg,** Jardin du Luxembourg (tel. 43 26 46 47). Mo. Vavin or Notre-Dame-des-Champs. Roofed-in theater. Such wonderful stories as the *Adventures of Pinocchio* and the *Three Little Pigs*. Usually Wed. and Sat.-Sun. 3:15 and 4:30pm. Call ahead for time changes. Admission 21F, groups 17F.

**Théâtre de la Petite Ourse,** Jardin des Tuileries, 8*ème* (tel. 42 86 03 34). Mo. Tuileries or Concorde. A classic marionette show within walking distance of the Louvre, for the ultimate in aesthetic contrasts. Call for times and titles. Admission 20F, children 15F. Wed. and Sat.-Sun. 3:30 and 4:30pm.

## CABARETS

Contrary to popular tourist belief, Parisian cabarets (officially called *revues)* are not exclusively for foreigners. The big names—the Moulin Rouge and the Folies Bergère—are frequented by as many cameras as people, but some of the less-publicized cabarets lure Parisians as well; stampedes of well-hoofed locals unwind at The Crazy Horse after work. Although the complete dinner package is prohibitively expensive, you might be able to watch from the bar while hanging on to your cash.

**Le Bal du Moulin Rouge,** pl. Blanche, 9*ème* (tel. 46 06 00 19). Mo. Blanche. The most famous of them all, this *revue* celebrated its centennial in 1989. Unfortunately, tourists—of the money-burning-a-hole-in-their-pocket variety—have replaced Toulouse-Lautrec and his leering disciples, who carefully selected their models from the comely performers on stage. Still, an impressive show with 100 dancers, singers, and castanet players. Opens at 8pm. Shows daily at 10pm and midnight. Reserve by phone 10am-7pm. Dinner and show from 670F. Show 465F.

**Crazy Horse Saloon,** 12, av. George V, 8*ème* (tel. 47 23 32 32). Mo. Alma-Marceau. More Parisians, fewer tourists; more flesh, less glamour. Crazy Horse just did some renovation and now has 380 seats. A pretty racy place. Dancers have names like Betty Buttocks and Funky Coconut. Shows Sun.-Thurs. at 9 and 11:35pm, Fri.-Sat. at 8pm, 10:30pm, and 12:50am. Reserve by phone 11am-6pm. Bar 195F, under 26 130F. Tables from 290F (2 drinks included).

**Les Folies-Bergère,** 32, rue Richer, 9*ème* (tel. 42 46 77 11). Mo. Cadet or Montmartre. Over 60 dancers and musicians in the music hall Manet immortalized with his strangely disturbing painting *Bar aux Folies-Bergère*. 105 years running. Shows Tues.-Sun. at 9:30pm. Reservations at box office daily 11am-6pm or by phone 11am-6:30pm. Seats 98F-399F.

**Le Monocle,** 60, bd. Edgar Quinet, 14*ème* (tel. 43 20 81 12). Mo. Edgar Quinet. This *cabaret feminin* (women's cabaret) caters to a sophisticated crowd. Transvestite revue starts at 9pm. Shows daily starting at 4pm. Drinks 100F and up.

## ■ Music

## CLASSICAL MUSIC, OPERA, AND DANCE

Paris toasts the classics under lamppost, spire, and chandelier. The city's squares, churches, and concert halls feature world-class performers from home and abroad. But visitors may find in France's cultural capital a giant with a limp, favoring classical music and opera in lieu of dance; the quality and quantity of classical repertoires here seem to follow the tastes of the city's patron, François Mitterrand. Acclaimed foreign and provincial dance companies swing into town to take up the slack; watch for posters and read *Pariscope*. Summer music and, to a lesser extent, dance festivals bring soloists from all over the world to a location near you. Connoisseurs will find the thick and indexed *Programme des Festivals* indispensable (free at *mairies* and at the tourist office). Paris offers cheap tickets to high culture in great quantities, thanks to a socialism that peddles the gentler arts to the masses. Beware, however, of rock-bottom prices. The Opéra Bastille suffers from an irremediable acoustical disease. While Balanchine may have said "see the music, hear the dance," you may not agree from the back row of the Opéra Garnier, Paris's ballet-only theater. Try to check a theater floor plan whenever possible. **ALPHA-FNAC,** 1-5, rue Pierre Lescot, Forum des Halles (tel. 40 41 40 00) is the popular booking agent (open Tues.-Sat. 10am-7:30pm, Mon. 1-7:30pm); call to find a FNAC near you. (See Festivals and Theater sections for details on annual events and last-minute tickets.)

**IRCAM, Institut de la Recherche et de la Coordination Acoustique/Musique,** Centre Pompidou, rue St-Martin, 4ème (tel. 44 78 48 16; for reservations 42 74 43 19). Mo. Rambuteau or Hôtel de Ville. Contemporary compositions sometimes accompanied by "film" or "theater." If it's weird and legit, it's here. Stop by the office near the Stravinsky fountain for schedules. (See also Museums.)

**Musée du Louvre,** 1er (tel. 40 20 52 99 for information; 40 20 52 29 for reservations). Mo. Palais-Royal/Musée du Louvre. Classical music in a classy auditorium. Tickets for individual concerts 100-250F, youth 80-200F. Open Sept.-June.

**Opéra de la Bastille,** pl. de la Bastille, 11ème (tel. 43 43 96 96). Mo. Bastille. The Opéra de la Bastille staged its first performance on July 14, 1989, the bicentennial of the French Revolution. Hailed by some as the hall to bring opera to the masses, decried by others as offensive to every aesthetic sensibility, this huge postmodern theater features classic opera, often re-interpreted to hum a materialist melody. The Bastille opera has acoustical problems, spread democratically throughout the theater, making this a bad place to go all-out for front row seats. Beware of seats in the 40s. Subtitles in English and French during impossible-to-understand lyrical performances. Tickets range from 50-560F. Call or write to obtain a free brochure of the season's events. Tickets can be purchased by writing and sending a check (foreigners can pay on arrival in Paris by presenting their letter of confirmation), by calling 44 73 13 00 Mon.-Sat. 11am-5:45pm, through minitel 3615 code THEA then Opéra Bastille, and at the opera house itself Mon.-Sat. 11am-6:30pm. Tickets go on sale on site 14 days before show. Opera reserves right to limit the number of tickets purchased. Reduced rush tickets for under 25, students, and over 65, often available 15 min. before show. Opéra-Bastille is wheelchair accessible; call 44 73 13 73 to make arrangements at least 15 days before the show. V.

**Opéra Comique,** 5, rue Favart, 2ème (tel. 42 86 88 83). Mo. Richelieu-Drouot. Operas on a lighter scale—from Rossini to Offenbach. Purchase tickets at the box office Mon.-Fri. 11am-6pm or reserve over the phone. Tickets 40-430F.

**Opéra Garnier,** pl. de l'Opéra, 9ème (tel. 40 17 35 35 for information, 47 42 53 71 for reservations). Mo. Opéra. The historic Opéra Garnier now hosts the Ballet de l'Opéra de Paris and visiting ballet troupes, as well as occasional operas and concerts by foreign companies and orchestras. Tickets available at the box office 2 weeks before each performance Mon.-Sat. 11am-6:30pm. Tickets 30-350F.

**Orchestre de Paris,** in the Salle Pleyel, 252, rue du Faubourg St-Honoré, 8ème (tel. 45 43 96 96). Mo. Ternes. The internationally renowned orchestra delivers first-class performances under the baton of music director Semyon Bychkov. Season runs Sept.-May; call or stop by for concert calendar. Tickets 50-250F.

**Théâtre des Champs-Elysées,** 15, av. Montaigne, 8ème (tel. 49 52 50 00, box office 47 20 36 37). Mo. Alma Marceau. Top international dance companies and orchestras. To play here is to "arrive" at the highbrow music scene. Buy tickets 3 weeks in advance. Box office open by telephone Mon.-Fri. 2-6pm; otherwise Tues.-Fri. 11am-7pm; Mon. and Sat. 11am-5pm. Tickets 40-500F.

**Théâtre Musical de Paris,** pl. du Châtelet, 1er (tel. 42 33 00 00). Mo. Châtelet. A superb 2300-seat theater normally reserved for guest orchestras and ballet companies. Magnificent acoustics. Call for a schedule. Tickets run 70-300F.

**Free concerts** are often held in churches and parks, especially when summer festivals scatter music throughout the city. These are extremely popular; get there early

# Let's Go wishes you safe and happy travels

These people are only a third of the 150 students who bring you the *Let's Go* guides. Most of us were still out on the road when this photo was taken, roaming the world in search of the best travel bargains.

Of course, *Let's Go* wouldn't be the same without the help of our readers. We count on you for advice we need to make *Let's Go* better every year. That's why we read each and every piece of mail we get from readers around the globe — and that's why we look forward to your response. Drop us a line, send us a postcard, tell us your stories. We're at 1 Story Street, Cambridge, Massachusetts 02138, USA. Enjoy your trip!

# LET'S GO®

if you want to breathe. Check the entertainment weeklies and the Alpha FNAC offices for concert notices. **AlloConcerts's** 24-hr. hotline provides info in French on free open-air concerts in the parks (tel. 42 76 50 00). The **American Church in Paris,** 65, quai d'Orsay, 7*ème* (tel. 47 05 07 89; Mo. Invalides or Alma Marceau), sponsors free concerts (Oct.-June Sun. at 6pm). **Eglise St-Merri** is also known for its free concerts (Sat. at 9pm and Sun. at 4pm, except in Aug.); contact Accueil Musical St-Merri, 76, rue de la Verrerie, 4*ème* (tel. 42 76 93 93; Mo. Châtelet).

Other churches, such as **Eglise St-Germain-des-Prés,** 3, pl. St-Germain-des-Prés, 6*ème* (Mo. St-Germain-des-Prés), **Eglise St-Eustache,** rue du Jour, 1*er* (Mo. Les Halles), and **Eglise St-Louis-en-l'Ile,** 19, rue St-Louis-en-l'Ile, 4*ème* (Mo. Pont Marie), stage frequent concerts that are somewhat expensive (70-100F for students), but feature fantastic acoustics and unbeatable atmosphere. For information about church concerts, call 43 29 68 68. **Ste-Chapelle** hosts concerts a few times per week in summer (sometimes free on Sun.). Contact the box office at 4, bd. du Palais, 1*er* (tel. 46 61 55 41; Mo. Cité; open daily 1:30-5:30pm; admission 110F, students 65F). Sunday concerts take place in the **Jardin du Luxembourg** band shell (tel. 42 37 20 00). Infrequent concerts in the Musée d'Orsay are free with a museum ticket.

## JAZZ

Some critics mourn that Paris is no longer the jazz center it once was. Although the big names find it more profitable to play the huge summer festivals in southern France and Switzerland, Paris still nourishes dozens of interesting clubs. While smoky cellars, blues, and booze may be a scene that students and backpackers want to explore, there is no shortage of chipper melodies to swing to. The Fête du Marias often features free big-band concerts; Parc de la Villette hosts jazz orchestras with a Latin beat in the summer. In the fall, the Jazz festival of Paris comes to town as venues high and low throw open their doors to celebs and lesser knowns (Oct. 19-Nov. 4). Not only do many fine, lesser-known American musicians play here, but the variety of music—including African, Antillean, Brazilian, and acid jazz—is astounding. For the most complete listings, pick up a copy of the monthly *Jazz Magazine* or check in one of the entertainment weeklies. Try to arrive on time, as many clubs stop seating people during the main show.

**Au Duc des Lombards,** 42, rue des Lombards, 1*er* (tel. 42 33 22 88). Mo. Châtelet. French jazz groups, with the occasional American singer or soloist. Dark, smoky, and packed with regulars, but don't feel intimidated; plenty of people come on nights without cover to hear the music and sit or stand for free. Jam sessions here are a treat. Call for prices. 1st drink about 60F. Open daily from 10:30pm.

**Café de la Plage,** 59, rue de Charonne, 11*ème* (tel. 47 00 91 60). Mo. Bastille. A 2-tiered club for a very trendy Bastille crowd. Upstairs African and Latin rhythms, downstairs acid jazz. *Cave* features DJ and live music. Upstairs open 8pm-2am. Downstairs 11pm-as long as you can stand. Obligatory 1st drink 100F.

**Caveau de la Huchette,** 5, rue de la Huchette, 5*ème* (tel. 43 26 65 05). Mo. St-Michel. Heavy on smoke and students. Nevertheless, still favored by Parisians who return for the eclectic programming—blues, swing, boogie, and gospel. The one-time tribunal, prison, and execution rooms here were used by Danton, Marat, St-Just, and Robespierre during the Revolution. Crowded on weekends. Min. age 18. Cover Sun.-Thurs. 55F, students 50F. Fri.-Sat. cover 60F. Drinks from 35F. Open Sun.-Thurs. 10pm-2:30am, Fri. 9:30pm-3am, Sat. 9:30pm-4am.

**Chica,** 71, rue St-Martin, 4*ème* (tel. 48 87 73 57). Mo. Châtelet. An excellent Brazilian restaurant (1st courses 45F, main dishes 90F). Devoted clients reserve tables downstairs in the *cave* for late-night samba. Live bands tune up at midnight. Fruit drinks 45F. Open Tues.-Thurs. and Sun. 8pm-2am, Fri.-Sat. 8pm-4:30am.

**Jazz O' Brazil,** 38, rue Mouffetard, 5*ème* (tel. 45 87 36 09). Mo. Monge. Excellent samba guitarists and new groups. Try the house drink *caitirissa* (lime juice and vodka). No cover. Drinks 55F. Open daily 9:30pm-2am.

**New Morning,** 7-9, rue des Petites-Ecuries, 10*ème* (tel. 45 23 51 41). Mo. Château d'Eau. 500 seats in a former printing plant. This place is about music, not ambience, so expect the best bookings in Paris, long lines, and a scramble for chairs. Attracts big names like Wynton Marsalis and Bobby McFerrin. All the greats have played here—from Chet Baker and Archie Shepp to Miles Davis. Open Sept.-July 9:30pm; times vary. Admission 110F.

**Le Passage du Nord Ouest,** 13, rue du Faubourg Montmartre, 9ème (tel. 40 22 92 66). Mo. Rue Montmartre. This 3-year old *art-et-essai* space books jazz from Brazil to the Mississippi, Egypt to Cameroon. Times vary with the event; call or stop by for a program. Admission around 120F.

**Le Petit Journal St-Michel,** 71, bd. St-Michel, 5ème (tel. 43 26 28 59). Mo. Luxembourg. A crowded but intimate establishment, where students mix with forty-somethings reminiscing about 1968. New Orleans bands and first-class performers play in this Parisian center of the "Old Style." Music Sept.-July Mon.-Sat. 10pm-2:30am. Obligatory 1st drink 100F, 40F thereafter.

**Le Petit Opportun,** 15, rue des Lavandières-Ste-Opportune, 1er (tel. 42 36 01 36). Mo. Châtelet. A relaxed and unpolished pub, where you can hear some of the best modern jazz around, including a lot of American bands and soloists. The club is tiny (60 seats), and so popular that it ought to seat 500. Come early. Open Sept.-July Tues.-Sat. from 11pm; bar open until 3am. 1st drink 100F, 50F thereafter.

**Slow Club,** 130, rue de Rivoli, 1er (tel. 42 33 84 30). Mo. Châtelet. Miles Davis's favorite jazz club in Paris. Big bands, traditional jazz, and Dixieland in a wonderful old-time setting. Expect dancing and a crowd in the 30s. Weekday cover 55F. Weekend cover from 70F. Women and students 5F less during the week. Drinks from 18F. Open Tues.-Thurs. 10pm-2:30am, Fri. 10pm-3:30am, Sat. 10pm-4am.

**Théâtre Dunois,** 28, rue Dunois, 13ème (tel. 45 84 72 00). Mo. Chevaleret. A newly renovated theater with 200 seats specializing in American avant-garde jazz. Bar serves drinks from 15-40F. Cover 80F. Open daily 10pm-2am.

# ■ Discos and Rock Clubs

Paris is not Barcelona, Montréal, or Buenos Aires; you won't find entire streets filled with young people waiting and struggling to get into discos. Instead, the clubs are small, private, and nearly impossible to find out about, unless you're a native. The discos that are "in" (or even in business) change drastically from year to year; only a few have been popular since the 1960s. Many Parisian clubs are officially private, which means they have the right to pick and choose their clientele. The management can evaluate prospective customers through peepholes in the handle-less front doors. Parisians tend to dress up more than North Americans for a night on the town; haggard backpackers might be wise to try a bar instead.

In general, word of mouth is the best guide to the current scene. Some of the smaller places in the *quartier latin* admit almost anyone who is sufficiently decked out. To access one of the more exclusive places, you need to accompany a regular. Otherwise, plan to look good, very good, don't publicize your foreignness, and be prepared to shell out a good amount of money. Many clubs reserve the right to refuse entry to unaccompanied men. Women often get a discount or get in free, but don't go alone unless you're looking for lots of amorous attention.

The French dance any way they please and often alone. The music is often mediocre, with fast-paced disco and new wave pop. Weekdays are cheaper and less crowded so you'll have a better chance of moving, but most of the action happens on weekends. **Les Bains** is still the best, but also most expensive and most exclusive. For a list of gay and lesbian dance clubs, see Bisexual, Gay, and Lesbian Paris.

**Les Bains,** 7, rue du Bourg l'Abbé, 3ème (tel. 48 87 01 80). Mo. Réaumur-Sébastopol. Ultra-selective and ultra-expensive, but worth it—if you can get in past the fearless bouncers. Prince established the joint's reputation with a surprise free concert a few years ago. Not only that, but it used to be a public bath that welcomed the likes of Marcel Proust into its midst. Lots of models and super-attractive people dressed to those proverbial nines. Cover and 1st drink 140F, 2nd drink 100F. Can you stand a 3rd? Open Tues.-Sun. 11:30pm-6am.

**Le Balajo,** 9, rue de Lappe, 11ème (tel. 47 00 07 87). Mo. Bastille. Formerly the favorite stage of Edith Piaf. Founded in 1936 by Jo France, hence the *Bal à Jo.* Jammed with a youthful crowd with a clear love of excitement. Cover and 1st drink 100F. Open Mon. and Wed.-Sat. 11pm-5am.

**La Casbah,** 18-20, rue de la Forge Royale, 11ème (tel. 43 71 71 89). Mo. Faidherbe-Chaligny. This funky dance club mixes pop music with Arabic music. Very elegant, but strict door policy. Cover 100F. Open daily 9pm-6am.

**Le Cirque,** 49, rue de Ponthieu, 8ème (tel. 42 25 12 13). Mo. Franklin D. Roosevelt. Currently one of the hottest clubs in Paris. Mixed gay and straight crowd. Mon-Thurs. nights no cover, Fri.-Sun 90F. Open daily 10:30pm-noon.

**Flash Back,** 18, rue des Quatre Vents, 6ème (tel. 43 25 56 10). Mo. Odéon. Two levels of unusual, secluded lounges and a small dance floor complete with mirrored walls and shiny disco ball. Tues. night is retro—70s and early 80s tunes. Thurs. night, there's a floor show featuring anything from Lola the showgirl to fly dancers. Comfortable, easy atmosphere among Paris's beautiful youth. Cover 65F, Sun.-Thurs. women free. Drinks 70F. Open Tues.-Sat. 11pm-6am (sunrise).

**Keur Samba,** 79, rue de la Boétie, 8ème (tel. 43 59 03 10). Mo. Franklin D. Roosevelt. This club is popular among Paris's West African community because of its wealth of music from the Congo, the Ivory Coast, and the Antilles. Very expensive but crazy fun. Cover 120F. Drinks 45-65F. Open midnight-6am.

**Le Palace,** 8, rue du Faubourg Montmartre, 9ème (tel. 42 46 10 87). Mo. Montmartre. A funky disco, although its days as the hottest club in Paris have gone by. If you hit a private party and still get in, the music and crowd can be very cool. Otherwise, the music is all too top-40.A mix of happy high school students wanting to "get together" and some older people wanting to get in on the action. Still, the place is huge (up to 2000 people per night), with multi-level dance floors, each with separate bars and different music. American cocktails and occasional rock concerts. Cover and 1 drink Tues.-Thurs. 100F, Fri.-Sat. 130F, Sun. 130F for men, women free. Subsequent drinks 85F. Open Tues.-Sun. 11:30pm-6am. The British owners also run **Le Central,** 102, av. des Champs-Elysées, 8ème (Mo. George V). Same prices, with older clientele and a higher percentage of foreigners.

**Le Saint,** 7, rue Saint-Séverin, 5ème (tel. 43 25 50 04). Mo. Saint-Michel. Plays a wide range of music, rap, soul, R&B, retro, reggae, and zouk. A small club, frequented by a crowd of regulars who like to get down and dance. Tues.-Thurs. Cover 50F, Fri. 70F, Sat. 80F. Drinks 15-50F. Open 11pm-6am.

**Scala de Paris,** 188bis, rue de Rivoli, 1er (tel. 42 61 64 00). Mo. Palais-Royal. Not as well-known or trendy as some of the other clubs, but becoming more and more popular as the others decline. Young (18-24) crowd dances to house and techno. Atmosphere changes a bit every night. Lots of foreigners. Cover Sun.-Thurs. 80F, women free, Fri. 80F, Sat. 90F. Additional drinks 45F. Open daily 11:30pm-6am.

**Le Tabou,** 33, rue Dauphine, 6ème (tel. 43 25 66 33). Mo. Odéon. An older, very chic crowd of *habitués* make this club somewhat difficult to get into. Being in pairs, and very well dressed (not clubby, more elegant) will give you a fighting chance. Music ranges from reggae to rock to house, depending on DJ. Cover and 1st drink Mon.-Thurs. 70F, Fri.-Sat. 80F. Drinks from 50F. Open daily 11pm-dawn.

For **folk music,** try the restaurant Au Limonaire (see Restaurants—12ème *arrondissement).* Also popular in France are clubs specializing in **Brazilian samba** and **African music:**

**Chez Félix,** 23, rue Mouffetard, 5ème (tel. 47 07 68 78). Mo. Monge. Eat on the top level; sway to the excellent Brazilian beat in the *caves.* Music 11pm-dawn. Cover and first drink 100F, subsequent drinks 50F. Open Sept.-July Tues.-Sat. 8pm-5am.

**La Plantation,** 45, rue Montpensier, 1er (tel. 49 27 06 21). Mo. Palais-Royal. Friendly place playing mostly African, Antillean, and salsa music. Dress well. Doesn't pick up until 2am. Cover and first drink 90F, subsequent drinks 50F. Open Tues.-Sun. 11pm-dawn.

**Le Tchatch au Tango,** 13, rue au Maire, 3ème (tel. 42 72 17 78). Mo. Arts et Métiers. Crowd dances to Antillean, African, salsa, and zouk music. Regulars all know each other. Wed. is salsa night; Fri.-Sat. and the eves of holidays are mostly zouk. Cover Wed. 50F, Fri. 40F, Sat. and eves of holidays 60F. Drinks 25-40F. Open Wed., Fri.-Sat., and eves of holidays 11pm-5am.

**Les Trottoirs de Buenos Aires,** 37, rue des Lombards, 1er (tel. 40 26 28 58). Mo. Châtelet. An old but popular club playing mostly tango, as well as other Latin-American rhythms. Live performances are common. Wed.-Sat. cover 100F. Sun and Tues. no cover but compulsory drink, 70F. Drinks 40-60F.

## ■ Bars

Apart from booze and chairs, there is no common denominator to the Parisian bar scene. Let *arrondissement* reputations be your guide. Bars in the 5ème and 6ème often cater to anglophone students, while the Marais and Bastille—the chic quarters of the moment—host lively crowds of Paris's young, hip, and friendly. Draught beer is *bière (à la) pression; kir* is a mixture of white wine and *cassis*. The bartender is the *bar-man*. As with cafés, expect two list prices for drinks; stand at the bar and pay less or sit and pay a few francs more for *ambiance*. Law dictates a price increase after 10pm, but no one really ventures out before this wee hour.

**Au Petit Fer à Cheval,** 30, rue Vieille-du-Temple, 4ème (tel. 42 72 47 47). Mo. St-Paul. A mainstay of the Marais crowd. Cozy up to the U-shaped zinc counter that gives the bar its name. People-watch from the terrace or head to the back room for a tête-à-tête. Beer 16F. Cocktails 35F. Try the *salade de petit fer à cheval* (58F). Open Mon.-Fri. 9am-2am, Sat.-Sun. 11am-2am. Last call 2:30am.

**Le Bar sans Nom,** 49, rue de Lappe, 11ème (tel. 48 05 59 36). Mo. Bastille. There's nothing cooler than this bar—cavernous, deep crimson, and packed with the hippest of the hip. Beer 20F. Cocktails 44F. Open daily 10:30pm-2am.

**Café de l'Industrie,** 16, rue St-Sabin, 11ème (tel. 47 00 13 53). Mo. Bastille. They think it's a café; we think it's a bar. Garage-sale assemblage of odd chairs, alligator skins, and tassled lamps alongside contemporary art and people too hip to try. Quick service and huge drinks. Beer 16-27F. Cocktails 25-40F. Good selection of food: *tagliatella carbonara* 42F. Open Sun.-Fri. 11am-2am.

**La Chope des Artistes,** 42, rue du Faubourg St-Martin, 10ème (tel. 42 02 86 76). Mo. Strasbourg St-Denis. Ochre-colored walls and chandelier frame a cozy piano bar. Theater-goers often head here for a cocktail (around 50F) and a musical evening, after 8pm. The young proprietor sets the tone; many an *artiste* while away the hours here. Open Tues.-Sat. 8am-2am.

**L'Entrepot,** 14, rue de Charonne, 11ème. Mo. Bastille. This authentic little bar pulsates with an electric Parisian crowd. A real pool table and loads of atmosphere—mostly chic, yuppie. Drinks from 50F. Open daily 7pm-2am.

**Finnegan's Wake,** 9, rue des Boulangers, 5ème (tel. 46 34 23 65). Mo. Jussieu or Cardinal Lemoine. A boisterous Irish pub set in a renovated 14th-century wine cellar. Pours the best pints of Guinness in the city (15-30F), and hosts a variety of Irish cultural events. Call about poetry readings, jig, and Gaelic lessons. A Bloomsday extravaganza, of course. During school year open Mon.-Fri. 8am-12:30am.

**James Joyce Pub,** 71, bd. Gouvion-St-Cyr (tel. 44 09 70 32), near the Palais des Congrès. Mo. Porte Maillot. The James Joyce is one of Paris's three most lively Irish pubs (next to Kitty O'Shea's (tel. 40 15 00 30) and Finnegan's Wake). The mahogany bar and tall green barstools create a warm backdrop to the daily and nightly crowd of Irish, British, and American expatriates downing a pint. A 50F lunch *menu* features boiled potatoes and smoked Irish salmon. Run by a friendly Irish staff, the pub is full of James Joyce paraphernalia, including a number of letters and pages penned in his own hand. Open daily noon-1:30am.

**La Micro Brasserie,** 106, rue de Richelieu, 2ème (tel. 42 96 55 31). Mo. Richelieu-Drouot. Possibly the best place for beer in Paris. You can choose from more than 60 kinds, but the best deals are on the beers they brew themselves. The Morgane should not be missed: slightly reddish, it is called in French a *bière rousse*. Also, try mussels and fries with your drinks (40F). You can visit the brewery downstairs Tues. and Thurs. 10am-8pm without paying extra. Before 10pm house beer is 12F at the bar or 13-14F at a table; after 10pm both beers go for 20F. Between 5 and 7:30pm, buy 1 beer and get 1 free. Open daily noon-midnight.

**La Perla,** 26, rue François-Miron, 4ème (tel. 42 77 59 40). Mo. Hôtel de Ville. The best of the Parisian Tex-Mex rage, La Perla mixes a superb margarita (48F). A star in the Marais nightlife, packed with laid-back, turned-out twenty-somethings. Beer on tap 20F, bottles 30F. *Quesadillas* 30-38F. *Fajitas* 42F. Open daily noon-2am.

**Polly Magoo,** 13, rue St-Jacques, 5ème (tel. 46 33 33 64). Mo. St-Michel. When the Violon Dingue closes at 2am, Polly's gets going. Super-friendly, amazingly lively crowd often bubbles over into the street. Beer on tap 12-19F. Open noon-5am.

**Pub St-Germain-des-Prés,** 17, rue de l'Ancienne Comédie, 6ème (tel. 43 29 38 70). Mo. Odéon. The place where they have to take you in, all night, every night. Perhaps the largest and least interesting pub in Europe, this 7-room mammoth bar is a long-time favorite for American students looking for a good time. Parisians go elsewhere. 100 types of whisky. 450 different types of bottled beer, with 24 on tap. Beers and cocktails start at an outrageous 75F per bottle. Open 24 hrs.

**Le Violon Dingue,** 46, rue de la Montagne Ste-Geneviève, 5ème. Mo. Maubert-Mutualité. Reminiscent of an American frat party with its American waiters, packed interior, and fast-flowing beer. C-SPAN and widescreen TV make this a good bet for Super Bowl Sunday. Bottled beer starts at 25F, on tap 32F. Cocktails from 30F. Open daily 6pm-2am.

# ■ Literary Life

If your French is good, Paris still offers the same range of intellectual pursuits that it did when Rousseau and Montesquieu jabbered about liberty and the state of nature. Many art museums sponsor conferences, lectures, and colloquia. The **Louvre,** for example, has an ongoing series of lectures and special colloquia on both the permanent collection and on visiting exhibitions in the Hall Napoléon. (Call 40 20 50 50 for more information.) The **Château de Versailles** offers an ongoing schedule of discussions and walking lectures by leading scholars on issues related to the Sun King, the French court, and Marie-Antoinette lore. (Call 30 84 76 18 for details.)

Many bookstores in the area offer free lecture series by visiting writers and poetry slams. The weekly publications always list walking tours of otherwise inaccessible *galleries, maisons,* and the like under the *Conférences* listings. These tours usually cost 30 to 60F and focus on the historical, architectural, social, artistic, or anthropological constructions surrounding a particular *quartier,* building, or time period.

**Le Club des Poètes,** 30, rue de Bourgogne, 7ème (tel. 47 05 06 03). Mo. Varenne. Dedicated to refreshing the stressed-out automata of Parisian society, former TV personality Jean-Pierre Rosnay hosts a nightly *"spectacle de poésie,"* beginning at 10:15pm. Artists read poetry, French and foreign, known and obscure alike in a cozy, country atmosphere. (See Restaurants for dinner information.) The proprietor also directs the 24-hr. poetry hotline called "Allô Poésie" (tel. 45 50 32 33).

**Finnegan's Wake,** 9, rue des Boulangers, 5ème (tel. 46 34 23 65). Mo. Jussieu Cardinal Lemoine. This intimate Irish pub on a small hilly street in the 5ème is renowned for its ongoing readings of Irish prose and poetry by James Joyce, W. B. Yeats, and other Irish writers. Call ahead for a schedule. Usually Irish folk music as well. Drinks 25-40F. Open Mon.-Fri. 10am-midnight, Sat.-Sun. 4pm-midnight.

**Maison de Radio-France,** 116, av. du Président Kennedy, 16ème (tel. 42 30 33 83). Mo. Passy, Ranelagh, or Mirabeau; RER Line C Av. du Pt. Kennedy/Maison de Radio-France. Yes, you too can sit in the audience and listen while French intellectuals debate away on live, prime-time radio! Programming and schedule varies with season. Call above number for details.

**Shakespeare and Co.,** 37, rue de la Bûcherie, 5ème. Mo. St-Michel. See Bookstores

**The Village Voice,** 6, rue Princesse, 6ème (tel. 46 33 36 47). Mo. Mabillon. This progressive English bookstore, run by the elegant Odile Héllier, sponsors readings by visiting writers. Call for details, or stop by and check out the guest collection of American and feminist literatures. Open Mon. 2-8pm and Tues.-Sat. 11am-8pm.

# ■ Offbeat Entertainment

*But ah, Paris! He who has not stopped in admiration of your dark passageways, before your glimpses of light, in your blind alleys deep and silent, he who has not heard your murmur between midnight and two in the morning, does not know your true poetry, not your strange and vast antitheses.*

—Honoré de Balzac

For a free show without the educational commentary, walk around the monuments at night. Everything from the Panthéon to the Eiffel Tower, Notre Dame, and Obélisque glows until midnight, taking on a whole new light. Pick up the pamphlet *Paris Illuminé* at the tourist office or your local *mairie* for a complete listing.

You've seen them slowly ploughing along the Seine in the darkness, then coming to life with their mega-watt spotlights and deafening speaker systems. Now it's time for you to experience them first-hand. A ride on the **bateaux-mouches** (tel. 42 25 96 10) river boats provides a classic, if highly goofy, tour of Seine-side Paris. Be prepared to laugh at the one-and-a-half hours of continuous sight-commentary in five languages and dozens of tourists straining their necks to peer over the next person. Why does the French version sound about twice as long? It's not your imagination—the translations are notoriously sparse. The ride is particularly worthwhile if taken at night. (Departures every ½hr. 10am-10:30pm from the Right Bank pier near Pont d'Alma. Mo. Alma-Marceau. 30F, under 14 15F.) **Vert Galant** boats (tel. 46 33 98 38) are another option. (Departures every ½hr. 10am-noon, 1:30-6:30pm and 9-10:30pm from the Pont Neuf landing. Mo. Pont-Neuf or Louvre. 40F, under 10 20F.) The **Canauxrama** (tel. 42 39 15 00) boat tours of Paris get excellent reviews for their 3-hour tour down the Canal St-Martin. The tour leaves at 9:15am from Bassin de la Villette, 5bis, quai de la Loire, 19ème (Mo. Jaurès) and at 2:30pm from Port de l'Arsenal facing 50, quai de la Bastille, 12ème (Mo. Bastille). (75F, students 60F, under 12 45F, under 6 free, weekends 75F.) Day-long trips along the Canal de l'Ourcq, through narrow locks, and to a small canal village leave the Bassin de la Villette at 8:30am Thursday through Tuesday (195F; reserve ahead; unsuitable for children). The **Batobus** (tel. 47 05 50 00) makes frequent stops along both sides of the river from April to September. A spin on this ridiculous form of transportation costs 10F (day pass 50F). Buy tickets on board.

For a low-stress lesson on the history of the City of Lights, head for 78bis, bd. des Batignolles (Mo. Villiers or Rome), where you can view a screening of **Paristoric: "Paris...le Film"** (tel. 42 93 93 46). This 45-minute multi-media spectacle combines a montage of superimposed photos and artwork of Paris past and present with classical music and modern French tunes. No summer vacation slideshow, this slick production is a private venture done with painstaking historical accuracy, primarily through consultation with an advisor from the Carnavalet Museum. The narration (headsets provide simultaneous translation in 7 languages) traces the 2000 years of Paris's history. Watch Paris's boundaries change and expand, roads widen, and landscape evolve, monument by monument, according to the whims, political leanings, and unabashed egoism of the countless rulers who have called Paris home. The technique is innovative, and the quotes and poetry sprinkled throughout are wholly entertaining. Good for a rainy day, that afternoon when you just can't make that *métro* trip to see one more monument, or as a preliminary introduction to Paris. (Shows daily on the hour 9am-9pm. 70F. Families or holders of weekly and monthly *métro* passes 50F, students and under 18 40F. Fully wheelchair accessible.)

The French have also invented a new art form—take an impressive building, add a light show, superimpose a recorded message about the glorious history of the building, the region, or the country, *et voilà:* **son et lumière.** Shown mostly in the suburbs, it's as tacky as it sounds, but that's half the fun.

# Festivals and Other Seasonal Events

The French love of celebration is most evident in Paris, where masses of people rush into the streets to drink, dance, and generally lose themselves in the spirit of the *fête* (festival) or *foire* (fair). The gatherings in Washington on July 4, in Times Square on New Year's Eve, on Parliament Hill on July 1, or in Auckland, ever, pale before the assemblages of humanity on hand for Bastille Day fireworks or the arrival of the New Year. The **tourist office,** 127, av. des Champs-Elysées, 8ème (tel. 47 23 61 72; Mo. Charles de Gaulle-Etoile), distributes the multilingual *Saisons de Paris 1994,* a booklet listing all the celebrations. The English information number (tel. 47 20 88 98 or 49 52 53 56) reports a weekly summary of current festivals. *Pariscope* lists *fêtes populaires* for the coming week. You can also get a listing of festivals from the **French National Tourist Office** (see Essentials)

**Foire du Trône,** Neuilly Lawn of the Bois de Vincennes. Mo. Porte Dorée. A gigantic amusement park. End of March-May. Open 2pm-midnight.

**Festival de Musique de St-Denis** (tel. 42 43 72 72). Late May-late June.

**Festival de Paris,** 38, rue des Blancs-Manteaux, 4ème (tel. 40 26 45 34). Mo. St-Paul. Great orchestras and choruses. Mid-May to late June. Admission 50-500F.

**Festival de Versailles** (tel. 30 21 20 20, *poste* 234). Ballet, operas, concerts, and theater. Prices vary radically from one event to another. Late May-late June.

**Les Trois Heures de Paris** (tel. 49 77 06 40). A day-long regatta on the Seine on a Sat. in May. Races between pont d'Austerlitz and Ile St-Louis.

**Festival de la Butte Montmartre,** 14bis, rue Ste-Isaure, 18ème (tel. 42 62 46 22). Mo. Jules Joffrin. Experimental drama, dance, and jazz. Mid-June to mid-July.

**Festival Chopin** (tel. 45 22 28 74). Concerts and recitals held at the Orangerie de la Bagatelle in the Bois de Boulogne. June-July.

**Festival Foire St-Germain** (tel. 43 29 12 78). Antique fair in pl. St-Sulpice, concerts in the Mairie du 6ème. Both free. Mid-June to early July.

**Festival du Marais,** 68, rue François Miron, 4ème (tel. 45 23 18 25). Mo. St-Paul. Classical and jazz music, theater, and exhibits. Early June-early July.

**Festival d'Orgue à St-Eustache** (tel. 45 22 28 74). Organ concerts in the beautiful St-Eustache church. Tickets 70-120F, on sale at ARGOS, 34, rue de Laborde, 8ème (Mo. St-Augustin). Mid-June to early July.

**Fête du Cinéma,** June 28. One movie ticket allows you to go from theater to theater until your head spins with movies. Three days.

**Fête de la Musique.** On June 21, the city celebrates the first day of summer with major rock concerts and audacious partying in all the big *places.* Free.

**Fêtes du Pont Neuf** (tel. 42 77 92 26). Mo. Pont Neuf. The bridge is opened for dancing, music, street artists, and minstrels. A weekend in late June.

**Musique en Sorbonne,** 47, rue des Ecoles, 5ème (tel. 42 62 71 71). Mo. Maubert-Mutualité. Classical music. Late June-early July. Admission 60-140F.

**Nuit de la St-Jean,** 18ème. Mo. Abbesses.For the Feast of St. John the Baptist, June 24. Magnificent fireworks at 11pm in front of the marble dome of Sacré-Coeur.

**Bastille Day,** July 14. *Vive la République,* and pass the champagne. The day starts with the army parading down the Champs-Elysées and ends with fireworks. Traditional street dances are held on the eve at the tip of Ile St-Louis (the Communist Party always throws its gala there), the Hôtel de Ville, pl. de la Contrescarpe, and of course, pl. de la Bastille, where it all began. Dancing continues the next night. Unfortunately, the entire city also becomes a nightmarish combat zone of leering men cunningly tossing firecrackers under the feet of unsuspecting bystanders.

**Festival Estival,** 20, rue Geoffroy-l'Asnier, 4ème (tel. 48 04 98 01). Mo. Pont Marie or St-Paul. Opera, chamber music. Early July to mid-Sept. Admission 25-40F.

**End of the Tour de France,** fourth Sun. in July. Expect a huge crowd.

**Festival d'Automne** (tel. 42 96 12 27). Drama, ballet, expositions. Late Sept.-Dec.

**Festival de l'Ile-de-France** (tel. 47 39 28 26). Late Sept.-late Dec.

**Fête de l'Humanité,** parc de la Courneuve. Take the *métro* to Porte de la Villette and then one of the special buses. The annual fair of the French Communist Party—like nothing you've ever seen. Entertainers in recent years have included

Charles Mingus, Marcel Marceau, the Bolshoi Ballet, and radical theater troupes. A cross between the Illinois State Fair, the Republican Convention, and Woodstock you don't have to be a Communist to enjoy it. 2nd or 3rd week of Sept.

**Festival d'Art Sacré,** 4, rue Jules-Cousin, *4ème* (tel. 42 77 92 26). Sacred music b Radio France Philharmonic Orchestra and Choir of Cologne. Early Oct.-Dec.

**Festival de Jazz de Paris,** 5, rue Bellart, 15*ème* (tel. 47 83 33 58). Mo. Ségu Everyone on the European circuit (Nice, Antibes, Montreux, etc.) should be here At the Théâtre Musical de Paris and the Théâtre de la Ville. Late Oct.-early Nov.

**Fête des Vendanges à Montmartre,** rue Saules, 18*ème*. Mo. Lamarck-Caulair court. Celebration of the harvest of the vineyards on Montmartre. First Sat. in Oct

**Rallye Paris-Deauville** (tel. 46 24 37 38). More than 100 vintage cars assemble a the Trocadéro fountains. 7am on a Fri. in early Oct. Race in Deauville on Sun.

**Concours International de Danse de Paris** (tel. 45 22 28 74). Week-long danc competition in mid-Nov.

**Festival Internationale de la Guitarre** (tel. 45 23 18 25). Concerts in many Par sian churches. Mid-Nov. to mid-Dec.

**Christmas Eve.** At midnight Notre-Dame becomes what it only claims to be th rest of the year: the cathedral of the city of Paris.

**New Year's Eve.** Bd. St-Michel and Champs-Elysées transform into pedestria malls, much to the dismay of the cops who still attempt to direct traffic.

# ■ Sports

## PARTICIPATORY SPORTS

You may find it hard to believe as you trudge around inner-city pavement, but Par and its surroundings teem with sporting opportunities. Your number one bes resource for information is the Mairie de Paris's sports hotline, **Allo-Sports** (tel. 4 76 54 54; open Mon.-Thurs. 10:30am-5pm, Fri. 10:30am-4:30pm). They also have a office called **l'Espace Information Jeunesse et Sports,** 25, bd. Bourdon, *4ème* (te 40 45 90 00). Many of the introductory courses offered by the city are for residen only, but if you're in town for an extended period, you may be able to talk your wa into one. Also for residents, the city coordinates summer introductory courses to variety of sports for kids. All such courses are offered in French only. *Pariscope* (se Essentials—Publications) has a 5-page *"Sports et Loisirs"* listing every week. *L'Off ciel des Spectacles* has a two-page sports spread as well, though not nearly as con prehensive a list. Also see *Paris Pas Cher* for lists of affordable gyms geared towar the long-term visitor. Hostels, hotels, and student services at the Université de Par may have suggestions for students.

The following are a grab-bag of activities and recommendations intended for th budget traveler. Sports facilities of all kinds form a ring around Paris, lining the inne and outer edges. While many house private clubs, specialized sports schools, c host pro events, some are open to the public.

**Jogging:** Joggers huff and puff around the park on their lunch hour and on wee ends. Warning: a person plugged into a Walkman and running around deserted c unknown areas may be a prime target for mugging. The **Champs de Mars,** 7*èm* (Mo. Bir Hakeim), is a popular in-city jogging spots, with a 2.5km path around th outside. The leafy **Jardin du Luxembourg,** 6*ème* (Mo. Cluny-La Sorbonne offers a 1.6km circuit. **Parc Monceau,** 8*ème* (Mo. Monceau), crawls with kic but remains serenely green; 1km loop. **Parc des Buttes Chaumont,** 19*ème* (Mc Buttes Chaumont), offers labyrinthine paths that feel uphill all the way. Th **Tuileries Gardens,** 1*er* (Mo. Concorde or Tuileries), provides a 1.6km route The **Canal St-Martin,** 10*ème*, is relatively safe and rather picturesque. The **Boi de Boulogne,** 16*ème*, has 35km of trails. Get a hold of a map before going in twisty routes can be confusing. Less renowned is the **Bois de Vincennes,** 12*èm* Or you can begin in the northeast at the medieval **Château de Vincennes** (Mc Château de Vincennes). For 250F, you can join the **Association culturelle d sport de plein air (ACSP),** stade de la Muette, 60, bd. Lannes, 16*ème* (tel. 45 2

74 87; Mo. Avenue Foch), which organizes runs in the Bois de Boulogne (Sat.-Sun. 10am-noon).

**Swimming:** The Mairie de Paris has created a network of public-access pools. Opening hours vary, but all are open in summer (Mon. 2-7pm, Tues.-Sat. 7am-7:30pm, and Sun. 8am-5pm). Call Allo-Sports to have a copy of *Les Piscines à Paris* sent to you, or pick one up at a *mairie*. It lists hours and services available at each pool. A warning on swimming laps in France: lane lines are not marked. Be prepared for confusion. Entry to any **municipal pool** 10F, under 17, over 64, or those accompanying children but not swimming 5F. Ask about 1-yr. passes and youth discounts. Under 8 must be accompanied by an adult. Last entry 30 min. before closing; pools are cleared 15 min. before closing. Some pools have a *"nocturne,"* 1 or 2 nights a week, when they are open past 8pm. **Municipale concédée** pools grant public time to the municipality and thus are a bit more expensive. They include the large, well-lit **Piscine des Halles,** level 3 of the Les Halles complex, 1er (tel. 42 36 98 44). Open Tues. and Thurs.-Fri. 11:30am-10pm, Wed. 10am-7pm, Sat.-Sun. 9am-5pm. Last entry 45min. before closing; pool cleared 30min. before closing. Admission 21F, under 16 16F. Pass for 10 entries 190F, under 16 150F. Wheelchair accessible. Also the **Piscine Pontoise-Quartier Latin,** 19, rue de Pontoise, 5ème (tel. 43 54 06 23; Mo. Maubert-Mutualité), a snazzy pool with a counter-current machine (admission 20F, students 18F, under 16 16F). Neither municipally owned nor *municipale concédée,* the **Piscine Deligny,** facing 25, quai Anatole France, 7ème (tel. 45 51 72 15; Mo. Chambre des Députés), was one of Paris's best-known and best-loved pools and the first place to allow topless bathing in the city. Built near the turn of the century on the hulls of two ships floating on the Seine, this pool was the centerpiece of the rollicking Deligny club. Unfortunately it sunk in 1993.

**Tennis:** Serious players should bring their equipment; Paris boasts of 170 municipal tennis courts in 45 "tennis centers," each open to the individual player. Free introductory lessons offered to children. To use the municipal courts, apply for a free **Carte Paris Tennis,** which enables you to reserve space through minitel. Court reservation is crucial, especially in summer. Pick up an application at one of the tennis centers scattered throughout the city. Cards take 5 weeks to process. For municipal courts, rates are low (25F/ hour).

**Gyms and Fitness: Alesia Club,** 143, rue d'Alésia, 14ème (tel. 45 42 91 05; Mo. Alésia), has a gym, sauna, and other facilities and will sell you a membership for the day (206F). If you feel the need of a beach, or perhaps just a sauna, jacuzzi, wavepool, and waterslide, find them at **Acquaboulevard,** 4, rue Louis Armand, 15ème (tel. 40 60 10 00; Mo. Balard or Porte de Versailles). Come early in the morning to avoid the crowds. (Open Sun.-Thurs. 9am-11pm, Fri.-Sat. 8am-midnight. Admission 68F for 4hr.; 75F on weekends. More facilities are available to club members: annual membership 1500F, classes supplement 100F per month.) Try the **Espace Vit'Halles**, 48, rue Rambuteau, 3ème (tel. 42 77 21 71), near Les Halles in place Beaubourg. Labelled "the American-style health club you've been looking for," Vit'Halles offers both long-term and short-term memberships (600F per month; open daily 10am-11pm). In the parks and gardens of the city, Sun. mornings (9:30am-noon) bring physical education monitors suggesting open-air exercises appropriate to your needs (free).

**Cycling:** The city proper is not a good place for a leisurely afternoon pedal, but cyclists happily while away the hours in the **Bois de Vincennes,** 12ème, around Lac Daumesnil (Mo. Porte Dorée) or deeper into the woods. The **Bois de Boulogne,** 16ème, officially boasts of 8km of bike paths, but any cyclist can make up an original route among the innumerable trees. The **canal de l'Ourcq** passes through the Parc de la Villette, 30, av. Corentin Cariou, 19ème (Mo. Porte de la Villette), and has a bicycle path alongside. English-language mountain bike tours of the sights of Paris are available for the adventuresome. For more information on bike rental and cycling around the city, consult the Essentials section under Getting Around—Bicycle. Long-distance cyclists may want to try the 109km ride out to **Ferté Milon** in the province of Aisne. Just follow the canal as far as it goes. The real test, of course, is getting back. Also consider the **Forêt de Fontainebleau** (see Daytrips).

SPECTATOR SPORTS

**Roller Skating:** Truly hip roller skaters perform slalom and other more death-defying feats in front of the Palais de Chaillot in the Jardins du Trocadéro. (Roller blades have yet to really hit Paris.) Rent skates at **La Main Jaune,** pl. de la Porte-de-Champerret, 17ème (tel. 47 63 26 47; Mo. Porte de Champerret). Open Wed. and Sat.-Sun. 2:30-7pm, Fri.-Sat. and holidays 10pm-dawn. Admission Wed., Sat. evening, and Sun. 40F, skate rental 10F; Fri. and Sat. night 70F, skate rental 15F.

**Fishing, Golfing, and Bowling:** The legendary, imperturbable Seine fishermen are gone, but sewer authorities hope to have the river fishable in a few years. For now, contact the **Annicale des Pêcheurs de Neuilly, Levallois, et environs,** Base Halientique de la Jatte, 19, bd. de Levallois prolongé, 92000 Levallois-Perret (tel. 43 48 36 34). They'll fill you in on angling in the Bois de Boulogne. Golf enthusiasts will find a wealth of possibilities in Paris. A number of golf courses in the city can sign you up immediately for as many holes as you want. Prices vary, but expect every place to be *cher.* Try **Club Rennes Raspail,** 149, rue de Rennes, 15ème (tel. 45 44 24 15); **Golf Club de l'Etoile,** 10, av. de la Grande Armée, 17ème (tel. 43 80 30 79); **l'Ecole de Golf de l'Aqua boulevard de Paris,** 4, rue Louis Armand, 15ème (tel. 45 57 43 06). Also try the Paris golf headquarters at the **Fédération de Golf,** 16ème (tel. 42 02 13 55). For bowling, head to the **Bowling de Paris** (tel. 40 67 94 00), in the Bois de Boulogne near the rte. Mahatma Gandhi entrance of the Jardin d'Acclimatation. Open daily 5pm-2am. Closed Mon. in Aug. Games Mon.-Fri. 20F, after 8pm 29F, Sat.-Sun. 30F. Obligatory bowling shoe rental 10F. After the park closes, you have to enter through the park's Mahatma Gandhi entrance, which remains open. Because the Bowling de Paris is inside the Jardin, you have to pay for admission to the Jardin even if you just want to go bowling.

## SPECTATOR SPORTS

If you think that Parisians are obsessed with only the very highest of high culture, think again. Parisians follow sports with fierce interest, reading between the lines of their own sports daily, *l'Equipe* (6F), as well as the sports section of other newspapers. Sports talk provides fodder for heated discussion on the *métro* and raucous play-by-play in bars; as for actually attending the real thing, it's almost a religious experience. Parisians' knowledge of sports is not limited to French and European teams—their fervor is of global proportions. Once again, Allo-Sports can tell you all you need to know. The **Palais Omnisports Paris Bercy,** 8, bd. de Bercy, 12ème (tel. 44 68 44 68; Mo. Bercy), hosts everything from opera and beach volleyball to figure skating and horse jumping beneath its radical, sod-covered roof. Ticket prices vary wildly according to the event.

**Soccer:** Soccer (called *"football"* or simply *"le foot"),* France's hands-down national sport, consumes Paris, especially during the big championships like the World Cup (*Le Mondial),* which takes place in the U.S. in 1994. Join the Parisian multitudes in waiting to see where *les bleus* will go from here. The **Club de Football Paris St-Germain** (tel. 40 71 91 91) is Paris's own professional *foot* team, splitting its time between road games and matches at the enormous **Parc des Princes** (recorded info 42 88 02 76; Mo. Porte de St-Cloud), the city's premier outdoor stadium venue. The finals of the Coupe de France take place in early May; the Tournoi de Paris is in late July. Tickets to all events can be purchased at the Parc des Princes box office and go on sale anywhere from 2 days to 2 weeks in advance. Games on weekends and some weekday evenings. Prices 50-170F, depending on the seat and the event. Box office open 9am-6pm when selling tickets for an event. The Parc des Princes also hosts **rugby** matches, including the Tournoi des Cinq Nations (Feb.-March) and the final of the Championnat de France de Rugby in early June. Call the box office for details.

**Cycling:** Even non-fans have heard of a fairly impressive road race called the **Tour de France,** which reached the age of 80 in 1993. Held in July, *Le Tour* pits 200 of the world's best cyclists against the Alps, the elements, and each other for 21 gruelling stages. Call *l'Equipe* (tel. 40 93 21 92), one of the tour's sponsors, for information about the race's itinerary. Spectators turn out in droves along the way, traipsing out to an obscure bend in the highway to cheer their favorite to victory.

Parisians and tourists alike line the Champs-Elysées for the triumphal last stage, usually between noon and 6pm. Show up early and be prepared for a mob scene; you may see more on TV. The women's Tour de France leaves Paris in mid-Aug. near the Eiffel Tower. Call 43 57 02 94 for information. The **Grand Prix Cycliste de Paris** is an annual time trial competition held in June at the Vélodrome Jacques Anguetil, Bois de Vincennes, 12ème (tel. 43 68 01 27; tickets 50F, available on site). Other events here are free, but may be canceled by rain.

**Tennis:** The *terre battue* (red clay) of the **Stade Roland Garros,** 2, av. Gordon Bennett, 16ème (Mo. Porte d'Auteuil), has ended more than one champion's quest for a Grand Slam. Two weeks each year (May 24-June 6 in 1993), **Les Internationaux de France de Tennis (The French Open)** welcomes the world's top players to Paris. Write to the **Fédération Française de Tennis** at the above address (tel. 47 43 48 00) in Oct., for information on tickets for the next spring's tournament. Also, ask your national tennis association; they sometimes have an extra supply of tickets. If in Paris and still out of luck, try your hotel, any ticket agencies, and the stadium itself. Sometimes there are surprises; the first three days of the tournament have sometimes produced last-minute tickets.

**Horse Racing:** Elegant dress, sleek beasts, fine food, and a day of seeing and being seen—of course Parisians love the races. The numerous hippodromes in and around town host races of all kinds throughout the year. Far from seedy, an afternoon at the track is a family affair. The level of classiness climbs a notch or two for the season's championship races. **Hippodrome de Vincennes,** 2, rte. de la Ferme, in the Bois de Vincennes, 12ème. Mo. Château de Vincennes. A hike through the woods from the *métro* stop takes you to the home of Parisian harness racing since 1906. Prix d'Amérique (late Jan.), Prix de France (early Feb.), and Prix du Président de la République (late June). Tickets 15-30F, even for the big races. **Hippodrome d'Auteuil,** in the Bois de Boulogne, 16ème (tel. 45 27 12 24). Mo. Porte d'Auteuil. Steeplechases (obstacle courses) since 1873; the stands date from 1921. For the big races in June and July, shuttles run from the *métro* and RER stations. Tickets about 22F during the week, 37F on Sun. **Hippodrome de Longchamp,** deeper in the Bois de Boulogne, 16ème (tel. 44 30 75 00). Mo. Porte d'Auteuil. On race days, shuttles run from nearby *métro* stops. **Hippodrome de Chantilly,** Chantilly (tel. (16) 44 57 02 54). See Daytrips.

# ▮ Shopping

In a city where everything is a "sight," where even walking becomes entertainment, where eating is a religion, one can only imagine what pleasures await the shopper. That Parisians pride themselves on dressing well is obvious from a short stroll down any major boulevard. Truly Parisian items, however, embody the utmost simplicity. They are made to last, never to go out of fashion.

Until the mid-19th century, the bourgeoisie shopped at small, specialized boutiques, which abounded in every neighborhood. Aristide Bouricaut opened Au Bon Marché in 1852, in a former lepers' hospital in the seventh *arrondissement.* Undeterred by the setting, shoppers flocked to the revolutionary store; its economies of scale resulted in prices far lower than those of the neighborhood stores. Most importantly, shoppers could browse through goods, and clothes were made **prêt-à-porter** (ready to wear) instead of custom-ordered at the local tailor. Today, French department stores are still going strong, though the shopping mall has already invaded Les Halles and La Défense. As for the aristocrats, they turned their nose up at "ready-made" clothes, and continued to purchase custom-made goods at ultra-expensive boutiques, the ancestors of the modern Hermès and Yves St-Laurent.

Although Paris is not a bargain hunter's paradise, even some of the most *haute* of the **haute couture** boutiques join in the twice-yearly *soldes* (major sales) that sweep the city in January and late June to early July. Non-Europeans are eligible to receive a refund of the Value Added Tax (VAT) if you spend more than 2000F in one store (see Essentials—Money for more information). Even if you don't spend 2000F, **souvenirs** are duty-free, and every Pierre, Jacques, and Etienne-Louis is selling them. Reasonable prices on t-shirts and the lovable mini-Eiffel Towers can be found on rue de Rivoli, near the Louvre, as well as on the Ile-de-la-Cité, near Notre-Dame. For quality perfume, watches, pens, clothing, and beauty products at a 30-40% discount, try **Honoré,** 316, rue St-Honoré, 1*er* (tel. 42 60 49 00; Mo. Tuileries; open Mon.-Sat. 9:45am-6:45pm). **Raoul et Curly,** 47, av. de l'Opéra, 2*ème* (tel. 47 42 50 10; Mo. Opéra), offers similar merchandise at similar prices, with an additional 20% discount for foreigners (open Mon.-Sat. 9:30am-6:30pm). **Perfume** is cheapest at the duty free shops at Charles de Gaulle and Orly, where the shops will often accept American or British currency at a favorable exchange rate.

A word of warning: all stores close on Sundays in Paris. Some of the smaller ones will close over the lunch hour on weekdays. When you walk into a boutique, many store owners will take that as a declaration of intention to buy. They will approach you immediately. If you want to browse, which they may not like, say, *"Merci. J'ai-merais seulement regarder"* (Thank you, I'd just like to look). Do not, of course, be coerced into buying something you don't want, but don't be surprised at reactions ranging from disdain to hostility should you leave without making a purchase.

## CLOTHING

Paris gowns have been in demand across the world since the days of the Bourbon kings and wax fashion-model dolls. Today's swankiest shopping districts are scattered all around Paris. Probably the most famous of these areas surrounds the exquisite **rue du Faubourg St-Honoré,** which runs northwest through the eighth *arrondissement.* This is the area of *haute couture* (custom-made, expensive clothing and accessories, as opposed to your normal, merely pricey, factory-made stuff). Gawk at the impeccably French scarves and bags at **Hermès** (no. 24), the outlandish solid knits at **Sonia Rykiel** (no. 70), the untouchables of all types at **Yves Saint Laurent** (no. 38), and the high fashion design of the Japanese **Ashida** (no. 34). **Karl Lagerfield, Pierre Balmain,** and **Versace** boutiques cluster nearby. Not far away, like webs ready to snag the oblivious passerby, the streets projecting from the **place des Victoires** (1*er* and 2*ème*) harbor another galaxy of *haute couture* boutiques.

Running southwest from the Rond Point des Champs-Elysées, **avenue de Montaigne** shelters the houses of **Christian Dior** (no. 32), **Chanel** (no. 42), **Valentino** (no. 17-19), and **Nina Ricci** (no. 39). The name **Pierre Cardin,** seemingly omnipresent in Paris, appears on a regal house in place François 1er. The windows in **place Vendôme** and along **rue de la Paix** (north to the Opéra) glitter with the designs of **Cartier, Van Cleef & Arpels,** and other offerings from the city's jewelry overlords.

Across the river on the Left Bank, boutiques tend to be smaller and occasionally less expensive, though no less stunning. A slew of shops (including **Sonia Rykiel, Kenzo,** and **Claude Montana)** display their goods in large open windows surrounding the streets of rue Bonaparte, rue du Four, rue de Grenelle, rue de Rennes, and rue de Sèvres. Find what you like on bd. St-Germain, but hunt around for better bargains around rue de Seine and the top of bd. St-Michel. Once the preliminary sightseeing mission is accomplished and you're ready to buy, head away from the big names and look for the smaller boutiques that cater to one particular style. Boutiques in the Marais and the Bastille tend more toward the funky and the trendy.

While most folks probably won't be able to afford the *vêtements* of these headquarters of fashion, there are a number of places where you can buy designer labels at lower prices. A unique Parisian shopping phenomenon is the *magasin du troc,* a large store that resells clothes bought and returned at the more expensive stores. Don't expect *troc* bottom prices, but given the retail prices of Chanel and Dior, bargains are astonishing nonetheless. Try **Troc Mod,** 230, av. du Maine, 14*ème* (tel. 45 40 45 93; Mo. Alésia; open Sept.-July Tues.-Sat. 10am-7:30pm; Aug. Tues.-Sat. 11am-7:30pm); **Troc'Eve,** 25, rue Violet, 15*ème* (tel. 45 79 38 36; Mo. Dupleix; open Tues.-Sat. 10am-7pm); and **Réciproque,** with three outlets at 95, 101, and 123, rue de la Pompe, 16*ème* (tel. 47 04 30 28; Mo. Pompe; open Tues.-Sat. 10am-6:45pm).

For the lowest prices on the newest shoe fashions, try the side streets surrounding pl. de la République and rue des Sts-Pères in the sixth *arrondissement.* Platforms are back—the Paris platform scene features shoes in multitudes of colors and materials. (Warning: during the 1970's, **Consumer Reports** condemned platforms as a health hazard.) As a matter of fact, the 70's are back; you'll find retro bell-bottoms and hot pants all over the city. Pseudo American wear is also popular, but that doesn't mean that Americans are automatically a hit; the fascination with the "cowboys" of the American West has never quite worn off.

A number of other discount stores offer designer labels and stock at used, returned, or discount prices: **Cacharel Stock,** 114, rue d'Alésia, 14*ème* (tel. 45 42 53 04); **Stock Daniel Hechter,** 16, bd. de l'Hôpital, 5*ème* (tel. 47 07 88 44); **Stock Chevignan,** 122, rue d'Alésia, 14*ème* (tel. 45 43 40 25).

## DEPARTMENT STORES

Paris has responded to the increasing demand for *prêt-à-porter* with a good number of department stores, offering the tourist (and throngs of Parisians) a more relaxed, American style of shopping. In sharp contrast to the tiny, exclusive boutiques that line the streets (presided over by the omnipresent salespeople-cum-guards), these *grands magasins* allow both the browser and serious shopper to slip into blissful anonymity while checking out the merchandise. Instead of cajoling you into buying not one but two of some trendy piece of work you wouldn't be caught dead in at home, the sales staff in these stores, while helpful, stay behind the counter and wait for you to approach them. With the pressure to purchase relieved, you can slyly look at the price tags and only your companion will witness the shock and utter disbelief that register on your face.

While the upper echelon of these stores maintains high prices, it is possible to get a real steal on top designers if you keep an eye out for sales. It is at this point that you will notice the peculiar Parisian sense of personal space. Be prepared to elbow your way through mobs of hell-bent bargain hunters. Practice your "*pardon*"s and "*excusez-moi*"s and fight to the death for that last size or color. Also keep in mind that many *grands magasins* are mini-malls; you can often get your hair cut, mail a letter, do your grocery shopping, and have lunch, all without leaving the store.

**Au Bon Marché,** 3, rue de Sèvres, 7ème (tel. 45 49 21 22). Mo. Sèvres-Babylone. Paris's oldest department store, and perhaps its best. As chic as Galeries Lafayette, but minus the tourists and most of the chaos. You'll find all the big designers, from Laura Ashley to Cachet. Especially amusing for travelers with children is the *Rentrée des Classes* section; you can get anything from a Tintin backpack to a model airplane. If you're hungry and feeling extravagant, go across the street to **la Grande Epicerie de Paris,** the food annex (see Groceries). Open Mon.-Fri. 9:30am-6:30pm, Sat. 9:30am-7pm. All major credit cards accepted.

**Au Printemps,** 64, bd. Haussmann, 9ème (tel. 42 82 50 00). Mo. Chaussée d'Antin. Also at 30, av. d'Italie, 13ème (tel. 40 78 17 17). Mo Italie. 21-25, cours de Vincennes, 20ème (tel. 43 71 12 41). Mo. Porte de Vincennes. 10, pl. de la République, 11ème (tel. 43 55 39 09). Mo. République. Bills itself as "the most Parisian of all the department stores," but when you see the international clientèle you may wonder why. Merchandise on par with Galeries Lafayette. Anything you could possibly want (but not necessarily need) at typical (high) department store prices. You will also find more people than you could possibly want to see in a lifetime. Haussmann store open Mon.-Sat. 9:35am-7pm. Check with branches for slightly different opening and closing times. All major credit cards accepted.

**BHV,** 52, rue de Rivoli, 4ème (tel. 42 74 90 00). Mo. Hôtel de Ville. The initials stand for Bazar de l'Hôtel de Ville, logical enough for a department store across the street from the Hôtel de Ville. Heavy on housewares, electronic equipment, and luggage, with less emphasis on trendy fashions. Less chic than Samaritaine. Open Thurs.-Tues. 9:30am-7pm, Wed. 9:30am-10pm. AmEx, MC, V.

**Galeries Lafayette,** 40, bd. Haussmann, 9ème (tel. 42 82 34 56). Mo. Chaussée d'Antin. Also at 22, rue du Départ, 14ème (tel. 45 38 52 87). Mo. Montparnasse. Prices are high, but not outrageous. Keep your eye out for *soldes*. Clothes are organized by designer, so you can get a taste of the most recent styles. Unfortunately, you'll be sharing this experience with unbelievable masses of tourists. So many Americans come here that it was considered highly unsafe during the terrorist attacks of the mid-80s. Take the time to admire the ornate Belle Epoque dome in the main building. Main store open Mon.-Sat. 9:30am-6:30pm. Rue du Départ branch open Mon.-Sat. 9:45am-7:15pm. All major credit cards accepted.

**Samaritaine** (tel. 40 41 20 20). Mo. Pont-Neuf, Louvre, or Châtelet. Spread across 4 large buildings between rue de Rivoli and the Seine, connected by tunnels. Not as chic as Galeries Lafayettes or Au Bon Marché, Samaritaine tends more toward home furnishings than endless racks of designer clothing. Building 2 has a beautiful roof with turquoise and ivory iron detailing and a peacock mosaic. You just might see more French people than Americans. Open Mon.-Wed. 9:30am-7pm, Thurs. 9:30am-10pm, Fri.-Sat. 9:30am-7pm. All major credit cards accepted.

**Tati,** 11, pl. de la République, 3ème (tel. 48 87 72 81). Mo. République. 106, rue Faubourg du Temple, 11ème. Mo. Goncourt. 140, rue de Rennes, 6ème (tel. 45 48 68 31). Mo. Montparnasse. 4, bd. de Rochechouart, 18ème (tel. 42 55 13 09). Mo. Anvers. The original bargain basement store (dresses 80-150F, T-shirts 15-40F, nightgowns 40-60F). In the cheapest department store in Paris, you must meet mayhem with an attitude, prepared to push through cramped displays and dig to the bottom of the bin for the elusive something-or-other-you-might-want-to-buy. With low prices, a good place for cheap clothes, but not a mecca for designer clothing. Get your sales slip made out before heading to cashier. Open Mon. 10am-7pm, Tues.-Fri. 9:30am-7pm, Sun. 9:15am-7pm. Eurocard, MC, V.

# BOOKS

Books in Paris, in either English or French, are much more expensive than in North American bookstores. New English-language books sell for about US$20 a novel (paperback). Scope the banks of the Seine, where *bouquinistes* sell their wares, peddling treasures in all languages and at all prices. Otherwise try second-hand shops where *livres d'occasion* (used books) go for 5-50F. The quest for a cheap, worthwhile read requires some patience, but for true bibliophiles, the search is half the fun. Almost all bookstores will order books for you, but the cost of mailing books from the U.S. can be apoplexy-inducing. Specialty bookshops also provide an excellent resource for information concerning specific ethnic groups in the city.

**Brentano's,** 37, av. de l'Opéra, 2*ème* (tel. 42 61 52 50). Mo. Opéra. An extensive selection, especially of American literature, and a wide display of guidebooks. Open Mon.-Sat. 10am-7pm.

**Chantelivre,** 13, rue de Sèvres, 7*ème*. Mo. Sèvres-Babylone. This literary playland defines excellence in children's bookstores. Full of old favorites for the young (Puss-in-Boots) and not so young (Dumas, Jack London), this place even vaunts an alcove where kids can draw or read. Everyone browses happily, poring over books, and the odd knapsack or game. Open Mon. 1-6:50 pm, Tues.-Sat. 10am-6:50pm. Closed 1 week in Aug. and on every other Mon. in summer.

**Galignani,** 224, rue de Rivoli, 1*er* (tel. 42 60 76 07; fax 42 86 09 31). Mo. Tuileries. A marvelous, wood-paneled bookstore, in the best of upper-crust literary traditions. "The First English Bookshop Established on the Continent," as the bookmarks declare. An excellent collection of beautiful British books you definitely can't turn down. Open Mon.-Sat. 10am-7pm.

**Gibert Jeune,** 5, pl. St-Michel, 5*ème* (tel. 43 25 70 07), near the Seine. Mo. St-Michel. *The* bookstore near bd. St-Michel, and also *the* place to go for French classics. Lots of reduced books for the short-on-cash. The same variety of books and stationery abounds at the branch at 15bis, bd. St-Denis, 2*ème* (tel. 43 26 82 84). Mo. Strasbourg-St-Denis. The store at 27, quai St-Michel (tel. 43 54 57 32; Mo. St-Michel), sells university texts.

**Gibert Jeune VALEC,** 7, rue Dupuytren, 6*ème* (tel. 46 33 43 18). Mo. Odéon. Right across from original locale of Sylvia Beach's legendary *librairie*. You'll find paperbacks in French at rock-bottom prices. Bins outside receive our applause: 5-10F. Books inside slightly more. Open Tues.-Sun. 10am-2pm and 3-7pm.

**La Librairie des Femmes,** 74, rue de Seine, 6*ème* (tel. 43 29 50 75). Mo. Odéon. The one-time home of feminist collective MLF; now a large, peaceful place to browse through the collection of women's literature. The *librairie,* together with the press it supports, has lost much of its former radical edge. Open daily 10am-7pm; late July-Aug. sometimes closed 12:45-2pm.

**Librairie Gallimard,** 15, bd. Raspail, 7*ème* (tel. 45 48 24 84). Mo. Rue du Bac. The main outlet of this famed publisher of French classics. A huge selection of Gallimard books at somewhat higher prices. Open Mon.-Sat. 10am-7pm.

**Librairie Gourmande,** 4, rue Dante, 5*ème* (tel. 43 54 37 27; fax 43 54 31 16). Mo. Maubert-Mutualité. Bookstore on the art of living, *par excellence*; new, old, and antiquarian volumes chronicle food and drink from Middle Ages to present day. Some English-language titles. Remainder bins offer bargains at around 30F. Open Mon.-Sat. 10am-7pm, Sun. 3-7pm. Closed Christmas and New Years Day.

**Librairies Ulysse,** 26, rue St-Louis-en-l'Ile, 4*ème* (tel. 43 25 17 35). Mo. Pont-Marie. Specializes in travel books and antiquarian maps. Owned and staffed by a *bon vivant* bibliophile and her friends. Used and out-of-print books. Open Tues.-Sat. 2-8pm.

**Les Mots à la Bouche,** 6, rue Ste-Croix-de-la-Bretonnerie, 4*ème* (tel. 42 78 88 30). Mo. Hôtel-de-Ville. The best gay and lesbian bookstore in town. French and English titles, magazines, postcards, and newsletters. An inside line on gay and lesbian nightlife and political and cultural events. Open Mon.-Sat. 11am-11pm.

**Presence Africaine,** 25, rue des Ecoles, 5*ème* (tel. 43 54 15 88). Mo. Maubert-Mutualité. French-language texts from Antilles and Africa put out by publishing house of the same name (tel. 43 54 13 74). Children's books, scholarly texts, poetry, and more. Paperbacks 30-70F. Also a helpful resource for travelers seeking businesses which cater to Black clientele. The proprietor keeps a stack of out-of-print guide books to Paris behind the desk. Open Mon.-Sat. 10am-7pm.

**Shakespeare and Co.,** 37, rue de la Bûcherie, 5*ème,* across the Seine from Notre-Dame. Mo. St-Michel. Run by George Whitman (alleged great-grandson of Walt), this shop seeks to reproduce the atmosphere of Sylvia Beach's establishment at 8, rue Dupuytren and, later, at 12, rue de l'Odéon, an extraordinary gathering-place for expatriates in the 1920s. Beach published Joyce's *Ulysses* from these quarters in 1922; avant-garde composer George Antheil wrote music for pianos and airplane propellers in his room upstairs. Quirky and wide-ranging new and used selection. Bins outside offer a mixed bag of bargains, including many French classics in English (30F). Profits support impoverished writers who live and work in this literary cooperative. The first *Let's Go* writer stayed at Shakespeare's; so did beatniks Allen Ginsberg and Lawrence Ferlinghetti. Check the window for information on upcoming readings. Open daily noon-midnight.

**W.H. Smith,** 248, rue de Rivoli, 1er (tel. 42 60 37 97; fax 42 96 83 71). Mo. Concorde. Find the latest publications from Britain and America here, including many scholarly works. Terrific selection of periodicals from *Car and Driver* to *New York Review*. And, of course, guides by *Let's Go*. Open Mon.-Sat. 9:30am-7pm.

**Tea and Tattered Pages,** 24, rue Mayet, 6ème (tel. 40 65 94 35). Mo. Duroc. The place to go for second-hand English-language fiction, cookbooks, sci-fi, and much more. The crazy-quilt selection is subject to barter and trade; sell books at 5F a paperback and get a 10% discount on your next purchase. If what you want isn't what they've got, sign the wish list and you'll be called if and when it comes in. Adjoining *salon de thé* serves up rootbeer floats, brownies, and American coffee with free milk and free refill. Open Mon.-Sat. 11-7pm.

**The Village Voice,** 6, rue Princesse, 6ème (tel. 46 33 36 47). Mo. Mabillon. An English bookstore with a terrific sci-fi section and a decent collection of feminist literature. Pick up *Let's Go: Europe* for 180F or *Lets Go: France* for 173F. Open Mon. 2-8pm, Tues.-Sat. 11am-8pm.

## MUSIC

Cassettes and compact discs are highly taxed in France, and are therefore *really* expensive (CDs 100F or more). Used LPs (*disques d'occasion*) can be found at the Marché aux Puces (see Markets). The good news is that you'll find a better sampling of certain types of music (especially French and African) than in North America. Look for recordings that never made it across the Atlantic. Each of the following megastores has helpful clerks, decent prices, and a huge selection.

**B.P.M.,** 1, rue Keller, 11ème (tel. 40 21 02 88; fax 40 21 03 74). Mo. Bastille. Catering to your rave needs, this address serves as a clubhouse, information point, and music store for house and techno fans. Rare and expansive collection. Check posters in the window for upcoming raves. Open Mon.-Sat. noon-8pm.

**Gilbert Jeune:** bd. St-Michel, 6ème. Mo. Odéon or Cluny-Sorbonne. This bookstore stocks new and used tapes, CDs, and LPs in the basement. Used CDs around 55F. LPs 20-200F. Open Mon.-Sat. 9:30am-7:30pm.

**FNAC (Fédération Nationale des Achats de Cadres):** Several branches. **Montparnasse,** 136, rue des Rennes, 6ème (tel. 49 54 30 00). Mo. Rennes. **Etoile,** 26-30, av. des Ternes, 17ème (tel. 44 09 18 00). Mo. Ternes. **Forum des Halles,** 1-7, rue Porte Lescot, 1er (tel. 40 41 40 00). Mo. Les Halles. Not only a huge selection of tapes, CDs, and stereo equipment, but also books and tickets for concerts and the like (see Entertainment). Montparnasse store open Mon.-Sat. 10am-7pm. Etoile and Les Halles branches open Mon.-Sat. 10am-7:30pm.

**Virgin Megastore,** 52-60, av. des Champs-Elysées, 8ème (tel. 40 74 06 48). Mo. Franklin Roosevelt. This music mecca includes an affordable restaurant and countless headphones that let you listen to the latest hits. If it's been recorded, it's likely to be at Virgin. Beware of free listening stations. They can be hard on your pocketbook since they invariably have recordings you've never heard of, but find you can't live without. Open Mon.-Thurs. 10am-midnight, Fri.-Sat. 10am-1am.

## ODDS AND ENDS

Paris is crawling with specialized boutiques, selling imports from the world over and hand-crafted goods representing centuries of tradition. Budget travelers beware: this is a prime way to stock up on those buy-on-impulse items that might leave you sleeping in the streets. But it's also a great opportunity to buy a unique souvenir or gift that will always remind you of Paris. For a cluster of these shops, try Ile St-Louis and the rue du Pont Louis-Philippe, both in the fourth *arrondissement.*

**Artisanat,** 52, rue St-André des Arts, *6ème* (tel. 43 25 44 45). Mo. Odéon. Eclectic proprietor imports handbags, fabric, ceramics, jewelry, and exquisite glass bottles from such places as South America, Indonesia, and Morocco. A fair share of European handicrafts as well. Open Mon. 3-7:30pm, Tues.-Sat. 11:30am-7:30pm.

**Clair de Rêve,** 35, rue St-Louis-en-l'Ile, *4ème* (tel. 43 29 81 06). Mo. Pont Marie. A winsome boutique with hand-crafted jewelry and beautiful, curious marionettes. Open daily 2:30-5:30pm.

**Galerie Bamyan,** 24, rue St-Louis-en-l'Ile, *4ème* (tel. 46 33 69 66). Mo. Pont Marie. Exquisite *objets d'art* and carpets from central Asia. Open daily 11am-8pm.

**Jule des Près,** 19, rue Cherche Midi, *6ème* (tel. 45 48 26 84). Mo. Rennes or St-Placide. The dried flower creations and loose herbs at this store appeal to many senses at once. The knowledgeable proprietor will explain the use and meaning of all the herbs she stocks, will help you create a potpourri, and will package and ship anywhere. Open Tues.-Sun. 2-6pm. Open mid-Aug to mid-July.

**Pentagram,** 15, rue Racine, *6ème* (tel. 43 26 99 99), directly across from the Ecole de Médicine. Mo. Cluny-Sorbonne. The perfect place to pick up a gift for a kid. An endearing collection of tiny wooden toys, kaleidoscopes, puppets, storybooks, and other goodies. For the adult in you, a small but impressive collection of books (in French) on gardening, art history, and literature. The *salle* above has expositions of contemporary art for sale. Open Mon.3-7pm, Tues.-Sat. 10:30am-7pm.

**Pylones,** 57, rue St-Louis-en-l'Ile, *4ème* (tel. 46 34 05 02). Mo. Pont Marie. Also at 7, rue Tardieu, *18ème.* Mo. Anvers. Lots of colorful and funky gadgets: clocks, funny ties, weird pens, and pins. A unique place.

**St-Louis Posters,** 23, rue St-Louis-en-l'Ile, *4ème* (tel. 40 46 91 65). Mo. Pont Marie. A classy shop with an array of *affiches,* old and new, postcards, prints, and cards. Open daily 11am-8pm.

## MARKETS

Paris's covered and uncovered markets often show the visitor a unique characteristic of daily life in the neighborhood. For a complete list of the locations and hours of Paris's 84 markets, ask for the brochure *Les Marchés de Paris* at the tourist office or your local *mairie.* For food markets, see Groceries in the Food section.

**Carreau du Temple,** on the angle of rue Dupetit Thouars and rue de Picardi, *3ème.* Mo. Temple. This structure of blue steel and glass is a neighborhood sports center in the afternoon and a clothes market in the morning. The market is especially strong in leather—coats, bags, and shoes—but also sells fur and other kinds of clothes. One of the last places in the capital where you can still bargain—usually you can get the price down by about 25%. Even if your French isn't up to bargaining, the starting prices are quite low. As in any public market, watch your wallets and pocketbooks. It gets crowded on weekends, so it's best to come during the week. Open Tues.-Fri. 9am-noon, Sat.-Sun. 9am-1pm.

**Marché aux Fleurs (flowers),** *4ème.* On the place Louis-Lépine just across from the Cité *métro* staircase. A flower market where it's as fun to look as it is to shop. Flower market open Mon.-Sat. 8am-7:30pm. On Sun., a bird market appears in its stead, supplemented by an unremarkable collection of goldfish, rabbits, and pet food stalls. Parakeets 500F. Rabbits 100F.

**Marché aux Timbres (Stamps),** on the Champs-Elysées at av. de Marigny. Thurs. and Sat.-Sun., during daylight hours.

**Quai de Mégisserie,** *1er.* Mo. Pont-Neuf or Châtelet. Established in the 17th century, this animal bazaar once bore the gloomy sobriquet "La Vallée de la Misère." One of the few open-air historical markets that continue to flourish in central Paris. Buy a turkey, pigeon, or rabbit, or come to browse. The shops in this section of the waterfront sell all manner of strange pets. Cages spill out from the stores onto the sidewalk. Open daily until sunset.

## PUCES DE ST-OUEN (ST-OUEN FLEA MARKET)

You may not find fleas at the **Puces de St-Ouen** (St-Ouen Flea Market), but you *will* find everything else, from spangled 1920s dresses to 18th-century wooden armoires and even used kitchen sinks, plus of course, plenty of pickpockets and con artists. The prices and quality of the merchandise vary as widely as the products, beginning at the dirt cheap, low-quality bargains found among the renegade stalls. At the other end of the spectrum, astronomically expensive, high-quality antique dealers use buzzers to ring in their preferred customers while keeping out the riff-raff. Antique itself, the market was formed during the Middle Ages, when merchants resold the cast-off clothing of aristocrats (crawling with the market's namesake insects) to peasant-folk on the edge of the city, and it has gradually developed into a highly structured, regular market alongside a wild, anything-goes street bazaar.

A rule of thumb for first-time visitors: bring as little money as possible, watch your wallet, and have something in mind before you go. There are no five dollar diamond rings here. If you find the maltese falcon mixed into a pile of schlock jewelry, the vendor probably planted it there. The one area, however, where peddlers seem not to know what they have is that of rare rock-and-roll recordings. If you know your stuff and have unlimited patience, this is the place—1960s and 70s garage bands, funk, and much more. Quite a large selection of blues as well, but don't expect to come away with a steal. Best deals are cut on rainy days and late afternoons.

If you take the *métro*, you'll encounter the street bazaar first. The 15-minute walk to the official market is jammed with tiny **unofficial stalls.** Most of these sell flimsy new clothes at exorbitant prices, but the leather jacket stalls have some good buys (suede jackets for 275F). Don't be turned off by the raucous hurriedness of the stalls; once you pass through to the real market you'll be able to browse leisurely. Pickpockets love this crowded area, and Three Card Monte con artists positively proliferate (don't be pulled into the game by seeing someone win lots of money— they're part of the con, there just to attract suckers to the crooked game).

The **regular market** comprises six markets, located on the rue des Rosiers and rue Jules Vallès. Rare finds linger at the Marché Malik (new and used clothing), Marché Vernaison (antique bric-a-brac), and Marché Paul Bert (antique bric-a-brac). The remaining three—Marché Biron (used valuable tableware: crystal glasses, etc., plus some gold and silver jewelry), Marché Dauphine (expensive antique furniture stores), and Marché Serpette (expensive antique furniture stores)—may be good for dreaming about what you'll buy when you're rich and famous. Wherever you shop, be prepared to bargain; sellers don't expect to get the starting price. The market is hard to navigate at first, and map fanatics will tear their hair out. The street names— rue des Rosiers, rue Jules Vallès, etc.—belong to the marketplace itself and not the 18*ème arrondissement* in which it is found. (Market open Sat.-Mon. 7am-7:30pm.)

If you want to stop for lunch while at the flea market, try a steaming bowl of *moules marinière* with *frites,* the uncontested specialty of restaurants in the area. Two restaurants in particular stand out: **Chez Louisette,** 130, av. Michelet (tel. 40 12 10 14), inside the Marché Vernaison allée no. 10, all the way at the back, where cigarette-puffing singers further enliven the already boisterous atmosphere. It's an eclectically decorated restaurant with classic French café *chansons*. Unfortunately, the secret is out, and you'll hear as much English and German as French. *(Moules* 58F. Open Sat.-Mon. 12:30-6pm.) A younger, less-touristy clientele frequents **Au Baryton,** 50, av. Jules Vallès (tel. 40 12 02 74), outside the Marché Malik, where people slurp up the *Moules-Frites* combo for only 54F while taking in the free live jazz and rock concerts. (Open Sat.-Mon. 8am-10pm. Music starts at 4:30pm.)

Other *marchés aux puces*, while less impressive, are also less crowded: **Vanves,** av. de la Porte-de-Vanves and av. Georges-Lafenestre, rue Marc Sanguier, 14*ème*, Mo. Porte de Vanves (open Sat.-Sun. 2-7:30pm); **Marché à la Ferraille,** rue Jean-Henri Fabre, 18*ème*, Mo. Clignancourt (open Sat.-Mon. 7am-7pm); **Montreuil,** av. de la Porte Montreuil, 20*ème*, Mo. Mairie de Montreuil (open Sat.-Mon.7am-7:30pm).

# Bisexual, Gay, and Lesbian Paris

## ■ Bisexual, Gay, and Lesbian Concerns

Next to London, Amsterdam, and Berlin, Paris has one of the largest gay populations in Europe: an estimated 100,000 gay and lesbian people. While Paris boasts a number of political action groups and service organizations that address issues concerning bisexual, gay, and lesbian people, the city lags behind communities in New York, Sydney, and San Francisco in of protest politics, public identity, and cultural visibility. The focus in Paris appears to be more on nightlife than on political action.

The recent disappearance of France's premier weekly gay magazine, *Gai Pied Hebdo,* the brutal 1990 murder of Pasteur Doucé, the director of a gay Christian center called Le Centre du Christ Libérateur, and the 1993 report that AIDS (called *le SIDA* in French) is now the second largest killer of Parisian men 24 to 44 years old, have signaled a growing concern that Gay Paris is as subject to gay-bashing and the ravages of HIV disease as other major cities in Europe and the U. S. But, thanks to the Socialist government, homosexuality is not illegal in France and bisexual, gay, and lesbian rights are protected by law.

Consult the encyclopedic *Guide Gai 1994* (45F at newsstands or in most American gay bookstores), which provides almost 400 pages of material in both English and French, to find out more about gay hotels, restaurants, nightlife, organizations, and services in both the capital city and the rest of France. For additional reading on gay and lesbian life and thought in France, read Monique Wittig's *The Lesbian Body* or Hervé Guibert's *Fou de Vincent* and *To the Friend Who Did Not Save My Life.* For information on HIV, AIDS, and safer sex, call the 24-hour free and anonymous AIDS information hotline, **SIDA Info Service** (tel. 05 36 66 36). For the names of other useful organizations, see Essentials—Specific Concerns, Essentials—Emergency, and the listings below.

**ACT-UP PARIS,** BP231 Paris Cedex 17 (tel. 42 63 44 78). The Paris chapter of ACT-UP (the AIDS Coalition to Unleash Power) meets Tues. 7:30pm at 106/112, bd. de l'Hôpital, 13ème, to discuss issues related to HIV, AIDS, and homophobia. Foreign members are welcome, but are expected not to take part in actions and protests that could lead to being arrested.

**Centre du Christ Libérateur,** 3bis, rue Clairaut, 17ème (tel. 46 27 49 36). Mo. La Fourche. Founded by Pasteur Doucé, this center provides cultural, medical, legal, and personal advice and counseling for bisexual, gay, and lesbian people.

**Ecoute Gaie,** (tel. 48 06 19 11). A gay hotline. Takes calls Mon.-Fri. 6-10pm.

**Fréquence Gaie,** 94.4 FM, 24-hr. gay and lesbian radio station providing news, music, and information in French and English.

**Maison des Femmes,** 8, Cité Prost, 11ème (tel. 43 79 61 91). Information and cultural center for lesbians and bisexual women.

**Maison des Homosexualités,** 25, rue Michel-le-Compte, 3ème (tel. 42 77 72 77). Mo. Rambuteau. Cultural center which provides information on gay and lesbian activities as well as information on HIV, AIDS, and conferences on sexuality. Open Mon.-Sat. 3-8pm.

**Les Mots à la Bouche,** 6, rue Ste-Croix de la Bretonnerie, 4ème (tel. 42 78 88 30). Mo. St-Paul or Hôtel-de-Ville. The best gay and lesbian bookstore in Paris. Carries the city's most extensive collection of gay and lesbian literature including novels, essays, books on art, and magazines in French, English, German, and Italian. Open Mon.-Sat. 11am-11pm.

**Le Projet Ornicar,** 56, rue de la Roquette, 11*ème* (tel. 48 09 22 10). Political action group which organizes protests, lobbying, and the dissemination of information regarding homophobia, discrimination, and public policy on gay, bisexual, and lesbian issues.

## ■ Bisexual, Gay, and Lesbian Entertainment

While the bisexual, gay, and lesbian communities of Paris may not be as politically active as those in New York or San Francisco, the scene is far from closeted. Let's face it, honey. This is Gay Paree, where Eartha Kitt is Queen Camp, where Jean-Paul Gaultier designs Madonna's cone-breasted *ensembles,* and where *everybody's* had a rough day at the gym. Lesbians are less visible here, and much of the entertainment is more widely scattered across the city.

The indisputable center of gay and lesbian life is still the Marais, known throughout gay and straight Paris as *the* chic-est part of the city. Here in the winding streets of the chic 4*ème arrondissement,* you will find elegant shops, focaccia bread, Perrier, gay cafés, lesbian bars, intimate restaurants, bookstores that stock bisexual, gay, and lesbian literature, and shops selling all the requisite pink triangle necklaces, Keith Haring lithographs, and other articles of Gay-Pride-wear. A few words of advice. Dress well. You're in Paris, honey. Work it. But also consider spending time at one of the quieter and more relaxing gay and lesbian hangouts, such as the numerous restaurants and cafés that line the rue Vieille-du-Temple.

The Marais is a relatively safe part of town and most gays and lesbians feel very comfortable here, even late at night. But despite the fact that gay-bashing is infrequent (or perhaps just infrequently reported) in Paris, you should be as careful here at night as you'd be in the Village, the Castro, or any other neighborhood in a major city.

A word on the current *mode.* While gay men in Paris may have a sense of fashion, they tend to be effeminophobic. You will find very few men here who sport long hair, who wear earrings or other jewelry, or who cross-dress. The butch aesthetic reigns, although you won't find the body-fascism here that you find at so many New York clubs. Lesbians cover a wide range of aesthetics, although lipstick lesbians are in greater abundance here than in many U.S. cities.

For the most comprehensive listing of gay and lesbian restaurants, clubs, hotels, organizations, and services, consult Gai Pied's *Guide Gai 1994* (45F at any kiosk or *papeterie*). *Lesbia's* ads are a good gauge of what's hot, or at least what's open (22F from kiosks).

**Au Petit Cabanon,** 7, rue Ste-Apolline, 3*ème* (tel. 48 87 66 53). Mo. Strasbourg-St-Denis. Classic French cuisine. Mostly female clientèle. 120F *menu* features *foie gras maison, terrines maison,* and *boeuf grillade aux échalotes.* Open Sun.-Wed. noon-2pm, Thurs.-Sat. noon-2pm and 8pm-midnight.

**Le Bar Central,** 33, rue Vieille-du-Temple, 4*ème* (tel. 42 72 16 94). Mo. Hôtel de Ville. On the ground floor of the Hôtel Central, this bar lives up to its name, standing in one of the most central and popular parts of Marais nightlife. Perhaps the only truly French gay bar. The Central features a long mahogany bar where regulars and visitors come to have a drink (20-60F), to check out the boys, and to worship the black marble torso over the back wall. Open daily 4pm-2am. Mostly men.

**Le Café Majéstic,** 34, rue Vieille-du-Temple, 4*ème* (tel. 42 74 61 61). Mo. Hôtel-de-Ville. An eclectic crowd of bisexual, gay, lesbian, and straight people come here to gaze at the Beautiful People. Beautiful men from Soho to Tokyo play out the nightly show of fashion fascism, smoky flirtation, and café seduction. Bring an attitude with you—you'll need it. Drinks 15-40F. Open daily 8am-2am.

**La Champmeslé,** 4, rue Chabanais, 2*ème* (tel. 42 96 85 20). Mo. Pyramides, Bourse. This intimate lesbian bar has comfortable couches, dim lighting, and a young and yuppie clientele. Cabaret show on Thurs. Come on the 15th of every month for the *soirée zodiaque;* if it's your birthday month, you get a free drink. No cover. Drinks 25-40F. Open Mon.-Sat. 6pm-2am, Sun. 5pm-2am. AmEx, MC, V.

**Le Club,** 14, rue St-Denis, 1*er.* Mo. Châtelet-Les Halles. Found in the less chic, but *très* gay area of Beaubourg, next to the Marais, this is a great place to just come and dance. Le Club is renowned for its frequent theme parties on Thurs. nights. Cover (48F) Fri.-Sat. only. Drinks 32-42F. Open daily 11:30pm-dawn. MC, V.

**Le New Monocle,** 60, bd. Edgar Quinet, 14*ème* (tel. 43 20 81 12). Mo. Edgard Quinet. This lesbian bar has been around since the days of Gertrude Stein, Natalie Barney, and René Vivier. Its name comes from the fashionable monocles worn by cross-dressed lesbians in the 1930s, a style that George Brassaï captured in his 1930s photos of Paris, and that Romaine Brooks captured in her paintings of lesbian women of the era. Drinks 20-45F. Open Tues.-Sat. 11pm-6am.

**Le Palace Gay Tea Dance,** 8, rue Faubourg-Montmartre, 9*ème* (tel. 47 70 75 02). Mo. Rue Montmartre. A fabulous place to meet on Sunday afternoons. Here, the Beautiful People sip coffee and drinks and discuss the week's events at the less swanky gay and lesbian establishments. Drinks 40-60F. Cover 40F before 6pm, 60F after 6pm. Men and women welcome. Open Sun. 5-11pm.

**Le Petit Fer à Cheval,** 30, rue Vieille-du-Temple, 4*ème* (tel. 42 72 47 47). Mo. Hôtel-de-Ville. Next to the Majéstic, this small café-bar-restaurant gets its name from the horseshoe shape of its bar. A busy café on the sidewalk, a crowded bar *à cheval,* and a small and hidden intimate restaurant in back make this a great place to meet with friends. The small menu includes a salmon pasta dish (67F) and a warm *chèvre salade* called, appropriately, *le salade du petit fer à cheval* (56F). Desserts include *mousse au chocolat* and cheesecake. The denim-shirted waiters here are zany and fun. Open daily 9am-midnight, but often later.

**Le Petit Prince,** 12, rue de Lanneau, 5*ème* (tel. 43 54 77 26). Mo. Maubert-Mutualité. Superb dining in this casual restaurant for lesbians and gays. The 82F and 146F *menus* feature *foie gras* and *filet de boeuf sauce béarnaise.* Delicious white-chocolate mousse 34F. Make reservations. Open daily 7:30pm-12:30am.

**Le Piano Show,** 20, rue de la Ververie, 4*ème* (tel. 42 72 23 81; fax 42 78 08 03). Mo. Hôtel-de-Ville. Welcome to the lipstick-smacking, falsies-wearing, wig-coiff-puffing world of drag. For over 10 years, this small restaurant-cabaret has been performing a drag cabaret that's sure to knock your pantyhose off! It may be a bit expensive, but divas cost and here's where you start paying—in sweat, tears, and hilarious laughter. Dinner consists of *rôti de veau brisé, filet de dinde,* and *banane brésilienne* ("*brésilien*" is a synonym for "gay" in French). Dinner and show Sun.-Thurs. 9-11:30pm. 260F. Reservations required.

**Le Piano Zinc,** 49, rue des Blancs Manteaux, 4*ème* (tel. 42 74 32 42). Mo. Rambuteau. According to some, this is *the* gay hangout in the Marais. Features a piano bar where campy performers pay homage to Judy, Liza, Eartha, Madonna, Bette, Grace Jones, and, of course, Edith Piaf. We're talking campy. Drinks 36-42F. Beer 16F. Piano Bar after 10:30pm. Open Tues.-Sat. 6pm-2am. AmEx, MC, V.

**Le Privilège,** 3, cité Bergère, 9*ème* (tel. 47 70 75 02). This nightclub is the place to go for a glam all-female crowd; dance all night and into the morning, when the club becomes an after-hours joint for the boys from the KitKat upstairs. Selective door policy. Drinks 100F. Open weekends 11:30pm-noon.

**Le Quetzal,** 10, rue de la Ververie, 4*ème* (tel. 48 87 99 07). Mo. Hôtel de Ville. Extremely popular but very intimidating, this modern, high-tech neon bar is actually 3 bars in one. Most men just stand around the bar or play pinball while checking out the plethora of beautiful boys. A mostly 30-something crowd of gay men, located across the street from the appropriately named rue des Mauvais Garçons, home to Paris's most renowned drag diva, Mme. Bijoux. Beer 12F. Drinks from 33F. Open Mon.-Fri. noon-2am, Sat.-Sun. 2pm-2am.

**Le Swing,** 42, rue Vieille-du-Temple, 4*ème* (tel. 42 72 16 94). Mo. Hôtel-de-Ville. This 50s-style bar features Richie Cunningham clientele and Elvis music. Beware the Fonz in the bathroom. Drinks 11-40F. Open Mon.-Sat. noon-2am, Sun. 2pm-2am. MC, V.

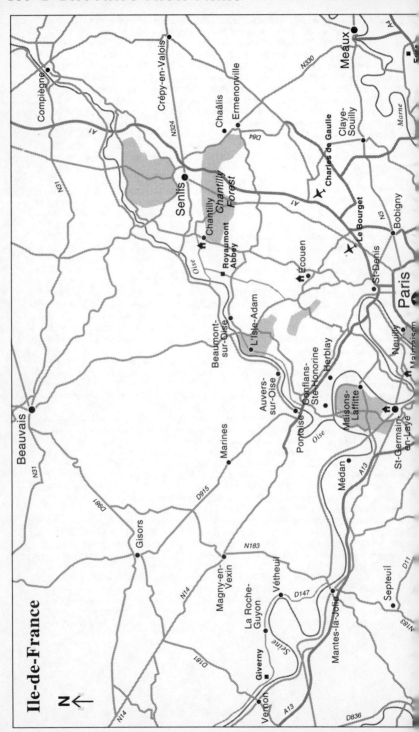

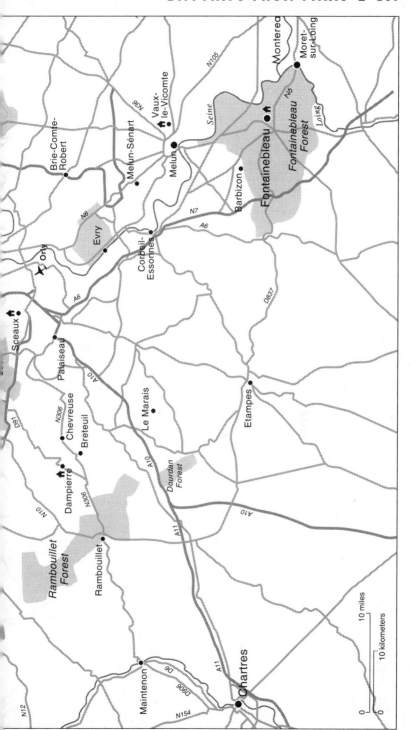

# ▪ Daytrips From Paris

Having taken all the time and expense to get to Paris, who would want to leav
Louis XIV, for one. Louis XVI, even more. But they didn't have the benefit of th
RER or SNCF that today can whisk you past the urban sprawl to some of the greate
monuments in France, barely a baguette's length from your home base in Pari
Whether you've got a few hours, a whole day, or an entire weekend to spare, the Il
de-France holds something for everyone. You can hike or rent a mountain bike
explore densely wooded forests, enjoy a peaceful picnic alongside a lazy cana
imagine what it would be like to hobnob with the aristocracy in the corridors an
gardens of ostentatious châteaux, or practice your French with Mickey and the gar
at Euro Disney® Resort. Spending time out of the city is the best way to recove
from the sensory overload that often accompanies a trip to Paris, whether it be yo
first or fifteenth, while giving you a taste of the France that exists beyond her sedu
tive capital.

## ▪▪▪ CHÂTEAUX

Venture forth to the many châteaux that surround Paris for a vision of the Frenc
aristocracy—and the French love of disciplined, ordered beauty—at its heigl
Although a château is literally a "castle," the magnificent structures that ring Pa
are by no means heavy defensive shields. Rather, they represent the greatest co
spicuous consumption in European history, all paid for by taxes inflicted on th
peasantry and townsfolk of France. Everything in these châteaux is intentional
from the carefully planned *parterres* and the "natural" English gardens, to th
restrained symmetry and Neoclassicism of the architecture and the idyllic "rura
quality of Marie-Antoinette's famous hamlet. Each of these buildings is a politic
statement in itself, a statement of wealth and power. They reflect the age of divin
right kings and aristocratic courts—more theatrical than the dramatists, from Raci
to Molière, which they sponsored.

Some helpful hints on château sight-seeing: in general, weekends are far busi
than weekdays, although Tuesdays (when most museums in Paris are closed) c
also get a bit hairy. On special occasions such as the fountain displays at Versaill
on Sundays, it may be worth braving the crowds. Keep on top of other spec
events—*son et lumière,* classical music concerts, temporary exhibitions, an
more—by reading the entertainment weeklies in Paris or by calling the châteav
directly. The main tourist office in Paris may also be of some assistance regardi
festivals and other annual events. Beware of groups of schoolchildren on weekda
although if you understand French, you might get the benefit of their guided tou
The morning is always a better time to arrive than the afternoon. Don't start a vi
45 minutes before the château closes for lunch—the guards will rush you by lockin
the door behind you each time you walk into a room. PLEASE leave your came
alone while you're inside the building. Flash pictures are forbidden for a good re
son; they slowly fade and discolor furniture, paintings, curtains, tapestries, e
Besides, unless you're a professional with a tripod and lighting equipment, your p
tures won't look nearly as good as the postcards you can buy for less money than
would cost to develop your film. Most of these sights are gargantuan in size and w
not fit into the view finder of the average camera—you'll only get bits and piec
anyway. Make a real effort to take your time, look around you at both the big pictu
and the delightful details, and revel in the history of these spectacular residence
hunting lodges, and summer homes.

# ■ Versailles

Built by the "Sun King," Louis XIV, because he was sick of the Louvre, the magnificent palace of Versailles, 20km from Paris, is unquestionably the most famous palace in the world. Everything else is compared to it. The palatial château, the luxurious rooms, the sparkling Hall of Mirrors, the stately bed-chamber of the Queen, and the expansive gardens remain as relics of the expensive fancies of a playboy king who loved lavish parties, theatrical extravaganzas, and mirrors, mirrors everywhere.

## HISTORY

Versailles embodies the Sun King's absolute power and his famous statement, *"L'Etat, c'est moi."* (I *am* the State.) Shunning Paris for its association with the power struggles of his youth, Louis XIV turned his father's hunting lodge into his royal residence, built and decorated mainly by Le Vau, Le Brun, and Le Nôtre, the team stolen from Vaux-le-Vicomte. The court became the center of noble life where more than a thousand of France's greatest aristocrats vied for the king's favor. In turn, Louis was able to keep the nobility away from Paris and their provincial power-bases and under his watchful eye. Busy vying for roles in the Sun King's wake-up *(levée)* and bed-going *(coucher)* rituals, the French aristocracy had no time for subversion. Ever the clever politician, Louis successfully destroyed their financial independence by forcing them to pay crippling taxes, which he used to support his own exorbitant expenditures.

The ostentatious rooms and endless gardens at Versailles represent the pinnacle of classical Baroque orchestration. No one knows just how much it cost to build Versailles; Louis XIV himself burned the accounts so no one would ever find out. At the same time, life there was less luxurious than one might imagine—courtiers wearing rented swords urinated behind statues in the parlors, wine froze in the drafty dining rooms, and dressmakers invented the color "puce" (literally, "flea") to camouflage the insects crawling on the noblewomen. Although Louis XIV and his palace number among the few monarchical successes of 17th-century Europe, the kind of mass extortion that Versailles represents would spark the French Revolution a century later. On October 5, 1789, 15,000 fishwives and National Guardsmen marched out to the palace and brought the royal family back with them. In 1871 the château regained its limelight as Wilhelm of Prussia became Kaiser Wilhelm I of Germany in the Hall of Mirrors. That same year, as headquarters of the Thiers regime, Versailles sent an army against its old rival, Paris, then ruled by the Commune. And in 1919, a vengeful France forced Germany to sign the ruinous Treaty of Versailles in the very room of its birth.

## THE MAIN TOUR

When you arrive at the Versailles Rive Gauche RER train stop, exit the station and take a right. At the first huge intersection look left and you'll see the immense outer courtyard of Versailles, surrounded by gilt grill fencing and centered around the equestrian statue of Louis XIV, decked out in long curls, lacy cuffs, hose, and high-heeled shoes. Towering over the courtyard is the façade of the terrace where Molière's *Tartuffe* debuted. The clock on the pediment used to be set to the time of death of the previous king. Above what appears to be the main entrance is the balcony of the **King's bedroom,** at the center of the east-west axis along which the château and gardens are laid out. The placement of the room was no mistake—the Sun King's place was at the center of the château system, and he rose each morning, to great ritual, in the east.

Signs in the courtyard point you to Entrance A, B, C, or D. Most of Versailles' visitors enter at **Entrance A,** located on the right-hand side in the North Wing. (Entrance B is for groups, Entrance C leads to the king's chamber, Entrance D is where guided tours start, and Entrance H is for visitors in wheelchairs.) Buy a ticket

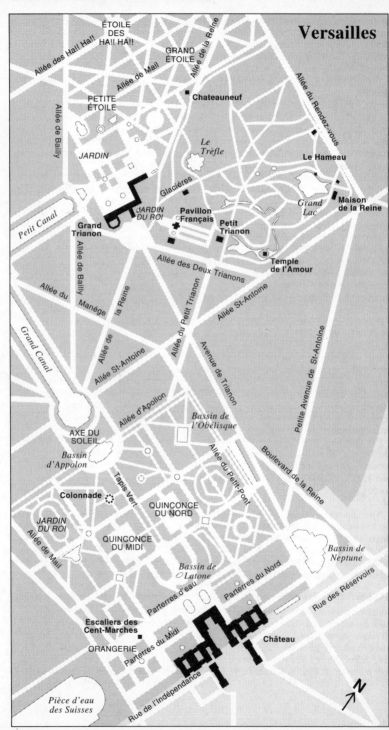

VERSAILLES

**Versailles**

ÉTOILE DES HA!! HA!!

GRAND ÉTOILE

Allée des Ha!! Ha!!

Allée de la Reine

Allée de Mail

PETITE ÉTOILE

Allée du Rendez-vous

■ Chateauneuf

Allée de Bailly

JARDIN

*Le Trèfle*

*Le Hameau*

Glacières

*Grand Lac*

JARDIN DU ROI

Pavillon Français

**Maison de la Reine**

**Grand Trianon**

Petit Trianon

Petit Canal

Temple de l'Amour

Allée des Deux Trianons

Allée de Bailly

Allée du Manège

Allée de la Reine

Allée St-Antoine

Allée du Petit Trianon

Allée St-Antoine

Grand Canal

Avenue de Trianon

Petite Avenue de St-Antoine

Allée d'Apollon

*Bassin de l'Obélisque*

AXE DU SOLEIL

*Bassin d'Appolon*

Allée du Petit-Pont

Boulevard de la Reine

Tapis Vert

**Colonnade**

QUINCONCE DU NORD

*Bassin de Neptune*

JARDIN DU ROI

QUINCONCE DU MIDI

Allée de Mail

*Bassin de Latone*

Parterres d'eau

Parterres du Nord

Rue des Réservoirs

**Escaliers des Cent-Marches**

Parterres du Midi

**Château**

ORANGERIE

Rue de l'Indépendance

*Pièce d'eau des Suisses*

N

for general admittance to the palace at Entrance A (40F; ages 18-25, over 60, and Sun. 26F; the economical Carte Musée includes admission to Versailles). General admission gains you entrance to the State Apartments of the King (in the North wing), the Galerie des Glaces (the famed Hall of Mirrors), and the State Apartments of the Queen (in the South wing).

The general admission ticket starts your visit in the **Musée de l'Histoire de France,** created in 1837 by Louis-Philippe to celebrate his country's glory. Against the backdrop of textured walls are hung portraits of men and women who shaped the history of France. The face of Louis XIV is ever-present; you may wonder if he spent his entire life sitting for portraits. Of particular interest are portraits by Philippe de Champaigne, pre-eminent court artist under Louis XIII. The 21 rooms, arranged in chronological order, try to construct an historical context from which to understand the château. The North Wing ground floor, in Louis XIV's day, was a bustling open-air market where men bought wigs and women ribbons. As you head into the (crowded) state apartments, imagine what living here as a not-so-elevated courtier would be like.

Each of the **Drawing Rooms** in the **State Apartments** is dedicated to a mythological god—Hercules, Mars and the ever-present Apollo, among others. Although less brilliant than you would expect, the gilt wood is still splendid, fresh from the five-year, $70 million restoration that ended in 1989. Note the integration of painting with bas-relief, sculpture, and furniture—as Le Brun's paintings meld with Le Vau's architecture. Shift your marble-mesmerized eyes toward the **Louis XIV statue** by Bernini in the **Diana Drawing Room.** A glimpse of his armor visible underneath the Baroque frenzy of clothing, the luxuriously coiffed Louis looks unflinchingly into the sun.

Framed by the **War and Peace Drawing Rooms** is the **Hall of Mirrors.** The hall was a somewhat gloomy passageway until Mansart added mirrors and doubled the light. Although many of the mirrors are old and cloudy, little compares to the impact of standing at one end of the Hall and gazing past the mirror-filled arches, gold figures, and many chandeliers. Le Brun's ceiling paintings tell the history of Louis XIV's heroism, culminating in the central piece entitled *The King Governs Alone.* Don't expect a wall of seamless mirrors—the Hall is a series of mirrored panels joined together and set in wooden frames. Each of these mirrors was the largest that 17th-century technology could produce; the ensemble represented an unbelievable extravagance.

The **Queen's Bedchamber,** which saw the public births of 20 members of the royal family, sports its floral summer décor—not the darker plush red and black velvet used during 18th-century winters. A version of David's painting depicting Napoleon's self-coronation dominates the **Salle du Sacré** (also known as the Coronation Room), in which the king used to wash the feet of 13 poor children on Holy Thursday.

You can rent a **cassette guide** in English for 28F (with ID deposit of passport) at the information desk behind the ticket booths. An excellent printed guide is Daniel Meyer's 50F color-photo guide to the palace called *Versailles Tour of the Château, Gardens, and Trianon,* on sale at the gift desk. This 96-page book, written by Versailles' curator, has dazzling photos and detailed explanations of the countless paintings, rooms, antiques, gardens, and fountains of Versailles.

## GUIDED TOURS

Consider starting your visit at **Entrance D,** where you can reserve a place on a guided tour, the only way to access many of the most interesting parts of the castle. All tours originate here, at the left-hand inside corner as you approach the palace. All cost the same (1-hr. tours 22F, ages 7-17 15F, under 7 free; 2-hr. tours 44F, ages 7-17 31F, under 7 free). Choose between seven tours of different parts of the château; only three are in English. Tours are primarily recommended for repeat visitors wish-

VERSAILLES

ing to go into detail about a specific part of the château. (Check at Entrance D for times.)

Don't miss the Opera and Chapel tour. The **Chapel** is visible from the general access area but you won't be able to appreciate the Rococo sculpture, the fresco of the Holy Ghost, or the floor's marble design from a distance. Church services were held regularly in this chapel dedicated to Saint Louis; Louis XV, far from a saint, yet not hypocritical enough to take communion while indulging with his mistresses, abstained from the rite for thirty years. In the chapel's last royal marriage, Marie-Antoinette and the 16-year-old Dauphin (future Louis XVI) were married here in 1770.

Architect Jacques-Ange Gabriel had been working on plans for the **Opéra** for 20 years when Louis XV demanded it be finished in a mere 21 months, in time for the marriage of the Dauphin. With 20,000 people working, it was finished the day before and held its first performance on the royal wedding night. The pink and blue oval room is a marvelous fake; though apparently marble or bronze, the restored Opéra is actually made of wood. Mirrors around the galleries reflect the chandeliers, making the theater seem larger than its actual size. Gabriel's 20 years of planning did not go to waste—many consider this one of the most beautiful theaters in the world. Many of Molière's plays premiered here, accompanied by the music of court composer Lully.

Most of the other tours take you through seemingly empty, if historically important, rooms. The tour of **Louis XV's Apartments** showcases a small collection of furnishings, instruments, and tapestries, while providing a history of Versailles under that monarch. You can see the room where Mozart played on his youthful visits (at ages 7 and 22) to Versailles and learn the origin of the name of the "voyeuses" chair. The visit to **Marie-Antoinette's Apartments** does not trail through as many lavishly decorated rooms as you would think. Some of the smaller rooms are hard to appreciate in a large group. Much of the tour is spent in rooms filled with portraits, learning the who's who for the Hapsburgs, Bourbons, and their ministers. True French Revolution buffs will not want to miss the door and passageway through which the Queen fled to rejoin her king on October 6, 1789, when a crowd of bloodthirsty Parisians flooded into her bedroom, demanding the head of the "Austrian whore."

The **King's Bedchamber** yields a look at the Sun-King's gold bed and balustrade, and more than a passing glance at Nocret's beautiful family portrait, featuring Louis XIV as Apollo and his brother, Philippe d'Orléans, as holder of the morning star. Philippe was the first after the morning chaplain to see the Sun King—Philippe was also kept in skirts until he was 18. (Tickets to the bedchamber sold at Entrance C.)

Other tours are fairly uninspiring. Unlike the Opera and Chapel tour, expect empty rooms with limited decoration—Versailles was completely sacked during the Revolution and only a tiny portion of its original glory has been restored. More portraits populate the visit to the **Apartments of Mesdames,** Louis XV's daughters, and the other French-only tours, including tours of the **Apartments of Mme. de Pompadour, Mme. du Barry,** and the **Dauphin and Dauphine.** Take these tours only if you are an addicted buff of the French aristocracy, or if you're looking for an oral history lesson, full of neat anecdotes, with some interesting background decoration.

Longer tours go to the **Gardens and Groves** and to the **Petit Trianon and English-Garden.** The Gardens and Groves tour, with considerable walking, provides the history of Le Nôtre's gardens and their countless fountains (June-Oct. Sat.-Sun. at 11:30am). Guided visits to the **Petit Trianon and the Jardin Anglais** illuminate this favored hangout of Marie-Antoinette (July-Sept. 1-hr. tour at 11am. 2-hr. French-only tour 4pm). Both tours leave from the entrance to the Petit Trianon (1-hr. tours of the gardens 22F, ages 7-17 15F, under 7 free; 2-hr. tours 44F, ages 7-17 31F, under 7 free).

# THE GARDENS

Versailles gardens are breathtaking, the perfect complement to the Sun King's huge palace. Numerous artists—Le Brun, Mansart, Coysevox—executed statues and fountains here, but it is the hand of master gardener André Le Nôtre that you see all over the grounds. Louis XIV, an amateur enthusiast of landscaping, wrote the first guide book to the gardens entitled the "Manner of presenting the gardens at Versailles." Start, as he suggests, on the terrace, pausing to study the layout of the gardens. During the summer, the grounds at Versailles have an overwhelming impression of green rare to this area of France. Even more rare are the wide paths and tall trees—you can feel quite alone, even with lots of people around. During the summer, the grounds are open until dusk. Come in the evening to see the immense château without people, like the empty stage of a grand opera. You will see the entire panorama of Versailles as it was originally conceived—a single work of art, bringing together artistic and natural media as a backdrop for the aristocrats who lived in its rigid, controlled beauty.

To the left of the terrace, the **Parterre du Midi** graces the area in front of Mansart's **Orangerie,** once home to 2000 orange trees. The temperature inside never drops below 6°C (42.8°F). In the center of the terrace, the **Parterre d'eau** boasts statues by the *ancien régime's* greatest sculptors. Below is one of the most extraordinary fountains, the **Bassin de Latone.** Latona, mother of Diana and Apollo, is seen shielding her children from the attack of peasants, whom Jupiter is turning into frogs. Part-human, part-frog figures belch water into the air when the fountains are turned on. The fountain can also be read as a thinly veiled political allegory—Latona as Anne d'Autriche, fleeing Paris and the Fronde with her children, Louis XIV (Apollo) and Philippe d'Orléans (Diana). Louis XIV appears as both victim (Apollo) and savior (Jupiter).

Past the *bassin* and to the left is the **Rockwork Grove,** built between 1681 and 1683. Once known as the ballroom because courtiers danced on the long-gone marble floor, the Grove shows off odiferous water cascading over shell-encrusted steps. The south gate of the grove leads to the magnificent **Bassin de Bacchus (or de l'Automne**), one of four seasonal fountains marking the intersection of pathways on either side of the main alley. The **Bassin du Miroir d'eau** spurts near the peaceful **Jardin du Roi** and the **Bassin de Saturne (or de l'Hiver),** an old man. The **Colonnade** is a 32-column peristyle, decorated by sculptures and 28 white marble basins, in the center of which the king used to take light meals. The north gate to the Colonnade exits onto the **Tapis Vert (Green Carpet),** the central strip of grass linking the château to the much-photographed **Bassin d'Apollon.** Pulled by the prancing of four horses, Apollo/Sun God/Louis XIV rises out of dark water to enlighten the world.

On the north side of the garden is Marsy's incredible **Bassin d'Encelade.** One of the giants who tried to unseat Jupiter from Mount Olympus, Enceladus cries in agony under the weight of rocks that Jupiter has thrown to bury him. When the fountains are turned on, a 25m jet bursts from Enceladus' mouth. Flora reclines more peacefully on a bed of flowers in the **Bassin de Flore (or du Printemps**), while Ceres luxuriates in sheaves of wheat in the **Bassin de Cérès (or de l'Eté**). The artificial grotto that houses the **Bains d'Apollon** was, surprisingly, not built under Louis XIV, but in 1778 under Louis XVI and shows, not surprisingly, nymphs fluttering around Apollo.

The **Parterre du Nord,** full of flowers, lawns, and sculpted trees, overlooks some of the garden's most spectacular fountains. The **Allée d'Eau,** lined with fountains held by child statues, provides the best view of the **Bassin des Nymphes de Diane.** At the end of Allée d'Eau roars the **Bassin du Dragon.** The dying beast vomits water 27m into the air, the highest of any jet in the gardens. The culmination of any visit to the gardens is the **Bassin de Neptune,** the largest of the fountains. Ninety-nine jets spray from urns and seahorns surrounding a fierce Neptune, trident thrust in front of him. (Gardens open sunrise-sundown. Free; May-Sept. Sun. 18F.)

VERSAILLES

Beyond the Petit Parc of Le Nôtre's classical gardens stretch wilder, more natural woods and farmlands. The **Grand Canal,** a large rectangular (and, like most of the park, entirely artificial) body of water lies beyond the Bassin d'Apollon. Rent a bike to the right (north) of the canal, just outside the garden gates, to appreciate Versailles' vast grandeur (35F/hr.). A *bateau-mouche* tours the Canal (25F, under 16 20F).

## THE TRIANONS AND MARIE-ANTOINETTE'S HAMEAU

Also within the grounds of Versailles are the two Trianons—"smaller" châteaux made of lavish pink, white, and black marble—and the Petit Hameau, an idyllic peasant village where Marie-Antoinette liked to milk the cows. Trianon was the name of the village the Sun King bought in 1668 in order to expand his estate. Built by Mansart, the single-story, marble-decorated **Grand Trianon** was intended as a meeker château in which, if need be, the king could reside alone with his family. Stripped of its furniture during the Revolution, the château was restored and inhabited by Napoleon and his second wife. Today past meets present as important state meetings, including the one that passed the constitutional amendment for Maastricht, are held at the Grand Trianon, and Versailles briefly becomes the capital of France once again.

The **Petit Trianon,** built for Louis XV and Mme. de Pompadour by Gabriel, was presented to Marie-Antoinette by Louis XVI. Restoration has closed off all but four rooms to the public—their cozy feel may not be worth the price of admission. The English Garden, made for Marie-Antoinette, and the Grand Trianon gardens provide calm away from the madding crowds closer to the château. Quainter still, and the opportune spot for a walk or some rest, is **Le Hameau** (the Queen's Hamlet), a collection of Normandy cottages built for Marie-Antoinette. The young queen of "Let them eat cake" fame liked to play peasant here, to the great disgust of the people who actually fit that description. None of the buildings is open to the public but they once contained drawing rooms of considerable, un-peasant-like elegance.

(Grand and Petit Trianons open daily 10am-6pm; Oct.-April Tues.-Fri. 10am-12:30pm and 2-5:30pm, Sat.-Sun. 10am-5:30pm. Admission to the Grand Trianon 20F, *tarif réduit* 13F; to the Petit 12F, *tarif réduit* 8F. Combined ticket to the palace and Trianons 60F, *tarif réduit* 45F, purchase before 12:30pm.) Shuttle trams from the palace to the Trianons and the Hameau leave from behind the main château most of the day (round-trip 27F). The train does a 35-minute circuit that allows you to get off, tour the Trianons, and get back on another train. But the commentary on the gardens only repeats what is written on the pamphlet. Otherwise, the walk takes about 25 minutes.

## SPECIAL EVENTS

Brave the crowds on Sundays from May through September to see (and hear) the **Grandes Eaux Musicales,** the only time the fountains are in full operation. Seeing Versailles with the fountains on completes the sensual experience that the palace was designed to be; the entire park comes alive with spouting water. A *grande perspective* is offered between 11:15 and 11:35am; the best time to circulate and visit each fountain is between 3:30 and 5pm, when the fountains spout and appropriately inspirational music plays. A free pamphlet lays out a suggested walking path; a more expensive 25F guide in English will not give you much more info than that already found in the Meyer guide. (Admission to park during *Grandes Eaux* 19F.)

The **Grand Fête de Nuit,** a musical and fireworks extravaganza, imitates the huge *fêtes* of Louis XIV. The garden at Versailles had to be finished in 1664 in time for one such party, the Fête of the Enchanted Isle, for which Molière wrote an up-to-the-minute *masque.* (Fêtes held at the Neptune Fountain July and Sept. Sat. nights rain-or-shine. 80min. 50-170F, reduced rates for children. Call the tourist office at 39 59 36 22 for dates and ticket info.) Tickets go on sale at the tourist office and certain agencies within Paris. Doors open 1½ hours before the show; enter at 2, bd. de la Reine.

The **Centre de Musique Baroque de Versailles** gives concerts, equestrian shows, masques, dance performances, and theater presentations in period costume, many focusing on the 18th-century French court, music, and drama (May-early Sept. Sat. 5:30pm; tickets 50-180F). Musical Thursday concerts by the Maîtrise Nationale of Versailles are held in the Royal Chapel (Nov.-June 5:30pm; tickets 20F). For more information call 39 50 36 22 in Versailles; in Paris call 42 60 58 31 or 43 59 24 60.

Versailles offers an ongoing lecture series called **Visites Thématiques** on issues such as "The Expression of Divine Right in the Décor of Versailles," "The Life of Marie-Antoinette at the Petit Trianon," and "Princes Who Would Never Become Kings." There is much here for the 18th-century French scholar and the Marie-Antoinette aficionado alike. (Lectures Sat. 10:30am, 2pm, and 2:30pm, Sun. 10am. Call 30 84 76 18 for more information.)

## PRACTICAL INFORMATION

Visiting Versailles is a mammoth undertaking; you may want to take two days to do it. Arrive early in the morning to avoid the worst of the crowds. Versailles is most crowded on Sundays when the fountains are turned on and in late June when the palace is swamped with French schoolchildren on field trips. (Château open daily 9am-6:30pm; Oct.-April 9am-5:30pm. Gardens open 7am-sunset. General admittance to the palace 40F; ages 18-25, over 60, and Sun. 26F; the **Carte Musée** includes admission to Versailles. For more information on the *carte*, see introduction to Museums.)

For more on Versailles, check out the **Ancienne Comédie Bookshop** in the *cour des Princes* next to the palace. Or call the **Office de Tourisme de Versailles,** Les Manèges, rue du Général de Gaulle (tel. 39 53 31 63), across from the train station, which has information about château events, other sights, lodging, and food. Food is both scarce and expensive at Versailles. There are two pricey restaurants: the **Caféteria** (tel. 39 50 58 62; open 9:30am-5pm) and **La Flotille** (tel. 39 51 41 58).

The RER has direct and frequent train service between Paris and Versailles. Trains run from the Invalides *métro* stop on RER Line C5 to the Versailles Rive Gauche station (every 15min.; 35-40 min.; 19F round-trip). From the Invalides *métro* stop, take trains whose label begins with "V." Buy your RER ticket *before* going through the turnstile to the platform, despite the fact that your *métro* ticket will get you through, because your *métro* ticket will not get you through the turnstiles to exit at Versailles.

## ■ Vaux-le-Vicomte

Some might consider **Vaux-le-Vicomte** a mere hut compared to Versailles. But as Le Vau, Le Brun, and Le Nôtre's first masterpiece, it is in many ways the more coherent creation. Nicolas Fouquet, Louis XIV's Minister of Finance, assembled the team of architect, artist, and landscaper to build Vaux for him between 1656 and 1661. In so doing, he financed the creation of a new standard of country château, in a uniquely French, Neoclassical Baroque style. To show off his new pad, Fouquet threw a *fête* to end all *fêtes* on August 17, 1661. Louis XIV and Anne d'Autriche were but two of the witnesses to a sensual orgy that provided poetry by La Fontaine, a new ballet by Molière, and concluded in a fireworks extravaganza featuring the King and Queen's coat of arms and pyrotechnic squirrels (Fouquet's symbol).

The celebration of Fouquet's impeccable grace, sophistication, and culture—he was surrounded by a circle of the finest artists and intellectuals—did not last long. Furious at being upstaged by his first minister, the young Louis ordered Fouquet arrested. Three weeks later at Nantes, d'Artagnan, the captain of the Musketeers immortalized by Dumas, arrested the hapless man for speculation. Behind Fouquet's downfall were hidden causes. Colbert, another minister, had been turning the monarch against Fouquet for years; Fouquet's ill-advised expression of affection for

Mme. de Lavallière, beloved of the king, didn't help matters either. And someone, even the man who had kept the French treasury solvent by raising funds against his own fortune, needed to be the fall guy for the state's abysmal financial condition. In a trial that lasted for three years, the judges in Fouquet's case voted narrowly for banishment over death; Louis XIV overturned the judgment in favor of life imprisonment. Pignerol, a dreary citadel, housed the fallen minister until his death in 1680, leading some to speculate he was the famous man in the iron mask. Louis did appreciate Fouquet's tastes; soon after the minister's arrest, the King confiscated many of Vaux's finest objects and hired the same trio—Le Vau, Le Brun, and Le Nôtre—to take their crafts to Versailles. Everything at Vaux-le-Vicomte has been orchestrated to create an impressive whole. The designers integrated painting and sculpture, architecture and décor, building and garden to please the viewer with ideal forms and harmony.

## THE CHATEAU

The château itself (tel. 60 66 97 09) recalls both the grandeur of a Roman past, with its rusticated columns, and a French fort, complete with squat walls and moat. Walk over the moat, invisible from the road, and appreciate Le Vau's sense of symmetry and his use of water to set off the building. With the Spanish war ended, Fouquet's entrance sends the message that peace unites art and prosperity. Although the tour begins to your left, upon entering, peek up at the dome in the Oval Room ahead and then out to the gardens. Vaux was designed to draw people inside, contain them within the cupola, and expel them into the seemingly infinite space of the gardens.

A thorough pamphlet, available in English, guides the visit to the château. For more detail and a brilliantly colored souvenir, buy the glossy guide in the gift shop (40F). Notice the ornate scripted Fs all round the château, and keep an eye out for the ever-present squirrel, Fouquet's industrious symbol, and for the tower with three battlements, his second wife's crest. The **Minister's Bedchamber** may lead you to wonder who the real monarch was in this kingdom. The opulent red and gold bed stands under an allegorical ceiling in which Apollo bears the lights of the world. (One begins to understand why he was arrested....) **Mme. Fouquet's Closet** once had walls lined with small mirrors, the decorative forerunner of Versailles' Hall of Mirrors. Le Brun's portrait of Fouquet, whose penetrating look overrides his general appearance of humility, hangs over the fireplace. Tear your eyes away from the beautiful 1877 billiard table in the **Square Room** to admire the exquisite beams of the Louis XIII-style ceiling. The vivid colors and engaging expressions of the nine muses in the **Room of the Muses** make this one of Le Brun's finest decorative schemes. Le Brun planned to crown the **Oval Room** (or Grand Salon) with a fresco entitled *The Palace of the Sun,* but Fouquet's arrest halted all activity. The tapestries once bore Fouquet's squirrel, but Colbert seized them and replaced the rodents with his own adders. The ornate **King's Bedchamber** (the balustrade gives it away) boasts an orgy of stucco, cherubs, and lions fluttering around the centerpiece of *Time Bearing Truth Heavenward.*

## THE GARDENS

Vaux-le-Vicomte presented André Le Nôtre with his first opportunity to create an entire formal garden. Three villages, a small château, and many trees were destroyed to open up space, though countless trees were later replanted to draw the all-important contrast between order and wilderness. Even a river was rerouted to provide the desired effect. With Vaux, Le Nôtre gave birth to a truly French style of garden—shrubs were trimmed, lawns shaved, bushes sculpted, and pools of water strategically placed to produce a kind of embroidered tapestry exuding classical harmony.

Start by considering the impressive panorama from the steps behind the château. The garden seems perfectly symmetrical and the grottoes appear to be directly behind the large pool of water. Closer inspection reveals otherwise. The right-hand *parterre* was a flowerbed in its original incarnation, but today is dominated by a statue of Diana. Its matching green area on the left side is actually wider and sunken. The **Pool of the Crown,** named for the gold crown at its center, is the most ornate of the garden pools. The **Round Pool** and its surrounding 17th-century statues mark an important intersection: to the left, down the east walkway, are the **Water Gates,** likely backdrop for Molière's performance of *The Annoyances* before Louis XIV. The **Water Mirror,** farther down the central walkway, was designed to reflect the château perfectly, but you may have some trouble positioning yourself to enjoy the effect. The Mirror also hides the sunken canal, known as **La Poêle** (the Frying Pan), fed by the Anqueuil River. Although somewhat smelly and scum-covered today, the canal is a reminder that Fouquet made his fortune in shipping. Climb to the **Farnese Hercules** (the vanishing point when you look out from the castle), and survey the land and imposing château before you. The old stables today house a carriage museum, **Les Equipages.** Magnificent carriages of all kinds come complete with piped-in music, dressed-up party-goers, and liveried footmen. Picnicking in the gardens is prohibited, but **L'Ecureuil** (squirrel) on the castle grounds provides good salads (35-40F) and cooked meat and vegetables (54-58F).

Vaux is exquisite; getting there is exquisite torture, which may explain the absence of crowds. Your best and cheapest option, if traveling with other people, is to rent a car. Take Autoroute A4 or A6 from Paris and exit at Val-Maubée or Melun, respectively. Head toward Meaux on N36 and follow the signs. Or take the train to Melun, a fairly large center on the SNCF *banlieue* line (every 15-30min. from Gare de Lyon, 45min., 62F round-trip). Unfortunately, the station is a smug 6km from the château. You can take a bike on the train free of charge, but riding on the undivided highway without shoulder next to big trucks is not advisable. It might be worth it to splurge and take a taxi. The 6km ride will cost you at least 66F one way (pick one up at the train station; call 64 52 51 50 from Vaux). Fit troopers might not mind the 70- to 90-minute hike for at least one part of the trip. The effort may pay off most handsomely on Saturday evenings from May to October (8:30-11pm) when candle-lit visits make the château seem almost homey. The fountains in Le Nôtre's gardens are turned on from 3 to 6pm every second and last Saturday of the month from April to October. The **tourist office,** 2, av. Gallieni, by the train station in Melun (tel. 64 37 11 31), can help you with accommodations, sight-seeing opportunities, and give you a free map—essential for those planning to walk (open Tues.-Sat. 10am-noon and 2-6pm).

(Château open Mon.-Sat. 10am-1pm and 2-6pm, Sun. and holidays 10am-6pm; Feb.-March, Nov., and Dec. 19-Jan. 4 Mon.-Sat. 11am-12:30pm and 2-4:30pm, Sun. and holidays 11am-5pm. *Equipages* open same hrs., but remain open during lunch and 30min. after the château closes. Gardens open same hrs. as the *équipages,* except Sun., when they are open an additional 30min. Admission 47F, students with ID and under 16 38F, under 6 free. Estate open May-Oct. Sat. 8:30-11pm for candle-lit evenings. Admission 65F, students with ID and under 16 52F. Admission to gardens 27F.)

# ■ Fontainebleau

What images do the words "hunting lodge" evoke in your mind? A rustic log cabin tucked away in the thick of the woods? Simple furnishings and a stone hearth? Stuffed deer heads on the wall? The men who commissioned and designed the Château de Fontainebleau had a slightly different vision; their efforts converged in this sprawling structure, deceptively simple when viewed from the main courtyard. Made from sandstone formed in the lush tangle of forest surrounding the château, Fontainebleau's warm yellow exterior, accented with red brick, hides the splendor and extravagance within. Not a bad place for a harried sovereign to get away from it all.

Like its name, believed to come from a certain Monsieur Bliaut who owned a local fountain, Fontainebleau is a composite of architectural and decorative styles. It has been a glorified hunting lodge for nearly 500 years, presenting a radically different

FONTAINEBLEAU

architectural statement from the unity of Vaux-le-Vicomte and Versailles. Kings of France have lived on these grounds since the 12th century, when the exiled Thomas à Becket consecrated Louis VII's manor chapel. In 1528, François I tore down and rebuilt the castle, to bring him closer to the "red and black furred animals" he so loved to hunt. Italian artists designed and decorated the palace, and their paintings, the *Mona Lisa* and the *Virgin in the Rocks* among them, filled his private collections. Subsequent kings had varying degrees of affection for the château, depending generally on their love for dead and dying furry animals. Most used their favorite designers to add at least one magnificent room, while some attached whole new wings. The château remained a happening place throughout. Louis XIII was born here in 1601, Louis XV was married here in 1725, and Louis XIV revoked the Edict of Nantes here in 1685. Fontainebleau was also the perfect place to welcome the Pope, who had come to crown Napoleon in 1804, and to imprison His Holiness between 1812 and 1814. Napoleon popped in to Fontainebleau frequently and it is presented as one of his main residences; in reality he only spent 194 days in the building whose eclectic blend of architecture led him to dub it *"La Maison des Siècles"* (the House of Centuries). **Cour des Adieux** was so named after serving as the scene of his dramatic farewell in 1814. Also known as the **White Horse Court,** it is used as the main entry to the château. Note the unique horseshoe-shaped stairway leading to the front door.

The **Grands Appartements,** the standard visitors' circuit, provides a lesson in the history of French architecture and decoration. Guides available in English will make the whole visit more meaningful: 15F will get you a pamphlet about the château and some of the gardens or one describing the Grands Appartements alone; 25F buys the glossy booklet with more complete descriptions. All labels in the rooms are in French. Dubreuil's **Gallery of Plates** tells the history of Fontainebleau on a remarkable series of porcelain plates, fashioned in Sèvres between 1838 and 1844. In the **Gallery of François I,** arguably the most famous room at Fontainebleau, muscular figures by Mannerist artist Il Rosso (known in French as Maître Roux) tell mythological tales of heroism and bravado, brilliantly illuminated by light flooding in from courtside windows. The **Ball Room's** magnificent octagonal ceiling, with complementary floor, reminds the visitor that much of Fontainebleau should be observed with a craned neck. The **King's Cabinet** (also known as the **Louis XIII Salon),** decorated under Henri IV, was the site of many an important meeting, as well as *le débotter,* the king's post-hunt boot removal. Gobelin tapestries and Savonnerie carpets line walls and floors throughout the palace—the four seasons, with floral hoops, are depicted on the wall of the **Empress's Antechamber.** Every Queen of France since the 17th century slept in the gold, green, and leafy **Queen's** (later Empress's) **Bed Chamber;** the gilded wood bed was built for Marie-Antoinette, who never used it. The $N$ on the throne is another testament to Napoleon's enduring humility; the red and gold velvet meets in a crown above the throne. **Napoleon's Bed Chamber** boasts predictably fancy decor, but the **Emperor's Small Bed Chamber,** complete with camp bed, seems more in the style of a military man. In the **Emperor's Private Room,** known today as the **Abdication Chamber,** Napoleon signed his abdication in 1814. (Grands Appartements open Wed.-Mon. 9:30am-12:30pm and 2-5pm. Last entry 11:30am and 4pm. Admission 30F; students, seniors, and Sun. 19F; under 18, teachers with ID, unemployed, and art students with ID free. 90-min. guided tours available in French and possibly English Wed. and Sat.-Sun. at 3pm; 32F; students, seniors, and Sun. 25F. Call 64 22 27 40 for details. Château is wheelchair accessible.)

The same ticket admits you to the **Musée Napoléon,** a collection of paraphernalia including his tiny shoes, his toothbrush, his field tent, and his son's toys. Not to be missed are the gifts (don't you wish you had enemies like this?) from Carlos IV of Spain. (Same tel. and hrs. as Grands Appartements. Last entry 11:30am and 4pm.)

The **Petits Appartements,** private rooms of Napoleon and the Empress Josephine, are accessible only by guided tours and only on certain days. If you are desperate to see these rooms, call ahead. (Admission 12F, under 26 and over 60 8F. Tours, on days they do take place, at 10am, 11am, 2pm, and 3pm. English-language tours may become available.) The **Musée Chinois de l'Impératrice Eugénie,** also in the château, offers a welcome respite from the sometimes crowded apartments upstairs. Reopened after restoration in 1991, these four rooms were remodeled in 1863 by the Empress to house the collection she herself called her *"Musée chinois"* (Chinese museum), a gathering of Far Eastern decorative art: porcelain, jade, and crystal. These pieces were brought to her after the 1860 Franco-English campaign in China and also by Siamese ambassadors received by Napoleon III in 1861. The rooms are quietly decorated in green and maroon and are among the few in the château that seem to have anything to do with real people living comfortably. (Open same hrs. as château. Last entry 11:30 and 4pm. Admission 12F; students, seniors, and Sun. 7F.)

Underkept and fairly unimpressive, the gardens at Fontainebleau still make for a pleasant stroll. Quieter and more refined are the **Jardin Anglais,** complete with rustic grotto and the famous Fontaine-belle-eau, and the **Jardin de Diane,** guarded by a statue of the huntress. (Gardens open daily sunrise-sunset. Jardin Anglais and de Diane open variably.) You can also cruise around the **Etang des Carpes** in a rented boat. (4-person max. per boat. Boat rental May 23-Aug. 31 daily 10am-12:30pm and 2-7pm; Sept. Sat.-Sun. 2-6pm. 38F/½hr., 58F/hr; 50F deposit.)

The **Forêt de Fontainebleau** is a thickly wooded 20,000-hectare preserve with hiking trails and the famous sandstone rocks used for training alpine climbers. If you're going to be around for a while and are up for it, you too can learn how to climb. Bikes can be rented in town. Maps of hiking and bike trails are available at the tourist office. Fans of 19th-century art will recognize the thick hardwoods and sandstones made famous by Rousseau and Millet, painters of the Barbizon school.

In the town itself, the **Musée Napoléonien d'Art et d'Histoire Militaire,** 88, rue St-Honoré (tel. 64 22 49 80), grew out of Louis Prost's (creator and conservator of the museum) childhood fascination with Napoleon and things military. This is the place to go if you've seen Fontainebleau but, like France, didn't get enough of Napoleon the first time. (Open Tues.-Sat. 2-5pm. Last entrance 4:30pm. Admission 10F.)

Fontainebleau's **tourist office,** 31, pl. Napoléon (tel. 64 22 25 68), across from the **post office** and near the château, organizes tours of the village surrounding the château and can help you with accommodations. (Open Mon.-Sat. 9am-12:30pm and 1:45-7pm; Oct.-May slightly shorter opening times.) A *petit train* (tel. 42 62 24 00) run by the tourist office, gives a 30-minute tour of the park, with multilingual commentary (Wed.-Mon. 10am-12:30pm and 2-6pm; 30F, children 15F). Hourly **trains** run to the town from the Gare de Lyon, *banlieue* level (45min., 74F round-trip). The château is a pleasant 20-minute walk or short bus ride. Take Car Vert A from the station (7F50). You can also rent a bike at the train station from **MBK** (tel. 64 22 36 14; fax 60 72 64 89). (For a basic model, 20F/hr., 40F/half-day, 80F/day. 3-speeds 30F/hr., 60F/half-day, 100F/day. Mountain bikes 40F per hour, 80F per half-day, 120F all day. Helmet rental 15F.) Ask about their generous student discounts. (Open daily 9am-7pm.)

## NEAR FONTAINEBLEAU: BARBIZON

On the edge of the Fontainebleau forest blossoms the rustic village of **Barbizon,** a favorite of 19th-century French landscape painters. Théodore Rousseau, Jean-François Millet, and Jean-Baptiste Camille Corot were the key figures in the Barbizon School, living and working in this artistic haven in the mid-1800s. Influenced at once by the writings of Jean-Jacques Rousseau and the 17th-century Dutch land-scapists, they were the spiritual and artistic predecessors of the Impressionists.

The **Musée Municipal de l'Atelier de Théodore Rousseau,** 55, rue Grande (tel. 60 66 22 38), showcases the work of the man who founded the Barbizon School and whose wooded scenes capture the dark beauty of the forest (open Wed.-Mon. 10:30am-12:30pm and 2-6pm; Oct.-March Wed.-Mon. 10:30am-12:30pm and 2-5pm;

admission 15F). The town's other museum, the **Maison et Atelier de Jean-François Millet,** 27, rue Grande (tel. 60 66 21 55), shifts focus to Millet, the best-known of the Barbizon masters, famous for his portrayal of the French peasantry as the great, the proud, the victimized, the simple, and the uncorrupted (open Wed.-Mon. 9:30am-12:30pm and 2-5:30pm; free). Galleries dedicated to the Barbizon School, as well as contemporary art, line the streets. The **Office du Tourisme,** 41, rue Grande (tel. 60 66 41 87), has all kinds of documentation on Barbizon and the surrounding area (open Wed. and Sat.-Mon. 10:30am-noon and 2-4pm, Fri. 2-4pm). The tourist office at Fontainebleau sells a 5F map of Barbizon and can provide a schedule for the *autocars verts* that connect the two towns; it is wise, however, to check before you arrive as the schedule is highly erratic. Biking to Barbizon is probably the cheapest option for those without a car; otherwise, a taxi from the Melun or Fontainebleau train station is the most practical (if highly extravagant) option.

# ■ Chantilly

Chantilly says a lot about unreality. The faux-Renaissance castle, built in the late 19th century, looms above a carefully-tended "natural" landscape, while a play village recalls the idealized view of peasant-life depicted by a medieval artist. The whole scene testifies to an aristocracy a bit removed from the real world. Fittingly, during World War I, French commander-in-chief Général Joffre established his headquarters here, whence he plotted grand strategy in blithe and happy ignorance of the magnitude of the slaughter taking place on the front.

Set in the magnificent gardens Le Nôtre sculpted from the surrounding forest, the **Château de Chantilly** drapes elegantly over its serene gardens, lakes, and canals. A Roman citizen named Cantilius built his villa here, leaving his name and a tradition of high property values. A succession of medieval lords constructed elaborate fortifications, but the château did not come into its own until the Grand Condé, cousin of Louis XIV, brought Le Nôtre to create the gardens and, eventually, commissioned the Grand Château. His château was razed during the Revolution; the present building is a reproduction built in the 1870s by its owner at that time, the Duc d'Aumale, fifth son of Louis-Philippe. As you approach, the dramatic Renaissance façade, lush greenery, and extravagant entrance hall whet your appetite for something truly remarkable.

Inside, the château houses the **Musée Condé** (tel. 44 57 08 00), crowded with the duke's private collection of elegant furniture and dusty paintings. For the castle's most sumptuous experience, head to the wood-paneled library, which displays medieval miniatures, a Gutenberg Bible, and a facsimile of the museum's most famous possession, the **Très Riches Heures du Duc de Berry,** a 15th-century manuscript showing the French peasantry and aristocracy engaged in the labors of the different months. The **Salle de Gardes** displays two Van Dyck paintings, along with a Roman mosaic of *The Rape of Europa* that was just the thing to hang over the duc d'Aumale's mantel. The galleries contain paintings by Raphael, Titian, Poussin, Gros, Corot, Delacroix, and Ingres—an impressive collection, but so crowded that it's hard to appreciate individual works. Think well before you pay the hefty 35F (25F *tarif réduit*) admission fee. For the dedicated royalist, it may be worth it, just to see the museum's collection of chairs taken from **Marie-Antoinette's** dressing room in Versailles.

Even if you skip the museum, consider taking a 15F wander through the **gardens,** the château's main attraction. For another 6F you can buy a map of the gardens with a suggested walking tour; free wandering, however, will lead you on a delightfully aimless tour of discovery. The central expanse, directly in front of the château, is in a typical French formal style, with neat rows of carefully pruned trees and calm statues overlooking geometrically shaped pools. To the right, hidden within a forest, the lovely "English" garden attempts to recreate the forms of nature, rendered more picturesque by the human element. Here, paths meander through woods and round pools where lone swans float along. Windows carved out in the foliage allow you to see fountains in the formal garden. You'll also find a play village, the inspiration for Marie-Antoinette's infamous hamlet at Versailles. Elsewhere, a statue of Cupid encased in a lovely gazebo reigns over the "Island of Love" with Dionysian ardor. (Château open Wed.-Mon. 10am-6pm; Nov.-March Mon.-Fri. 1-5pm and Sat.-Sun. 10:30am-5:30pm. Admission 35F, reduced 25F. Admission to grounds 15F.)

The approach to the castle passes the **Grandes Ecuries**, immense stables that housed 240 horses and hundreds of hunting dogs from 1719 until the Revolution. The stables were originally ordained by Louis-Henri Bourbon, who hoped to live in them when reincarnated as a horse. These stables now house the **Musée Vivant du Cheval** (tel. 44 57 13 13 or (16) 44 57 40 40), a huge museum dealing with all things equine: on display are saddles, horseshoes, merry-go-rounds, and horse postcards and sculptures. The horses themselves are here only for your viewing pleasure—no touching, no riding. The museum also puts on magnificent horse-training demonstrations (in French), a must-see for all horse lovers. (April-Oct. daily at 11:30am, 3:30pm, and 5:15pm. Museum open Mon. and Wed.-Fri. 10:30am-6:30pm, Sat.-Sun. 10:30am-7pm; May-June also Tues. 10:30am-5:30pm; July-Aug. also Tues. 2-5:30pm. Admission to museum and show 45F, students and seniors 35F. Special show Sun. 4pm. Admission 1-4:30pm 50F.) Two of France's premier horse races are held here in June—the **Prix de Diane** and the **Prix du Jockey Club. Polo at the Hippodrome**, September 18 to 19, is free to the public (matches at 11am, 12:30pm, 2pm, 3:15pm, and 4:30pm).

The **tourist office** is stabled at 23, av. du Maréchal Joffre (tel. 44 57 08 58; open Wed.-Mon. 10am-12:30pm and 2-5:30pm., Sun. 9am-2pm). **Trains** run to Chantilly from Paris's Gare du Nord (35min., 72F round-trip). Call ahead for the schedule: many trains to Chantilly run only on weekends. To reach the château from the station, take the shuttle bus (6F, ask at the station for times), or walk down rue des Otages and turn left in front of the tourist office (2km). Rent **bikes** at **Cycle Aventure Chantilly** (tel. 44 57 73 72), located across from the château.

# ■ Senlis

Tiny **Senlis,** a 10-minute bus ride from Chantilly, basks in the ineffable glory of being the quaintest and best-preserved village in the Ile-de-France. Its cobblestone streets, friendly residents, and intimate atmosphere are the closest you'll get to the France of storybooks. The **Cathédrale de Notre-Dame,** begun in 1191, is a prime example of early Gothic architecture. Its Grand Portal influenced the designs of Chartres and Notre-Dame in Paris. Across the *place* from Notre-Dame, the **Eglise St-Frambourg,** founded around 900 by the merciful Queen Adélaïde, also deserves a quick look. Reconstructed in 1177 by Louis VII and ransacked during the Revolution, this beauty found its most recent savior in the great pianist Girogy Cziffra, who restored the church as an international music center, now called, appropriately, the Fondation Cziffra. Enter the park next to the tourist office to reach the **Château Royal,** a hunting lodge for monarchs from Charlemagne to Henri IV, now converted to a hunting museum. The remains of Gallo-Roman fortifications, with 31 towers, surround the town (open April-Sept. Thurs.-Mon. 10am-noon and 2-6pm, Wed. 2-6pm; admission 15F, reduced 10F). The old town is a network of medieval alleyways winding up and down cobblestone hills between several of the original gates. Senlis's **tourist office**, pl. du Parvis Notre-Dame (tel. (16) 44 53 06 40), has information on concerts and exhibitions (open March-Nov. Mon. and Wed.-Fri. 2-6pm, Sat.-Sun. 10am-noon and 2-6pm). Erratic SNCF buses meet most trains to Chantilly for the 10-minute ride to Senlis (14F one-way; railpasses valid).

# ■ Malmaison

Pack lunch and travel to the **Château de Malmaison**, 1, av. du Château (tel. 47 49 20 07), for a trip backstage in the Napoleon and Josephine affair. Bought with borrowed funds in 1799 on the eve of Napoleon's rise to power, the château served as a love nest for the newlyweds, later to become Josephine's own Elba after their divorce in 1809. The house itself was built in 1622 on the site of a former leper colony—thus its name *"Mal-Maison"* (house of sickness).

Part temple to Napoleon, part temple to Nature, Malmaison is a mélange of his and hers; the restored Empire interiors combine *trompe l'oeil* marble and sarcophagus-inspired *fauteuils* with a smattering of Romantic landscape paintings, many of the château itself. Private and public apartments feature paintings of the emperor by David, Greuze, Gros, and others. Josephine furnished them in the height of the Empire style: chairs with Egyptian motifs, square tables, short, tentlike beds. Especially interesting is Napoleon's study, decorated to look like a tent, reminiscent of council-rooms on a Napoleonic campaign. In contrast, the museum at Malmaison is more about the Napoleon we never knew, following him off the battlefield and into the boudoir. Curators appear to have emptied the contents of his overnight bag; view his toothbrush, tweezers, and the handkerchief he carried at Toulon, behind glass.

The house itself overflows with Josephine memorabilia: her jewels, her shoes, her colossal dress bills, her harp, her perfumes (together, of course, with souvenirs of *"le petit corporal,"* including his death mask and the bed on which he died). Josephine's suite attests to her passion for the groomed outdoors. She preferred the modestly sized, sunny bedroom to the lavish one she had for show; at a corner of the house, its two walls of windows look out on the Malmaison grounds.

Left by Napoleon for a Hapsburg after she failed to produce an heir, Josephine lived out her remaining years here, cultivating her gardens in plush seclusion. A devotee of the natural sciences, she consulted botanists worldwide about her gardens and collected exotic animals; camels, zebras, and kangaroos once walked these grounds. Josephine, née Rose—she changed her name to please her husband—devoted much attention to the rose gardens which now surround the château. In sharp contrast to the Mondrian/Rubic's cube surfaces of the Tuileries, these English-style plantings are as much worth the trip as Malmaison itself. On vine and bush hundreds of varieties bloom in the early summer months. On these grounds is also a memorial to Eugène-Louis-Jean-Joseph Bonaparte, the Prince Imperial, son of Napoleon III.

The **Ancienne Roseraie,** to the left as you enter the château, is a restful place to sit, contemplating the ends of this illustrious pair. While you're at the château, head to the adjoining park of **Bois-Preau.** One of the few places in Paris where you can walk on the grass, the park contains a statue, erected to Josephine. (Château open Wed.-Mon. 10am-noon and 1:30-5pm. Admission 26F; students, seniors and Sun. 17F. Park open June-Sept. 10am-7pm; Oct.-March Wed.-Mon. 10am-5:30pm; free.)

To get to Malmaison and Bois-Preau, take the RER or *métro* to La Défense and change to bus #258. (Make sure not to take the bus or *métro* to Rueil-Malmaison which is quite far from the museum.)

# ■ St-Germain-en-Laye

A swift RER ride from Paris, St-Germain-en-Laye treats the visitor to small-town charm. It offers an eclectic sample of reasonably sized museums (for those travelers on fine arts overload), a rambling garden, and a stunning view of Paris.

Regardless of the tourist office's sales pitch, this town may be less remarkable for what it is now than for what it once was. Louis VI le Gros built the first castle here in the 12th century, near the site where his ancestor Robert the Pious had constructed a monastery dedicated to St-Germain. Rebuilt by Charles V after destruction during the Hundred Years War, the castle took on its present appearance in 1548 under François I. Lover of all things Italian, François I ordered his architects Chabiges and Delormé to construct a Renaissance palace—the current *château vieux*—on the foundations of the old church and castle. Henri IV added the *château neuf,* Louis XIII made it his home, and in 1638, his son, the future Louis XIV, was born there. The Sun King retreated to St-Germain during the Fronde and while waiting for Versailles to be finished. Even after the court moved to Versailles, St-Germain was used for important ceremonial occasions. An impressive list of names graced these two châteaux—among them Colbert, Mme. de Sévigné, Rousseau, Molière, and Lully (the last two wrote plays and poems performed at the châteaux). James II of England died here in exile in 1701. But the 18th century was not kind to the estate. The *château neuf* was torn down; during the Revolution, the Empire, and the July Monarchy St-Germain was alternately used as a prison, a cavalry school, and a military prison. The Austro-Hungarian Empire was formally dismantled here in 1919. In 1955, the *château* saw the independence of Morocco agreed to within its halls.

Napoleon III decided to make the castle into a museum of antiquity. Today, the **Musée des Antiquités Nationals** (tel. 34 51 53 65) claims to have the richest collection of its kind in the world. At first, the display looks a bit like someone's pet rock collection, but the work gets more sophisticated as you move through the eras (100,000 BC to the 8th century AD), and by the time you get to the Iron Age, you can believe these relics were made by the ancestors of the French artists we know and love. The highlight may be the ancient tombs complete with dirt, bones, and burial loot. Despite the lack of explanation, the museum might interest the curious, well-informed viewer. (Open Wed.-Mon. 9am-5:15pm. Admission 20F; students, seniors, and Sun. 13F. Wheelchair accessible.) If used tools don't thrill you, wander along the **garden terrace** (open daily 8am-10pm), designed by the omnipresent Le Nôtre. His gardens were destroyed along with the *châteaux neuf* at the end of the 18th century; the terrace survived. While lacking the extraordinary orchestration of Versailles, the gardens and nearby forest make for a pleasant stroll and panoramic view of Western Paris and *banlieue*. A map of forest trails is available from the tourist office.

Across from the château stands the **Eglise St-Germain**, consecrated in 1827 on the site of the 11th-century priory that gave St-Germain its name. The modern white pillars and piped-in religious music give the church a Southern evangelical atmosphere, but the 14th-century stone statue of **Notre-Dame-de-Bon-Retour** is one of the most venerated images in St-Germain. The statue was called Our Lady of the Safe Return because it was found buried deep underground when they dug the foundations for the church in 1775. (Church open daily 8:30am-noon and 2-7pm.)

Spend an afternoon at the two-room museum of the **Maison Claude Debussy,** 38, rue Au Pain (tel. 34 51 05 12), the Impressionist composer's birthplace. An autographed copy of *Prélude à l'après-midi d'un faune* (a work which was later interpreted in a ballet by Nijinsky) and a revealing survey he completed for a young girl—he wrote Hamlet down as his hero in fiction—are among the eclectic array of documents and pictures about the man who said, "I want to dare to be myself and to suffer for my truth." According to evidence in the museum, he also caused suffering to those close to him—he was quite a philanderer and twice drove his first wife Lilly to the brink of suicide. (Open Tues.-Sat. 2-6pm. Free.)

The fascinating **Musée Départemental du Prieuré,** 2bis, rue Maurcie-Denis (tel. 39 73 77 87), is dedicated to the works of painter Maurice Denis (1870-1943), the Symbolists, and the Nabis. Built in 1678 for the Marquise de Montespand and used as a hospital, *Le Prieuré* (The Priory) was purchased by Denis in 1914. He decorated the chapel with his interpretation of the Beatitudes. Today, you can visit his house and workshop and see the work of such artists as Vuillard, Bonnard, and Moret who, like Denis, received Gauguin's challenge to "risk everything." (Open Wed.-Fri. 10am-5:30pm, Sat.-Sun. and holidays 10am-6:30pm. Admission 25F, students 15F, children under 12 free.) Linger in the peaceful garden or at the *salon de thé*.

Eat at any of a number of places. **Le Collignon,** 7, rue Collignon (tel. 34 51 48 56), serves French fare (65F *menu;* open Tues.-Sat. noon-3pm and 7-11pm, Sun. noon-3pm). The **Office Municipal de Tourisme,** Maison Claude Debussy, 38, rue Au Pain (tel. 34 51 05 12), provides lists of restaurants and hotels, and a map in English.

(Open Mon.-Sat. 9am-12:30pm and 2:15-6:30pm; June-Sept. also open Sun. 10am-1pm.)

You can rent a bike at the RER station (in the parking garage). (Open Sat.-Sun. and holidays 9am-7pm; daily July-Aug. 3-speed bikes 25F/hr., 80F/day. 1000F deposit. Mountain bikes 40F/hr., 150F/day. 1500F deposit.)

St-Germain is 45 minutes from downtown Paris by RER Line A1 (11F there, 14F50 back).

## ■ St-Cloud

The town of **St-Cloud**, 3km southwest of Paris, is well worth a half-day visit. Built on a steep hill across the Seine from Paris, St-Cloud harbors a beautiful park, the former site of a château. Framed by orderly hedges and trimmed with rectangular beds of more than 30 varieties of flowers and 30 types of rosebushes, the multi-terraced park marches its way down the hillside, stretching almost all the way to the Seine below. By consulting horticultural guides of the 19th century, modern-day gardeners have painstakingly reconstructed the floral arrangements in the fashion of the court of Napoleon III during his stays at St-Cloud.

The **Château de St-Cloud** was the scene of the assassination of Henri III in 1589 and Napoleon's coup d'état in 1799, when troops loyal to the rising general invaded the chambers of the legislature in session there. In 1870 marauding Prussians burned the château; nothing remains but Le Nôtre's magnificent park. To orient yourself, consult the large marble slab in the center of the park. A map of the grounds in 1811, the slab shows clearly the parts of the original park that still remain, the parts that were destroyed, and the exact location of the château. To the left of the park gates, the **Musée Historique** offers drawings, paintings, and a short film tracing the history of the château. (Grounds open daily 7am-9pm. Museum open Wed. and Sat.-Sun. 2-5:30pm. Free.)

Stroll around the town of St-Cloud. The quiet streets are lined with small shops and pretty houses, interspersed with the occasional modern apartment building. Nearing the top, the streets are so steep that some of them become stairways, leading to the *centre-ville*, a classic French town square with the Hôtel de Ville and the modest but charming Romanesque **Eglise St-Cloud.** To get to St-Cloud, take the *métro*, bus #72 from the Hôtel de Ville, or bus #52 from Madeleine to "Boulogne-Pt. de St-Cloud." There you can either take a local bus across the Pont de St-Cloud or walk (15min.) across. After you cross the river, the park is to your left, the town is straight ahead and up; look for the spire of Eglise St-Cloud.

## ■ Sceaux

The peaceful, upscale suburb of **Sceaux**, 10km south of Paris, is one of the most fashionable places to live outside of Paris itself. Three hundred years ago, Sceaux was home to Colbert, Louis XIV's finance minister. His resplendent mansion, built by Claude Perrault, was expanded and embellished by his son, then sold to the Duc du Maine whose wife turned it into a much sought-after literary salon where such greats as Voltaire enjoyed spending time. During the Revolution, the château was confiscated, then later abandoned and destroyed during the first years of the 19th century. Only Le Nôtre's gracious gardens remain. In the 19th century, the Duc de Trévise inherited this property and built the charming (if more humble) **Château de Sceaux** (RER: Bourg-la-Reine or Parc de Sceaux), which now houses the **Musée de l'Ile de France** (tel. 46 61 06 71), dedicated to the *haute culture* and *traditions folkloriques* of the region surrounding Paris. Unlike the hulking, imposing, often tasteless structures that dot the landscape around France, this château is small (relatively), elegant, and inviting. To one side dips the **Grande Cascade** (with 20th-century additions by Rodin) which spills into Le Nôtre's graceful Octagon pool. Slightly to the southwest is a long stretch of the tree-lined grand canal. In front of the château is an immense lawn—the **Plaine des Quatres Statues.** You may have to hunt for these four; they are dwarfed by the expanse of green that precedes them. You'll know you're not in Paris anymore when you lie on the grass without a green-clad *gardien* whistling at you and yelling *"pelouse interdite."* (Museum open Mon. and Fri. 2-6pm, Wed.-Thurs. 10am-noon and 2-7pm; off-season until 5pm. Admission 10F, students and seniors 5F. Park open daily 6:45am-9:30pm. Free.)

If you take the RER to Parc de Sceaux, the park is to the west. If you get off at Bourg-la-Reine, walk straight ahead out of the *gare,* past the Mairie, take a right on av. du Général LeClerc, then a right onto the shady Allée d'Honneur. The park entrance is straight ahead.

# ■■■ CATHEDRALS

While most people think of demonic gargoyles, dank corners, dark medieval architecture, and the horrors of the Inquisition, the cathedrals of Paris and the Ile de France can offer some of the brightest moments of your stay. The dark gray interiors of Notre-Dame, Chartres, Beauvais, and St-Denis serve only as a somber contrast to the explosions of color that burst from the cathedrals' intricate rose windows and other masterpieces of stained glass. Despite the ravages of the Hundred Years' War, nine centuries of weather, political upheaval and war, including the Revolution and the bombs of two world wars, these ornate structures still stand as a testimony to human faith, architecture, and yes, technology. Most were built during the Gothic period of the Middle Ages by thousands of skilled sculptors, artisans, stone masons, iron smiths, and hard laborers who worked without the help of complex machinery or electricity.

The word "cathedral" literally means the "place of the cathedra," which is the Archbishop or Cardinal's seat (roughly equivalent in symbolic weight to a throne). A cathedral serves as the mother church for an archdiocese, a geographical county within the Roman Catholic Church. Cathedrals from the Middle Ages are most often built in the form of a cross and consist of the nave (the vertical section of the cross) and the transept (the horizontal section). Aside from these basics, cathedrals can be as architecturally diverse as museums and palaces. Some, like Notre-Dame, feature elegant and massive flying buttresses; others show off tall bell towers. Still others, like St-Denis, serve as the burial ground for royalty, saints, and other well-known national figures.

Cathedrals can be a welcome break from the hot sun and the stressful bustle of busy Paris streets. They're also always open on Sundays, but realize that although it is considered perfectly acceptable to take pictures and comment to your friends about the interior, you are still visiting an active place of meditation and prayer. Be respectful of silent prayer areas and schedules for mass. For the most radiant view of the rose windows and stained glass, visit in the mid-morning or in the mid-afternoon when the sun is at its most direct slant. Check the bulletin boards at the back of the cathedral for information on concerts (choral, orchestral, and organ) and events (such as plays or opera performances), many of which are free or inexpensive. Don't be alarmed if some cathedrals charge a small admission fee. They use this money for much needed restorations and upkeep, and the fee, if any, is never more than 12-15F.

# ■ Saint-Denis

The home of the famed **Basilique St-Denis,** the burial place of France's kings and queens, this town is named after the bishop missionary Denis. According to legend, Denis was beheaded by the Romans in Montmartre in 250 AD and walked north carrying his head until he reached the town and was buried here in a plowed field. Today, St-Denis (Mo. St-Denis-Basilique) is a pleasant and busy working-class town with a large and vibrant population of West and North African immigrants. Ironically, although ancient kings tried to keep out English invaders, the town now flourishes because of an influx of ethnic immigrants from many points beyond France's borders.

Ever since 768, the Basilica has been home to the remains of almost all of the kings and queens of France, whose funerary monuments form a progression from medieval simplicity to 19th-century extravagance. As importantly, its delicate 12th-century ambulatory (the cloistered passageway encircling the choir at the church's east end) is *the* first example of Gothic architecture in all of Europe. Toward the year 475, a little church was built to honor St-Denis's grave. About two centuries later, King Pepin destroyed that church to make way for a larger one, perhaps because he wanted to be buried there—he was, in 768. Vestiges of both of these early churches can be seen in today's crypt. Other early Frankish kings followed Pepin's lead, and at the end of the 10th century the church became the official necropolis of French royalty.

In 1136 Abbot Suger began the rebuilding of the basilica in a revolutionary style that would open the hallowed area of the basilica to the "light of the divine." Suger was dissatisfied with dark and heavy Romanesque interiors, with their small windows and forests of thick columns. Instead, he brought together already-known architectural elements to create an unprecedented openness in the suddenly spacious nave. In the final Gothic creation, function melded with aesthetic form—the vaulted arches of the nave, essential to the cathedral's effect of verticality and weightlessness, funneled the weight of the roof into a few points, supported with long, narrow columns and flying buttresses outside. Freed from the burden of supporting the roof, the walls could be pierced with the huge stained-glass windows that became the style's trademark.

These developments had a complex theological counterpart: the play of light from the stained-glass windows in the church's vast interior became the symbolic presence of God, as expressed in the Book of John: "In the beginning was the Word and the Word was the Light of the world." Appreciation of earthly beauty allowed the soul to commune with the Absolute. "Thus," declared Abbot Suger, "when—out of my delight in the beauty of the house of God—the loveliness of the many-colored gems has called me away from external cares...then it seems to me that I see myself dwelling, as it were, in some strange region of the universe which neither exists entirely in the slime of the earth nor entirely in the purity of Heaven; and that, by the grace of God, I can be transported from this inferior to that higher world."

Whatever opinion one may hold on Suger's metaphysics, there is indeed something awe-inspiring in the church he created. In an age before skyscrapers and neon lights, the stained glass and human-dwarfing nave must have seemed like a miracle. Suger's contemporaries were flabbergasted and quickly worked to outdo him with their own cathedrals, building ever more intricate interiors, larger stained-glass windows, loftier vaults, and higher towers—the age of the Cathedral had been born.

Suger himself died in 1151, well before most of his basilica had been rebuilt. His successors altered his plans, but did not stray from the Gothic pattern he had set. They created an unusually wide transept, complete with magnificent rose windows. The extra space was needed to accommodate the ever-growing number of dead monarchs. In 1593, underneath the newly spacious nave, Henri IV converted to Catholicism with his famous statement: *"Paris vaut bien une messe"* (Paris is well worth a mass). St-Denis's royal connection brought upon it the wrath of the Revolution. Most of the tombs were desecrated or destroyed, and the remains of the Bourbon family were thrown into a ditch. With the restoration of the monarchy in 1815, Louis XVIII ordered that the necropolis be reestablished. Louis XVI and Marie-Antoinette were buried here with great pomp. The remains of the other Bourbons were dug out of their ditch and placed in an ossuary inside the crypt. Tombs that had survived the Revolution were returned from the National Museum of Monuments (see Sights—6ème arrondissement), where they had been displayed. Louis also added funerary monuments from churches that had been completely destroyed during the Revolution.

Admission to the necropolis includes a pair of headphones with a recorded tour (available in English). The headphones don't come with a tape recorder, but pick up infrared signals from a number of "islands." This whiz-bang technology makes for an enjoyable visit. Don't miss the little room on the left side of the church (outside of the necropolis area). It contains the splendid funerary garments (literally, "regalia") of the royal family. (Basilique open daily 10am-7pm; Oct.-April 10am-5pm. Admission 26F, seniors and students 17F, under 18 6F. Ticket booth closes ½hr. before the Basilica. Guided tours in French daily at 3pm. Free organ concerts Sun. 11:15am.)

For a bite to eat before you head back to Paris, try one of the reasonably priced restaurants that cluster around the park in front of the Basilique. **The Restaurant Campile,** 14, rue Jean Jaurès (tel. 48 20 74 31), in the galleries near the *métro* station serves an excellent salad bar menu of *grillade de boeuf*, salad, cheese, and dessert (open daily 6:30-9:30am, noon-2pm, and 7:30-10pm).

The helpful **tourist office,** at 2, rue de la Légion d'Honneur (tel. 42 43 33 55) has lots of information on the Basilique and the town of St-Denis (open Mon.-Sat. 9:30am-12:30pm and 2-6:30pm, Sun. 10am-12:30pm and 2-6:30pm). It also has information about St-Denis's museums including the Musée d'Art et d'Histoire, 22bis, rue Gabriel-Péri (tel. 42 43 05 10, open Mon.-Sat. 10am-5:30pm, Sun. 2-6:30); the Musée de l'Orfèvrerie, 112, rue Ambroise-Croizat (tel. 49 22 40 00, open Mon.-Fri. 10am-noon and 2:30-5pm); and the nearby Château de St-Ouen, 12, rue Albert-Dhalenne, Parc Abel-Mézières, St-Ouen (tel. 40 11 65 79, open Mon. and Wed.-Sat. 2-6pm). The tourist office also provides information on the annual **Festival de St-Denis** (tel. 42 43 77 72) which brings world-class orchestras and musicians such as conductors Seiji Ozawa and Charles Dutoit and the Orchestre National de France to the Basilica in June.

# ■ Chartres

## THE CATHEDRAL

The **Cathédrale de Chartres** survives today as one of the most sublime creations of the Middle Ages. The existing structure is the fifth to occupy this site—three different churches stood here before the year 1000. In 876, Charlemagne's grandson, Charles the Bald, made a gift to Chartres of the *Sancta Camisia,* the cloth believed to have been worn by Mary when she gave birth to Christ. Pilgrims have been flocking to the cathedral ever since to see the sacred relic and benefit from its supernatural powers. In 911 its magic was confirmed when the citizens of Chartres, under attack from Vikings, placed the relic on view at the top of the city wall. The infidels ran away; their leader Rollin converted to Christianity and became the first duke of Normandy.

The cathedral became a foremost center of learning, led by the brilliant Fulbert who arrived in 990 and supervised the building of the fourth church, a fine Romanesque cathedral. Disaster struck in 1194 when the third fire in 200 years burned all but the crypts, the west tower, and the Royal Portal. When they discovered that Mary's relic (hidden in the crypt by three loyal priests who stayed with it, sweating out the fire) had emerged unsinged, the villagers took it as a sign of not only Mary's love but her desire for a more worthy cathedral. Clerics took advantage of the miracle to solicit funds on a grand scale and building proceeded at a furious pace: most of the cathedral was completed by 1223 and consecrated in 1260. The stained-glass windows soon gained fame for their clarity and beauty, as did the magnificent sculptures adorning each of the main portals. Since then, in a series of miracles as great as the survival of the *Sancta Camisia* in 1194, the Cathédrale de Chartres has emerged intact from Protestant iconoclasm, the clergy's decision to "modernize" in the 18th century, the Revolution's attempt to turn it into a Temple of Reason, and two world wars.

Few cathedrals rival Chartres in size and majesty. A masterpiece of finely crafted detail, the cathedral will appeal to the aesthete in anyone. Imagine yourself a 12th-century farmer who set down the hand plow for a day of sculpture and stained glass. While the cathedral remains a showcase for the massive, the tall, and the glorious, its minute detail is equally worthy of attention. At the time it was built, Chartres served as a stage for cutting-edge contemporary artisanry. Sculpture and stained glass here tell the story of Christ, set in medieval castles and lordly dress. (Perhaps as remote to modern visitors as a fig leaf or a hairshirt, this is the rough equivalent of Jesus in the Trump Tower.) On the other hand, in the slouching figure of sloth or the tunicked and tempted St. Anthony, 13th-century visitors might have recognized themselves.

The cathedral is an extraordinary fusion of Romanesque and Gothic architectural elements. Built in a record-breaking 29 years (compared to 163 years for Notre-Dame de Paris) the cathedral stands as one of the most harmonious of medieval buildings. The famous twin-steepled silhouette is visible miles around the town, rising up above the flat wheat fields that surround it. The flying buttresses, connected to the vaulting inside, fulfill both a functional and aesthetic role: they take the weight of the roof away from the walls (allowing the wall to open to the magnificent stained glass) and provide an elegant outside expression of the cathedral's interior structure. Towering over the surrounding town, the cathedral is a powerful embodiment of a time when the Church controlled every aspect of the daily routine and the tallest buildings in existence were its cathedrals. The famous 12th-century statues of the Royal Portal present an assembly of Old Testament figures at the height of late Romanesque sculpture. Those in the central bay, attributed to the "Master of Chartres," are especially beautiful: their elongated figures have a stillness and elegance that invites the visitor to leave the material world behind as they enter the divine space of the cathedral.

The 13th-century North and South Porch, representing the life of Mary and Christ triumphant, are highly expressive examples of Gothic sculpture. Notice, for example, the face of John the Baptist on the North Porch; an expression of sorrow is traced from the downcast eyes to the disc he holds with the lamb and cross, symbols of Christ's coming. In the left bay, the figures of Mary and Elizabeth turn to greet each other, telling the story of the Visitation, resembling two nuns, chatting privately during mass. Inside, the process is continued in the beautiful Renaissance choir screen, begun by Jehan de Beauce in 1514 and finished in the 18th century, which tells Mary's story from her birth, through the life of Christ, to her death and ascension.

Most of the glass dates from the 13th century and was preserved through both world wars by town authorities, who dismantled over 3000 square meters and stored it piece by piece until the end of hostilities. The merchant sponsors of each window are shown in the lower panels, providing a valuable record of daily life during the 13th century. The famous "Blue Virgin" window, an object of pilgrimage and one of the few pieces of 12th-century glass to survive the fire, is visible at the first window of the choir, on the right. Bring binoculars if you can; many of the stories told by the stained glass are barely visible with the naked eye.

World-renowned tour guide Malcolm Miller, an authority on Gothic architecture, has brought the cathedral to life for English-speaking visitors for the past 35 years. Miller composes each tour individually to explain the cathedral's history and symbolism. Miller knows everything about the religion and daily routine that the windows depict. His presentation is intelligent, witty, and enjoyable for all ages, although somewhat too fast—consider taking notes. He will tell you about the labyrinth on the floor, which provided a path for the penitent pilgrim to follow on hands and knees, as well as the sloping floor which permitted the cathedral to be washed after becoming a hostel for pilgrims every night. If you can, take both of his tours. They are worth it, and Miller is careful to discuss different aspects of the cathedral on each one. You may want to invest in a 29-35F guide as well. (1¼ hr. tours April-Jan. Mon.-Sat. noon and 2:45pm. Admission 30F, students 20F. Avoid Sat.

and Tues.—busy days in the high season. Private tours available on request: tel. 37 28 15 58; fax 37 28 33 03.)

The sacred relic is now on display in the cathedral's **treasury,** at the east end, along with other significant garments and objects from the building's history. (Open Mon.-Sat. 10am-noon and 2-6pm, Sun. and holidays 2-6pm; Oct. 16-March 15 Mon.-Sat. 10am-noon and 2:30-4:30pm, Sun. and holidays 2-5pm. Free.) Climb the north tower, **Tour Jehan-de-Beauce,** named after its architect and completed in 1513, for a magnificent view of the cathedral roof, the flying buttresses, and the city below. The tower itself is a wonderful example of flamboyant Gothic, a late medieval style named after the flame-like nature of its decoration. Built to replace a wooden steeple which continuously burned down, it provides a fascinating counterpart to its more sedate neighbor (and predecessor by three centuries), the octagonal steeple built just before the 1194 fire. (Open April-Sept. Mon.-Fri. 9:30-11:30am and 2-5:30pm, Sat. 9:30-11:30am and 2-4:30pm, Sun. 2-4:30pm; Nov.-Feb. Mon.-Sat. 10-11:30am and 2-4pm, Sun. 2-4pm. Admission 20F; students, big families, and seniors 13F; under 6 free.)

Parts of Chartres's **crypt,** one of the largest in Western Christendom, date back to the 9th century. You can only enter the subterranean crypt as part of a tour that leaves from *La Crypte,* the store opposite the cathedral's south entrance. The tour (tel. 37 21 56 33 for info) is in French but information sheets are available in English. Even if you can't follow the narration you'll see the numerous old chapels, the staircase that allowed the relic to be saved from fire, a 4th-century wall, and the well down which a band of Vikings tossed the bodies of their victims after an 858 raid. The wooden statue of virgin and child is a 19th-century copy of the 16th-century original, burnt by Revolutionaries in front of the cathedral (while they hid the relic). Look for the ethereal forms of statues from the Royal Portal, copied and transferred to the crypt after severe weathering had almost erased their features. (Tours last 30min., daily at 11am (except Wed.), 2:15pm, 3:30pm, 4:30pm, and in summer 5:15pm. Admission 10F.)

The cathedral is open daily in summer from 7:30am to 7:30pm and in winter from 7:30am to 7pm. No casual visits are allowed Saturdays from 5:45pm to 7pm or Sundays from 9:15am to 11am because of religious services. If you want the true Chartres experience, however, try attending one of these services. Call the tourist office (see below) for information on concerts in the cathedral, as well as the annual student pilgrimage in late May and other festivals throughout the year.

## THE TOWN

Rightly called a *ville d'art* (artistic city), Chartres celebrates the medieval crafts showcased in the cathedral. In addition to the workshops and galleries, the downtown area is itself a vision to behold. The charming *vieille ville* (old town) has the cobblestone staircases, gabled roofs, timbered houses, and iron lamps of a village that likes its past. Old streets, named for the trades once practiced there—rue de la Poissonerie being home to the fishmongers—run into one another. Charming stone bridges cross the Eure River. Although the town is surrounded by flat wheat fields, Chartres is built on a hill, and some of the best views of the cathedral are found by walking down along the well-marked tourist circuit. Maps are available from the tourist office (see below).

**Le Musée des Beaux Arts** (Museum of Fine Arts), 29, cloître Notre-Dame (tel. 37 36 41 39), next door to the cathedral, resides in the former Episcopal Palace. Built mainly in the 17th and 18th centuries on the site occupied by bishops since the 11th century, the palace houses a rich collection of painting, sculpture, and furniture. Zurbaran, Holbein, and Vlaminck all figure prominently, as do local scenes and medieval wood polychrome statues from the 13th century on. (Open Wed.-Mon. 10am-6pm; Nov.-March 10am-noon and 2-6pm. Admission 10F, students and seniors 5F. For temporary exhibits 20F, students and seniors 10F.)

La Galerie du Vitrail (Gallery of Stained Glass), 17, rue du Cloître Notre-Dame (tel. 37 36 10 03), provides information on the cathedral's stained glass as well as showcasing and selling contemporary pieces. Films (8-25min.) on the history and production of stained glass and on Chartres in the Middle Ages are shown free upon request in English, French, or German (open Tues.-Sun. 9:45am-7pm; Nov.-March Tues.-Sat. 9:45am-1pm and 2-6:30pm). The **Centre Internationale du Vitrail,** 5, rue du Cardinal Pie (tel. 37 21 65 72), hosts temporary exhibitions on stained glass, both historical and contemporary. The 12th-century barn in which it is housed was once used to store wine and grains received by the clergy from surrounding farmers. Note the 14th-century wood rafters and the 12th-century vaulting downstairs (open 9:30am-7pm; Oct.-March 10am-12:30pm and 1:30-6pm). Anticipate a stylistic, topical range from 16th-century flat-faced supplicants to late 20th-century machine dreams, with an emphasis on Art Nouveau and Art Deco. "Compagnon, Cuzin, Revel," an exposition focusing on stained-glass abstracts, runs from November 1993 to January 1994.

**Eglise St-Aignan,** on rue des Greniers, was rebuilt in the 16th century, but boasts feudal origins. The Romanesque **Eglise St-André** sits on a street by the same name overlooking the banks of the Eure River. Fires have ravaged it, but the church has been a part of Chartres since the 12th century. During the 16th and 17th centuries, its gallery was extended to cross the river; one of the arches on which it was supported is still visible. **Eglise St-Pierre** in the place St-Pierre is a delicate Gothic, 13th-century masterpiece. Once the church of the Benedictine monastery of St-Père-en-Vallée, St-Pierre was renamed during the French Revolution when the monastery was disestablished. (All churches open in season daily 9am-7pm; Oct.-June 10am-5pm.)

Worth the walk across the river (which offers the best view of the cathedral), up rue St-Barthelémy and down rue du Repos past the cemetery is the **Maison Picassiette,** 22, rue du Repos (tel. 37 34 10 78). From 1928 until his death in 1964, Raymond Isidore decorated his house and garden with mosaics made from broken china and colored glass. Beginning with the kitchen, the former graveyard groundskeeper worked with abandon and no preconceived plan, filling courtyards and building shrines, reconstituting Paris and Chartres on wall, planter, and rooftop. A bricolage fairy tale, Isidore's weekend hobby continues to baffle art critics and locals alike. When asked "Why?" Isidore responded, "I built it for shelter." Japanese gardens, Eiffel Towers, giraffes, and magi make Picassiette a walk through one man's imagination (open April-Oct. Wed.-Mon. 10am-noon and 2-6pm; admission 10F, students 5F).

Chartres seems to be more confident than many French towns that its history is untainted; filled with streets with names like bd. de la Résistance, the town boasts a monument to **Jean Moulin,** the famous resistance hero who worked closely with de Gaulle. *Préfet* of Chartres during World War II, Moulin attempted suicide rather than be forced to sign a document maintaining that French troops had committed atrocities. Tortured and then killed by the Gestapo in 1943, he was eventually buried in the Panthéon. To get to the monument, walk from the Cathédrale down rue Cheval Blanc until it turns into rue Jean Moulin; the monument will be on your right.

## PRACTICAL INFORMATION

The **tourist office** (tel. 37 21 50 00), opposite the cathedral's main entrance, helps find accommodations in and near Chartres (20F fee). They also have a list of restaurants, brochures, and an excellent map with a walking tour marked. For 35F, one or two people can use a headphone guide (in English, French, or German) to see the old city. (Tour lasts 1½-2 hr. and is worth it. Available while the office is open.) The tourist office staff speaks excellent English, as well as other languages. (Open Mon.-Fri. 9:30am-6:45pm, Sat.-Sun. 9:30am-6pm; March-May and Oct. Mon-Sat. 9:30am-6pm, Sun. 10am-noon and 3-6pm; Nov.-Feb. Mon-Fri. 9:30am-6pm, Sat. 9:30am-5pm.)

For **food**, try sandwich or *brasserie* fare in rue de Cygne or place Marceau, open-air pedestrian areas with musicians and great atmosphere. **La Passacaille**, 30-32, rue Ste-Même (tel. 37 21 52 10), offers filling pizza (28-53F) in tasteful surroundings (open June-Aug. daily 11:30am-10:30pm; around mealtimes rest of the year). **Le Pélage,** place Châtelet (tel. 37 36 07 49), serves ample portions of standard meat and potatoes fare (49-60F; *menus* at 69F50 and 81F50; open Mon.-Sat. noon-2pm and 7-11:30pm).

Chartres is accessible by frequent **trains** from Gare Montparnasse (1hr., round-trip 122F. In Paris call 45 82 50 50 for info; in Chartres call 37 28 50 50). Many trains run only on certain days or occasions—call ahead.

## NEAR CHARTRES: ILLIERS-COMBRAY

Proust fans should bite the cookie and take the half-hour train ride from Chartres to **Illiers-Combray,** the author's childhood vacation home and the setting for much of *A la recherche du temps perdu (Remembrance of Things Past).* In Proust's own words, the town remains "a church epitomizing a town, speaking of it and for it to the horizon." Uncut lawns, medieval ruins, half-timbered façades, and sloping roofs mark the town as an unhurried vestige from a French past, best seen by tourists armed with *Swann's Way* and a bicycle. In 1971, the Proust centennial year, the town came out of hiding, changing its name from Illiers to Combray, its literary pseudonym. Visitors should proceed from the train station down rue de Chartres. Buy a map of the town at the *papeterie* across from the Eglise St-Jacques (10F). The map is a pilgrim's necessity, with Swann's way, the Guermante's way, and other fondly remembered promenades clearly marked. Visit **Maison de Tante Léonie,** 4, rue Docteur Léonie (tel. 37 24 30 97), the home of Proust's much loved invalid aunt who "had gradually declined to leave, first Combray, then her bedroom, and finally her bed." Mementos from his life displayed here may be seen by tour only (Wed.-Mon. at 2, 3, 4, and 5pm—times subject to change; call ahead to verify and to ferret out foreign-language tours on weekday mornings; admission 25F). **Trains** to Illiers leave from Chartres irregularly, around midday and early evening. Pick up a schedule before you begin your trip; trains vary with the days of the week and with holidays. The trip costs 48F round-trip.

## ■ Beauvais

Home to the Gothic Cathédrale St-Pierre and the Galerie Nationale de la Tapisserie, the small town of Beauvais offers *un beau tour* (a lovely excursion) into French life of the Middle Ages. Unfortunately, the 20th century has not been so kind to this fairly quiet town 130km northwest of Paris. Largely destroyed in the shelling of World War I, the town of Beauvais has not fully recovered. Originally known as Caesaromagus—Ceasar's market—the town was an important Gallo-Roman settlement until Germanic invasions destroyed it in the 3rd century AD. Along with the rest of Ile-de-France, the city thrived in the 12th century, and decided to rebuild its cathedral in the trendy Gothic style. The mammoth **Cathédrale Saint-Pierre** still stands proud on rue St-Pierre. Its Gothic chancel, tallest in the world, is the product of architectural ambition pushed beyond reason and engineering principle. In the late Gothic race to build a tower and prestige, this was the ultimate contender—and the most dramatic failure.

First begun in 1225, the chancel was finished in 1272 and collapsed dramatically in 1284. Despite numerous attempts to rebuild, most notably one in the 16th century, the spire would not stay intact. Construction of the nave never began; the slate-covered wooden panel that blocked off the opening from the transept has been "temporarily" in place for the past 400 years. A pricey 40F guide, available in English, helps to illuminate the finer details of the church.

Venture out the back door to the green, seemingly ancient cloister. The buildings that border the courtyard are known as the **Basse-Oeuvre** and are the only remains of the 10th-century Carolingian church that once stood on the site. The cathedral also flaunts an impossibly complex **Astronomical Clock.** Crafted between 1865 and 1868 by clockmaker Louis-Auguste Vérité, the clock has ninety thousand pieces which work synchronously to power one of the world's most complete and most beautiful astronomical timepieces. A 25-minute *son et lumière* highlights the different facets of the impressive decorative scheme. (Explanations of the clock daily at 10:40am except Sun. in summer, 2:40pm, 3:40pm, and 4:40pm. Admission 15F, children 5F. Call Association *"ESPACES"* at (16) 44 48 11 60 for any further info. Cathedral open daily 9am-12:15pm and 2-6:15pm; in winter 9am-12:15pm and 2-5:15pm.)

Beauvais also boasts three museums with collections of painting, sculpture, ceramics, and tapestries from the Middle Ages. In the former Bishop's Palace, the **Musée Departemental de l'Oise,** 1, rue du Musée (tel. (16) 44 06 37 37), displays an eclectic ensemble of painting, furniture, and sculpture dating from the 16th century onward, plus a few fossils and focusing on regional artists. While the collections are not exceptional, occasional gems do surface: the seven canvases in Nabi painter Maurice Denis's *l'Age d'Or* series (1912), the ceramic plates (Beauvais's specialties), and the 16th-century wood rafter sequence on the third floor. (Open Wed.-Mon. 10am-noon and 2-6pm. Admission 16F; students, under 18, and over 65 8F; Wed. free.)

On the other side of the cathedral, across from the ruins, the modern **Galerie Nationale de la Tapisserie** (tel. (16) 44 05 14 28), rue St-Pierre, pays homage to the Gobelins factory built here in 1664 under the watchful eye of Colbert. Because it is a gallery and not a museum, the display is continually changing, but always constitutes an interesting collection of tapestries dating from the ancient and historical to the contemporary and abstract. *The King Visiting the Gobelins Factory,* woven between 1673 and 1680, features the Sun King, Colbert, Charles Le Brun—both the designer of the work and the first director of the factory—and countless workers scrambling to look occupied. Gallo-Roman ramparts and a tower dating from the late 3rd and early 4th centuries jut into the basement as an added historical touch. (Open Tues.-Sun. 9:30-11:30am and 2-6pm; Oct.-March Tues.-Sun. 10-11:30am and 2:30-4:30pm. Last entry ½hr. before closing. Admission 21F; students, seniors, and under 18 13F.)

The **Manufacture Nationale de la Tapisserie,** 24, rue Henri Brispot (tel. 44 05 14 28), spent 49 years in exile during and following World War II. Installed again in Beauvais, this time in a former slaughterhouse, modern weavers continue the tradition of producing stunning tapestries. You can see them at work and are even encouraged to question them about their craft. (Open Tues.-Thurs. 2-4pm. Admission same price as the Galerie. You do not gain admission to both for one fee—you must pay again.)

The **Office de Tourisme,** 1, rue Beauregard (tel. 44 45 08 18), near the cathedral, offers countless brochures on the surrounding area, a list of hotels and restaurants, and an invaluable map of the town. (Open Tues.-Sat. 9:30am-7pm, Sun.-Mon. and holidays 10am-1pm and 2-6pm; in winter closed Sun.) On the last weekend in June (June 26-27 in 1994), the **Fête de Jeanne Hachette** celebrates the bravery of Jeanne Hachette, the town's patron who led the resistance against the onslaught of Charles the Bold's Burgundian army in 1672. Townspeople trundle through the streets dressed in medieval garb, and the central *place* is transformed into a medieval market.

Roughly 12 **trains** daily head to Beauvais from Paris's Gare du Nord, *grandes lignes* platform (75-90min., express, Paris-Beauvais, 118F round-trip). For more information, call the Beauvais train station (tel. 44 21 50 50). To reach the cathedral from the train station, follow bd. du Général de Gaulle past the garden and turn left on rue des Jacobins. Walk through the pedestrian area and if you can't see it by now...

# ■■■ OTHER DAYTRIPS

## ■ Euro Disney® Resort

It's a small world after all; it's a small, small world. When the Euro Disneyland® Park opened on April 12, 1992, it joined its fellow Disney communities in California, Florida, and Japan in bringing the magic of Mickey Mouse, Minnie, Cinderella, Snow White, Beauty and the Beast, and Peter Pan to people across countless languages, cultures, continents, and time zones. (Of course, most Europeans find it cheaper to fly to Disneyworld in Florida.) It is an exciting place to spend a day (if you've seen everything else in Paris), even for the budget traveler—every show, attraction, and ride is included in the (rather hefty) admission price.

The Euro Disney® Resort's designers (called "Imagineers") and staff (called "Cast Members") have created a resort which celebrates imagination, childhood, fantasy, creativity, technology, and fun. The fanfare of publicists tout Euro Disney® Resort as a vast entertainment and resort center, the largest on the continent, covering an area one-fifth the size of Paris. But though Disney may eventually develop its 600 hectares, the current theme park doesn't even rank the size of an *arrondissement*. From the gate it takes only ten minutes to walk to the farthest point inside the park, nothing like the vast reaches of Florida's Disneyworld. On the other hand, this Disney park is the most technologically advanced yet, and the special effects on some rides are enough to knock your Reeboks off. And the high quality of Disney service means that you will be greeted with a warm smile and efficient and courteous help.

Despite the whines of Euro Disney® Resort's early critics who wrote countless editorials on the resort, going so far as to call it a "Cultural Chernobyl," the park has been a hit, and Disney has had to close the ticket windows repeatedly for hours at a time to keep lines down. Try to get there on a weekday—Tuesdays and Thursdays are the least crowded. Otherwise, expect to spend most of your time fighting to keep your place in line, rather than having fun. Masses of people practice the French national custom of line-cutting, as whole families duck under barriers and worm their way up front. To make things worse, devious architecture hides the true length of the lines. A line just emerging from a building may be just the tail end of a 90-minute wait inside. The crowds thin out toward 5pm, when the kiddies start crying to go home, reducing the wait in line to as little as 15 minutes. Saving the bigger rides for the evening is probably the best way to go, and considering that the park closes at midnight during the summer, you'll still have plenty of time to do all your favorite rides several times over. Euro Disney® Resort has started offering a discounted admission after 5pm (150F), which helps defray the cost if you want to spend hours here later in the day.

## ORIENTATION AND PRACTICAL INFORMATION

Everything in the Euro Disney® Resort is in English and French. The staff is extremely helpful, and the detailed guide called the *Euro Disneyland® Guest Guidebook,* which you'll receive when you enter the park, has information on everything from restaurants, to attractions, to bathrooms, to first aid.

**Tickets:** Instead of selling tickets, Euro Disneyland® Park issues *Passeports,* available at the 50 windows located on the ground floor of the Disneyland Hotel. You can also buy *Passeports* at the Paris tourist office on the Champs-Elysées (see Paris—Once There). Pursue this option if you plan on coming out on a weekend day, so you won't risk wasting a couple of hours while the windows remain closed due to the crowds. Admission 250F, under 12 175F. Open daily 9am-11pm. Hours subject to change during the winter. Discount ticket for only 150F if you arrive after 5pm.

**Restaurants:** Pick up a restaurant guide at City Hall or consult your *Euro Disneyland® Guest Guidebook*. The elegant but pricey **Auberge de Cendrillon** (Cinderella's cottage) in Fantasyland features mouth-watering salmon, tender veal, and chocolate *gâteaux à la sauce anglaise*. For less expensive fare head for the very British fish and chips at **Toad Hall Restaurant**, the frontier grub and saloon show at **Lucky Nugget Saloon**, or the burgers at Discoveryland's **Café Hyperion**.

**Hotels:** The resort has six hotels, each designed on a particular theme celebrating a region of the United States. The **Sequoia Lodge** is surrounded by sequoia trees imported from California, the **Hotel Santa Fe** is modelled on the adobes of New Mexico, and the **Hotel Cheyenne** is built to look like a frontier town. A group of four could comfortably and affordably stay for a weekend at the Hotel Cheyenne for 475F per night, or at the Hotel Santa Fe (unpopular with the French because it looks like a French housing project) for only 375F per night during off-season. The Resort also has a campground called the **Davy Crockett Ranch,** which is being converted into a resort village. For more information call in Paris tel. 49 41 49 10, in the U.K. tel. (071) 753 29 00, or in the U.S. tel. (407) W-DISNEY (934-7639).

## SIGHTS AND ACTIVITIES

The park can be divided into five areas. **Main Street,** the first area you'll pass through after the gate, is home to City Hall and the highest concentration of stores. The **Château de la Belle au Bois Dormant (Sleeping Beauty's Castle)** contains one stupendous high-tech smoke-breathing dragon in the dungeon, and a shop where you can buy the crown jewels for a paltry 3200F. It makes one heck of a landmark. Exiting out the back of the château, you fall into **Fantasyland.** Although the rides are tame, **Peter Pan's Flight,** and **It's a Small World** merit a spin; **Alice's Curious Labyrinth** is a hedge maze, replete with squirting fountains and a bong-smoking caterpillar.

Off to the left, **Adventureland** awaits both the intrepid explorer and the weary parent with a mix of themes from "adventurous" regions: the Middle East, West Africa, and the Caribbean. **Pirates of the Cambeau** presents 15 minutes of frighteningly life-like corsairs and a fantastic water-dungeon set. Be warned: the line outside is only a fraction of the total wait. Mosey on down to the rough and ready zone of **Frontierland** where **Thunder Mesa,** a towering sunset-colored reproduction of a New Mexican desert mesa, hosts the park's most breathtaking ride, **Big Thunder Mountain.** At high noon, the line is almost as deadly as the ride, but the marvelous robot llamas and donkeys that border the track, and the bumpy trip itself, are superb. Set apart on a scraggly hill, the creaky **Phantom Manor** is the park's classic haunted house. While the Haunted Mansion at Disneyland in Florida is a huge scary fortress, the architecture had to be changed in Europe, where fortresses and châteaux are common; this haunted Manor is based instead on the Victorian mansion in the film *Psycho*.

In addition to the rides, Disney also puts on three daily special events: a **Disney character parade** with myriad elaborate floats; the **Main Street Electrical parade** (for the best view of the parades stand to the left at the top of Main Street near the pseudo-rotary—that's where the special effects on the floats are timed to go off); and a fantastic **fireworks** show, set against the background of the château.

Five new attractions opened in 1993. **Indiana Jones**™ **et le Temple du Péril** is a roller coaster that features the first 360° loop ever on a Disney park ride. Three more attractions are set to open in 1994 and 1995: **Casey Jr. le Petit Train du Cirque** and **Le Pays des Contes des Fées,** both of which feature tours of fairy tales, and **Space Mountain,** Euro Disneyland® Park's third roller coaster. Disney has also opened an entirely separate resort village called **Festival Disney,** located to the left as you exit the RER station. This resort includes countless restaurants on American themes plus cafés, dancing, nightlife, shopping, a French tourist office, and a post office.

## GETTING THERE

The easiest way to get to the Euro Disney® Resort is by taking the **RER** A4 from Paris. Get on at either Mo. Gare de Lyon or Châtelet-Les Halles and take the train (direction: "Marne-la-Vallée") to the last stop, "Marne-la-Vallée/Chessy." Before boarding the train, check the illuminated electric boards hanging above the platform to make sure there's a light next to the Marne-la-Vallée stop; otherwise the train won't end up there (every 30min., 50min., 66F round-trip). The last train to Paris leaves Disney at 12:22am, but you may have trouble getting the *métro* at the other end. By **car**, take the A4 highway from Paris and get off at exit 14, marked "Parc Euro Disneyland," about a 30-minute drive from the city. You can park for 30F in any one of the 11,000 spaces in the parking lot. **Euro Disney® Buses** make the rounds between the terminals of both Orly and Roissy/Charles de Gaulle airports and the bus station near the Marne-la-Vallée RER (every 45-60 min., 40min., 65F, 6:45am-10pm).

# ■ Giverny

Halfway between Paris and Rouen, the small village of **Giverny** would have fallen off the map by now had Claude Monet not decided to purchase a small garden here. The impoverished painter surely would not recognize today his quaint pink and green house and his small, tangled garden. Landscapers now tend the famed impressionist flora for six months a year, and the house witnesses a barrage of tourists to rival that of Versailles. The Japanese-style bridge and water lilies are indeed quite beautiful, but the site has been methodically converted into a tourist trap of the first degree, called the **Musée Claude Monet** (tel. 32 51 28 21). The steep admission fees now finance six months of continuous blooms, something Monet, who spent nearly as much time writing rent-forgiveness letters to his landlord as he did painting, might well find incredible. The most famous paintings have been scattered around the world's great museums, but with a little imagination, it's possible to disregard the tourists and appreciate the inspiration of Monet's water lilies.

The water garden is the definite top attraction of Giverny, made famous by Monet's paintings of *Les Nymphéas*, now hanging in the Musée de l'Orangerie (see Museums). There are several connecting pools, full of water lilies of several varieties, and shaded by enormous weeping willows. A winding path around the pools, traversed at several points by famous Japanese bridges, is reminiscent of Monet's later paintings as well as the Japanese prints that inspired him both in his gardening and his painting. The house itself is lovely, with a façade of pink crushed brick. Inside, the walls are lined with Monet's collection of 18th- and 19th-century Japanese woodblock prints, imported en masse after the opening of Japan in 1853. (House and gardens open April-Oct. Tues.-Sun. 10am-6pm. Admission 35F, students with cards 25F. Gardens only 20F. Arrive early as the line quickly becomes a two-hour wait.)

Along the rue Claude Monet sits the **Musée Américain Giverny** (tel. 32 51 94 65) which contains work of American artists who were influenced by French Impressionists (open April-Oct. Tues.-Sun. 10am-6pm; admission 30F, students 20F). Within walking distance is the **Ancien Hôtel Bauddy (Musée)** (tel. 32 21 10 03). Once home to artists such as Renoir, Rodin, and Americans John Singer Sargent and Mary Cassatt, it has recently been renovated and will soon contain a gallery of contemporary works. Gardens climb the hill in dense splendor with benches at all levels and tables at the bottom. Bring food from one of the shops on the rue d'Albufera and picnic here. (Open April-Oct. Tues.-Sun. 10am-6pm. Admission 25F, students 20F.)

Thanks to their popularity, Giverny and its lilies are easily accessible by public transportation. **Trains** run from Paris to Vernon several times a day (every 2hr., 45min., from Gare St-Lazare, 60F each way). The train station of **Vernon** is across the river and a 6km hike from the museum. To get to Giverny, rent a bike from the station (55F per day, 1000F deposit), or take a bus from the front of the station (3 per day each way; 10min.; 10F, round-trip 16F). Consider a climb up the valley into the **Forêt de Vernon,** alongside Giverny, to see some of the beautiful poppy-covered countryside. The Vernon **tourist office,** 36, rue Carnot (tel. 32 51 39 60) distributes maps of hiking trails in the area. (Open Mon. 2:30-6:30pm, Tues.-Sat. 9:30am-12:15pm and 2:30-6:30pm.) Frequent signs lead the way from the Vernon station to the tourist office and to Giverny. Finally, the **Musée de Vernon,** 12, rue du Pont (tel. 32 21 28 09), exhibits an eclectic but interesting collection. Besides the predictable series on Giverny (only one is a Monet), this museum displays archaeological relics found near Vernon and animal art. (Open Tues.-Sun. 2-6pm. Admission 15F, students free.)

## ■ Auvers-sur-Oise

*I am entirely absorbed by these plains of wheat on a vast expanse of hills like an ocean of tender yellow, pale green, and soft mauve, with a piece of worked (farmed) land dotted with clusters of potato vines in bloom, and all this under a blue sky tinted with shades of white, pink, and violet.*
—*Vincent Van Gogh, 1890*

The beautiful town of Auvers-sur-Oise, located 30km north-west of Paris, is known as a birthplace of Impressionism. During the late 19th century, painters like Daubigny, Cézanne, and Van Gogh came to this small wooded town, surrounded by wheatfields and the river Oise, to experiment with the technique of painting that would come to be known as Impressionism. Their use of long brush strokes and their manipulation of color and light necessitated natural landscapes outside of the dark crowded streets of Paris. Pre-Impressionist painter **Charles-François Daubigny** (1817-1878) built a studio for himself here in 1864 and invited a number of famous painters to stay with him. His home, the Atelier de Daubigny at 61, rue Daubigny (tel. 34 48 03 03), can be visited today (Wed. and Fri.-Sun., 2-6pm, admission 20F, 15F *tarif réduit*).

**Docteur Gachet** (1828-1909) was perhaps more instrumental in placing Auvers on the artistic map; a doctor, painter, and patron of the arts, he supported painters like Vincent Van Gogh in Auvers. Gachet's own work is on display at the Musée d'Orsay. On May 20, 1890, **Vincent Van Gogh** accepted Docteur Gachet's invitation and moved to Auvers-sur-Oise, where he rented a room at the **Auberge Ravaux,** known today as the **Maison de Van Gogh** (at 52, av. du Général de Gaulle). The Maison was under renovation in summer 1993; the completion date is yet unknown. During the 70 days that he spent here, Van Gogh produced more than 60 sketches, *études*, and paintings, including the famous painting of Auver's Eglise de l'Assumption, which now hangs in the Musée d'Orsay. On the night of July 27, 1890, the 37-year-old Van Gogh shot himself in the fields of Auvers, returned to the *auberge*, and died two days later, attended by his close friend Dr. Gachet, and his much loved younger brother Théo. Both brothers are buried in the **Cimetière d'Auvers** on rue Daubigny. Vincent's grave lies next to his brother's grave against the far wall of the cemetery. From here, there is a lovely view of the church that Van Gogh immortalized.

The **Office de Tourisme d'Auvers-sur-Oise** (tel. 30 36 10 06), in the Manoir des Colombières, is in the parc Van Gogh, rue de la Sansonne (open Mon.-Fri. 9am-noon and 2-6pm, Sat.-Sun. 10am-noon and 2-6pm; 1½-hr. tours of Auvers on selected days at 3pm). Take the train from the Gare St-Lazare or the Gare du Nord to Pontoise, then switch to the Creil line to the Gare d'Auvers-sur-Oise (several trains/day, 1hr., 42F).

# ■ Compiègne

Tranquil Compiègne (pop. 45,000) has tripped through twelve centuries of diplomatic notoriety, without being much affected by it. The town emerged as a diplomatic capital in the 8th century, welcoming Frankish and Byzantine officials to the banks of the Oise. The English captured Jeanne d'Arc here in 1430 during a siege in yet another round of the Hundred Years' War. The armistice ending World War I was signed on November 11, 1918 in a forest clearing about 6km away; in 1940 Adolf Hitler forced the French to surrender at the same spot. Beech trees, landscaped grounds, and the 17th-century château make today's Compiègne a quaint town with a few skeletons hidden in the *armoire*; under the German occupation, Compiègne served as one of France's largest detention centers for Jews on their way to concentration camps farther east. It was from the train station in Compiègne that the "death train" to the concentration camps left—a train ride that ended in the death of more than half of its passengers. This dark period in the town's history is carefully neglected by most tour guides, and visitors can enjoy Compiègne's 17th-century château, three unusual museums, and web of hiking trails in peaceful ignorance. Remember that towns as well as people look gentler as they age. A walk through the compact center and proximate periphery will lead you past medieval spires, half-timbered façades, decaying monasteries, and, more prominently, architectural remains from the Second Empire.

The **Palais National,** just beyond the Hôtel de Ville and behind the Eglise St-Jacques, is a souped-up version of the hunting lodge that served French kings since Charles IX. The Estates General met here in 1382. Compiègne later served Louis XIV as one of the three royal abodes, a folksy time-out from Versailles and Fontainebleau. Fond of its rustic charms, Louis would quip, "I am lodged as king at Versailles, as gentleman at Fontainebleau, as peasant at Compiègne." With the original manor house too small for the royal entourage, ministers and servants stayed with villagers and at neighboring châteaux. Louis XV showed less of a taste for its humble charms and in 1751 started the building of a large palace; it forms the outline of what we see today.

Compiègne did not truly achieve its current status until the 19th century, when it served as second home to Napoleon, and later as autumn residence for Second Empire pomp, circumstance, and guests. Napoleon III played emperor here before a rotating circle of distinguished friends. The château's interior bears the mark of his ostentatious tastes, an often kitschy ensemble of nude nymphs and stuffed chairs.

Anyone who was *anyone* was there; each stayed in a particular room for a particular amount of time depending on social status. The elite of Paris elite spent their days hunting in 16th-century costume and living in terror of making a *faux-pas*. As Théophile Gautier told the Goncourts, "everybody behaves very awkwardly: the whole atmosphere is one of embarrassment. They aren't used to it....The only people who are completely at their ease are the old servants, the remnants of dynastic varletry, handed down from Charles X and Louis-Philippe. They are the only people who look as if they knew what a court was like." Painted ceilings by Redouté, tapestry from Beauvais, and a *trompe l'oeil* bag of tricks—secret doors, fake marble, and the like—make the château of Compiègne a period piece well worth the hour train ride from Paris.

This era is further recalled by the **Musée du Second Empire** (tel. 44 40 02 02) and the **Musée de la Voiture** (Carriage Museum, tel. 44 40 04 37) which features an 18th- and 19th-century sampling of coaches and omnibuses, including those used by Napoleon I and III. Perhaps the most impressive set of wheels to be found here is that of an anonymous 19th-century charlatan and traveling dentist, a surrey with a fringe on top painted with lions, horned beasts, and harpies. The Palais National may only be visited by guided tour (in French, every 15min., Wed.-Mon. 9:30am-5pm; last entry 4:30pm). Conference visits to the emperor's and empress's private apartments, not included in the standard tour, fall on weekends only (Sat. 3pm, Sun. 11am-3pm; admission to palace and museums 30F; students, seniors, and Sun. 19F).

No visit to the palace is complete without a tour of the grounds designed at Napoleon's request in 1811. These gardens are in the process of being restored to their original state; they should be finished in 1996. Meandering walkways, shade trees, and flower beds *à l'anglaise* complement a picnic or tryst. And while, officially, the *grande pelouse* (great lawn) is forbidden territory, the tolerant grounds crew don't seem to notice. Just beyond this vast expanse of manicured grass lies the untamed **Forêt de Compiègne,** a more adventurous setting for a bike ride or hike. Check with the tourist office for details about hunting season.

Six km into the forest is the **Clairière de l'Armistice** (Armistice Clearing). The Ludendorff Offensive of 1918 put Compiègne on the frontline between the French and German forces, so it was here that the Supreme Commander of the Allies, Maréchal Foch, brought his railway carriage for the signing of the Armistice in November. In June 20, 1940, Hitler ordered that the leader of France's delegation of surrender be driven all the way from Tours so he could be presented with the German terms for peace in the very same railway carriage, in the very same clearing. Hitler himself arrived and sneered at the monument to French victory, showing, in the words of eyewitness William Shirer, his "burning contempt for this place now and all that it has stood for in the 22 years since it witnessed the humbling of the German Empire." After the capitulation was signed two days later, Hitler destroyed the monument and took the railway carriage to Berlin as a trophy. It was destroyed there by Allied bombing; a sturdy replica is now berthed here in a small **museum** (tel. 44 40 09 27) with a simple monument (open Wed.-Mon. 9am-12:30pm and 2-6:30pm; Oct.-March Wed.-Mon. 9am-noon and 2-5:30pm; admission 3F).

The **Musée de la Figurine Historique,** in the annex of the Hôtel de Ville (tel. 44 40 72 55), contains a charming collection of toy kings, soldiers, and commoners reenacting highlights of French history. Its highlight is a fully staged battle of Waterloo (open Tues.-Sun. 9am-noon and 2-6pm; Nov.-Feb. 9am-noon and 2-5pm; admission 11F, students 5F, students on Wed. free).

Before starting your visit, head to the **tourist office** (tel. 44 40 01 00), in the Hôtel de Ville, which provides maps (furnished with a one-hour walking tour of historic monuments) and info on music festivals, bike rentals, and forest hiking trails. To get to the office, take a right from the train station, turn left and cross the canal, then head straight uphill to the most important-looking building in town, on the left side of the street (open Easter-Oct. Mon.-Tues. and Thurs.-Fri. 9am-noon and 1:45-6pm, Wed. and Sat. 9am-noon and 1:30-6pm, Sun. 9:30am-12:30pm and 2:30-5:30pm).

The town is easily accessible by **trains** from Paris's Gare du Nord (1hr., 55F). The train station is across the river from the center of town. To reach the center, cross place de la Gare in front of the station, turn right, and then turn left onto the bridge

# ■ Jouy-en-Josas

Situated southwest of Paris at the base of the plateau des Metz (altitude 170m), **Jouy-en-Josas** was the 18th-century production center of the luxurious linen material known as les *Toiles de Jouy*. Today, it is home to one of the largest collections of post-modern sculpture and one of France's most prestigious universities.

Located in the 18th-century Château de L'Eglantine, the **Musée Municipal de la Toile de Jouy** at 54, rue Charles de Gaulle (tel. 39 56 48 64), houses what remains of the vibrant fabric manufacturing industry which produced the famous *toile de jouy*, an ornately printed floral fabric, highly popular in 18th-century French fashion, especially of the court. Swiss designer Christophe-Philippe Oberkampf (1738-1815) founded the industry in 1760 in response to a royal decree to find other materials for French fashion which would not come from the already saturated and costly silk industry. Today, the **Château d'Eglantine** houses a museum showcasing pieces and clothing made from this exquisite material (open Tues.-Sun. 10am-noon and 2-5pm; Nov.-March Tues. and Thurs. 2-5pm; admission 25F, *tarif réduit* 15F).

At 3, rue de la Manufacture des Toiles de Jouy, the **Fondation Cartier pour l'Art Contemporain** (tel. 39 56 46 46), founded in 1984 by Alain Dominique Perrin, the president of Cartier Internationale (of jewelry fame), showcases some of the funkiest examples of late 20th-century sculpture in France. Larger-than-life sculptures such as Arman's *Long-Term Parking,* César's *Homage to the Eiffel Tower,* and Jean Pierre Reynaud's *La Serre* are scattered throughout the château and outside on the grounds (Fondation open daily noon-6pm; admission 35F).

Founded in 1881, the institution of **Hautes Etudes Commerciales (HEC)** (Advanced Business Studies), 1, rue de la Libération (tel. 39 67 70 00), one of France's Grandes Ecoles, educates the top French students in business management. The Jouy campus, complete with halls, dormitories, and green spaces is the closest thing in France to resemble an American (or Oxbridge) university campus; most French universities are non-residential colleges, without a defined campus.

French literature fans may want to see the house on rue Victor Hugo where the writer lived for a short period. Visits of the interior are not allowed, but there is a plaque on the house's left corner that commemorates its once resident genius.

Jouy-en-Josas is within close reach of a few 18th- and 19th-century châteaux, such as the **Château Mallet** at 5, rue de la Libération, the **Château du Bois des Rochers,** the **Château Vil Vert,** and the **Château de Canrober** at 54, rue Charles de Gaulle. The **Mairie de Jouy-en-Josas,** av. Jean Jaurès (B.P. 33, 78354 Jouy-en-Josas cedex; tel. 39 20 11 11; fax 39 56 17 98), can give you info (open Mon.-Fri. 8:30am-noon and 2-5pm, Sat. 8:30am-noon). To get to Jouy-en-Josas, take the train from the Gare St. Lazare to the Gare de Chanile Rive Droite (several trains/day, 45min., 27F).

# ■ L'Abbaye de Royaumont

Located 35km north of Paris, the Abbaye de Royaumont (tel. 30 35 40 18; fax 34 68 00 60); Asnières-sur-Oise, 95270) is one of the oldest and best preserved medieval monasteries in Europe. Despite seven centuries of war, political turmoil, and natural disaster, this cloistered abbey stands as a monument to medieval architecture, monastic life, and years of literature, music, and learning. Today, the *abbaye,* with its expansive Gothic arches, verdant courtyards, chapel, abbot's residence, and monastic chamber rooms, cells, and script rooms, houses the celebrated **Fondation Royaumont.** This international cultural organization sponsors summer and fall concert festivals and a center for medieval studies. Throughout the year, the *abbaye* hosts seminars and conferences for scholars on topics from Gregorian Chant to monastic writings.

Founded by St-Louis (King Louis IX of France) in 1228 and completed in 1235, the *abbaye* was devoted to the order of Cîteaux (Cisterian Order). The king provided the plentiful funds necessary to establish the monastery, and brought learned and devoted men to dedicate their lives to prayer and scholarship within the *abbaye's* walls; the king's brother, three of his sons, and two of his grandsons studied here.

The monks of the Abbaye de Royaumont were divided into two vocations: those who dedicated their lives to a mere 10 hours of daily prayer, called *Réligieux de Coeur,* and those who dedicated their time and energy to scholarship and script-copying. St-Louis invited one of the most celebrated medieval monk-scholars in Europe, Vincent de Beauvais, to lecture on his work, the *Speculum Majus,* an encyclopedia of world leaders, historical figures, and scholars. It was the very first *Who's Who* and, at several thousand pages, was one of the most comprehensive—a prime example of the high quality of European medieval monastic scholarship.

During the Revolution, the *abbaye* was ravaged by patriots seeking to eliminate the politically powerful and corrupt church. In 1791, the *abbaye's* church was demolished by revolutionaries. Used alternately as a prison, a hospital, and a seat of local government, the monastery eventually fell into the hands of Isabel and Henry Goüin-Lang (between 1900-1964), who, in 1977 donated the monastery to the newly created Fondation Royaumont "for the progress of human arts and sciences."

Inside the *abbaye* you can tour the *réfectoire,* where the monks ate in silence while a designated reader recited from the scripture. In the *anciennes cuisines,* the beautiful 14th-century statue of the Vierge de Royaumont stood (and still stands) watching over the monks who prepared the meals. Visitors can also see the *palais abbatial*, the abbot's formal residence, designed by Louis Le Masson. (Abbaye open daily 10am-12:45pm and 2-6pm; in winter daily 10am-12:45pm and 2pm-sundown. Admission 20F; students, scholars, and over 60 14F. Free tours on weekends only.) For more information or a schedule of concerts (held usually in Aug.-Oct.), seminars, or conferences, call 30 35 88 90 or 34 68 05 50, or write to the Fondation Royaumont. Come for a weekend of rest in the abbey's rooms, where you can sleep in considerably more comfort than the monks who once occupied the same spartan cells.

To get to the Abbaye de Royaumont from Paris, take the Paris-Nord-Luzarches line from the Gare du Nord line and get off at the Gare de Viarmes (several trains daily, 40min., 46F; call 30 35 30 16 for train schedules).

# Appendices

## Glossary

Here you will find a compilation of some of the French terms Let's Go has used. The glossary is followed by some phrases you might find helpful.

| | | | |
|---|---|---|---|
| **l'abbaye** | abbey | **la fête** | celebration |
| **l'allée** | lane, avenue | **la forêt** | forest |
| **l'aller et retour** | round-trip | **la galerie** | gallery, passageway |
| **aller simple** | one-way | **la gare** | station |
| **l'auberge** | inn, tavern | **l'hôtel (particulier)** | mansion (town house) |
| **la banlieue** | suburbs | **l'île** | island |
| **le bateau** | boat | **la librairie** | bookstore |
| **BCBG** | French Yuppie | **la mairie** | mayor's office |
| **la bibliothèque** | library | **le marché** | market |
| **le billet** | ticket | **le mur** | wall |
| **le bois** | forest | **le musée** | museum |
| **la boîte (de nuit)** | night club | **le palais** | palace |
| **la boulangerie** | bakery | **la papeterie** | stationery store |
| **la cave** | cellar | **le parc** | park |
| **la chambre** | room | **la pâtisserie** | pastry shop |
| **la charcuterie** | butcher's shop | **la place** | square |
| **le cimetière** | cemetery | **le pont** | bridge |
| **le cours** | tree-lined walk | **la porte** | gate; entry to the city |
| **la douane** | customs | **le quartier** | section (of town) |
| **l'école** | school | **la rue** | street |
| **l'église** | church | **tarif réduit** | reduced fee |
| **l'escalier** | stairway | **la tour** | tower |
| **le faubourg** | quarter | | |

## Helpful Phrases

| | | | |
|---|---|---|---|
| please | *s'il vous plaît* | I don't want | *Je ne veux pas* |
| thank you | *merci* | to rent | *louer* |
| hello | *bonjour* | The bill, please. | *L'addition, s'il vous plaît.* |
| good evening | *bonsoir* | Where is/are | *Où est/sont?* |
| How are you? | *Comment allez-vous?* | the bathroom? | *les toilettes* |
| goodbye | *au revoir* | the police | *la police* |
| Excuse me. | *Pardon.* | to the right | *à droite* |
| (to get s.o.'s attention) | *Excusez-moi.* | to the left | *à gauche* |
| Do you speak English? | *Parlez-vous anglais?* | up | *en haut* |
| I don't understand. | *Je ne comprends pas.* | down | *en bas* |
| I'm sorry. | *Je suis désolé.* | straight ahead | *tout droit* |
| how much? | *combien?* | a room | *une chambre* |
| what? | *comment?* | double room | *une chambre pour deux* |
| who | *qui* | single room | *une chambre simple* |
| why | *pourquoi* | with | *avec* |
| when | *quand* | without | *sans* |
| What is it? | *Qu'est-ce que c'est?* | a shower | *une douche* |
| I would like | *Je voudrais* | included | *compris* |
| I need | *J'ai besoin de* | | |

## Numbers

| | | | |
|---|---|---|---|
| one | *un* | twenty | *vingt* |
| two | *deux* | thirty | *trente* |
| three | *trois* | forty | *quarante* |
| four | *quatre* | fifty | *cinquante* |
| five | *cinq* | sixty | *soixante* |
| six | *six* | seventy | *soixante-dix* |
| seven | *sept* | eighty | *quatre-vingt* |
| eight | *huit* | ninety | *quatre-vingt-dix* |
| nine | *neuf* | one hundred | *cent* |
| ten | *dix* | | |

## ■ Menu Reader

| | | | |
|---|---|---|---|
| agneau | lamb | frites | french fries |
| bar | sea bass | fromage | cheese |
| beurre | butter | gâteau | cake |
| bien cuit | well done | glace | ice cream |
| bière | beer | grenouille | frog (legs) |
| bifteck | steak | haricot vert | green bean |
| blanc de volaille | breast of chicken | jambon | ham |
| bleu | very rare, blood red | lait | milk |
| boeuf | beef | lapin | rabbit |
| boissons | drinks | légume | vegetable |
| brioche | buttery bread, almost like pastry | magret de canard | breast of duck |
| canard | duck | mille feuille | "thousand-layered" pastry with cream; a Napoleon |
| champignon | mushroom | | |
| Chantilly | whipped cream sweetened with sugar | moutarde | mustard |
| | | nature | plain |
| chaud | hot | navarin | lamb or mutton stew with potatoes and turnips |
| chèvre | goat cheese | | |
| choix | choice | ouef | egg |
| citron | lemon | oignon | onion |
| confit | duck or goose cooked and preserved in its own fat | pain | bread |
| | | petit déjeuner | breakfast |
| | | poisson | fish |
| côte | rib or chop | pomme | apple |
| crème fraîche | fresh heavy cream | pomme de terre | potato |
| croque-monsieur | toasted, open-faced ham and cheese sandwich | potage | soup |
| | | poulet | chicken |
| crudités | raw vegetables, usually with a dressing | salade verte | green salad |
| | | saucisson | large dried sausage |
| | | saumon | salmon |
| déjeuner | lunch | tartare | chopped raw meat topped with a raw egg |
| dîner | dinner | | |
| échalote | shallot | | |
| entrée | first course (appetizer) | tarte tatin | caramelized upside-down apple pie |
| | | thé | tea |
| escargot | snail | viande | meat |
| foie gras | liver of a fattened goose | vichyssoise | cold cream soup with leeks and potatoes |
| forestière | with mushrooms | | |
| frais | fresh | vin | wine |
| fraise | strawberry | | |

# Index

# Paris Metro

•The stations Liège and Rennes are closed after 8pm and/or Sundays and holidays.

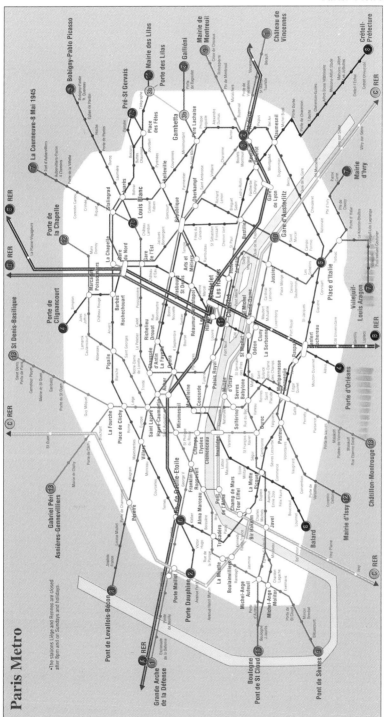

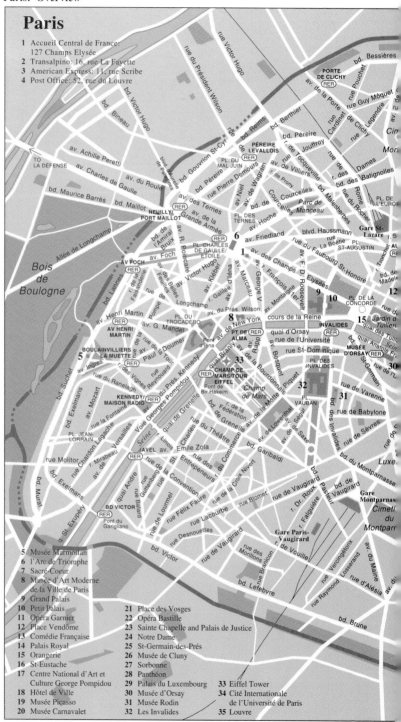

# Paris

1 Accueil Central de France:
127 Champs Elysée
2 Transalpino: 16, rue La Fayette
3 American Express: 11, rue Scribe
4 Post Office: 52, rue du Louvre

5 Musée Marmottan
6 l'Arc de Triomphe
7 Sacré-Coeur
8 Musée d'Art Moderne
de la Ville de Paris
9 Grand Palais
10 Petit Palais
11 Opéra Garnier
12 Place Vendôme
13 Comédie Française
14 Palais Royal
15 Orangerie
16 St-Eustache
17 Centre National d'Art et
Culture George Pompidou
18 Hôtel de Ville
19 Musée Picasso
20 Musée Carnavalet

21 Place des Vosges
22 Opéra Bastille
23 Sainte Chapelle and Palais de Justice
24 Notre Dame
25 St-Germain-des-Prés
26 Musée de Cluny
27 Sorbonne
28 Panthéon
29 Palais du Luxembourg
30 Musée d'Orsay
31 Musée Rodin
32 Les Invalides

33 Eiffel Tower
34 Cité Internationale
de l'Université de Paris
35 Louvre

**9e**

Rue Chaussée d'Antin

Richelieu

Rue St-Lazare

R. d'Amsterdam

Ⓜ St Lazare

Chaussée
d'Antin Ⓜ

Ⓜ

Havre-
Caumartin Ⓜ

Boulevard Haussmann

**Bd. Haussmann**

Ⓜ

Rue Auber

**Opéra**

Boulevard des Italiens

Rue Pasquier

Rue Tronchet

Rue Auber

Rue

Scribe

Auber (RER)

Bd. des
Capucines

Ⓜ Opéra
(RER)

Rue du Quatre Sep

Ⓜ

Quatre
Septembre

Bd. de la
Madeleine

Rue des
Capucines

Rue de la Paix

Rue des Petit Champs

**Bibli
N**

**Madeleine**

Rue Boissy d'Anglas

Madeleine Ⓜ

Ⓜ

**La Colonne**

PLACE
VENDÔME

**Pyramides** Ⓜ

Avenue de l'Opéra

Rue Royale

Rue St-Honoré

**8e**

**Musée Bouilhet
Christofle**

Rue de Castiglione

Rue St-Honoré

Rue des Pyramides

**1er**

Ⓜ Concorde

Ⓜ

Rue de Rivoli

**Tuileries** Ⓜ

PLACE
ANDRE
MALRAL

**Jeu de Paume**

Palai

PLACE DE
LA CONCORDE

*JARDIN DES
TUILERIES*

PLAC
CARR

**L'Orangerie**

Quai des Tuileries

Pt. de la
Concorde

*Seine*

Pont
Solférino

Pont
Royal

Pont du
Carrousel

Quai Anatole France

Quai Voltaire

**Assemblée
Nationale**

Chambre des
Deputés

Ⓜ

**Musée
D' Orsay**

(RER)

**Musée
d'Orsay**

Rue de Lille

Bd. St-Germain

**7e**

Rue de l'Université

| 0 | | 1/8 mile |
| 0 | | 125 meters |

Solférino Ⓜ

Ecole Na
Superie
Bea

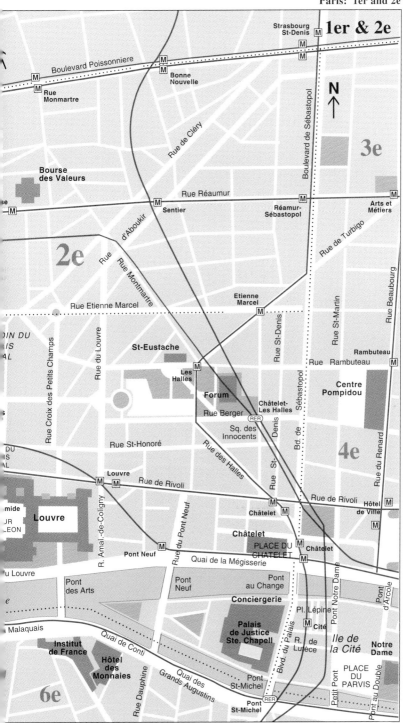

Palais
du Louvre

Pont Neuf

Châtelet M

Quai du Louvre

**1er**

Pont
des
Arts

Pont
Neuf

Pont au
Change

Pont du
Carrousel

Conciergerie

Cité

Quai Malaquais

Quai de Conti

Ste-
Chapelle

Palais du Pt

Ile de
la Cité

Hôte
Dieu

Ecole Nationale
Superieure des
Beaux Arts

Institut
de France

Hôtel des
Monnaies

Quai des
Grands
Augustins

Pont St-Michel

Rue de la Cité

R. Bonaparte

Rue Jacob

Rue de Seine

Rue Mazarine

Rue Dauphine

Pont
St-Michel

St-Michel

RER

Rue des Sts-Pères

M

St-Germain
Des Prés

Rue St-André des Arts

Pl.
St-Michel

Rue St-Jaques

R. de l'Abbaye

PLACE
ST-GERMAIN-
DES-PRÉS

Rue Danton

M

Bd. St-Germain

St-Germain
des Prés

M

Mabillon

Odéon

Bd. St-Germain

**7e**

R. du Four

Rue de l'Odéon

Boulevard

Musée
du Cluny

R. de Sèvres

R. du Vieux
Colombier

R. du Saint Sulpice

Rue de Tournon

Rue Racine

Sorbonne

R. du Cherche Midi

R. de Rennes

PLACE
ST-SULPICE

St-Sulpice

PLACE DE
L'ODÉON

PLACE
DE LA
SORBONNE

St-Michel

R. d'Assas

M

St-Sulpice

Palais du
Luxembourg

Rue Soufflot

Bd. Raspail

Rue de Vaugirard

M

Luxembourg

Rennes

**6e**

Rue Gay-Luss..

St Placide

M

JARDIN
DU
LUXEMBOURG

Rue du Montparnasse

Notre-Dame
des Champs

M

Rue d'Assas

Boulevard St-Michel

Rue Vavin

Rue Notre-Dame des Champs

Montparnasse
Bienvenüe

M

Vavin

M

Boulevard du Montparnasse

Avenue de

Port Royal

M

Rue St-Jaques

R. du Depart

**14e**

Boulevard Raspail

la Observatoire

Edgar
Quinet

M

Boulevard Edgar Quinet

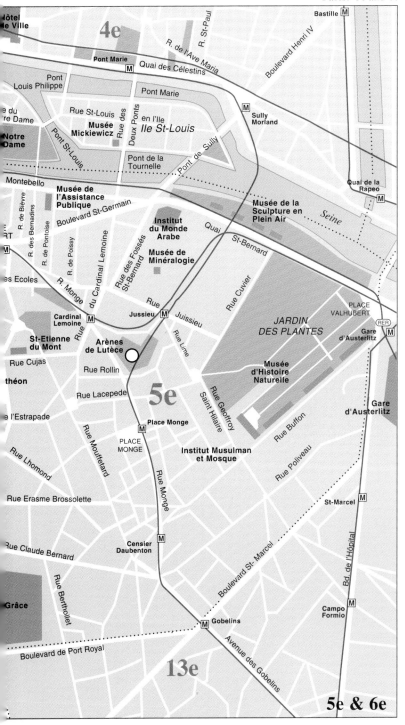

Bastille Ⓜ

4e

R. St-Paul

R. de l'Ave Maria

Boulevard Henri IV

Pont Marie Ⓜ
Quai des Célestins

Hôtel de Ville

Pont Louis Philippe

Pont Marie

Rue St-Louis

Rue des Deux Ponts

en l'île Ile St-Louis

e du re Dame

Musée Mickiewicz

Pont St-Louis

Notre Dame

Sully Morland Ⓜ

Pont de la Tournelle

Pont de Sully

Montebello

Musée de l'Assistance Publique

R. de Bièvre

R. des Bernadins

R. de Pontoise

R. de Poissy

Boulevard St-Germain

Institut du Monde Arabe

Musée de Minéralogie

Quai

Musée de la Sculpture en Plein Air

Seine

Quai de la Rapeo Ⓜ

St-Bernard

RT Ⓜ

es Ecoles

R. Monge

R. du Cardinal Lemoine

Rue des Fossés St-Bernard

Rue Cuvier

PLACE VALHUBERT

RER

Cardinal Lemoine Ⓜ

Jussieu Ⓜ

Juissieu

JARDIN DES PLANTES

Gare d'Austerlitz

St-Etienne du Mont

Arènes de Lutèce ●

Rue Lime

Rue Cujas

Rue Rollin

5e

Musée d'Histoire Naturelle

Gare d'Austerlitz

théon

Rue Lacepede

Rue Geoffroy

Saint Hilaire

e l'Estrapade

Rue Mouffetard

Place Monge Ⓜ

Rue Buffon

Rue Lhomond

PLACE MONGE

Institut Musulman et Mosque

Rue Poliveau

Rue Erasme Brossolette

Rue Monge

St-Marcel Ⓜ

Rue Claude Bernard

Censier Daubenton Ⓜ

Bd. de l'Hôpital

Rue Berthollet

Boulevard St-Marcel

Gobelins Ⓜ

Campo Formio Ⓜ

Grâce

Boulevard de Port Royal

13e

Avenue des Gobelins

5e & 6e

# Paris: RER

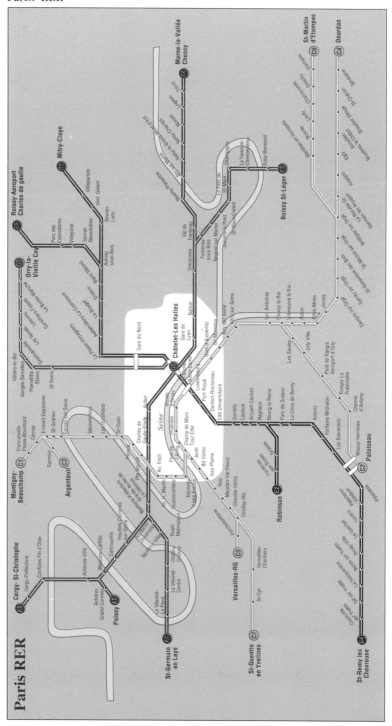

Paris RER